D1357339

TECHNOLOGY
AND
COPYRIGHT
Sources and Materials

edited by

George P. Bush
and
Robert H. Dreyfuss

Foreword by Lowell H. Hattery

Revised Edition

Lomond Books
Mt. Airy, Maryland
1979

LC Catalog Number: 79-656-35
ISBN: 0-912338-17-2 (Clothbound)
ISBN: 0-912338-18-0 (Microfiche)

Composition by Barbara J. McGiffin and Jeanne Moran.
Printing by Universal Lithographers, Inc.   Jacket design by Markey Graphics.

Lomond Publications, Inc.
P.O. Box 56
Mt. Airy, Maryland 21771

FOREWORD

This book will be a very useful guide to thought, information and experience which illuminates the background and issues of the relationships between technology and copyright law.

Three elements in the book's design contribute to its usability. Nearly three hundred fifty annotations to selected references are grouped under major topics to facilitate both searching and browsing. Significant amplifications and explications are contained in a set of carefully selected reprinted documents. Together they comprise a concise encyclopedia on the subject. Finally, name and subject indexes provide thorough finding tools for those with specific questions.

The impact of technology on copyright remains as challenging a subject as ever, even though the new Copyright Act which became law on January 1, 1978 clarified some issues. Many issues were not met in the language of the new law, and compromise language produced new ambiguities. The dynamics of new technology continuously changes the environment in which copyright law must function.

Therefore, the importance of continuing to monitor and evaluate technology-copyright interrelationships is unabated.

The first edition of this book was prepared by the distinguished bibliographer, technologist and academician, the late Dr. George P. Bush. He had an unflagging curiosity about the nature of technological change and its effect on information transfer processes. It was long after retirement from military and academic careers that he undertook the preparation of *Technology and Copyright: Annotated Bibliography and Source Materials.* He completed the manuscript at the age of 81.

Professor Bush approved the invitation to Robert H. Dreyfuss to update and revise the book and counseled with him in the early stages of the work.

Mr. Dreyfuss was a happy selection. He had shared an office with Professor Bush when a graduate student in Public Law. He has subsequently pursued a productive career in various aspects of information transfer processes, especially legal information retrieval systems and technical editing. His understanding of legal documentation and information technology and an intellectual curiosity about the nature and significance of their intersection are the qualities which have produced an excellent new volume on *Technology and Copyright: Sources and Materials.*

The new volume consists of 80% new references and resource documents. When coupled with the 1972 edition, the user has a comprehensive historical and contemporary review of the subject.

Lowell H. Hattery
American University

PREFACE

During the six years since the first edition, the Congress has enacted a new Copyright Law. The law, which became effective on January 1, 1978, was a compromise among many competing interests. As with most compromises, the resultant product is complex.

The purpose of this book is to present the reader with references and resource materials which will not only inform and educate, but will also provide a sense of the debate centering on the provisions of the Copyright Law relating to technology and copyright. The scope of this work is fairly narrow: the impact of technology on copyright law and vice versa. However, this narrow area had much to do with delaying final passage of a new law and has generated much debate about its application.

The bibliography is not intended to be complete. The goal is to include representative citations of the views which have been expressed on the provisions of the new law, before and after final passage. Of the originals 305 entries, 125 have been retained resulting in this edition having a total of 359 references.

Because the book appears at the juncture of two laws, many of the references refer to various Copyright Revision Bills. In most instances the provisions of the Copyright Act which was passed are similar to the versions of the bills reviewed in the entries presented.

Three new categories have been added in this edition: CONTU (National Commission on New Technological Uses of Copyrighted Works), Permissions and Payments, and Basic References. One category, Systems, has been eliminated and the entries which would have come under that heading have been distributed among other, more specific categories. The coverage of two categories has been broadened. Computer Systems now includes references pertaining to the copyright eligibility of computer software, while Libraries, Networks, and Information Systems includes references to library networks and document distribution systems. Author, subject, and case indexes are provided.

Although this book is concerned primarily with copyright law in the United States, references do appear on relevant copyright activities within other nations and on international copyright activities.

As anyone who edits a book of this nature, I could not have come this far alone. My sincere thanks are extended to Catherine Brauner and Diane Ward for their editorial assistance, and to Barbara McGiffin for typing the manuscript. Special thanks go to Douglas Price, Deputy Director of the National Commission on Libraries and Information Science, for allowing me to use his document collection. My deepest gratitude goes to Lowell H. Hattery, whose patience, guidance, and faith has brought me to this point. His friendship is truly valued. Of course, I take responsibility for any errors of omission or commission that may appear herein.

Although Professor Bush and I corresponded during the initial stages only of the research for this edition, it is my hope that the end result would have met with his approval and does nothing to tarnish his legacy of fine craftsmanship.

Robert H. Dreyfuss
Editor, Second Edition

CONTENTS

PART I

ANNOTATED BIBLIOGRAPHY

A. TECHNOLOGY

Under this category are references that bear upon the several mechanisms used in the knowledge process. The items under this heading do not pertain to any one type of technology (i.e., computers, reprographic equipment, cable television, etc.), but rather to technology, in general, and the effect technology has on copyright law and vice versa.

Because specific technologies are categorized under separate headings, the reader is referred to those headings, specifically B. Computer Systems; C. Reprography; D. Video Communications; and E. Microforms. Of special importance to those interested in the effects of present and future technology on copyright are the references appearing in Section F. CONTU.

Selected Material related to Technology will be found in Part II: CRC SYSTEMS INCORPORATED, *Impact of Information Technology on Copyright Law in the Use of Computerized Scientific and Technological Information Systems.*

Bailey, Herbert S., Jr. *The Art and Science of Book Publishing.* **New York: Harper & Row, 1970. 216 p. (Especially pp. 103-173).**

"[T]he economics of publication of an individual book, with particular attention to the determination of print order, the price, the discount, the royalty rate, and the budget for operating costs related to the book." (page 104). Technology and copyright are treated briefly on pages 167 and 169.

CRC SYSTEMS INCORPORATED. Impact of Information Technology on Copyright Law in the Use of Computerized Scientific and Technological Information Systems. In *Copyright in Computer-Readable Works: Policy Impacts of Technological Change,* **by R.G. Saltman, Appendix A. Washington: National Bureau of Standards, 1977.**

This report studies major judicial decisions relating to technology and copyright law and reviews the changes in the old copyright laws which have occurred as a result of technological developments. The report considers the recent computerized Scientific and Technological Information (STI) Systems; the impact this new technology may have on existing copyright laws; the arguments favoring licensure prior to inputting copyrighted materials into computer systems; the arguments advocating royalty payment only upon the output of the copyrighted material; and the potential licensing and clearinghouse mechanisms.

Cunningham, Dewey J.   Information Retrieval and the Copyright Law. *Bulletin of the Copyright Society of the U.S.A.* **14: 22-27. October 1966.**

A discussion of the impact of technology upon certain aspects of the copyright law, with stress upon the valid interests of the authors who create and the publishers who disseminate. At the same time the author recognizes that "we cannot operate the world of information exchange in the future according to the rules of the past. It is not the same world. Thus, we must be able to retrieve particular accumulated information to meet the needs of the readers if we are to have progress. Indeed, the scientists and engineers who create the scientific and technical literature have the same need of any other reader." (page 27).

Eltgroth, George V.   Technology and the Copyright Law: The Systems Approach. In *Automated Information Systems and Copyright Law,* edited by Lowell H. Hattery and George P. Bush. (Reprinted in U.S. Congress. *Congressional Record,* **90th Cong., 2nd sess., 1968, 114, pt. 13: 17285-17286. July 13, 1968).**

A discussion of the problems which have arisen from the proposed copyright law revision in the light of growth patterns of data processing and other new technology.

Harvey, William B.   Orphans of the Storm. *Scholarly Publishing* **1: 299-305. April 1970.**

This article concerns the new technology: how it could help to keep more scholarly books, falling out of print every day, on publishers' lists. The proposal involves certain provisions of the fair use doctrine.

Hattery, Lowell H. and George P. Bush, editors. *Technological Change in Printing and Publishing.* **Rochelle Park, New Jersey: Spartan Books, 1973. 275 p.**

The essays in this book reflect on conditions and trends within the printing and publishing industry. The papers discuss the issues associated with managing and planning for the new technologies and the procedures that will continue to influence and affect the industry. Among the topics addressed are computer typesetting, video editing, and microform publishing. A 250-item annotated bibliography and an index are provided.

Heilprin, Laurence B. **Technology and the Future of the Copyright Principle.** *Phi Delta Kappan* **48**: 220-225. **January 1967.**

The background of copyright, the need for copyright revision, technology and copyright control, and users' need for new technology are reviewed along with conflicting valid principles and possible solutions.

Henry, Nicholas. *Copyright-Information Technology-Public Policy Part I: Copyright-Public Policies.* **New York: Marcel Dekker, Inc., 1975. 140 p.**

The new communication technologies which have been developed within recent years (e.g., photoduplication, microreproduction, computers, and cable television) are changing the nature of publishing. In the future copyright may not be the proper method to ensure the creation and dissemination of information. "Neopublishing technologies not only have undercut owners' control of information, but in the process have reduced the potency of the state to enforce its own laws." (page 54). The ways in which the executive, legislative, and judicial branches of the Federal government have circumvented copyright in order to be able to disseminate information more readily are considered. The observation is made that as the Copyright Office becomes more political, its functions will change from registration to regulation.

Henry, Nicholas. *Copyright-Information Technology-Public Policy, Part II: Public Policies-Information Technology.* **New York: Marcel Dekker, Inc., 1976. 166 p.**

The political history of the effort to revise the 1909 Copyright Law is reviewed in terms of the way this law is affected by the advancements in neopublishing technologies (e.g., photocopying and computer storage and retrieval). Consideration is given to the transformation of the copyright revision effort from "noetic politics" to interest group politics. The positions of some of the lobbies involved in the revision process are examined. The position taken is that copyright users have more political resources (and thus power) than copyright owners. The 1973 Copyright Law Revision Bill

(S. 1361) is reviewed, with an emphasis on the provisions relating to neo-publishing technologies. Such provisions include fair use, library photocopying, and computers.

Henry, Nicholas.   Copyright: Its Adequacy in Technological Societies. *Science* **186: 993-1004. December 1974.**

Copyright as an adequate policy for the production and dissemination of information in societies in which information technology is highly developed is questioned. Although copyright may have been a worthwhile policy when only a few persons possessed the means for printing, it may not be valid today in societies where almost anyone can gain access to a printing medium, such as a photocopying machine. The article describes some of the "dysfunctions of copyright," specifically copyright as a censor, the for-profit limitation, and the fair use doctrine. Alterations and alternatives to the present copyright structure are proposed.

Henry, Nicholas.   Copyright, Public Policy, and Information Technology. *Science* **183: 384-391. February 1, 1974.**

The term "neopublishing" is employed to describe the use of computers and photocopying equipment in information dissemination. The effect that these two technologies have had, and possibly will have, on producers and users of copyrighted information is analyzed. The author indicates those factors which should be considered when formulating Federal policies in this area.

Kaplan, Benjamin. *An Unharried View of Copyright.* **New York: Columbia University Press, 1967. 142 p.**

The James S. Carpentier Lectures delivered by Professor Kaplan at the Columbia University School of Law in March 1966. "His counsel that greater emphasis should be placed on the public's interest in the free accessibility of ideas is particularly appropriate in an era when freedom of expression is frequently under attack and when the means of dissemination of ideas are increasingly concentrated in fewer hands." (page viii).

Linden, Bella L.   Copyright, Photocopying, and Computer Usage. *Bulletin of the American Society for Information Science* **1(10): 12-14. May 1975.**

Photocopying and computer technology are simply means of efficiently disseminating information rather than the substance of copyright. The resolution of the problems which have developed between copyright and the use of the new technologies lies in ensuring a fair economic return to the creators and owners of artistic and literary property. Some of the arguments involved in the debate between the users of the new technologies and the copyright owners are reviewed. It is observed that the users of the new technologies (e.g., librarians, educators, and scientists) do have budgetary constraints, but without an economic incentive there will be little of value created on which to utilize the new technologies. It is further suggested that the National Commission on New Technological Uses of Copyrighted Works (CONTU) can play an important role in resolving the problems associated with the competing interests.

Markham, Jesse W. et al. *An Economic-Media Study of Book Publishing.* New York: American Textbook Publishers Institute and the American Book Publishers Council, 1966. 283 p.

The four parts of this study are titled: I An Economic Analysis of the New Information Technologies; II Federal Programs and Commercial Book Publishing; III The Impact of Technology on Publishing; and IV Copying and Duplicating Practices in American Education. References to *copyright* appear on the following pages: 7 to 14, 25, 32, 54, 59, 62, 88 and 91.

Publishers Study the Management of Change(1). *Publishers Weekly* 191(18): 22-27. May 1, 1967.

This was the topic of a two-day seminar, April 4-5, at Tarrytown, N.Y., held for members of the American Book Publishers Council. The topic: "The Forces of Change" was presented by Putney Westerfield, who "foresaw that, by 1980, most major commercial printing will be from 'digital storage' and that document storage on film will also play a dominant role . . . computer-based systems for each major discipline are in prospect by 1980 . . . The new world of information . . . will mean 'instantaneous, simultaneous involvement' of the individual—and there will be a problem of an 'information overload.' . . . " (pages 22-23).

Ringer, Barbara A. Copyright in Its Historical and Philosophic Setting. In *Copyright and Related Protections for Information Age Products.* Proceedings and Related Documents of the Meeting of the Information Industry Association Held at Airlie House, Virginia on July 18 and 19, 1969, pp. 7-20. Bethesda, Maryland: Information Industry Association, 1969.

A brief review of the history and philosophy of copyright law, with emphasis upon the relationship to present day situations and problems, is presented.

Of interest is an explanation of French copyright law as contrasted with Anglo-Saxon theories. The question and answer period was very productive, and it is this which justifies the reader to search out this paper for its concern with the implications of the new technology.

Scientific and Technical Communication: A Pressing National Problem and Recommendations for its Solution. **Washington: National Academy of Sciences, 1969. (Especially pp. 217-238).**

A review of the principal scientific-and-technical-information-handling processes in which new technologies play an increasingly prominent role; information systems that involve the concerted use of such technologies; and the resulting problems of law and equity. It is the latter portion which relates to copyright. Topics discussed are: Scope of copyright coverage; Exemptions from copyright; Copyright and new technology; and Proposal for a National Commission.

Stedman, John C.   Copyright Developments in the United States. *AAUP Bulletin* **62:** 308-319. October 1976.

The technological developments since the 1909 Copyright Law which have made it difficult to establish an equitable balance between the interests of the copyright owners and those of the users of copyrighted materials are outlined. Specifically, the advent of CATV, the advancements in reprography, and the development of computers are discussed. It is proposed that a Technology Commission, such as the (then-recently established) National Commission on New Technological Uses of Copyrighted Works (CONTU), study the economic and technological impact of these new technologies on creators and users and then advise the Congress on policy.

Tebbel, John. Book Publishers' Salvation? *Saturday Review* **49(30): 32-33. July 23, 1966.**

"Why new technology not only represents no basic threat to print media, but may be its long-term benefactor." (page 32).

"For the book audience, the new technology can be expected to enable publishers to make better books, at lower prices, to be distributed to readers far more efficiently than is possible today . . . " (page 33).

B. COMPUTER SYSTEMS

Although computer software appears to be protected by the 1976 Copyright Law, the debate as to the desirability of this has continued. Furthermore, the Congress has left for future determination, and possible legislation, the extent of protection to be provided copyrighted works which are used within computer systems. Both of these areas, as well as the protection of new works created by computer, were within the congressionally mandated scope of study of the National Commission on New Technological Uses of Copyrighted Works (CONTU).

References within this section pertain to copyright protection for machine-readable data bases, for computer software, and for works created with the assistance of the computer. References also appear concerning the use of copyrighted works in conjunction with computer systems (and the discussion of whether protection should be provided at the input and/or output stages). Related references appear under such categories as A. Technology; G. Fair Use; I. Libraries, Networks, and Information Systems; J. Permissions and Payments; K. Legislation/Legal; and L. International. Of course, many of the items categorized under F. CONTU pertain directly to this area.

Selected Materials related to Computer Systems will be found in Part II: CRC SYSTEMS INCORPORATED, *Impact of Information Technology on Copyright Law in the Use of Computerized Scientific and Technological Information Systems* (Section A.4); Jeffrey Squires, *Copyright and Compilations in the Computerized Era: Old Wine in New Bottles*; Yale M. Braunstein et al., *Economics of Property Rights as Applied to Computer Software and Data Bases* (Overview of Issues); John Hersey, *Dissent from CONTU's Software Recommendation;* and International Bureau of the World Intellectual Property Organization, *Model Provisions on the Protection of Computer Software* (Introduction).

Allan, Steven et al. New Technology and the Law of Copyright: Reprography and Computers. *UCLA Law Review* 15: 939-1030. March 1968.

Among the topics discussed are the physical properties of the computer, input and output, rights of authors versus needs of readers, the "fair use" doctrine, permission and payments, and home TV in the future in its relation to the library.

Application of Copyright on Computer Usage. **Washington: National Academy of Sciences, December 1, 1967. 26 p.**

Summary of main findings: 1. Computer information processing is of growing importance, and in a multitude of ways involves dealing with what is copyrightable material. 2. The Copyright Revision Bill does not deal directly with many vital aspects of computer information processing. We feel that enacting it into law in its current form could lead to difficulties of interpretation. 3. We recommend further study of the copyright issue, and support in general the proposal to create a study commission on copyright law. We find that the Panel is divided on the advisability of enacting the present bill in its current form, pending the outcome of the Commission's study. Panel participants: Albert V. Crewe—chairman, Robert M. Hayes, Benjamin Kaplan, William F. Miller, Charles G. Overberger, W. B. Wiley, F. Karl Willenbrock and Charles P. Bourne—executive director.

Banzhaf, John F. III. Copyright Law Revision: A Recent Amendment Favors Information Storage and Retrieval—A Report of the Data Processing Community. *Computers and Automation* **15(12): 10-11. December 1966.**

A brief statement related to H.R. 4347, 89th Congress, and the impact of computers and computer programs on copyright law is presented.

Banzhaf, John F. III. When a Computer Needs a Lawyer. *Dickinson Law Review* **71: 240-256. Winter 1967.**

The purpose of this article is to sensitize the reader to the legal problems which may occur in the operation of a computer so that he can, with foresight, take steps to avoid the difficulties before they happen. At the same time it illustrates some of the fascinating and unresolved legal problems computer usage has created. To dramatize some of these problems each area is considered in terms of a particular hypothetical situation.

Beard, Joseph J. Cybera: The Age of Information. In *Copyright Law Symposium: Number Nineteen* **by the American Society of Composers,**

Authors and Publishers, pp. 117-142. New York: Columbia University Press, 1971.

Mr. Beard states his purpose: ". . . to examine the proposed revision [of the Copyright Act of 1909] and to evaluate its potential effectiveness to deal with the problems created by computer-based information systems and those that may be developed over the next several decades." (page 121). He offers as a finale to his conclusion: "It is only by collecting a royalty at the point at which the material is input that the author can survive in an era when the user will deal not in documents but in ideas and facts and the system will write 'two-thousand-word essays'." (page 142).

Bigelow, Robert. Copyrighting Programs—1978. *Computer Law Service.* Volume 3. Chapter 4. Section 4-3. Article 4. Chicago: Callaghan & Co., 1975.

The eligibility of computer programs for copyright protection under the 1976 law is reviewed by outlining the positions of both the Copyright Office and the National Commission on New Technological Uses of Copyrighted Works (CONTU). The registration and deposit requirements for computer software and data bases are presented, as are the proposed copyright notice regulations.

Bigelow, Robert and Susan H. Nycum. *Your Computer and the Law.* Englewood Cliffs, New Jersey: Prentice-Hall, Inc., 1975. 283 p. (Especially Chapter 8).

This book is designed to enable the computer manager to recognize situations in which the services of an attorney should be employed and to provide the manager with enough background to allow him to work effectively with counsel. Among the topics examined are proprietary rights in computer software (including copyright protection), contract law, and computer abuses. The appendix includes the Copyright Office's registration requirements for computer programs.

Braunstein, Yale M. et al. *Economics of Property Rights as Applied to Computer Software and Data Bases.* Washington: National Commission on New Technological Uses of Copyrighted Works, June 1977. 131 p. (Available from National Technical Information Service, Springfield, Virginia. Order No: PB-268 787).

Economic theory is used to analyze the question of whether trade secrecy or copyright is the best form of protection for computer data bases and computer software. Economic analysis is also used to study the issue of whether exemptions from paying copyright royalties should be allowed for various classes of users and to determine the optimal length of time that copyright should subsist in computer data bases and software. Formulas are presented for determining the optimal term of protection. It is stressed that although a copyright system ideally balancing both proprietor and user needs can be theoretically designed, reality requires that compromises be made.

Computer Programs and Proposed Revisions of the Patent and Copyright Laws. *Harvard Law Review* **81: 1541-1557. May 1968.**

In this note the first part is titled: Programs and Programming and is concerned with two themes: (A) The program's functional relation to the computer; and (B) Programming. The second part is titled: The Programming Industry and is concerned with: (A) The current state of the industry; and (B) Industry problems. The third part is: Copyright, Patent, and Trade Secrecy Protection For Computer Programs and is concerned with: (A) The industry's attitude toward protection; and (B) Copyright (pages 1548-1552). Subsection (1) is titled: The efficiency of copyright as a protective device against plagiarism; while subsection (2) is titled: The effect of copyright on the programming industry.

Corasick, Margaret J. and Brian G. Brockway. Protection of Computer-Based Information. *Albany Law Review* **40: 113-153. 1975.**

Copyright, patent, and trade secret laws are not adequate to protect computer-based data. A new registration procedure based on the copyright registration system is proposed, as are penalties for infringement.

Dorn, Philip H.   Programs Are Not Books. *Datamation* **23(11): 231-233. November 1977.**

Computer programs are not analogous to books. The author outlines six points of difference between programs and books to defend the argument that copyright should not be extended to computer programs.

Duggan, Michael A. *Computer Aspects of Copyright and Patents, Working Paper 75-6.* **Austin, Texas: University of Texas, Graduate School of Business, University of Texas at Austin, November 1977. 12 p. (Distributed by the Bureau of Business Research, University of Texas at Austin.)**

There is a great deal of uncertainty as to the extent patent and copyright laws protect computer programs or protect against the use of copyrighted works in computers. It is noted, for instance, that given the present expense associated with computerized information storage and retrieval systems as compared to manual alternatives (especially in the area of data reproduction) the use of copyrighted works within such systems would presently be considered a fair use. A brief review of some of the relevant case and statutory law is presented.

Duggan, Michael A., compiler. *Law and the Computer: A KWIC Bibliography.* **New York: Macmillan Information, 1973. 323 p.**

A comprehensive bibliography covering the interrelationship between law and the computer is presented. The 6,310 items represent those references known to the compiler as of January 1, 1972. The Main Entry Section is primarily arranged by author, but also includes items under the section headings Anonymous Authors, Legal Cases, Conferences, Journals, Patents, and U.S. Congressional Documents. A Key-Word-In-Context (KWIC) index of the titles and an author index are provided.

Duggan, Michael A.   Viewpoint of the Computer Scientist. In *Copyright: Current Viewpoints on History, Laws, Legislation,* **edited by A. Kent and H. Lancour, pp. 66-103. New York: R.R. Bowker Co., 1972.**

Arguments for and against copyright liability for using copyrighted material as input into, or output from, computer systems are presented. In addition, the factors involved in determining whether a work that is produced by the computer (e.g., musical tones) can be copyrighted are reviewed. One of the conclusions reached is that, at present, the computer input and output of copyrighted material would be considered fair use because the use of computerized systems does not pose an economic threat to authors and publishers. As computers become more economical, this could change. A bibliography on protection of proprietary rights in software accompanies the text. The 206 citations refer to materials published no later than December 1968.

Freed, Roy N. *Computers and Law: A Reference Work.* **Fifth Edition. Boston: Roy N. Freed, 1976. 648 p. (For copies of the book, write the author at: Powers & Hall, 30 Federal Street, Boston, Massachusetts 02110.)**

This work, a compilation of major articles and cases, touches upon many facets of computers and the law. Consideration is given to the protection of proprietary programs and computer data bases and files; computers and communications regulation; and computers and the paramount issue of privacy. The author provides a Table of Cases and references to such items as bibliographies, glossaries of computer terms, journal and newspaper articles, and conference proceedings.

Freed, Roy N. **Copyrighting Programs is Unwise.** *Datamation* **23(11): 227-231. November 1977.**

The title of this brief article presents its conclusion. The essay explains why trade secret protection is better for computer programs than copyright protection.

Galbi, Elmer W. **Copyright and Unfair Competition as Applied to the Protection of Computer Programming.** *Computer Law Service.* **Volume 3. Chapter 4. Section 4-3. Article 1. Chicago, Illinois: Callaghan & Co., 1975.**

"This article first discusses the background and philosophical nature of copyright protection and shows how the general purpose and nature of copyright law is well suited to the type of protection which the creators of computer programs require. Second, the specific application of copyright law to the protection of computer programming [is] discussed. Third, the close relationship between copyright and unfair competition law and the manner in which unfair competition law can be used to protect computer programming will be analyzed." (page 1).

Greenbaum, Arthur J. **Computers, Copyrights and the Law.** *Bulletin of the Copyright Society of the U.S.A.* **15: 164-173. February 1968.**

A talk on the law as it exists today [July 19, 1967] with respect to whether it is infringement to convert copyrighted works into machine-readable form for use as computer input; (2) computer output and fair use; and (3) copyrightability of computer programs. It includes: a discussion of the Apollo case; the Fortnightly Corporation case; Lawlor's: "Copyright Aspects of Computer Usage"; and fair use, especially the study by Alan Latman: "Fair Use of Copyrighted Works."

Greenbaum, Arthur J. **Copyright and the Computer: Why the Unauthorized Duplication of Copyrighted Materials For Use as Computer Input Should Constitute Infringement. In** *Automated Information*

Systems and Copyright Law, edited by Lowell H. Hattery and George P. Bush. (Reprinted in U.S. Congress. *Congressional Record,* 90th Cong., 2nd sess., 1968, 114, pt. 13: 17042-17043. July 12, 1968).

"The purpose of this paper is to explain why I believe that the conversion of copyrighted works into machine-readable form for use as computer input should be considered copyright infringement." (page 17042).

Holmes, Edith. Copyrights Urged for Software Protection. *Computerworld* 11(11): 1, 6. March 14, 1977.

Two subcommittees of the National Commission on New Technological Uses of Copyrighted Works (CONTU) recommend that copyright, rather than patent, be used to protect computer software and commercial data bases. Copyrights are less expensive to obtain and easier to administer than patents. For protecting computer software, copyright is preferred to trade secret laws because trade secret laws vary from state to state while there is a Federal, and therefore uniform, copyright law.

Holmes, Grace W. and Craig H. Norville, editors. *The Law of Computers.* **Ann Arbor, Michigan: Institute of Continuing Legal Education, 1971. 332 p.**

This book documents the issues involved in the increased use of computer technology. Among other chapters is one titled: *Computers and Copyrights.* Of the four appendixes, one is titled: Public Law 91-555, S.T.R. 230, Copyright Protection in Certain Cases.

Jeanneret, Marsh. Information Retrieval and the Decision to Publish. *Scholarly Publishing* 1: 229-243. April 1970.

The author expresses the fear that computer input will impair the incentive to create new works. Licensing is necessary at the input stage.

Keplinger, Michael S. The Case for Invisible Copies. In *The Information Conscious Society.* **Proceedings of the American Society for Information Science, Volume 7, edited by Jeanne B. North, pp. 241-243. Washington: American Society for Information Science, 1970.**

"The problem of control of the use of copyrighted works in computerized information storage and retrieval systems is discussed. It is concluded that

such input may be considered copyright infringement under the current
Copyright Revision Bill as interpreted through the teachings of recent court
decisions, as well as being an infringement under the current [1909]
copyright statute." (page 241).

**Keplinger, Michael S.   Computer Intellectual Property Claims: Computer
Software and Data Base Protection.** *Washington University Law Quarterly*
1977: 461-467. Summer 1977.

Following an outline of the National Commission on New Technological
Uses of Copyrighted Works' (CONTU's) mandate and a review of the issues
to be investigated by the Commission, the author presents the contents and
recommendations of the reports produced by CONTU's Software and Data
Base Subcommittees.

**Kernochan, John M.   Subject Matter of Copyright; Rights in General;
Rights in Relation to Computers. In** *Current Developments in Copyright
Law 1977.* **Volume One, by Morton David Goldberg, chairman, pp.
49-67. New York: Practising Law Institute, 1977.**

The portions of the 1976 Copyright Law and the 1976 House Report dealing
with the subject matter of copyright are reviewed. Also discussed are Section
106 of the 1976 law, which describes the exclusive rights provided copyright
owners, and Section 117, which maintains the status quo for using
copyrighted materials in computer systems until the deliberations of the
National Commission on New Technological Uses of Copyrighted Works
(CONTU) are finished. Although computer programs and computer data
bases are eligible for copyright protection under provisions of the 1976 law,
the use of copyrighted works in computer systems is to be governed by
existing law (as of December 31, 1977) as that is defined by the courts.
However, it is suggested that provisions in the 1976 law and House Report
might provide guidance in litigation involving Section 117 or the 1909 law.

Levy, Howard A.   Copyright Law and Computerized Legal Research.
Bulletin of the Copyright Society of the U.S.A. **20: 159-180. February
1973.**

"This essay [examines] the copyright problems raised by computerized legal
research systems, particularly those of the input, index, abstracts and
editorial aids, the transmission from print to tape, and journals. Economic
consequences of the use of computerized legal research [are] also . . . considered, with a view toward the problems of cost, the limitations of antitrust

law, and the feasibility of a clearinghouse for legal 'data.' Finally, the essay [explores] the competing interest groups and legal policies, and [assesses] the directions in which computerized legal research may go." (page 161).

Lorr, Richard. Copyright, Computers and Compulsory Licensing. *Rutgers Journal of Computers and the Law* 5: 149-169. 1975.

The purpose of this article is to examine constitutional and statutory issues which could affect the determination of whether computer programs are eligible for copyright protection. Computer programs appear to satisfy the authorship and writing requirements of the Constitution. A compulsory license for computerized uses of copyrighted works is advocated.

Lowry, W. Kenneth. Use of Computers in Information Systems. *Science* 175: 841-846. February 25, 1972.

This is primarily a description of the in-house computer-based information system at Bell Telephone Laboratories. The author states: "Despite these problems, the computer will continue to strengthen its kinship with information systems and may prove to be the most important development for dissemination of information since the time of Johann Gutenberg." (page 846).

Mooers, Calvin N. Computer Software and Copyright. *Computing Surveys* 7: 45-72. March 1975.

This article, which is designed to educate the creators and owners of computer programs about the desirability of using copyright to protect their software, reviews what is and what is not copyrightable, the ways in which copyright can be infringed, and the areas wherein copyright appears to be most applicable (e.g., programs, documentation, translation from one language to another, and compilers). Copyright protection will encourage both the "portability" and "standardization" of computer programs.

Mooers, Calvin N. Legal Protection of Software. In *Encyclopedia of Computer Science,* edited by A. Ralston and C. L. Meek, pp. 771-775. New York: Petrocelli/Charter, 1976.

Various methods of protecting computer software are reviewed. The kinds of protection examined are simple secrecy, obfuscation, contract, trade secret, remedies for unfair trade practices, patent, trademark and service mark, and copyright. It is recommended that simple secrecy be used during software development, but that copyright be used during the marketing phase. Trademark or service mark protection should be used for the product name.

National Academy of Sciences. *Report on the Application of Copyright on Computer Usage.* **Washington: National Academy of Sciences, December 1, 1967. 26 p.**

Summary of main findings of a study by the National Academy of Sciences Panel on the Application of Copyright on Computer Usage.
"1 Computer information processing is of growing importance, and in a multitude of ways involves dealing with what is copyrightable material."
"2 The copyright revision bill does not deal directly with many vital aspects of computer information processing . . ."
"3 We recommend further study of the copyright issue, and support in general the proposal to create a study commission on copyright law."

Oberman, Michael S.   Copyright Protection for Computer-Produced Directories. In *Copyright Law Symposium: Number Twenty-Two,* **by the American Society of Composers, Authors and Publishers, pp. 1-52. New York: Columbia University Press, 1977.**

The question of whether computer-produced directories should be eligible for copyright protection is explored. The essay, which won the 1972 Nathan Burkan Memorial Competition, uses computer-produced directories as an example to investigate the applicability of copyright to the products of the new technologies. The questions of whether these directories meet the requirements of originality (i.e., authorship) and whether these products fall within the restriction against monopolizing words and ideas are explored, and the limits of copyright protection for directories are analyzed.

Pataki, Louis Peter, Jr.   Copyright Protection for Computer Programs Under the 1976 Copyright Act. *Indiana Law Journal* **52: 503-516. Winter 1977.**

The applicability and scope of copyright protection for computer programs are discussed. The author views computer programs as similar to form books and architectural plans which also are developed for practical use. Court cases pertaining to these types of works are examined to determine the possible limits of copyright protection which can be expected to be afforded computer programs.

Saltman, R.G. *Copyright in Computer-Readable Works: Policy Impacts of Technological Change.* **Washington: National Bureau of Standards, 1977. 267 p.**

In arriving at the conclusion that both computer-readable data bases and computer programs should be eligible for copyright protection, the author applies the theory of public goods. Judicial decisionmaking in copyright cases is analyzed, as are the basic principles underlying copyright. An appendix presents a detailed study of the way in which copyright law has adapted to technological change.

Scafetta, Joseph, Jr. **Computer Software Protection: The Copyright Revision Bills and Alternatives.** *The John Marshall Journal of Practice & Procedure* **8: 381-399. Spring 1975.**

Neither patent protection nor copyright registration offers adequate protection for computer software. Because computer software may be construed as part of the computer hardware and as not the "writing of an author," programs may be determined to be uncopyrightable. Furthermore, many programs do not meet the level of inventiveness required by patent law. A new "petty patent" is recommended for protection of computer programs.

Squires, Jeffrey. **Copyright and Compilations in the Computer Era: Old Wine in New Bottles.** *Bulletin of the Copyright Society of the U.S.A.* **24: 18-46. October 1976.**

Copyright protection afforded machine-readable bibliographic data bases under the 1909 Copyright Law and under the 1976 Copyright Revision Bill is examined. There is some doubt whether the 1909 Act could have protected machine-readable data bases which were frequently updated, primarily because of the Act's strict notice and deposit requirements. The Revision allows the Register of Copyrights some leeway in issuing regulations concerning both the placement of copyright notice onto copies of a work and the requirements for deposit.

Stork, Philip. **Legal Protection for Computer Programs: A Practicing Attorney's Approach.** In *Copyright Law Symposium: Number Twenty,* **by the American Society of Composers, Authors and Publishers, pp. 112-139. New York: Columbia University Press, 1972.**

The scope and limitations of protection afforded computer programs under the trade secret laws, copyright laws, and patent laws are surveyed in an article which concludes that the programmer's attorney should select the most suitable form of protection based on the expected use of each program.

Wittenburg, Pauline.   Computer Software: Beyond the Limits of Existing Proprietary Protection Policy. *Brooklyn Law Review* **40: 116-146. Summer 1973.**

The question of whether computer software falls within the domain of copyright or patent protection is explored. It is pointed out that copyright seems inadequate because it protects only the physical expression of the idea and not the idea itself. Doubts are raised about whether computer programs are patentable and whether state trade secret laws are applicable to computer programs in the event that programs cannot be copyrighted or patented. Finally, an IBM proposal for a combination system involving features from both the copyright and patent laws is briefly examined.

C. REPROGRAPHY

Although the majority of references under this category pertain to photocopying, the term "reprography" is used because it is a more generic term related to any means of producing a "visually perceivable facsimile copy" (*Report of the Committee to consider the Law on Copyright and Designs,* p. 55). In addition to photographic copying, methods of producing facsimile copies include microfilming, holography, computer-output-microfiche, and others.

Lesser references which in most instances relate to how the copies are used, rather than the way in which they are made, can be found under such headings as A. Technology; E. Microforms; F. CONTU; G. Fair Use; H. Education; I. Libraries, Networks, and Information Systems; J. Permissions and Payments; K. Legislation/Legal; and L. International.

Selected Materials related to Reprography will be found in Part II: CRC SYSTEMS INCORPORATED, *Impact of Information Technology on Copyright Law in the Use of Computerized Scientific and Technological Information Systems* (Section A.2.5); *Copyright and Designs Law: Report of the Committee to consider the Law on Copyright and Designs* (Chapter 4); Maurice Line and D.N. Wood, *The Effect of a Large-Scale Photocopying Service on Journal Sales;* and E. van Tongeren, *The Effect of a Large-Scale Photocopying Service on Journal Sales.*

Arntz, Helmut. Reprography and Copyright. *Copyright* 11: 95-102. April 1975.

Because there is no efficient method of verifying the number of copies produced, advancements in reprographic processes (e.g., microfilming and computer storage and retrieval) make it impractical to charge for the number of reproductions of copyrighted material. This article suggests that instead of paying at the copying stage, a small surcharge should be levied on the reprographic equipment at the time of purchase. Such a charge would provide the owner of the intellectual property a return, while ensuring that the dissemination of information was not impeded.

Breslow, Marc, Allen R. Ferguson and Larry Haverkamp. *An Analysis of Computer and Photocopying Copyright Issues from the Point of View of the General Public and the Ultimate Consumer.* **Washington: The Public Interest Economics Center, June 1977. 161 p.**

This report studies the desirability of providing copyright protection for computer-based information (i.e., software, data bases, and computer-created works) and photocopying and considers the way in which that protection would affect the ultimate user of this information. The primary question underlying the study concerns what level of cost to the consumer and what level of inducement to producers of information will be required to provide the optimal availability of information in the future. Although the concept of copyright protection for computer-based information is generally supported, the researchers conclude that royalty payments are not desirable for photocopying except in cases where the copies would be offered for resale.

Culliton, Barbara J.   Photocopying Habit in Jeopardy. *Science* **176: 265. April 21, 1972.**

A brief news report on the Williams & Wilkins vs. National Institutes of Health and the National Library of Medicine case. The author in the final paragraph refers to "express license," which ". . . refers to a privilege that the government has had since 1965 that allows it to stipulate that publications about research funded with federal money cannot be copyrighted under any provisions that preclude the government's copying or translating them without paying royalties . . ." (page 265).

Gipe, George A. *Nearer to the Dust: Copyright and the Machine.* **Baltimore: Williams & Wilkins Co., 1967. 290 p.**

"The purpose of this book is to describe, in layman's language, these basic unsolved problems [subsequent to the expected passage of a revision of the Copyright Law in 1967] and their relevance to the average person in our society." (page xvii).

Chapter 4 is concerned with the invention of xerography and its impact upon the office copier field. Chapter 5 is concerned with "fair use" of copies by students and librarians. Chapter 6 is a discussion of several aspects of the concept of "fair use." Chapter 12 expresses views of various interested parties in the conflict between copyright and computerized storage, retrieval, and dissemination of information. Chapters 12, 13 and 14 discuss the efforts toward revision of the Copyright Law. Chapter 15 discusses permissions and payments, as related to some type of clearinghouse. Three appendixes relate to Chapter 15. An index is provided.

Graham, Gordon. U.K.'s Whitford Report: Faith, Hope, Clarity. *Publishers Weekly* **211(17): 49. April 25, 1977.**

A summary of that portion of the Whitford Committee's Report which pertains to reprography is presented. In addition to advocating a blanket licensing system, the Report makes no distinction between single and multiple machine copying. Photocopying for educational purposes would not be exempted from the licensing provisions that a new copyright law for the United Kingdom should contain.

Hattery, Lowell H. and George P. Bush, editors. *Reprography and Copyright Law.* **Arlington, Virginia: American Institute of Biological Sciences, 1964. 204 p.**

This book is derived from presentations at a symposium in 1963 sponsored by The American University, which explored the reprography-copyright problem, its varied interests, viewpoints, proposed solutions, and outlook. It includes a summary chapter, three appendixes, and a selected bibliography.

Heilprin, Laurence B., editor. *Copyright and Photocopying: Papers on Problems and Solutions, Design for a Clearinghouse, and a Bibliography,* **Student Contribution Series Number 10. College Park, Maryland: University of Maryland, 1977. 158 p.**

Of the three items in the compilation of student papers, two study and evaluate potential solutions to the problem of balancing the rights of users and owners of copyrighted material when this material is used in conjunction with photocopying equipment. The first essay summarizes and evaluates the range of possible solutions, while the second paper presents a detailed study of one possible solution: the private, nonprofit, voluntary copyright clearinghouse. The third entry in this collection provides an annotated, selected bibliography of items about photocopying of copyrighted works with a subsection devoted to documents relating to the *Williams & Wilkins* case.

Holroyd, Michael. The Wrongs of Copyright. *Library Journal* **101: 1081-1083. May 1, 1976.**

Many manuscripts needed by historians are not readily accessible because the private owner of the manuscripts remains anonymous or because the manuscripts have been sent to several libraries. The resolution of the problems associated with copying is the key to resolving most of the difficulties in dealing with manuscripts. Three recommendations are offered to help increase the dissemination of information in manuscript form: (1) a computerized index of English language manuscripts which lists information concerning the sale of the manuscripts, including information on the purchaser and the identity of the copyright holder (if known), should be established; (2) following the author's death, the burden of establishing copyright or conditions for copying should be transferred to the executors, whose names should be maintained in a register; and (3) firms that market photocopying equipment should pay an annual fee, to be distributed to authors.

Line, Maurice B. and D.N. Wood.   The Effect of a Large-Scale Photocopying Service on Journal Sales. *Journal of Documentation* **31: 234-245. December 1975.**

Although the volume of photocopying by the British Library Lending Division (BLLD) has increased greatly in recent years, there is no evidence that this photocopying has had an adverse effect on the sale of scholarly journals. It is true that British libraries are beginning to cancel journal subscriptions, but this is due in large part to the lack of money available to maintain journal collections. The journals being cancelled tend to be those for which the demand is small or those which have large circulations and libraries maintain multiple copies. Even if the activities of the BLLD were halted, there is no evidence that libraries could afford to subscribe to more journals. Although the BLLD maintains an extensive collection of journals, the copying it does is confined to a relatively small number of journals with large circulations and the number of copies of articles from issues still in print is small.

Nasri, William Z. *Crisis in Copyright.* **New York: Marcel Dekker, Inc., 1976. 174 p.**

The impact of reprography on subscriptions to scientific and technical journals is evaluated. Based on the results of a small survey of potential subscribers to the four journals involved in the *Williams & Wilkins* case, it is tentatively concluded that photocopying does not have a significant influence on a subscriber's decision to drop a journal subscription. Constraints on the user's time, as well as his budget limitations and narrowed interests, are the main reasons for dropping or reducing the number of subscriptions. In addition to this empirical study, chapters on trends in copying and on the economics of publishing primary journals are presented.

Parker, Mary Lou. Photocopying in University Libraries and the Canadian Law of Copyright. *APLA Bulletin* **32: 41-50. June 1968.**

A synopsis of copyright law and practice in Canada with comments and recommendations in view of the ease of copying, particularly by the Xerox process; spells out in detail the classes of libraries whose librarians may be permitted to copy.

Photocopying and the Law: A Guide for Librarians and Teachers and Other Suppliers and Users of Photocopies of Copyright Work. **Sydney, Australia: Australian Copyright Council, 1970. 7 p. (Available from ERIC Document Reproduction Service, Arlington, Virginia. Order No: ED-054 784.)**

Some possible uses to which the photocopying of copyrighted works can be put under the Copyright Act of 1968 are explored. The law, as interpreted by those who have used it, is not unduly restrictive. Nevertheless, there must be a limit on the unlicensed photocopying of copyrighted works.

Tallman, Johanna E. An Affirmative Statement on Copyright Debate. *Journal of the American Society for Information Science* **25: 145-150. May-June 1974.**

The proposition that it "shall not be considered a copyright infringement for research purposes to make copies of all or parts of publications when they resulted directly from work supported in whole or in part by the Government through grants, page charges, or other funding mechanisms" is supported. (page 145).

van Tongeren, E. The Effect of a Large-Scale Photocopying Service on Journal Sales. *Journal of Documentation* **32: 198-204. September 1976.**

This article is a reply to the article, "The Effect of a Large-Scale Photocopying Service on Journal Sales." (See abstract above.) That article, written by Maurice Line and D.N. Wood, asserted that the photocopying activities of the British Library Lending Division (BLLD) did not adversely affect subscriptions to scientific journals. The reply attempts to refute the conclusions of Messrs. Line and Wood, claiming that they were not specific enough and did not differentiate between the large scale circulation journals, which address a national audience and carry general articles, and small circulation journals which provide the "core" for reporting the results of advanced research. The author believes that the photocopying services rendered by the BLLD are causing the significant increase in cancellations of journal subscriptions by academic libraries. In a rebuttal following this reply (pp. 204-206), Messrs. Line and Wood claim that most academic libraries would agree that their journal cancellations have not been caused by the BLLD.

Weinberg, Louise.   The Photocopying Revolution and the Copyright Crisis. *The Public Interest* **38: 99-118. Winter 1975.**

Library photocopying services, such as the one at the National Library of Medicine and secondary services, such as *Current Contents* and MEDLINE, encourage users to photocopy articles instead of subscribing to the journals. It is argued in this article that "what may be fair use in the individual case may seem less so when advanced technology can multiply the transactions endlessly." (page 108). A royalty system for publishers is advocated.

Zaaiman, R.B.   Copyright and its Implications for Reprography. *South African Libraries* **44: 139-152. April 1977.**

Following a brief review of the history of copyright, the author outlines the provisions of the South African Copyright Act of 1965 which relate to library photocopying. Libraries in South Africa are classified by type such as libraries connected to universities, libraries which lend books to the public free of charge, and profit-making libraries. Each class must fulfill regulations issued pursuant to the law regarding photocopying. One of the problems with the current South African law is that it is based on the British law. Many technological developments, including the introduction of electrostatic photocopying and fast information services, have occurred since the drafting of the British law in the early 1950's. The South African law is undergoing revision. A suggestion is made that a separate law be passed which would deal solely with reprography.

D. VIDEO COMMUNICATIONS

This heading includes references primarily concerned with cable television (CATV) and videocopying. The sudden, rapid expansion of CATV had great impact upon the Copyright Law revision process. Recently, the exponential growth of the video cassette recorder market has created new conflict between users and owners of copyrighted works. References to the Copyright Royalty Tribunal, the duties of which include the distribution of royalty fees paid to the Copyright Office by cable operators, are included under section J. Permissions and Payments.

Other related references to this category can be found under Sections H. Education; I. Libraries, Networks, and Information Systems; K. Legislation/Legal; and L. International.

Selected Materials related to Video Communications will be found in Part II: **CRC SYSTEMS INCORPORATED,** *Impact of Information Technology on Copyright Law in the Use of Computerized Scientific and Technological Information Systems* (Section A.2.6); Susan C. Greene, *The Cable Television Provisions of the Revised Copyright Act;* Steven Brill, *Will Betamax Be Busted?*

Besen, Stanley M., Willard G. Manning, Jr., and Bridger M. Mitchell. Copyright Liability for Cable Television: Compulsory Licensing and the Coase Theorem. *The Journal of Law & Economics* **21: 67-95. April 1978.**

The essay uses a theorem developed by R.H. Coase which provides that "under certain circumstances, the allocation of resources in the economy is unaffected by the manner in which the rights to property are distributed" (page 79) and the "public-good" aspects to television programming to support the argument that signal importation will increase the revenue of program suppliers if cable systems are subject to full copyright liability rather than to the compulsory licensing scheme instituted under the 1976 Copyright Law. Because the compulsory license does not reflect the true value of the program to the consumer, the resultant revenues will be in many cases too low to provide the incentive necessary for program suppliers to produce new programs.

"Betamax" Trial Gets Underway: Judge Breaks Case into Three Separate Issues. *VideoNews* 9(3): 1. January 31, 1979.

A report on the beginning of the trial in the Betamax case is presented. The judge has defined three issues, each of which will evidently be tried separately. The issues are whether off-the-air recording of copyrighted television programs is infringement; if so, whether MCA's and Disney's charges are "valid as to their control of rights;" and whether antitrust is an issue in the litigation.

Bobbit, Philip C.   Cable Television and Copyright Royalties. *The Yale Law Journal* 83: 554-579. January 1974.

The position taken in this paper is that the courts should adopt an "outcome analysis" approach in determining copyright infringement in suits involving cable television operations. That is, the courts should consider the policy implications of their decisions. The author outlines some of the factual issues which would be relevant in determining copyright infringement.

Brill, Steven.   Will Betamax Be Busted? *Esquire* 89(11): 19-20,22. June 20. 1978.

This article presents a brief analysis of the issues in the Sony Betamax home video recording suit. The defense lawyers for Sony will use home taping of phonograph records as an analogy but the plaintiffs, Universal City Studios and Walt Disney Productions, contend that it is not clear that copying phonograph records is not an infringement. The defense claims that there is a "home use" exception which allows recording for private, home viewing. The plaintiffs refute that any home use exception appears in the copyright law. However, Sony is expected to rely heavily on a "public interest" defense. The judge will have a number of options even if Sony is found to have infringed. The author concludes that the law as currently written supports the plaintiffs' allegations.

de Freitas, Denis.   Audio Visual Systems. *Bulletin of the Copyright Society of the U.S.A.* 18: 304-312. April 1971.

An examination of the implications of the systems currently being developed in the United States, Europe and Japan, for recording and presenting via conventional television sets, combined sound and visual programs. Topics discussed: Areas of use; The recording right; Commercial recordings of television programs; Recording of Films; Specially produced AVRP (Audio

Visual Recording Presentation) programs; Contractual problems; The performing right.

Dreher, Nancy C. Community Antenna Television and Copyright Legislation. In *Copyright Law Symposium: Number Seventeen,* by the American Society of Composers, Authors and Publishers, pp. 102-132. New York: Columbia University Press, 1969.

This paper won fourth prize in the 29th Annual Nathan Burkan Competition. The principal topics are: The public policy to be served; The economics of the industries; and Proposed revision—a suggestion. The author presents a suggested solution to the problem previously mentioned: The legislation should be as flexible as possible; it must be less complex than heretofore presented; and, the several opposing interests need to be equitably balanced.

Gerlach, Gary G. Toward the Wired Society: Prospects, Problems, and Proposals for a National Policy on Cable Technology. *Maine Law Review* 25: 193-240. 1973.

This essay criticized the lack of planning in developing a national telecommunications policy, especially one that concerns the use of cable technology. It also proposes that a Presidential commission be appointed to study and design a blueprint for such a policy, and outlines the services which cable television can provide to promote the development of both rural and urban areas. It is observed that "the quibbling over who gets what distant signals or who gets copyright for how much has stolen valuable time and energy from the exploration of cable's larger promise for fundamental community service." (page 196).

Greene, Susan C. The Cable Television Provisions of the Revised Copyright Act. *Catholic University Law Review* 27: 263-303. Winter 1978.

Following a discussion of the major judicial decisions relating to secondary transmissions under the 1909 Copyright Act, the author reviews the FCC signal carriage rules, including the "syndicated exclusivity" rules, and the provisions of the 1976 Copyright Law governing copyright liability for secondary transmissions (Section 111). Possible conflicts in wording between the 1976 Copyright Act and the FCC rules pertaining to cable systems are outlined. The responsibilities of the Copyright Royalty Tribunal are also explained.

Introducing the "Computer Tele Journal". *Modern Data* 2: 58-60. **April 1969.**

The *Computer Tele Journal* (CTJ) is the first audio-visual trade magazine and will be published in the form of an Electronic Video Recording (EVR)—a film cartridge, designed for use with the CBS-developed attachment player, that makes possible the playing of high-resolution miniaturized film on any television set.

Jones, Joanne G.   Community Antenna Television versus Copyright Rights: An Unresolved Controversy. *Howard Law Journal* 16: 553-574. **Spring 1971.**

This article deals with the efforts of the courts, the Federal Communications Commission and the Congress in grappling with the problems involved in reconciling the conflicting interests between CATV systems and TV broadcasting systems and in attempting to solve the ultimate issues.

Jones, Peter.   UNESCO Home Dubbing Verdict: Urge Royalty Fee on Tape and Recorders. *Billboard* 90(40): 1,71. **October 7, 1978.**

An international meeting sponsored by UNESCO, the World Intellectual Property Organization, and the International Labor Organization was held in Paris from September 13-20, 1978, to consider the copyright problems associated with home audio and audiovisual recording. The conferees decided that a royalty on the recording equipment and on the blank tapes used for audio and audiovisual recording was the most efficient means of compensating the copyright owner of the material being recorded.

Kachigian, Mark.   The New Copyright Law and Cable Television, Interpretation and Implications. *Performing Arts Review* 7: 176-195. **1977.**

After a brief review of CATV under Federal Communications Commission regulations and under the 1909 Copyright Law, including a review of some of the major court decisions, the author describes the provisions of the 1976 Copyright Revision relating to cable television. The impact that the new law should have on cable operators is also discussed.

Kallal, Edward W., Jr.   Betamax and Infringement of Television Copyright. *Duke Law Journal* 1977: 1181-1218. **January 1977.**

Arguments are developed on both sides of the issue of whether the home recording of copyrighted television programs for private use should be considered an infringement of copyright. Through a review of the history of legislation concerning sound recordings and a review of the case law supporting an exemption for de minimus violations of copyright, the author favors an emerging corollary to fair use—the "home use exception." The author contends that the Congress reformulated its view of the economic impact factor in determining infringement. Under the traditional approach of determining infringement, the cumulative economic effect on the copyright was taken into account. The Congress' intent under the 1976 law is to only measure the individual impact on the value of the copyright. In presenting the opposing arguments for a determination of copyright infringement for non-commercial, home video recording, the author reviews the CATV cases.

Keane, J. Timothy. **The Cable Compromise: Integration of Federal Copyright and Telecommunications Policies.** *St. Louis University Law Journal* 17: 340-354. **Spring 1973.**

The contention of this article is that the courts have not provided a balance among the competing interests of the cable television operators, the broadcast stations and networks, and the copyright owners, and that the decisions have tended to undermine the copyright holders. Much of the essay concentrates on the emergence of a judicial definition of "performance" as that concept relates to cable operations. The article briefly examines the cable compromise worked out by the Federal Communications Commission and the President's Office of Telecommunications Policy.

Krasnow, Erwin G. and John C. Quale. **Developing Legal Issues in Cable Communications.** *Catholic University Law Review* 24: 677-691. **Summer 1975.**

This article serves as an introduction to the symposium, Developing Legal Issues in Cable Communications. "To provide a fuller understanding of the issues addressed by the symposium, this article discusses recent governmental actions and pending proposals for regulation of cable television in three key areas. These areas are regarded by many cable television operators as capable of making or breaking the industry in the 1970's—copyright, pay cable, and state regulation." (page 679).

Larsen, Brent A. **Narrowing the Scope of the Copyright Act:** *Twentieth Century Music Corp. v. Aiken. Utah Law Review* 1975: 752-765. **Fall 1975.**

This article presents a criticism of the "functional" analysis approach relied upon in deciding *Aiken* and the CATV cases and proposes a two-part test for determining copyright infringement in cases like *Aiken, Fortnightly,* and *Teleprompter.* The first part of the test involves determining whether the retransmission of a broadcast constitutes a performance. Rather than determining whether a performance has occurred on the basis of how the equipment functions, the court should examine the potential economic impact of the conduct in question on the value of the copyright. If the court determines that a performance has occurred, it should then consider whether there is a license implied-at-law which would allow the party to perform the material in question without infringement liability.

Lipper, Jerome.   The Congress, The Court, and the Commissioners: A Legacy of *Fortnightly.*   *New York University Law Review* **44: 521-539. May 1969.**

This article concerns relations among copyright owners, broadcasters, community television (CATV) operators, and the public. Mr. Lipper enumerates the elements necessary to balance copyright and communications policies and emphasizes the importance of early congressional action. The headings comprise: (I) *Fortnightly* Revisited; (II) The Proposed Regulations; (III) Validity of the Proposed Rules; (IV) Validity of Customer Restriction Provisions; and (V) Conclusions. The author's proposal to balance the competing interests involved is stated on page 539.

Magnetic Video Plans to Propose VCR Industry Anti-Piracy Effort. *VideoNews* **8(18): 6. August 30, 1978.**

A procedure for encoding video tapes so that they cannot be copied illegally is described.

Meyer, Gerald.   The Feat of Houdini or How the New Act Disentangles the CATV-Copyright Knot. *New York Law School Law Review* **22: 545-571. 1977.**

Following a brief review of the background of copyright legislation regarding CATV, the author outlines the provisions of the new Copyright Law relating to secondary transmissions.. Those transmissions exempted from a compulsory license and copyright liability and those secondary transmissions subject to compulsory licensing are indicated. The basic formula for determining the royalty payment is provided, as is an example of the way in which the formula is applied. It is noted that small cable systems are provided certain considerations which lessen their financial burden regarding royalty payments. The discussion also covers the way in which the Copyright Law and the Federal Communications Commission's regulations interface, the function of the Copyright Royalty Tribunal, and the remedies provided for infringement.

Meyer, Gerald. The Nine Myths of CATV. *Federal Bar Journal* 27: 431-450. Fall 1967.

The author is a partner in the law firm which represented the plaintiff in the copyright test case, *United Artists Television, Inc. v. Fortnightly Corporation.* In this article he presents eight myths which over the years have grown up around the CATV controversy. These myths, pro and con, "are affirmed by their followers with great earnestness and zeal, an attitude which has been maintained in defiance of scientific, technical and economic evidence to the contrary." (page 431).

Oney, Steve. The Videodiscs: TV Goes on the Record. *The Washington Post* 102(20): D1, D16. December 25, 1978.

A brief description of the videodisc player is presented. The article notes that the videodisc player is functionally different from the video cassette recorder (VCR) in that the videodisc player cannot record. The author feels that the MCA-Universal company's suit against VCR manufacturers might have delayed the introduction of its videodisc player which is only now being test marketed.

Popham, James J. The 1971 Consensus Agreement: The Perils of Unkept Promises. *Catholic University Law Review* 24: 813-832. Summer 1975.

The complaint voiced in this article is that the cable television industry has not abided by the provisions of the 1971 Consensus Agreement as adopted by representatives of the broadcast, cable, and copyright interests and as subsequently adopted by the Federal Communications Commission (FCC). The author claims that the FCC has not enforced the copyright liability provisions of the Consensus on the cable television industry, while at the same time CATV is benefiting from the liberalized signal carriage provisions agreed to by the broadcast industry under the Consensus.

Schlafly, Hubert J. CATV, Information and Communications Policy. In *Copyright and Related Protections for Information Age Products.*

Proceedings and Related Documents of the Meeting of the Information Industry Association Held at Airlie House, Virginia on July 18 and 19, 1969, pp. 53-61. Bethesda, Maryland: Information Industry Association, 1969.

This talk concerns the relationship of CATV with the so-called "information explosion." Of particular interest are seven declarative statements, appearing on pages 60-61, which are in the nature of predictions or assumptions relative to the field. For example: "1. I am optimistic about a copyright settlement, although possibly not in time to pass this session of the Congress. When it comes, I think many of the regulatory problems will fall into place as side issues of the copyright question." (page 60).

Seiden, M.H. & Associates, Inc. *The Economic Impact of the Proposed Copyright Law upon Educational Television Broadcasters.* A report to Educational Television Stations, a division of the National Association of Educational Broadcasters. Washington. April 1967. 20 p.

"The proposed copyright law will have a far reaching effect upon the organization and character of educational broadcasting. This effect will flow from the costs of copyright clearance and the effect which these costs will have upon the sources and content of educational programs." Includes: cost components; administrative costs; the process of copyright clearance; copyright fees; summary of costs; structural impact of proposed law. Eight tables.

Smith, E. Stratford.   CATV—A Tainted Virgin? *Federal Bar Journal* 27: 451-480. Fall 1967.

This paper is a synthesis of the arguments contained in the briefs filed by the defendant in *United Artists Television, Inc., v. Fortnightly Corporation,* and in its petition for review in the U.S. Supreme Court, September 15, 1967. " . . . the Congress . . . is the only body in our legal system equipped to tailor the law to balance the interests of the copyright proprietors and the CATV operators to protect and achieve the public interest." (page 480).

Smith, R.H.   New Copyright Challenge to Cable Television. *Publishers Weekly* 200(15): 40. October 11, 1971.

A brief report and comment on the case *Columbia Broadcasting System et al. vs. Teleprompter Corporation,* the issue being whether cable television is subject to the payment of performance royalties.

Tewlow, Jules S. Exploring the Way to CATV Publishing. *Book Production Industry* **46: 42-45. November 1970.**

Cable television is already a publishing medium carrying original programming. No one knows for certain how important it will become. A leading communications specialist examines what publishers stand to gain or lose.

Wallace, William. Impact of New Technology on International Copyright and Neighboring Rights. *Bulletin of the Copyright Society of the U.S.A.* **18: 293-303. April 1971.**

This talk deals with two principal subjects: (1) The dissemination of copyrighted works by means of computers (beginning on page 294) and (2) The impact on international copyright of the communication satellite (beginning on page 299). In the first instance much of the discussion concerns fair use (in Britain termed "fair dealing"). In the second instance emphasis is placed on broadcasting, TV, CATV, and the Rome Convention. The author points out that other disseminators raise problems, such as cassettes, phonograms and reprography.

Warren, Albert. The Coming Cable TV War. *Saturday Review* **49(24): 90, 93, 101. June 11, 1966.**

"But CATV has possibilities that make AT&T uncomfortable. With its potentially unlimited access to homes, what's to stop CATV from providing many services other than TV? Facsimile newspapers? Shopping from the home? Library references? Channels of background music? Telegrams? Mail delivery? Maybe—who knows—telephone service itself, not only aural, but visual?" (page 101).

"Presumably, copyright holder [of TV programs] could exert powerful forces on the development of CATV—granting or withholding distribution rights." (page 101).

E. MICROFORMS

It has been said by Arthur E. Gardner, in speaking of the future of the printing industry, that "The names of the game, as they say, will be electronics and computerization, information storage and retrieval, micrographics, data transmission, electrostatics, and all of the other so-called 'buzz-words' now buzzing around."* Micrographics as used in this context consist of: microforms, microbooks, micropublishing, readers and reader-printers. Some lesser references may be found in C. Reprography; and I. Libraries, Networks, and Information Systems.

No Selected Materials in Part II relate primarily to Microforms. However, reference may be found in CRC SYSTEMS INCORPO-RATED, *Impact of Information Technology on Copyright Law in the Use of Computerized Scientific and Technological Information Systems* (Section A.2.7), and in Madeline Henderson, *Copyright Impacts of Future Technology.*

----

*The Future Isn't What it Used to Be. In *Proceedings of the ASIS Workshop on Computer Composition,* edited by Robert M. Landau, p. 5. Washington: American Society for Information Science, 1970.

Deutsch, Alvin.   Microfilm Copyright Problems. *Microfiche Foundation Newsletter* 27: 3-10. March 1974.

The micropublisher faces two problems when microreproducing copyrighted works on an international level: (1) obtaining permission from the copyright owner to create a microform edition and (2) international piracy of the microform edition itself. Both of these issues are examined and potential solutions are offered. An international clearinghouse system is proposed for administering and distributing payments from micropublishers to copyright proprietors.

Montagnes,   Ian.   Publishing   the   Pre-Shrunk. *Publishers Weekly* 200(21): 13-15. November 22, 1971.

The University of Toronto Press issues its books simultaneously in hard copy and microfiche. The decision to publish on microfiche rested primarily on three factors: (1) information will increase faster than available library shelving space needed for books; (2) the acceptance of microfiche in North America; and (3) the greater efficiency of using microfiche over using microfilm for research involving books rather than serials, such as newspapers. The use of reader-printers to make inexpensive hard copies of the projected page and the availability of printers which can reproduce the microfiche itself could erode the author's or publisher's copyright protection.

Powell, David J. **The Law of Copyright in Relation to Publications on Microfilm.** *MICRODOC* 13(2): 34-37. 1974.

The 1956 British Copyright Act does not specifically refer to microfilm. This article examines several areas which will require clarification in future legislation, including the status of microfilms of copyrighted works, the copyright status of the microfilm itself (e.g., the question of whether the organization of the images on the microfilm can be copyrighted), requirements for the legal deposit of microfilms, requirements for the legal deposit of paper copies produced from microfilm, and fair dealing and educational uses of microfilm.

Williams, Bernard J. S. **Microforms in Information Retrieval and Communication Systems.** *Aslib Proceedings* 19: 223-231. July 1967.

"I intend in this paper to draw attention to microform developments likely to have a substantial influence on library and communication technology in the near future. The major microforms at present in use, or coming into use, and their areas of application are as follows: 16mm roll . . ., 35mm roll . . ., aperture cards . . ., microfiches . . ., micro opaques . . ., PCMI . . ., 8mm roll . . ., 70mm roll . . ., magnetic tape . . ."

F. CONTU

The congressional mandate to the National Commission on New Technological Uses of Copyrighted Works (CONTU) was to study and compile data on the use of copyrighted works in conjunction with computer and machine reproduction systems, and to recommend to the Congress any changes required in the Copyright Law to ensure a proper balance between the rights of owners and users of copyrighted works which are used in conjunction with these technologies.

This section forms a bridge between the previous sections which concentrated on processes and on the technological aspects of copyright, and the following sections which are primarily concerned with areas that are affected by and which use these technologies and processes, e.g., libraries, educational institutions, and copyright payment centers. Under this section are references to the transcripts of the hearings held by CONTU, the reports issued by the Commission, and one item written about the Commission.

Unless otherwise indicated, the author of the items referenced below is CONTU. Lesser references to CONTU appear in Sections B. Computer Systems and K. Legislation/Legal.

Selected Material related to CONTU's work will be found in Part II: John Hersey, *Dissent from CONTU's Software Recommendation.* Other items appearing in Part II which were prepared in whole or in part under CONTU's sponsorship are Yale M. Braunstein et al., *Economics of Property Rights as Applied to Computer Software and Data Bases* (Overview of Issues); King Research, Inc., *Library Photocopying in the United States: With Implications for the Development of a Copyright Royalty Payment Mechanism* (Summary); and Bernard Fry et al., *Survey of Publisher Practices and Present Attitudes on Authorized Journal Article Copying and Licensing* (Project Background and Summary of Findings).

TRANSCRIPTS

Editor's Note: There were 24 meetings of CONTU, 21 of which are cited below. The transcripts of meetings 22, 23, and 24 were not available when this book went to press. Meetings 22 and 23 included discussion among the Commissioners on the content and wording of the *Final Report,* while Meeting 24 was a ceremonial closing of CONTU's business.

Meetings 1 through 5. **October 1975 through April 1976. 113 p. (Available from National Technical Information Service, Springfield, Virginia. Order No: PB-253 757).**

A summary of the Commission's first five meetings is presented. The first session defined the scope of the Commission's work, the procedures to be followed in conducting its business, and its operating budget. At the second meeting the commissioners heard from an ad hoc committee appointed at the first meeting. That committee was charged with outlining the issues to be studied relating to photocopying. The third, fourth, and fifth sessions were devoted to educating the commissioners on the technologies and issues involved in CONTU's areas of responsibility.

Meeting Number 6. **May 1976. 186 p. (Available from National Technical Information Service, Springfield, Virginia. Order No: PB-254 765).**

The sixth session was primarily concerned with copyright protection for computer software. Among the questions the witnesses were requested to address were whether computer programs should be copyrightable, whether the type of protection should vary according to the nature of the program, what constitutes the copying of a program, whether more protection than is available for programs under the present (1909) law should be provided, how additional protection could be granted to computer programs without causing the monopolization of ideas, and whether increased copyright protection would increase sales and decrease reliance on restrictive licensing agreements.

Meeting Number 7. **June 1976. 225 p. (Available from National Technical Information Service, Springfield, Virginia. Order No: PB-254 766).**

After a brief discussion of how to approach the problem of establishing photocopying guidelines for libraries under Section 108(g)(2) of S. 22, the Copyright Revision Bill, the Commission continued to hear testimony on the protection of computer software.

Meeting Number 8. **September 1976. 367 p. (Available from National Technical Information Service, Springfield, Virginia. Order No: PB-259 749).**

The commissioners heard testimony relating to the protection of information contained in data bases. Some of the recommendations received pertained to controlling output. Works created by computer and the problems associated with data base and program security were also discussed. The Commission continued its refinement of the guidelines pertaining to interlibrary arrangements under Section 108(g)(2) of the 1976 Revision.

Meeting Number 9. **October 1976. 227 p. (Available from National Technical Information Service, Springfield, Virginia. Order No: PB-261 947).**

Testimony concentrated on centralized systems and networks for photocopying and distributing periodical articles through interlibrary loans. Among the witnesses were Vernon Palmour, who reported on a study investigating the feasibility of establishing a three-tiered national periodicals system, and representatives of libraries that do significant amounts of photocopying in furtherance of interlibrary loan programs.

Meeting Number 10. **November 1976. 197 p. (Available from National Technical Information Service, Springfield, Virginia. Order No: PB-261 946).**

The first day of this two-day meeting was devoted to the question of whether computer programs should be eligible for copyright protection. In addition to feeling that computer programs should be protected, Mr. Daniel McCracken, the only witness on the first day, believed that there should be protection against the unauthorized use of computer programs. During the second day, the commissioners heard the reports of the Commission's subcommittees. The subcommittee considering copyright protection for computer software felt that programs could be accommodated within the framework of the 1976 law and did not merit a separate chapter or statute. One member of the subcommittee considering copyright protection for computer data bases offered his personal suggestion concerning the extent to which copyright protection should be afforded computer data bases. The subcommittee on photocopying outlined its desire to hold hearings on devices which can be incorporated into photocopying machines to determine the type of photocopying occurring and to hear testimony regarding clearinghouse proposals.

Meeting Number 11. **January 1977. 289 p. (Available from National Technical Information Service, Springfield, Virginia. Order No: PB-263 160).**

Meeting number 11 was devoted to a discussion of the clearinghouse solution to photocopying that goes beyond fair use. Such a solution would involve copy satisfaction centers or royalty payments and distribution centers. A witness from the National Technical Information Service (NTIS) testified about a proposal to establish a copy satisfaction clearinghouse within NTIS for articles from selected periodicals. This proposal was opposed by other witnesses who favored a clearinghouse run by the private sector. The thrust of their argument was that the government should only become involved in situations where the private sector is unable or unwilling.

Meeting Number 12. **February 1977. 193 p. (Available from National Technical Information Service, Springfield, Virginia. Order No: PB-265 765).**

The Commission heard from its subcommittees concerned with software, data bases, and photocopying. The discussion of the Software Subcommittee concentrated on the issue of whether computer programs should come under the Copyright Statute or should be protected by other means, if at all. Members of the Data Base Subcommittee felt that the 1976 Copyright Law adequately covered data bases, although they did indicate that recommendations should be made concerning the deposit of data bases with the Copyright Office. Finally, a question was raised by a member of the Photocopying Subcommittee concerning the possibility that it would be more economical for a user to pay for every copy of a periodical article than to keep records of which copies fall within the exemptions provided by the fair use and library photocopying provisions of the 1976 Copyright Law.

Meeting Number 13. **April 1977. 347 p. (Available from National Technical Information Service, Springfield, Virginia. Order No: PB-266 277).**

The first day of this two-day session concentrated on a discussion of payment clearinghouses. Charles Lieb, counsel for the Association of American Publishers, testified on the proposed structure and function of the Copyright Clearance Center whose initial membership would be composed primarily of technical-scientific-medical journal publishers. The Clearance Center would provide payments to publishers from users who photocopy beyond the limits of the fair use or the library photocopying provisions of the 1976 Copyright Act. Bernard Korman and Edward Cramer testified on the operation of the music clearinghouses ASCAP and BMI, respectively. On the second day of this session Ed Brown, president of the Newsletter Association of America, testified on the economic effects of photocopying on newsletter publishers. Mr. Brown recommended that newsletters be exempted from the Copyright Act's fair use provisions, except for non-profit users, e.g., students. Finally, the Commission heard testimony from Allen Ferguson, president of the Public Interest Economic Center, who argued that the greater the royalties paid to producers of information, e.g., authors, the greater is their incentive to produce; the availability of existing information to consumers, however, will decrease.

Meeting Number 14. **May 1977. 117 p. (Available from National Technical Information Service, Springfield, Virginia. Order No: PB-267 332).**

The draft reports of CONTU's Software and Data Base Subcommittees were discussed. Commissioner John Hersey disagreed with the Software Subcommittee's recommendation that programs be eligible for copyright as are any other written descriptions of a process. Mr. Hersey's contention was that the programs are part of the mechanical process of the computer and are, therefore, not works of authorship subject to copyright protection. The discussion on data bases centered on the deposit requirements specified in the Copyright Law. The Photocopying Subcommittee presented an oral report on its activities. It recommended that the Subcommittee foster discussion among interested parties who want some of the provisions of Section 108 of the new Copyright Law clarified.

Meeting Number 15. **July 1977. 270 p. (Available from National Technical Information Service, Springfield, Virginia. Order No: PB-271 326).**

The findings of several studies on photocopying, computer software, and computer data bases are reviewed. Among the studies reviewed were an updated Palmour study the purpose of which was to determine the point at which it becomes more economical for a library to subscribe to a journal than to "borrow" through interlibrary loan; a new report by the Indiana University Graduate School of Library Science which surveyed the present practices and attitudes of research and scholarly journal publishers regarding the supplying of copies of journal articles; and the results of an investigation by the Public Interest Economics Center (PIE-C) which studied copyright relating to computer software, computer data bases, and photocopying from the perspective of the ultimate consumer. PIE-C concluded that there should be no royalties for photocopying not for resale and that there should be royalty charges for using computer software and data bases.

Meeting Number 16. **September 1977. 362 p. (Available from National Technical Information Service, Springfield, Virginia. Order No: PB-273 594).**

Witnesses gave testimony on the preliminary reports drafted by CONTU's Data Base and Software Subcommittees. Although most of the testimony favored the conclusions of the reports, dissenting viewpoints (especially concerning the Software Report) are presented, as are suggested modifications to the Subcommittees' preliminary recommendations. Appended to the testimony are the reports of the Data Base and Software Subcommittees and any additional views offered by the commissioners. Commissioner Hersey's detailed dissent from the Software Report is also included. During the second day of this session, CONTU heard testimony on the findings of the study on library photocopying done by King Research, Inc., along with a description of a study being conducted by University Microfilms involving a mechanized method of accounting for copies made of journal articles which are on microfiche. The mechanism could be used to automatically determine royalty payments owed to copyright owners.

Meeting Number 17. **October 1977. 281 p. (Available from National Technical Information Service, Springfield, Virginia. Order No: PB-275 786).**

The views of library, author, and publisher groups on Section 108 (the library reproduction section) of the 1976 Copyright Law were heard. Although disagreeing as to the meaning and applicability of the law, all three groups agreed that CONTU should not make any recommendations to the Congress for changes in the law. However, the publisher and author representatives did favor CONTU's assistance in bringing the three groups together to establish further photocopying guidelines, in addition to those already promulgated for interlibrary arrangements. Testimony was also heard from the Institute for Scientific Information (ISI) and from the National Technical Information Service (NTIS) on their journal article fulfillment programs and from Mr. Ben Weil on progress toward establishing the Copyright Clearance Center (CCC). Among the items appended to the testimony are two handbooks (one for serial publishers and one for organizational users) which describe the procedures for using the CCC.

Meeting Number 18. **November 1977. 171 p. (Available from National Technical Information Service, Springfield, Virginia. Order No: PB-278 329).**

Included in this meeting are a panel discussion on the future of computer technology and an analysis of potential copyright problems created by these advances in technology. The second session of the meeting examined a survey of firms producing software. The purpose of the survey was to ascertain opinions on the effectiveness of various types of legal protection for computer software.

Meeting Number 19. **January 1978. 217 p. (Available from National Technical Information Service, Springfield, Virginia. Order No: PB-280 052).**

Most of the nineteenth meeting was devoted to reviewing the reports and findings of the Software, Data Base, and Photocopying Subcommittees. However, one witness from the field of chip technology was heard. He argued in favor of copyright protection for the layout of chips, protection that the Copyright Office had refused to recognize. The appendixes to this session include a statement prepared by the Association of American Publishers and the Authors League outlining their own guidelines for permissible photocopying by corporate libraries, and two documents prepared by the Special Libraries Association and the Medical Library Association, respectively, concerning the sections of the 1976 law relating to library photocopying.

Meeting Number 20. **February 1978. 171 p. (Available from National Technical Information Service, Springfield, Virginia. Order No: PB-283 876).**

The commissioners heard testimony in support of copyright protection for computer software and on the progress of the Copyright Clearance Center during its first month of operation. The Commission also considered the Photocopying and Software Subcommittee Reports, and adopted the Data Base Subcommittee Report. The discussion of the Photocopying Subcommittee Report focused on the copying done by "photocopying mills" and the need for legislation pertaining to this type of for-profit photocopying. The use of the term "adaptation" with respect to modifying a program for use on a machine other than the one for which the program was created was the central topic of discussion during the Commission's review of the Software Subcommittee Report.

Meeting Number 21. **April 1978. 198 p. (Available from National Technical Information Service, Springfield, Virginia. Order No: PB-281 710).**

The testimony and discussion on the first day of this two-day session focused on the Photocopying Subcommittee's Report. One of the concerns expressed by the witnesses was the Report's recommendation that some application of fair use be applied to commercial copiers but not to a National Periodicals Center. There is also a need for a definition of systematic photocopying. On the second day the full Commission discussed the report of the New Works Subcommittee which recommended, in part, that copyright be available to a product of a computer if the programmer had the end work in mind when creating the program. The Commission also approved the Software Subcommittee Report which recommended that computer programs be eligible for copyright.

REPORTS

Dix, William S., John Hersey, and Dan Lacy. *The Photo-Copying Issue.* Washington: National Commission on New Technological Uses of Copyrighted Works, 1975. 25 p. (Unpublished).

This early statement by three members of the Commission attempts to narrow the areas of controversy by "indicating areas of agreement and disagreement" among the concerned parties, primarily libraries and publishers. The Commission is presented with potential questions which it should investigate and offered possible solutions worthy of consideration. A brief background of the photocopying issue is also presented.

National Commission on New Technological Uses of Copyrighted Works. *Final Report of the National Commission on New Technological Uses of Copyrighted Works.* Washington: National Commission on New Technological Uses of Copyrighted Works, July 31, 1978. 365 p. (Available from National Technical Information Service, Springfield, Virginia. Order No: PB-284 141).

This is the culmination of three years of work by the Commission. The mission of CONTU was to recommend to the President and to the Congress changes needed in the copyright law to more effectively balance the rights of creators and users of copyrighted works used in conjunction with computers and machine reproduction (i.e., photocopying). Related to these concerns were the matters of the copyrightability of computer software and new works created with the assistance of a computer. Although no significant changes were recommended in the current law, the Commission does recommend repealing the current Section 117 and enacting a new Section 117 limiting the exclusive rights of copyright in computer programs. Of special interest is the eloquent and well-reasoned dissent of Commissioner Hersey from the Commission's recommendation that computer software be given copyright protection. The section of the Report on machine reproduction reviews the numerous studies and reports that have been issued concerning photocopying, specifically library photocopying.

National Commission on New Technological Uses of Copyrighted Works. *Preliminary Report.* Washington: National Commission on New

Technological Uses of Copyrighted Works, October 8, 1976. 55 p. (Available from National Technical Information Service, Springfield, Virginia. Order No: PB-260 373).

A review of CONTU's first-year activities and proposed research plan is presented. The report outlines the Commission's initial hearings on the copyrightability of computer software and CONTU's role in developing photocopying guidelines for interlibrary arrangements. The statute creating the Commission, brief biographical sketches of the commissioners, a list of witnesses who appeared before the Commission and the topics on which they spoke, CONTU's research plan and proposed timetable, and the photocopying guidelines in support of interlibrary arrangements are appended.

ARTICLE

Keplinger, Michael S. and Robert W. Frase. Role of CONTU in Computers and Photocopying. *IEEE Transactions on Professional Communication* PC-20: 167-170. November 1977.

The legislative history and the purpose of establishing the National Commission on New Technological Uses of Copyrighted Works (CONTU) are discussed. The role of CONTU's subcommittees on software, computer-created works, data bases, and photocopying is outlined. In addition to describing its participation in formulating guidelines with respect to receiving copies of articles through interlibrary arrangements, the authors briefly describe various studies relating to photocopying which are being conducted under CONTU's auspices. In the discussion following the article, Mr. Frase gives his reasons for his opinion that the photocopying practices of the National Institutes of Health and the National Library of Medicine as presented in the *Williams & Wilkins* case would be in violation of the 1976 law.

G. FAIR USE

The judicially developed criteria for determining whether a particular use of a copyrighted work is fair was incorporated, almost unaltered, into the 1976 Copyright Law. The criteria are "(1) the purpose and character of the use . . . ; (2) the nature of the copyrighted work; (3) the amount and substantiality of the portion used in relation to the copyrighted work as a whole; and (4) the effect of the use upon the potential market for or value of the copyrighted work." Related references may be found in Sections A. Technology; B. Computer Systems; C. Reprography; F. CONTU; H. Education; I. Libraries, Networks, and Information Systems; J. Permissions and Payments; K. Legislation/Legal; and L. International.

Selected Materials related to Fair Use will be found in Part II: Stephen Freid, *Fair Use and the New Act*; and *Williams & Wilkins Company v. The United States*.

Freid, Stephen.   Fair Use and the New Act. *New York Law School Law Review* 22: **497-519. 1977.**

The two most important criteria in determining whether a use of a copyrighted work is fair are the purpose of the use and the economic effect of the use on the copyrighted work. When the economic effect is not detrimental to the copyright owner and the purpose of the use is positive, or, if there is a detrimental economic effect and the purpose of the use is not particularly beneficial to society, the courts have an easy task in determining fair use. It is when these two factors are at odds where the courts have the more difficult task of balancing the benefits to the user with the rights of the copyright owner. The *Williams & Wilkins* case should have been an example of the latter situation. However, the Court of Claims determined that the publishing firm had not shown any actual economic damage and that the use did advance medicine and medical research. This article suggests that to recover statutory damages the copyright owner need only show that the probable economic effect of the use is detrimental to sales. Judicial decisions are used to support this contention. The author feels the 1976 Copyright Act retains this flexibility when determining economic effect.

The Gentlemen's Agreement of 1935. In *Reprography and Copyright Law,* edited by Lowell H. Hattery and George P. Bush, pp. 157-158. Arlington, Virginia: American Institute of Biological Sciences, 1964.

This is a statement of agreement, signed by Robert C. Binkley and W. W. Norton, representing respectively the Joint Committee on Materials For Research and the National Association of Book Publishers, concerned with the growing use of photographic methods of reproduction. Reference is made to an article by Jackson S. Saunders: "Origin of the 'Gentlemen's Agreement' of 1935" which is listed in the present bibliography.

Harvell, Michael C.   Copyright—Fair Use—Government Photocopying of Medical Journals Does Not Infringe Journal Copyright. *Boston University Law Review* 54: 689-701. May 1974.

The Court of Claims in *Williams & Wilkins* is criticized for placing on the defendant the burden of proving substantial financial injury by unauthorized photocopying and for not allowing the plaintiff to take the loss of licensing revenue into account in proving financial harm. It is argued that "such an approach alters the traditional focus of the copyright law from protection of the [copyright] holder's financial interests to a balancing test which weighs the potential harm to science of infringement liability against the harm to the holder [of copyright] of infringement. Such an alteration is within the orbit of congressional, rather than judicial, responsibility." (page 701).

Lieb, Charles H.   The Computer and Copyright: The Next Five Years. *Bulletin of the Copyright Society of the U.S.A.* 15: 13-18. October 1967.

The author seeks to correlate the interests and needs of producers of works of authorship with those who want to use them in the computer for education, scholarship and research. In his words: "The question before us is how to reconcile the present need of the publisher to control the computer use of his copyrighted work beyond existing standards of fair use with the need asserted by educators and others for broad computer rights." (page 16).

Marquis, John C.   Conscience vs. Copyright. *America* 119: 326-27. October 12, 1968.

A sort of homily and plea to copyists to abide by the doctrine of "fair use." Several examples are invoked from various fields of endeavor in an attempt to get the copyist to weigh the act in the scales of his own conscience.

McCormick, Marilyn G., compiler. *The Williams & Wilkins Case: The Williams & Wilkins Company v. The United States,* **Volume One. New York: Science Associates/International, Inc., 1974. 275 p.**

The first section of this book contains those documents which are part of the record of *Williams & Wilkins* in the United States Court of Claims. The first document is the Report of Commissioner James F. Davis to the Court of Claims favoring the Williams & Wilkins Company's copyright infringement claim. Others, in chronological order, are the Defendant's Exceptions to the Commissioner's Report, the defendant's and plaintiff's briefs, and the *Amicus Curiae* briefs of those associations which maintain an interest in the outcome of the suit. The first part concludes with the decision rendered by the full United States Court of Claims, rejecting the conclusions of the Commissioner's report. The second part presents, in chronological order, those documents filed before the United States Supreme Court. Included are the plaintiff's Petition for *Writ of Certiorari*, the *Amicus Curiae* briefs of the associations which favored granting the Petition, and the Brief for the United States in Opposition.

Nimmer, Melville B. **Photocopying and Record Piracy: Of Dred Scott and Alice in Wonderland.** *UCLA Law Review* 22: **1052-1065. June 1975.**

Of special interest is the first half of this article. Professor Nimmer criticizes the opinion of the Court of Claims in the *Williams & Wilkins* case in which the Court of Claims relied upon the publisher's ability (or lack of ability) to show actual damages. The issue should have been whether the photocopying practices of the defendant would hurt Williams & Wilkins' potential market. The author reviewed the Supreme Court's split decision upholding the Court of Claims decision. He provides evidence to indicate on which side of the issue Justice Blackmun, the nonvoting justice in this case, would fall in a subsequent photocopying case.

Passano, William M. **How Photocopying Pollutes Sci-Tech Publishing.** *Publishers Weekly* 197(5): 63-64. February 2, 1970.

An account of the Williams & Wilkins Co. suit against the United States involving the National Library of Medicine and the National Institutes of Health, charging infringement of copyright by making photocopies of articles which appear in journals published by the Williams & Wilkins Co.

Perlman, Harvey S. and Laurens H. Rhinelander. *Williams & Wilkins Co v. United States:* **Photocopying, Copyright, and the Judicial Process. In *The**

Supreme Court Review, 1975, **edited by Philip B. Kurland, pp. 355-417. Chicago: University of Chicago Press, 1976.**

The history of the copyright-photocopying controversy and the failure of both the courts and the Congress to resolve that controversy are reviewed. The essay also describes and analyzes the functions of copyright, discusses the origin and judicial development and use of the fair use doctrine, and examines the unfair competition cases which provide an analogy for the fair use controversy presented in *Williams & Wilkins.* It is concluded that the copyright-photocopying controversy should be resolved by the Congress, not by the courts, because the exclusive right to copy was a congressional grant to copyright owners.

Pforzheimer, Walter.   Historical Perspective on Copyright Law and Fair Use. In *Reprography and Copyright Law,* **edited by Lowell H. Hattery and George P. Bush, pp. 18-35. Arlington, Virginia: American Institute of Biological Sciences, 1964.**

A short study of the background of the U.S. Copyright Law and a notation of the steps in its development to 1964 is presented.

Photocopying and Fair Use: An Examination of the Economic Factor in Fair Use. *Emory Law Journal* **26: 849-884. Fall 1977.**

The traditional method of interpreting the fair use doctrine is critically examined. Using the traditional approach courts will normally consider the fair use defense if the use promotes learning rather than advance primarily commercial ends. Although the essay agrees that the economic criterion is the most important in establishing whether a particular use is fair, it argues that the party claiming infringement should have to show actual economic injury rather than presumed economic harm. If the First Amendment right to receive information is applied to copyright, then the copyright holder must prove economic harm before the use of the copyrighted material could be restricted.

Rosenfield, Harry N.   The Constitutional Dimension of "Fair Use" in Copyright Law. *Notre Dame Lawyer* **50: 790-807. June 1975.**

The thesis of the article is that fair use is protected by the First and Ninth Amendments of the U.S. Constitution, whereas copyright protection is statutorily conferred on its holder. "Since copyright conveys only a statutory privilege while fair use enjoys constitutional protection, the burden

of proof must shift from the alleged infringer to the alleger of infringement."
(page 807).

Rosenfield, Harry N.   Customary Use as "Fair Use" in Copyright Law.
Buffalo Law Review **25: 119-140. Fall 1975.**

This article suggests that for non-commercial research and educational uses
the doctrine of fair use rests on custom and should not depend on statutory
provisions. Considering customary use as fair use would create greater
stability in the law than judging each case of alleged infringement on the
four criteria listed in the Revision Bill. Under a doctrine of customary use,
the question of whether a particular use had a detrimental economic effect
on the copyright owner would be irrelevant. However, the criteria for
determining fair use, as enumerated in the Revision Bill, should be applicable
to commerical interests. This thesis is supported with passages from cases
and other relevant literature.

Saunders, Jackson S.   Origin of the "Gentlemen's Agreement" of 1935. In
Reprography and Copyright Law, **edited by Lowell H. Hattery and
George P. Bush, pp. 159-174. Arlington, Virginia: American Institute of
Biological Sciences, 1964.**

This article traces the development of a compromise between copyright
holders and "researchers" and their respective interests relative to
photocopying.

Seltzer, Leon E. *Exemptions and Fair Use in Copyright: The 'Exclusive
Rights' Tensions in the New Copyright Act.* **Cambridge, Massachusetts:
Harvard University Press, 1978. 199 p.**

The attempt and apparent failure by the Congress to adequately and to
precisely define "fair use" in the 1976 Copyright Act is critically examined.
The statute provides little guidance to the courts in ranking by importance
the four judicially created factors to be considered in determining fair use.
The essay, which offers a refined definition of fair use, reflects an ordering
of these factors which puts primary importance on the author's expected
economic rewards. A distinction is made between fair use and exempted use,
the former not coming within the scope of copyright protection, the latter
coming within this protection but excluded for technological or public
policy reasons. The essay reviews the exemptions under the new Copyright
Act and provides a detailed analysis of the provisions on library
photocopying. Appendixes include selected sections from the Copyright Act

of 1976, the congressional committee reports on the fair use and on the library reproduction sections, a portion of the 1965 Supplementary Report of the Register of Copyrights on the General Revision of the U.S. Copyright Law, and the 1935 "Gentlemen's Agreement." An index is provided. [This item originally appeared, without the appendixes and index, in the *Bulletin of the Copyright Society of the U.S.A.* 24: 215-277, 279-337. April and June 1977.—editor's note.]

Sharp, Roy C.   Copyright—Shield or Shroud. *Copyright* **11: 113-118. May 1975.**

An argument against the doctrine of fair use, including photocopying for research and educational purposes, is presented. Included is a proposal for a blanket licensing system whereby the authors or publishers would be reimbursed in direct relation to the use of their works.

Sophar, Gerald J. *Williams and Wilkins versus U.S. Government* **A Memorandum dated September 30, 1970, addressed to members of Proprietary Use/Rights Committee/ASIS (American Society for Information Science). Washington. September 30, 1970. 5 p.**

A statement relative to Case 73-68 in the United States Court of Claims involving the National Institutes of Health Library and the National Library of Medicine. The author indicates an opinion that this case is "destined to become a landmark case in copyright law—at least until Congress writes and passes a revision bill to replace the copyright Act." (page 1).

Sophar, Gerald J. and Laurence B. Heilprin. *The Determination of Legal Facts and Economic Guideposts with Respect to the Dissemination of Scientific and Educational Information as It is Affected by Copyright—A Status Report.* **Washington: U.S. Department of Health, Education, and Welfare, Office of Education, Bureau of Research, 1967. 86 p.**

This report is "organized by chapters of which the first four are introductory to the fifth, which contains the substance of the report and conclusions." Chapter 5—Findings and Analysis: Analysis of Current Practices of Libraries and Information Centers and the Resulting Size of the Problem Due to these Practices. Section One treats such subjects as "Fair Use;" Aborted or Curtailed Library Services Due to Action of Copyright Owner; ERIC; Do Libraries Profit from Copying Facilities and Services?; Inter-library and Intra-library Networks; Clearinghouse System Question; and the proposed National Commission on New Technological Uses of Copyrighted Works. Section Two presents the Economics on Copying of Copyrighted Works.

Stevenson, Iris Caroline.   The Doctrine of Fair Use as it Affects Libraries.
Law Library Journal **68: 254-273. August 1975.**

The purpose of this article is to trace a series of cases which have delineated the criteria and boundaries of fair use beginning with *Folsom v. Marsh* in 1841 and ending with the *Williams & Wilkins* case (decided by the full Court of Claims in 1973). Appendix I includes a table of copyright cases, a brief statement of the fact situations involved in each, and the holding (i.e., the ruling as to whether the contested use was "fair" or "unfair").

Sword, Larry F.   Photocopying and Copyright Law—*Williams & Wilkins Co.*
   v. United States; **How Unfair can "Fair Use" Be?** *Kentucky Law Journal*
   63: 256-278. 1974-1975.

A point-by-point refutation of the Court of Claims' decision holding for the United States is presented. Among the points directly addressed are the Court's interpretation of whether periodicals were to be included in the 1909 Copyright Act's prescription against copying; the Court's attention to the nonprofit character of the alleged infringers; and the Court's balancing of the potential harm to be done to medical science, if photocopying of the type described in the current case were deemed unfair, and the harm to be done to publishers, if the photocopying were allowed to continue.

The Williams & Wilkins Company v. The United States, **487 F.2d 1345 (Ct.
   Cl. 1973).**

The full Court of Claims reversed the opinion of the Trial Judge and held that the photocopying practices of the National Library of Medicine and the National Institutes of Health library were "fair." In arriving at this conclusion the court reasoned that 1) there was inadequate evidence that the photocopying practices adversely affected the financial situation of the publisher, 2) medical research would be seriously harmed if such copying were deemed infringing, and 3) the balancing of the interests of science and those of copyright owners should rest with the legislature. [An equally divided Supreme Court upheld the decision of the full Court of Claims (420 U.S. 376).—editor's note].

The Williams & Wilkins Company v. The United States, **No. 73-68 (Ct. Cl.,
   filed February 16, 1972).**

This is the opinion in the first instance of the first case involving massive unauthorized photocopying of copyrighted works. Commissioner James F.

Davis found in favor of the publisher against the U.S. Department of Health, Education and Welfare and its National Institutes of Health (NIH) and the National Library of Medicine (NLM). ". . .The issues raised by this case are but part of a larger problem which continues to plague our institutions with ever-increasing complexity—how best to reconcile, on the one hand, the rights of authors and publishers under the copyright laws with, on the other hand, the technological improvements in copying techniques and the legitimate public need for rapid dissemination of scientific and technical literature." (page 31). [Opinion was overturned by the full Court of Claims whose opinion was affirmed by an equally divided U.S. Supreme Court.—editor's note].

H. EDUCATION

Education is a primary user of intellectual property and it is more and more a user of the technologies previously mentioned. One of the great needs was for a compromise between these two aspects of the copyright problem, so that the teacher could know how one could use the technologies and still remain within the law. The doctrine of fair use loomed large in this problem and an exemption for multiple copying for classroom use was included in the fair use provision of the 1976 law. Additionally, guidelines pertaining to the copying of periodical articles and portions of books were developed by representatives from educator, author, and publisher groups. These guidelines became part of the legislative history of the 1976 Copyright Law. To date, however, no agreement has been reached in the increasingly important area of off-the-air copying of audiovisual works.

Related references may be found in Sections G. Fair Use; I. Libraries, Networks, and Information Systems; and J. Permissions and Payments.

Selected Material related to Education will be found in Part II: Stephen Freid, *Fair Use and the New Act.*

American Association of School Librarians and American Library Association, Washington Office. *Copyright, Media, and the School Librarian: A Guide to Multimedia Copying In Schools.* **Chicago: American Association of School Librarians, Spring 1978. 16 p. (Reprinted from** *School Media Quarterly.* **Spring 1978).**

This booklet explains in simple language the 1976 Copyright Law as it pertains to copying works from a variety of media formats including audio discs, cassettes, tape recordings, printed materials, microforms, films, filmstrips, photographs, printed music, television, and radio. Examples of permissible and impermissible copying are provided emphasizing that copying which may, or may not, be done by the student and individual teacher. The pamphlet also addresses multiple copying for classroom use. The guidelines for classroom copying and for educational uses of music are appended.

American Library Association, National Council of Teachers of English, and National Education Association. *The New Copyright Law: Questions Teachers & Librarians Ask.* **Washington: National Education Association, 1977. 76 p.**

After a brief introductory chapter on the 1976 Copyright Act, this primer for teachers and librarians in academic institutions examines fair use; educational media, especially off-the-air taping of television and radio programs; library copying; and, penalties and remedies for infringement. Each chapter begins with a short discussion of one of the topics which is followed by a series of questions and answers on the subject.

Association for Educational Communications and Technology, and Association of Media Producers. *Copyright and Educational Media: A Guide to Fair Use and Permissions and Procedures.* **Washington: Association for Educational Communications and Technology, and Association of Media Producers, April 1977. 28 p.**

The provisions of the 1976 Copyright Law which relate primarily to fair use, library reproduction, and noncommercial broadcasting are examined to provide guidance for educational users of such copyrighted audio-visual aids as motion pictures, film strips, sound recordings, and videotapes in determining the legal boundaries of reproduction without obtaining permission from copyright owners. One of the topics addressed is off-the-air copying of network, public, and instructional programs. Agreements allowing rerecording of certain public and instructional programs are reprinted. Also included is a series of hypothetical situations involving the use of copyrighted materials. Following each item is an opinion as to whether the activity described is a fair use. Because many uses of copyrighted audio-visual works will not be considered "fair" under the new law, an explanation of the procedures to be followed in obtaining permission from copyright owners is presented. The appendix includes the "Agreement on Guidelines for Classroom Copying in Not-For-Profit Educational Institutions" and the "Guidelines for Educational Uses of Music."

Bender, Ivan R. *Overview of P.L. 94-553 (Copyright Law Revision).* **Washington: Association of Media Producers, February 25, 1977. 10 p.**

An overview of the 1976 Copyright Law is presented emphasizing those provisions relating to the production and distribution of educational audio-visual aids.

Benjamin, Curtis G. *Computers, Copyrights and Educators.* **An address before the 75th Annual Meeting, American Society for Engineering Education, Michigan State University, June 19-22, 1967. Unpaginated.**

This address concerns the emerging problem of computer uses of copyrighted materials. Topics include: Permissions and payments; Input-Output; Clearinghouse; EDUCOM; ERIC. "So I can heartily endorse the widely favored suggestion that Congress should enact the present copyright bills without more specific legislation on computer uses, but with a provision for the appointment of a study commission to investigate the impact of the developing new technology on the creators, publishers, and users of copyrighted works."

Billings, Roger D., Jr. Off-The-Air Videorecording, Face-To-Face Teaching, and the 1976 Copyright Act. *Northern Kentucky Law Review* **4: 225-251. 1977.**

The copying rights and the performance rights provided instructors by the 1976 Copyright Act are analyzed to determine the extent to which educators may copy audiovisual works off-the-air for teaching purposes. The lack of explicit definitions in the Act has made the relevant provisions difficult to interpret. The author favors guidelines under which the owners of audiovisual works would outline what and how much material could be copied.

Copyright Law Revision: Its Impact on Classroom Copying and Information Storage and Retrieval Systems. *Iowa Law Review* **52: 1141-1169. June 1967.**

This note is comprised of two principal parts: (I) Classroom Copying and the Copyright Law; and (II) Information Storage and Retrieval Systems and the Copyright Law. The first part is comprised of (1) The Doctrine of Fair Use; (2) Education's Position on Classroom Copying; and (3) The Publishers' Position on Classroom Copying (pages 1147-1158). The second part is comprised of (1) The Computer Program; (2) Protection of Computer Input; (3) Computer Output and Fair Use; and an extensive conclusion. "The proposed copyright law does not create that balance between the copyright proprietor and the computer user." (p. 1169).

Copyright Office and Ford Foundation. *Conference on Video Recording for Educational Uses.* **Washington: Library of Congress, Copyright Office, 1978. 206 p.**

The proceedings of the Conference on Video Recording for Educational Uses held in Airlie, Virginia, from July 19 to 22, 1977 are reprinted. The purpose of the conference was to discuss the current practices and the future direction of off-air video recording in the educational context. The conference began with the presentation of several papers, including one on the "Impact of Copyright Law on Video Recording" and another on the "Impact of Video Recording on Copyright Law." Each conferee was assigned to one of five working groups, each group charged with presenting a report covering generally five topics: 1) Consideration of present practices; 2) What do people think is going to happen; 3) Does anyone think that all off-air taping should either be completely free from copyright restrictions (even if commercial) or be completely restricted (including no fair use); 4) Assuming some fair use exists, what should be its dimension in the educational/archive area; and 5) Assuming that copying is beyond fair use, what is the solution. The discussions of the interim reports and the final reports are reprinted. The conference ended with panelists discussing the issues from the point of view of their respective constituencies. The names of the participants and a bibliography of materials provided attendees are appended.

The Ethics and Legality of Off-Air Videotaping. *Audiovisual Instruction* **21(4): 50-51. April 1976.**

The letters presented here were written in response to a column written by Harold Hill, president of the Association for Educational Communications and Technology that stated that off-air videotaping is obviously illegal.

Gilkey, Richard. Copyright: Technology, Ethics, and Instruction. *The Clearing House* **44: 255-56. 1969.**

This short article seeks to reconcile the diverse interests of the new technology with, particularly, school teachers and their sense of ethics. Technology will be increasingly employed near or in the classroom. Such vehicles of instruction enhance creativeness and individualization. Yet, "conflict will occur only if these two sectors of society see their purposes in opposition instead of in support of one another." (page 256).

Henry, Nicholas. The New Copyright Act, or How to Get into a Heap of Trouble Without Really Trying. *PS* **10: 6-8. Winter 1977.**

A brief account of how the political scientist is affected by the 1976 Copyright Law in his or her role as author, researcher, and teacher is presented. Among the provisions discussed are those dealing with the Federal preemption of common law copyright, computers and photocopying.

Klein, Harold S., chairman. Symposium—Copyright and Educational Media. *Performing Arts Review* 7: 1-90. 1977.

The proceedings of a May 1975 symposium on copyright and educational media are presented. Among the opinions expressed during the symposium were that there should be no general exemption for educational users and that licensing the use of educational media has advantages over outright sale. Licensing, through the use of contracts, would provide the copyright owner greater control over copies.

Krasilovsky, M. William. The Effect of Copyright Practices on Educational Innovation. *Teachers College Record* 70: 413-427. February 1969.

"Mr. Krasilovsky . . . charts a course for educators through a normally complicated terrain. Interested in technological innovation and the possibilities of teachers' maintaining the initiative when using new devices, he calls for the development of a reasonable and informed approach to the problem of arranging for the use of copyrighted materials." (page 413). Discussed are the basic economics of accommodation licenses; sound recordings; inadequacy of the fair use doctrine; threat of compulsory licensing; voluntary practices; educational goals.

Martell, Charles. Copyright Law and Reserve Operations—An Interpretation. *College & Research Libraries News* 39(1): 1-6. January 1978.

The impact that the 1976 law and the *Guidelines for Classroom Copying in Not-for-Profit Educational Institutions* will have on both teachers and librarians in maintaining reserve collections is reviewed. The author outlines those practices associated with traditional reserve operations which must be discontinued. One conclusion reached is that although a single copy of an entire journal article may conditionally be placed on reserve, seldom will the teacher be able to place multiple copies on reserve. A summary sheet listing the photocopying activities in which teachers and librarians may and may not engage follows the text.

May, Jill P. Copyright Clearance Problems in Educational Television: Children's Materials. *Journal of Education for Librarianship* 17: 149-160. Winter 1977.

The difficulties of obtaining permission from copyright holders to videotape material from various types of educational media in support of classroom instruction are discussed. The author summarizes some of the reasons given for denying permission.

Miller, Arthur R.   The Copyright Revision Bill in Relation to Computers. A statement approved by the Board of Trustees and the Task Force on Legal and Related Matter of the Interuniversity Communications Council (EDUCOM). *Communications of the ACM* **10: 318-321. May 1967.**

This statement refers to Senate Bill 597, which would generally revise the Copyright Law of the United States. "It is submitted that these provisions in their present form will seriously hamper the educational programs of the nation. The following statement examines the impact of the bill upon the development of the use of computers in instruction and research and suggests measures and means which will fairly protect authors and publishers and which will at the same time permit the full application of the genius of the computer to the advancement of the nation's educational program." (page 318).

Miller, James G.   EDUCOM: Interuniversity Communications Council. *Science* **154: 483-488. October 28, 1966.**

Institutions have joined forces to foster application to higher education of the burgeoning information sciences. A brief account of the founding, the objectives, and the current [October 1966] operations of the Interuniversity Communications Council is presented. Mention is made (page 486) of the establishment of a Committee on Copyright.

Pitt, Don L.   Education and the Copyright Law: Still an Open Issue. *Fordham Law Review* **46: 91-138. October 1977.**

The provisions of the 1976 Copyright Law affecting educators, especially fair use, are reviewed. Although the new law and accompanying guidelines have clarified some of the issues confronting educators, several unsettled issues remain. The discussion considers educational uses of copyrighted works which remain of questionable legality. Instead of "explaining" fair use through the use of guidelines, an education section, similar to the one pertaining to libraries, should be enacted. Such a section would codify the rights and limitations of educational uses of copyrighted works while retaining the flexibility of the fair use provisions. A proposed education section is appended.

Schuster, Nancy and Marc J. Bloch. **Mechanical Copying, Copyright Law, and the Teacher.** *Cleveland-Marshall Law Review* **17: 299-323. May 1968.**

This article deals with the infringement problems encountered by a teacher in duplicating copyrighted material for his/her class. These authors conclude that: "Each case, as it always has in theory, must be tried on its own merits in light of the circumstances surrounding it. These must include the prospective harm to the author, the state of mind of the copier, and the benefit to education. All in the light of the real reason for copyright in this country: to benefit the arts and sciences by encouraging the author and scholar to produce." (page 323).

Siebert, Fred S. *Copyrights, Clearances, and Rights of Teachers in the New Educational Media.* **Washington: American Council on Education, 1964. 62 p.**

The purpose of this study is to explore and, wherever possible, recommend solutions for three groups of problems growing out of the use of the new instructional media in American education: (1) methods of protecting educational material through copyright; (2) identifying materials which may infringe the rights of others; and (3) analysis and evaluation of compensation policies in the new media and teacher relationships.

Stedman, John C. **Academic Library Reserves: Photocopying and the Copyright Law.** *AAUP Bulletin* **64:142-149. September 1978.**

Using the library photocopying and, especially, the fair use sections of the 1976 Copyright Law, the author analyzes the permissibility of copying items for library reserve collections. The author argues that the classroom guidelines developed in support of the fair use provision set forth the minimum photocopying practices in which educators may engage and that the guidelines are binding only on the parties who agreed to them. Practices which go further than the guidelines may still be considered fair use under the four factors determining fair use, especially the fourth one concerning market effects. The author supports multiple copying for library reserve collections within reasonable limits. Appendixes include excerpts from the 1976 Copyright Law and the "Agreement on Guidelines for Classroom Copying in Not-For-Profit Educational Institutions."

Stedman, John C. **The New Copyright Law: Photocopying for Educational Use.** *AAUP Bulletin* **63: 5-16. February 1977.**

The provisions of the 1976 Copyright Law relating to educational photocopying are examined. Reliance upon voluntary guidelines over statutory requirements is favored because guidelines offer greater flexibility than statutes and can be altered more easily as more information regarding the effects of modern technology on the user-copyright proprietor relationship becomes available. The fair use and the library reproduction provisions of the new law (Sections 107 and 108, respectively) are reprinted in the appendixes. A copy of a letter from the president of the American Association of University Professors (AAUP) to the chairman of the House Subcommittee on Courts, Civil Liberties and the Administration of Justice which criticizes the guidelines for classroom photocopying developed by representatives from educational and author-publisher groups is also appended. AAUP was not represented in the guideline-development process.

Stedman, John C.   Statement on Copyright Law Revision. *AAUP Bulletin* **53: 127-132. Summer 1967.**

The statement refers to Senate Bill 597. Topics include: Traditional Education-Copyright Relationship, and Modern Developments Affecting This Relationship; Provisions of S. 597 Relating to Education—and the Premises that Underlie Them; Summary and Conclusions; Specific Recommendations.

Taylor, Joe D.   Off-The-Air Video Taping for Educational Purposes—Fair Use or Infringement: *Air Force JAG Law Review* **17: 90-99. Spring 1970.**

An analysis of the off-the-air taping problem at the Air University and how it was resolved. Numerous cases are referenced and deductions made, mostly with reference to the doctrine of fair use. The author concludes: "For these reasons, as long as the facts and circumstances in our educational environment remain the same, there would be no copyright infringement in off-the-air taping and replaying of commercial television programs for educational purposes." (page 99).

Teaching Machines: The Impact of New Devices on Educational Publishing. *Publishers Weekly* **189(10): 103-105, 108, 109. March 7, 1966.**

Speakers at a recent meeting in Boston analyzed the threat of photocopying and duplicating machines in the school to conventional graphic arts techniques. Mr. Richard B. Gladstone of Houghton Mifflin Company, the final speaker, is quoted as saying: "Before almost any major instructional innovation can establish itself in these [State] sections of the country, change must take place not only in custom but in law . . . I foresee little change for some time to come and books should continue to rule the roost indefinitely." (page 109).

Troost, F. William. The Controversy Over Off-Air Videotaping: Does Videocopying Constitute Unprofessional Conduct for Educators? *Phi Delta Kappan* 58: 463-465. February 1977.

Both sides of the controversy concerning off-air videotaping of network television programs for nonprofit educational purposes are reviewed. The author offers three solutions to the problem: licensing, governmental control of the manufacturing process so that videotape recorders can no longer copy, and the public service concept which would grant the copyright holders of the program a tax write-off in return for allowing schools to videotape the program.

Troost, F. William. Off-The-Air Videotaping: An Issue of Growing Importance. *Audiovisual Instruction* 21(6): 60-63. June-July 1976.

The issues involved in off-air videotaping of commercial television programs for classroom use are both legal and ethical in nature. There are currently no clear answers as to the permissibility of this activity. Arguments on both sides of the issue are reviewed and possible solutions to the problem—e.g., payment of a fee to the program producers for the privilege of videocopying, government prohibition of the copying ability of videotape recorders, and a tax write-off for producers and/or networks who permit schools to videocopy their programs—are discussed.

I. LIBRARIES, NETWORKS, AND INFORMATION SYSTEMS

Libraries are increasingly becoming users of the technologies mentioned earlier. Computer-assisted library networks are no longer ideas for the future. The conflict over library photocopying was not entirely put to rest with the passage of the 1976 Copyright Law. Although library, author, and publisher groups were able to develop numerical guidelines for "lending" copies of periodical articles and other short works not older than five years through interlibrary arrangements, they were not able to reach agreement on any of the remaining problems which face them.

Related references may be found in Sections B. Computer Systems; C. Reprography; F. CONTU; G. Fair Use; H. Education; J. Permissions and Payments; and L. International.

Selected Materials related to Libraries, Networks, and Information Systems will be found in Part II: Madeline Henderson, *Copyright Impacts of Future Technology*; King Research, Inc., *Library Photocopying in the United States: With Implications for the Development of a Copyright Royalty Payment Mechanism* (**Summary**); **Richard De Gennaro**, *Copyright, Resource Sharing, and Hard Times: A View from the Field*; and **James M. Treece**, *Library Photocopying*.

Ad Hoc Task Group on Legal Aspects in National Information Systems. *Copyright Law as it Relates to National Information Systems and National Programs.* **Washington: Federal Council for Science and Technology, Committee on Scientific and Technical Information (COSATI), 1967. 73 p. (Available from National Technical Information Service, Springfield, Virginia. Order No: PB-175 618).**

The study concerns three areas: (1) Ready access to copyrighted material; (2) Conversion of copyrighted material into machine readable form as a possible infringement of copyright; (3) Exemptions from copyright by nonprofit users.

American Library Association. Special Issue of ALA Washington Newsletter on New Copyright Law. *ALA Washington Newsletter* **28(13). November 15, 1976. 70 p.**

Those provisions in the 1976 Copyright Law which relate to libraries and librarians are reviewed and explained. Among the major provisions discussed are those concerning fair use and the making of reproductions by libraries and archives. Appendix I includes relevant sections from the 1976 law, while Appendix II is composed of excerpts from the reports of the House Judiciary Committee and of the Conference Committee on S. 22, the Copyright Revision Bill.

Aronofsky, Julius S. and Robert R. Korfhage. Telecommunication in Library Networks: A Five-Year Projection. *Journal of Library Automation* **10: 5-27. March 1977.**

A review of those developments in the computer and, especially, in the telecommunications industries which have made networking feasible follows a brief description of current library networks. Six model network designs are described and evaluated.

Artigliere, Ralph. The Impact of the New Copyright Act on Photocopying by Law Firms. *The Florida Bar Journal* **52: 528-535. July/August 1978.**

The fair use and the library copying provisions of the 1976 Copyright Law are reviewed as they apply to the photocopying practices of law firms and their libraries. Suggestions on the ways in which law firms can comply with the law are presented within the text and in the appendixes following the article.

Association of American Publishers, Inc., and Authors League of America, Inc. *Photocopying by Academic, Public and Nonprofit Research Libraries.* **Washington: Association of American Publishers, Inc., May 1978. 42 p.**

The Association of American Publishers and the Authors League of America present their own Interim Guidelines relating to photocopying of journal articles and other short works by nonprofit libraries. The guidelines offer numerical limits on the copying done by libraries for their own patrons from their own materials. Limits also are provided for articles older than five years which are borrowed through interlibrary loan. Definitions of "reasonable effort" and "fair price," as used in Subsections 108(c) and 108(e) of the

1976 law pertaining to lost, damaged, or stolen works, and pertaining to out-of-print works, respectively, are provided. A question and answer section is also included.

Association of American Publishers, Inc., and Authors League of America, Inc. *Photocopying by Corporate Libraries: A Statement of Position with Respect to the Photocopying of Journal Articles and Other Short Works by Corporate Libraries Under the New Copyright Law, and Answers to Some Questions Frequently Asked.* **Washington: Association of American Publichers, Inc., January 1978. 14 p.**

The general copying rights of corporate libraries as presented in Sections 107 and 108 of the 1976 law are provided followed by the organizations' numerical guidelines for copying which fall outside the CONTU guidelines. Specifically, this includes making copies of articles for interlibrary loan purposes from journal issues older than five years, copies made by corporate libraries for its own users from a journal it owns, copying done at unsupervised machines, and copying done at multiple libraries of the same company. Following the statement of numerical guidelines, a question and answer section appears.

Baynham, Robert J. and Marian G. Gallagher.   Copyright: Colloquium Notes. *The Serials Librarian* **1: 83-98. Fall 1976. (Especially pp. 90-98).**

Of primary interest is the section of this paper by Marion G. Gallagher. This section examines the fair use provisions presented in S. 22 (the 1976 Copyright Revision Bill) and the way they relate to libraries. Of special concern to librarians are sections 108-A through 108-I of the Bill.

Becker, Joseph.   Information Network Prospects in the United States. *Library Trends* **17:306-317. January 1969.**

This article is devoted to the prospect of a national information network in the United States, which implies the interconnection of existing systems and library systems. The author traces the developments in this area in the past; indicates that which should be expected of such a network; and how it might well be planned. In his conclusion one notes: "The object is to remove these impediments [various constraints] to knowledge by developing mechanisms such as networks that will facilitate the extraorganizational distribution and communication of information in all forms." (page 317).

Benadie, R.B.   The Problem of Copyright in the University Library. *LIBRA* **10: 33-41. 1975.**

The provisions of the South African Copyright Act of 1965 relating to library photocopying are outlined. Librarians are uncertain of the Act's application, because it offers no clear definition of "fair dealing." Because the Act is difficult to interpret and to apply, a combination of various solutions—e.g. that the Act be revised, that a royalty system be instituted, and that a code be established for research practices—is proposed.

Brown, Ralph S., Jr.   Copyright: An Overview. In *Libraries at Large,* **edited by Douglas M. Knight and E. Shepley Nourse, pp. 229-236. New York: R.R. Bowker Co., 1969.**

This paper concerns the availability of cheap and easy reproduction of all kinds of documents, either by copying techniques or by electronic storage and retrieval. The involvement of copyrights on this material generates vexing problems for the librarian. There follows a discussion of some of the issues: reprography and computers; the concept of limited copyright; clearinghouse proposals; and what is next.

Burchinal Lee G.   Copyright Impacts of and on Government Programs. *Journal of Chemical Information and Computer Sciences* **16: 70-71. May 1976.**

The types of information dissemination activities supported by the Federal government are reviewed, including direct Federal dissemination, dissemination in private journals and other private outlets, copyrighted distribution of data compilations, and photocopying of copyrighted materials by Federal libraries. The proposed copyright revision will not have much effect on these activities, except in the area of library photocopying, where issues involving "fair use" versus "systematic" photocopying and the limits of interlibrary loans must be resolved.

Butler, Meredith.   Copyright and Reserve Books—What Libraries Are Doing. *College & Research Libraries News* **39: 125-129. May 1978.**

A small survey designed to ascertain the attitudes and practices of university libraries as they relate to reserve collections was conducted. A synopsis of the different approaches libraries are using to comply with their interpretations of the new law and the accompanying guidelines is presented.

Carter, Launor F.   The Scientific User: The Library and Informational Service Needs of Scientists. In *Libraries at Large,* **edited by Douglas M.**

Knight and E. Shepley Nourse, pp. 143-151. New York: R.R. Bowker Co., 1969.

All kinds of scientists are dependent on documents and reports, as well as upon books. Timeliness and availability are of great importance. Thus documentation services with information storage and retrieval have flourished in the years since 1960. Many such systems are discipline-oriented, such as MEDLARS, as operated by the National Library of Medicine. Even larger, comprehensive systems are envisioned, such as a COSATI System by the Federal Council for Science and Technology. Such systems are dependent upon the new technology.

Carter, Launor F. et al. *National Document-Handling Systems for Science and Technology.* **New York: John Wiley & Sons, Inc., 1967. 356 p.**

"The book grew out of a study undertaken for the Committee on Scientific and Technical Information (COSATI) by the System Development Corporation." (The original study report, containing COSATI recommendations, is available from National Technical Information Service, Springfield, Virginia. Order No: AD-624 560).

Cerutti, Elsie and Jane C. Tucker. *Impact of the New Copyright Law on Interlibrary Loan in a Research Library.* **Washington: National Bureau of Standards, January 26, 1978. 16 p.**

The results of a study designed to assess the economic impact of the CONTU guidelines on interlibrary arrangements on the library of the National Bureau of Standards is presented. A determination of the point at which it becomes less expensive to purchase than to borrow is included.

Clapp, Verner W. *Copyright—A Librarian's View.* **Prepared for the National Advisory Commission on Libraries. Washington: Association of Research Libraries, Copyright Committee, August 1968. 40 p.**

Includes such topics as: copying services; author's rights; the "for profit" principle; mass-dissemination v. normal use; the rights of owners of copies of copyrighted works to use their copies. The appendix is comprised of 12 items and is titled: Copyright and Library Copying/Photocopying.

Copyright Office. *Circular R21: Reproduction of Copyrighted Works by Educators and Librarians.* **Washington: Library of Congress, Copyright Office, 1978. 26 p.**

This booklet excerpts portions of the 1976 law, the congressional reports and debates, and the Copyright Office regulations for use by educators, librarians and archivists engaged in the reproduction of copyrighted works for the purposes of teaching, research, interlibrary arrangements, and archival preservation.

Copyright Office and the National Commission on Libraries and Information Science, cosponsors. *Conference on Resolution of Copyright Issues: Transcript of Proceedings.* **First Meeting. Washington: Library of Congress, November 16, 1974. 109 p. (Unpublished).**

The first meeting of the Conference on Resolution of Copyright Issues concentrated on defining the areas of discussion for a working group to be selected from among the participants composed of representatives of author, publisher, and library interests. (These representatives became known as the Upstairs/Downstairs Group.) Library photocopying within the context of Sections 107 and 108 of the Revision Bill and possible licensing and clearance arrangements were to be the working group's prime areas of examination.

Copyright Office and the National Commission on Libraries and Information Science, cosponsors. *Conference on Resolution of Copyright Issues: Transcript of Proceedings.* **Second Meeting. Washington: Library of Congress, February 5, 1975. 83 p. (Unpublished).**

The report of the Working Group selected to consider library photocopying was presented to the full Conference. Although no consensus was reached concerning any obligation of libraries to compensate copyright owners for copying journal and periodical articles, the Working Group did recommend that the development of clearance mechanisms be investigated by either the same or a reconstituted Working Group. A procedure and framework for conducting this further study was discussed.

Copyright Office and the National Commission on Libraries and Information Science, cosponsors. *Conference on Resolution of Copyright Issues: Transcript of Proceedings.* **Third Meeting. Washington: Library of Congress, April 24, 1975. 112 p. (Unpublished).**

The purpose of this session was to discuss the report of the Working Group selected to study possible clearance and licensing procedures for libraries that photocopy journal articles. In addition to reviewing the report, the Conference participants considered a proposal to conduct a study of certain types of library photocopying and to test a possible payments mechanism.

De Gennaro, Richard. Copyright, Resource Sharing, and Hard Times: A View from the Field. *American Libraries* **8: 430-435. September 1977.**

This award-winning article argues that library resource sharing, through such mechanisms as interlibrary loan, consortia, and "centralized libraries' libraries," is not causing publisher revenues to decrease significantly, nor will this sharing solve the budgetary problems libraries are and will be experiencing. Data are presented to illustrate that such resource sharing does not constitute a significant amount of library photocopying. Libraries are encouraged to use all the rights granted under the 1976 Copyright Law which, in effect, reinforces most of the current library practices.

Diaz, Albert James. On-Demand Publishing—The Clearinghouse Concept. In *Levels of Interaction Between Man and Information.* **Proceedings of the American Documentation Institute Annual Meeting, Volume 4, pp. 238-241. Washington: Thompson Book Co. 1967.**

This paper describes in detail the Clearinghouse for Sociological Literature, an organization based on the "demand publishing concept." Also stated are the advantages of the system and answers to questions which may arise. Small organizations in the sociological field "simply deposit all research reports with the Clearinghouse and subsequently refer any inquiries to it." (page 241).

Flacks, Lewis I.   Living in the Gap of Ambiguity; An Attorney's Advice to Librarians on the Copyright Law. *American Libraries* **8: 252-257. May 1977.**

After outlining the provisions of Section 108 of the 1976 Copyright Law dealing with library reproduction, the author provides answers to or commentary on a series of questions frequently asked by the library community. Among the topics addressed are 1) the question of whether libraries are responsible for potential infringement by patrons using coin-operated copiers; 2) the problem of obtaining replacement copies for missing journal issues; 3) the legal force of the guidelines on interlibrary arrangements; 4) the applicability of fair use to library copying along with the legal status of the activities involved in the *Williams & Wilkins* case; 5) recordkeeping requirements under the interlibrary loan provisions of the new law; and 6) off-the-air taping of television programs.

Fraser, Walter J.   Publishers Versus Libraries: Some Hidden Dimensions in the Current Debate. *IEEE Transactions on Professional Communication* **PC-18: 200-206. September 1975.**

A discussion focusing on librarians' concerns about publishers' desires to obtain a fee for photocopying journal articles is presented. It is suggested that libraries, which already pay the higher institutional subscription rates, should not be forced to charge users for copies. Such charges could impede access to scientific and technical information. This practice could in turn hinder scientific progress.

Fry, Bernard M., Herbert S. White, and Marjorie Shepley. *Publishers and Libraries: A Study of Scholarly and Research Journals.* Lexington, Massachusetts: Lexington Books, 1976. 167 p.

This study, which is based on data from 1969 through 1973, examines the economic factors involved in publishing research and scholarly journals and in subscribing to research and scholarly journals by academic, public, and special libraries. The publisher sample is stratified by type of publisher (commercial, society, university, and other not-for-profit publishers) and by discipline (pure science, applied science and technology, humanities, and social sciences). The effects of increased publication costs and static or decreasing library budgets on journal subscriptions are examined. Fifty-seven tables are included. Appendixes include the methods used for identifying and stratifying the library and publisher samples and a brief explanation of the pretest of the survey instruments. A bibliography and an index are also included.

Gifford, Woody, Carter & Hays. *Library Photocopying and the U.S. Copyright Law of 1976: An Overview for Librarians and Their Counsel.* New York: Special Libraries Association, 1978. 90 p.

A practical discussion of each relevant provision of the 1976 law relating to library photocopying is accompanied by excerpts from the statute, as well as from the House, Senate, and Conference reports. The argument is made that the library copying rights provided in Section 108 of the 1976 law are additional to any rights granted in Section 107, fair use. The "warning of copyright" issued by the Copyright Office to be used on copying order forms and to appear at supervised photocopying machines is appended.

Golub, Melinda V. **Not by Books Alone: Library Copying of Nonprint, Copyrighted Material.** *Law Library Journal* 70: 153-170. May 1977.

An attempt is made to determine how the courts would rule on library copying of nonprint, copyrighted materials using case analogies from the photocopying and CATV fields. Additionally, a parallel is drawn from Vanderbilt University's activities involving the copying of live network news broadcasts. It is noted that the 1976 Act takes a restrictive view toward library copying of nonprint material. However, the author is optimistic about the future.

Graham, Margaret H.   Copyright Impacts on Chemical-Industry Users and Information Centers. *Journal of Chemical Information and Computer Sciences* **16: 68-69. May 1976.**

Industrial technical-information centers need to make available to their users copies of journal articles, many of which are located outside any particular center. Support is given to a "fair access" system which would allow these information centers to photocopy journal articles or to request photocopies from other libraries in return for a royalty payment for each item copied.

Hattery, Lowell H. and George P. Bush, editors. *Automated Information Systems and Copyright Law.* **A Symposium of The American University. (Reprinted in U.S. Congress.** *Congressional Record,* **90th Cong., 2nd sess., 1968, 114, pt. 13: 16852-16858, 17042-17045, 17285-17292, 17337-17347. July 11-14, 1968).**

The following is quoted from a speech by Hon. Robert W. Kastenmeier in Congress on June 11, 1968: "Accordingly, I include the report on the symposium in the *Record* so as to be readily available to Members and others interested in this subject matter." The Table of Contents includes: Copyright Law Revision; Post-Gutenberg Copyright Concepts; Copyright and The Computer; Economics, Automation and Copyright; Electronic Computers; Technology and The Copyright Law; Authors' Rights; Permissions and Payments in Automated Systems; A Code for The Unique Identification of Recorded Knowledge and Information; The Publishers' Rumplestiltskin; Summary and Analysis; Conclusions and Recommendations; Selected Bibliography.

Hattery, Maxine.   British Bring IR to Home TV. *Information Retrieval and Library Automation* **13(7): 1-3. December 1977.**

An interactive home information service called Viewdata (since renamed Prestel) is described. The service, which is being developed by the British Post Office and which is still in the experimental stage, uses a slightly modified television set to provide information-on-demand in a variety of subject areas, including community services, sports, news and weather, and buying advice. Programmed learning can also be provided. Plans are being made to connect the service to world telex.

Henderson, Madeline M. **Copyright Impacts of Future Technology.** *Journal of Chemical Information and Computer Sciences* **16**: 72-74. **May 1976.**

Libraries must respond to higher costs and budgetary constraints by developing more economical and efficient means of acquiring and disseminating information. Developments and trends in computer, communication, reprographic, and micrographic technologies leading towards the creation of information and library networks are examined. The development and use of these technologies must be combined with a concern that the rights of the owners and producers of the information are protected.

Holley, Edward G. **A Librarian Looks at the New Copyright Law.** *American Libraries* **8**: 247-251. **May 1977.**

This article primarily reviews those provisions of the 1976 Copyright Law that deal with the period of copyright, fair use, and copying by libraries for interlibrary loans. Although it appears that the legal burden is on the borrowing library, the guidelines developed to clarify the meaning of the interlibrary copying provision are vague. Therefore, it is recommended that both the lending and borrowing libraries maintain accurate records of interlibrary loan transactions requiring journal copying. The author reviews that literature which he feels best explains the 1976 law as it affects libraries.

Hoskovsky, A.G. and H.H. Album. **Toward A National Information System.** *American Documentation* **16**: 313-322. **October 1965.**

"Our objective is to offer a general plan for the construction of a comprehensive national technical information system. The system we will consider will deal exclusively with the published scientific literature." (page 313).

Illinois State Library Task Force on Copyright Guidelines. *A Fair Shake: Photocopying Rights for ILLINET Participants Under the Copyright Revision Act of 1976.* **Springfield, Illinois: Illinois State Library, December 1977. 12 p.**

This pamphlet, prepared for the members of the Illinois Library and Information Network (ILLINET), outlines in simple language the permissible limits of library photocopying under the fair use and library reproduction sections of the 1976 Copyright Law. The booklet instructs on the extent to which single and multiple copies can be made either for local use or for interlibrary loans. The requirements for ensuring compliance with the CONTU guidelines on interlibrary arrangements are briefly described.

King Research, Inc. *Library Photocopying in the United States: With Implications for the Development of a Copyright Royalty Payment Mechanism.* **Washington: National Commission on Libraries and Information Science, October 1977. 251 p.**

Academic, public, Federal, and special libraries were surveyed to determine the amount of serial photocopying done for local use, intrasystem loans, and interlibrary loans. Among other purposes, the data collected were analyzed to determine the eligibility of photocopies for royalty payments under various interpretations of the 1976 Copyright Law and the CONTU guidelines on interlibrary arrangements. Libraries indicated a preference for four royalty collection mechanisms: higher subscription rates which would include the right to make copies; a surcharge on photocopying machines; the use of coupons or stamps; and the purchase of multiple copies from a central sales source. Publishers, who were surveyed in another study, seemed to prefer to license photocopying directly rather than to go through a clearinghouse. In addition to a table of contents, there are lists of tables and figures which reference the 97 tables and 31 figures, respectively. The appendixes include the survey instruments used and material on the method used to survey the photocopying activities of the libraries studied, and a method to estimate the amount of photocopying done per serial title. A 13-page summary of the report is included in the full report; it is also available separately.

Lazowska, Gene.   Photocopying, Copyright, and the Librarian. *American Documentation* **19: 123-130. April 1968.**

This paper explores the subject of copyright as it relates to photocopying in libraries. Mention is made of the several attempts made to resolve the various issues. "Undoubtedly, copyright will become an increasingly difficult problem for librarians for sometime to come. The revolution in communications technology is going to require some revolutionary thinking about copyright, but evidently this has not yet generally occurred." (page 129).

Legal Information Retrieval Systems and the Revised Copyright Law. *Valparaiso University Law Review* **1: 359-380. Spring 1967.**

"To illustrate the potential copyright problems of a legal information retrieval system, the following hypothetical example is presented." (page

360). There follows a heading, Legal Research in 1985. Later, one notes the headings: The legal monopoly of copyright; Does the legal information retrieval system's copying qualify as fair use?; Author's rights vs. public interest; Revision of the Copyright Law; and solution to the copyright problem. ". . . the courts should not expand fair use to include unauthorized duplication of portions of copyrighted works by a legal information retrieval system. It is suggested that any copying by the system should be held to constitute an infringement." (pages 379-380).

Lenny, David.   Copyright Infringement Problems of a Network/Home Cable Record Selection and Playing System. *Rutgers Journal of Computers and the Law* **5: 51-96. 1975.**

Potential copyright problems associated with the development of a network/home cable record selection and playing system (RSPS) are studied. An RSPS will utilize a central computer facility at which sound recordings are stored. Individual recordings would be selected by communicating with the central computer facility using the same cable attached to a cable television and the music from this computer facility would be piped into homes, classrooms, and other facilities. It is observed that although the Congress should enact legislation specifically designed for RSPS, analogies can be drawn from present legislation dealing with photocopying, cable television, and jukeboxes. Possible legal solutions to copyright problems created by RSPS are suggested.

Lieb, Charles H.   Library Photocopying Under the 1976 Copyright Law. *Bulletin of the Copyright Society of the U.S.A.* **25: 243-249. February 1978.**

A review of library photocopying rights under the sections of the 1976 Copyright Law pertaining to fair use and library reproduction is presented. Among the conclusions are that the law requires institutions serving as centralized sources of photocopies in support of interlibrary arrangements to obtain permission from the copyright holders and that almost all photocopying of copyrighted works by libraries in for-profit institutions will require clearance.

Lukac, George J., editor. *Copyright—The Librarian and the Law.* **New Brunswick, New Jersey: Rutgers University, Graduate School of Library Service, 1972. 220 p. (Distributed by Rutgers University Press).**

The proceedings of a 1970 Rutgers University symposium whose central issues were library photocopying and fair use. The document includes lectures delivered by each of the five participants, among whom were representatives of authors, publishers, and libraries, and panel discussion by the symposium participants. The Copyright Law, revised to July 1, 1967, and a facsimile of an application for copyright are two of several appendixes.

Marke, Julius J.   Copyright Revision and Issues of Continuing Concern to the Librarian. In *The Bowker Annual of Library & Book Trade Information,* 22nd Edition, edited by Nada Beth Glick and Sarah L. Prakken, pp. 159-163. New York: R.R. Bowker Co., 1977.

The major sections of the 1976 Copyright Law pertaining to the activities of librarians are reviewed. Among the provisions examined are those concerning the subject matter of copyright, rights granted to copyright owners, the fair use doctrine, library reproduction, and the mandated review of the library reproduction provision in 1982. Because of the author's concern that the National Commission on New Technological Uses of Copyrighted Works (CONTU) was attempting to develop additional guidelines on photocopying periodical articles more than five years old and on intralibrary photocopying, he advises librarians to develop a single position of permissible library practices under the 1976 law.

Marron, Harvey and L.G. Burchinal.   ERIC—A Novel Concept in Information Management. In *Levels of Interaction Between Man and Information.* Proceedings of the American Documentation Institute Annual Meeting, Volume 4, pp. 268-272. Washington: Thompson Book Co., 1967.

ERIC refers to the Educational Resources Information Center which is a national information system dedicated to the progress of education through the dissemination of educational research results and research related materials. This article describes the overall concept, a system description, the clearinghouse, research in education, lexicography, copyright considerations, and future plans.

Martin, Susan K. *Library Networks, 1976-77.* White Plains, New York: Knowledge Industry Publications, Inc., 1976. 131 p.

The author reviews the scope and potential of library networks. Descriptions of the Ohio College Library Center (OCLC) and other existing networks are included in this state-of-the-art report. The efforts to create a national network, and the issues and problems associated with network management are also outlined. The appendix presents information on the locations, membership, status, and plans for 25 operational networks.

McQueen, David.   Copyright. *Canadian Library Journal* **32: 433-449. December 1975.**

This essay, an economic view of copyright, examines copyright as a property right and discusses the dilemma which develops between those institutions interested in producing information and those involved in information dissemination, specifically libraries. The dilemma is that the practices of those institutions disseminating information may adversely affect the production of information and vice versa. A concern is voiced that with the advent of advanced technologies, there may be fewer and fewer book publishers which might result in censorship.

Medical Library Association, Inc.   *The Copyright Law and the Health Sciences Librarian.*   **Chicago: Medical Library Association, Inc., 1977. 27 p.**

After outlining the provisions of the 1976 Copyright Law affecting librarians, the essay examines the pertinent statutory sections, common library practices, and recordkeeping requirements relating to particular services within the library (i.e., audiovisual learning centers, collection maintenance, interlibrary loan, photocopying services, and reserve collection). Appendixes include the full text of the relevant provisions of the law, the guidelines on copying for educational purposes and interlibrary arrangements, limitations on copyright in works supported by the U.S. Public Health Service and the National Institutes of Health, and an explanation of the revised interlibrary loan form. An index is provided.

Overhage, Carl F.J. and R. Joyce Harman, editors. *INTREX.* **Report of a Planning Conference on Information Transfer Experiments. Cambridge, Massachusetts: MIT Press, 1965. 276 p.**

The object of those experiments is to provide a design for evolution of a large university library into a new information transfer system that could become operational in the decade beginning in 1970. Such a system will result from a confluence of three streams: (a) the modernization of current library practices, (b) a national network of libraries and other information centers, and (c) the extension of on-line, interactive computer communities into domains of libraries and other information centers.

Palmour, Vernon E., Marcia C. Bellassai, and Robert R.V. Wiederkehr. *Costs of Owning, Borrowing, and Disposing of Periodical Publications.* **Arlington, Virginia: Public Research Institute, October 1977. 65 p.**

A mathematical model is used to determine the point at which borrowing journal articles through interlibrary loan becomes more expensive than subscribing to the journals. The model is used to determine the "cross-over point" at which the cost of borrowing equals the cost of owning. Among the appendixes are the cost elements for using the decision model and the methodology used for the collection of library cost data.

Panel on the Legal Aspects of Information Systems. Legal Aspects of Computerized Information Systems. *The Honeywell Computer Journal* **7: 3-96. 1973.**

Parts VII and VIII of this report to the Committee on Scientific and Technical Information (COSATI) from its Panel on Legal Aspects of Information Systems are particularly relevant to copyright problems associated with the new technologies. Part VII primarily covers the problems of ready access versus compensation for those creators whose copyrighted works are used in storage and retrieval systems. Although no definite solutions are offered, some basic objectives of a new copyright law in relation to the new technologies are set forth. Part VIII describes efforts on the international level to define copyright protection for satellite transmissions, library photocopying, and computer storage and retrieval of copyrighted works.

Phelps, Ralph H.   Factors Affecting the Costs of Library Photocopying. *Special Libraries* **58: 113. February 1967.**

The author provides answers to some questions relative to the factors which bear upon setting rates for photocopying materials in the Engineering Societies Library. They seem to be relevant to other library situations.

Ramey, Carl R.   A Copyright Labyrinth: Information Storage and Retrieval Systems. In *Copyright Law Symposium: Number Seventeen,* **by the American Society of Composers, Authors and Publishers, pp. 1-23. New York: Columbia University Press, 1969.**

This paper won first prize in the 29th Annual Nathan Burkan Competition. The focus of this paper is on the potential infringement aspects of information storage and retrieval systems. The principal topics treated are: Copyright Law; The Stages of Information Handling; Fair Use or Infringement—The Competing Interest; and Legislative Reform. In his conclusion Mr. Ramey states: "What is needed at this stage is fruitful discussion to bring these interests into closer harmony." (page 21).

Recommendations for National Document Handling Systems in Science and Technology. Washington: Federal Council for Science and Technology, Committee on Scientific and Technical Information (COSATI), November 1965. Three Volumes. (Available from National Technical Information Service, Springfield, Virginia. Order No: AD-624 560).

These three documents represent a comprehensive attempt to develop guidelines for planning at a high level in the Federal government, so that the information activities within each department and agency as well as nongovernmental components may be knit into a national network. (See also Carter, Launor F. et al. *National Document-Handling Systems for Science and Technology.* New York: John Wiley & Sons, Inc., 1967. 356 p.).

Ringer, Barbara A. *The Use of Copyrighted Works in Information and Retrieval Systems.* An address delivered at the Max Planck Institute on October 10, 1967.

This address concerns the problem of how to deal with copyrighted works as both input to and output from information systems, as proposed in the revision of the U.S. Copyright Law of 1909. Particular emphasis is placed upon the implications of computer applications of the future and the possible effects upon the authors of intellectual property as well as the prospective users thereof.

Roberts, Matt. Copyright and Photocopying: An Experiment in Cooperation. *College and Research Libraries* 30: 222-229. May 1969.

This article seeks to clarify for librarians some guidelines for copying copyrighted materials. Fair use is explained and quotations and opinions gathered from experienced practitioners. One notes the wording: ". . . libraries not only are privileged, but are obligated to photocopy reasonable parts of copyrighted works in order to fulfill their responsibility to scholarship and to 'promote the Progress of Science and Useful Arts'." (page 222).

Roberts, Matt. *Copyright: A Selected Bibliography of Periodical Literature Relating to Literary Property in the United States.* Metuchen, New Jersey: The Scarecrow Press, Inc., 1971. 416 p.

This bibliography includes 6,215 citations published in English, arranged under 26 subject headings which provide approximate access to various aspects of copyright. The cut-off date is 1968. Literary property in this case refers to books.

Smailes, A.A.   The Future of Scientific and Technological Publications.
  Aslib Proceedings **22: 48-54. February 1970.**

". . . the next significant steps in accessibility and presentation of scientific information to be: 1. By 1975 there will be selective on-line document storage and retrieval facilities available on a commercial basis; but at a cost . . . 3. Optical character recognition devices . . . will be developed by 1980 . . . 4. Copyright agreements will be streamlined with authors and publishers accruing royalties for each document stored, scanned and retrieved. 5. Between 1980 and 1990 electromagnetic circulation of local printing of newspapers and periodicals to be a commonplace but . . . 6. By 1990 national bibliographic data and information banks for major disciplines will be developed and these will later merge into international banks. 7. Finally . . . on-line interrogation systems . . ."

Smith, R.H.   Comment by D.M. Lacy. *Publishers Weekly* **190(6): 22-23.**
  August 15, 1966.

Ways in which publishers and librarians agree on copyright are provided.

Tallman, Johanna E.   Implications of the New Copyright Law for Libraries
  and Library Users. *IEEE Transactions on Professional Communication*
  PC-20: 178-184. November 1977.

The provisions of the 1976 Copyright Law and accompanying guidelines as they relate to photocopying within academic and special libraries are reviewed. Precautions which libraries should follow when allowing photocopying either at attended or unattended machines are outlined. If the copying machine is attended, the attendant should ascertain the purpose to which the copies are to be put. Suggested methods of complying with the 1976 law when the copying exceeds the fair use and library copying provisions are outlined. An index referencing the photocopying provisions of the law, the House Report, the CONTU guidelines on interlibrary arrangements, and the guidelines on copying for classroom use is appended.

Treece, James M.   Library Photocopying. *UCLA Law Review*
  24: 1025-1069. June-August 1977.

The legislative balance between copyright owners and library users of copyrighted works is examined. Following an outline of the library-related provisions of the 1976 Copyright Law, the impact of these provisions on the services offered by libraries and on the cooperative arrangements of library networks and consortia is discussed. A rule of thumb for determining when library photocopying substitutes for a purchase or subscription is offered. Beyond this limit the library should order another subscription to the journal or purchase another copy of the compilation. The 1976 law also seems to preclude the sharing of copyrighted works among libraries in a network using computerized methods. Furthermore, libraries that "rationalize" acquisitions by determining the holdings of the other libraries in a network or consortium by technological methods may do so only under license from the copyright owners. The author concludes that the Congress did equitably balance the interests of both the libraries and the copyright owners.

Trezza, Alphonse.   Impact on Emerging Networks, Consortia, and the National Plan. In *The Copyright Dilemma,* **edited by Herbert S. White, pp. 179-192. Chicago: American Library Association, 1978.**

This analysis explains why the new Copyright Law will facilitate the development of networks and a "national periodicals access program."

UNISIST Study Report on the Feasibility of a World Science Information System. **Paris: United Nations Educational, Scientific and Cultural Organization, 1971. 161 p.**

This Study Report describes a world science information system and the conclusion is reached that the establishment of such a system is not only necessary, but also feasible. The subject of copyrights is discussed on pages 77 and 117. "The matter of copyright is of particular concern . . . reprography . . . [and] that publishers are now expected to provide input to computer-based distribution systems . . " (page 77). "The national scientific information agencies . . . should stimulate revisions of national copyright laws in order to better conciliate public interests in document availability . . . and . . . evolve an international doctrine of fair use in this area." (page 117).

Urbach, Peter F.   Access to Journal Article Copies through NTIS. *IEEE Transactions on Professional Communication* **PC-20: 176-178. November 1977.**

The proposal made by the National Technical Information Service (NTIS) for providing copies of journal articles is detailed. The NTIS clearinghouse would provide copies of articles to requesters for a single fee, regardless of the length of the article. NTIS would not maintain an extensive collection of journals for this purpose; instead, existing collections held by other institutions would be used to obtain copies. The proposed methods for ordering and payment are also described.

van der Wolk, L.J.   Teletype and Telecode for Libraries. *Unesco Bulletin for Libraries* **20: 170-176. July-August 1966.**

This article concerns library cooperation through union catalogs, teletype systems, and reprography. "Libraries nowadays can buy only a small segment of the literature collection they should have to satisfy really all the demands of the clientele by themselves. Consequently, they need a fast and reliable means of communication in order to continue their good service to their clients. It is here that teletype in combination with reproduction methods, especially with microfiche (which can be sent in an air-mail envelope) offers a solution." (page 172).

Voigt, Melvin J.   EURONET. *Library Journal* **101: 1183-1185. May 15, 1976.**

EURONET, a scientific and technical information network serving the member countries of the European Community, is expected to be fully operational by 1985. EURONET plans to use existing European information facilities rather than to develop an independent network, and eventually expects to provide access to data bases from all parts of the world. The problem of interrogating data bases in different languages must be resolved, as must the difficulties associated with obtaining licenses which do not restrict the use and dissemination of any particular data base to users in only one country (a stipulation of some of the present licensing agreements).

Weil, Ben H.   Private Information Center Aspects. *IEEE Transactions on Professional Communication* **PC-18: 222-223. September 1975.**

Because information centers within private industry cannot expect to maintain all the journal subscriptions necessary to satisfy their users' needs, these centers want "fair access" to copyrighted journal articles. Under a fair access system, information centers would be able to obtain the desired copyrighted material from a variety of sources upon payment of a fee which would ensure the publisher an equitable return in relation to use.

Weinstock, Melvin.   Network Concepts in Scientific and Technical Libraries. *Special Libraries* **58: 328-334. May-June 1967.**

"National information networks of the future will formalize and by augmentation and expansion of existing facilities will strengthen the existing fabric of interrelationship between central national libraries and the technical library community. Computers will play an important role in such networks to the extent that they are used in document retrieval systems, and give users access to the total resources of the national document handling system . . ."

White, Herbert S., editor. *The Copyright Dilemma.* **Chicago: American Library Association, 1978. 212 p.**

Papers given at a conference sponsored by the Indiana University Graduate Library School are reprinted. Participants representing government, authors, professional societies, libraries, and secondary information services offered their interpretations of the way in which the 1976 law would affect their interests. A focal point of the conference was library photocopying.

Woledge, G. Copyright and Library Photocopying: The Practical Problems. *Aslib Proceedings* **19: 217-222. July 1967.**

"The present paper, based on an address to an Aslib Winter Meeting and on the very useful discussion which followed it, concentrates on the kinds of cases that trouble the librarian most frequently, and approaches them practically rather than theoretically." Topics treated: Periodical articles—single copies; Books—single copies; Interlibrary copying: Copying by individuals; Multiple copies; and The influence of xerography.

Wright, Gordon H. The Canadian Mosaic—Planning for Shared Partnership in a National Network. *Aslib Proceedings* **30: 88-102. February 1978.**

This article on library networks in Canada concentrates on the computer-based information services offered by the Canada Institute for Scientific and Technical Information and the services provided by the University of Toronto Library Automation Systems. The difficulties faced by the National Library of Canada in forming a computer-based network for resource sharing are discussed.

J. PERMISSIONS AND PAYMENTS

The 1976 Copyright Law created the Copyright Royalty Tribunal and established the need for other mechanisms for collecting, recording, and distributing royalties. The citations under this heading explain the purpose, function, and procedures of these mechanisms. Lesser references appear under Sections A. Technology; B. Computer Systems; C. Reprography; D. Video Communications; F. CONTU; G. Fair Use; H. Education; I. Libraries, Networks, and Information Systems; and L. International.

Selected Materials related to Permissions and Payments will be found in Part II: Barbara Ringer, *Copyright in the 1980's*; CRC SYSTEMS INCORPORATED, *Impact of Information Technology on Copyright Law in the Use of Computerized Scientific and Technological Information Systems* (Section A.4.6); King Research, Inc., *Library Photocopying in the United States: With Implications for the Development of a Copyright Royalty Payment Mechanism* (Summary); and Bernard Fry et al., *Survey of Publisher Practices and Present Attitudes on Authorized Journal Article Copying and Licensing* (Project Background and Summary of Findings).

Association of American Publishers, Inc. *Explaining the New Copyright Law: A Guide to Legitimate Photocopying of Copyrighted Materials.* **New York: Association of American Publishers, Inc., 1977. 15 p.**

This brief guide introduces the layman to the provisions of the 1976 Copyright Law pertaining to fair use and library photocopying of copyrighted works. Additionally, the guide presents the various guidelines which have been issued relating to those provisions; suggestions on procedures to obtain permission from copyright owners for uses exceeding fair use; and a sample letter requesting permission.

Association of American Publishers, Inc., and the Information Industry Association. *Essential Elements of a Copyright Clearinghouse.* **Proceedings of a Conference, February 11-12, 1976. Bethesda, Maryland: Information Industry Association, 1977. 136 p.**

These conference proceedings cover the practices and policies which have made a clearinghouse for photocopying payments necessary; existing and proposed copy fulfillment and royalty payment mechanisms; and the copyright clearance practices in the music industry. The meeting, which was attended by members of the publishing community, recommended a task force composed of publishing industry representatives to develop the mechanisms and the structure of a copyright clearinghouse. Included in an appendix is *A Handbook for Serial Publishers: Procedures for Using the Programs of the Copyright Clearance Center, Inc.* An index is also provided.

Association of American Publishers, Inc., TSM Copy Payments Center Task Force. *Program for the Provision of Technical-Scientific-Medical Journal Articles and for Related Information-Service Copying.* **New York: Association of American Publishers, Inc., March 17, 1977. 8 p.**

A not-for-profit Copy Payments Center (CPC) is being established to provide journal publishers with a mechanism which will allow them to collect royalties for articles photocopied from their journals. Initially, the program will concentrate on technical-scientific-medical (TSM) journals, but others will be permitted to participate. A description of the requirements for both the publisher and user organizations is presented. The main feature of the program is an identification and price-per-copy code which will appear on the first page of each article. This code will provide the information necessary to distribute the royalties to the participating publishers.

Association of American Publishers, Inc., TSM Copyright Clearance Center Task Force. *A Handbook for Serial Publishers: Procedures for Using the Programs of the Copyright Clearance Center, Inc.* **New York: Copyright Clearance Center, Inc., August 1977. 18 p.**

This manual for serial publishers provides instructions for joining the Copyright Clearance Center. Included are directions for constructing the article-fee codes which provide the Center with the information needed to distribute payments to publishers; instructions on the way in which publishers may collect royalties through the Center for pre-1978 articles; and an explanation of charges by the Center for providing this service. Sample registration forms are appended.

Botein, Michael. **The New Copyright Act and Cable Television—A Signal of Change.** *Bulletin of the Copyright Society of the U.S.A.* **24: 1-17. October 1976.**

Section 111 of the 1976 Copyright Law Revision governs the compulsory licensing and royalty payment requirements of cable television systems. This article reviews Section 111 and the Federal Communications Commission's regulations that have a direct impact on it.

Brennan, Thomas C.   The Copyright Royalty Tribunal. *Bulletin of the Copyright Society of the U.S.A.* **25: 196-197. February 1978.**

This brief review of the functions of the Copyright Royalty Tribunal uses cable television as an illustration.

Broady, Barbara et al. Proposed Solutions to the Problem of Photocopying Copyrighted Material: A Survey. In *Copyright and Photocopying: Papers on Problems and Solutions, Design for a Clearinghouse, and a Bibliography,* **Student Contribution Series Number 10, edited by Laurence B. Heilprin, pp. 1-37. College Park, Maryland: University of Maryland, 1977.**

A survey of proposed solutions to the photocopying problem in relation to copyright law is presented. Each solution is evaluated on the basis of fifteen criteria. A matrix is created for ranking each solution based on the established criteria. The advantages and disadvantages of each solution are outlined. Among those solutions ranked highest are (1) the "Statutory Option" which, if adopted by law, would provide the copyright owner the option of either retaining all rights to copy or granting the user such copying rights as stated in the copyright notice; (2) the "Contract Agreement" which would allow limited photocopying by copying organizations in return for royalty payments to copyright owners; and (3) the "Non-Profit, Voluntary Clearing House," which would provide a centralized center for the collection of royalties from user-member organizations and would provide for the distribution of royalties to copyright-owner members. The study updates an earlier report issued by the Committee to Investigate Problems Affecting Communication in Science and Education (CICP).

Brylawski, E. Fulton.   The Copyright Royalty Tribunal. *UCLA Law Review* **24: 1265-1286. June-August 1977.**

Because there is not much discussion of the Copyright Royalty Tribunal within the congressional hearings and reports, the 1976 Act becomes the only guide. This article covers the evolution and function of the Tribunal, the procedures to be followed by the Tribunal, and some of the potential problems and conflicts the Tribunal may encounter.

Cairns, Robert W. **Copyright Impacts on Chemical Journals and Data Bases.** *Journal of Chemical Information and Computer Sciences* 16: 64-65. May 1976.

Libraries and individual users have resorted to more photocopying as journal subscription costs have increased. The American Chemical Society (ACS) offers a variety of services which provide alternatives to hard-copy subscriptions to journals. These services will aid publishers in receiving the revenue necessary to continue production. Among the services offered are a "single article service," whereby a user can order individual papers which have been printed in ACS journals, and a microfilm service, whereby ACS leases microfilm versions of its journals to organizations. This leasing arrangement involves a licensing fee which allows the lessees to photocopy for dissemination within their own organizations. ACS also supports the concept of a clearinghouse for collecting photocopying royalties.

Copyright Clearance Center, Inc. *Handbook for Libraries and Other Organizational Users Which Copy From Serials and Separates: Procedures for Using the Programs of the Copyright Clearance Center, Inc.* **New York: Copyright Clearance Center, Inc., October 1977. 20 p.**

Procedures for membership in the Copyright Clearance Center (CCC) by organizations whose copying activities exceed the fair use and library copying provisions of the 1976 Copyright Law are outlined. Included are instructions for obtaining a CCC User-Registration Number, and explanations of the codes used on post-1977 articles, the Center's copying reporting requirements, the methods of payment, and the frequency of those payments. Forms which can be used for reporting copying activities for coded and uncoded articles and a sample CCC User-Organization Registration Form are appended.

Curtis G. Benjamin Urges Higher Permissions Fees. *Publishers Weekly* **194(14): 35-36. October 7, 1968.**

A review of a talk on "Permissions: A Reappraisal for the 1970's" given by Curtis G. Benjamin before the New York Rights and Permissions Group on September 19, 1968. Mr. Benjamin indicated that publishers need and will need more income from reproduction rights, and will have to make special efforts to keep pace with new technology. Publishers tend to charge each other too little. The technological explosion is going to increase the demand for reproduction rights dramatically. There will be an increasing use of material in computer-based systems, such that publishers must insist on copyright protection at the input stage.

Dotterweich, Earl J. et al.   Copyright Clearinghouse: In-Depth Study of a Proposed Solution to the Copyright Photocopying Problem. In *Copyright and Photocopying: Papers on Problems and Solutions, Design for a Clearinghouse, and a Bibliography,* **Student Contribution Series Number 10, edited by Laurence B. Heilprin, pp. 39-81. College Park, Maryland: University of Maryland, 1977.**

A detailed analysis of the design, organization, startup, and maintenance of a voluntary clearinghouse for the collection and distribution of royalties resulting from photocopying copyrighted works is presented. User-member organizations, such as libraries, would pay a fixed fee per copyrighted page copied. Distribution of royalties would be weighted based on the per-page cost of production by the most frequently copied individual publishing house members. These heavily photocopied publishers would receive payment based on the actual number of pages copied. Those publishers whose copyrighted works are only rarely copied will be paid a fixed amount annually. The advantages and disadvantages of the clearinghouse approach are outlined.

Fry, Bernard M., Herbert S. White, and Elizabeth L. Johnson. *Survey of Publisher Practices and Present Attitudes on Authorized Journal Article Copying and Licensing: Analysis of Returns to Questionnaires Developed by and Distributed for the National Commission on New Technological Uses of Copyrighted Works (CONTU).* **Washington: National Commission on New Technological Uses of Copyrighted Works, June 1977. 211 p. (Available from National Technical Information Service, Springfield, Virginia. Order No: PB-271 003).**

This study surveyed the practices and attitudes of publishers of scholarly and research journals regarding various methods of providing copies of articles to users. Journal publishers were broken down by circulation size, subject matter, and, where applicable, commercial versus nonprofit status. The publishers were asked whether they would allow nonprofit users more copying liberties than commercial users, whether they would rather distribute copies directly or through agents, and whether they would be more lenient in allowing photocopying of back issues of a journal than of current issues. There were two types of questionnaires sent to each publisher, a publisher questionnaire and a journal questionnaire. The methodology for determining the journal population is included. Statistical analysis is presented for each question in both questionnaires in prose and tabular form. Among the items included in the appendixes are the survey instruments used.

Hamann, H. Frederick. Comments on the Copyright Aspects of Automatic Information and Retrieval Systems. *Bulletin of the Copyright Society of the U.S.A.* **15: 9-12. October 1967.**

The practical aspects of information utilization in automatic information storage and retrieval systems; the negotiation of agreements with each copyright proprietor; the mere storage in memory; the doctrine of fair use; some centralized licensing authority; the nature of the stored material; its character, too, such as title, author and key words; even the amount of material could affect fair use. Some system is needed "which compensates the copyright owner and provides some measure of control while allowing the . . . system to be developed and used in an environment free of unnecessary uncertainties and impractical legal restraints." (page 12).

Hilton, Howard J. A Code for the Unique Identification of Recorded Knowledge and Information. In *Automated Information Systems and Copyright Law,* **edited by Lowell H. Hattery and George P. Bush. (Reprinted in U.S. Congress.** *Congressional Record,* **90th Cong., 2nd sess., 1968, 114, pt. 13: 17289-17291. July 13, 1968).**

This paper explains the need for a system which will uniquely identify recorded knowledge and information by means of a universal code. An application to the processing of permissions and payment of copyrighted materials is set forth. Another application concerns the identification of materials in automated information systems.

Horty, John F. Computers and Copyright: A Third Area. *Bulletin of the Copyright Society of the U.S.A.* **15: 19-23. October 1967.**

The 'third area' in the title refers to users of the system versus the makers of the information system, such a maker not allied with either a publisher or a computer company. The author favors reasonable payment for use of copyrighted materials in any kind of information system. Whether such payment should be upon input or output is a question of mechanics. Discussed is the question of negotiation for permission to input and this brings up the clearinghouse proposal, one which the author is not willing to endorse at the time. He does heartily endorse the concept of a National Commission to study the problem.

Karp, Irwin. Authors' Rights. In *Automated Information Systems and Copyright Law,* **edited by Lowell H. Hattery and George P. Bush. (Reprinted in U.S. Congress.** *Congressional Record,* **90th Cong., 2nd sess., 1968, 114, pt. 13: 17286-17288. July 13, 1968).**

A discussion of permissions and payments for the use of books and other intellectual property in automated systems of communication; "what kind of permission will be required; what type of consideration will be paid when storage and retrieval systems ingest the information and cultural output of our society . . ." (page 17286). And manipulate and disseminate it?

Karp, Irwin.   A "Statutory" Licensing System for the Limited Copying of Copyrighted Works. *Bulletin of the Copyright Society of the U.S.A.* 12: 197-209. April 1965.

Misgivings regarding possible application of ASCAP procedures to a clearinghouse are presented.

A Licensing System: A Proposal by the Authors League of America, Inc. *Library Journal* 91: 892-893. February 15, 1966.

This proposal is a system under which authors and publishers would license the making of copies of material from books and periodicals on a royalty basis.

Lieb, Charles H.   Economics, Automation and Copyright. In *Automated Information Systems and Copyright Law,* edited by Lowell H. Hattery and George P. Bush. (Reprinted in U.S. Congress. *Congressional Record,* 90th Cong., 2nd sess., 1968, 114, pt. 13: 17043-17044. July 12, 1968).

A discussion of how to assure an adequate reward to publishers and authors when full use is made of computer technology for education, for information storage and retrieval, and for any other purposes that are found for this technology.

MacLean, Ann W.   Education and Copyright Law: An Analysis of the Amended Copyright Revision Bill and Proposals for Statutory Licensing and a Clearinghouse System. In *Copyright Law Symposium: Number Twenty,* by the American Society of Composers, Authors and Publishers, pp. 1-35. New York: Columbia University Press, 1972. (Especially pp. 21-35).

Of particular interest is the part of this award-winning essay which identifies the need for a central clearinghouse to distribute royalty payments to copyright owners for the use of copyrighted material by educational institutions and then outlines a proposal for such a facility. It is suggested that although a clearinghouse should distribute the royalty payments, the Register of Copyrights should grant the licenses and collect the payments. The author supports an annual fee, rather than a per-copy fee, because an annual-fee system would alleviate the need to determine whether any particular use of a copyrighted work is fair.

Passano, William M. **The Photocopying Menace.** *Johns Hopkins Magazine* 18: 30-33. Fall 1967.

"Many academic journals may be doomed to extinction by the widespread, illegal use of photocopying machines, says a prominent medical publisher." The gist of this article concerns payments and permissions for copying copyrighted materials, particularly on the part of libraries and educators. Suggestions are made for resolving the dilemma.

Perle, E. Gabriel. **Commentary on Access to Copyrighted Materials by Information Storage and Retrieval Systems.** *Bulletin of the Copyright Society of the U.S.A.* 15: 4-8. October 1967.

A discussion of the several interested parties relative to input and output for computers. The author makes the point that payment is not and cannot be the sole factor and condition of use of another's copyright. Parties at interest, either alone or in concert, must arrive at an agreement with users as to the conditions and terms of access. This relationship should evolve with the utilization of systems based upon needs for such access.

Richardson, John M. **Copyright Law.** *Bulletin of the American Society for Information Science* 1(10): 25-26. May 1975.

An attitudinal change on the part of owners of copyrighted works is needed in order that the law can adapt to photocopying and computer technology. Until owners do change their position—from one of controlling and restricting copying so that revenue can be obtained from the sale of literary works to one of supporting the concept of allowing copying without advance permission as long as a fair return is guaranteed to the author or copyright owner—no accommodation can take place. A method for ensuring a fair return from photocopying is described.

Ringer, Barbara A. **Copyright and the Future of Authorship.** *Library Journal* 101: 229-232. January 1, 1976.

Copyright law has failed to keep pace with the developments in communication technology and the effects that these changes have on individual authorship. Compulsory licensing appears to be supplanting exclusive rights as the vehicle for ensuring a monetary return to authors. However, there is a danger that compulsory licensing, which includes government involvement, will erode the freedom of the individual author.

Ringer, Barbara A. *Copyright in the 1980s.* **Sixth Donald C. Brace Memorial Lecture. March 25, 1976. (Reprinted in** *Information Hotline* **8(10): 28-31. November 1976).**

In this lecture the Register of Copyrights asserts that the rapid development of technology may be detrimental to independent individual authorship. The advent of compulsory licensing, whereby a tribunal determines the royalty rate which an author should receive for the use of a particular work, is described. Two dilemmas are noted. One is that authors may not be able to guarantee themselves a fair return for their works without joining a collective bargaining unit for royalties. However, this will cause them to lose some of their independence. The other dilemma is that although the Register does not want the Copyright Office to become a regulatory agency—a move which could lead to government control over authorship—she does not want to sit idly by and watch others take the initiative to assert such control.

Sharp, Roy C.   Licensing the Photocopier. *Scholarly Publishing* **1:245-253. April 1970.**

The author suggests a new, assignable photocopying right, on a "per use" basis licensing system, coupled with computer use for accounting purposes, with a central collection agency.

Sophar, Gerald J.   Vestigiality of Fair Use. *IEEE Transactions on Professional Communication* **PC-18: 220-221. September 1975.**

The "fair use" concept is not clear enough to cover the use of copyrighted works in large computer systems and networks. A clearinghouse system for obtaining permission to use copyrighted material in these computerized networks could handle the large number of transactions anticipated.

Stabler, Charles N.   Copiers and Copyrights: Growing Reproduction of Books, Periodicals Is Worrying Publishers. *Wall Street Journal* **169(85): 1,12. May 2, 1967.**

A popularly written piece about the dilemma of permissions and payments, against a background of automation, technology and electronics.

Weil, Ben H. **Copying Access Mechanisms.** *IEEE Transactions on Professional Communication* **PC-20: 171-173. November 1977.**

A brief description of the then-proposed procedures of the Copyright Clearance Center (CCC) is presented. Methods which user organizations could employ to pay royalties to the Center for copying which exceeded the fair use and the library copying provisions of the 1976 law are described.

Wigren, Harold E. **Permissions and Payments in Automated Systems. In** *Automated Information Systems and Copyright Law,* **edited by Lowell H. Hattery and George P. Bush. (Reprinted in U.S. Congress.** *Congressional Record,* **90th Cong., 2nd sess., 1968, 114, pt. 13: 17288-17289. July 13, 1968).**

The author discusses the need for teachers and learners to be able to use the new educational technology in their teaching and learning. He also presents the changing character of teaching and its relation to the proposed Copyright Bill. Furthermore, he presents reasons both for and against a clearinghouse or statutory licensing system, with the related process of permissions and payments.

K. LEGISLATION/LEGAL

The references under this section are concerned with the legislative and judicial processes leading to the revision of the 1909 Copyright Law. The citations below trace the history of the legislative process and provide analysis of various aspects of the Revision before and after its enactment into law. Related references may be found in Sections A. Technology; C. Reprography; D. Video Communications; and L. International.

Selected Material related to Legislation/Legal will be found in Part II: CRC SYSTEMS INCORPORATED, *Impact of Information Technology on Copyright Law in the Use of Computerized Scientific and Technological Information Systems.*

American Bar Association Copyright Symposium. Computers and Copyright: The New Technology and Revision of the Old Law. *Bulletin of the Copyright Society of the U.S.A.* **15: 1-28. October 1967.**

Includes papers by M.D. Goldberg, E.G. Perle, H.F. Hamann, C.H. Lieb, J.F. Horty, and T.C. Brennan. The introductory remarks by Mr. Goldberg indicated a principal concern with H.R. 2512, 90th Congress, and a companion bill S. 597, which appeared to make both computer input and computer output more clearly infringements, other than under the doctrine of fair use.

Brady, Ed.   Copyright and Standard Reference Data Publications. In *Copyright and Related Protections for Information Age Products.* **Proceedings and Related Documents of the Meeting of the Information Industry Association Held at Airlie House, Virginia on July 18 and 19, 1969, pp. 21-26. Bethesda, Maryland: Information Industry Association, 1969.**

The Congress has granted the Bureau of Standards the right to take copyright in certain of its publications and the author discusses this relationship.

Brennan, Thomas C. Some Observations on the Revision of the Copyright Law from the Legislative Point of View. *Bulletin of the Copyright Society of the U.S.A.* **24:** 151-160. February 1977.

The provisions pertaining to cable television and library photocopying were among the items causing the most interesting controversies during congressional consideration of the 1976 Copyright Revision. The author briefly reviews the legislative resolution of these two issues.

Brennan, Thomas C. S. 2216, To Establish the National Commission on New Technological Uses of Copyrighted Works. *Bulletin of the Copyright Society of the U.S.A.* **15:** 24-28. October 1967.

This paper discusses the issues involved toward the establishment of a National Commission on New Technological Uses of Copyrighted Works, and the various steps taken toward the passage of S. 2216 by the Senate on October 12, 1967. The issues included: COSATI, computers, "Fair Use," a clearinghouse, community antenna television systems (CATV), its location, and membership.

Breyer, Stephen. The Uneasy Case for Copyright: A Study of Copyright in Books, Photocopies, and Computer Programs. *Harvard Law Review* **84:** 281-351. December 1970.

The author examines the moral and economic rationale for copyright in books; considers proposals to lengthen the term of protection and increase its scope in relation to photocopies and computer programs; and concludes that copyright should not be abolished, but that its extension is unnecessary and would be harmful. Photocopying is treated on pages 329-338; Research with computer on pages 338-340; Computer programs on pages 340-350. The author's conclusions are explicitly stated on pages 350-351. They apply to all parties at interest in the revision process.

Brown, Ralph S., Jr. *Cases on Copyright, Unfair Competition, and Other Topics Bearing on the Protection of Literary, Musical, and Artistic Works.* Third Edition. University Casebook Series. Mineola, New York: Foundation Press, Inc., 1978. 910 p.

This text is the third edition of a casebook originally by Benjamin Kaplan and Ralph S. Brown, Jr. For readers particularly interested in only the impact of technology on the principle of copyright, the casebook offers an excellent detailed table of contents as well as an index. The appendix includes such items as the 1909 and 1976 Copyright Laws, the first Copyright Act of the United States (approved in 1790), and the Statute of Anne.

Brown, Ralph S., Jr., Benjamin Kaplan, and Dan Lacy. Property Rights Under the New Technology. In *Computers, Communications, and the Public Interest,* **edited by Martin Greenberger, pp. 189-224. Baltimore: Johns Hopkins Press, 1971.**

This is a panel discussion with Brown as speaker and Kaplan and Lacy as discussants. The subject headings for Brown include: The New Technology; The Spheres of Patent and Copyright; Patents for Computer Programs; Copyrights for Computer Programs; An Application Right for Programs; Secrecy; Copyright Works in Computers; Compulsory Licensing; Observations in Conclusion. Kaplan stressed a question related to Xerox copying, while Lacy emphasized the problem of the copyright structure which should govern and foster the production of works intended principally for use in conjunction with the new technology. A general discussion followed.

Cambridge Research Institute. *Omnibus Copyright Revision: Comparative Analysis of the Issues* **Washington: American Society for Information Science, 1973. 280 p.**

The focus of this book is S. 1361, the immediate predecessor of S. 22, the 1976 Copyright Revision Bill. The discussion opens with a history of copyright law both in the United States and other countries. Subsequent material reviews recent attempts to revise the 1909 Copyright Law, analyzes specific sections of S. 1361, including those concerned with library photocopying, fair use, cable television, and computers; discusses some of the issues and controversies which were involved in the efforts to revise the 1909 law; and presents a table which provides a section-by-section comparison of the 1909 law with S. 1361. An analysis of any differences is provided.

Cary, George D. The Quiet Revolution in Copyright: The End of the 'Publication' Concept. *George Washington Law Review* **35: 652-674. May 1967.**

"It is the purpose of this article to briefly examine the background of that revolution, some cases which illustrate the need for a change, and the innovation brought about by the new bill." (page 653).

"In sum, the 'most serious defect' of the present Copyright Law has been quietly excised from the law in the bill as reported favorably by the House Judiciary Committee . . . [It] is probable that the death of the 'publication' concept will not be mourned by anyone." (page 674).

Cohen, Richard E. **Communications Report/Copyright Changes Given Impetus by New Technology.** *National Journal Reports* **6: 659-667. May 4, 1974.**

A brief history of copyright legislation since 1966 and an examination of some of the major provisions of S. 1361 (a predecessor of the bill which became the 1976 Copyright Law Revision) are presented. The review concentrates on the provisions relating to cable television and photocopying. Among the views represented concerning cable television are those of the cable operators, the broadcasters, and the Antitrust Division of the Justice Department. The positions of libraries, publishers, and authors are reviewed in connection with the photocopying provisions of the bill.

Commerce Clearing House, Inc. *Copyright Revision Act of 1976.* **Chicago: Commerce Clearing House, Inc., 1976. 279 p.**

The book's three parts consist of an explanation of the 1976 Copyright Revision Law; the full text of the law; and selected portions of the Senate, House, and Conference reports. Where applicable, cross-references are provided from the explanatory section to the appropriate sections of the law and to pertinent portions of the congressional reports. A topical index is included.

Copyright and Related Protections for Information Age Products. **Proceedings and Related Documents of the Meeting of the Information Industry Association Held at Airlie House, Virginia on July 18 and 19, 1969. Bethesda, Maryland: Information Industry Association, 1969. 99 p.**

Includes papers by: William T. Knox, Barbara Ringer, Ed Brady, Bella Linden, Alan Latman, Hubert J. Schlafly, Elmer W. Galbi, Fred Ensleg, Eugene Garfield, Jeffrey Norton and Norton Goodwin.

Copyrights Act, **Public Law No: 94-553, 90 Stat. 2541 (1976).**

Of particular interest to the readers of this statute, the 1976 Copyright Law, are those provisions pertaining to exclusive rights in copyrighted works

(Section 106); fair use (Section 107); library reproduction (Section 108); secondary transmissions (Section 111); the use of copyrighted works in conjunction with computers (Section 117); notice, deposit, and registration (especially Sections 401,407, 408, and 411); copyright infringement and remedies (Sections 501-510); and the Copyright Royalty Tribunal (especially Sections 801, 804, and 810). Transitional and supplementary provisions are also included. The law is codified as Title 17 of the *United States Code.*

Goldberg, Morton David. Recent Judicial Developments in Copyright Law. *Bulletin of the Copyright Society of the U.S.A.* **13: 378-401. August 1966.**

Originally a paper delivered before the Section of Patent, Trademark and Copyright Law of the American Bar Association at Montreal, Canada, August 10, 1966. Mr. Goldberg discusses the CATV case *United Artists Television, Inc. v. Fortnightly Corp.* and comments briefly upon three scores of lesser cases.

Gosnell, Charles F. The Copyright Grab-bag. Observations on the New Copyright Legislation. *ALA Bulletin* **60: 46-55. January 1966.**

These reflections are based on the author's testimony before the congressional committees working on copyright legislation. Topics include: History of copyright; What actually is copyrighted; Photocopying; Fair use; Joint Libraries Committee on Fair Use in Photocopying; Current efforts for revision of the Copyright Law; and the ALA Committee on Copyright Issues.

Gosnell, Charles F. The Copyright Grab Bag, II. A New Kind of Lend-Lease. *ALA Bulletin* **61: 707-712. June 1967.**

Reference is made to a previous article (*ALA Bulletin* 60: 46-55. January 1966). "Since then, several copyright bills have been introduced in both the House and the Senate, together with a substantial report by the House Committee on the Judiciary. It is now appropriate to assess the current trend and to issue a warning accordingly." (page 707). Topics include: Fair use; Duration; Not-for-profit; Proposals for a clearinghouse and a regulatory commission.

Henn, Harry G. Copyright Law Revision: Paragon or Paradox. *New York University Law Review* **44: 477-520. May 1969.**

Technological developments have posed many new problems which the Copyright Act of 1909 did not envision. The author examines the proposed revision of this Act and finds that its draftmanship results in inflexibility. The headings include: (I) Copyright Revision Program, 1955-1969; (II) Present American Dual Copyright System; (III) Proposed Revision of American Copyright System; (IV) Widened Incompatibility with Copyright Systems of Other Intellectually Advanced Nations; and (V) Conclusions: Paragon or Paradox? One should read part V in its entirety.

Johnston, Donald F. *Copyright Handbook.* **New York: R.R. Bowker Co., 1978. 309 p.**

Following a brief overview of the 1976 Copyright Law, detailed chapters appear on such topics as copyrightable subject matter, notice, exclusive rights, infringement remedies, international considerations, fair use, library reproduction, compulsory licenses, and others. Because of the complexity of the law's provisions concerning cable television and computers, the coverage of these areas is not as comprehensive. Among the extensive appendixes are the full texts of the 1909 and 1976 laws, the fair use and library reproduction guidelines, tables cross-referencing the old and new law, sample copyright registration forms, and selected regulations of the Copyright Office. A detailed table of contents and an index are included.

Kastenmeier, Robert W. **Revision Revisited.** *Bulletin of the Copyright Society of the U.S.A.* **16: 269-277. June 1969.**

The author's intent is to present some idea of the vicissitudes necessarily undergone by legislation intended to revise and bring up-to-date Federal law governing the relations between users and owners of copyrighted materials. To this end he has divided the paper into three phases: Study and Report, being the years 1955 to 1961; Revision in the House of Representatives, being 1964-1966; Revision in the Senate, being from April 1967 to about May 9, 1969. During the 1964-1966 phase several topics are discussed: fair use; the duration of copyright; a single Federal system; government works; CATV; performance right; computer uses; and the floor debate.

Latman, Alan. **A Glimpse at the New Copyright Act.** *Bulletin of the Copyright Society of the U.S.A.* **24: 77-84. December 1976.**

In this brief examination of the 1976 Copyright Act special emphasis is placed on Sections 107 through 118, which limit the exclusive rights of the copyright holder to make and distribute copies of the copyrighted work.

Lehman, Bruce A.   Legislative Background. *Bulletin of the Copyright Society of the U.S.A.* **25: 192-195. February 1978.**

The resolution of the most problematic issues hindering passage of a new copyright law is briefly described. The role compromise played in final passage is emphasized.

Lieb, Charles H.   Journal-Related Aspects of the New Copyright Law. *IEEE Transactions on Professional Communication* **PC-20: 155-159. November 1977.**

This article briefly reviews those portions of the 1976 law which are of most interest and concern to journal publishers, authors, and users. Among the sections of the law outlined are those relating to the copyrightability of works done by employees of the United States government, or of government contractors, and "fair use." The discussion following the body of the article focuses on the questions of when is permission required to copy and from whom must this permission be obtained.

Lieb, Charles H. *New Copyright Law: Overview.* **New York: Association of American Publishers, Inc., 1976. 18 p.**

A synopsis of those provisions of the 1976 Copyright Law which most affect book publishers is presented. Among the sections of the law reviewed are those pertaining to the period of copyright, the manufacturing clause, photocopying, public broadcasting, and rights in contributions. Included at the end of the summary are a chart of the transitional provisions relating to the duration of copyrights already in effect and various agreements which have been reached concerning classroom copying, educational fair use for music, interlibrary photocopying in lieu of interlibrary loan, and the fair use of nondramatic literary works in public broadcasting programs.

Linden, Bella.   Copyright Revision—Issues and Interests. In *Copyright and Related Protections for Information Age Products.* **Proceedings and Related Documents of the Meeting of the Information Industry Association Held at Airlie House, Virginia on July 18 and 19, 1969, pp. 27-45. Bethesda, Maryland: Information Industry Association, 1969.**

A quotation indicates the general tenor of this paper: "It is the attempt to resolve and include in an existing legal structure this revolutionary processing of information *subsequent* to its storage as well as its retrieval in non-traditional forms that is causing the greatest dilemma to all concerned with the proposed revision of the 1909 Copyright Act." (page 28).

Marke, Julius J. *Copyright and Intellectual Property.* **New York: Fund for the Advancement of Education, 1967. 108 p.**

A study of the public domain issue as raised by the U.S. Office of Education policy with related matters such as government-financed research and its accessibility, and copyright and reprography. Of particular interest is the last chapter: The Information Explosion and the New Technology, pp. 88-105.

Marke, Julius J. Copyright Revisited. *Wilson Library Bulletin* **42: 35-45. September 1967.**

A discussion is presented of the basic problem of whether copyright law can respond to the new techniques of electronic document-storage and computerized information, as well as the emerging possibilities of miniaturization and remote transmission of data.

Marke, Julius J. **United States Copyright Revision and Its Legislative History.** *Law Library Journal* **70: 121-152. May 1977.**

Following a brief review of the early history of copyright law in the United States, the author describes the legislative developments leading up to the enactment of the 1976 Copyright Act. The essay concentrates on the development of those provisions concerning the use of new technologies, primarily cable television and photocopying, especially library photocopying. The activities and responsibilities of the Conference on Resolution of Copyright Issues and its "Working Group," and those of the National Commission on New Technological Uses of Copyrighted Works (CONTU) are described. The essay concludes with a summary and analysis of the major provisions of the 1976 Act.

New York Law School Law Review. *The Complete Guide to the New Copyright Law.* **Dayton, Ohio: Lorenz Press, Inc., 1977. 448 p.**

This collection of articles was originally published in the *New York Law School Law Review.* The first part contains articles pertaining to various aspects of S. 22, the Copyright Revision Bill, while the second part reviews the 1976 law as signed by the President. Of particular interest are those articles covering the fair use and the CATV provisions of the 1976 law. The text of S. 22 is included in the appendix to part I, while the 1976 law (P.L. 94-553) is reprinted in the appendix to part II.

Oettinger, Elmer R. *Copyright Laws and Copying Practices.* **Chapel Hill, North Carolina: University of North Carolina, Institute of Government, March 1968. 35 p.**

The treatment of this subject is "selective and oriented to those who have specific need to copy and spread copyrighted materials, especially as an adjunct to teaching, research, and publishing." (page iii).

Peters, Marybeth. *General Guide to the Copyright Act of 1976.* **Washington: U.S. Copyright Office, September 1977. 142 p.**

Of particular interest in this guide to the Copyright Act of 1976 are chapters 8 and 9. The former reviews the provisions of the law relating to fair use (Section 107) and library reproduction (Section 108), while the latter outlines the provisions concerning cable television (Section 111) and the Copyright Royalty Tribunal (Sections 801-810). The Tribunal is responsible for the distribution of royalties paid by cable operators to copyright owners. Included in the appendixes are the CONTU guidelines on interlibrary arrangements and the educational fair use guidelines.

Questions and Answers About the New Copyright Law. Supplement to *Legal Briefs for Editors, Publishers, and Writers* **1(2). July 1977. 68 p.**

Part Four, "Rights Accorded to Copyright Owner and Limitations and Restrictions on Those Rights," and Part Five, "Cable Television, Public Broadcasting, and the Copyright Tribunal," are particularly relevant to persons interested in technology and copyright. Among the provisions of the Act reviewed are those concerning fair use and its application to educational library photocopying, compulsory licensing requirements for cable television and public broadcasting, and the responsibilities and duties of the Copyright Royalty Tribunal.

Ringer, Barbara A. *Annual Report of the Register of Copyrights for the Fiscal Year Ending September 30, 1977.* **Washington: Library of Congress, 1978. 34 p.**

Of special interest is the brief history of the revision process leading to the passage of the 1976 Copyright Law. The Register reviews the activities of the Copyright Office's Revision Coordinating Committee whose task it was to prepare the Copyright Office for implementing those provisions of the law for which it had responsibility. The *Report* also reviews relevant judicial opinions and international developments. A table which illustrates the copyright relationships the United States maintains with other independent nations is appended.

Ringer, Barbara A. *Annual Report of the Register of Copyrights for the Fiscal Year Ending June 30, 1975.* **Washington: Library of Congress, 1976. 19 p.**

In addition to reviewing the administrative activities of the Copyright Office for fiscal year 1975, this report outlines the progress made on the general revision of the copyright law. Also discussed are the mission of the newly created National Commission on New Technological Uses of Copyrighted Works (CONTU) and the legal problems which confronted the Copyright Office, including the problem of library photocopying. Finally, the *Report* highlights activities related to international copyright and reviews Supreme Court opinions, including *Williams & Wilkins.*

Ringer, Barbara A. **Copyright Law Revision: History and Prospects. In** *Automated Information Systems and Copyright Law,* **edited by Lowell H. Hattery and George P. Bush. (Reprinted in U.S. Congress.** *Congressional Record,* **90th Cong., 2nd sess., 1968, 114, pt. 13: 16853-16856. July 11, 1968).**

A short history is provided of the several events between 1924 and 1967 during which the Copyright Law of 1909 was under prospective amendment. Prophetically, Ms. Ringer stated: ". . . I view the enactment of a revised copyright law in the near future as a probability but by no means a certainty." (page 16853).

Technology vs. Copyright: Form vs. Content. *Publishers Weekly* 196(6): 18-20. August 11, 1969.

"How does a publisher protect his informational product from infringement when the utility of that product is a function of its *form* rather than its *content?*" A report on the meeting at Airlie, Va., July 18 and 19, 1969: "Copyright and Related Protections For Information Age Products," sponsored by the Information Industry Association (IIA).

Tyerman, Barry W. **The Economic Rationale For Copyright Protection for Published Books: A Reply to Professor Breyer.** *Bulletin of the Copyright Society of the U.S.A.* **19: 99-128. December 1971.**

The author focuses upon the essential features of Professor Breyer's article (The Uneasy Case For Copyright: A Study of Copyright in Books, Photocopies, and Computer Programs. *Harvard Law Review* 84: 281-351. December 1970) and then proceeds to furnish a reply to each of them in turn.

U.S. Congress. House. Committee of Conference. *General Revision of the Copyright Law, Title 17 of the United States Code: Conference Report.* **94th Cong., 2nd sess., 1976, H. Rept. 94-1733. 82 p.**

Following the text of the substitute Revision Bill, those sections wherein disagreements between the House and Senate versions appeared are outlined. Where there were disagreements, the Report presents the Senate version, the House version, and the Conference substitute. The CONTU guidelines on photocopying for interlibrary arrangements are accepted as a "reasonable interpretation" of Section 108(g)(2), but the Report notes that they are not intended to be "determinative in themselves."

U.S. Congress. House. Committee on the Judiciary. *Copyright Law Revision: Hearings on H.R. 2223.* **94th Cong., 1st sess., May 7-December 4, 1975. Three Volumes.**

The hearings, held before the House Subcommittee on Courts, Civil Liberties, and the Administration of Justice, considered the House equivalent of S. 22, the Senate bill which became the new Copyright Revision Law. Of particular interest is the testimony presented in Parts 1 and 3. The testimony in Part 1 discusses the history of attempts to revise the 1909 law; the library photocopying issue; the problem of educational uses of copyrighted material; the performance rights in jukebox performances; and the cable copyright problem. The testimony in Part 3 includes a summary by Barbara Ringer, the Register of Copyrights, of the provisions of the bill and some of the controversies surrounding such provisions as library photocopying.

U.S. Congress. House. Committee on the Judiciary. *Copyright Law Revision: Report to Accompany H.R. 2512.* **90th Cong., 1st sess., 1967, H. Rept. 90-83. 253 p.**

A favorable report on H.R. 2512 for the general revision of the Copyright Law, Title 17 of the *United States Code* with a recommendation that the bill be passed. The first 144 pages are devoted to a summary of the principal provisions. Pages 145 to 251 are tabulations of the proposed changes in existing law. The last two pages state dissents.

U.S. Congress. House. Committee on the Judiciary. *Copyright Law Revision: Report to Accompany S. 22.* **94th Cong., 2nd sess., 1976, H. Rept. 94-1476. 368 p.**

The House version of S. 22, the Copyright Revision Bill, is presented along with a section-by-section analysis. Included in this Report is a parallel table comparing the texts of the Senate version of S. 22, Title 17 of the *United States Code* (the then-current Copyright Law), and the House version of the bill.

U.S. Congress. Senate. Committee on the Judiciary. *Copyright Law Revision: Hearings on S. 597.* **90th Cong., 1st sess., March 15-April 28, 1967. Four Volumes.**

The Subcommittee on Patents, Trademarks and Copyrights resumed the public hearing on legislation to provide for a general revision of the Copyright Law. It considered all sections of S. 597 with the exception of CATV.

U.S. Congress. Senate. Committee on the Judiciary. *Copyright Law Revision: Report to Accompany S. 22.* **94th Cong., 1st sess., 1975, S. Rept. 94-473. 169 p.**

The Report includes the text of S. 22, the Senate's version of the Copyright Revision Bill; a brief outline of the history of the copyright legislation; and a sectional analysis of the provisions of the Revision Bill.

L. INTERNATIONAL

The issues involved in technology and copyright have been actively considered within the last few years in other countries as they have been in the United States. This section provides references which illustrate how other countries have been seeking to balance the rights of users of the new technologies with those of copyright owners. Additionally, multinational groups, such as the Berne Union and Universal Copyright Convention, have been searching for international solutions to the same problems. Related references may be found in Sections A. Technology; C. Reprography; and I. Libraries, Networks, and Information Systems.

Selected Materials related to technology and copyright on an International level will be found in Part II: International Bureau of the World Intellectual Property Organization, *Model Provisions on the Protection of Computer Software* (Introduction); and *Copyright and Designs Law: Report of the Committee to consider the Law on Copyright and Designs* (Chapter 4).

Advisory Group of Non-Governmental Experts on the Protection of Computer Programs. Second Session, Geneva, June 23 to 27, 1975. Note. *Copyright* **11: 183-185. September 1975.**

The Advisory Group recommended that a special form of legal protection for computer software should be developed which would include protection for both the program's code and accompanying documentation. The group reserved for further study the question of whether there should be any principle of fair use associated with computer programs. The possibility of an international register for computer programs was also considered.

Benjamin, Curtis G. Photocopying: World Bodies Decide Against International Guidelines. *Publishers Weekly* **208(7): 28. August 18, 1975.**

A commentary on the meeting of two subcommittees of UNESCO and the World Intellectual Property Organization (WIPO) is presented. It was decided in the joint meeting not to recommend guidelines for the organizations' members in adopting regulations for photocopying copyrighted works covered by the Universal Copyright and the Berne Conventions. Despite that decision, this essay applauds the conference for realizing that finding an equitable solution to the photocopying problems on the national level is very difficult and that it would be premature to establish international guidelines before the problems at the national level had been resolved. The final resolution of the conference is outlined.

Benjamin, Curtis G. Regulation of Photocopying: A World-Wide Quandary. *Library Journal* **100: 1481-1483. September 1, 1975.**

A brief survey of the way in which selected foreign countries regulate photocopying, especially that done for educational purposes, is presented. The discussion focuses on photocopying regulations in Sweden, West Germany, France, the United Kingdom, the Netherlands, and Australia. It is suggested that each country has its own set of circumstances on which the solution to the problem of photocopying rests. The magnitude of the problem increases in those countries with a large number of copying machines.

Committee to consider the Law on Copyright and Designs. *Copyright and Designs Law: Report of the Committee to consider the Law on Copyright and Designs.* **London: Her Majesty's Stationery Office, 1977. 272 p.**

This Committee, chaired by Mr. Justice Whitford, was established to review the British Copyright Act of 1956 and the Design Copyright Act of 1968 to determine whether changes were desirable. Of particular interest in the Committee's Report are those chapters pertaining to reprography, audio and video recording, diffusion (which includes cable television), and computers. The material on computers covers computer software, data bases, and works created by computer. Each chapter begins with a discussion of the current situation in Great Britain followed by a review of the way in which other countries and international conventions handle the subject. Also included in each chapter is a review of some of the views received by the Committee during the course of its study and the Committee's recommendations. The Report includes a summary chapter listing the recommendations as they appear at the end of each chapter. An index is provided.

Commonwealth Secretariat. *Copyright in the Developing Countries.* **Second Edition. London: Commonwealth Secretariat, 1976. 24 p.**

A review of those provisions of international copyright agreements which relate to the dissemination of copyrighted materials in the developing countries is presented. Special emphasis is given to the provisions of the Berne and Universal Copyright Conventions. Part A examines general questions of copyright, such as copying and photocopying of copyrighted materials and compulsory licensing, while Part B examines the usual conditions included in publication agreements between authors and publishers.

Gerbrandy, S.   The Netherlands Solution to the Problem of Reprography. *Copyright* **11: 47-51. February 1975.**

Legislation regulating reproduction by reprography has been enacted in the Netherlands. The effects of the law on individuals, public service institutions (including libraries and educational facilities), and businesses are examined. Public service institutions and enterprises are required to pay royalties set by royal ordinance. The effect of this legislation on the other members of the Berne Convention is also discussed.

Gotlieb, Allan, Charles Dalfen, and Kenneth Katz.   The Transborder Transfer of Information by Communications and Computer Systems: Issues and Approaches to Guiding Principles. *American Journal of International Law* **68: 227-257. April 1974.**

The balance between "informational sovereignty" and the free flow of information across national borders is analyzed. Specifically, the essay examines the effect broadcasting satellites, remote-sensing satellites, and the transmission and computer storage of data outside the country of origin has on this balance. The authors suggest that each nation should have some authority to protect its national interests and those of its citizens by exerting some control over the information entering or leaving the country. However, such authority should be based on bilateral or multilateral agreements and should not be unilateral or arbitrary.

Gotzen, Frank.   Copyright and the computer. *Copyright* **13: 15-21. January 1977.**

There is a trend on the international level toward developing a protection system for computer programs that is based on aspects of both patent law and copyright. Some of the provisions of both patent law and copyright relating to computer programs are reviewed, along with copyright problems associated with the storage and retrieval of copyrighted works and the issue of whether computer-generated works should be afforded copyright protection. The conclusion reached is that copyright will continue to protect literary and artistic property which, in turn, will continue to adapt to technological changes.

Heaps, Doreen M. and G.A. Cooke. National Policies, National Networks, and National Information Studies in Canada. In *The Information Conscious Society.* **Proceedings of the American Society for Information Science, Volume 7, edited by Jeanne B. North, pp. 199-203. Washington: American Society for Information Science, 1970.**

This paper outlines briefly the more significant Canadian studies of information networks, the influence upon and interaction with national policy and their implications for the education of information scientists.

International Bureau of the World Intellectual Property Organization. *Model Provisions on the Protection of Computer Software.* **(Reprinted in** *Law and Computer Technology* **11: 2-27. First Quarter 1978).**

The Model Provisions on the Protection of Computer Software, which were developed by the International Bureau of the World Intellectual Property Organization, are presented and discussed. These model provisions, the result of six years of effort, create a potential international standard for minimum protection of computer programs. By providing protection to the proprietor and/or creator of computer programs, this protection would aid developing countries in gaining access to computer software. The form of protection offered in the model provisions closely parallels copyright. Each of the sections of the model law is followed by comments on the provision. Appended to the presentation and analysis of the model law are the names of those non-governmental experts, governments, and intergovernmental organizations that participated in the sessions leading to the model provisions.

Karp, Irwin. Downgrading the Protection of International Copyright. *Publishers Weekly* **200(13) 143-147. September 27, 1971.**

The revised texts of the 1952 Universal Copyright Convention and the Berne Convention and the purpose of the revisions are discussed. The degree to which international copyright protection is affected by the revision conferences held in Paris in July 1971 will want to be the subject of study for both "developed" and "developing" nations.

Kerever, Andre.   Cable Distribution and Copyright in French Law and in the International Conventions. *Copyright* **13: 48-57. February 1977.**

Cable distribution has not yet been used extensively in France, but it can be expected to be used more often in the future. The legal provisions governing cable distribution under French copyright law and under the Berne Convention are reviewed.

Kerever, André.   The International Copyright Conventions and Reprography. *Copyright* **12: 188-196. July-August 1976.**

The provisions of the Berne Union and the Universal Copyright Convention relating to reprography are analyzed. In June 1975 representatives from both Conventions met in Washington, D.C., to study methods of protecting authors' and publishers' economic interests in the area of photocopying. Although the ultimate responsibility for resolving the problems associated with reprography resides with the separate states, a number of alternatives for resolving the photocopying issue were examined. The participants seemed to prefer collective systems over other alternatives, such as a surcharge on equipment.

Keyes, A.A. and C. Brunet. *Copyright In Canada. Proposals for a Revision of the Law.* **Hull, Quebec: Consumer and Corporate Affairs Canada, April 1977. 245 p.**

Proposals and recommendations for the revision of the Canadian Copyright Act are presented. Part I reviews the history of the Canadian experience with copyright law and outlines the reasons for revision, while Part II analyzes the economic significance of copyright. Recommendations addressing the issues which have caused the need for revision are presented in Part III. Part IV deals with administrative details resulting, in part, from the recommendations set forth in Part III. Of special interest are those sections relating to fair dealing, photocopying, cablecasting, the use of copyrighted works in conjunction with computer systems, and copyright protection for computer programs.

Klaver, Franca.   The Legal Problems of Video-Cassettes and Audio-Visual Discs. *Bulletin of the Copyright Society of the U.S.A.* **23: 152-185. February 1976.**

The copyright problems relating to the public, semi-public (educational), and private uses of video-cassettes and audio-visual discs are delineated. Also discussed is the position of performers, authors, and producers of copyrighted works in relation to the use of these devices under the Berne and Universal Copyright Conventions. Because much policy discretion is left to the member countries, the relevant provisions of national copyright acts are reviewed, specifically those of Australia, Canada, Japan, the United States, and the European countries.

Klaver, Francesca. Satellites. Communication-Satellites and International Copyright. *Gazette* **20: 57-72. 1974.**

The evolution and the provisions of a draft "Convention relating to the distribution of programme-carrying signals transmitted by satellite" are reviewed. The purpose of the Convention was to prevent pirating of broadcast signals transmitted by satellite.

Kolle, Gert. Computer Software Protection—Present Situation and Future Prospects. *Copyright* **13: 70-79. March 1977.**

Following a description of existing forms of software protection (i.e., contracts, trade secrets, patent law, and copyright law), the provisions of a proposed model law specifically designed by the World Intellectual Property Organization (WIPO) for protecting computer software are reviewed. The protection afforded by the model law would be executed by the national laws of the subscribing countries.

Lahore, James. Photocopying in Australian Libraries: Developments in Copyright Law. *International Journal of Law Libraries* **4: 32-37. March 1976.**

This article reviews the decision in the landmark Australian copyright case, *University of New South Wales* v. *Moorhouse and Angus & Robertson (Publishers) Pty. Ltd.* [(1975) 6ALR 193], which held that a library may be held liable for the infringing photocopying done by its patrons on unsupervised machines if adequate safeguards against infringement are not implemented.

Lottman, Herbert R. Photocopying: How is Europe Handling the Problem? *Publishers Weekly* **206(22): 26-27. November 25, 1974.**

A brief review of photocopying policies in Sweden, Austria, France, the Netherlands, West Germany, and Italy is presented. While Sweden, West

Germany, and the Netherlands have each implemented royalty payment plans for photocopying (with exemptions), West Germany and the Netherlands appear most concerned with the copying of scientific periodical articles by commercial firms.

National Science Foundation. Office of Science Information Service. *U.S.-U.S.S.R. Copyright Negotiations on Scientific and Technical Journals.* **Washington: National Science Foundation, June 1974. 52 p.**

The results of a survey designed to determine the attitudes of American publishers toward the royalty rate offered by the Soviet Union in return for the right to reproduce and distribute scientific and technical journals published in the United States are reported. The majority of respondents thought the rate offered was inequitable. Only 18 percent of the publishers surveyed had completed agreements with the U.S.S.R.; 54 percent of these publishers accepted the Soviet standard agreement. A breakdown of the responses, the Statute of the Copyright Agency of the U.S.S.R. (VAAP), and a sample Soviet Agreement for Reproduction Rights to U.S. Journals are appended.

Report of the Working Group on the Legal Problems Arising from the Use of Videocassettes and Audiovisual Discs. **UNESCO/WIPO/VWG/I/8. February 25, 1977. 9 p.**

The Working Group examined the legal position of "videograms" in relation to the Berne and Universal Copyright Conventions and reached the conclusion that the current provisions of both Conventions would adequately cover the use of videograms.

Ringer, Barbara A. Role of the United States in International Copyright—Past, Present and Future. *Georgetown Law Journal* **56: 1050-1079. June 1968.**

"International copyright is facing a crisis, and the directions it takes will influence, if not determine, the future intellectual climate and cultural achievements of the entire world." (Page 1051). Principal headings: Historical Background; Developments 1952-1967; The Stockholm Conference; and The Aftermath of Stockholm. "Unless copyright owners in the developed countries go forward soon with programs involving major concessions to the developing countries, . . . they are likely to find their works being used in those countries without permission or payment." (page 1079).

Soroka, Allen and Françoise Hébert, coordinators. CACUL Copyright Workshop. *Canadian Library Journal* **33: 87-117. April 1976.**

The purpose of this Canadian workshop was to review different aspects of copyright and to increase librarians' awareness of the effect of the Canadian Copyright Law on them. Of particular interest were the panel "Copyright and the Non-print Media," which discussed such topics as fair dealing and compulsory licenses to copy material, and the "Mock Copyright Trial," which presented similar facts as those in *Williams & Wilkins*. However, this trial used the current Canadian Copyright Law. No verdict is presented.

Ulmer, Eugen. Automatic and, In Particular, Computerized Information and Documentation Systems and the Copyright Law. *Copyright* **11: 239-246. December 1975.**

This article reviews the formation of information and documentation centers with emphasis on the data components to be included in national and international information systems. The use of electronic data processing (EDP) in conjunction with microforms in disseminating bibliographic and copyrighted information is described and the copyright implications of these developments in relation to the international conventions are outlined.

Ulmer Eugen. Copyright Problems Arising from the Use of Copyright Materials in Automatic Information and Documentation Systems. *Copyright* **14: 66-70. February 1978.**

American, British, and Canadian proposals relating to the use of copyrighted works in conjunction with computerized information systems are reviewed. Although believing that provisions in both the Berne and Universal Copyright Conventions can cover the use of copyrighted works with computerized systems, the author feels that the issue should be resolved in the jurisdictions noted above before an international solution is recommended.

United Nations Educational, Scientific and Cultural Organisation. *Guidelines for the Creation of National and Regional Copyright Information Centers.* **(Reprinted in** *Information Hotline* **9(10): 9-11. November 1977).**

The International Copyright Information Centre of the United Nations Educational, Scientific and Cultural Organisation (Unesco) drafted these Guidelines in an effort to facilitate the use of copyrighted works by developing countries. The Guidelines include both recommendations and essential elements for establishing a regional or national copyright information center. The goal of each center would be to obtain and exchange information on producers, creators, and publishers of copyrighted works and to arrange favorable terms for the use of these works by users from developing countries.

Wallace, William C.M.G. The Impact of New Technology on International Copyright and Neighboring Rights—The Ninth Annual Jean Geiringer Memorial Lecture on International Copyright Law. *Bulletin of the Copyright Society of the U.S.A.* **18: 293-303. April 1971.**

This talk focuses on computer storage and retrieval of copyrighted works and on the impact on international copyright of communication satellites. The former topic is discussed with primary emphasis on existing British law. The author believes that current British law provides protection against unauthorized computer input of copyrighted works. Communication satellites are discussed in relation to current international agreements, primarily the Rome Convention of 1961.

Wilson, A.J. Photocopying: "Fair Dealing" Under the Copyright Act 1968. *University of Western Australia Law Review* **12: 181-198. December 1975.**

The Australian case of *Moorhouse and Angus & Robertson (Publishers) Pty. Ltd. v. University of New South Wales* [(1974) 3 ALR 1 (Supreme Court of NSW, Equity Division); (1975) 6 ALR 193 (High Court)] is examined in the light of the "fair dealing" provisions of the Australian Copyright Act. The High Court ruled that the "various measures adopted by the University, even when considered cumulatively, do not appear . . . to have amounted to reasonable or effective precautions against an infringement of copyright by use of the [University Library's] photocopying machines." Although the Act permits photocopying for research and private use, this does not include substantial copying. Substantiality should be determined primarily arithmetically.

M. BASIC REFERENCES

The references appearing below are to sources which regularly discuss the issues involved within the scope of this book. No attempt has been made to provide a complete list of references on copyright. For such an authoritative list the reader is referred to Luciana Chee, "How to Research Copyright Law," *Law Library Journal* 70: 171-183, May 1977.

Bulletin of the Copyright Society of the U.S.A. **Published every two months by The Copyright Society at the Law Center of New York University, New York.**

Each issue of the *Bulletin of the Copyright Society of the U.S.A.* contains articles on several aspects of copyright law. The *Bulletin* also includes bibliographical coverage of national and international legislative and administrative developments in copyright law; conventions, treaties, and proclamations; and judicial developments in literary and artistic property. An extensive annotated bibliography covering books, treatises, and articles from law reviews and trade magazines appears in each issue.

Bush, George P., editor. *Technology and Copyright: Annotated Bibliography and Source Materials.* **Mt. Airy, Maryland: Lomond Publications, Inc., 1972. 454 p.**

This book is the first edition of the present volume. Part II, Source Material, provides documents of historical significance. Among the items included in Part II are Stephen Breyer's essay "The Uneasy Case for Copyright: A Study of Copyright in Books, Photocopies, and Computer Programs;" Walter L. Pforzheimer's "Historical Perspective on Copyright Law and Fair Use;" Jackson S. Saunders' "Origin of the 'Gentlemen's Agreement' of 1935" which reprints the text of the Agreement; and the complete Trial Judge's opinion in the *Williams & Wilkins* case. Topical, name, and case indexes are provided.

Computer Law Service, **edited by Robert Bigelow. Chicago: Callaghan & Co., 1975.**

The *Computer Law Service* is a multi-volume set composed of articles, appendixes, and cases relating to the following nine areas involved in the relationship between law and computer technology: (1) The Law and the Computer; (2) Legal Problems of Systems Design; (3) Computer System Procurement; (4) Protection of Proprietary Rights; (5) Liability Aspects of Computer Usage and Other Litigation Problems; (6) Data Communications; (7) Other Governmental Aspects; (8) Legal Aspects of Particular Industry Applications; and (9) International Aspects. The articles and appendixes are included in updatable compression-bound volumes, while the court decisions are issued in the hardbound *Computer Law Service Reporter*. A looseleaf *Current Reporter Volume* contains advance sheets of court decisions as well as finding aids for the other volumes.

Copyright. **Published monthly by the World Intellectual Property Organization (WIPO), Geneva, Switzerland.**

Copyright reports on the activities of the Berne Union and on the various copyright and neighboring rights conventions administered by the World Intellectual Property Organization (WIPO). In addition, information on those conventions not administered by WIPO is presented. Each issue normally contains at least one feature article highlighting some aspect of international copyright or neighboring rights. Book reviews and a calendar of WIPO meetings are also included.

Copyright Law Symposium. **Published annually for the American Society of Composers, Authors and Publishers by the Columbia University Press, New York.**

The winning essays of the annual Nathan Burkan Memorial Competition, sponsored by the American Society of Composers, Authors and Publishers (ASCAP), are presented. The essays, which are written by law students, must relate to some aspect of copyright.

Copyright Management. **Published monthly by the Institute for Invention and Innovation, Inc., Arlington, Massachusetts.**

This monthly newsletter is designed to provide practical information to authors, publishers, librarians, individuals in data processing, and others involved in the management of intellectual property. Among the features included are announcements of upcoming seminars and new publications, and brief reviews of events relating to intellectual property management.

Henry, Nicholas. *Copyright, Congress and Technology: The Public Record Volume I: The Formative Years, 1958-1966.* **Phoenix, Arizona: The Oryx Press, 1978. 46l p.**

This volume, the first of a scheduled four-volume set, reprints selected portions from the annual reports of the Register of Copyrights (1958 through 1966) along with several studies produced for the early efforts to revise the 1909 Copyright Act. Selections from the 1961 *Report of the Register of Copyrights on the General Revision of the U.S. Copyright Law* and from the early congressional hearings are also included. The emphasis of this volume and the following volumes is on the legislative process involved in the revision of those portions of the 1909 Copyright Act concerning the "neo-publishing" technologies (e.g., photocopying and computers). Among the items to be reprinted in the three succeeding volumes are portions of the annual reports of the Register of Copyrights for the years 1967 through 1976, portions of the congressional hearings, the six CONTU-sponsored studies, and the complete text of the 1976 Copyright Law.

Information Hotline. **Published 11 times yearly by Science Associates/International, Inc., New York.**

Information Hotline presents national and international news on all aspects of the information industry. The newsletter also includes the full text of speeches, regulations, guidelines, and other material which conveys important developments or ideas in the information field; course and conference announcements; announcements of recent grants and contracts awarded by the National Science Foundation; lists of papers presented at recent information-oriented conferences; and references to new publications, with a special section devoted to reports available from the National Technical Information Service (NTIS).

Nimmer on Copyright, **by Melville B. Nimmer. Four Volumes. New York: Matthew Bender & Company, Inc. 1978.**

This is a complete revision of the significant legal treatise on copyright law. The first three volumes contain an analysis of copyright under the 1976 law. This analysis is supported by references to the case law and to the congressional reports which accompanied the 1976 Copyright Act. The final volume contains, among many other items, the text of the 1976 law, the House and Conference reports, the texts of international copyright conventions, Copyright Office regulations issued pursuant to the 1909 and

1976 laws, a table of cases cited in the text, and an index. [While mainly an exposition on the law, this work provides insight and guidance in many areas in which readers of this book would have substantial interest.—editor's note].

Publishers Weekly. **Published weekly by the R.R. Bowker Co., Whitinsville, Massachusetts.**

Although primarily a trade magazine for the publishing industry, *Publishers Weekly* has regularly reported new developments in copyright law which affect the industry.

PART II
SELECTED MATERIALS

INTRODUCTION TO SELECTED MATERIALS

In the lead paper, *Copyright in the 1980's,* Register of Copyrights Barbara Ringer voices her fears about the trend "to expand the concept of compulsory licensing into every new form of use of copyrighted works created by changes in communications technology." In the paper which follows, *Impact of Information Technology on Copyright Law in the Use of Computerized Scientific and Technological Information Systems,* judicial decisions are used to trace the role of technological developments in changing the copyright law.

The three topics which best seem to exemplify the tension between the new technologies and the rights of copyright owners are computers, video communication (including cable television and off-the-air recording), and reprography. The Congress, when it enacted the Copyright Act of 1976, left for future consideration many of the issues associated with computer technology. The National Commission on New Technological Uses of Copyrighted Works (CONTU) was established to study the use of copyrighted works in conjunction with computer systems and reproducing equipment. In July 1978 CONTU presented its recommendations to the Congress. (See heading, "CONTU," in Part I.)

In *Copyright and Compilations in the Computerized Era: Old Wine in New Bottles,* Jeffrey Squires, who was an attorney with CONTU, examines the copyright status of machine-readable compilations of bibliographic information. He concludes that "machine-readable data bases, which are functionally identical to their hard copy counterparts, should not be denied proprietary protection to which the latter are entitled." (It should be noted that references to the "present Copyright Act" in that article refer to the 1909 Act.)

Much of the debate concerning computers and copyright has focused on the copyrightability of computer software. The issues involved in an economic analysis for determining whether copyright is the best form of protection for computer software and data bases and for arriving at the optimal term of protection are presented in the overview of *Economics of Property Rights as Applied to Computer Software and Data Bases.*

Agreement that computer software (programs) is deserving of copyright protection is not unanimous. Author John Hersey, who served as a commissioner of CONTU, expresses his opposition to affording copyright protection to computer programs in his *Dissent from CONTU's Software Recommendation.* CONTU recommended that computer software be eligible for copyright protection. However, Commissioner Hersey is not opposed to protecting computer software through other forms of protection; he objects only to the idea of providing this protection through copyright law which he feels is the province of writings which communicate with humans, rather than with machines.

The need for software protection is recognized on an international level. To this end, the World Intellectual Property Organization (WIPO) has developed *Model Provisions on the Protection of Computer Software.* These provisions essentially follow a copyright law approach. A summary of the provisions and an analysis of the need for such protection are included in Part II. The stated purpose of these provisions is to eliminate the "uncertainty as to the protection of computer software under various legal systems."

The Register of Copyrights has stated that the cable television issue "has been the reef on which copyright law revision foundered for seven years." Susan Greene in her essay, *The Cable Television Provisions of the Revised Copyright Act,* sorts out and explains the complexities of the cable provisions of the 1976 Copyright Law.

An issue of growing importance and of continuing controversy is the extent to which private individuals can record copyrighted television programs off-the-air for later viewing. Steven Brill, in his article *Will Betamax Be Busted?,* reviews the issues involved in a major court case on home video recording.

The document selected to provide a background and an overview of the relation reprography (primarily photocopying) has to copyright law is a chapter on reprography from the British report *Copyright and Designs Law* prepared by the Committee to consider the Law on Copyright and Designs, better known as the Whitford Committee. The committee was established to determine whether changes to the British Copyright Act of 1956 and the Design Copyright Act of 1968 were desirable. The Chapter provides a clear definition of reprography and offers a view of how other countries are dealing with the issues raised by photocopying and reprography, in general. The reader should pay special attention to the committee's recommendation that there should be no exemption for fair use or library photocopying once blanket licensing arrangements can be established.

The information and communication technologies described in the items cited above have had a significant effect on the development of information and library networks. New networks are constantly being created, while older ones are being expanded. Madeline Henderson explains in *Copyright Impacts of Future Technology* that higher costs and budgetary constraints have forced libraries to look for more economical and efficient means of acquiring and disseminating information. She examines the development and trends in computer, communication, reprographic, and micrographic technologies leading toward the creation of networks.

The impact that the 1976 Copyright Law would have on libraries produced much debate and controversy during the development of the law. The issue of library photocopying caused the most controversy. During the years immediately preceding enactment of the 1976 law, representatives from the copyright proprietors (i.e., publishers and authors) and the library community had been largely unsuccessful in reaching agreement on permissible photocopying practices.

The National Commission of Libraries and Information Science was the primary sponsor of a study of the kinds and amounts of photocopying occurring in academic, public, Federal, and special libraries, and on possible royalty payment mechanisms. The result of this effort is the King Research study on *Library Photocopying in the United States: With Implications for the Development of a Copyright Royalty Payment Mechanism,* the summary of which is reprinted in this section. Also included is the summary of a CONTU-funded study, *Survey of Publisher Practices and Present Attitudes on Authorized Journal Article Copying and Licensing,* which surveyed publishers of research and scholarly journals on various methods of providing copies of articles to users.

The effect of library photocopying on publisher revenues is still unclear, particularly on the sale of journal subscriptions. In their article, *The Effect of a Large-Scale Photocopying Service on Journal Sales,* Maurice Line and D. N. Wood of the British Library Lending Division (BLLD) claim that there is no evidence that the photocopying done by the BLLD has adversely affected the sale of scholarly journals. Mr. E. van Tongeren contends in his reply, which is rebutted by Line and Wood, that the BLLD photocopying services are causing significant increases in journal subscription cancellations by academic libraries.

Domestically, the same theme has been raised by those who believe library resource sharing (including interlibrary loan, consortia, and centralized libraries' libraries) has caused academic libraries to cancel journal subscriptions. Richard De Gennaro argues in his award-winning article, *Copyright, Resource Sharing, and Hard Times: A View from the Field,* that resource sharing among libraries has not caused significant decreases in publisher revenues. He also points out that this sharing will not solve the budgetary problems libraries are experiencing. In general, he believes that rising costs and changing market conditions, not library photocopying, are responsible for the revenue problems of publishers.

Those who framed the provisions of the 1976 law on library photocopying sought a balance between copyright proprietors and library users. James Treece examines this balance in *Library Photocopying* and offers a rule of thumb for determining the point beyond which library photocopying substitutes for a purchase of a journal subscription. Treece believes that the law precludes the sharing of copyrighted works or "rationalizing" acquisitions through library networks without obtaining a license from the copyright owners.

Closely related to library photocopying is the subject of "fair use." The fair use doctrine developed in the case law. The Congress codified the concept in the 1976 legislation. Stephen Freid examines the application of the criteria used by the courts in determining whether a particular use is fair. He argues that the two most important criteria for determining fair use are the purpose of the use and the economic effect of the use on the copyrighted work. He examines the judicial application of these criteria and concludes that the Court of Claims did not properly apply the criteria in the *Williams & Wilkins* case.

Williams & Wilkins Co. v. United States is the only major copyright case involving fair use and photocopying. The opinion of the Trial Judge finding that the photocopying practices of the National Institutes of Health (NIH) and the National Library of Medicine (NLM) did infringe Williams & Wilkins' copyright in its journal articles is reprinted in the first edition of *Technology and Copyright*. In November 1973, the full Court of Claims overturned the Trial Judge's opinion on a four to three vote. The court decided that the publisher had not shown actual economic loss from the contested photocopying practices of NIH and NLM. (Mr. Freid argues that showing actual loss is not required.) Furthermore, the court argued that medical research could be seriously harmed if such copying were deemed infringing. An equally divided Supreme Court upheld the opinion of the Court of Claims in February 1975. The Court of Claims' majority opinion and part of the dissent are reprinted.

These selections provide an overview of the major technology-related issues and concerns confronting copyright owners and the users of their works. The 1976 Copyright Law is complex. It is hoped that if these items cannot resolve the complexities associated with the 1976 law, they can at least help to explain why the complexities exist.

COPYRIGHT IN THE 1980's

by Barbara Ringer*

When Paul Gitlin called to invite me to deliver the Sixth Donald C. Brace Memorial Lecture, he did me more honor than he knew. Donald Clifford Brace was a truly outstanding publisher, who brought to the American public the works of some of the greatest English authors of the Twentieth Century. Among them is the single writer whose works and voice and life have spoken to me more directly than that of any other: George Orwell.

In 1946 Orwell wrote to his agent, Leonard Moore:

> You mentioned in your last letter something about giving Harcourt Brace an option on future books. It's a bit premature as I have no book in preparation yet, but I should think Harcourt Brace would be the people to tie up with, as they had the courage to publish *Animal Farm*. But of course they may well be put off the idea if the book flops in the USA, as it well may. I am not sure whether one can count on the American public grasping what it is about. You may remember that [a certain publisher] had been asking me for some years for a manuscript, but when I sent the MS of *AF* in 1944 they returned it, saying shortly that "it was impossible to sell animal stories in the USA." . . . So I suppose it might be worth indicating on the dust-jacket of the American edition what the book is about. However, Harcourt Brace would be the best judges of that.

Harcourt Brace did, in fact, go on to publish Orwell's next work, one whose literary and historical significance, and whose ultimate social influence, cannot be exaggerated. The title of Orwell's work, "1984" has become a symbol and, I fear, a political slogan of exactly the kind he was attacking in the book. The popularity of the title as a catch

---

* Register of Copyrights. The views of the author are personal and are not intended to reflect any official positions of the Copyright Office or of the Library of Congress. No copyright is claimed in this lecture.

SOURCE: Sixth Donald C. Brace Memorial Lecture presented March 25, 1976.

phrase has obscured and distorted the meaning of the work itself. Orwell, who was dying when the novel was published in 1949, cast his story in terms of the utmost pessimism, but his intention was the opposite of despair. "1984" is a kind of hymn to what Erich Fromm has called the very roots of Occidental culture: the spirit of humanism and dignity. Most of all it is a warning that the values on which our culture is based—of individualism, idealism, and free expression—are in the most immediate possible danger, not from any particular ideology or political system, but simply from the juggernaut of technology. Orwell was powerfully and desperately trying to warn us of the new barbarism just around the corner, of "the new form of managerial industrialism in which," to quote Fromm's trenchant essay, "man builds machines which act like men and develops men who act like machines"—of "an era of dehumanization and complete alienation, in which men are transformed into things and become appendices to the process of production and consumption."

For publishing this book, and for publishing George Orwell at all, Donald Brace deserves to be thanked and honored. The message Orwell was seeking to convey affected the lives and actions of some members of my generation very profoundly. And yet today, less than eight years from the date Orwell chose as his particular doomsday—when everything he predicted is coming true, and not just in other countries—we accept these horrors as inevitable or even acceptable, and spend most of our time looking for personal anodynes.

When he first called to ask me about making this lecture, Paul Gitlin had just seen a piece I wrote for the Centennial Issue of the *Library Journal* titled "Copyright and the Future Condition of Authorship." He said he found the tone of my essay pessimistic, and he rather implied that I might do well to make this lecture a little more up-beat. As I told him, my own feeling is not one of despair, and I certainly have no wish to plunge anyone into a blue funk over what is happening to copyright and the condition of authorship. But in copyright, which is the particular field I am called upon to plow, I do believe that people should be made to recognize the dangers and to realize that there is still a chance to do something toward averting them.

I am making these remarks at a time that may prove to be a major turning point in the history of American copyright law. In February the bill for general revision of the copyright law, which has been pending in Congress for nearly 12 years, passed the Senate unanimously by a vote of 97 to nothing. Progress in the House of Representatives has been slow, and I see enormous difficulties in the months ahead, but I still believe it is safe to predict enactment of the bill this year. If I am wrong, if the efforts to reform the present copyright statute of 1909 have to continue into the 1980's in the face of on-rushing technological change, I am afraid the picture I am painting will be much darker and bleaker than I anticipate.

I prefer to look on the brighter side. I base my analysis of copyright in the 1980's on the assumption that S. 22 of the 94th Congress will be in effect before the start of that decade, and that the impact of its changes will already have been felt. These changes will certainly lay the basis for the conditions of authorship and the dissemination of authors' works during the last quarter of this century.

When I began to frame the outline of this lecture I first thought I would take the specific provisions of S. 22 and project them into the 1980's, in an attempt to analyze how they should work out in practice. It did not take me long to realize that this approach would be both too difficult and too easy: too difficult because of the amount of complex detail and imponderabilia involved, and too easy because it is always simpler to analyze the trees and ignore the forest and the surrounding terrain. Instead, and with considerable misgivings, I will try to take the trends I see working upon and through the domestic revision bill—and in international copyright—and to project what may emerge from them in the next decade. I will try to deal with these trends under four general headings: 1) The nature of copyrightable works and the methods of their dissemination; 2) The nature of rights in copyrightable works; 3) The situation of individual authors; and 4) The role of the state in copyright and authorship.

The nature of copyrightable works and the methods of their dissemination

I believe, with Orwell, that mankind is changing the world through technology and that technology in its turn is changing mankind into technological beings. Where does this leave the creative individual and his ability to present his ideas and creations to others?

It seems almost superfluous to observe that the technological revolution in communications is a pivotal event in the history of mankind, and that its full impact has not yet been felt. Among the plethora of electronic marvels now arrayed for our use, there are those that are merely transitory toys and gadgets, but there are others that seem to some people to have god-like qualities. It is certain that, amid all the electronics and advertising, the quality of human life is changing, and that the real impact of the change has not yet been felt.

Anyone who sits down and thinks about what has happened to mass communications since 1909 can come up with quite a list. Silent and later sound motion pictures; radio and later television and still later cable and pay-television; computers and their ability to assimilate, generate, and manipulate limitless amounts of information; satellites and their potential for reaching and linking everyone on earth; sound recordings and later audio and video tape recordings; photocopying and microreprography; and automation in the composition and reproduction of printed matter. This certainly does not exhaust the list, and many of these developments combine and interact, providing nationwide and worldwide networks for quick or instantaneous dissemination of what passes for information and entertainment. And there is evidently no end to this process: a satellite is already making direct transmissions into individual receiving sets in India; holography is beginning to lose its mystery; and lasers are being used for all sorts of things: for data storage, for communications channels into homes, and as part of commercial video disk players soon to enter the consumer marketplace.

On the face of it, all this opens tremendous new channels for creative endeavor and new ways of reaching huge audiences of readers, and viewers, and listeners, and information seekers. Like the invention of movable type and of painting techniques and musical instruments during the Renaissance, technology is bringing a whole new breed of creators into the communications arts. It is also allowing traditional creators to fix their works permanently and literally to get them into the hands of anyone who wishes to see or hear them. The 80's should see some startling developments in one-way, two-way, and unlimited wireless communications.

Despite the cynicism and alienation that we see everywhere today, most people still welcome each technological "advance" as some sort of miracle and rush to buy and use it for purposes that, if pressed, they might have trouble articulating. Yet, unless I misjudge the signs, there is a growing realization that all this machinery has done less than nothing to improve human life, and the more voracious our craving for technological advance, the more individual people suffer. Instead of fostering perfection in the arts and the creation of masterpieces, the communications revolution has already maimed a number of traditional forms of expression and is destroying our standards, our ability, and our desire to judge our own culture.

I remember someone predicting a few years ago that, if the present trends continue, by the end of the century we will have a great many more birds than we have now, but that they will almost all be either pigeons and *(sic)* starlings. I have the same feeling about the effect of technology on copyright: a great many more works are going to be copyrighted in 1986 than in 1976, but their intrinsic value will continue to decline.

I believe that the courts and the Congress will continue to expand the subject matter protected by copyright and to cover the new uses of copyrighted works made possible by the expanding technology. But if the effect of this limitless expansion is to destroy incentives to truly creative work, to substitute remuneration for inspiration, and to make great creative works compete unequally with vastly increased quantities of trash and propaganda, we will have lost much more than we have gained.

The nature of rights in copyrightable works

Throughout the whole range of national and international copyright regimes since 1950, a single concept insistently recurs: it is usually called compulsory licensing, although in its various guises it may be referred to as "obligatory," "statutory," "legal" or "agreed" licensing. Characteristically, it is offered as a compromise to copyright controversies in two situations: where technology has created new uses for which the author's exclusive rights have not been clearly established, and where technology has made old licensing methods for established rights ponderous or inefficient.

Under a typical compulsory licensing scheme, the author loses the right to control the use of his work, and cannot grant anyone an exclusive license for a certain specified purpose. Instead, his work is lumped with thousands or millions of other works, and the author also becomes a unit in a large collective system under which blanket royalties are received and distributed. The government is involved in operating the system, and the individuality of both authors and works tends to be lost. Authors may be paid well for the use of their works, but their participation in the system is, by definition, compulsory rather than voluntary.

It may come as a shock to realize that S. 22, as it now stands, contains four full-fledged compulsory licenses involving rate-making by a Government tribunal. A separate piece of legislation, which will be pushed very hard in the House, raises the possibility of a fifth, and others may emerge before the bill is finally enacted. As we go into the 1980's, copyright is becoming less the exclusive right of the author and more a system under which the author is insured some remuneration but is deprived of control over the use to which his words are put.

In 1908, Congress was confronted with a peculiar dilemma of either giving exclusive rights to musical copyright owners, and thereby allowing the creation of what they referred to as a giant music trust, or of withholding these rights and thereby causing a great injustice to creators. Congress devised what, to my knowledge—and I have never been challenged on this statement—is the first compulsory license in history, section 1(e) of the present law. There may well have been intellectual antecedents to this under specific court decisions or in private, blanket licensing arrangements; but, as far as statutory, across-the-board, arrangements are concerned, I believe that the copyright royalty for sound recordings was the first compulsory license in the world.

It was copied almost immediately in the copyright statutes of other countries, in the same context of mechanical royalties for recording music. The situation as it evolved in the statute meant that a two-cent limit was imposed on the amount of royalties a copyright owner could get for having a song recorded. Once the owner of the copyright in a musical composition licensed his work for recording, everyone else had a right to make a recording by paying two cents per song per record. This is still the law, all these years later, and it is getting on towards 70 years now.

It would seem, on the basis of a great deal of experience, that this compulsory license is as firmly rooted in our copyright law as anything can be. I suspect that, by the time S. 22 is enacted into law, the two-cent rate will have been raised somewhat, but it is probably too late to raise any philosophical questions about compulsory licensing in this context. Indeed, the trend is exactly the reverse: to expand the concept of compulsory licensing into every new form of use of copyrighted works created by changes in communications technology. This seems certain to be true in the case of jukebox performances and cable television transmissions.

The cable issue, in particular, has been the reef on which copyright law revision foundered for seven years. In 1967, the House Subcommittee, confronted by this new and highly controversial issue, tried as forthrightly as possible to solve the problem through a rather simple form of compulsory license, and without imposing the heavy hand of government regulation. This effort was doomed to failure. The reason was that no one knew what the liability of cable systems was under the law, as construed in 1967. They do now: the Supreme Court has twice held in favor of cable and against exclusive rights under the copyright statute.

Cable became a roaring issue in 1967 and, as a result, when the House passed the bill, the whole cable provision was simply wiped away and the problem was passed to the Senate.

The Senate, in turn, evolved a whole new concept of protection for cable uses of copyrighted works which rested upon a compulsory license and added a new and very significant institution, a copyright royalty tribunal. This new device, which was inevitable when the House approach of 1967 failed, would create a government-associated body empowered to make decisions with respect to the practical running of the compulsory licensing system. Rates would be subject to review by this tribunal and decisions would be made with respect to the distribution of fees.

All three of these compulsory licenses—the so-called mechanical royalty, the jukebox compulsory license, and the compulsory license for cable television—seem certain to be enacted in some form. All three are very deeply rooted in the bill, and they are all related, in one way or another, to a copyright royalty tribunal that would be involved in rate-making and in the distribution of fees.

In 1969, the Senate Subcommittee added a fourth compulsory license for the performance of sound recordings. This turned out to be one of the most controversial provisions in the bill. It was knocked out in the Senate in September of 1974 and has not yet been reintroduced. Interestingly, for a generation or more the organized musicians turned their back on copyright protection and sought to protect their interests through collective bargaining and a controversial trust-fund device. Now, in a complete turnabout, the whole AFL-CIO has joined with the record industry in a concerted effort to enact a copyright law establishing a royalty for the performance of sound recordings in radio and other media. Of course, this is being fought vigorously by the broadcasting industry, and the fight will probably go right down to the House floor, promising a dramatic confrontation.

I am supporting this proposal in principle because I think it is unfair that individual performers have rarely received any of the benefits from the great technological developments that have, to a large extent, actually wiped out their profession. Fairness indicates that it is wrong that they not get paid for performances of their works, and I believe that sooner or later this right will be recognized under some form of compulsory licensing.

When this provision was in the bill the public broadcasters said, "Well, for heaven's sake, if all these commercial interests are going to get something like this compulsory license, why shouldn't we? We public broadcasters are not paying any copyright royalties now, but we recognize that we should. But, even if we have to pay something, we cannot put ourselves in the position of having to get individual clearances for all the music we play, all the graphic works that we show on the screen, and all of the literary works that we read over public radio and on the tube."

They took their problems to Senator Mathias and apparently made a persuasive case, because we now have a new Section 118 in the bill as it passed the Senate. It would create a rather amorphous compulsory license for the public broadcasting of musical compositions, nondramatic literary works, and pictorial, graphic and sculptural works. It would leave to the proposed royalty tribunal the problem of setting the terms, rates, and the entire mechanism for running the compulsory license.

I am opposed to this provision, and particularly its impact on the whole range of nondramatic literary works. At the same time, I am aware of the vast political power of public broadcasters, and I think the chances of facing compulsory licensing in this area in the 1980's are better than ever.

What we have seen demonstrated in the evolution of these five compulsory licensing schemes, and others that seem to be right around the corner, is a kind of inexorable historical process.

- First you have a copyright law that was written at a particular point in the development of communications technology, and without much foresight.

- Then you have technological developments, which create whole new areas for the creation and use of copyrighted works.

- Business investments are made and industries begin to develop.

- The law is ambiguous in allocating rights and liabilities, so no one pays any royalties.

- A point is reached where the courts simply stop expanding the copyright law and say that only Congress can solve the problem by legislation.

- You go to Congress, but you find that you have hundreds of special interests lobbying for or against the expansion of rights, and the legislative task is horrendous.

- So Congress, looking for a compromise, turns to compulsory licensing. On its face, a compulsory licensing system looks fair to each side: the author and copyright owner get paid, but the user, who has made a strong argument that what he is doing represents the public interest, cannot be prevented from using the work.

We have reached the point where any new rights under the copyright law apparently cannot be exclusive rights. If a new technological development makes new forms of exploitation possible, compulsory licensing seems to offer the only solution. This is happening in the United States and it is happening just as much internationally. Compulsory licensing systems represent key provisions in the 1971 revisions of both the Berne and Universal Copyright Conventions, and in recent copyright laws in other countries.

Before the present program for general revision of the copyright law began in 1955, the United States had endeavored successfully to develop an international convention which would provide multilateral copyright relations between Western Hemisphere countries and the European countries members of the Berne Convention. The result was the Universal Copyright Convention, which was signed in Geneva in 1952 and came into effect in 1955.

In its origins the Universal Copyright Convention was considered a low-level transitional treaty which would dry up and blow away as more and more of its members accepted the principles of the Berne Convention. The confident assumption twenty-five years ago was not only that the level of protection reached at the Brussels revision of the Berne Convention in 1948 constituted the norm in international copyright, but that even its relatively high level of protection would continue to rise and expand.

These expectations, have proved false, for at least three interrelated reasons:

- First, the technological revolution in communications and the compulsory licensing demands that it has spawned in practically all countries.

- Second, the needs of developing countries. At crucial conferences in Stockholm in 1967 and Paris in 1971 the developing countries made a persuasive case for an international copyright system that gives them ready access to the materials they need to combat illiteracy, provide educational, and scientific and technical information for their peoples, at prices they can afford to pay. Whether the 1971 revisions of the two conventions have achieved this goal as a practical matter remains to be seen.

  The concessions made in the Paris revisions of both the UCC and Berne Convention, in a general sense, are an attempt to preserve the principles of copyright in the face of the needs of states with limited resources, confronted with difficult and pressing development choices in allocating their expenditures. In this light, the Paris revisions looked towards greater interdependence and cooperative trading relationships within the world copyright community. Whether this approach is realistic in an increasingly inflationary world economy is far from certain.

- Third, the impact of socialist legal thinking. The adherence by the USSR to the 1952 text of the UCC, effective on May 27, 1973, was a dramatic illustration of a trend already apparent in international copyright. Increasingly, the status of an author as an individual controlling definite rights, and the concept of copyright as a form of private property, are being questioned and challenged.

  Socialist attitudes toward property generally have made deep inroads into the fabric of international law. To an extent, it is even something of a misnomer to call them "socialists," since they are frequently attitudes shared and enunciated forcefully by nonsocialist developing states. The 19th Century capitalist tradition of unqualified individual property rights and full freedom of contract disappeared from the West long before the same principles came under attack internationally. The gradual disappearance of colonies has largely produced a reworking of those notions of property and contract which underlay mercantile capitalism. The constitutions and legislation of developing states are replete with provisions which stress that the notion of private property is qualified in all cases by social welfare and necessity. As unique a form of property as copyright is, it has not proved immune from these pressures.

The situation of individual authors

All of these forces seem to be combining throughout the world to substitute compulsory licensing and various forms of state control for exclusive copyright control, and to substitute remuneration for voluntary licensing arrangements. Individual authors, standing alone, are helpless to protect themselves in a situation like this. Ironically, in order to preserve their own independence as authors, they will inevitably be forced to unite in collective bargaining organizations, and to allow their representatives to speak for them.

Authorship, by which I include all kinds of creative endeavor, is in an extra-ordinary state of flux. For some two hundred years, from the end of the patronage system in the late 17th Century to the emergence of the new technology in the beginning of the 20th Century, authors enjoyed something like a direct one-to-one relationship with their readers through their publishers. This relationship has ceased to exist entirely in some creative fields, and is fast disappearing in others. Authors are losing their ability to speak directly to readers, listeners and viewers, and must now deal with increasing hordes of middle-men who control the communications media or the access to them. In this situation it is quite possible to envision the emergence of societies in which there is little individual or independent authorship; most creative work would be done as part of collective endeavors, merged together anonymously, and whatever individual writing remains would be done under the patronage and control of the state.

Copyright is obviously caught up in a social tidal wave. In trying to preserve independent, free, authorship as a natural resource, one must be aware of the changes that are taking place and cautious about the methods adopted and deal with them. Some ideas that are put forward as solutions to practical problems of copyright clearance and access to information may turn out to be more destructive to our society than the problems they are supposed to solve.

I confess that at this point I come to the first of two dilemmas in my present thinking about the next 20 years—questions that I consider of immense importance but to which I can see no clear-cut answers. The first is what individual authors can do to protect themselves from this onslaught of technology. We have already reached a turning point in several areas, and are fast approaching it in others, where the individual creator simply cannot assure himself of fair remuneration for the use of his works unless he joins a collective organization of some sort. ASCAP and BMI are examples of one sort of collective organization in which authors pool their copyrights but maintain some degree of individual ownership and control over their use. The other most common type of organization is a trade union, which represents its members as employees and bargains for them on a collective basis.

There is, quite obviously, a loss of independence in both cases, and for some authors and for some types of work this may prove an intolerable sacrifice. But what are the alternatives? A continuing alliance with publishers or equivalent middle-men in which the individual author's voice cannot be heard? Direct government control over licensing? Direct government patronage?

These are the questions that will inevitably have to be faced and answered in the 1980's, and I find it astonishing that so far there is very little awareness or discussion of them. The discussion should be undertaken by the authors and creators themselves, not by lawyers or government types like me, and not by publishers or film producers or information industry representatives. But a movement toward clearinghouse arrangements and collective licensing has already started, and unless the implications and alternatives are carefully examined, patterns may become established that authors will soon find themselves powerless to change.

The role of the state in copyright and authorship

The most critical question arising from all of these trends involves the role that government will play in the operation of the copyright systems of the 1980's. In the United States that role is clearly expanding. It seems inevitable that the government will shortly be involved in setting regulatory standards and royalty rates, in settling disputes over distribution of statutory royalties, and in establishing means by which individual authors organize for the payment of royalties. How far this process is allowed to go, and how irreversible it is allowed to become, will depend on decisions that must be taken in the immediate future.

My second dilemma thus involves the Copyright Office and what is to become of it. Recognizing what happens whenever bureaucratic nature is allowed to take its course, I feel that the office must resist the lure of embracing new regulatory powers over copyright licensing which could easily grow into government control over the conditions of authorship. Yet, I feel just as strongly that the Copyright Office cannot simply walk away from the problem, leaving it to other would-be government regulators or communicators or patrons to fill the vacuum. The decisions on this question, whatever they are, must be taken in full realization of the dangers facing independent authorship in the next decade, and in full determination to surmount them.

IMPACT OF INFORMATION TECHNOLOGY ON COPYRIGHT LAW IN THE USE OF COMPUTERIZED SCIENTIFIC AND TECHNOLOGICAL INFORMATION SYSTEMS

CRC Systems Incorporated

EXECUTIVE SUMMARY

A.1.1 BACKGROUND

The National Bureau of Standards (NBS) retained CRC Systems Incorporated, 125 Church Street, Suite 202, Vienna, Virginia 22180 to perform an analysis of the impact of information technology on copyright law in the use of computerized Scientific and Technological Information Systems (STI). The purpose of this report is twofold: First, to identify and describe the recent (1900-1970) impacts of technology upon copyright law and second, to present and discuss the potential impact of STI systems upon copyright law.

The accelerated pace of technological change and development during the twentieth century has required major adaptations and adjustments in the body of copyright law that was set forth in the statutes previously enacted. The courts have to a large degree been called upon to adapt the pre-existing copyright statutes by interpretation, to the issues arising from the later development of technologies. By reviewing the more significant decisions, this report attempts to develop for the reader an understanding of the underlying principles and philosophies of the copyright statutes and the court decisions applying to them. With this background and framework of the adaptation heretofore of the copyright law to new technologies, the authors focus upon the new computerized STI technology and the issues that this technology may bring to bear upon the body of copyright law in existence at the time of writing this report.

SOURCE: Originally appeared as Appendix A in Roy G. Saltman's *Copyright in Computer-Readable Works: Policy Impacts of Technological Change.*

A.1.2 SCOPE OF THE STUDY

Although the history of copyright law in the United States dates from 1790, the rapid development of technology, especially electronic-based technologies, has occurred mainly after 1909. In that year the copyright law was rewritten, and it was not until recently (1976) that it was again rewritten. This report therefore will examine the changes, interpretations, and modifications to the 1909 law, and the ramifications of the new 1976 Copyright Law, as they relate to technological changes. The scope of this report is bounded by issues that developed as a direct or indirect consequence of the introduction of new technologies.

A.1.3 MAJOR FINDINGS AND CONCLUSIONS

This section summarizes the major findings and conclusions of this report.

A.1.3.1 Technological Innovation. Among the more important innovations in information technology which have had important effects on the applicability, interpretation, and enforceability of copyright law in the twentieth century are:

- Motion Pictures
- Sound Recordings
- Radio and Television Broadcasts
- Photocopying
- Cable Television Systems
- Microfilm, Videotape, and Computer Programs

A.1.3.2 Major Historical Issues. Each of the above new technologies has resulted in adaptation of the copyright statutes to the new products and processes growing out of the new technologies developed after the statutes were enacted. With regard to the technologies examined in this report several basic questions arose which required judicial, legislative, or Copyright Office intervention. Among the more important issues raised were:

√ (1) Is the new product copyrightable? (Motion pictures, sound recordings, microfilms, videotapes, computer programs.)

√ (2) What rights are covered by the copyright in the new product? (Motion pictures, sound recordings, computer programs.)

✓ (3) Are new devices for using copyrighted works subject to the copyright? (Motion pictures, sound recordings, radio and television broadcasts, photocopying, cable television.)

These issues were dealt with and resolved principally by court decisions, of which the most significant are reviewed and analyzed in this report. Some relatively simple issues have been resolved as a practical matter by industry practice or by Copyright Office interpretation of the statute. The same issues have been dealt with finally in the new Copyright Act of 1976.

A.1.3.3 Conclusions Relating to Adaptation of Copyright Law to New Technologies. We believe the following observations and conclusions may be drawn from all of these sources concerning the adaptation of the copyright statutes to the new products and processes growing out of new technologies developed after the statutes were enacted. These are not, of course, the only conclusions that might be drawn from the cases and events cited:

1. It seems certain that technologies now in their infancy or now unknown will, at some future time, result in new products or processes that will raise copyright questions not provided for specifically in the Copyright Act of 1976 (or the earlier statutes). The 1976 Act attempted to take into account recently developed technologies and their foreseeable applications affecting copyright. Even here the new Act did not succeed completely: As is shown in Section A.4 of this report, the problems concerning uses of copyrighted works in computer systems (which were discussed during the Congressional hearings in 1965 and 1967 on the copyright revision bills in the light of what was then known or anticipated as to such computer uses) were considered not sufficiently crystallized or understood to allow the formulation of legislative rules; instead, Congress provided (in P.L. 93-573 enacted in 1974) for the establishment of a National Commission (CONTU) to study these problems and make recommendations for appropriate legislation. And there will no doubt be other copyright problems raised hereafter by new technologies of the future that are completely unforeseen now.

2. Past experience indicates that the problems raised in the future by new technologies will be brought before the courts for decision as to how the terms of the 1976 Act are to be construed in their application to the new situations. The courts will be expected to make definitive rulings on many new issues involving such questions as the copyrightability of works produced in new ways or in new forms, and

the rights of copyright owners and users with respect to uses made of copyrighted works by new methods or in new media.

3. The courts will probably differ among themselves in the basic approach they take to the application of the 1976 Act to the new situations. The decisions reviewed illustrate two main approaches:

(a) One is to expound the philosophy that the copyright law is intended to stimulate the creation and dissemination of works of authorship by giving to authors (and their successors as copyright owners) the economic rewards that are afforded by the market for the various uses that may be made of their works; the courts taking this approach have looked for analogies between the situations clearly provided for in the statute and the new situations, and, finding such analogies, have tended to hold that the new situation comes within the intended scope of the statutory provisions.

(b) The opposite approach has been to construe the statute narrowly as referring to the situations known at the time of its enactment; the courts starting with this premise have generally been concerned with the restrictions that copyright was seen to impose on socially beneficial new developments, if applied to them, and have considered that the extension of the statute to these new developments should be left to Congress.

The review of the court decisions in this study can be taken to indicate that, on the whole, the courts have been more inclined to take the first approach, particularly in the usual case where the issue appeared to be capable of satisfactory resolution by deciding simply whether the work or the use involved was or was not subject to copyright under the statute. The courts have taken the second approach when they were faced with a choice between holding for complete copyright liability or none, against an important new industry or use whose development or very existence was thought to be jeopardized if complete liability were imposed, and where legislation on the issue appeared imminent. (The majority opinions in the *White-Smith* case, in the Court of Claims decision in the *Williams and Wilkins* case, and in the Supreme Court decisions in the *Fortnightly* and *Teleprompter* cases illustrate the second approach; all the other decisions reviewed—excluding some district court decisions that were reversed on appeal—illustrate the first approach.)

4. Where the courts have held that the earlier copyright statutes extend to the products or uses resulting from new technologies developed later, Congress has generally adopted the same position in

subsequent legislation. Where the courts have refused to extend the earlier statutes to new uses of copyrighted works because of the danger that imposing full copyright liability would result in unduly harmful consequences to the users or to the public. Congress has provided in subsequent legislation that such uses are to be brought under copyright, but subject to special exceptions or special conditions and limitations designed to forestall those harmful consequences, while giving copyright owners the measure of protection still possible or, at least, compensation for the new uses of their works.

5. Where a clear yes-or-no answer on a question of copyright protection or copyright liability will solve a problem raised by new technology, the problem can be, and is likely to be, resolved by judicial decisions construing the existing statutes. But where the problem is quite complex, with compelling economic or social interests on both sides to be safeguarded and reconciled, the slow and cumbersome process of legislation may be required to formulate a multifaceted set of basic rules together with special conditions, limitations, exceptions, etc., peculiarly tailored to fit the differing needs of the several interest groups concerned. And it may be extremely difficult to enact legislation of this nature unless and until the interest groups are ready to agree or to accept the main features of the proposed legislation. (These observations regarding legislation are illustrated by the provisions in the 1976 Act on photocopying and on cable television.)

6. On some questions of how the existing statutes apply to the products of new technology, where the question is fairly uncomplicated and the justice of the answer given is fairly clear, a ruling by the Copyright Office or a practice adopted by an industry group may be sufficient to settle the question for all concerned.

A.1.3.4 Providing Technological Expertise to the Judiciary. When courts have needed to be informed concerning matters of esoteric technology, they have generally been provided with the technological expertise pertinent to the issues in the case before them through such established procedures as the testimony of expert witnesses, physical demonstrations of technical devices or processes, briefs or memoranda presented by counsel, and research conducted by the court or its aides. Those procedures have apparently been found adequate in most litigation, including the usual run of copyright cases.

If other means were considered to be necessary, in extraordinary cases, to provide technological expertise to the judiciary, several other mechanisms might be given consideration:

1. The establishment of a special court or system of courts to deal with cases involving highly complex and sophisticated technological issues. Prototypes of such courts now exist in the Court of Customs and Patent Appeals, the United States Tax Court, and the special State courts established to deal with juvenile and domestic relations cases.

2. Having specialists in the fields of science or technology involved attached to the staff of the court or available to serve as consultants to the court. Many of the juvenile and domestic relations courts now employ specialists in the medical, behavioral, and social sciences as staff members or consultants.

3. Making available to the courts the expertise of the wide range of scientific and technological specialists employed by the various Government agencies.

We do not believe any such special mechanisms are needed in copyright litigation involving new technologies. The judicial decisions in copyright cases dealing with new technologies—as exemplified by those reviewed in this study—indicate that the courts have been adequately informed, through the judicial procedures now used, concerning the new technologies involved, to reach intelligent and appropriate judgments.

A.1.3.5 STI Systems and Copyright Law. The authors, after reviewing the general principles that the courts have applied to copyright issues, and the historical impact of new technologies upon the copyright statutes, examined computerized STI systems in relation to the copyright law.

A.1.3.6 Groups Interested in STI Systems. The interest groups having, primarily and most directly, a financial, professional or service interest in the copyright issues relating to the generation, dissemination, or use of STI systems include:

-- Authors of various kinds of works, principally textual and graphic works in the field of science and technology.

-- Commercial and nonprofit publishers of journals and of books and monographs of a scholarly or informational character.

-- Producers and publishers of compilations of bibliograhic and factual data.

- Libraries, especially large research, university, and industrial libraries.

- Educators and students, especially at the college and university levels.

- Industrial and nonprofit research organizations and individual researchers.

- Producers of computer hardware and software.

- Organizers and operators of computerized information service systems.

- Commercial indexing and data search services.

These groupings could, of course, be arranged in other ways, and there is considerable overlap among the groups as listed above.

A.1.3.7 Orientation of Suppliers and Users of STI Systems. From the standpoint of their copyright interests, the various groups may be divided into two broad categories: (1) authors, producers, publishers, and other suppliers of copyrightable materials, who are interested in having copyright protection and in receiving compensation for the uses of their works; and (2) researchers, educators, scholars, libraries, and other users of copyrightable materials, who are interested in having access to and use of those materials.

The differing needs of copyright owners on one hand and users of copyrighted materials on the other hand, are usually met by contracts negotiated in the open market. The desire of copyright willingness of owners to derive revenue from the market for their works, and the willingness of users to pay reasonable fees for the use of those works, have generally operated to make the market place responsive to the needs on both sides. In most situations the system of freely negotiated contracts should work to meet the needs of the owners and users of copyrighted works used in computerized STI systems.

In certain situations involving the use of copyrighted works in other media, problems of accommodating the needs of both owners and users have called for special treatment, either through voluntary systems for centralized or blanket licensing or through statutory provisions for compulsory licensing. These special methods of accommodation are discussed in the report as outlined below.

3 Copyright Law and its Impact upon Computerized STI
ıs. Among the conclusions reached in this study concerning the
application of the copyright law to computerized STI systems are the
following:

A.1.3.8.1 Copyright Protection for Computer Programs. Computer
programs generally are subject to copyright protection. The protection
afforded by copyright is limited to reproduction of the program in its
substance. Copyright would not protect the processes or techniques
revealed in the program.

A.1.3.8.2 Copyright Protection for Data Bases.

(1) In general, data bases, whether in printed or machine-
readable form, are copyrightable as compilations.

(2) Complying with the requirements of copyright notice and
deposit of copies, as may be necessary for effective
copyright protection, may call for some special procedure in
the case of data bases in machine-readable form, and in the
printout of material from data bases, but no insuperable
difficulties in this regard are seen.

A.1.3.8.3 The Production of Data Bases.

(1) The indexing of documents in order to compile a
bibliographic data base can be done manually or by using a
computer. If done by computer, the indexer must have the
documents in machine-readable form. If the documents are
copyrighted, the indexer would apparently have to obtain
machine-readable copies from the publishers, or to obtain
permission from the publishers to make and use his own
machine-readable copies, for indexing. It has been argued
that where the publishers cannot supply machine-readable
copies, an indexer should be permitted by law to make his
own, for the sole purpose of indexing, as a fair use or,
alternatively, under a compulsory license.

(2) The typical abstracts in data bases are no more than brief
identifying statements of the subjects covered in the
document; making such abstracts of copyrighted works is
not an infringement. However, a so-called "abstract" that is
actually a digest of the substance of a copyrighted work for
the work itself, would constitute a derivative work, and
making such would infringe the copyright.

A.1.3.8.4 The Use of Copyrighted Data Bases in Computerized Systems.

(1) Where a system operator obtains a machine-readable data base from the publisher, the lease agreement between them will generally include (expressly or impliedly) a license for the operator's use of the data base in his system. Such agreements will usually serve to settle the copyright questions that would otherwise be expected to arise. Where the publisher offers machine-readable copies, a system operator who makes his own copy instead of obtaining one from the publisher should be considered an infringer.

(2) Where the publisher of a copyrighted compilation of data does not offer machine-readable copies, an operator who wishes to place that compilation in his data base system should be expected to ask the publisher to make and supply a machine-readable copy or to permit the operator to make one for use in his system. Where the publisher then refuses or fails to accede to such request, a valid argument could be made for a compulsory license.

(3) It can be assumed that the publishers of machine-readable copies of copyrighted compilations of data will generally lease them, but not sell them, to system operators. An operator who is offered such a copy from a third person should therefore be suspicious of its legitimacy, and should be held liable if he acquires such a copy that was made or supplied to him in violation of the copyright.

(4) If a system operator makes his own machine-readable copy of a copyrighted compilation or acquires a copy legitimately from a third person, he will need to obtain a license from the publisher to use it in his system. There are good arguments for requiring the operator in this situation to obtain such a license before putting the data into his system.

(5) If a license for the use of a copyrighted data base in a system has not been obtained earlier, the operator would need to obtain a license for the output of material from the data base. In the absence of a license, the extraction of a small fragment of a data base by a user of the system on one occasion would appear to qualify as a fair use; but the aggregate of the output of fragments on many occasions

would appear to constitute an infringement by the operator of the system.

(6) If a user of a system were to extract from it an entire copyrighted data base or a major part of it, he would be infringing the copyright. Practical arrangements for preventing and detecting such infringements seem feasible.

A.1.3.8.5 <u>Exclusive and Compulsory Licenses for the Use of Data Bases</u>. In order to facilitate the development of computerized systems that will contain all the data bases needed for comprehensive coverage of any subject area, and also to prevent the monopolization of data base search services by one or two systems, consideration should be given to a scheme for precluding exclusive licenses for the use of data bases in individual systems. One such scheme would be a statutory provision for the compulsory licensing for use in all systems, of a data base licensed for use in any one system.

A.1.3.8.6 <u>Full-Text Storage and Retrieval of Documents in Computerized Systems.</u>

(1) The questions as to input and output of copyrighted documents are substantially the same as those pertaining to the input and output of copyrighted data bases. The discussion and conclusions in this study relating to data bases are applicable generally to the computer storage and retrieval of the full text of documents.

(2) There has been considerable discussion as to whether the input of copyrighted documents should be free, with a license and payment to the copyright owner being required for output, or whether a license should be required before input. The arguments advanced on both sides are presented in this report. The authors of this report are impressed most by the argument that, since a license will admittedly be required for output, practical considerations suggest that the terms of the license, including the basis for assessing fees, should be settled between the parties before the operator of the computer system begins the process of using the material.

A.1.3.9 <u>Unique Characteristics of Computerized STI Systems.</u> It can be deduced from the analysis of copyright questions relating to the use of copyrighted works in computer systems that such uses present special characteristics not present in the traditional ways of using copyrighted material. The following special features of computer uses seem particularly significant:

(1) Copyrighted works in their usual form of printed pages are usable in that form in other media, but must be converted to machine-readable form for use in computer systems.

(2) The availability to researchers and other users of the works placed in a computerized STI system will tend to displace the market that would otherwise exist for the sale of copies of the works to them.

(3) Computerized STI systems, to realize their potential value for research, must seek to include comprehensively the whole body of works extant in any particular field of science or technology.

(4) Exclusive licensing of copyrighted works for use in one STI system could have two undesirable results: (1) It would prevent other systems from attaining comprehensive coverage of the whole body of works in a particular field, thus putting researchers to the inconvenience of searching through several systems; and (2) It would tend to foster the monopolization of STI system services to one or two giant systems.

The first two of these special features would seem to indicate that the copyright law should recognize, as it now appears to do, that the conversion of copyrighted works into machine-readable form and their input and output in the operation of computerized STI systems require the consent of the copyright owner. The last two of these special features would seem to indicate that there may be a need to establish, at least in some situations, either voluntary "clearinghouse" systems for the blanket licensing, on a nonexclusive basis, of the use of copyrighted works in computer systems, or a statutory system of compulsory licensing for the use of such works in those systems.

A.1.3.10 Clearinghouses and Compulsory Licenses. The clearinghouses operated by the American Society of Composers, Authors, and Publishers (ASCAP) and by Broadcast Music, Inc. (BMI) for the blanket licensing of public performances of musical compositions, have frequently been cited as possible models that might be adaptable for the blanket licensing of reproduction rights in journal articles and other works. The operation of these two organizations and the factors that have contributed most importantly to their effectiveness are outlined in this report. Some of the major problems that would be faced in attempting to establish a clearinghouse for the reproduction of journal articles are mentioned and some approaches for meeting those problems are suggested in the report.

Provisions for a compulsory license for the recording of copyrighted musical compositions were enacted in the Copyright Act of 1909. That compulsory license was designed to prevent the establishment of a monopoly in making recordings of music under exclusive licenses that would otherwise have been granted. One of the practical consequences of these compulsory licensing provisions, incidentally, has been the voluntary establishment by music publishers of a centralized agency (the Harry Fox Office) for the issuing of negotiated licenses on standard terms for the music of most of the major publishers.

The Copyright Act of 1976 provides for compulsory licenses of a different character in three additional situations: for the performance of music in jukeboxes, for CATV retransmissions of broadcasts of copyrighted material, and for the use of certain works in noncommercial broadcasting. These three compulsory licensing systems are examples of blanket, non-exclusive licensing established by statute. The purpose of the compulsory license in these three instances is not to prevent a monopoly, but is to avoid the difficulties and high transaction costs that would be entailed if the user groups had to obtain licenses from and pay fees to the individual copyright owners.

If a voluntary clearinghouse satisfactory to both copyright owners and users can be organized, that would seem to be preferable over a statutory compulsory licensing scheme. Among other reasons mentioned for this preference, perhaps the most important is the greater flexibility of a voluntary arrangement and its easier accommodation, by negotiations between the groups concerned, to experience and changing circumstances.

A.2 ADAPTATION OF THE COPYRIGHT LAW TO NEW TECHNOLOGIES

A.2.1 IN GENERAL

Since the enactment of the first United States copyright statute by the First Congress in 1790, the copyright law has had to be added to, modified, revised, and interpreted to meet changing conditions brought about in large part by new technological developments. The statutes were completely rewritten in 1831, 1870, 1909, and just recently, in 1976. In the intervals between those comprehensive revisions, the statutes were amended in some particulars, and they were further adapted to changing conditions by judicial interpretation and, to some extent, by business practice.

Adaptation of the copyright law to changing conditions brought about by new technology has been especially necessary in the twentieth century, primarily for the obvious reason that the rate of technological development has accelerated rapidly. And, because of the long interval of more than 65 years from the 1909 revision, with the statute being amended during that period in only relatively minor respects, the courts have been called upon to take a large part in adapting the law, by interpretation, to meet the problems emanating from the new technologies.

An analysis of the more significant court decisions dealing with those problems, particularly as the decisions reveal the basic principles and philosophical approaches adopted by the courts in construing the copyright statutes, may contribute to an understanding of how the copyright law has been shaped and reshaped to fit new conditions flowing from technological innovations, and may be useful in indicating approaches to the solution of similar problems that may be raised by the newer and emerging technologies of today and the foreseeable future.

In this section we shall seek to show how the copyright law has been adapted to resolve the questions raised by the new technologies of the twentieth century that were not dealt with specifically in the statutes because they were just beginning to emerge or were unknown when the statutes were enacted. Among these new technologies are:

- motion pictures, silent and with accompanying sound;

- sound recordings and sound reproducing mechanisms;

- radio and television transmission and reception;

- rapid, efficient copying machines;

- cable television systems;

- microfilm, videotapes, and computer programs.

We shall review principally the adaptations of the copyright law in court decisions, but some attention will also be given, in passing, to industry practice and to the regulations and practices of the Copyright Office. In addition, we shall summarize the adaptation to the several new technologies reflected in the copyright law revision enacted in 1976.

A.2.1.1 Philosophical Basis of Copyright. To understand how the copyright law has developed and has been adapted to meet new issues, it is important to keep in mind the fundamental philosophy underlying copyright. The basis of copyright is stated in broad terms in the clause of the United States Constitution empowering Congress—

> To Promote the Progress of Science and useful Arts, by securing for limited Times to Authors and Inventors the exclusive Right to their respective Writings and Discoveries.

We deduce from the Constitution that the end purpose of copyright is to "promote the progress of science and useful arts," that is, to stimulate the growth and spread of learning and culture for the benefit of society at large; and that, as a means toward achieving this end, authors are to be given exclusive rights in their works; thus, the creation and public dissemination of works of authorship are to be fostered by giving to authors the legal means to realize the economic value of their contributions to society.

The United States Supreme Court has expressed the underlying purpose of copyright as follows:

> The primary object in conferring the monopoly (of copyright) lie(s) in the general benefits derived by the public from the labors of authors. A copyright, like a patent, is "at once the equivalent given by the public for benefits bestowed by the genius and meditations and skill of individuals, and the incentive to further efforts for the same important objects." (*Fox Film Corporation* v. *Doyal*, 286 U.S. 123, 1932)

> The economic philosophy behind the clause empowering Congress to grant patents and copyrights is the conviction that encouragement of individual effort by personal gain is the best way to advance public welfare through the talents of authors and inventors in "Science and Useful Arts." Sacrificial days devoted to such creative activities deserve rewards, commensurate with the services rendered." (*Mazer* v. *Stein*, 347 U.S. 201, 219, 1954)

We move on now to a review of how the courts have dealt with the issues raised by the new technologies for which the statutes then in effect made no specific provisions.

*   *   *

A.2.5 PHOTOCOPYING

In common usage, the duplication of a printed page by modern copying machines is referred to as "photocopying" whether the process used by the machines is photographic or is of another kind such as a thermal or xerographic process. As the making of copies by such machines became easier, faster, more effective, and less costly, the practice of using those machines to provide copies of copyrighted material for persons engaged in study, research, teaching, and other activities, created serious and difficult problems concerning the application of the copyright law to such copying.

The 1909 Copyright Act (like all the earlier acts) made no provision allowing any copying of copyrighted material without the copyright owner's permission. The Act gave the copyright owner the exclusive right to make copies of his work, without qualification. The courts, however, over a long period of time, had developed the doctrine of "fair use" which, stated in broad terms, allowed the copying of small portions of copyrighted works, for a legitimate purpose, in circumstances where such copying would have no appreciable effect upon the copyright owner's market for his work. The court decisions dealt mainly with short quotations from the work of one author in the later works of other authors; how far the doctrine of fair use extended to photocopying for research or scholarly purposes remained problematical.

At an early stage when the photocopying processes were less proficient and more costly, the processes then in use being mainly photostatic and mimeographic, copies made by libraries for scholars and researchers were relatively few in number and short in length and were made in response to isolated and occasional requests. Even then the existence of a copyright problem was recognized, and the first efforts to resolve the problem were made by members of the groups concerned—publishers, scholarly and research organizations, and libraries—who sought to work out an agreement defining the area and limits of permissible photocopying. In 1935 members of those groups adopted a statement known as the "Gentlemen's Agreement" which stated that a library owning copyrighted books or periodicals "may make and deliver a single photographic reproduction or reduction of a part thereof to a scholar representing in writing that he desires such reproduction in lieu of loan of such publication or in place of manual transcription and solely for the purpose of research."

The "Gentlemen's Agreement" had no binding effect for several reasons: Among others, the persons signing it were not representative of the generality of the groups concerned. Nevertheless, it suggested guidelines that were followed thereafter by many libraries, and that were to be referred to as a basis for working out a solution to the copyright issue concerning library photocopying. It is also significant as an example of attempts to adapt the copyright law to a new technology by a practical agreement negotiated between the opposing interest groups.

The photocopying problem became acute as copying machines became highly proficient in producing excellent reproductions rapidly and at steadily declining cost. During the 1960's and early 1970's the volume of copyrighted material being photocopied by libraries, as well as in schools and elsewhere, ballooned continuously to the point, and beyond the point, where publishers—especially of scientific and technical journals and of educational texts—expressed the fear that the resulting loss of subscriptions and sales might force them to discontinue publication of some of those materials.

The problem was given attention in the preliminary stages of the program looking toward the general revision of the copyright law*, but the groups concerned were agreed, when the first revision bill to be considered by Congress was introduced in 1965, that no specific rules for library photocopying should be incorporated in the bill; they were all willing to leave the photocopying issue for resolution by agreement among themselves or by the courts under the general principles of the fair use doctrine.

Meanwhile, a suit was instituted in the U.S. Court of Claims, *Williams and Wilkins Co.* v. *United States*, in which the plaintiff, a publisher of medical journals and books, charged two Government libraries, the National Institutes of Health library and the National Library of Medicine, with having infringed the copyright in several of its medical journals by supplying photocopies of articles in those journals to the staff researchers of NIH and to medical libraries, research institutes, and

---

* See the *Report of the Register of Copyrights on the General Revision of the U.S. Copyright Law*, published as a House Judiciary Committee Print in July, 1961, at p. 25.

practitioners throughout the country. The main defense (among others) argued on behalf of the libraries was that their photocopying was a fair use. The case was a particularly difficult one because it presented a situation of copying on such a large scale as to strain the usual limits of fair use and perhaps jeopardize the economic viability of publishing such journals; but, on the other hand, copying for a noncommercial social purpose—to supply medical and related scientific information to those engaged in medical research and health maintenance—as worthy and essential as any that could be thought to justify copying as a fair use.

In both the initial opinion of the Commissioner of the Court of Claims (172 USPQ 670, 1972) and the subsequent decision by the full Court (487 F. 2d 1345, 1973), it was noted that fair use is a judicially-created doctrine that cannot be defined with precision, and that the House Judiciary Committee, in its Report (No. 83, 90th Cong.) on the copyright law revision bill then pending had stated that the principal factors in determining what constitutes a fair use were:

> (a) the purpose and character of the use, (b) the nature of the copyrighted work, (c) the amount and substantiality of the material used in relation to the copyrighted work as a whole, and (d) the effect of the use on a copyright owner's potential market for and value of his work.

The Commissioner held that the photocopying practices of the two Government libraries were not within the bounds of fair use but constituted infringement of the copyrights. As he saw it:

> Defendant's photocopying is wholesale copying and meets none of the criteria for "fair use." The photocopies are exact duplicates of the original articles; are intended to be substitutes for, and serve the same purpose as, the original articles; and serve to diminish plaintiff's potential market for the original articles since the photocopies are made at the request of, and for the benefit of, the very persons who constitute the plaintiff's market.

The full Court divided 4 to 3 on the issue. The majority stressed the social importance of making information readily available for medical research and played down the potential damage to the copyright owner, concluding that the photocopying practices of the two libraries were fair use. Quoting from the majority opinion:

> While, as we have said, this record fails to show that plaintiff (or any other medical publisher) has been substantially harmed by the

photocopying practices of NIH and NLM, it does show affirmatively that medical science will be hurt if such photocopying is stopped. Thus, the balance of risks is definitely on defendant's side—until Congress acts more specifically, the burden on medical science of a holding that the photocopying is an infringement would appear to be much greater than the present or foreseeable burden on plaintiff and other medical publishers of a ruling that these practices fall within "fair use."

The majority opinion wound up by calling for Congressional resolution of the problem:

Finally, but not at all least, we underline again the need for Congressional treatment of the problem of photocopying . . . . The Courts are now precluded, both by the Act and by the nature of the judicial process, from contriving pragmatic or compromise solutions which would reflect the legislature's choice of policy and its mediation among the competing interests . . . . Hopefully, the result in the present case will be but a "holding operation" in the interim period before Congress enacts its preferred solution.

The three judges of the Court of Claims who dissented from the majority opinion expressed their agreement with the Commissioner's view of the case, saying:

What we have before us is a case of wholesale, machine copying, and distribution of copyrighted material by defendant's libraries on a scale so vast that it dwarfs the output of many small publishing companies . . . .

It is indisputed that the photocopies in issue here were exact duplicates of the original articles; they were intended to be substitutes for and they served the same purpose as the original articles. They were copies of complete copyrighted works within the meaning of Sections 3 and 5 of the Copyright Act. This is the very essence of wholesale copying and, without more, defeats the defense of fair use.

The minority opinion sought to counter the fear expressed by the majority that a holding of infringement in this case would result in stopping entirely the furnishing of photocopies needed by medical researchers; the minority suggested that those needs could be met by arrangements for licensing photocopying.

The *Williams and Wilkins* case was accepted for review by the Supreme Court where, after the arguments were heard, the Court split 4 to 4 without an exposition of the reasoning on the two sides (420 U.S. 376, 1975). The case thus came to an inconclusive end.

A.2.5.1 <u>The Copyright Act of 1976.</u> During the proceedings for general revision of the copyright law, the question of photocopying came up primarily and most importantly in two contexts; in connection with copying by teachers for classroom use in schools, and with copying by libraries for the use of scholars and researchers. The proposals for legislation in each of these contexts were subjects of major controversy. Two sets of provisions evolved in the successive revision bills; section 107 dealing with fair use generally and containing special references to copying for purposes of teaching, scholarship, or research; and section 108 dealing specifically with copying by libraries.

Section 107, providing that "the fair use of a copyrighted work . . . is not an infringement of copyright," specifies that:

> In determining whether the use made of a work in any particular case is a fair use the factors to be considered shall include—
>
> (1) the purpose and character of the use, including whether such use is of a commercial nature or is for nonprofit educational purposes;
>
> (2) the nature of the copyrighted work;
>
> (3) the amount and substantiality of the portion used in relation to the copyrighted work as a whole; and
>
> (4) the effect of the use upon the potential market for or value of the copyrighted work.

As noted in the Congressional committee reports on the revision bills, this statement of the determining factors is a distillation of those stated by the courts in the line of decisions that developed the fair use doctrine, except for the phrase in clause (1) reading "including whether such use is of a commercial nature or is for nonprofit educational purposes." This added phrase was thought to be within the spirit of the court-developed doctrine and was added to the bill as a concession to the educators.

Section 107 also specifies, as examples of uses that may be fair use (if they come within the stated criteria):

> The fair use of a copyrighted work, including such use by reproduction in copies or phonorecords or by any other means . . . ,for purposes such as criticism, comment, news reporting, teaching (including multiple copies for classroom use), scholarship, or research . . . .

It may be noted that the parenthetical phrase was added to the bill in the late stages of the Congressional proceedings as a further concession to the educators.

The language of section 107 pertaining to copying for educational purposes reflects agreements reached between the educator and copyright owner groups over a period of time. In addition, the Reports of the Congressional Committees on earlier versions of the revision bill (House Report No. 83, 90th Cong., and Senate Reports No. 93-983 and No. 94-473) contained an explanatory discussion in considerable detail of how the four criteria of fair use stated in section 107 would apply to copying by teachers for classroom use, which also reflected an understanding between those groups. Further, and with more finality, the House Committee Report (No. 94-1476 at pages 67-71) sets forth the texts of agreements between educator groups on one hand and representatives of authors and publishers of books, periodicals, and music on the other, stating in precise terms, as guidelines, the minimum standards of fair use copying for educational purposes. These agreements were reached at the urging of the Congressional committees, after a series of meetings between the interested groups.

The more far-reaching problem raised by modern photocopying devices—that of copying by libraries for scholars and researchers—is dealt with in section 108 of the new statute. (That section also provides for copying for certain internal library purposes but we are not concerned with that here.) In main substance, section 108(d) and (e) permits libraries to make, for any user requesting it, a single copy of no more than one article or other contribution to a copyrighted collection or periodical issue or of a small part of any other work (such as a book), or a single copy of an entire work or a substantial part of it if the library has first determined that a copy cannot be obtained from trade sources at a fair price. (This right of a library to make single copies for users is subject to certain specified conditions and exceptions which we need not detail here.)

To preclude multiple copying under the guise of repeated single copying, section 108(g) states that, while the right of a library to make copies extends to "the isolated and unrelated reproduction . . . of a single copy . . . of the same material on separate occasions," it does not extend to "the related or concerted reproduction . . . of multiple copies . . . of the same material, whether made on one occasion or over a period of time, and whether intended for aggregate use by one or more individuals or for separate use by the individual members of a group;" and to preclude wholesale copying under a systematic program whereby one library would serve as the source of material for a number of other libraries or persons who might otherwise subscribe for or purchase copies, section 108 states further that the right of a library to make copies does not extend to "the systematic reproduction . . . of single or multiple copies," with the proviso that this does not prevent a library "from participating in interlibrary arrangements that do not have, as their purpose or effect, that the library . . . receiving such copies . . . for distribution does so in such aggregate quantities as to substitute for a subscription to or purchase of such work."

This latter provision of section 108 excluding "systematic reproduction" had been objected to strongly by library groups, and the proviso to permit "interlibrary arrangements" was added in an effort to meet those objections. The proviso, however, was thought to be too vague in its reference to "such aggregate quantities as to substitute for a subscription to or purchase of such work." Accordingly, the National Commission on New Technological Uses of Copyrighted Works (CONTU) undertook to bring the interested parties together to see if agreement could be reached on a practical definition of that phrase, and it succeeded in formulating a set of guidelines that were accepted by the several groups concerned. These guidelines are set forth in the Conference Report (H. Rept. No. 94-1733, at pages 71-73) on the bill which was then enacted. In essence, the guidelines state that the "aggregate quantities" limitation in the proviso would permit, for any requesting library within any calendar year, not more than five copies of articles published in any given periodical during the preceding five years, and not more than five copies of any other material from any given work (including a collective work) during the entire period of copyright.

So it was that the complex and multi-faceted resolution of the problem of adapting the copyright law to the availability of modern copying machines was achieved through the legislative process. The one appeal to the courts to resolve the issue—the *Williams and Wilkins* case—proved to be futile. As the Court of Claims observed, the problem of photocopying in its broad and varied aspects did not lend itself to judicial resolutions; the Court could do no more than to decide whether the photocopying done in the particular circumstances of the case before it was or was not an infringement of copyright under the existing law; Congressional action was needed to examine the wide range of situations in which photocopying could be a useful practice, and to arrive at policy determinations that in certain circumstances and under certain conditions photocopying should be permitted free of copyright while other circumstances and conditions called for subjecting photocopying to copyright restrictions. On the foundation of the fair use doctrine developed earlier by the courts, the principles underlying the "Gentlemen's Agreement" worked out initially by some of the interested groups, and the practical and equitable considerations presented by the needs of the several interested groups, Congress was able to establish sets of basic principles and subsidiary conditions and exceptions to resolve the issues in the variety of situations that had arisen or could be foreseen. In this process Congress was aided by the spirit of compromise and accommodation in which the interested groups negotiated agreements among themselves on the principles of the legislative provisions and on practical guidelines for their application.

A.2.6 CABLE TELEVISION SYSTEMS

During the early 1960s commercial enterprises began to be organized to bring to subscribers, by means of new technologies, using special antennas located on high points and a network of cables and amplifiers, television broadcasts of stations whose signals could not be received satisfactorily by the subscribers off-the-air because of the distance or the hilly terrain between the station and the location of the subscribers. By the middle of that decade such commercial enterprises, known as cable television or CATV systems, were proliferating rapidly and expanding their operations to carry more, and farther distant, broadcasting stations; and it had become apparent that a copyright problem of considerable magnitude was involved in their operation. Television broadcast programs commonly included performances of copyrighted motion pictures, plays, music, and other works, for which broadcasters obtained licenses from the copyright owners. Was the retransmission of the broadcast programs by a cable system to its subscribers to be treated as a further performance of the copyrighted works which infringed the copyright owners' exclusive right of public performance?

The existence of this problem and its economic importance for copyright owners and the operators of cable systems, and indirectly for broadcasters, had come to the attention of the House Subcommittee by the time it held its first hearings, in 1965, on the initial bill for general revision of the copyright law. The testimony at the hearings demonstrated that the issue was highly controversial, and that it involved many ramifications pertaining to the economic position and potential growth of cable systems, and their potential impact upon broadcasters as well as copyright owners. It was also evident that the copyright problem was complicated by being intertwined with the problems of communications policy relating to the nation's broadcasting system that were dealt with by the Federal Communications Commission.

In 1966, after its hearing had been completed, the House Subcommittee formulated a complex set of provisions for inclusion in the revision bill by which it proposed to reconcile the divergent views and needs of the interested parties. The Subcommittee recognized that the copyright problem could not be resolved by a uniform rule under which all cable retransmissions would be an infringement, or not an infringement, of copyright; it proposed that in some situations retransmissions by a cable system would be exempt from copyright, in certain other situations their retransmissions would be subject to copyright, in still other situations their retransmissions (of broadcasts from another area) would become subject to copyright only if they were given advance notice that a local broadcasting station had an exclusive license to show the program in the local area, and in yet other situations (where they brought the broadcasts of distant stations into an area not adequately served by local stations) they would be liable only for payment of a reasonable license fee.

Meanwhile, the problem was brought before the courts in the case of *United Artists Television, Inc.,* v. *Fortnightly Corp.* where a cable system brought to its subscribers the television programs of several stations whose signals could not be received satisfactorily by the subscribers because of the intervening mountainous terrain. The copyright owners of motion pictures shown in the broadcasts retransmitted by the cable system sued the system for infringement. The District Court (255 F. Supp. 177, S.D.N.Y. 1966) held that the retransmission constituted infringement of the copyright owner's exclusive right of public performance. On appeal, the Circuit Court of Appeals reached the same conclusion (377 F. 2d 872, 1967). Both the District and Circuit Courts considered this case to be parallel with those decided a generation earlier, particularly the *Remick, Jewell-LaSalle,* and *SESAC* cases (reviewed above in the portion of this report dealing with radio and television broadcasts); in those earlier cases, broadcasts of copyrighted works, and the public diffusion of receptions of such broadcasts, were held to be infringing public performance. Of particular interest here is the philosophical approach stated in the District Court opinion in the *Fortnightly* case as to the judicial application of the 1909 Copyright Law to the new technology of cable retransmission of broadcasts:

> The updating of statutory language to accommodate it with current technological advances is part of the genius of our law to adapt and to grow. The achievements of modern science and technology surpass the imagined marvels of the philosopher's stone and Aladdin's lamp. The practical necessities of such an age require judicial recognition of the contemporary meaning of the words of the Copyright Act . . .

It is hardly conceivable that Congress intended the statute to be read with a strangling literalness so as to require it to be amended on a month-to-month basis as the means of keeping pace with science and technology. The responsibility of keeping the Copyright Law a living law devolves primarily, though not exclusively, upon the courts whose traditional function of statutory interpretation and construction, if effectively performed, will achieve in great measure the desirable object of accommodating the statute to the realities of modern science and technology.

The decision of the District and Circuit Courts in this case was destined, however, to be reversed by the Supreme Court: *Fortnightly Corp.* v. *United Artists Television, Inc.*, 392 U.S. 390 (1968). To the surprise of most commentators, the Supreme Court held, in a 5 to 1 decision, that the retransmission of broadcasts by the cable system to its subscribers did not constitute a performance of the works in the broadcast within the meaning of the Copyright Act. The Supreme Court approached the question by saying:

At the outset it is clear that the petitioner's systems did not "perform" the respondent's copyrighted works in any conventional sense of that term, or in any manner envisaged by the Congress that enacted the law in 1909. But our inquiry cannot be limited to ordinary meaning and legislative history, for this is a statute that was drafted long before the development of the electronic phenomena with which we deal here. In 1909 radio itself was in its infancy, and television had not yet been invented. We must read the statutory language of 60 years ago in the light of drastic technological change.

Nevertheless, the Court held that the cable retransmission was not a "performance" under the Act. It reasoned:

Broadcasters have judicially been treated as exhibitors, and viewers as members of a theater audience. Broadcasters perform. Viewers do not perform. Thus, while both broadcasters and viewers play crucial roles in the total television process, a line is drawn between them. One is treated as active performer; the other, as passive beneficiary.

When CATV is considered in this framework, we conclude that it falls on the viewer's side of the line. Essentially, a CATV system no more than enhances the viewer's capacity to receive the broadcaster's signal; it provides a well-located antenna with an efficient connection to the viewer's television set.

In his lone dissent, Justice Fortas agreed with the lower courts that the precedents of the *Jewell-LaSalle* and *SESAC* decisions should be followed here. He observed that any decision of the Court—either that CATV systems were liable for copyright infringement, or that they were not—had dangerous implications for one party or the other, and commented:

> Our major object, I suggest, should be to do as little damage as possible to traditional copyright principles and to business relationships, until the Congress legislates and relieves the embarrassment which we and the interested parties face.

Justice Fortas said that the majority opinion abandoned the teachings of the precedents "in an attempt to foster the development of CATV," and he had noted earlier that "it is darkly predicted that the imposition of full liability upon all CATV operations could result in the demise of this new, important instrument of mass communications." The majority opinion, in a footnote, said that the result of following the *Jewell-LaSalle* decision here would be such "as retroactively to impose copyright liability where it has never been acknowledged to exist before." These brief quotations suggest a plausible explanation of the surprising result reached by the majority, namely, the argument which was made by the cable system in this case that a holding of infringement would subject existing cable systems generally to retroactive liability of such aggregate magnitude as to destroy many of them.

It should be noted specifically that both the majority and dissenting opinions in the Supreme Court decision in *Fortnightly*, as well as the lower court decisions, took cognizance of the ongoing consideration by Congress of the copyright problem of cable retransmissions, in the context of the general revision of the copyright law, and suggested that the problem in its complex and varied aspects called for resolution by Congress in the manner permitted by the flexibility of legislative improvisation. (We have already seen the same thought echoed in the Court of Claims decision in *Williams and Wilkins*.)

A few years later, in 1974, another case involving the copyright liability of CATV systems was before the Supreme Court. In this case, *Teleprompter Corp.* v. *CBS*, 415 U.S. 394, the cable system, using microwave relay equipment, brought to its subscribers the signals of far distant broadcast stations that could not have been intended to be received by them. (We leave aside the other issues in this case that are not relevant here.) The District Court in which this case began held (*CBS* v. *Teleprompter*, 355 F. Supp. 618, S.D.N.Y. 1972) that the Supreme Court decision in *Fortnightly* applied here; it considered the function of the cable system in importing distant signals to be no different in essential character from the function of the system in the

Fortnightly case as analyzed by the Supreme Court. The Circuit Court of Appeals held otherwise (476 F. 2d. 338, 2d Cir. 1973); it thought that the *Fortnightly* decision of the Supreme Court established the governing rule where the CATV served to bring the signals of a local broadcasting station to persons in the adjacent community who were prevented from receiving them directly only because of topographical conditions. When the CATV imported distant signals, the Circuit Court held, it did more than merely providing an antenna service; it brought the broadcast programs to a new audience that could not have received them even with an advanced antenna such as CATV used in the community, and in doing this it was "functionally equivalent to a broadcaster and thus should be deemed to 'perform' the programming distributed to subscribers on these imported signals."

The Supreme Court, in its majority opinion, agreed with the District Court's view that its ruling in the *Fortnightly* case applied to the CATV importation of distant signals since, it thought, the function of the CATV in providing viewers with the means of receiving broadcast signals is essentially the same. The majority opinion also rejected the argument that copyright liability should be imposed upon the importation of distant signals because the CATV was thereby diluting the value of the copyright owner's market for licensing broadcasts by stations in the area to which the distant signals were imported.

Three Justices dissented strongly, two of them not having participated in the *Fortnightly* decision. The dissenters indicated that they thought the *Fortnightly* decision itself was wrong, but that, accepting that decision now, the importation of distant signals presented a different case in which the CATV was functionally equivalent to a broadcaster. In one of the two dissenting opinions, by Justice Douglas with the concurrence of Chief Justice Burger, it was said:

> The Copyright Act . . . gives the owner of a copyright "the exclusive right" to present the creation "in public for profit" and to control the manner or method by which it is "reproduced." A CATV that builds an antenna to pick up telecasts in Area B and then transmits it by cable to Area A is reproducing the copyright work not pursuant to a license from the owner of the copyright but by theft. That is not "encouragement to the production of literary (or artistic) works of lasting benefit to the world" that we extolled in *Mazer* v. *Stein* . . .
>
> . . . Rechanneling by CATV of the pirated programs robs the copyright owner of his chance for monetary reward through advertising rates on rebroadcasts in the distant area and gives those monetary rewards to the group that has pirated the copyright.

Again in the several opinions in the *Telepr[ompter]* [and] *Fortnightly*, the courts called for Congressional [action to] resolve the complex issues of cable TV transm[ission of] programs. As the Circuit Court of Appeals put it:

> The complex problems represented by the issues [are not] readily amenable to judicial resolution . . . We ho[pe Congress] will in due course legislate a fuller and more flexible accommo[dation of] competing copyright, antitrust, and communications policy considerations, consistent with the challenge of modern CATV technology.

What we see reflected in these disparate decisions in the *Fortnightly* and *Teleprompter* cases is, first of all, the realization that the basic issue of the copyright liability of cable systems for their transmission of broadcast programs cannot be resolved satisfactorily by the simple yes-or-no answer of a judicial decision, but requires a multi-faceted formulation that can be molded only through the legislative process. Further, inasmuch as the courts must decide particular cases presented to them in the meantime, we see a conflict among the judges between the desire to extend the principles of the copyright law as it exists so as to give the copyright owners the benefit of the economic value of their works as used in a new medium, and the desire to promote the development and growth of the new medium for the benefit of the public by shielding it from the heavy burden that would be imposed by holding it fully and retroactively liable for copyright infringement.

A.2.6.1 <u>The Copyright Act of 1976</u>. As we have already noted, bills for the general revision of the copyright law, including proposed provisions on the CATV problem, were under consideration by Congress during the time that the *Fortnightly* and *Teleprompter* cases were making their way through the courts. The controversy over the CATV issue was so intense that when the revision bill first reported out by the House Judiciary Committee was debated by the full House in 1967, the opposition to the CATV provisions was strong enough to force the proponents of the bill to agree to deleting the entire section dealing specially with CATV transmissions, and the bill was passed by the House without any resolution of the issue. For several years thereafter the revision bill languished in the Senate, mainly because of the intractable dispute over the CATV issue.

We will not trace the twists and turns taken in the provisions of the successive revision bills dealing with the CATV problem; they were changed substantially from the version in the bill of one year to the bill of the next. Nor will we recount the series of regulations proposed and by the FCC to control the carriage of broadcasts by cable ms or the steps by which the interested parties—copyright owners, TV operators, and broadcasters—ultimately reached agreements on the essential points of a legislative solution. What finally emerged was a complex and highly detailed set of provisions in section 111 of the revision bill based on two main premises: That commercial cable systems should have a compulsory license for those retransmissions of broadcasts that were authorized by the Federal Communications Commission, and that they should pay copyright royalties in a lump sum under a formula fixed initially in the statute. Omitting many of the details in the complicated structure of section 111, the Copyright Act of 1976 provides in main substance that:

- A cable system may obtain a compulsory license to retransmit the broadcasts of those stations whose signals the system is authorized to carry by the FCC. It obtains the license by filing certain pertinent information in the Copyright Office.

- A cable system will be fully liable for copyright infringement if it willfully or repeatedly retransmits the signals of a broadcast station that the FCC has not authorized it to carry, or if it willfully alters the content of a broadcast program or the accompanying commercial advertising.

- Under the compulsory license the cable system must deposit semiannually with the Register of Copyrights a statement of account giving the specified information needed to determine the sum it is required to pay as the royalty fee for the preceding six months. The royalty fee is computed on the basis of specified percentages of the gross receipts of the cable system from its subscribers for its retransmission service; the percentages are fixed on a sliding scale according to the number and character of distant stations whose nonnetwork programs are imported by the cable system, with a special fee schedule provided for smaller systems.

- The aggregated royalty fees are to be distributed, as determined by the Copyright Royalty Tribunal (established under sections 801-810 of the Act), among the copyright owners who file claims for their works that were included in the nonnetwork programs of distant broadcast stations carried by the cable systems. The Copyright Royalty Tribunal is also authorized to review and adjust the royalty rates from time to time under standards stated in the Act.

A.2.7 MICROFILM, VIDEOTAPE, AND COMPUTER PROGRAMS

When the Copyright Office first received, as a deposit for copyright registration, copyrightable textual material on microfilm, it had to make a decision on what appeared, at least at first glance, to be a doubtful question: In view of the 1908 decision of the Supreme Court in the *White-Smith* case—holding that a "copy" of a work had to be visually perceptible—could microfilm reproductions of a work qualify as the "copies" required by the 1909 statute to be deposited for registration? The effect of the *White-Smith* ruling had been avoided in subsequent legislation and court decisions dealing with sound recordings, but the ruling itself had never been overturned.

The work could not, of course, be read from the microfilm with the naked eye. It could, however, be made plainly visible and readable by placing the microfilm in a reader, a device that magnified the text in the microfilm. On this ground the Copyright Office decided that the *White-Smith* ruling on piano rolls of music, which could not have made the music visually perceptible by any means and was not intended to do so, did not preclude its acceptance as a "copy," of a microfilm from which the textual work was intended to be, and could be, made visually readable with the aid of a device readily available for that purpose.

The Copyright Office was presented with the same question again when it first received, for copyright registration, a motion picture produced on videotape. Nothing could be seen on the videotape itself, but when used in a projector designed for the purpose the videotape would reproduce plainly the visual images constituting the motion picture. Following its reasoning with respect to copyrightable text on microfilm, the Copyright Office concluded that it would accept videotape recordings as deposit "copies" of motion pictures for purposes of copyright registration.

The Copyright Office was faced once more with a similar question when it was asked to register copyright claims in computer programs embodied in magnetic tape. On the preliminary question of whether the program itself, consisting of a series of instructions by which a computer could be made to operate as directed, was a copyrightable work, the Copyright Office took the position, in substance, that if the instructions would constitute a copyrightable work if printed in the form of a book, they would be copyrightable in the form of a computer program. The question remained of whether the program in the form of punched card or magnetic tape, from which the instructions could not be read, was acceptable for copyright registration in view of the *White-Smith* ruling. The Copyright Office concluded that its reasoning with respect to microfilms and videotape should be extended to the punched cards or magnetic tape bearing the copyrightable program, since the copyrightable series of instructions could be made readable by the human eye in the printout or projection from the computer. It may be noted that the Copyright Office announced its conclusions regarding the acceptance of computer programs for copyright registration in a circular (No. 61, issued initially in 1964) expressing some doubt about its conclusions in the absence of any court ruling on the precise questions involved, and stating that it would require the deposit of a printout or other readable form of the program, in addition to copies of the form in which the program was published, in order to identify the copyrighted content of the program.

The foregoing account illustrates how the Copyright Office may play a role in the adaptation of the copyright law to new technologies. Its conclusions concerning the copyrightability and registrability of works embodied in microfilms, videotapes, punched cards or magnetic tape have not been tested in the courts but have generally been accepted and followed in practice by the groups concerned.

The new Copyright Act of 1976 removes any lingering doubt as to copyright protection or registrability of works embodied in forms in which the work is not visually perceptible but from which it can be made perceptible by the use of a machine or device. As we have noted earlier, the new Act, in section 101, defines "copies" as meaning:

> material objects . . . in which a work is fixed by any method now known or later developed, and from which the work can be perceived, reproduced, or otherwise communicated, either directly or with the aid of a machine or device.

A.3 PROVIDING TECHNOLOGICAL EXPERTISE TO THE JUDICIARY

The following discussion is responsive to the task as stated in these terms:

> Discuss the utility of institutionalizing, by any appropriate new means, the provision of technological expertise to the judiciary with specific application to copyright litigation.

It is inherent in our judicial system that the courts may be called upon to render judgment in an infinite variety of cases involving some element of technology based on the various physical and social sciences. Thus, in particular cases the court may need to be informed, on an ad hoc basis, of the fundamental theories and operating principles and mechanisms of a scientific technology involved in the issues it must decide.

Over the years procedures have been instituted whereby such information, to the extent considered necessary, is furnished to the courts. It is characteristic of the adversary process in our judicial system that the parties to litigation are expected, through their counsel, to present testimony to the court—including testimony by experts in a specialized field of knowledge where necessary—explaining the salient facts in the case, the issues they raise, and the rationale advanced for the proposed decision. Witnesses offered as experts in a particular field of knowledge are required to be qualified as such, and their examination and cross-examination, including questioning by the judge, are expected to elicit the technical intelligence needed by the court to render an informed decision. Also, in the course of a trial or hearing, the court may be given a physical demonstration of the operation of a technological device or process.

Courts are also given memoranda and briefs prepared for counsel for the parties, which purport to explain fully and persuasively the factual data—including the technical information considered pertinent—as well as the legal analysis and arguments, that make up the case for each party. And the court, if it feels the need for further information, may call for the submission of additional memoranda or briefs on specified subjects. In cases of general importance the courts often receive informative memoranda and briefs also from interested persons or organizations other than the parties to the case. And, of course, judges may gain the information they need through their own research or through research conducted for them by their aides.

The procedures mentioned above comprise those most generally used to inform the courts of the facts and issues that must be known to them as the bases for their judgments, and those procedures have apparently been found adequate for the purpose in most litigation, including the usual run of copyright cases in which such technologies as may be involved are old and so well known as to be taken for granted.

If, in extraordinary cases, other means are needed to provide technological expertise to the judiciary, there are several prototypes that might be adapted to serve that need. Thus, in a few areas of the law where the cases involve technical questions of a specialized character, special courts have been established to decide controversial issues: for example, there is a special Court of Customs and Patent Appeals for the review of contested rulings by the Patent Office on the validity of patent claims, as well as rulings by the Customs Bureau on customs matters; and a special Tax Court has been established to decide cases involving liability for Federal taxes. Special courts have also been established in the States to deal with certain classes of social problems, notably juvenile and domestic relations courts. Judges of these special courts are expected to be or to become experts in the particular field within their jurisdiction.

Another means that might be employed to provide the courts with expertise in scientific or other technical fields is to have specialists in those fields attached to the staff of the court or otherwise serving as consultants to one or a group of courts on a regular basis. As an instance of this, many juvenile and domestic relations courts and some criminal courts have specialists, such as physicians, psychologists, and social workers, serving as members of their staff or as consultants to conduct examinations or investigations and advise the judges. It may not be practicable to staff the Federal courts with experts in the various branches of science and technology, but perhaps they could be called in as consultants as and when needed.

The evolution of regulatory and similar administrative agencies of the Government also suggests ways that might be developed to provide the courts with technical information. Those agencies are somewhat comparable to courts in that they exercise quasi-judicial functions in interpreting the broad provisions of statutes and applying them to specific situations. To assist in their performance of these functions the agencies employ specialists in various fields to assemble information on technical subjects and to evaluate the significance of that information for the guidance of the agency in making decisions. It might be feasible to make arrangements whereby the expertise of the various Government agencies could be made available to the courts in a regularized manner.

Are special institutions or procedures such as those mentioned above needed in copyright litigation involving new technologies for the production or use of copyrighted works? This comes down to a matter of opinion on which analysts of the question may differ. We believe the answer is: no. As we see it, the judicial decisions in copyright cases, as exemplified by those reviewed earlier in this study—(and they are more concerned with technological aspects than are the bulk of copyright cases)—indicate that the courts have been adequately informed, through the judicial processes and procedures now used, on the new technologies involved, to enable them to reach intelligent and appropriate judgments.

It is evident that patent law, for example, deals essentially with products and processes of the physical sciences and technology, so that a fairly thorough knowledge of those fields is required in deciding many of the questions that arise under the patent law. But the copyright law is quite different in the nature of its subject matter—works of authorship—and in its central concerns with the reproduction and dissemination of such works; the technologies involved in the means of reproduction and dissemination appear to be no more than incidental to the main issues which relate to the economic and social values of such works and their uses. So, it is generally enough, in copyright cases, for the court to be informed of the basic features of the technologies involved; the court does not need to acquire the detailed knowledge in depth of an expert in the technology.

This last observation is well illustrated by the *Fortnightly* case: The District Court devoted twelve pages of its opinion to a detailed exposition on the technological processes involved in the cable system's retransmission of broadcast signals, as throwing light on the question of whether the cable system merely relayed those signals or transformed them into new signals constituting a new performance of the content of the program (though this was not the sole basis for the District Court's decision). Both the Circuit Court of Appeals and the Supreme Court disavowed this technological analysis as a basis for deciding the issue; instead, they looked at the functional purpose and effect of the retransmission to decide whether it was a performance comparable to that of a broadcaster (as the Circuit Court held) or was merely a passive aid to the viewer's reception of the broadcast (as the Supreme Court held).

Commentators have criticized some court decisions in one copyright case or another as reflecting the court's lack of understanding of certain principles of the copyright law; but it would be hard to find any complaints that the courts have reached erroneous conclusions because they did not understand the technologies involved in the use of copyrighted works.

In sum, as we see it, the technology employed in the reproduction or dissemination of copyrighted works would rarely, if ever, be decisive of the issues in copyright cases, and the means now used to bring the pertinent facts of a case to the attention of the court are adequate to provide the court with as much information as it needs concerning the technologies involved.

4   THE COPYRIGHT LAW IN RELATION TO COMPUTERIZED
    INFORMATION SYSTEMS

A.4.1   BACKGROUND

A.4.1.1 <u>Legislative History</u>. During the initial hearings in the House of
Representatives in 1965 on the bill for general revision of the copyright
law, some sketchy testimony was presented on the problems then
anticipated concerning the use of copyrighted works in computer
systems (Hearings on H.R. 4347, 89th Cong.). In its Report in 1967
based on those hearings (House Report No. 83, 90th Cong.) the House
Judiciary Committee said:

> Although it was touched on rather lightly at the hearings, the problem
> of computer uses of copyrighted material has attracted increasing
> attention and controversy in recent months. Recognizing the profound
> impact that information storage and retrieval devices seem destined to
> have on authorship, communications, and human life itself, the
> committee is also aware of the dangers of legislating prematurely in this
> area of exploding technology.

Even while it spoke of legislating prematurely, the Committee went on
to express these opinions:

> Thus, unless the doctrine of fair use were applicable, the following
> computer uses could be infringements of copyright under section 106:
> reproduction of a work (or a substantial part of it) in any tangible form
> (paper, punch cards, magnetic tape, etc.) for input into an information
> storage and retrieval system; reproduction of a work or substantial parts
> of it, in copies as the "print-out" or output of the computer;
> preparation for input of an index or abstract of the work so complete
> and detailed that it would be considered a "derivative work"; computer
> transmission or display of a visual image of a work to one or more
> members of the public. On the other hand, since the mere scanning or
> manipulation of the contents of a work within a system would not
> involve a reproduction, the preparation of a derivative work, or a public
> distribution, performance, or display, it would be outside the scope of
> the legislation.

These problems of computer uses of copyrighted works were discussed
thereafter at much greater length during the Senate hearings in 1967 on
the general revision bill (Hearings on S. 597, 90th Cong.). The
testimony at those hearings on behalf of authors and publishers
generally argued in support of the opinions stated in the House

Committee Report (No. 83). The testimony on behalf of user groups, especially academic users, was critical of those opinions; suggested that some uses of copyrighted material in computer systems should be exempt from copyright control, and insisted that it was premature to reach any legislative conclusions on the issues. There were suggestions by some witnesses on both sides that many of the controversial aspects of the problem could be resolved if a central "clearinghouse" system could be established to license computer uses of copyrighted works on a mass basis upon payment of preestablished royalties.

Subsequently a consensus developed among the interested groups that the problems of computer use required further study before they could be dealt with satisfactorily in legislation. Two legislative provisions emerged from that consensus. One was the provision to establish the National Commission on New Technological Uses of Copyrighted Works (CONTU) which was enacted on December 31, 1974 as part of Public Law 93-573. This act states:

> The purpose of the Commission is to study and compile data on:
>
> > (1) the reproduction and use of copyrighted works of authorship—
> >
> > > (A) in conjunction with automatic systems capable of storing, processing, retrieving, and transferring information, and
> > >
> > > (B) by various forms of machine reproduction . . .
> >
> > (2) the creation of new works by the application or intervention of such automatic systems or machine reproduction.

The Commission is to make a final report within three years (by December 31, 1977) with its recommendations as to "such changes in copyright law or procedures that may be necessary to assure for such purposes access to copyrighted works, and to provide recognition of the rights of copyright owners."

The second provision resulting from the consensus among the parties concerned was section 117 of the new Copyright Act of 1976, providing in substance that the law pertaining to computer uses of copyrighted works in effect on December 31, 1977 (the day before the new Act becomes effective) would continue to be in effect under the new Act. Section 117 states that the new Act—

> does not afford to the owner of copyright in a work any greater or lesser rights with respect to the use of the work in conjunction with

automatic systems capable of storing, processing, retrieving, or transferring information, or in conjunction with any similar device, machine, or process, than those afforded to works under the law, whether title 17 or the common law or statutes of a State, in effect on December 31, 1977, as held applicable and construed by a court in an action brought under this title.

What the applicable law now in effect may be is uncertain, but it appears to be unlikely that any major issue of computer use of copyrighted works will require a decision in the very near future.

A.4.1.2 Interested Groups. The wide range of interest groups having a financial, professional, or service interest in the generation, dissemination or use of scientific and technical information that might be used in computerized systems is reflected in the list of persons and organizations by or for whom testimony was presented on the issues of computer uses, or whose interests were referred to, during the Congressional hearings on the copyright revision bills. The interest groups identified in those hearings and in other literature on the subject include:

   – Authors of textual, graphic, and other kinds of works in the various fields of science and technology.

   – Commercial publishers and nonprofit publishers (such as scientific societies) of journals in the various fields of science and technology. These journals appear to be the copyrighted works most used in scientific and technical research.

   – Commercial publishers and nonprofit publishers (such as university presses) of books, monographs, graphic and other materials of a scholarly or informational character. Included here would be the publishers of cyclopedic works and educational materials.

   – Producers and publishers of compilations of bibliographic and factual data.

   – Libraries, especially large research, university, and industrial libraries.

   – Educators and students, especially at the college and university levels.

- Industrial and nonprofit research organizations and individual researchers, including professional practitioners and societies, in the various fields of science and technology.

- Producers of computer hardware and software.

- Organizers and operators of computerized information service systems.

- Commercial indexing and data search services.

- Other specialists in computer and information technologies.

These groupings could, of course, be arranged in many other ways, and there is considerable overlap among the groups as listed above. For example, educators or researchers may also be authors; some journal publishers also publish compilations of data; and a future may be envisioned in which publishers or libraries are also the operators of computerized information service systems.

A.4.2 SCOPE OF THIS SECTION

A.4.2.1 Computer Programs. We have referred above, in section A.2.7 of this report, to the availability of copyright protection for computer programs. The broad question of protection for computer programs was not intended to be a primary subject of this report; but it is tangential to some of our main subjects; and we will supplement the earlier reference to their copyrightability with a brief review below, in section A.4.3, of the extent of protection afforded to computer programs by copyright. Because, as we shall see, copyright protection is limited essentially to copying the program as written, broader protection under patent principles, extending to the process or algorithm embodied in the program, has been advocated by some parties but has been opposed by others. The issues of protecting computer programs under patent principles, or by contracts based on the law of trade secrets which some program producers have relied upon, are completely outside the scope of this report.

A.4.2.2 Data Bases. The much-heralded "information explosion"—the massive proliferation of published material during the last few decades—has greatly emphasized the need of scientific and technical researchers for two capabilities; first, they must be enabled to learn of, and to segregate from the steadily growing flood of published material, principally journals, those particular articles that appear to be pertinent to their fields of research and to their current inquiries; and second, having identified the articles that appear to be pertinent, they must be enabled to obtain copies of those articles for study.

The conventional effort to meet the first need—identifying the pertinent articles—has been to compile and publish in printed form various kinds of bibliographic indexes and abstracts of the mass of published articles. These bibliographic publications have been indispensable research tools; but even in any one specialized field, a researcher seeking comprehensive coverage of the pertinent sources would need to review a number of indexes and collections of abstracts, which he would generally not be able to do efficiently and might often not be able to do at all, because of the high cost of acquiring all or most of the relevant bibliographic publications, and because it would take too large a portion of his working time to review all of the accessible bibliographic publications and identify the articles of interest to him.

Computer technology has offered a means of solving this problem. Bibliographic indexes and abstracts can be prepared or reproduced in the form of machine-readable data bases and placed in computerized information systems. Such computerized systems make it possible for a researcher to find and select, quickly and with a high degree of accuracy, from the mass of articles indexed and abstracted in the data bases, those which appear to pertain to the particular subject of his research. A large assemblage of data bases, coupled with a modern telecommunication system and available terminals, can enable researchers located at a distance to make a fairly comprehensive search, in a very short time, of the published articles in their specialized fields.

Several such data base systems are now in operation and some of them include copyrighted data bases leased by the system from the copyright owners. Data base systems of this character present prime examples of computerized information systems using copyrighted material. Many of the copyright questions that are seen as likely to arise in connection with the use of copyrighted material in computer systems can be posed in the context of data base systems. Those questions will be considered in relation to data base systems in section A.4.4 of this report.

A.4.2.3 Supplying Copyrighted Documents. The second of the researcher's needs—to obtain the full text of the articles he finds pertinent—presents a different situation. Even though the costs of computer storage of textual materials can be expected to be reduced very substantially over the next decade or two, the cost of full-text computer storage might still be extremely high as compared with other effective means of storing a library of many articles from which copies could be provided as needed. Such other methods would include, for example, the storage of articles in microform from which reproductions (either in microform or in printed pages) could be supplied readily and at small cost by mail.

It seems highly probable that the supplying of copies of journal articles as needed by researchers will continue, for a long time to come, to be a function primarily of the publishers or their licensees. Several commercial organizations, operating under licenses from a large number of publishers, are now in the business of supplying copies of documents on order. A few of these organizations provide a data base search service, and supply copies of documents in conjunction with that service. Such arrangements will probably expand.

Insofar as publishers and their licensees do not fulfill the function of supplying copies of documents adequately and expeditiously, libraries will no doubt continue to be called upon to supply "photocopies." (Perhaps a library maintaining a large collection of journals will be an adjunct to a computerized data base system.) In that case, the copyright questions relating to the supplying of copies of articles to researchers will be those pertaining to library photocopying. We have already referred briefly to the copyright aspects of library photocopying in section A.2.5 of this report. Further consideration of that subject is beyond the scope of this report, except for the related matter (which pertains also to computer storage and retrieval of copyrighted works) of the possibility of establishing central clearinghouses for the mass licensing of copyrighted works for reproduction. The subject of clearinghouses will be considered in section A.4.6 of this report.

As indicated above, it does not seem likely that computer storage of any large mass of documents will be common in the foreseeable future. However, there have been a number of instances of full-text input of copyrighted works into computers for various purposes such as analysis or indexing of the work, or reproduction of all or parts of the work for review. And there are a few instances of computer storage for retrieval of a fairly large volume of documentary material. Some computerized law research services, for example, contain the full text of many statutes and court decisions (which, it may be noted, incidentally, are not subject to copyright) together with related notes, abstracts, and commentaries (which may be subject to copyright).

ill assume that full-text input of some kinds of copyrighted
| will become more common eventually. As previously
mentioned, many of the copyright questions that might arise in
connection with full-text storage of copyrighted works will be similar
to those that will be discussed in the context of data base systems in
section A.4.4 below. The questions that we see pertaining specially to
full-text storage and retrieval will be reviewed in section A.4.5.

A.4.3 COPYRIGHT PROTECTION FOR COMPUTER PROGRAMS

As we have noted earlier, in section A.2.7 of this report, computer
programs (i.e., the series of instructions which are considered to
constitute a literary work) are subject to copyright protection. The
doubt that was previously expressed about their copyrightability
(stemming from the fact that in the machine-readable form in which
programs are distributed they are not visually perceptible) has been
removed by the new Copyright Act of 1976, especially by section
102(a) which reads:

> Copyright protection subsists, in accordance with this title, in original
> works of authorship fixed in any tangible medium of expression, now
> known or later developed, from which they can be perceived,
> reproduced, or otherwise communicated, either directly or with the aid
> of a machine or device.

The protection afforded to computer programs by copyright, however,
is limited. The exclusive rights of a copyright owner to "copy" and
"publish" his work, as provided in section 1 of the 1909 Copyright Act
still in effect, would apply to computer programs. These same rights are
embraced by the provisions in section 6 of the new 1976 Act giving the
copyright owner the exclusive rights to "reproduce the copyrighted
work in copies" and to "distribute copies . . . of the copyrighted work
to the public."

What constitutes "copying" or "reproduction" may be a matter of fine
distinctions. Infringing reproduction would, of course, include full,
literal copying of the work as written, but it is not confined to this.
Copying of a substantial and material part of a work would be an
infringement, and so would copying with slight changes. Tracking of
the substance and sequence of the steps set forth in a program may
constitute infringement, even though many superficial changes are
made (as in an effort to disguise the fact of copying).

On the other hand, it is a basic principle of copyright law that the ideas or concepts embodied in a work, even if they are original with the author, are not protected against use in the independent work of another author. In other words, it is only the author's original "expression" or exposition that is protected against copying. Copyright does not preclude others from using the know-how they learn from a copyrighted work in their own works. Thus, in the case of computer programs, copyright would not protect the processes or techniques developed to make the program operative and revealed in the program. This is reflected in the provision in section 102(b) of the new 1976 Act reading:

> In no case does copyright protection for an original work of authorship extend to any idea, procedure, process, system, method of operation, concept, principle, or discovery, regardless of the form in which it is described, explained, illustrated, or embodied in such work."

The protection afforded by copyright against reproduction may be of little or no significance with respect to programs designed specially for a particular user. Such protection may be quite valuable, however, for a program that would have a market of many users and could be reproduced cheaply in the absence of copyright.

A.4.4 DATA BASE SYSTEMS

A.4.4.1 Copyright Protection for Data Bases

A.4.4.1.1 Copyrightability. Data bases are compilations of data consisting typically of bibliographic indexes—words and phrases identifying the subject content of published documents—and abstracts of documents describing their subject content more fully. Data bases may also consist of compilations of factual data such as mathematical or scientific formulas or statistical tables. Compilations of various kinds of data are traditional subjects of copyright protection. Both the Copyright Act of 1909 (in sections 5(a) and 7) and the new Act of 1976 (in section 103) mention compilations explicitly as a category of copyrightable works. In section 101 of the Act of 1976 a "compilation" is defined as "a work formed by the collection and assembling of pre-existing materials or of data that are selected, coordinated, or arranged in such a way that the resulting work as a whole constitutes an original work of authorship."

As reflected in this definition, the authorship that makes a compilation copyrightable lies in the labor, skill, and judgment involved in selecting the pertinent data and organizing and arranging the mass of selected data into a systematic and useful whole. Thus, while the individual items in a compilation are not subject to copyright in themselves, the collection as a whole, or any segment of it large enough to be the product of selection and organization by the author, would be protected by the copyright against unauthorized reproduction.

Compilations of various kinds of data—including bibliographic indexes and abstracts—are well known as printed publications and have generally been copyrighted in that form. A number of them are now being issued also in machine-readable copies and this trend seems to be growing. It is now possible also to compile indexes and other data by the use of computers, and there is no apparent reason why a data base so compiled, in machine-readable form, would not be copyrightable.

As reported in the February 1977 issue of *Information Action* (a publication of the Information Industry Association): "the number of data bases available for on-line access has doubled in the last year . . . In 1965, 24 machine-readable, bibliographic data bases covering 880,000 documents existed. In 1975, the total was over 160 covering 46 million documents."

Many of the existing data bases are covered by copyright but others are not. Several of them have been produced by the U.S. Government and are therefore not copyrightable. Some producers of data bases apparently rely upon their contractual arrangements with the systems to which their data bases are leased for protection of their proprietary rights.

A.4.4.1.2 Copyright Notice on Data Bases. In order to maintain copyright protection, the published copies of a work are required by the statute to bear a notice of copyright in a prescribed form, "affixed to the copies in such manner and location as to give reasonable notice of the claim of copyright" (Act of 1976, section 401). Some commentators have anticipated difficulty in meeting this requirement in the case of machine-readable copies such as magnetic tapes. Their concern on this score may have been due in large part to the less flexible language of the notice provisions in the 1909 statute (section 20) which was phrased in terms of printed publications. In any event, we see no real difficulty in affixing the required notice to the magnetic tapes (or other machine-readable copies). The notice could be incorporated in the system software so that it would appear in any printout. And even assuming that an eye-readable notice should be affixed to the tape copies, it seems reasonable to expect the tape copies, or a container in which they are housed, to bear an eye-readable label showing the title which identifies the work on the tape; the copyright notice could readily be placed on that label. It might be added that any special problems regarding the placement of the notice on tape copies could be resolved under the Act of 1976 by the Register of Copyrights who is authorized (by Section 401(c)) to prescribe "specific methods of affixation and positions of the notice on various types of works that will satisfy this requirement."

A similar problem concerning the copyright notice occurs when some part of a data base is printed out from a computerized system in response to a user's inquiry. It is not clear whether the notice would be necessary on each reproduction of a relatively small number of items in a data base. It is arguable, we believe, that the reproduction of a small part of the collected data is not such a published copy of the work as would call for the notice; and this argument would be more cogent where the subscribers to the computer system's service were informed in advance that certain of its data bases were copyrighted. If it is thought to be necessary or advisable to have the notice appear on each printout of any part of a data base, this appears to be feasible. The data base would normally be identified by its title in the printout, and the computer could be programmed to include the copyright notice in every printout of the title.

A.4.4.1.3 <u>Deposit of Copies for Registration</u>. Registration of a copyright may be essential to its effective enforcement against infringers. Under the Act of 1909, registration is a prerequisite to maintaining a suit for infringement (section 13) and it facilitates proof of the validity of the copyright claim (section 209). The 1976 Act has provisions to the same effect (sections 411 and 410(d)), and provides in addition that awards of statutory damages and attorney's fees (special remedies that make enforcement of the copyright more effective) are to be granted only when registration has been made (section 412).

To make registration, the deposit of two copies of the work as published is required under both the 1909 Act (section 13) and the 1976 Act (section 408(b)). That requirement has been met readily for printed compilations of data, and printed copies would apparently suffice for deposit where the compilation has also been produced as a data base in machine-readable form. But if a data base were prepared only in machine-readable form, the deposit of copies could be troublesome, or at least burdensome, if, as the 1909 Act has been thought to require, the copies deposited had to be visually perceptible. The resolution of this problem has been made possible by the provisions in the Act of 1976 (section 408(c)) reading--

The Register of Copyrights is authorized to specify by regulation the administrative classes into which works are to be placed for purposes of deposit and registration, and the nature of the copies or phonorecords to be deposited in the various classes specified. The regulations may require or permit, for particular classes, the deposit of identifying material instead of copies or phonorecords . . .

A.4.4.1.4 Supplements to Update Data Bases. Bibliographic data bases must be brought up to date from time to time by adding to them new index entries and citations for more recently published articles. Some observers have seen difficulties in complying with the requirement for deposit of copies with respect to such supplemental additions. Printed publications with supplements issued serially, such as loose-leaf information services, are well known. The usual procedure for them has been to publish each supplemental issue as a new work in itself with its own copyright notice, and to deposit copies of each supplemental issue for registration as a separate work. Alternatively, an entire new edition of the work as revised to include the supplemental additions could be published, and copies of the new edition could then be deposited. Either of these procedures would seem to be feasible for supplements compiled periodically for addition to a data base, though the latter procedure of publishing an entire new edition may be expensive.

It might be noted also that when supplemental items are merged into a computer-stored data base, coverage of the new material by copyright might require changing the year date in the copyright notice appearing with the data base in its earlier form. But even if the notice is left unchanged, copyright protection of the content of the data base in that earlier form would not be affected, and this may be adequate protection for all practical purposes as long as the newly added material could not be used without some of the earlier material. When the volume of new material added by updating over a long period of time becomes a major part of the entire data base, reissue of the data base in a new edition might be found appropriate.

A.4.4.2 Compiling Data Bases

A.4.4.2.1 Bibliographic Indexes. The process of compiling bibliographic indexes involves the following steps: obtaining copies of the documents to be included in the index, scanning those documents and selecting from them the key words and phrases to be listed in the index as subject headings, perhaps inserting other subject headings judged by the compiler to be needed as cross-references, and arranging the subject headings together with citations to the documents in an alphabetical or other orderly arrangement. Traditionally, this process has been, and generally still is, performed manually through the exercise of human effort and skill, and the completed index is published in printed form.

It is now possible to perform this process and prepare an index of some quality by using a properly programmed computer, but with this difference: The documents to be indexed must be in machine-readable form to be processed by the computer.

As long as the indexer uses authorized copies of copyrighted documents, there is ordinarily no copyright problem in the manual compilation of a bibliographic index. Scanning of the copies, the extraction of key words and phrases as subject headings, and the arrangement of those headings with citations to the documents, do not constitute infringement of the copyright. No copy of the substance of the document is made in this process, nor would the resulting index be considered an infringing copy or derivative work since it would not convey the essence or meaning of the work embodied in the document.

Similarly, if a machine-readable copy of a copyrighted document used for indexing by a computer was obtained from the publisher,* preparation of the index by the computer would seem to involve no infringing act. A publisher who supplies a machine-readable copy of a work to a computer operator would impliedly authorize the use for which it was intended: Its input into the computer. The subsequent processing of the document by the computer in indexing it would be the same in character as the processing done in manual indexing, which, as pointed out in the preceding paragraph, would not involve any infringement of the copyright.

When a machine-readable copy is made available by the publisher, it would seem reasonable to expect the computer operator to acquire such a copy for his machine indexing. But if, instead, he chose to make his own machine-readable copy (which would seem to be unlikely since making his own would usually cost more than obtaining one from the publisher), he would then be making a reproduction of the document in apparent violation of the copyright owner's exclusive right to "reproduce the copyrighted work in copies" (Act of 1976, section 106 (1)).

---

* The references made here and below to the publisher as the supplier of copyrighted material assume that he is the copyright owner or the agent of the copyright owner.

If a machine-readable copy is not made available by the publisher of a copyrighted document, an indexer would appear to be unable to use a computer in indexing that document unless he obtained permission from the publisher to make and use a machine-readable copy. To seek permission from a large number of individual publishers could be a very time-consuming and costly procedure, so much so perhaps as to discourage computer indexing of any large number of documents. Some persons interested in fostering the development and use of computers have suggested that in this situation, the making of a machine-readable copy and its input into the computer for the sole purpose of preparing an index should not be regarded as an infringement but should be treated as a fair use. They argue that, as long as the publisher does not offer such copies, making one for a use which is not itself an infringement would not injure the copyright owner in any way and would not displace the potential sale of a copy of the work. In fact, they say, the inclusion of the work in the index would create some demand for copies. Alternatively, some of the same persons suggest, the statute should provide for a compulsory license to make and use a machine-readable copy in situations of this character.

A.4.4.2.2 Abstracts in Data Bases. Bibliographic data bases may include, in addition to index headings and citations, abstracts of the contents of the cited documents. These abstracts aid the researcher in determining more precisely the relevance to his subject of the documents cited in connection with the pertinent index headings. Typically, the abstracts in a data base are similar to a table of contents in that they are brief identifying statements of the subjects dealt with in the document. Such abstracts of copyrighted works do not reproduce the substance of the work and would not be a substitute for the work in conveying the essential information to be derived from reading the document itself. Accordingly, it would seem that such abstracts, like indexes, may be made freely without regard to the copyright in the work.

On the other hand there are so-called "abstracts" that are really synopses or digests of the substance of the document, conveying that substance so fully that a researcher's need for the information in the document might be satisfied by his reading of the "abstract" alone. This kind of synoptic abstract would seem to constitute a derivative work under the definition in section 101 of the Act of 1976 reading in part:

> A "derivative work" is a work based upon one or more pre-existing works, such as . . . (an) abridgement (or) condensation . . .

A person who makes an "abstract" amounting to a condensation of a copyrighted work infringes upon the exclusive right of the copyright owner to "prepare derivative works based upon the copyrighted work" (Act of 1976, section 106 (2)).

It is evident that there will be difficulty in some borderline cases in determining whether a particular abstract would be considered a mere non-infringing identifier of the subjects covered in a document, or an infringing condensation of the document.

The author abstracts accompanying many copyrighted articles are often sufficiently full in themselves to be protected as a copyrighted component of the work, so that their unauthorized reproduction would infringe the copyright.

In sum, the compiler of a data base would risk being charged with copyright infringement if his data base included abstracts prepared by him that could be considered condensations of copyrighted works, or included author abstracts of some length.

A.4.4.3 Putting Copyrighted Data Bases into Computer Systems

A.4.4.3.1 Where Publishers Offer to Supply Machine-Readable Copies. As shown by the preceding examination of the operation of existing computerized information systems, machine-readable data bases are being produced by many of the publishers of the compiled indexes and abstracts making up the content of those data bases, and the computer systems obtain their data bases from the publishers. Under this established business practice, the rights of the system to use the data bases and supply information extracted from them to their subscribers, and the compensation to be paid to the publishers, are settled by the contracts between the parties. As such contracts become common, a standard pattern of terms and conditions, shaped by the industry needs and experience, can be expected to evolve. The recognized copyright problems that would otherwise be involved in the use of copyrighted data bases in computerized systems would generally be resolved by such contracts. Nor would these copyright problems arise in those instances where the computer systems are operated by the publishers themselves.

To be most effective, a bibliographic data base system should cover the literature in any particular field of information as comprehensively as possible. The rapid expansion of published information has been, and no doubt will continue to be, accompanied by a corresponding expansion in compiled indexes and abstracts. As computerized data base systems become more highly developed and more commonly used, the publishers of more of the printed compilations of bibliographic data will no doubt make them available in machine-readable form to meet the demand for their use in computerized systems. To the extent that this occurs, the copyright problems pertaining to the use of data bases in such systems will continue to be settled by contractual arrangements.

Where the publisher offers to supply a machine-readable copy of a copyrighted data base wanted by an operator for inclusion in his system, we suggest that the operator should be expected to obtain it from the publisher. For the operator to make his own machine-readable copy in that situation should constitute an infringement.

A.4.4.3.2 Where Publishers Do Not Offer Machine-Readable Copies. It may be supposed that instances will arise in the future when a large computerized information system, seeking comprehensive coverage of some field, will wish to include in its data bases certain copyrighted compilations of bibliographic data that have been published only in printed copies. No more than a few publishers would be involved at any particular time and the system operator could identify them readily. It would therefore seem reasonable in such cases to expect the system operator to deal directly with the individual publishers. The operator could ask the publisher to make and supply a machine-readable copy of the compilation for the operator's use under a contract, or, as an alternative, to grant permission to the system operator to make his own machine-readable copy for such use. It seems probable that one or the other of such requests would be acceded to by the publisher upon terms mutually agreed to.

But suppose further that the publisher refuses to accede to either request, or simply fails to respond to the system operator's inquiry. In light of the value for research of having comprehensive coverage in data base systems, there would seem to be a valid argument in favor of providing some kind of compulsory license to permit a system operator to make and use a machine-readable copy of a copyrighted compilation of data where the publisher refuses or fails to provide such a copy or to grant permission to the operator to make one for his own use, within a reasonable period of time after being requested to do so. Under the compulsory license, of course, the system operator would be required to pay equitable compensation to the publisher.

A.4.4.3.3 Where Third Persons Offer to Supply Machine-Readable Copies. A machine-readable copy of a copyrighted data base is not likely to be available to the operator of a computerized system from a source other than the publisher (or his agent). Publishers who supply machine-readable copies for use in such systems will normally not sell a copy to a system operator so as to give him ownership of it, but will lease it to him under an arrangement which expressly confines its use to that system and precludes its being made available to anyone else. This practice is necessary because of the so-called "first sale doctrine" which is well established in the copyright law. Under that doctrine, the copyright owner's control over the distribution of copies of his work ends, with respect to any particular copy, when he makes the first sale of that copy. The doctrine is reflected in section 109(a) of the Copyright Act of 1976 which reads:

> . . . the owner of a particular copy or phonorecord lawfully made under this title, or any person authorized by such owner, is entitled, without the authority of the copyright owner, to sell or otherwise dispose of the possession of that copy or phonorecord.

How the "first sale doctrine" operates is best illustrated in the familiar setting of the sale of a copy of a book by the copyright owner. The purchaser of that copy becomes its owner. He is precluded by the copyright law from reproducing the work in other copies (either in its original form or in a derivative form) and from performing or displaying the work publicly (except as specially permitted by the copyright statute); but as the owner of the particular copy purchased, he is free to sell, lend, destroy, or otherwise dispose of that particular copy as he sees fit.

Machine-readable data bases have no use other than in computerized information systems, and the number of prospective customers for copies is limited. The publisher must therefore seek to prevent the system operator to whom he supplies a machine-readable copy from passing that copy on to another system operator. This is done by leasing copies under specified restrictions against allowing others to use them.

If leasing copies in this manner, rather than selling them, is known to be the usual practice, a system operator who is offered a machine-readable copy of a data base by another system operator, or by anyone other than the publisher, would have reason to be suspicious of the legitimacy of such offer. He would therefore be required to investigate the offeror's right to claim lawful ownership of the copy and to dispose of it, and he would subject himself to liability if he obtained the copy from an offeror who was acting in violation of the rights of the copyright owner.

Even assuming that a system operator could lawfully obtain a machine-readable data base for use in his system from someone other than the publisher, he would probably have little or nothing to gain from doing so. He would still need to input the data base into his system and to provide the output of material from the data base to the users of his system. It seems virtually certain that at some stage during these operations he would have to deal with the publisher to obtain a license for these uses of the data base. The terms of the license might well be much the same as if he had leased the data itself from the publisher.

A.4.4.3.4 <u>Input of Data Base as Use Subject to Copyright</u>. As we have observed above, in the usual case where the operator of a computerized information system obtains a machine-readable data base from the publisher, the copyright license he might need to use the data base in his system would no doubt be included in his lease agreement with the publisher. This would apparently be true also in the situation mentioned above where a system operator arranges with the publisher of a printed compilation of data to make his own machine-readable copy for use in his system.

There may be some special circumstances in which a system operator acquires a machine-readable copy of a copyrighted data base without having obtained a license for its use in his system. As an example of this unusual situation, we have mentioned above the possibility of an operator's acquiring a machine-readable data base from a person other than the publisher. The question would then arise as to whether the system operator should be required to obtain a license from the publisher before he puts the data base into his system or need only arrange thereafter to pay the publisher for output.

In the extended discussion of a similar question heretofore (in relation to full-text input of documents), it has generally been agreed that the copyright owner of works placed in and retrieved from computer systems should be entitled to compensation for such use of his works. Differing views have been expressed, however, as to whether the copyright owner should be entitled to payment for input or only for output. The arguments advanced in the past discussion for free input have been concerned largely with the input of documents for experimental purposes during the developmental stages of computer systems, or for non-infringing purposes such as analyzing or indexing a work which do not entail any reproductive output of the work.

With regard to bibliographic data bases, the only purposes of their input into a computerized system is to make them available for output in pertinent portions in response to inquiries. Assuming that the copyright owner is entitled to payment, at some stage of the input-output process, for the use of his data base in the system, three considerations seem to us to be of prime importance:

(1) It is more practical for the parties concerned to agree upon the payment to be made, and the other conditions relating to the use of the data base in the system, before the process of use begins—that is, before input. This would be true even if the amount to be paid were made dependent in part upon the volume of output. To defer negotiating the terms and conditions of use and payment until after the operator has incurred the trouble and expense of input could be awkward and perhaps abortive if the parties then find it difficult to reach an agreement.

(2) Where the data base is not obtained from the publisher, he would not be assured of learning of its use in the system, and would not be able to exercise any control over its use, unless the system operator is required to deal with him before input takes place.

(3) There may be room for dispute as to whether the output, which would ordinarily consist of no more than a fragment of the content of the data base, amounts to a fair use rather than an infringing reproduction of the work. (We shall have more to say about this later.)

These three considerations, among others, would seem to justify the conclusion that a license to use a copyrighted data base in a computer system should be negotiated before input.

A.4.4.4 Output from Data Base

A.4.4.4.1 Normal Output. The output of material from a data base in a computerized system may be in the form of a printout ("hard copy") or in the form of a display on a cathode ray tube (CRT). There was formerly some question as to whether a CRT display of copyrighted material would constitute an infringement of the copyright owner's exclusive right to make a "copy" of his work. But the new Copyright Act of 1976 provides, in section 106(5), that the public "display" of a work, such as would appear on a CRT, is among the exclusive rights of the copyright owner; and under the definition in section 101, a display is made "publicly" if (among other things) it is transmitted "to the public, by means of any device or process, whether the members of the public capable of receiving the . . . display receive it in the same place or in separate places and at the same time or at different times."

The output of material from a data base will usually consist, in each individual instance, of no more than a few of the great mass of index entries, citations, and abstracts making up the copyrighted compilation of data. As mentioned earlier, it may be contended that the extraction of a few such items from a data base is a fair use rather than an infringement of the copyright. To appraise this contention, the criteria of fair use as stated in section 107 of the Act of 1976 should be recalled:

> In determining whether the use made of a work in any particular case is a fair use the factors to be considered shall include—
>
> (1) the purpose and character of the use, including whether such use is of a commercial nature or is for nonprofit educational purposes;
>
> (2) the nature of the copyrighted work;
>
> (3) the amount and substantiality of the portion used in relation to the copyrighted work as a whole; and
>
> (4) the effect of the use upon the potential market for or value of the copyrighted work.

It may be conceded that the taking of a few items from a data base by an individual researcher on any one occasion may meet the criteria of fair use. The posture of the system operator, however, appears to be quite different in this regard. The operator is supplying many portions of the work, though each may be small in itself, to many persons; the aggregate is quite substantial. He does so for commercial purposes. The repeated use of the work in small portions is the normal use for which the work was intended. And finally, since such output fulfills the user's need for the work, it displaces what might otherwise be potential sales of copies of the work.

In sum, while the output of a small fragment of a data base on any one occasion would have the indicia of fair use, the aggregate of the output of fragments on many occasions in the operation of a computerized system can be seen to constitute an infringing activity for which a license from the copyright owner should be required.

Here again, the matter of copyright infringement by the system operator will be set at rest where the operator contracts with the publisher for use of the data base in his system. It may be assumed that such a contract would cover output as well as input. In the lease agreements known to us for the use of data bases in computerized systems, provision is made for an initial payment to the publisher for the lease of the data base and additional periodic payments based upon the volume of output.

A.4.4.4.2 <u>Extraction of Bulk of Data Base by User of System</u>. A different question may arise in relation to the users who extract data base material from a computerized system. The system will ordinarily provide users with the capability of extracting as much of the material in a data base as they wish and are willing to pay for. It is conceivable that an individual user might take out an entire data base, or so much of it as to constitute an infringing reproduction usable as an abbreviated data base in itself. He might do so, for example, in order to have his own data base for his future use, or to supply a data base for use by others.

The act we are assuming here by the user may be characterized as a theft of the data base and is clearly an infringement of the copyright. The problems are practical ones: what can be done to prevent such a theft, and how can it be detected?

The answers appear to lie in the way the system deals with its users and the way it monitors the volume of their uses. In current practice, as we understand it, a system will make some provision, in its agreement with each user, that purports to limit the extent of the material to be taken from any data base, and to restrain the user from supplying the material taken to anyone else. Moreover, since the fees charged for use of each data base in the system are based on the length of time that the user is on-line, or on the number of items included in an off-line report, the system must keep records of the extent of uses made of each data base. If the recorded use of a data base seems suspiciously excessive, the system could report the facts to the publisher for further investigation. Publishers might require, in their contracts with system operators, that such cases be reported to them.

Another factor serving to inhibit the theft of a data base by the on-line user of a computerized system, under present-day conditions, is the very high cost of using the system for the length of time it would take to do so. It might be less expensive to lease the whole data base from the publisher.

A.4.4.5 <u>Exclusive and Compulsory Licenses for Use of Data Bases</u>. In some instances publishers of data bases have leased them exclusively for use in one computerized information service system, thereby making them unavailable for use by any other such system. This practice of exclusive licensing may have either of two results that might eventually prove to be undesirable.

First, if each of several competing systems has its own exclusive group of data bases in some particular subject area, no one system will be able to provide researchers with comprehensive coverage of that area. The consequent necessity for searching through more than one system—perhaps through several of them—will probably diminish the convenience and effectiveness and increase the cost of bibliographic searches, as compared with a single search through one comprehensive system.

Second, exclusive licensing of data bases may tend to foster the monopolization of data base search services by one or two giant systems. Whether the prevention of such a monopoly or the regulatory control of a permitted monopoly as a public service organization would be preferable is an open question.

From the standpoint of providing maximum service for researchers, and at the same time preventing the development of a monopoly in the business of providing bibliographic search services, the ideal situation might be the development of a number of competing systems each of which can offer comprehensive coverage of any subject area. One way of encouraging such a development would be to provide for a compulsory licensing scheme under which a data base made available for use in any one system would thereupon become available for use in all other systems.

A compulsory license of this character would be similar to the one (the first of its kind) that was established by the Copyright Act of 1909 for the making of mechanical sound recordings of copyrighted music. (See sections A.2.3.1 and A.2.3.2 of this report.) In that precedential case the compulsory license scheme was prompted by the threat of a monopoly being established in the manufacture of such recordings of music. This and other compulsory licensing schemes will be discussed later in section A.4.6.3 of this report.

Whether a compulsory licensing scheme for the use of data bases in computerized information systems is needed, and whether it would be desirable, are debatable issues. There is no doubt much to be said in favor of allowing market forces to operate normally in the leasing of data bases and the development of information systems. We merely mention the proposition of compulsory licensing here as a possibility that may be worth consideration in the future.

A.4.5 FULL-TEXT STORAGE AND RETRIEVAL OF DOCUMENTS

A.4.5.1 <u>Preliminary Observations</u>. A few years ago there was a good deal of speculative discussion of the possibility that, at some time in the future, computer technology will have developed to such a far-reaching extent that computer systems might become the principal storehouse of the world's published knowledge. In this dream of a brave new era, computer systems were pictured as replacing printed copies of books and journals as the primary means of recording and disseminating works of authorship. Computer systems, in conjunction with modern communications technology, would then become the main source of documents for reference or reading.

By now, this dream has receded into the far distant future. It is generally acknowledged that the full-text storage of a large mass of documents in a computer system would be far too costly to be feasible now or in the predictable future. And as long as copies of documents are made readily available in some other manner—as in printed or photocopied pages or in microform reproductions—there would be no apparent reason to incur the very high cost of using computers for full-text storage and retrieval of a vast collection of documents.

To a limited extent, however, some complete documents are now being put into computer systems for various purposes, and this practice may well expand rapidly in the coming years. Moreover, it may be important to consider now the problems that can be anticipated with respect to the future possibility of computer storage and retrieval of the full-text of copyrighted documents on a large scale.

The anticipated problems relating to the use of copyrighted documents in computer systems have been discussed at some length in the Congressional hearings on the copyright revision bills, especially in the Senate hearings in 1967, and in more recent articles. The discussion of those problems has been concerned primarily with the following questions:

> (1) Under what conditions should the input of copyrighted documents into a computer system be deemed to infringe the copyright?

    (2) Under what conditions should the output of such documents or portions of them from the computer system be deemed to infringe the copyright?

    (3) Where permission from the copyright owner is required for the use of a document in a computer system, should such permission be obtained before input, or should it suffice to obtain permission before output?

A.4.5.2 <u>Input and Output of Documents as Infringement</u>. It will be perceived that, in the main, the questions concerning the input and output of copyrighted documents are substantially the same as those pertaining to the input and output of copyrighted data bases. In fact, data bases are a category of complete documents in themselves. Accordingly, the discussion of these questions above in relation to data bases would be applicable to the storage and retrieval of the full text of copyrighted documents in computer systems. As to input, see sections A.4.4.2.1 and A.4.4.3.1 through A.4.4.3.4. As to output, see sections A.4.4.4.1 and A.4.4.5.

One difference, however, may be noted. Whereas the output from a data base will usually consist of a few only of the mass of items in the copyrighted compilation of data, the output in the case of a document will ordinarily be of the entire work. In the latter case there would be no question of fair use. However, the user of a computer system could not be charged with infringement for his extraction from it of a complete copy of a copyrighted document as long as the system is authorized to provide its users with such documents. But if he then used the copy so extracted to make further copies of the document, he would thereby be infringing the copyright. And if a person not entitled to use the system did so surreptitiously to produce copies of copyrighted documents, he would be committing an infringement of the copyright as well as an offense against the system itself. It seems likely, however, that wrongful acts of this nature would often escape detection. (Cf. section A.4.4.4.2.)

One more point is in order here. We suggest that a publisher would be well advised, when he licenses the input and output of copyrighted documents in a computer system, to require the system to have its computer programmed to reproduce the copyright notice on each reproduction of the work as output. (Cf. section A.4.4.1.2.)

A.4.5.3 <u>Input or Output as Occasion for Obtaining License</u>. We have adverted earlier to the discussion, in the 1967 Senate hearings on the copyright revision bill and elsewhere, of the question whether the input of a copyrighted document into a computer system should require a license from the publisher, or whether input should be free though a license will be required for output. The arguments advanced for free input, enunciated mainly by members of the academic community, may be summarized as follows:

(1) Works may be put into computers for the purpose of a noninfringing manipulation of the work within the computer that will not result in any output of the work itself. Known examples include the analysis of the text of a work to show the characteristics of an author's style or the frequency of word uses, or the preparation of a concordance or index. Input for such noninfringing purposes should be exempt from copyright.

(2) Input should be regarded as being merely the means of making a work available to users, i.e., as being comparable to the noninfringing act of placing a copy of a work on the shelves of a library.

(3) Even when a work is input for the purpose of making it available for output, its output may never be requested.

(4) Input of itself does not affect the publisher's market for copies of the work.

(5) The copyright license fees payable to the publisher should be based on the volume of output. No separate fee should be charged in addition for input.

In refutation of those arguments, and in support of the proposition that a license should be obtained before input, the following contentions have been made on behalf of authors and publishers:

(1) Input for any purpose entails the machine-readable reproduction of the work. Such reproduction and input of the work constitute a valuable use of the work, whatever the purpose may be. There is no valid basis for exempting such reproductions from the exclusive right of the copyright owner to make copies of his work.

(2) Libraries are generally expected to buy copies of the published works they place on their shelves. Likewise, computer systems should be expected to obtain the machine-readable copies they need for input, or to obtain

licenses to make them, from the publishers. If free input implies that computer systems are free to make their own machine-readable copies, the publisher's potential market for such copies would be destroyed.

(3) When output is contemplated, input of itself, by making copies of the work available as output, displaces potential sales of printed copies of the work.

(4) Licensing before input is necessary to enable the publisher to know that the work is being used in the system and to see that appropriate arrangements are made to compensate him for such use.

(5) Since a license will admittedly be required for output, practical considerations dictate that the terms of the license, including the basis for assessing fees, should be settled between the parties before input is effected.

As may be perceived from our earlier discussion relating to the input of data bases, in section A.4.4.3.4, we are inclined to believe that the weight of the argument comes down on the side of requiring licenses to be obtained before input.

A.4.6 BLANKET LICENSING AND COMPULSORY LICENSING FOR REPRODUCTION OF DOCUMENTS

A.4.6.1 Need for Blanket Licensing Mechanism. The ideal of providing researchers, through computeirzed data base systems, with bibliographic data relating comprehensively to all the published documents pertaining to any particular fields of science and technology has been mentioned in section A.4.2.2 of this report. Also mentioned there and in section A.4.2.3 is the further need of the researcher to be able to obtain expeditiously copies of the documents he identifies as being pertinent to his inquiry. And we noted that the documents needed for scientific and technical research are now mainly articles published in journals.

If and when computer storage of documents should become practicable on a sufficiently large scale to comprise complete libraries of virtually all the documents in any subject area, there will be a compelling need for some mechanism that will facilitate obtaining the licenses required for input and output of the mass of copyrighted documents in such a comprehensive library.

Meanwhile, the problem of supplying researchers with copies of documents on a comprehensive scale through other, existing sources, including libraries and other information centers, is already with us. (We have suggested earlier, in passing, that the time may not be too far off when such document supply centers will be operated in conjunction with, or as adjuncts to, computerized data base systems.) A few commercial organization now supplying copies of copyrighted journal articles have succeeded in arranging for licenses from a large number of publishers. Libraries have been supplying photocopies of articles from journals in their collection but, with respect to copyrighted material, they have usually purported to do so within the limited scope of fair use.

It is generally recognized that, for a document supply center wishing to provide copies of articles from a large number of journals, the process of seeking out, and obtaining licenses individually from, each of the many publishers involved could be so time-consuming and costly as to be impracticable. (At any rate, this is the widely and firmly held consensus notwithstanding the success of at least two commercial suppliers of copies of journal articles—University Microfilms and the Institute for Scientific Information—in obtaining such licenses for a large number of journals.) It is also generally agreed that the publishers of copyrighted journals are entitled to be paid for reproduction of their articles (except for the limited reproduction permitted as fair use).

With two objectives in mind—namely, to facilitate the mass licensing of copyrighted material for reproduction by document supply centers, and at the same time to provide for compensation to the publishers—it has been urged that "clearinghouses" be organized through which blanket licenses could be obtained for an entire catalog of the copyrighted journals of as many publishers as can be brought within the organization, and lump-sum payments could be made for distribution among the publishers.

There are two existing types of blanket licensing mechanisms in other areas that might serve as prototypes for the blanket licensing of reproduction of copyrighted journal articles. One is a voluntary type of clearinghouse established by the copyright owners of musical compositions for licensing public performances. The other is a compulsory license plan established by the new copyright statute to permit the use of copyrighted works en masse, upon payment of lump-sum royalties, by CATV systems, jukebox operators, and educational broadcasters. We shall now look at these two types of blanket licensing mechanisms in turn.

A.4.6.2 <u>Voluntary Clearinghouses</u>. Possibilities for establishing a voluntary clearinghouse for the blanket licensing of copyrighted journal articles for reproduction have been under discussion, off and on, for a number of years. The development of an acceptable plan has been found to be beset with many difficulties. Two or three fairly detailed plans have been proposed in outline and put aside as unsatisfactory. The discussions so far have hardly gone beyond attempts to explore some of the possible bases on which such a clearinghouse might be organized and operated, and to expose the difficulties that might be encountered in establishing a workable mechanism.

A.4.6.2.1 <u>ASCAP and BMI as Models</u>. In the discussions referred to above, the clearinghouses operated by the American Society of Composers, Authors and Publishers (ASCAP) and Broadcast Music, Inc. (BMI), have frequently been cited as possible models that might be adaptable for the blanket licensing of reproduction rights in journal articles.

ASCAP is a voluntary membership association of writers and publishers of copyrighted music. It was established to license and enforce the rights of its members collectively in public performances of their music. A few statistics taken from recent reports will indicate the size and effect of its operation. Its membership consists of about 18,500 writers and 5,300 publishers of music. Its catalog of musical compositions is constantly growing, and the number of compositions covered by its licenses (a figure that is not announced) must now be well in excess of a million. Its gross revenues from domestic licenses is now over 80 million dollars per year, and from foreign licenses is over 13 million dollars per year. Its cost of operations in recent years has run to about 19 or 20 per cent of its gross revenues. The remainder of about 80 per cent is distributed among its writer and publisher members under a rather complex formula in which the principal basis for allocation is the estimated number of performances of each member's works.

ASCAP issues licenses to a number of different classes of users. The largest users, from which it derives a major portion of its revenues, are the radio and television networks. Other classes of users include local broadcasters, music and dance halls, orchestras and bands, hotels and restaurants, wired music services, business establishments, etc. ASCAP announces periodically a schedule into which its users are divided. As required by consent decrees of the United States District Court for the Southern District of New York, it must license all qualified applicants, all licensees in the same class are charged the same fees, and any licensee or applicant may request the Court to review the fees charged.

The royalty fee payable by a user is a flat sum per year for a blanket license permitting his performance of any and all of the music in ASCAP's catalog. Broadcasting networks supply ASCAP with logs identifying the compositions performed by them, and ASCAP conducts a sampling of performances by some of its other licensees, and these are the bases for ASCAP's determination of the allocation of its net revenues among its members.

Two other organizations also license performances of music on a blanket basis in much the same manner as ASCAP. One of them is Broadcast Music, Inc. (BMI), which rivals ASCAP in the size of its operation. BMI is an incorporated organization which represents about 30,000 writers and 10,000 publishers of music in licensing a collective catalog of their copyrighted music. Its catalog is reported to contain one million compositions, and its gross revenues are about 50 million dollars per year. Its payments to its members are based on contracts which are designed to distribute among them the net revenues of BMI after deductions from the gross for its expenses and reserves. Its fees charged users, like those of ASCAP, are a lump sum per year and are uniform for all the users in any class.

The third organization licensing performances of a collective catalog of music is SESAC, Inc., a commercial company that contracts with another smaller group of writers and publishers to license their copyrighted music. Its catalog is a relatively small one of special kinds of music. Statistics concerning the size of its operation have not been determined. Its fees charged licensees are also fixed at a lump sum per year.

The effectiveness of ASCAP and BMI may be attributable in large part to the following factors:

(1) The copyright owners of music have realized that they cannot enforce their performance rights individually. They have therefore felt compelled to join in collective organizations that can monitor and license performances for all of them as a group. As a result, the combined membership of ASCAP and BMI, together with the relatively small number of those affiliated with SESAC, comprise the copyright owners of virtually all music copyrighted in the United States.

(2) Users who obtain a license from each of the three organizations are virtually assured of the right to perform (except for dramatic performances which these organiza-

tions do not license) any and all of the compositions they might choose to perform.

(3) Licensees are not burdened by the necessity for maintaining records of the compositions they perform. Fortunately for ASCAP and BMI, the largest source of their revenue from licenses, the broadcasting networks, do maintain logs of the compositions they perform and supply those logs to the organizations. Those logs, plus a limited amount of sampling of the performances by other licensees, are sufficient for allocation of the fees collected by ASCAP and BMI among the individual copyright owners.

(4) Licensees are required to pay only a lump-sum royalty fee annually in a predetermined amount.

How far can these factors—universal coverage; ease for users in obtaining licenses and in accounting and paying for their uses; and the ability of the organization without too much cost, to distribute its revenues among the copyright owners on an equitable basis—be duplicated in an organization for the blanket licensing of copyrighted journal articles? The answer to that question may determine the feasibility of establishing such an organization.

A.4.6.2.2 Problem Areas. Attempts to plan a clearinghouse for the blanket licensing of reproductions of journal articles run into a number of problems. We are not undertaking to offer solutions to those problems, or to propose any plan for such a clearinghouse. We shall merely mention some of the major problems and some suggested approaches to meeting them.

Perhaps the most difficult set of problems relate to reconciling several imperatives: The basis on which licensees pay fees must be kept simple to avoid expensive record-keeping; some information as to the identity of the journals used and the number of uses may be needed to determine how the fees collected are to be distributed among the publishers; the operating expenses of the clearinghouse must not be so high as to consume too much of the fees collected.

Assuming that the sum to be paid by a licensee as fees is to be related to the volume of reproductions made by him, how is that sum to be assessed? To require licensees to keep records of each reproduction of individual articles would probably be excessively burdensome. For the purpose of assessing the fees, perhaps it would suffice to have the licensee report only the total number of units (e.g., articles or pages) reproduced by him from all of the journals in the aggregate.

This would leave the problem of how the clearinghouse is to determine what portion of its net receipts is to be distributed to each of the publishers. Perhaps a limited amount of sampling would be enough for this purpose. For example, each licensee might be asked to keep records of the articles he reproduces during a short period of time such as one or two weeks each year. Or those licensees only who are known to be the large volume users might be asked to keep such records for somewhat longer periods of time. Or perhaps such records kept by the licensees could be dispensed with entirely if it were assumed that the proportionate volume of reproductions by all users from any one journal is roughly equivalent to the proportionate volume of its subscriptions or sales. And other alternatives could no doubt be thought of.

If record-keeping by the clearinghouse as well as by the licensee can be kept to a minimum, there would seem to be a fair prospect that, with fees fixed at appropriate but reasonable amounts, the clearinghouse would have enough net revenues to give publishers a significant return.

Several other problems that may need to be resolved can be mentioned:

- The publishers of scientific and technical journals (which we assume to be the material for which a clearinghouse is most urgently needed) will have to be persuaded to join the clearinghouse. Inclusion of nearly all of them may be necessary to provide adequately comprehensive coverage. If it can be shown that the proposed clearinghouse is likely to become profitable within a few years, it should not be difficult to enlist the publishers.

- Some library groups have objected that blanket licensing may result in their paying for what are now fair use reproductions. Perhaps the license fees can be so adjusted as to overcome this objection.

- A clearinghouse licensing reproductions from most of the existing copyrighted journals may be charged with operating as a monopoly under the antitrust laws. This problem might be resolved by appropriate legislation granting an exemption, or by negotiations with the Department of Justice. Precedents for a statutory exemption from the antitrust laws are now found in the Copyright Act of 1976 (sections 111(d)(5)(A), 116(c)(2), 118(b) and 118(3)(1)), with respect to copyright owners or users acting as a group, or through a common agent, in negotiating and agreeing upon royalty rates and the distribution of lump-sum royalty receipts among the members of the group.

A.4.6.3 Compulsory Licensing. Compulsory licensing was originally provided for in the Copyright Act of 1909 as a device for preventing the establishment of a monopoly. One manufacturer of phonorecords of music, anticipating that the law would be revised to give the copyright owners of music a new exclusive right to make recordings of their music, had obtained agreements from the major music publishers to give him exclusive rights to record all the musical works in their catalogs. To prevent this potential monopoly, Congress provided in Section 1(e) of the Act of 1909 that once the copyright owner permitted one company to make a recording of his music, anyone else was permitted to make a similar recording upon payment of two cents per composition for each record manufactured.

One result of this compulsory license provision has been the establishment of a central agency—the Harry Fox Office—through which most of the music publishers issue licenses for the recording of individual compositions. Record companies generally obtain such licenses from the Harry Fox Office instead of exercising the compulsory license under the terms of the statute, because the licenses issued by that Office are more favorable than the statute in several respects.

The Harry Fox Office is an example of a centralized agency for licensing the works of a number of publishers. It is no doubt more convenient for licensees than would be the case if (without the compulsory license) they had to negotiate for licenses with each publisher separately. But it should be noted that the Harry Fox operation is not an example of blanket licensing. It issues licenses for individual compositions as requested. It has a standard form of license agreement and a fixed schedule of royalty fees applicable to all the compositions alike, but licensees may, and often do, negotiate with the Office for reduced fees in special cases.

The new Copyright Act of 1976 provides for compulsory licenses of a different character in three situations: For the performance of music in jukeboxes, for CATV retransmissions of broadcast programs, and for the use of certain works in noncommercial broadcasting. These are examples of blanket licensing. The purpose of the compulsory license in these three instances is not to prevent a monopoly, but is to avoid the difficulties that the user groups would encounter if they had to obtain licenses from and pay fees to the individual copyright owners.

A.4.6.3.1 <u>The Compulsory License for Jukeboxes</u>. The Copyright Act of 1909 contained a specific exemption for the performance of music on coin-operated machines (popularly called "jukeboxes"). This has been cited for many years since as an outstanding example of shortsighted legislation. During the hearings in the 1960s on the copyright revision bills, it became evident that the Congressional committees had concluded that jukebox operators should pay for their use of copyrighted music. Obtaining licenses would present no great problem for jukebox operators since they could obtain blanket licenses from the three performing rights licensing organizations (ASCAP, BMI, and SESAC). But, as the jukebox operators demonstrated, to require them to keep records of their performances of each composition would impose a tremendous and costly burden on them.

To avoid this difficulty, Congress provided, in section 116 of the Act of 1976, for a compulsory license under which jukebox operators may use any copyrighted music in their machines, for which they are to pay annually a single lump-sum royalty. To obtain the compulsory license, the jukebox operator is required to file in the Copyright Office information identifying himself and his machines, and to deposit the royalty payment with the Register of Copyrights. The operator is then given a certificate for each machine which he must affix to the machine.

The royalty is fixed in the statute at $8 a year per machine. The Copyright Royalty Tribunal (established under sections 801-810 of the Act) is authorized to adjust the royalty rate periodically upon petition by any of the interested parties.

Distribution of the accumulated royalty fees among the copyright owners (after the deduction of certain expenses) is to be made by the Copyright Royalty Tribunal on the basis of claims filed with it by the copyright owners. There is a provision in the statute allowing persons who may have claims to have access to the licensed machines and the opportunity to obtain information, "by sampling procedures or otherwise," pertinent to their claims.

It may be observed that the appropriate distribution should not be difficult to determine in this case because the great bulk of the royalties will be payable to the three performing rights licensing organizations, and specific provision is made for an agreement among them as to their respective pro rata shares. The three organizations have indicated that they are confident of being able to reach such an agreement.

A.4.6.3.2 <u>The Compulsory License for CATV Systems</u>. We have already outlined, in section A.2.6.1 of this report, the provisions of section 111 of the Copyright Act of 1976 under which cable television systems are given a compulsory license for their retransmissions of broadcast programs containing copyrighted works. To recapitulate the essential features of the compulsory licensing arrangement:

- The compulsory license covers the broadcasts of all stations whose signals the cable system is authorized by the FCC to carry.

- To obtain the compulsory license, the cable system is required to file in the Copyright Office a statement identifying its owner and the broadcasting stations whose signals are regularly carried by it. The Register of Copyrights may, by regulation, require the filing of further information if found to be necessary.

- The cable system is to deposit with the Register of Copyrights semiannually a statement of account showing (1) the number of its channels used for retransmissions and the broadcasting stations whose programs were retransmitted, and (2) the number of its subscribers and the gross amounts paid by them to the system for its retransmission service. The Register of Copyrights may by regulation, require additional data to be furnished.

- The cable system is to pay to the Register of Copyrights for each semiannual period a single royalty fee computed on a sliding scale of specified percentages of its gross receipts from subscribers for its retransmission service.

- The aggregated royalty fees (after certain expenses are deducted) are to be distributed by the Copyright Royalty Tribunal on the basis of claims filed by copyright owners whose works were included in the nonnetwork programs of distant stations carried by the cable systems.

- The Copyright Royalty Tribunal is authorized to review and adjust the royalty rates from time to time, under standards stated in the Act, upon petition by any interested party.

The task of the Copyright Royalty Tribunal in determining how the aggregated fees are to be distributed among the claimants will probably be more difficult here than in the case of jukeboxes. The copyright owners whose works are used in broadcast programs are large in number, and their works are diverse in character. This problem may be eased somewhat by a provision in the statute that claimants may lump their claims together and may agree among themselves as to their division of the aggregate sum paid on their claims.

A.4.6.3.3 The Compulsory License for Noncommercial Broadcasting. The Copyright Act of 1976 makes noncommercial broadcasters liable for their performances and displays of copyrighted works (with certain exceptions not pertinent here) for which they have heretofore claimed to be exempt from liability. The noncommercial broadcasters argued before the Congressional committees considering the revision bills, that with respect to certain kinds of works at least, the process of obtaining licenses for their use of copyrighted works individually would be extremely difficult and costly. Congress was persuaded to include in the 1976 Act, in section 118, a compulsory license for the use by noncommercial broadcasters of published nondramatic musical works and published pictorial, graphic and sculptural works (and for certain educational uses of recordings of their broadcast programs containing such works).

The compulsory license provisions in section 118 of the Act for noncommercial broadcasting are quite different from those relating to jukeboxes and CATV systems. The terms and conditions of the compulsory license under section 118 are not spelled out in the statute, but are left for the Copyright Royalty Tribunal to establish.

Section 118 contemplates that copyright owners and noncommercial broadcasters, or groups of them on either side, may negotiate their own licensing agreements, and these are given effect. For those instances where no such voluntary agreement is made, the Royalty Tribunal is to establish the "rates and terms" for the permitted uses of the specified categories of copyrighted works by the broadcasters, after considering proposals submitted to it by any interested parties and the rates for comparable circumstances under existing voluntary license agreements. The rates and terms for the compulsory license are to be reviewed and prescribed anew by the Tribunal every five years.

No express provision is made for the collection and distribution of royalty payments. It is provided that the Tribunal is to establish "requirements by which copyright owners may receive reasonable notice of the use of their works under this section, and under which records of such use shall be kept" by the broadcasters. Apparently, the copyright owners or their group agencies are expected to collect their own royalties.

A.4.6.4 <u>Concluding Comments.</u> If a voluntary clearinghouse satisfactory to both copyright owners and users can be organized, that would seem to be preferable over a statutory compulsory licensing scheme. A voluntary clearinghouse would be more nearly in accord with the basic philosophy of copyright which contemplates that the author should have control over the use of his work. Congress seems to have demonstrated its preference for voluntary licensing arrangements in the provisions of section 118 of the Act of 1976, suggesting that the copyright owners and noncommercial broadcasters should try to negotiate voluntary agreements between themselves, and giving such agreements effect over the compulsory licensing scheme to be devised by the Copyright Royalty Tribunal. Perhaps the most important consideration is the greater flexibility of a voluntary arrangement and its easier accommodation, by negotiations between the groups concerned, to experience and changing circumstances.

COPYRIGHT AND COMPILATIONS IN THE COMPUTER ERA: OLD WINE IN NEW BOTTLES*

By Jeffrey Squires**

The collector of information about subjects both trivial and profound, who systematically arranges and sets it out in print for others to see, can claim protection against unauthorized copying of his work under the law of copyright.[1] The first general revision of the copyright law in over 65 years is now pending in Congress, and if enacted in its present form will continue to endow the compiler of such printed works with the right to exclude others from copying and distributing an original presentation of facts.[2] This is true despite the fact that the contents of such collections consist solely of information that is in the public domain and over which no one may exert exclusive control.[3] The collector of such information, however, has not

---

*This article was delivered to the printer immediately before the Copyright Revision Bill, S.22, 94th Cong., 2d Sess. (1976) was passed by both houses of Congress and signed by the President on October 19, 1976. All references to the Revision Bill as "pending" should therefore be understood to apply to that Act which will, as of January 1, 1978, be the governing federal copyright legislation.

**Mr. Squires is a member of the Bar of the District of Columbia. He is a Staff Attorney for the National Commission on New Technological Uses of Copyrighted Works. The views herein expressed are those of the author and do not represent the position of the Commission.

[1] 17 U.S.C. § 5(a) provides for registration of copyright in:
  Books, including composite and cyclopedic works, directories, gazetteers, and other compilations.

[2] S. 22, 94th Cong., 2d Sess. [hereinafter cited as "S. 22"] as passed by the Senate on February 19, 1976, contains the following:
  § 103(a). The subject matter of copyright as specified by Section 102 includes compilations and derivative works.
  H.R. 2223, 94th Cong., 2d Sess., (1976) [hereinafter cited as "H.R. 2223"] contains this identical provision. While numerous aspects of general copyright revision are controversial, creating the possibility that they will not be enacted in the form found in the pending bills, there is no controversy over the inclusion of compilations as copyrightable works.

[3] *See* cases cited in notes 21-27, *infra*.

SOURCE: Reprinted from the *Bulletin of the Copyright Society of the U.S.A.* 24: 18-46 (October 1976) by permission of the copyright holder. Copyright © 1977 by the Copyright Society of the U.S.A.

been neglected by those scientific and technological advances which are fast transforming every aspect of our existence: collections of information useful in broad areas of inquiry and research, which in the past were protected against piracy by copyright, are more and more often being published as machine-readable data bases, capable of being perceived by human users only in conjunction with a computer.[4] Technically, machine-readable data bases are a subset of the universe of data bases, the vast majority of which are not in machine-readable form. Every dictionary, for example, is a data base. Machine-readable data bases, however, by virtue of capabilities for use in conjunction with the modern automatic data processing machine, have applications which functionally distinguish them from mere human-readable collections of information. The concern of this article is with machine-readable information, and it is that to which the term "data base" herein refers.

The present Copyright Act has not demonstrated the capacity to adjust comfortably to technological advances that, to date, have made available new media for the presentation of the work product of intellectual creativity. Sound recordings of music were long kept out of the domain of copyright.[5] The performance of copyrighted works on commercial radio and television, and the development of modern photocopying, none of which were anticipated by the Copyright Act of 1909, have outdistanced the scope of protection the courts found available by copyright.[6] Works recorded on magnetic tape and disc for

---

[4] Such collections, referred to as "data bases," have been defined as

> [O]rganized set[s] of machine-readable records containing bibliographic or document-related data.

Williams, *Uses of Machine-Readable Data Bases,* 9 ANNUAL REVIEW OF INFORMATION SCIENCE AND TECHNOLOGY 221 (C. Cuadros, ed. 1974) [hereinafter cited as "Williams"].

[5] Pursuant to the Supreme Court's decision that a piano roll, being illegible, was not a "copy" of copyrighted music in the case of White-Smith Publishing Co. v. Apollo Co., 209 U.S. 1 (1908), it was long recognized that phonograph records were not subject to protection under the Copyright Act of 1909. Not until enactment of the Sound Recording Act of 1971, Pub. L. 92-140, 85 Stat, 391, codified in 17 U.S.C. §5(n), were phonograph records entitled to statutory copyright protection.

[6] In Fortnightly Corp. v. United Artists, 392 U.S. 390 (1968), programming relayed to subscribers by community antenna television (CATV) systems was found not to be a performance and therefore not an infringement of the copyright in motion pictures which had been licensed to commercial broadcast stations. This holding was shortly thereafter applied to retransmission of distant signals by CATV in Teleprompter Corp. v. Columbia Broadcasting System, Inc., 415 U.S. 394 (1971). In Twentieth Century

use in conjunction with computers are but the most recent examples of inventive achievements which will pose copyright problems in the future.

Certainly the potential that an extension of copyright protection to works transmitted over newly developed media would contribute to monopoly-like control over the dissemination of information is a major concern and has contributed to a narrowing of the scope given copyright proprietors' rights.[7] This concern may not, however, justify the contortions which have been engaged in by the judiciary to limit the scope of a copyright proprietor's rights. The denial of protection in this area raises the spectre of increased government control over the dissemination of works of authorship which has given rise to Professor [now Justice] Kaplan's fears over the continuing relevance of copyright protection.[8]

Bibliographic, machine-readable data bases contain the same information that has traditionally been published in hard copy format, transposed into a new medium made functional by technological advance. Nevertheless, though a substantial body of case law exists describing the protection provided by copyright to compilations in hard copy, the present copyright law and that likely to be enacted leave uncertain the scope of protection afforded to large collections of data which are first published or exist only in machine-readable form. If copyright is to continue as a patron for the encouragement of the sharing of ideas, it must be willing to recognize that which is not engraved in stone as deserving of its attention.

Music Corp. v. Aiken, 422 U.S. 151 (1975), the playing of commercial radio over four loudspeakers by the owner of a restaurant was held not to be an infringing performance of the copyrighted content of the broadcast. The question of whether, and to what degree, photocopying of copyrighted works constitutes infringement was addressed, but not resolved, by the Supreme Court in Williams & Wilkins v. United States, 487 F.2d 1345 (Ct. Cl. 1973), *aff'd by equally divided Court*, 420 U.S. 516 (1975). The Register of Copyrights, even prior to these cases, made clear that technological advances were the major impetus for the now long-awaited Copyright Revision Bill. *See* Kaminstein, *Preface*, REPORT OF THE REGISTER OF COPYRIGHTS ON THE GENERAL REVISION OF THE U.S. COPYRIGHT LAW at ix (1961).

[7] *See* Silverman, *CATV and Copyright Liability: Teleprompter Corp. v. Columbia Broadcasting System, Inc. and the Consensus Agreement*, 26 HAST. L.J. 1507 (1974).

[8] B. KAPLAN, AN UNHURRIED VIEW OF COPYRIGHT at 120-21 (1966). [hereinafter cited as "Kaplan"].

I. AUTOMATION AND INFORMATION RETRIEVAL

The information requirements of those engaged in such fields as law, medicine, science, engineering, business and government—be they for legal precedent, the results of medical and scientific research, or current business and government statistics—have traditionally been satisfied with bibliographic and encyclopedic reference material contained in hundreds of printed volumes.[9] These materials, in conventional printed form, often are protected by copyright.[10] The continuing practical value of such reference works, however, is subject to serious doubt. It is convincingly argued that hard copy bibliographic reference works neither adequately comprehend the universe of information pertaining to specific areas of advanced research nor pro-

---

[9] Lawyers are, of course, familiar with publications such as CORPUS JURIS SECUNDUM, AMERICAN JURISPRUDENCE, and AMERICAN LAW REPORTS, all of which appear in several editions comprising hundreds of volumes of encyclopedic material. SHEPARD'S CITATIONS is but another form of legal bibliographic reference. In the medical field, the National Library of Medicine publishes INDEX MEDICUS, the annual compilation of references to journal articles concerning medical science in some 2,500 periodicals, and the NLM CURRENT CATALOGUE, which references all titles cited in INDEX MEDICUS since its inception in 1879. CHEMICAL ABSTRACTS and ENGINEERING INDEX MONTHLY serve the chemical and engineering communities with a bibliographic tool for finding published information. The National Technical Information Service ("NTIS") of the U.S. Department of Commerce has published since 1968 the GOVERNMENT REPORTS ANNOUNCEMENTS and GOVERNMENT REPORTS INDEX of research projects carried out under the auspices of the federal government. These represent but several well-known examples of bibliographic reference tools.

[10] The law encyclopedias and digests referred to in note 9, *supra*, are published with notice of copyright, and it is beyond dispute that such volumes are copyrightable. *See* West Publishing Co. v. Edward Thompson Co., 176 Fed. 833 (2d Cir. 1910). The actual text of judicial decisions reported in thousands of volumes from state and federal jurisdictions, are not copyrightable, but the brief abstracts of these decisions, commonly referred to as "headnotes," are likely copyrightable by their creators. *See* Opinion of the Attorney General of the State of New York, 142 U.S.P.Q. 288 (July 21, 1964). Abstract and indexing compilations such as CHEMICAL ABSTRACTS and THE ENGINEERING INDEX are protected by copyright. Government publications such as those published by the National Library of Medicine and NTIS, are not copyrightable under 17 U.S.C. § 7, and are not eligible for copyright under section 105 of the Copyright Revision Bill as passed by the Senate, S.22, *supra* note 2. However, an amendment to section 105 of the Revision Bill presently pending in the House of Representatives, H.R. 2223, *supra* note 2, would provide five year copyright protection for material published by NTIS.

vide means for accessing that information within acceptable time limitations, and that they thus fail to fulfill the requirements for complete and current awareness of those engaged in information-intensive activities.[11]

The automatic data processing machine—the computer—has wrought radical changes in the methods and speed of information transfer in our contemporary, technologically advanced society.[12] These changes have created for institutions and people engaged in information-intensive undertakings the capability of obtaining access to the spiralling quantity of both published and unpublished information which may have bearing on their work.[13] Access to such information, traditionally obtained with the assistance of bibliographic reference material published in hard copy, is now being made available through a variety of data bases in machine-readable form. These data bases include both factual and bibliographic information and can be accessed "on-line" by users at locations remote from computers where the information is stored.[14] The existence of these data bases is a re-

---

[11] The vast increases in quantity of scientific and technical publications, and alternative means of recording and disseminating this information which are feasible in light of modern computer and telecommunications technology, are the subjects of a current study conducted under the auspices of the National Science Foundation. A CLAYTON AND N. NISENOFF, THE INFLUENCE OF TECHNOLOGY UPON FUTURE ALTERNATIVES TO THE SCIENTIFIC AND TECHNICAL JOURNAL, 3 vol. (Forecasting International, Ltd., Arlington, Va. 1975).

[12] The increases in speed, efficiency and accuracy of operation of automatic data processing equipment, along with the diminishing costs of these operations, are measured in order of magnitudes rather than simple numerical terms. *See* R. TURN, COMPUTERS IN THE 1980's (1974). An earlier work in which the technological capabilities of the computer for information transfer were analyzed with similar findings, is J. BECKER AND R. HAYES, INFORMATION STORAGE AND RETRIEVAL (1963).

[13] The existence of an information-explosion is well-documented. The fact that the existing store of published knowledge has been growing exponentially, particularly in the natural sciences, was documented and discussed in D. DE SOLLA PRICE, LITTLE SCIENCE, BIG SCIENCE (1963) and F. MACHLUP, THE PRODUCTION AND DISTRIBUTION OF KNOWLEDGE IN THE UNITED STATES (1962). Although these studies are over 10 years old, the general logarithmic projections therein made still appear valid. *See* R. LAPP, THE LOGARITHMIC CENTURY (1973).

[14] For example, data bases containing reported legal decisions are available from LEXIS, and data bases containing the abstract "headnotes" of such decisions are available with West Publishing Company's WESTLAW system. The National Library of Medicine's MEDLINE is a machine-readable version of INDEX MEDICUS which can be accessed "on line". CHEMICAL ABSTRACTS and ENGINEERING INDEX MONTHLY are likewise available for

cent phenomenon, and the number and uses of such materials are rapidly expanding.[15]

Demand for such information retrieval capabilities has created a growing industry, comprised of data base publishers, distributors and users.[16] One writer has predicted that the gross revenues generated by the data base industry would more than double between 1975 and 1980, from $165 million to $350 million annually.[17] This estimate appears already to be outdated.[18] The existence of this industry has increased concern about the legal rights the creators of data bases have in relation to those who would reproduce the fruit of their efforts, without incurring costs of developing the product or accepting the risks inherent in manufacturing and marketing an untested commodity. These are concerns shared with all those seeking copyright protection for computer software. It has long been contended on behalf of software developers that legal protection presently available for software is insufficient to deter misappropriation of valuable products, and that as a result the software industry has been unable to attract investment capital to finance continued development and quality improvement of the software sector.[19] One possible source of propriet-

---

on-line searches under the names CHEMICAL ABSTRACTS CONDENSATES and COMPENDEX. The GOVERNMENT REPORTS ANNOUNCEMENT published by NTIS was made available in machine-readable form for on-line searches in 1974. In addition, business-service organizations such as Standard & Poor's are compiling business statistics data bases.

[15] See Elias, *An Overview of the Data Base Industry Including Generation, Design and Production Factors,* in INFORMATION SYSTEMS AND NETWORKS 21 (J. Sherrod, ed. 1975) [hereinafter cited as "Elias"]. Currently available data bases are listed in Williams, *supra* note 4 at 224-30, and demographic information about the current state of data base development is found in R. CHRISTIAN, THE ELECTRONIC LIBRARY: BIBLIOGRAPHIC DATA BASES 1975-76 (1975) [hereinafter cited as "Christian"].

[16] A sampling of published data bases is provided in note 14, *supra.* Williams, *supra* note 4 at 224-30, and Christian, *supra* note 15 at 90-112, provide current lists of available data bases, which now number over 120. A number of organizations now provide central access to numbers of data bases, by contracting for distribution rights with the publishers. The two largest organizations engaged in such enterprise are Lockheed Information Sciences and System Development Corporation.

[17] Elias, *supra* note 15 at 22.

[18] Dr. Vincent Giuliano of Arthur D. Little, Inc. estimates that the commercial data base industry, exclusive of government and not-for-profit association publications, would generate $1.2 billion in 1976. Conversation with Dr. Vincent Giuliano, April 19, 1976.

[19] See Statement of Dr. Ruth M. Davis, HEARINGS OF THE GOVERNMENT ACTIVITIES SUBCOMMITTEE OF THE HOUSE COMMITTEE ON GOVERNMENT OPERATIONS, May 16, 1972, pp. 12-13. The issue of legal protection for com-

ary protection for data bases exists in federal statutory copyright law.[20]

II. COPYRIGHT PROTECTION FOR HARD COPY COMPILATIONS AND DIRECTORIES

A wide variety of collections of factual information has been determined properly subject to copyright as directories or compilations under 17 U.S.C. § 5(a). Such works include interest and discount tables,[21] city telephone directories,[22] catalogues of trademarks,[23] lists of restaurants compiled in an eating guide,[24] insurance forms,[25] lists of words contained in a code book,[26] consolidated indexes of freight tariffs,[27] and catalogues containing lists of products for a wide variety

---

puter software has produced a spate of journal literature advocating patent and trade secret, as well as copyright protection for such programs. *See, e.g.* Beard, *The Copyright Issue* 9 ANNUAL REVIEW OF INFORMATION SCIENCE AND TECHNOLOGY 381 (C. Cuadros, ed. 1974); Galbi, *Proposal for New Legislation to Protect Computer Programming,* 17 BULL. CR. SOC. 280 (1970); Bender, *Trade Secret Protection of Software,* 38 G.W.U.L. REV. 909 (1970); *Note: Computer Programs and Proposed Revision of the Copyright Laws,* 81 HARV. L. REV. 1541 (1968). These articles are by no means exhaustive of the literature on the subject. *See also* articles cited in note 49, *infra.*

[20] The present federal copyright statute is essentially that enacted as the Copyright Act of 1909, codified in 17 U.S.C. §1 *et seq.* Federal statutory copyright differs from common law copyright, commonly referred to as the right of first publication, which protects an author against unauthorized copying of his work until such time as the work is published at the author's behest. At the time of publication the author must either secure copyright protection under the federal statute, or lose any proprietary interests by virtue of publication dedicating the work to the public. Common law rights are specifically preserved in the present Act, 17 U.S.C. §2. However, the proposed Copyright Revision Bill abolishes common law copyright, and provides that only statutory protection will be available pursuant to enactment of the law. Section 301, S.22, *supra* note 2. As a practical matter, common law copyright is not significant as a method of protection for data bases, even under the present Act, as misappropriation of a data base prior to commercial usage sufficient to constitute publication is not likely to occur.

[21] Edward & Deutsch Lithographing Co. v. Boorman, 15 F.2d 35 (7th Cir.), *cert. denied,* 273 U.S. 738 (1926).

[22] Leon v. Pacific Tel. & Tel., 91 F.2d 484 (9th Cir. 1937).

[23] Jeweler's Circular Publishing Co. v. Keystone Publishing Co., 281 Fed. 83 (2d Cir.), *cert. denied,* 259 U.S. 581 (1922), *aff'g* 274 Fed. 932 (S.D.N.Y. 1921).

[24] Adventures in Good Eating v. Best Places to Eat, 131 F.2d 809 (7th Cir. 1942).

[25] Continental Casualty v. Beardsley, 253 F.2d 702 (2d Cir. 1958).

[26] American Code Co., Inc. v. Bensinger, 282 Fed. 829 (2d Cir. 1922).

[27] Guthrie v. Curlett, 36 F.2d 694 (2d Cir. 1929).

of commercial uses.[28] Such examples of copyrightable works are notable for their practical and commercial rather than their literary or artistic value.[29]

It has been held that little, if any, originality in the contents or style of a collection of facts, all of which may be in the public domain, is necessary to entitle a compilation to copyright. Although some judges have glorified the creative aspects of a compiler's work, as did Circuit Judge Chase in praising the "treatment . . . thought, arrangement, and style . . ." evidenced in a schedule of freight tariffs held copyrightable,[30] many compilations and directories contain little more than lists of names and products and are not noteworthy for any creativity in style or form of expression.[31] This is entirely consistent

---

[28] Further, but by no means exhaustive, citations of cases involving copyright in compilations are found in NIMMER ON COPYRIGHT, § 43 n. 53 at 175.1 (1976).

[29] Copyright is not uniquely confined to works of art, be they literary or visual. The history of copyright indicates that copyright was initially intended as an incentive for the printing as much as for the authoring of written works. See generally R. BOWKER, COPYRIGHT, ITS HISTORY AND ITS LAW (1912). As Justice Holmes indicated in Bleistein v. Donaldson Lithographic Co., 188 U.S. 239 (1902), the law does not contemplate that copyright depend on an evaluation of whether any particular work has or lacks artistic value. There referring to a decorative circus poster, Justice Holmes said:

> It would be a dangerous undertaking for persons trained only to the law to constitute themselves final judges of the worth of pictorial illustrations, outside of the narrowest and most obvious limitations . . . . Yet if [such works] command the interest of any public, they have a commercial value—it would be bold to say that they have not an aesthetic and educational value—and the taste of any public is not to be treated with contempt. Id. at 251-52.

[30] Guthrie v. Curlett, 36 F.2d 694 (2d Cir. 1929).

[31] As the District Court recognized in List Pub. Co. v. Keller, 30 Fed. 772 (S.D.N.Y. 1887), a case involving the alleged copyright infringement of plaintiff's social directory "The List" by defendant's "The Social Register", directories of that sort "are original to the extent that the selection is original". 30 Fed. at 773. This case was cited with approval in the leading case of Jeweler's Circular Publishing Co. v. Keystone Publishing Co., 281 Fed. 83 (2d Cir.), cert. denied, 259 U.S. 581 (1922), aff'g 274 Fed. 932 (S.D.N.Y. 1921). In affirming the validity of copyright in a catalogue of trademarks, the Court of Appeals said:

> The right to copyright a book upon which one has expended labor in its preparation does not depend upon whether the materials which he has collected consist or not of matters which are publici juris, or whether such materials show literary skill or originality, either in thought or in language, or anything more than industrious collection. The man who goes through the streets of a town and puts down the name of each of the inhabitants, with their occupations and their street

with the fact that little in the way of originality has ever been required to entitle the physical emanation of human effort to copyright.

Originality, as a precondition of copyright, derives from the requirement of authorship contained in the constitutional clause empowering Congress to legislate

> To promote the Progress of Science and useful Arts, by securing for limited Times to Authors and Inventors the exclusive Rights to their respective Writings and Discoveries.[32]

In the case of *Burrow-Giles Lithographic Co. v. Sarony*,[33] the Supreme Court interpreted this constitutional grant of power to permit a photograph of Oscar Wilde to be the proper subject of copyright:

> An author in [the constitutional] sense is "he to whom anything owes its origin; originator; maker, one who completes a work of science or literature.[34]

Justice Holmes, in accord with this broad reading of the Copyright Clause, authored the majority opinion upholding the copyrightability of a decorative circus poster in *Bleistein v. Donaldson Lithographic Co.*[35] He there cited the decision in *Sarony, supra,* and proceeded to remark that "the least pretentious picture has more originality in it than directories and the like, which may be copyrighted".[36] Thus the level of originality required to support a copyright in work of this type has been held to be minimal.

The generally recognized prohibition against granting copyright to mere facts has never been specifically controverted.[37] The practice of granting copyrights to certain compilations of facts is apparently best explained by considering copyright as a reward for labors which result in a commercially valuable product.[38] Because of this minimal standard of originality, litigation involving alleged infringement of copyright in compilations and directories has consistently turned on

---

number, acquires material of which he is the author. He produces by his labor a meritorious composition, in which he may obtain a copyright. 281 Fed. at 88.

[32] U.S. CONST. Art. I, sec. 8, cl. 8.

[33] 111 U. S. 53 (1881)

[34] *Id.* at 58.

[35] 188 U.S. 239 (1902).

[36] *Id.* at 250.

[37] In International News Service v. Associated Press, 248 U.S. 215 (1918), copyright as a basis of protection for news, which the Associated Press claimed had been pirated, was quickly dismissed. *Id.* at 234.

[38] *See* note 31, *supra.*

the nature and extent of copying involved, rather than the copyright-ability of the allegedly infringed work.[39] Traditional analysis has focused on the type and amount of original work undertaken by a subsequent compiler, whose compilation of information is identical with or similar to that contained in a previously copyrighted work. One view, never of great significance and now apparently discarded, would permit subsequent compilers to use information contained in a previously copyrighted directory as a guide for actual fact-gathering efforts for the purpose of publishing the same information. No recent decisions, however, have condoned this practice, commonly referred to as "slipping".[40] The majority view holds, rather, that subsequent compil-

[39] In Consumer's Union of United States v. Hobart Mfg. Co., 189 F. Supp. 275 (S.D.N.Y. 1960), copyright in the contents of a magazine containing product evaluations was upheld, the court saying:
> The directory cases are exceptions to the rule that facts are not a proper subject of copyright. 189 F. Supp. at 278.

The court, however, refused to enjoin the defendant from quoting the plaintiff's publication in sales literature on the ground that:
> That exception does not go so far, however, as to prohibit non-competitive uses of facts set forth in a copyrighted collection. *Id.*

See also cases cited in notes 21 through 27, *supra.* In each the defense was raised that the allegedly infringed work was not copyrightable subject matter, and in each instance the work was held copyrightable. In most cases, it was then necessary to determine whether the defendant's work did, as a factual matter, infringe plaintiff's copyright.

[40] In Edward Thompson Co. v. American Law Book Co., 122 Fed. 922 (2d Cir. 1903), the defendant was found entitled to use citations contained in plaintiff's law encyclopedias as guides to the cases for preparation of its own law encyclopedia. The court there cited with approval the English case of Moffat v. Gill, 86 L.T.R. 465 (C.A. 1902) in which "slipping" had been approved. The facts in *Thompson,* however, did not constitute true slipping, as the court pointed out: the defendant used the citations in plaintiff's encyclopedias solely for direction to the original source, and did not copy the contents or arrangement of plaintiff's book. 122 Fed. at 924.

Nevertheless, the decision in *Thompson* was interpreted to permit a subsequent compiler to include names set forth in another's business directory without subsequent verification in Dunn v. International Merchantile Agency, 127 Fed. 173 (S.D.N.Y. 1903). This decision appears to be aberrant, however. Other cases referring to *Thompson* have voiced disapproval of the actions of subsequent compilers who used prior publications to verify the results of their own efforts and made corrections on the basis of the earlier compilation without independently confirming the information found in the earlier compilation. *See, e.g.* Hartford Printing Co. v. Hartford Directory and Pub. Co., 146 Fed. 332 (D. Conn. 1906). The lack of judicial approval of "slipping" without subsequent verification has been documented by other commentators. *See* Lurvey, *'Verifying' from Prior Directories—'Fair Use' or Theft*, 13 BULL. CR. SOC. 271 (1966), which contains a thorough review of both English and American developments in copyright protection of fact compilations and directories.

ers may use information contained in a copyrighted compilation only to verify that information gathered and reproduced as result of independent effort. Any discrepancy between newly obtained information and that obtained from an already subsisting compilation may be corrected only by verification from the actual source, rather than from the prior compilation.[41]

As discussed above, a minimum amount of originality of expression is required to entitle works containing listings of names or commercial information to statutory copyright protection. Copyright in such instances provides the basis for a financial reward for the creation of something of purely utilitarian value. It appears that the utilitarian and commercial value of such works best explains the limited use a subsequent compiler may make of a prior collection of facts in producing a new collection serving an identical or like purpose.[42]

---

[41] Judge Learned Hand referred to a conflict in opinions over the permissible use of a copyrighted collection of facts by a subsequent compiler in the lower court decision in Jeweler's Circular Publishing Co. v. Keystone Publishing Co., 281 Fed. 83 (2d Cir.), *cert. denied*, 259 U.S. 581 (1922), *aff'g* 274 Fed. 932 (S.D.N.Y. 1921):

> Everyone concedes that a second compiler may check back his independent work upon the original compilation, but there has been some dispute whether he may use the original compilation after simply verifying its statements, or whether he must disregard the assistance of the original, except in subsequent verification. 274 Fed. at 935.

Judge Hand found it unnecessary to reach that issue, however, determining that the defendant had initially appropriated the contents of plaintiff's catalogue of trademarks without independently acquiring the information from the initial sources. *Id.*

The issue adverted to but not answered by Judge Hand in the District Court was addressed on appeal by the Court of Appeals for the Second Circuit, which voiced approval of a rule enunciated in several earlier cases, Sampson & Murdock Co. v. Seaver-Radford Co., 140 Fed. 539 (1st Cir. 1905) and List Publishing Co. v. Keller, 30 Fed. 772 (S.D.N.Y. 1887), permitting a subsequent compiler to use an earlier compilation only to verify the results of completely independent labors. 281 Fed. at 90-92. This must be considered the governing rule today. Although the issue of "slipping" has not been idrectly addressed by a court in recent years, the general proclivity of the courts to enforce rights of proprietors in copyrighted compilations reflects adherence to a rule which narrowly circumscribes the use a subsequent compiler may make of prior compilation. *See, e.g.* Leon v. Pacific Tel. & Tel., 91 F.2d 487 (9th Cir. 1937).

[42] In Gorman, *Copyright Protection for the Collection and Representation of Facts*, 76 HARV. L. REV. 1569 (1963), the author asserted, at 1586-87, that the permissible use made of a prior copyrighted compilation by a subsequent compiler is narrower when the subsequent compiler is a competitor of the former:

The use of a prior compilation to obtain an unfair competitive advantage in a purely commercial enterprise is that which is prohibited, in such cases, by copyright.[43] Apparently, in the case of compilations, collections of information in the public domain may be held to infringe a prior copyrighted work solely because of the economic harm such subsequent collection may cause to the copyrighted work, for reasons not directly related to any act of copying of that which is original in the former work.

This rationale for carefully circumscribing the non-infringing uses a subsequent compiler may make of a subsisting copyrighted compilation explains and harmonizes several judicial decisions which might be considered discordant with general principles of copyright law. In *Leon v. Pacific Tel. & Tel. Co.*,[44] for example, defendant's directory of telephone numbers listed in numerical sequence, commonly known as a "criss cross", was held to have infringed the copyright in plaintiff's alphabetical city directory. The court referred to the labor and expense undertaken by plaintiff in publishing its directory, upheld the validity of its copyright, and dismissed defendant's contention that its inversion of names and numbers for use in its numerical listings constituted "fair use" of plaintiff's work, citing language in several English cases referring to the unfair economic advantage obtained by similar practices.[45]

As the use approaches the point of possible competitive disadvantage to the copyrighted works—or at least dilution of its reputation or uniqueness—the courts will be less inclined to condone unverified copying.

The author referred to both Leon v. Pacific Tel. & Tel., 91 F.2d 484 (9th Cir. 1937) and Jeweler's Circular Publishing Co. v. Keystone Publishing Co., 281 Fed. 83 (2d Cir.) *cert. denied,* 259 U. S. 581 (1922), *aff 'g.* 274 F. 932 (S.D.N.Y. 1921) in support of his theory. *Id.* at 1587-88.

[43] Several cases in which a subsequent compiler was found to have infringed a prior copyrighted work have apparently turned on whether the infringer obtained an unfair economic advantage. *See, e.g.,* Leon v. Pacific Tel. & Tel. 91 F.2d 484 (9th Cir. 1937) (telephone directory); Hartfield v. Peterson, 91 F.2d 998 (2d Cir. 1937) (cable and telegraphic code). This does not comport precisely with the scope of protection normally considered to be afforded by statutory copyright, which provides an author exclusive rights to "copy" a work classified as a "Book" under 17 U.S.C. §5(a), and provides also for injunctive and monetary relief for infringement under 17 U.S.C. §101 without evidence of actual monetary damages suffered by the copyright proprietor. *See* Jewell-LaSalle Realty Co. v. Buck, 283 U.S. 202 (1930); Westerman Co. v Dispatch Printing Co., 249 U.S. 100 (1918).

[44] 91 F.2d 484 (9th Cir. 1937).

[45] *Id.* at 485-87. The court there referred to the efforts of plaintiff deserving of copyright protection:

The decision in *Leon*, has not met with universal approval. Professor Nimmer, while recognizing the economic basis of copyright protection in telephone directories and the like, argues that such works are lacking in the originality required for copyright. He states:

> One who explores obscure archives and who finds and brings to the light of public knowledge little known facts or other public domain materials has undoubtedly performed a socially useful service, but such service in itself does not render the finder an "author." Protection for the fruits of such research may in certain circumstances be available under a theory of unfair competition. But to accord copyright protection on this basis alone distorts basic copyright principles in that it creates a monopoly in public domain materials without the necessary justification of protecting and encouraging the creation of "writings" by "authors." The situation is quite different with respect to an original combination or arrangement of such public domain materials. Such combination or arrangement may in itself constitute an original contribution of authorship and should be protectible [*sic*] against appropriation under copyright principles. However, the fact that an author has made such an original contribution is no basis for protecting the public domain materials per se if the original combination or arrangement is not copied.[46]

It is here suggested that compilations of fact materials of the sort dealt with in *Leon*, are the proper subject of copyright under applicable copyright principles. Subsequent compilations which capitalize upon the efforts undertaken in the creation of a prior work by reproducing the same material, albeit in a slightly different arrangement, are properly enjoined, and damages are properly awarded to the proprietors of copyright in the infringed work, in accord with provisions of the Copyright Act.[47]

It is obvious from this evidence that the business of getting out a directortor is an expensive, complicated, well-organized endeavor, requiring skill, ingenuity, and original research. *Id* at 485-86.
No credit was given to the originality of form or expression employed in plaintiff's directories.

[46] NIMMER ON COPYRIGHT §41 (1975) at 171-72.

[47] Remedies of injunctive relief and money damages are provided those whose copyrights are infringed under 17 U.S.C. § 101. Similar provisions are contained in Sections 502 and 504 of the Copyright Revision Bill, S.22, *supra* note 2; and H.R. 2223, *supra* note 2.

III. COPYRIGHT PROTECTION FOR DATA BASES APPEARING IN MACHINE-READABLE FORM

Although machine-readable data bases serve generally the same purpose as their hard copy counterparts, the technological advances embodied in machine-readable data bases create serious obstacles to their protection under the law of copyright. As is the case with computer software, data bases exist in machine-readable form, not intended to be read directly by human beings. The form in which data bases appear may preclude full compliance with the notice requirements for obtaining a valid copyright. In addition, data bases are constantly being updated to reflect recent additions to the particular area of information they catalogue, which may prevent the proprietor of copyright in a data base from being able to comply with registration requirements of the copyright law. Also, those uses of data bases which are exclusive to the proprietor of copyright are uncertain. It is here suggested that machine-readable data bases, which are functionally identical to their hard copy counterparts,[48] should not be denied proprietary protection to which the latter are entitled.

A. Data Bases in Machine-Readable Form Constitute Copyrightable Subject Matter

A considerable body of literature exists on the issue of copyright for computer software.[49] "Software" and "program" are generic terms for the sets of instructions in machine-readable form which direct the operations of a computer. Doubts have been expressed as to whether

---

[48] That is, they are intended to serve the same function, although the intervention of a computer may facilitate operations of a speed and accuracy which would not be possible with the use of solely hard copy reference material.

[49] In addition to those articles cited in note 19, *supra, see,* Lorr, *Copyright Computers and Compulsory Licensing,* 5 RUTGERS J. OF COMP. & LAW 149 (1975) [hereinafter cited as "Lorr"]; Oler, *Statutory Copyright Protection for Electronic Digital Computer Programs: Administrative Considerations,* 7 LAW & COMP. TECHNOLOGY 96 (1974) [hereinafter cited as "Oler"]; Wittenberg, *Computer Software: Beyond the Limits of Existing Proprietary Protection Policy,* 40 BKLYN. L. REV. 116 (1973); Wild, *Computer Program Protection: The Need to Legislate a Solution,* 54 CORN. L. REV. 586 (1969); Breyer, *The Uneasy Case for Copyright: A Study of Copyright in Books, Photocopies and Computer Programming,* 84 HARV. L. REV. (1970); Miller, *Computers and Copyright Law,* 46 MICH. ST. BAR J. 11 (1967); *Note: Copyright Protection for Computer Programs,* 64 COL. L. REV. 1274 (1964); *see also,* Mooers, *Computer Software and Copyright,* 7 COMPUTING SURVEYS 46 (March 1975); Henry, *Copyright: Its Adequacy in Technological Societies,* 186 SCIENCE 993 (1974).

computer software constitutes copyrightable subject matter under the present Copyright Act. One source of these doubts, which applies with equal force to machine-readable data bases, lies in the pre-1909 Act decision of the Supreme Court in the case of *White-Smith Publishing Co. v. Apollo Co.*[50] There the Court determined that piano rolls, utilized in conjunction with a mechanical player piano, were not tangible, legible expressions of music which had been copyrighted in sheet music form, and thus were not infringing copies of the sheet music.[51] The decision strongly implied, moreover, that piano rolls were not "writings," in themselves susceptible to copyright protection, because they could not be experienced by humans without the intervention of a player piano.[52]

The Supreme Court's interpretation of "writings" in *White-Smith* was found to have been incorporated in the 1909 Copyright Act by the United States Court of Appeals for the Second Circuit in the case of *Capitol Records v. Mercury Records Corp.*[53] There phonograph records were held not to be copyrightable under the *White-Smith* test for "writings" under 17 U.S.C. §4.[54] It is this interpretation of "writings" which is the primary source of doubt as to whether a work of intellectual labor most commonly recorded in electronic impulses—such as computer programs or data bases—would come within the coverage of the present Copyright Act.[55]

In spite of this concern, the Copyright Office announced in May, 1964, that it would accept computer programs for registration.[56] This

---

[50] 209 U.S. 1 (1908).

[51] *Id.* at 16-18.

[52] *Id.* at 17.

A musical composition is an intellectual creation which first exists in the mind of the composer; he may play it for the first time upon an instrument. *It is not susceptible of being copied until it has been put in a form which others can see and read* (emphasis supplied).

17 U.S.C. § 4 provides that copyright may be secured in "all the writings of an author." Copyright protection is extended under the provisions of 17 U.S.C. §5, however, to such "non-writings" as maps, photographs and works of art.

[53] 221 F.2d 657 (2d Cir. 1955).

[54] *Id.* at 660-61. *See* note 5, *supra.*

[55] *See, e.g.,* Lorr, *supra* note 49; Oler, *supra* note 49.

[56] *Announcement, Copyright Registration for Computer Programs,* 11 BULL. CR. SOC. 361 (1964) [hereinafter cited as "Announcement"]. An article accompanying that announcement indicated that programs would be accepted for registration in spite of doubt as to whether a reproduction of a program constituted a copy acceptable for registration under 17 U.S.C. § 13. Cary, *Copyright Registration and Computer Programs,* 11 BULL. CR. SOC. 362 (1964). The applicability of registration requirements to data bases will be discussed, *infra.*

practice has been mentioned with apparent approval in at least one judicial opinion,[57] and has not been challenged in the courts. Data bases, which consist of information contained in the same medium as computer programs, might be considered copyrightable subject matter according to the principle enunciated by the Copyright Office. The Copyright Office Announcement declaring computer programs to be registrable defined a computer program as "either a set of operating instructions for a computer or a compilation of reference information to be drawn upon by the computer in solving problems."[58] This could be interpreted to encompass machine-readable data bases. Several significant distinctions between programs and data bases do exist, however, which might indicate that data bases were not intended to be included in this definition. Data bases are not merely stores of information "to be drawn upon by the computer in solving problems."[59] Rather, they consist of information available in machine-readable form which is sought out in a process directed by a set of operating instructions—a program—and presented as the solution to the problem. Moreover, the information contained in a data base is intended to be made available for human perception on a cathode ray tube with the aid of a computer, while ordinary computer programs are intended only to be "read" by the computer in the course of its operations. Even if data bases are copyrightable, however they may not be registrable as a practical matter under the terms of the Copyright Office Announcement, which requires deposit of copies of the program "in a language intelligible to human beings" as a precondition to registration.[60] While human-readable print-outs of computer programs are prepared and deposited with the machine-readable material for which registration is sought, this is not practical in the case of data bases, which often contain more information than the normal computer program and are constantly being updated.[61]

Any remaining question as to whether a machine-readable data base qualifies as copyrightable subject matter would be resolved by

---

[57] Harcourt, Brace & World v. Graphic Controls Corp., 329 F. Supp. 517 (S.D.N.Y. 1971) involved an infringement of copyrighted test answer sheets. In finding these answer sheets copyrightable, the court adopted an expansive interpretation of "writings", in support of which was mentioned the Copyright Office practice of accepting computer programs for registration.

[58] Announcement, *supra* note 56.

[59] *Id.*

[60] *Id.* Procedures for registering computer programs are set forth in COPYRIGHT OFFICE CIRCULAR 61 (U.S.G.P.O. 1975) [hereinafter cited as "Circular 61"].

[61] *See* discussion of notice and deposit requirements, notes 77-90 and accompanying text, *infra*.

enactment of the pending Copyright Revision Bill, which provides that copyright protection be available for

> original works of authorship fixed in any tangible medium of expression, now known or later developed, from which they can be perceived, reproduced or otherwise communicated, either directly or with the aid of a machine or device.[62]

The Senate Report accompanying this Bill makes unequivocal the legislative intent to confer copyright on materials, such as data bases, which exist in machine-readable form.[63] Difficulties in obtaining copyright protection for data bases would then lie solely in complying with formalities of notice and registration of works for which copyright protection is sought, and in determining what uses of a data base are protected under the law of copyright.

B. Limits on the Protection Afforded Data Bases by Copyright.

Although data bases may constitute copyrightable subject matter under existing federal copyright legislation, and certainly would under the proposed Copyright Revision Bill, data base proprietors may be unable to secure copyright in their creations because of an inability to comply with notice and registration formalities. Under current law, one must comply with the notice requirements contained in Section 10 of the Copyright Act[64] as a precondition of obtaining statutory copyright in a published work.[65] Generally, publication is

---

[62] S. 22, *supra* note 2, §101; H.R. 2223, *supra* note 2, §101.

[63] S. Rep. 94-473, 94th Cong., 1st Sess. (1975) states that §102(a) of the Revision Bill:

> is intended to avoid the artificial and largely unjustifiable distinctions, derived from cases such as White-Smith Publishing Co. v. Apollo Co., 209 U.S. 1(1908), under which statutory copyrightability in certain cases has been made to depend upon the form or medium in which the work is fixed. Under the bill it makes no difference what the form, manner, or medium of fixation may be—whether it is in words, numbers, notes, sounds, pictures, or any other graphic or symbolic indicia, whether embodied in a physical object in written, printed, photographic, sculptural, punched, magnetic, or any other stable form, and whether it is capable of perception directly or by means of any machine or device "now known or later developed." *Id.* at 51.

[64] 17 U.S.C. § 10.

[65] Statutory copyright in unpublished works is provided for in Section 12 of the present Act, 17 U.S.C. § 12. *See* Hirshon v. United Artists Corp., 243 F.2d 640 (D.C. Cir. 1957). Notice requirements pertain only to published works. *Id.*

held to take place when a work is made available for commercial distribution to the public.[66] A data base would, under this rationale, be published when made available for purchase or lease by those desiring to employ its retrieval functions. The related question of whether a data base is published by its "performance", i.e. its use in conjunction with a computer, would be mooted by the fact that it would not likely be "performed" publicly until it had been made commercially available.[67] In addition, one must comply with the registration requirements of Section 13 of the Act[68] in order to claim remedies for infringement established by the Act.[69] Machine-readable data bases would likely not satisfy either the notice or registration requirements under the present Act; nor would this situation be remedied by enactment of the Copyright Revision Bill in its present form.

1. Notice Requirements for obtaining copyright in data bases.

Publication of copyrightable subject matter must be accompanied by notice of copyright[70] in the form[71] and location[72] prescribed by the Copyright Act in order to vest the proprietor with a valid statutory copyright. Failure to comply with the statutory notice requirements has resulted in placing many works in the public domain.[73] While

---

[66] *See* NIMMER ON COPYRIGHT §49 (1975) at 194, and cases cited therein.

[67] *See id.* at §53, p. 208.

[68] 17 U.S.C. § 13. Registration is a prerequisite only of seeking relief under the terms of the Act, and is not necessary to obtain statutory copyright, which is accomplished by publication of copyrightable matter with proper notice. Washingtonian Publishing Co. v. Pearson, 306 U.S. 30 (1939).

[69] 17 U.S.C. § 101 *et seq.*

[70] Section 10 of the Act, 17 U.S.C. § 10, provides:

Any person entitled thereto by this title may secure copyright for his work by publication thereof with the notice of copyright required by this title; and such notice shall be affixed to each copy thereof published or offered for sale in the United States by authority of the copyright proprietor, except in the case of books seeking ad interim protection under section 22 of this title. *Id.*

[71] Section 19 of the Act, 17 U.S.C. § 19, specifies the required contents of a valid copyright notice. Notice must include the word "copyright" or an approved abbreviation or symbol in its place, the name of the copyright proprietor, and the year of first publication or the year in which registration was secured as an unpublished work under Section 12, 17 U.S.C. § 12. *See* Marx v. United States, 96 F.2d 204 (9th Cir. 1938).

[72] Section 20 of the Act, 17 U.S.C. § 20, prescribes the proper location of copyright notice in the copyrighted work. In the case of books, copyright notice must appear on the title page or the page immediately following. The location of notice in certain other types of works is also therein specified.

[73] *See* Thompson v. Hubbard, 131 U.S. 123 (1889), where the failure of an assignee of copyright to include notice in editions of a work he published

under certain circumstances unintentional, slight deviations in the form of notice have been found not to divest a proprietor's copyright, the failure to include notice will unquestionably work such a divestiture.[74]

Under current Copyright Office practice, computer programs are accepted for copyright registration only if copies in human-readable form bearing copyright notice have been published. The proprietor of an extensive data base, however, would be unable to comply with such a notice requirement, which preconditions the right to statutory copyright under present law and practice.[75] Such data bases "appear" directly in machine-readable form; no print-out in human-readable form is prepared as a normal by-product of a bibliographic data base, as in the case of computer programs, and thus there is no tangible medium in human-readable form on which copyright notice could appear. The print-outs which accompany computer programs serve an independent function, e.g. testing a program for errors to make certain it is directing the computer's operations correctly. There is no such necessity for a hard copy print-out of a machine-readable data base. The lack of notice in human-readable form is a defect which,

---

was held to bar an action for infringement under the Act of 1874. It has consistently been recognized that rights provided by federal copyright legislation are purely statutory, and that failure to comply with the notice requirements of the statute will deprive a proprietor of statutorily created rights. *See e.g.*, Puddu v. Buonamici Statuary, Inc., 450 F.2d 401 (2d Cir. 1971).

[74] *See* National Comics Publications v. Fawcett Publications, 191 F.2d 594 (2d Cir. 1951). There it was held that notice which gave the substance of what was required by 17 U.S.C. § 19 would not divest the proprietor of his copyright, when the date of publication, the letter ©, and a trade name under which the proprietor did business, were present in the notice. *See also* the discussion of notice requirements in Nimmer on Copyright, §§ 84-88 (1975) at 304.1-331.

[75] Circular 61, *supra* note 60, states that registration for a computer program will be considered if

The program has been published with the required copyright notice, that is, "copies" (i.e. reproductions of the program in a form perceptible or capable of being made perceptible to the human eye) bearing the notice have been distributed or made available to the public.

While this could be interpreted to accept notice in machine-readable form on data bases, which can be made "perceptible to the human eye" with the aid of a computer, while requiring a human-readable "print-out" of a computer program, which is not made perceptible to a human by the computer it operates, both the content of Circular 61 and present Copyright Office practices indicate that unless a human-readable print-out of the machine-readable information is presented with the required notice, the information will not be registered. *See* note 86, *infra*.

under the governing statute and regulations, would work a forfeiture of statutory copyright.[76]

The pending Copyright Revision Bill would ease the harsh penalty of forfeiture which has resulted from failure to comply strictly with the notice requirements of the present Act.[77] Moreover, section 401 of the Revision Bill, consistent with the Bill's general recognition of copyright protection in machine-readable works, would eliminate the requirement that notice be in a form legible to the human eye.[78] Nevertheless, the Bill leaves ambiguous what, if any, form of notice on a machine-readable data base would comply with the statutory requirement for notice.

It is uniformly recognized that the purpose of requiring that copyright notice be affixed to a work is to make the general public aware of the proprietor's rights in the work.[79] Even were copyright notice affixed both in human-readable form on a label attached to the container in which a machine-readable data base was packaged, and in machine-readable form at the initial section of the data base, there is some question as to whether the purpose of requiring notice would be fulfilled. While entire duplications of a data base may be produced for dissemination to secondary distributors or to users of the entire work,

---

[76] While the Copyright Office's refusal to register a work for lack of properly affixed notice is not dispositive of the cause as to whether the work is entitled to copyright protection, *see* Bouvé v. Twentieth Century-Fox Film Corp., 122 F.2d 51 (D.C. Cir. 1941) (Register's refusal to register collected contributions to a periodical as a book held unjustified), its regulations and practices are normally afforded respect by the courts, in the absence of an abuse of the Register's rulemaking and administrative functions. *Id.*

[77] S. 22, *supra* note 2, §§ 405 and 406, replaces the strict notice requirements of the present Act with a rule which would not work a forfeiture in instances of unintentional omission of notice, and permits a copyright proprietor to correct unintentional errors. These sections also provide that innocent infringers, misled by faulty notices, will be excused from liability for infringements occurring prior to being placed on actual notice of registration of the work. In accord is H.R. 2223, *supra* note 2, §§ 405 and 406.

[78] S. 22, *supra* note 2, §401 and H.R. 2223, *supra* note 2, §401 both provide:
    (a) GENERAL REQUIREMENT—Whenever a work protected by this title is published in the United States or elsewhere by authority of the copyright owner, a notice of copyright as provided by this section shall be placed on all publicly distributed copies from which the work can be visually perceived, *either directly or with the aid of a machine or device* (emphasis supplied).

[79] Even in light of the tendency to construe the notice requirements of the present Copyright Act strictly, *see* note 73, *supra,* the underlying rationale for requiring notice is to inform the public of the existing copyright in the work. *See, e.g.,* Uneeda Doll Co. v. Goldfarb Novelty Co., 373 F.2d 851 (2d Cir. 1967), *cert. denied,* 389 U.S. 801 (1968).

the primary use of a data base is that associated with a "search" for a selection of information on the basis of a specified need. A user in such an instance will be apprised only of selected responses appearing on a cathode ray tube at a terminal linked to a computer's central processing unit where the entire data base is stored, and might never be aware of copyright notice affixed only at the beginning of the data base. It can be contended that notice should appear on every image projected on the cathode ray tube in response to a data base user's request, if the statutory purpose of requiring notice is to be fulfilled. While this may be technologically feasible, it is certainly a burdensome and unprecedented requirement.[80]

There does exist a mechanism under the Copyright Revision Bill for clarifying the methods of affixing notice which would also assure compliance with the statutory notice requirements. Section 401 of the Bill requires the Register of Copyrights to:

> prescribe by regulation, as examples, specific methods of affixation and positions of the notice on various types of works that will satisfy this requirement . . . .[81]

In accord with this authority, the Register may enact regulations prescribing an appropriate location where notice is to be affixed to machine-readable data bases, and clarifying the form of the notice, i.e., that the notice should be capable of display on a cathode ray tube in the same visual form as required for all copyright notices. By so doing, the Register could eliminate a problem that might otherwise result in pointless litigation, and which undoubtedly would create needless uncertainty about the formalities involved in obtaining copyright protection for data bases.

2. Deposit Requirements for Registering Copyright in Data Bases

After having secured copyright by publication with required notice, a copyright proprietor may register his claim to copyright with the Copyright Office, as provided in Section 11 of the Copyright

---

[80] It has long since been determined, for instance, that copyright notice need be affixed only to the initial frames of a series of photographs constituting an early motion picture to fulfill the statutory requirements. Edison v. Lubin, 122 Fed. 240 (3d Cir. 1903). And one notice at the beginning of a book in which are compiled a number of different cartoon strips protects all the individual strips. Bouvé v. Twentieth Century-Fox Film Corp., 122 F.2d 51 (D.C. Cir. 1941).

[81] S. 22, *supra* note 2, § 401; H.R. 2223, *supra* note 2, § 401.

Act.[82] Registration, along with the deposit of two copies of the work for which registration is sought, is a condition precedent to the right to invoke the statutory remedies for infringement provided by the Copyright Act.[83] This practice would continue largely unchanged under the pending Copyright Revision Bill.[84]

The proprietor of copyright in a machine-readable data base could not complete the deposit of copies required for registration under registration practices enforced pursuant to the present Act. Section 13 requires deposit of "two complete copies of the best edition thereof then published" in fulfillment of the registration requirements.[85] The machine-readable copies of programs deposited for registration must be accompanied by reproductions, such as print-outs, in human-readable form, to satisfy the Register's requirements.[86] Not

---

[82] 17 U.S.C. § 11.

[83] 17 U.S.C. § 13 sets forth the mechanics of depositing copies of a published work for which registration is sought. In most instances, two complete copies of a work must be deposited. The Register of Copyrights is therein authorized to prescribe regulations permitting modifications of the deposit provisions when, for reasons related to the size or monetary value of the copies, deposit of two copies is "impracticable." *Id.* That section also provides that:

> No action or proceedings shall be maintained for infringement of copyright in any work until the provisions of this title with respect to the deposit of copies and registration of such work shall have been complied with. *Id.*

It has been determined by the Supreme Court that deposit of copies may be made long after publication of the work occurs, so long as it precedes an action for infringement under the Act. Washingtonian Publishing Co. v. Pearson, 306 U.S. 30 (1939).

[84] S. 22, *supra* note 2; H.R. 2223, *supra* note 2. Both versions of the Bill provide, in section 411, for registration as a precondition to the right to bring an infringement action, and deposit of copies is required as one of the formalities of registration under section 408, much as deposit is required under the present Act. Section 408 also provides that:

> Subject to the provisions of section 405 (a), such registration is not a condition of copyright protection. *Id.* § 408.

Section 408 is on that point contradicted by section 411, for effective protection implies the right to bring an infringement action. While under the present Act one can bring an action to enforce common law copyright, there would be no such common law right of action after enactment of the Revision Bill, which in section 301 abolishes all common law rights within the subject matter of copyright. *Id.* § 301.

[85] 17 U.S.C. § 13.

[86] Circular 61, *supra* note 60, states, in pertinent part:

> Registration for a computer program will be considered if:
> The copies deposited for registration consist of two complete copies of the program in the form as first published. If the first publication was

only do data bases generally appear only in machine-readable form, thus failing to meet the requirement for deposit of "visually perceptible reproduction[s] or descriptions[s],"[87] but data bases, by virtue of their function as means of retrieving a constantly expanding body of information,[88] are themselves constantly being modified to include recent additions to the body of literature therein referenced. Machine-readable data bases are best described as ever-changing, ever-distinct derivative works, containing much material common with their predecessor, underlying works, yet including a certain amount of new material in the most recent "editions".[89]

This fluid characteristic of the contents of data bases makes difficult, if not impossible, compliance with the deposit requirements for copyright registration under the present Act. In order to comply with the registration requirements, a data base proprietor would have to deposit and register anew the data base whenever there was an addition of new material to its corpus. While the Register of Copyrights has limited discretion under the present Act to modify the deposit requirements with regard to certain works, this discretion is strictly limited and does not apply to data bases.[90] A data base proprietor is thus effectively prevented from complying with the registration provisions

---

in a form (such as machine-readable tape) that cannot be perceived visually or read by humans, a visually perceptible reproduction or description (such as a print-out of the program) must also be deposited.

[87] *Id.* Because of their size and purpose, data bases are not "printed out" in human-readable form, as are many computer programs.

[88] *See* notes 11-14, *supra.*

[89] Derivative works are those which incorporate certain material from a prior work, and supplement such material with new matter to create a new work. A common example of a derivative work is a motion picture or dramatic production based on a novel. *See, e.g.,* G. Ricordi v. Paramount Pictures, 189 F.2d 469 (2d Cir. 1951). A translation or new edition of a book would also be a derivative work, presenting a closer analogy to a modified data base.

[90] 17 U.S.C. § 13 provides that:

if the work belongs to a class specified in subsections (g), (h), (i) or (k) of section 5 of this title, and if the Register of Copyright determines that it is impractical to deposit copies because of their size, weight, fragility, or monetary value he may permit the deposit of photographs or other identifying reproductions in lieu of copies of the work as published under such rules and regulations as he may prescribe with the approval of the Librarian of Congress.

37 C.F.R. § 202.16 incorporates the intent of this statute in Copyright Office Regulations. The categories of works to which this statue, and the regulation promulgated thereunder, apply are limited to works of art, and could not be applied to data bases.

of the present Act, and cannot obtain statutory protection for a data base.[91]

Deposit of copies, although in machine-readable form without the additional requirement of human-readable print-outs,[92] would continue to be a requirement of copyright registration and of the right to enforce one's rights by bringing an action for infringement, under the proposed Copyright Revision Bill.[93] Nothing in the Revision Bill speaks directly to the unique problems confronted by those who desire to register claims to copyright in material, such as data bases, which are constantly being modified to include new material. Proprietors of copyright in such data bases will thus be left uncertain under the language of the Revision Bill as to what, if any, protection exists for their works under the copyright law.

However, the Register of Copyrights is given greater discretion under the proposed Revision Bill than under the present Act to administratively modify the deposit requirements for copyright registration.[94] Under the provisions of section 408 of the Bill, the Register has authority to promulgate regulations which would govern the deposit requirements for all copyrighted works, including data bases, and thus clarify any uncertainty as to the effect of those requirements on the protection afforded data bases under the pending Bill.[95] In ac-

---

[91] It could be contended that the failure to deposit a copy of a data base corresponding to each revision would not be a serious concern to the data base proprietor, who would be unprotected only with regard to recently added material. Although this may be the case, such a contention overlooks the fact that the copyrightable element of a data base likely is its systematic organization and selection of material, rather than the content, which may be in the public domain. *See* notes 40-43, *supra*. It is conceivable that the failure of a proprietor to deposit a completely updated copy of a data base which was allegedly infringed could deprive the proprietor of his statutory action. *Cf.* Hoyt v. Daily Mirror, Inc., 31 F. Supp. 89 (S.D.N.Y. 1939) ("block-outs" of portions of photographs deposited with Copyright Office held to disqualify copies for registration purposes and deprive proprietor of rights to maintain statutory infringement action).

[92] *See* notes 60 and 62 and accompanying text, *supra*.

[93] *See* note 83, *supra*.

[94] S. 22, *supra* note 2, § 408; H.R. 2223, *supra* note 2, § 408.

[95] *Id.* Section 408 (c) (1) provides:

The Register of Copyrights is authorized to specify by regulation the administrative classes into which works are to be placed for purposes of deposit and registration . . . The regulations may require or permit, for particular classes, the deposit of identifying material instead of copies or phonorecords, the deposit of only one copy or phonorecord where two would normally be required, *or a single registration for a group of related works.* This administrative classification of works has no exclusive rights. *Id.* (emphasis supplied).

cord with this authority, the Register could promulgate regulations permitting the deposit of identifying material in lieu of the entire data base for which registration is sought. In addition, the Register could rule that registration for a data base would protect all modifications in that data base for a specified period of time, at the end of which period registration, including deposit of identifying material, would have to be updated. Promulgation of such regulations would appear to be within the scope of the Register's discretion intended by the Revision Bill and provided under generally recognized principles of administrative law.[96] This would assure proprietors of machine-readable data bases that copyright protection, which is available to compilations of information in hard copy, would not be denied for the same information in machine-readable form. A contrary result would penalize the economies and efficiencies created by the capability of the computer, by elevating technical formalities over the substantive protection offered by copyright.

3. What Constitutes Infringement of Copyright in a Data Base?

There remains the necessary, and perplexing, task of determining what activities will violate the exclusive rights of a copyright proprietor in a machine-readable data base. Analogies with works made possible as a result of past technological advances, such as motion pictures and television, present themselves, but do not resolve all issues related to the unique characteristics of data bases. Yet it is no more acceptable in copyright than any other body of law to have a right without knowledge of the limits of that right; accordingly, an attempt to define the scope of copyright in a data base must be undertaken.

The proprietor of a data base would likely be concerned with two distinct unauthorized uses of his work against which copyright could offer protection: 1) the actual misappropriation of the information in the data base for the purpose of duplicating or compiling a sub-

---

[96] The 1974 Senate Report accompanying the Revision Bill makes clear the intention of Section 408 to give the Register discretion "consistent with the principle of administrative flexibility underlying all the deposit and registration provisions . . ." S. Rep. 94-473, 94th Cong., 1st Sess. (1975). Such discretion is consistent with the deference properly shown by the judiciary to the interpretation given a statute by the agency charged with its administration. *See* Udall v. Tallman, 380 U.S. 1 (1965). Such deference will be shown to the actions of the Register of Copyrights in determining compliance with statutory formalities of copyright registration, absent reliance on a statutory interpretation which is clearly erroneous as a matter of law. *Cf.* Bouvé v. Twentieth Century-Fox Film Corp. 122 F.2d 51 (D.C. Cir. 1941).

sequent work without compensation to the proprietor and 2) an unauthorized use, or "search", of the data base to obtain the information found therein for one's own research or commercial purposes. There is no reason why the former activity should not be considered an infringement of copyright according to the same criteria applied to the use of a prior hard copy directory by a subsequent compiler.[97] The latter use presents the more difficult question of whether employing a computer to locate and display on a cathode ray tube a small amount of the total information contained in a data base should constitute an infringing act.

Yet the scope of protection provided by copyright need not remain fixed by the state of the art of hard copy publishing. The exclusive rights appurtenant to copyright have not remained unaffected by the passage of time and the recognition that new forms of intellectual creation were appropriately subject to copyright. The exclusive right to print copies of books was all that was expressly granted by the first modern copyright legislation, the British Statute of 8 Anne.[98] The first federal copyright statute enacted in the United States closely followed the language of its English progenitor, while expanding the coverage of copyright to include maps and charts.[99] By the time of enactment of the present federal copyright law,[100] copyright had grown to protect plays, musical compositions, works of art and photographs,[101] and provided for exclusive rights in making

---

[97] See discussion of Copyright Protection for Hard Copy Compilations and Directories, Section II of this article, supra. A related question is whether the placement of a data base in a computer without the authorization of the copyright proprietor is itself an infringing act. Considering such unauthorized actions to be infringement might have the advantage of making somewhat easier the enforcement of rights against one who "drains off" a major segment of a data base by making injunctive relief available as soon as unauthorized access is found. It would not, however, insure protection against the damage which would occur as a result of such infringements. In order to be adequately compensated, one whose rights were infringed would still have to prove financial injury caused by the individual acts, or resort to the statutory damages provision of the Act which would not necessarily provide adequate monetary relief. A discussion of the debate as to whether input of a computer program or data base should be an act of infringement is found in Project, New Technology and the Law of Computers: Reprography and Computers, 15 U.C.L.A. L. Rev. 939 (1968).

[98] Statutes at Large, 8 Anne, c. 19 (1709).

[99] Act of May 31, 1790, ch. 15, 1 Stat. 124.

[100] The Act of March 4, 1909, ch. 320, 35 Stat. 1075, now codified as 17 U.S.C. §1 et seq.

[101] 17 U.S.C. §5(e), (g), and (j).

new versions or derivative works, and giving public performances of works such as dramatic or musical compositions.[102] Since then, the Copyright Act has undergone further amendment to include motion pictures,[103] and sound recordings.[104] In most instances the statutory recognition of rights was in response to judicially created law. For example, photographs were recognized as subject to copyright protection by the Supreme Court in *Burrow-Giles Lithographic Co. v. Sarony,* [105] but sound recordings were found not to be copyrightable under the Act of 1909 in *Capitol Records v. Mercury Records Corp.* [106] Neither the fact that use of a data base does not result in the production of a tangible copy, nor the fact that only a small portion of the data base is actually displayed, should preclude such use being considered a violation of copyright.

A search to locate desired information or the source of such information is the function most often associated with a data base.[107] In response to a request communicated to the computer in which a data base is stored, pertinent information is either printed out and delivered to the person making the request or, as is the case in searches conducted "on-line" from terminals linked to the computer from remote locations, the information is displayed on a cathode-ray tube screen at the terminal site. While in the latter instance a "copy" of information viewed by a data base user may appear only for a matter of seconds or minutes on a screen, and then disappear, this should not affect the exclusivity of the right granted by copyright. Motion pictures, in the same fashion, appear but briefly on a screen, and it is not seriously disputed that the unauthorized projection of a motion picture under copyright protection, whether termed a performance, a display, or—when shown on television—a broadcast, is an infringing act.[108]

---

[102] 17 U.S.C. §1(b), (d) and (e).
[103] Act of Aug. 24, 1912, 37 Stat. 488, ch. 356.
[104] Sound Recording Act of 1971, Pub. L. 92-140, 85 Stat. 391.
[105] 111 U.S. 53 (1884).
[106] 221 F.2d 657 (2d Cir. 1955).
[107] *See* note 14, *supra.*
[108] Motion pictures were specified as copyrightable works in the Act of Aug. 24, 1912, 37 Stat. 488, ch. 356, and in Patterson v. Century Productions, Inc., 93 F.2d 489 (2d Cir. 1937) a motion picture projected on a screen was held to be an infringing copy of the copyright proprietor's work. While Professor Nimmer questions this holding, NIMMER ON COPYRIGHT § 101.4 (1975) at 380, the fact that the projection of a motion picture can constitute an infringement of copyright, despite the evanescence of the image on the screen, is not contested in actual litigation. *See, e.g.,* Rohauer v. Killiam Shows, Inc., 379 F. Supp. 723 (S.D.N.Y. 1974).

One could also cogently argue that the search of a data base will often result in the retrieval of but a small fraction of the data therein contained, and that unless the entire data base or a substantial segment of it is displayed, no infringement occurs because there has been a copying only of that which is in the public domain. Closely related to such a contention would be that retrieval of a small amount of information from a data base constitutes fair use. Neither contention ought to preclude the unauthorized use of a data base from constituting an infringement of copyright.

Fair use is invoked to permit the unauthorized use of copyrighted works in instances when overriding public values are thereby served,[109] or when such copying is sufficiently minimal and causes so little economic harm to the proprietor of copyright that the use falls under a principle similar to that of *de minimus non curat lex*.[110] While a wide variety of criteria for determining fair use have been identified,[111] it is generally recognized that the tendency of an unauthorized copy to diminish or prejudice the commercial value of a copyrighted work is the key to whether no infringement will be found because of fair use.[112] Economic damage to the proprietor of a data base is precisely that which would result from an unauthorized search: the amount of information actually retrieved has little if anything to do with recognition of the proprietor's rights.

Nor should the fact that the information retrieved by searching a data base is itself in the public domain mitigate the infringing nature of an unauthorized search. It is the organization of information and the capacity to provide that information in response to a request that constitutes the copyrightable element of a directory in hard copy,[113] and it should not affect the scope of copyright protection that the information contained in a directory is embodied in machine-readable media and retrieved by what is, in effect, an automated indexing system. While a data base may not be a work of enduring literary value, it nevertheless merits the protection of copyright, and we can be certain that the application of copyright principles to raw data stored and reproduced with the use of a computer today will determine the ap-

---

[109] *See* Time Inc. v. Bernard Geis Associates, 293 F. Supp. 130 (S.D.N.Y. 1968), in which copyrighted photographs of the 1963 Kennedy assassination published in Life Magazine were held to be fair use because of the public significance of events surrounding the occurrence.

[110] *See* Latman, *Fair Use of Copyrighted Works*, COPYRIGHT LAW REVISION STUDY No. 14 (U.S.G.P.O. 1958).

[111] *Id.* at 15.

[112] *See* NIMMER ON COPYRIGHT § 145 (1975) and cases cited therein.

[113] *See* notes 42 and 43, *supra*.

plication of principles of copyright to literary works made available with the use of a computer in the future.

IV. CONCLUSION

Data bases contain information that has traditionally been printed and protected by copyright in hard copy format. The present state of technology has made possible, and considerations of time and cost economies now demand, that access to this information be obtained with the use of computers. Extensive collections of resource and reference material created in machine-readable format are now being produced and marketed to those engaged in professional and scholarly research of all kinds. There is reason to believe that machine-readable data bases will largely replace their hard copy counterparts in providing direction and access to information for private organizations and public institutions with substantial research needs.[114]

This development is occurring just as enactment of the first general revision of the federal copyright law since 1909, motivated largely by a concern that copyright legislation had been outpaced by technology, appears imminent. Doubt has been expressed by some, notably Benjamin Kaplan, as to whether copyright will continue to have a significant role to play in the creation and dissemination of intellectual works.[115] If copyright is to remain a vital source of stimulus to and protection for those who create literary and artistic works which communicate ideas to others, be they in written, graphic or machine-readable format, the likely soon-to-be enacted Copyright Revision Bill must provide protection for bibliographic data bases.

---

[114] *See* notes 11-15, *supra.*

[115] *See* Kaplan, *supra* note 8. Professor [now Justice] Kaplan there predicted a bleak future for copyright:

> For many of the uses available through the machine, exaction of copyright will be felt unnecessary to provide incentive or headstart—especially so when the works owe their origin, as so many will, to one or another kind of public support. *Id.* at 120-21.

ECONOMICS OF PROPERTY RIGHTS AS APPLIED TO COMPUTER SOFTWARE AND DATA BASES

Yale M. Braunstein, Dietrich M. Fischer, Janusz A. Ordover, and William J. Baumol

OVERVIEW OF ISSUES

A. Historical Perspective

Since the passage of the 1909 copyright act (and in some ways, since the enactment of the first U.S. copyright law in 1790) it has been necessary for the courts and the Copyright Office to interpret that act in the light of technological and business advances. Two trends have emerged: First, utilitarian (non-artistic) creations and compilations of data such as interest tables and telephone books have been found to be copyrightable.[1,2] Second, the relationship of the copyright act to the products of and information transmitted by new technologies has frequently created difficult cases and often bad, or at least unclear, law. Among these technological advances have been sound recordings, radio and television broadcasts, photocopying, and cable television.[3]

Although the Supreme Court has expressed "the conviction that encouragement of individual effort by personal gain is the best way to advance public welfare through the talents of authors and inventors . . ."[4] the decision concerning new techniques has

---

[1] *Edwards and Deutch Lithographing Co. v. Boorman,* 15F. 2a 35(7th Cir. 1926).

[2] *Leon v. Pacific Tel. & Tel. Co.,* 91 F. 2d 484 (9th Cir. 1937).

[3] Among the more distinctive cases are: *White-Smith Music Publishing Co. v. Apollo Co.,* 209 U.S. 1 (1908) (Piano roll not a copy of copyrighted music); *Capitol Records, Inc., v. Mercury Records Corp.,* 221 F. 2d 657 (2d Cir. 1955) (phonograph record not copyrightable); *Williams & Wilkins Co. v. United States,* 420 U.S. 376 (1975) (Wholesale governmental photocopying no infringement); and *Fortnightly Corp. v. United Artists Television Inc.,* 392 U.S. 390 (1968) (CATV system does not "perform" works it makes available to its customers.)

[4] *Mazer v. Stein* (347 U.S. 201, 1954).

sometimes appeared to ignore that conviction. (*Fortnightly* and *Williams and Wilkins* are perfect examples.) As a result several copyright revision bills have in recent years been considered by Congress; these addressed various parts of the issue of the proper scope of copyright protection in light of new technology.[5] The 1969 revision bill (S. 543) and the version finally enacted in 1976 (P.L. 94-553) each contained a section (§ 117) that stipulated that the case law on the use of copyrighted works in computer systems would be unaffected by the new law. In an action which may have permitted the passage of the new copyright act, the National Commission on New Technological Uses of Copyrighted Works (CONTU) was established to recommend legislation in the area of the reproduction and use of copyrighted works by computer and photocopying systems.[6]

In general terms the conflict to be resolved is that between the desire for a free flow of ideas, on one hand, with the establishment of incentives for the creation of ideas on the other. This balance is addressed by the copyright and patent laws, both of which grant, under certain circumstances, limited monopolies to the creators of inventions, books, and other forms of products of intellectual creativity.

B. Specific Issues in the Area of Computer-based Information

There are three basic questions that underlie this discussion of the proper scope of copyright protection:

(1) What is the product, i.e., what exactly is copyrightable in the context of items used with the aid of a computer system?

(2) How do we define usage in this context?

(3) How do we detect and monitor such usage?

These questions obviously do not pertain only to information used in a computer or automatic data processing system. There are natural parallels, say, to the use of copyrighted phonographic recordings by radio stations or the transmission of copyrighted still or motion pictures by means of television. But in the computer field these questions can not simply be answered by analogy with other forms of communication.

Although the Commission has received considerable testimony and advice on whether input to, storage in, or output from a computer would constitute usage,[7] we shall take a step back to the basic underlying principle which has given rise to these questions:

---

5   For example, see H.R.2512 and S.597 (1967), S.543 (1969).

6   P.L.93-573, enacted on Dec. 31, 1974. The Commissioners were appointed on July 25, 1975.

7   See, e.g., Data Base Subcommittee report, Feb. 18, 1977.

Principle 1.1   The more complete and certain the specification of property rights, the greater the level of economic efficiency that is possible.

It is because of this principle that one seeks to define what is meant by property in reference to information used by a computer system. As the Data Base Subcommittee has indicated, it seems clear that the intention of Congress was that computer data bases be considered a proper subject for copyright.[8] However in the discussions of proprietary rights in computer programs and software, arguments have been made for protection by means of copyright, patent, or the trade secret laws.[9] It is in the comparison between protection by means of copyright and reliance on trade secrecy and restrictive licensing that the contrasts are most apparent. Copyright promotes disclosure while trade secrecy results in minimal disclosure and dissemination (if it works).

We shall examine the economic issues such as the trade-off between the incentives to create and the incentives to use new information or products. Although we shall not be able to disregard completely many of the legal issues, they shall not be in the forefront of our discussion.

C. Introduction to the Economic Analysis

The subject of copyright gives rise to a number of complex economic issues. After pointing out some fundamental relationships that will underlie our discussion, it is well to begin with a survey of these issues. From there we turn to a brief indication of the evaluation of these issues to which one is led by economic analysis. Our report then turns to a rather more probing discussion of a number of these matters, and ends up with a careful description of a novel and powerful method by which one can evaluate one of the key issues in the area—the optimal length of copyright.

The need for copyright or some substitute arises from what economists call difficulty of exclusion from the use of printed material, software, and various other such products whose initial cost of production is quite high but for which the cost of replication is very small. Ability to exclude means that the producer of such an item can prevent a potential user from employing it unless that person is willing to provide payment for the item. Difficulty of exclusion means that people can help themselves to the item without payment and with little or no fear of untoward consequences. Such goods, particularly when

---

8   Ibid., p.1.

9   For example, see D. Bender, "Trade Secret Protection of Software,"*G. Washington Law Review* 38:909 (1970); C.N. Mooers, "Computer Software and Copyright," *Computing Surveys* 7 (March 1975), 45-72; and O.R. Smoot, "Development of an International System for Legal Protection of Computer Programs," *Communications of the ACM* 19 (April 1976), 171-174.

they are expensive to produce, normally will find no private suppliers. Firms will surely be discouraged from investing in new software if the products will be immediately available to anyone for the taking. To prevent this is, of course, the purpose of copyright. It is intended to protect the investment of firms that put resources into valuable new products, not only as a means to protect the interests of those firms, but perhaps even more important from the social viewpoint, to encourage the production of valuable items from whose use it would be difficult to exclude anyone without such protection.

However, there is another side to the matter which will play an important role later in the analysis. These same products which seem to require statutory protection are also, generally, items which, in the view of economists, should be offered with maximal encouragement of widespread use. That is, these items generally involve a heavy (sunk) cost of development to which little or nothing is added when there is an increase in number of users. This is in sharp contrast with other products such as food or clothing in which additional usage requires substantial additional use of resources—additional users are not free. Thus, economists argue, while goods like shirts or potatoes should have a high price reflecting the high costs imposed by additional users, there is something undesirable about a commensurately high price for the use of a software package since that high price will discourage widespread use even though such added use costs society little or nothing over and above the sunk cost of development of the package.

D. Issues in Copyright Policy

Having discussed the logic of the underlying problem we can turn next to a listing of the issues which must be faced by copyright policy. In the following section we will see how the analysis which has just been summarized helps us to provide a fruitful evaluation of these issues.

The most obvious issue that arises in this area is whether copyright is the only way to go about dealing with the problem that copyright protection is designed to solve. As a matter of fact there are several alternatives to copyright, and the issue is to determine whether anyone of them is generally better than the others, or, what may be more likely, whether some work well in some circumstances while others are better suited under different conditions.

Since copyright is intended to protect the interests of those who invest in the design of certain types of new products and to encourage that sort of investment, an obvious alternative to copyright is the provision of added protection to industrial secrets. If a potential investor in a software package can be made to feel reasonably confident that others will be unable to discover the secrets underlying his product so that he will be able to retain a monopoly over its use, then that may perhaps be as effective a stimulus to this sort of investment as copyright protection.

There is also a third possibility where neither secrecy nor copyright protection is applicable or effective, then private investment will obviously be discouraged. In that case the substitute possibility is investment by the public sector. This helps to explain the heavy investment of government agencies in a wide variety of types of research, most notably in basic research which is preponderantly carried out under government sponsorship.

Thus there are alternatives to copyright, and we will see in the next section that for each of them there are areas in which it promises to be more appropriate than the others.

The second set of issues that arises in the area of copyright policy is the nature of the terms that should be permitted. Here several issues arise immediately:

(1) Over how long a period should the copyright extend?

(2) Should the length of copyright be uniform for all items protected?

(3) Should there be any restrictions upon the monopoly power conferred upon the holder of a copyright?

(4) In particular, should there be compulsory licensing of the copyrighted product?

(5) If there is compulsory licensing, how should the price be set?

(6) Should there be classes of uses or classes of users of copyrighted products who are exempted from the copyright provisions?

Finally, there are a variety of issues that arise in carrying out copyright policy in light of the complications inevitably injected by reality. These force policy-makers to accept compromises which can be avoided altogether only in theoretical discussions. Only two examples will be offered, both of them arising because of problems of enforcement.

First, are there types of use which should be exempted from copyright protection, not because their exemption is inherently desirable but because the cost of entering copyright protection in these areas exceeds the potential benefits of enforcement? If so what can one say about the nature of such exemptions? (This is one of the issues addressed by the "fair-use" section (§107) of the 1976 Copyright revision.)

Our second example relates to charges for the use of copyrighted material. Here the question is whether the imposition of charges based directly on use is always practical, and if not, what alternatives constitute a second-best solution.

This brief disucssion has been intended to provide a short list of the main economic issues involved in copyright policy. It certainly does not pretend to be exhaustive nor does it even begin to suggest the noneconomic (e.g., legal, political and social) issues. This list should, however, serve as an adequate working framework for our discussion.

We proceed now to a brief commentary upon each of these issues, indicating how economic analysis suggests they should be viewed. After that, we will turn to a somewhat more extensive examination of several of the more crucial topics.

E. Copyright and Its Alternatives

We have indicated that copyright is only one of three avenues to encourage investment in the development of the pertinent new products, trade secrecy and direct government investments being the two prime alternatives. What is the appropriate role of each of these instruments?

Later we will discuss in some detail the differences in the consequences of secrecy and copyrighting. But, in brief summary, secrecy necessarily restricts the range of direct users of the product involved, whereas copyright does not necessarily do so and certainly does not do it where there is compulsory licensing at reasonable prices. Second, resort to secrecy does encourage expenditure on product features which inhibit discovery of the secrets. There are other costs, extending even to outlays on espionage which this process encourages. On the other hand, if the copyright remains valuable as its expiration date approaches, this can encourage research expenditures whose only purpose is to discover product variations just sufficient to justify a new copyright, an exercise which obviously has little payoff to society.

Secrecy is likely to work most effectively where the uncopyrighted product is an intermediate good which is itself used in the production of other goods, e.g., if it is a computer program used to process other people's data. When this is the case it is easier for the investor to earn the cost of his investment without revealing his secret because his product need never leave his hands. On the other hand, if the investor must rely for his earnings on the sale of the uncopyrighted product itself (e.g., by selling the program itself to users) then it is very difficult to retain secrecy. This distinction naturally suggests the sort of item in which innovation can be expected in the absence of copyright protection, and the sort of product which requires copyright if private investment in development is to be obtained.

But there are reasons why the third way of obtaining this sort of investment—direct government financing—should at least sometimes be utilized. We saw earlier that for at least some potentially copyrightable products the cost of serving additional users is negligible, so that a high price which discourages use is undesirable socially. However a very low price is likely to be incompatible with recovery of initial investment outlays for its development. Where this is a significant consideration (and precise conditions for this case can be enunciated)[10] then neither copyright nor secrecy will be in the social interest, for both operate via the extraction of prices sufficiently high to bring a return that will be attractive to private investment. It is clear that in such a case, if the investment in the product is worthwhile to society but compensatory pricing is not, then the only alternative is goverment financing. Even if one were to think of another method of making such investment attractive financially to private enterprise, it would, by definition, be no more satisfactory than the use of copyright or reliance on secrecy.

F. Terms of Copyright

We come next to the issue of which conditions should be applied to the granting of a copyright where that is the procedure adopted.

The first issue to be considered is the period of time over which the copyright should remain valid. It is shown in detail in this report that this is an issue which need not be settled *ad hoc*, on the basis of tradition or compromise. There are strong economic considerations which can serve as an underpinning for an analysis of optimal copyright life. The point is that a very short copyright period will fail in its purpose by being insufficient to attract any significant amount of investment into the development process. On the other hand a very long copyright period can extract an excessive price from society by granting monopoly powers to investors for an excessive period. The optimality calculation consists of a balancing of these two considerations to determine that duration of copyright which maximizes its net contribution to social welfare.

This immediately indicates that, at least in principle, the optimal period of protection will vary from case to case. It will depend on the annual profitability of the investment, the magnitude of the monopoly price extracted from the public, the "natural" rate of obsolescence of the product of the investment[11] and a variety of other such

---

10 Baumol, W.J. and Ordover, J.A., "On the Optimality of Public-Goods Pricing with Exclusion Devices," Kyklos 30 (1977) Fasc. 1, pp 5-21.

11 In general, for example, the optimal period of protection will be less than the useful economic life of the item covered. This is necessary in order to make sure that the net gains from the project are shared by the investor and by the general public. Obviously, the latter's gains are limited until after the expiration of the copyright since before that time the copyright holder may be able to use the monopoly power it confers to extract the bulk of the gains flowing from the copyrighted product.

considerations which are indicated specifically in detail later in our analysis. That means that one industry or one type of product may call for a copyright life different from another. A computer program may be encouraged most effectively by a copyright lasting x years while a novel may call for a y year copyright. Obviously, a case-by-case approach to copyright period is totally impractical, but it is certainly worth considering whether the establishment of, say, two or three different categories of materials eligible for copyright protection, each with its own copyright period, may not be desirable and feasible administratively. Often it has proven to be true that where administrative simplicity calls for uniformity while other efficiency considerations call for variability, a very small number of categories adds very little to administrative costs and yet contributes enormously to efficiency—sometimes capturing the bulk of the gains that are potentially available. It is because of this possibility that this report devotes so much space to a model for the evaluation of optimal copyright duration. Should it be determined that the possibility of several copyright periods is worth further exploration, our model indicates just how this issue should be investigated.

Other potential provisions of the copyright that require comment are the idea of compulsory licensing, the possibility of restrictions upon pricing and the notion of exemptions from the terms of the copyright of certain categories of use or certain categories of users.

All of these possibilities share one common feature. Each of them constitutes some restriction upon the avenues which the holder of the copyright can use to pursue profits. This means that, if statutory protection is to serve as an incentive for investment in the production of material subject to that protection, any provision of the sort now under discussion must weaken this incentive.[12] To achieve any given degree of stimulation of such investment, a price ceiling, a requirement of licensing or other such restrictions must be offset by a commensurate improvement in some other inducement, e.g., it may call for a countervailing increase in length of the period of copyright protection. But we have seen that a lengthening of this period is not without its social cost, so that the decision becomes a trade-off in which the advantages expected to flow from the restrictions in the copyright holder's monopoly power are balanced against the social cost of the lengthened protection period.

Compulsory licensing and restrictions upon the price charged for a license obviously must constitute a gain to those who decide to acquire a license as well as to the customers for their products. This will necessarily be so since those who obtain a license do so voluntarily, and hence to them it must be worth its price. Without compulsory licensing they would be deprived of this gain.

---

12 This argument only considers the economic incentives for investment in the production of intellectual works. There are, of course, other incentives.

But one must be careful not to jump to the conclusion that this is a net gain to the community. It is equally certain that compulsory licensing must constitute a net loss to the holder of the copyright, at least in his own view of the matter, for otherwise there would be no need to compel him to issue licenses. There is, in general, no easy way to judge whether the net result will be a social gain or a social loss.

Since one of the purposes of the copyright is to protect the interests of the initial investors in the new product and stimulate investment in this area, this all counsels the desirability of proceeding with caution before adopting measures that erode these gains.

There is another argument that suggests a similar view, the near universal evidence that increasing complexity of regulatory provisions tends to undermine the effectiveness of the regulatory process. When that process is impeded by a complex body of special exceptions, complex provisos and intricate modifications, the workings of the process are all too often sidetracked into concentration on administrative detail rather than substance.

This becomes even clearer when one considers the possibility of exceptions—should certain classes of users be exempted from copyright restrictions either because they are considered particularly meritorious or simply because they cannot afford the fees? There may be cases where the political realities or some other special considerations justify such exemptions. However, there are two important reasons such general exemptions are difficult to justify on economic grounds.[13] First, every such exemption means in effect that the burden is then shifted to someone else. Generally, if the prices of the product are to remain compensatory every exemption will require a rise in the prices paid by other users. It may be highly desirable that society provide subsidies, say, to certain classes of nonprofit users, but there seems to be no reason to require the burdens to be borne by other users of the same copyright. Economists are not opposed to all subsidies, but where they support them they prefer general subsidies that are provided openly and explicitly and financed by the community as a whole through the tax system, rather than subsidies which are concealed and extracted from some fortuitously chosen group from whom it happens to be convenient to obtain the funds.

There is a second reason why economists generally do not favor broad exemptions of particular classes of users. As we have noted earlier, a price for the use of some copyrighted material always tends to discourage its use—the higher the price, the less use will generally be made of the product. Now a zero price to one group of users

---

13 In the following section of this report we will however encounter a case in which such exemptions are justified by the high cost of collection of fees for certain types of use.

compensated by a higher price to other users will cause a lopsided change in demand patterns which generally cause a larger overall social loss than a balanced spread of the price increases. There are carefully worked out principles in economic analysis which indicate how the social losses from such distortions can be minimized, and these principles are generally inconsistent with broad exemptions.[14]

G. Compromises Required in Practice

As has already been noted, even if an ideal copyright system can be designed in theory one can be sure that it will require considerable compromise to make it workable in practice. Thus, we noted that while ideally the length of the copyright should vary from product to product, in reality such lattitude could only result in an administrative nightmare.

At least two other compromises also suggest themselves immediately, though others will undoubtedly arise in practice.

First, the economic principles of optimal charging which were discussed in the preceding section call not only for payments to be borne by all classes of producer, but also for payments to be required for every use. For example, if a charge is imposed upon photocopying of materials protected by copyright, such a charge should, ideally, be required for every such act. Yet (aside from the issue of fair use) with current technology it is literally impossible to monitor every instance of photocopying done in a library or elsewhere. Consequently, user charges for the photocopying of copyrighted material can only be approximated at best. One may be able to impose a flat fee on a photocopying machine or upon a library, or one can base a payment upon the number of recorded uses of a photocopier. However, these all involve three serious compromises: First, there is no way of knowing whether it is the individual who uses the copyrighted material who actually bears the cost. Such a crude payment process must bear as heavily upon the person who copies his own handwritten page as upon the person who copies a journal article to avoid buying that journal. Second, payment will generally not correspond closely to the amount of use of material under copyright. Finally, there is no way of allocating the payments among the producers of the copyrighted materials in proportion to their use. One is driven instead to resort to some sort of pooling arrangement such as the one used to compensate composers of music. Fixed annual payments for performances of recorded music are, for example, made by the television networks to

---

14 See for example, Y. Braunstein, "An Economic Rationale for Page and Submission Charges by Academic Journals," Center for Applied Economics Discussion Paper, New York University (1976).

the composers' organization which then divides these proceeds among the composers on the basis of some rule of thumb. This is all a very crude approximation to the theoretical ideal of payment proportioned to use, but enforcement and administrative problems leave no choice except some such compromise arrangement. This type of accommodation may frequently have to characterize payment under copyright in the future.

A second compromise which seems unavoidable is the exemption of very limited usage, for example the photocopying of a single reproduction of a short passage from a journal. The main argument for such an exemption from the viewpoint of the economist is not that such a limited use is "fair," but rather that potential gains from payment for such limited use are likely to be swamped by the administrative and policing costs.

The main issue raised by the necessity of compromises such as have been discussed is whether they should be written into the rules of copyright with an attempt to fix the boundaries of permitted compromise, or whether one prefers to permit time and usage to soften the working rules formulated without exceptions. But this is a choice which lies outside the economist's area of special competence. It is therefore appropriate to turn from this outline of the general issues, to a more careful examination of those directly amenable to economic analysis.

DISSENT FROM CONTU'S
SOFTWARE RECOMMENDATION

John Hersey

This dissent from the Commission Report on computer programs takes the view that copyright is an inappropriate, as well as unnecessary, way of protecting the usable forms of computer programs.

Its main argument, briefly summarized, is this:

In the early stages of its development, the basic ideas and methods to be contained in a computer program are set down in written forms, and these will presumably be copyrightable with no change in the 1976 Act. But the program itself, in its mature and usable form, is a machine control element, a mechanical device, which on Constitutional grounds and for reasons of social policy ought not to be copyrighted.

The view here is that the investment of creative effort in the devising of computer programs does warrant certain modes of protection for the resulting devices, but that these modes already exist, or are about to be brought into being, under other laws besides copyright; that the need for copyright protection of the machine phase of computer programs, quite apart from whether it is fitting, has not been demonstrated to this Commission; and that the social and economic effects of permitting copyright to stand alongside these other forms of protection would be, on balance, negative.

The heart of the argument lies in what flows from the distinction raised above, between the written and mechanical forms of computer programs: Admitting these devices to copyright would mark the first time copyright had ever covered a means of communication, not with the human mind and senses, but with machines.

SOURCE: Reprinted from the *Final Report of the National Commission on New Technological Uses of Copyrighted Works*.

ARE MATURE PROGRAMS "WRITINGS"?

Programs are profoundly different from the various forms of "works of authorship" secured under the Constitution by copyright. Works of authorship have always been intended to be circulated to human beings and to be used by them—to be read, heard, or seen, for either pleasurable or practical ends. Computer programs, in their mature phase, are addressed to machines.

All computer programs go through various stages of development. In the stages of the planning and preparation of software, its creators set down their ideas in written forms, which quite obviously do communicate to human beings and may be protected by copyright with no change in the present law.

But the program itself, in its mature and usable form, is a machine control element, a mechanical device, having no purpose beyond being engaged in a computer to perform mechanical work.

The stages of development of a program usually are: a definition, in eye-legible form, of the program's task or function; a description; a listing of the program's steps and/or their expression in flow charts; the translation of these steps into a "source code," often written in a high-level programming language such as FORTRAN or COBOL; the transformation of this source code within the computer, through intervention of a so-called compiler or assembler program, into an "object code." This last is most often physically embodied, in the present state of technology, in punched cards, magnetic disks, magnetic tape, or silicon chips—its mechanical phase.

Every program comes to fruition in its mechanical phase. Every program has but one purpose and use—one object: to control the electrical impulses of a computer in such a particular way as to carry out a prescribed task or operation. In its machine-control form it does not describe or give directions for mechanical work. When activated it does the work.

An argument commonly made in support of the copyrightability of computer programs is that they are just like ordinary printed (and obviously copyrightable) lists of instructions for mechanical work. The Computer Report calls programs "a form of writing [which] consists of sets of instructions." But this metaphor does not hold up beyond a certain point. Descriptions and printed instructions tell human beings how to use materials or machinery to produce desired results. In the case of computer programs, the instructions themselves eventually become an essential part of the machinery that produces the results. They may become (in chip or hardware form) a permanent part of the actual machinery; or they may become interchangeable parts, or tools, insertable and removable from the machine. In whatever material form, the machine-control phase of the program, when activated, enters into the computer's mechanical process. This is a device capable of commanding a series of impulses which open and close the electronic gates of the computer in such order as to produce the desired result.

Printed instructions tell how to do; programs are able to do. The language used to describe and discuss computer programs commonly expresses this latter, active, functional capability, not the preparatory "writing" phases. For example, this Commission's Report on New Works uses the following verbs to characterize the doings of various programs in computers: "select," "arrange," "simulate," "play," "manipulate," "extract," "reproduce," and so on. It is not said that the programs "describe" or "give instructions for" the functions of the computer. They control them. This is the mechanical fact.

The Issue of Communication

The Commission Report on Computer Programs suggests that musical recordings also do work, analogous to what we have been describing. "Both recorded music and computer programs are sets of information in a form which, when passed over a magnetized head, cause minute currents to flow in such a way that desired physical work gets done."

But these are radically different orders of work. And the difference touches on the very essence of copyright.

We take it as a basic principle that copyright should subsist in any original work of authorship that is fixed in any way (including books, records, film, piano rolls, video tapes, etc.) which communicate the work's means of expression.

But a program, once it enters a computer and is activated there, does not communicate information of its own, intelligible to a human being. It utters work. Work is its only utterance and its only purpose. So far as the mode of expression of the original writing is concerned, the matter ends there; it has indeed become irrelevant even before that point. The mature program is purely and simply a mechanical substitute for human labor.

The functions of computer programs are fundamentally and absolutely different in nature from those of sound recordings, motion pictures, or videotapes. Recordings, films, and videotape produce for the human ear and/or eye the sounds and images that were fed into them and so are simply media for transmitting the means of expression of the writings of their authors. The direct product of a sound recording, when it is put in a record player, is the sound of music—the writing of the author in its audible form. Of film, it is a combination of picture and sound—the writing of the author in its visible and audible forms. Of videotape, the same. But the direct product of a computer program is a series of electronic impulses which operate a computer; the "writing" of the author is spent in the labor of the machine. The first three communicate with human beings. The computer program communicates, if at all, only with a machine.

And the nature of the machine that plays the sound recording is fundamentally and absolutely different from that of the machine that uses software. The record player has as its sole purpose the performance of the writing of the author in its audible form. The computer may in some instances serve as a storage and transmission medium for writings (but different writings from those of the computer programmer—i.e., data bases) in their original and entire text, in which cases these writings can be adequately secured at both ends of the transaction by the present copyright law; but in the overwhelming majority of cases its purposes are precisely to use programs to transform, to manipulate, to select, to edit, to search and find, to compile, to control and operate computers and a vast array of other machines and systems—with a result that the preparatory writings of the computer programmer are nowhere to be found in recognizable form, because the program has been fabricated as a machine control element that does these sorts of work. It is obvious that the means of expression of the preparatory writing—that which copyright is supposed to protect—is not to be found in the computer program's mechancial phase.

An appropriate analogy to computer programs, in their capacity to do work when passed over a magnetized head, would be such mechanical devices as the code—magnetized cards which open and close locks or give access to automated bank tellers. These are not copyrightable.

But a more telling analogy, since it speaks to the supposed instructional nature of programs, is afforded by that relatively primitive mechanical device, the cam. A cam, like a mature computer program, is the objectification of a series of instructions: "Up, down, up, down . . . " or, "In, out, in, out . . . ." A cam may be the mechanical fixation of rather intricate and elegant instructions. A cam controlling a drill may embody such instructions as, "Advance rapidly while the hole is shallow, pause and retract for a short distance to clear chips, advance more slowly as the hole goes deeper, stop at a precise point to control the depth of the hole, retract clear of the hole, dwell without motion while the work piece is ejected and another loaded; repeat procedure." (Computer programs can and do embody precisely similar instructions.) But although such a cam was originally conceptualized, described, and written out as this series of instructions for desired work and is, in its mature form, the material embodiment of the instructions, capable of executing them one by one, no one would say (as the Commission now says of another form of "instructions," the mature computer program) that it is a literary work and should be copyrighted.

To support the proposition that programs are works of authorship the Report says that "the instructions that make up a program can be read, understood, and followed by a human being," and that programs "are capable [emphasis theirs] of communicating with humans . . . ." Programmers can and sometimes do read each other's copyrightable preparatory writings, the early phases of software, but the implication of these statements is that programs in their machine form also communicate with human "readers"—an implication that is necessarily hedged by the careful choices of the verbs "could be" and "are capable of"; for if a skilled programmer can "read" a program in its mature, machine-readable form, it is only in the sense that a skilled home-appliance technician can "read" the equally mechanical printed circuits of a television receiver.

It is clear that the machine control phase of a computer program is not designed to be read by anyone; it is designed to do electronic work that substitutes for the very much greater human labor that would be required to get the desired mechanical result. In the revealing words of the Report programs "are used in an almost limitless number of ways to release human beings from . . . diverse mundane tasks . . . ."

The Commission Report thus recommends affording copyright protection to a labor-saving mechanical device.

IS COPYRIGHT PROTECTION NEEDED?

We can agree with a memorandum of the Commission's Software Subcommittee that computer programs "are the result of intellectual endeavors involving at least as much human creativity as the preparation of telephone books or tables of compound interest"—or, we might add (thinking of the mechanical phases of programs), as the design of high-pressure valves for interplanetary rockets or of special parts for racing cars for the Indianapolis 500. The investment in these endeavors, often dazzling in their intricacy and power, does indeed warrant legal protection of the resulting devices.

But is copyright a necessary form of protection? According to the evidence placed before the Commission it is not.

In all the months of its hearings and inquiries, this Commission has not been given a single explicit case of a computer "rip-off" that was not amenable to correction by laws other than copyright. Interestingly, this exactly parallels the experience of the World Intellectual Property Organization (WIPO) in its search for a model form of protection for computer programs. Alastair J. Hirst, attending the WIPO discussions as representative of the International Confederation of Societies of Authors and Composers, noted in an article of June, 1978: [1]

---

1   CISAC document no. CJL/78/45.266, p.2

At no stage in the meetings of the Group was any convincing case ever made out for the proposition that computer software did actually <u>need</u> any additional legal protection; the most the representatives of the computer industry could say was that they "would <u>like</u> some further form of legal protection." No documented instances of piracy were adduced; and there was no serious suggestion that technological progress in the software field had been inhibited by any shortcomings there might be in the legal protection presently available.

CONTU has had precisely the same lack of evidence on this score. A book recently published,[2] describing a large number of computer crimes committed in this country, cites no single piracy or other misappropriation that would have fallen under copyright law. A study of 168 computer crimes by the Stanford Research Institute,[3] made available to the Commission, also failed to turn up any single such case.

It appears that the existing network of technological, contractual, non-disclosure, trade-secret, common-law misappropriation, and (in a few instances) patent forms of protection, possibly to be joined soon by Senator Abraham Ribicoff's Computer System Protection Act[4]—to say nothing of laws on fraud, larceny, breaking and entering, and so on—will be wholly adequate, as they apparently have been up to now, to the needs of developers.

We will discuss below the ways the various forms of protection will likely affect the issue of access versus secrecy.

LEGISLATIVE INTENT AND THE CONSTITUTIONAL BARRIER

"It was clearly the Congress' intent," the Report says "to include computer programs within the scope of copyrightable subject matter in the Act of 1976." This intent was by no means clear. It is true that in several places in the legislative reports there are passing references to computer programs which seem to assume their copyrightability under the 1909 Act and, by extension, the 1976 Act. Prior to these reports, the only authority for considering them potentially copyrightable was the Register of Copyright's letter of May 19, 1964—itself hedged with doubt whether programs were within the category of "writings of an author" in the Constitutional sense. And even these legislative reports contain cautionary language on computer programs, to the effect that they would be copyrightable only "to the extent that they incorporate authorship in the programmer's expression of original ideas, as

---

2 T. Whiteside. *Computer Capers: tales of electronic thievery, embezzlement and fraud* (1978).

3 D. Parker. *Computer Abuse* Stanford Research Institute (1973).

4 S. 1766, 95th Cong., 1st Sess. (1977).

distinguished from the ideas themselves."[5] Section 117 of the new copyright law provided for a moratorium precisely awaiting the conclusions of this Commission, and it indicates beyond a doubt that Congress has not reached the point of clear intention at least with respect to the use of copyrighted works.

The legislative history of the new law can give little comfort to any who would suggest that a thoughtful legislative judgment had been made about the propriety of copyright protection for computer programs. Where the Commission Report finds the legislative history disconcerting, it simply avers, on its own authority, that the House Report "should be regarded as incorrect and should not be followed."

Even if the legislative intent were unmistakable, there would remain the distinct possibility of a Constitutional barrier to the copyrighting of computer programs. It is an underlying principle of copyright law, expressed in Section 102 (b) of the 1976 Act, that copyright does not extend to "any idea, procedure, process, system, method of operation . . . regardless of the form in which it is described, explained . . . or embodied in such work." This section of the statute is intended to recognize the distinction between works conveying descriptions of processes and works which are themselves the embodiment of a system or process. In *Baker v. Selden* (101 U.S. 99 (1879)), the Supreme Court found that, as a matter of Constitutional law, the latter are not protected by copyright.

That decision has been consistently applied to deny copyright to utilitarian works—not those, like phonorecords, which contain expression made perceptible by the use of a machine, but rather those which exist solely to assist a machine to perform its mechanical function. Professor Nimmer, while criticizing some interpretations of the *Baker v. Selden* decision, recognized that it properly bars copyright protection for a work embodying a method of operation when duplicated of necessity in the course of its use.[6] This dissent urges the view (to which Commissioner Nimmer's concurrence seems to lend further weight) that computer programs are exactly the type of work barred from copyright by these considerations.

DISTORTION BY SHOEHORN

We now come to two technical points that arise in the Commission's position on computer programs, matters that we stress here at some length as two examples of the forcible wrenching that is involved in fitting the mature computer program into copyright law—and consequent distortions of traditional copyright usages. It is urged that

5 *House Report,* *Supra* note 1, at 54.
6 1 *Nimmer on Copyright* § 37.2 (1976).

such distortions, with the formidable power of the computer industry behind them, must in the long run tend to corrupt and erode the essential purposes of copyright.

Copies?

In its attempts to justify the copyrighting of mechanical devices—the mature phases of computer programs—the Commission's Software Subcommittee was obliged, at successive stages, to resort to certain euphemisms.

The first draft of its report described the usable, mechanical phases of computer programs as "derivative works"—a term traditionally used, with respect to the printed word, for condensations, dramatizations, translations, and so on (each of which has always had to be copyrighted separately from the parental work). When the invalidity of this suggestion became evident, the second draft of the Report characterized the programs in their usable machine forms, equally with their written forms, as "literary works." When the difficulty in maintaining that the mechanical commands on punched cards, magnetic tapes, disks, and printed circuits in chips were identical with programs' preparatory writings had been considered, the third draft of the Report brought yet another shift of terms. The mechanical phases of programs were now described as "copies."

On several grounds this euphemism proves as unserviceable as the previous ones. (And so, in this view, will every euphemism that attempts to justify the copyrighting of a machine control element.)

"Copies," for the control of which the rights vested in copyright were devised, are defined in the 1976 Act as:

> material objects, other than phonorecords, in which a work is fixed by any method now known or later developed, and from which the work can be perceived, reproduced, or otherwise communicated, either directly or with the aid of a machine or device.[7]

This definition has always referred to one form or another of reproduction of an original work, for the purpose of dissemination to, and perception by, human beings. In plain language: books, monographs, films, prints, and other such replications we all recognize as copies in the true copyright sense. Their uses always involved perception by one human sense or another of the linguistic intentions, the images, or the sounds of the original works. A data base, when keyed or run into a computer, is being copied in this sense, for the data are maintained in the copy as data, and they issue as data for human

---

7 17 U.S.C. § 101.

use in the end product. But a program, when keyed or run into a computer, is transformed by a compiler program into a purely machine state. The term "copy" is meaningless for the reason that in this transformation the means of expression of the original work becomes totally irrelevant. All that matters is the program's functional use.

Furthermore, many programs (in fact, a greater and greater proportion of commercial programs) never are "input" into computers in the conventional sense. They are distributed already transformed into their purely mechanical form, as printed circuits on chips in microprocessors. They are, in all but name, hardware. They are no more copies in the copyright sense than are repeatedly stamped-out solid-state circuits of television sets. These programs in microprocessors are built into, or can be clipped into, automobiles, airplanes, telephone and television sets, microwave ovens, games, and an ever-growing number of industrial and home gadgets. How can this vast class of machine control elements ever be considered "copies" of "literary works"?

We are dealing here with an entirely new technology, one with a highly intricate multiplicity of means of fixation, of transformation, of movement from one medium (of communication) to another (of mechanical function) and back again. The fact that some of these many intricate fixations and changes enable a human-readable version of a program to be stored in a computer parallel to its mechanical variant, or to be reconverted to eye-readable form from its mechanical variant, does not mend at all the basic distortion that arises from this abuse of the term "copies."

In discussing "copies," the Commission Report admits the central difficulty to which this dissent addresses itself:

> [T]he many ways in which programs are now used and the new applications which advancing technology will supply may make drawing the line of demarcation [between the copyrightable form of a program and the uncopyrightable process which it implements] more and more difficult. To attempt to establish such a line in this Report written in 1978 would be futile. Most infringements, at least in the immediate future, are likely to involve simple copying. In the event that future technology permits programs to be stated orally for direct input to a computer through auditory sensing devices or permits future infringers to use an author's program without copying, difficult questions will arise.

It is the thesis of this dissent that all such difficulties, present and future, disappear if the euphemism in the work "copies" is recognized for what it is, and if a clear line is drawn forthwith. The line can and should be drawn in 1978. The line should be drawn at the moment of the program's transformation, by whatever present or future technique, to a mechanical capability. This is the moment at which the program ceases to communicate with human beings and is made capable of communicating with machines.

Here is dramatized, in our view, the central flaw—and the subtle dehumanizing danger—of the Commission's position on programs. To call a machine control element a copy of a literary work flies in the face of common sense. Ask any citizen in the street whether a printed circuit in a microprocessor in the emission control of his or her car is a copy of a literary work, and see what answer you get. But if our government tells the citizens in the street that this is so, and makes it law, what then happens to the citizen's sense of distinction between works that speak to the minds and senses of men and women and works that run machines—or, ultimately, the citizen's sense of the saving distinction between human beings themselves and machines themselves?

Adaptations

A particularly serious blurring of valid traditional distinctions lies in the Report's extension of copyright protection to adaptations of programs. There is not merely a question here of unfairness to all other sorts of adaptations, which must be re-copyrighted (as in the case, for example, of a telephone directory, which is annually adapted—and must be re-copyrighted each year). What is shocking, in its transparency, is the reason given by the Report for authorizing these adaptations—"to facilitate use."

The transparency lies in the fact that the means of expression of the original program—the only thing in which copyright is reposed—is here again totally irrelevant. The only test the user is required to meet is whether the machine phase of the program, having been adapted, will then work. And what will make it work is certainly not its means of expression but its mechanical idea, which remains constant however expressed.

In his testimony before CONTU in Cambridge, Mass., on November 17, 1977, Professor J.C.R. Licklider of M.I.T. raised as one of his concerns about the idea of copyrighting the mechanical phases of programs precisely this matter of adaptation.[8] He gave the example in which a protracted program may be taken from "machine language, or FORTRAN, or whatever level . . . to a higher level and back to a lower level," and stressed that all that survives from one version to the other is "the essential underlying idea, not the mode, not the form of expression."

---

8 *See Transcript CONTU Meeting No. 18* at 130-132.

In the present reality of computer usage, particularly in sophisticated operations, a great deal of programming ingenuity goes precisely into various kinds of adaptation, commonly called "program maintenance": new mechanical functions may be added to an existing program; a program may be modified, possibly extensively, to make it workable in a different or more up-to-date computer; or a program may be changed to mesh with other programs in a complex multi-processor. Under these and many other circumstances, the protection would remain in effect for an underlying idea that was itself being adapted, or perhaps even being transformed into something quite different from the original idea. The mode of expression of the original writing would be long, long gone. As Professor Licklider pointed out, only the "effect of the action of the program" is of consequence in a series of such changes; programmers, he said, "don't care a thing for the particulars of the expression."[9]

The limitations on adaptations suggested in the Commission Report will, in the real world of program maintenance, be unthinkably difficult to police.

By the admission of this word, "adaptation," in this new sense, with no means test except workability, the Commission has bypassed a fundamental distinction of copyright from other forms of protection, and may well have opened the way for covert protection, in the name of copyright, of the underlying mechanical idea or ideas of a program, rather than of its original means of expression.

SOCIAL EFFECTS

Access

The Commission Report has based much of its case on its conclusion that copyright would assure greater public access to innovative programs than would continued reliance on trade-secrecy law.

The evidence the Commission has received casts considerable doubt on this argument.

In the first place, the testimony CONTU has heard makes it quite clear that the industry would have no intention of giving up trade-secrecy protection in favor of copyright; to the contrary, every indication is that it would fight hard to assert its undeniable continuing right to the former.

It is obvious that the industry, faced with a choice between secrecy and dissemination, as represented in the choice between trade-secrecy laws and copyright, has overwhelmingly opted for the former. From 1964, when the Register first received programs for registration, to

---

9 *Id* at 131.

January 1, 1977, only 1205 programs have been registered (and two companies, IBM and Burroughs, accounted for 971 of them). According to International Computer Programs, Inc., which publishes a newsletter on the programming industry, something in the order of 1,000,000 programs are developed each year (taking into account adaptations of existing programs so radical as to make them new programs). There are roughly 300,000 programmers in the United States who spend at least part of their time developing new programs. These figures show how miniscule has been the industry's interest in copyright, and they strongly suggest that such registration as has taken place has been in the nature of bet-hedging, reflecting efforts of major hardware manufacturers to assert any possible colorable claim to protection, regardless of its real legal merits.

The Commission Report recognizes that "the availability of copyright for computer programs does not, of course, affect the availability of trade secrecy protection." It suggests leaving all future "difficult questions" for settlement by the courts on a case-by-case basis.

The uncertainty resulting from this situation, as Robert O. Nimtz of the Bell Laboratories has pointed out in a response to the Commission's Draft Report, "would have the unfortunate consequence of driving computer program owners into even deeper secrecy"—by encryption, physical barriers to access, contractual restraints, nondisclosure agreements, and further innovative technical tricks for locking out pirates, thieves, and competitors. "Secrecy will be seen as the only effective protection for their creations."[10] Such being the case, public access to innovative programs would likely be inhibited rather than eased by the addition of the copyright solution to those that already exist and that would continue to exist.

Indeed, it is evident that, with eased requirements for deposit and disclosure, copyright itself would be used as one more device to prevent, rather than enable, access to innovative programs—one more device of industrial security. The entitlement of copyright protection to "adaptations" of programs might, under these circumstances, even further inhibit access, insofar as it provided owners with a covert means of protecting the underlying ideas of their program. And the lengthy term of 75 years for corporate ownership of copyright would be a negative balance, at the very least, against the presumed "thinness" of the protection.

Economic Costs

All of this, rather than reducing the transaction costs of using and protecting programs, as the Commission argues, would in fact raise the

---

10 Nimtz Comment, letter to CONTU, August30, 1977, at 9.

costs—for producers, transacting copyright while spending more and more money looking harder than ever for new and surer forms of secrecy; for users, to whom the added costs of this search and its found devices would be passed along in higher prices; and for the tax-paying public, which would have to bear the costs of the added burdens of the Copyright Office and the courts.

A more likely prospect for the reduction of money costs would lie in the exclusion of usable computer programs from copyright. This would eliminate or diminish the uncertainty as to legal protection available for computer programs. All questions of the Constitutionality of such protection would become moot; some of the guesswork which would otherwise have colored all business planning for securing software would be voided.

An additional consideration would be the easing of the administrative burden on the Copyright Office. The Office, already monstrously overloaded by administration and regulation of the new law, is presently unsuited for making evaluations of computer programs which might be registered for copyright. Eliminating this responsibility would save a public expenditure and place the costs of commercial protection on those enterprises seeking its benefits.

Concentration of Economic Power

While it has always been the case that corporate entities could be copyright proprietors, the picture CONTU has been given, when rights in computer programs are concerned, is that the proprietor is almost invariably corporate. If there is an individual "author," it will be an author for hire, whose creativity is in strict harness and whose property rights are nonexistent.

The sheer bigness of the corporate enterprise in computers is staggering. According to testimony by Peter McCloskey, President of Computer and Business Equipment Manufacturers' Association (CBEMA), the combined revenues of the 42 members of that association of manufacturers of computers and related business equipment rose in 1976 to 32.7 billion dollars; as to software, we heard at one point an estimate of 17 billion dollars of production in the next three years.[11] The art is growing and changing with blinding speed. In his testimony Ralph Gommery of IBM suggested, with perhaps a pinch of hyperbole, that if the automobile industry had progressed on the same curve as computers in the last 15 years, we would now have been able to buy for $20 a self-steering car that would attain speeds up to 400 m.p.h. and be able to drive the length of California on one gallon of gasoline.

---

11 *Transcript CONTU Meeting No. 6* at 11.

In a study funded by this Commission, Harbridge House concluded that the availability of copyright protection for computer software is "of monumental insignificance to the industry."[12] It is important for us to bear in mind that the universe of this study consisted almost entirely of smallish, independent corporate producers. The two trade associations that were most active in pressing their views on this Commission, the above-mentioned CBEMA and the Information Industry Association, represent primarily major industrial corporations. The Association of Data Processing Service Organizations, which more than any other trade association represents independent computer program producers, was conspicuously absent from Commission appearances and limited its participation to a written response in support of the Software Subcommittee's recommendations. Such perfunctory participation certainly tends to support the Harbridge House view as to the interest of the independents.

On this point, the WIPO experience strikingly parallels CONTU's. Alastair J. Hirst writes that a one-sided approach in the WIPO search:

> was more or less inevitable, given the composition of the Group. It is important to distinguish between the names shown on the list of participating organizations, and the individuals who were most active in directing and moulding the discussion as it proceeded. Of the latter, the most frequent and the best informed grouping was that composed of patent agents and lawyers in the employ of the large computer companies such as ICL and IBM. Even amongst those representing the computer industry, there was a singular lack of representation from the smaller independent software houses, who were intended to be the chief beneficiaries of the new software right: those who had the most influence on the discussions were in fact the representatives of the large companies who are in many ways the economic adversaries of these intended beneficiaries.[13]

Congress is urged to take careful note of this difference. Why do the large industrial corporations press for copyright, while it seems to be a matter of much less concern to the small independents? Is it not evident, from testimony CONTU received, that the big companies want, by availing themselves of every possible form of protection, to lock their software into their own hardware, while the independents want to be able to sell their programs for use in all the major lines of hardware?

Thus a warning appears to be in order that the copyrighting of the machine phases of programs would be likely to strengthen the position

---

12 *Legal Protection of Computer Software: An Industrial Survey* Harbridge House (1977) iii.
13 *Supra* note 148.

of the large firms, to reinforce the oligopoly of these dominant companies, and to inhibit competition from and among small independents.

The country has lately seen an alarming trend toward the concentration of economic power in all the communications industries. One company dominates telephonic communication. One company (IBM) dominates the computer hardware field, while three others (Burroughs, Honeywell and Sperry-Univac) join with IBM to manufacture over 85% of large-scale computers. One company (Xerox) dominates photocopying, and again three other companies (IBM, Kodak and 3M) outstrip all others. Three networks dominate television. There are now but six major film distributors. Paperback publishing has become the backbone of the book industry, and there are now but seven leading paperback lines. Industrial conglomerates are buying up these communications leaders horizontally: e.g., Gulf and Western owns both Paramount Pictures and Simon and Schuster, which in turn owns Pocket Books.

If there are social benefits to our nation, as we have always believed, in pluralism, in diversity, in lively competition in the marketplace, and in the rights of the individual to maximum freedom of choice within the limits of the social contract, and above all to maximum freedom of speech, then this increasing concentration of corporate power in that most sensitive area in a democracy—the area of communication from one human being to another, from leaders to citizens and vice versa—should surely be a matter of greatest concern.

COMMUNICATION—HUMAN AND MECHANICAL

The aim of all writing, be it for art or use, is communication. Up to this time, as we have seen, copyright has always protected the means of expression of various forms of "writing" which were perceived, in every case, by the human sense for which they were intended: written words by the human eye, music by the ear, paintings by the eye, and so on. Here, for the first time, the protection of copyright would be offered to a "communication" with a machine.

This pollution of copyrighted "writings" with units of mechanical work would affect not only creators but also the general public. Placed beside such traditional end products as books, plays, motion pictures, television shows, dance, and music, under the aegis of copyright, what end products of computer programs would we find?

The overwhelming majority of program applications are mechanical and industrial: the monitoring of an assembly line in a factory; microprocessors in an automobile; the aiming device of a weapons system; the coordination of approach patterns at an airport. An entire branch of the program industry is devoted to systems software—new techniques for more efficient uses of machines, for more efficient industrial processing.

Progress is progress, and we can guess that we must have all these products of human ingenuity to keep one jump ahead of entropy. It can reasonably be argued, as the Commission Report does, that they reduce the load of human labor. But a definite danger to the quality of life must come with a blurring and merging of human and mechanical communication.

As one step in its education, this Commission has had the benefit of a book written by one of our witnesses, Professor Joseph Weizenbaum of M.I.T., entitled *Computer Power and Human Reason*—a work which is both intricately technical and profoundly humanistic. Something that Professor Weizenbaum keeps emphasizing over and over again is the extent to which computer scientists, especially those who have worked on so-called artificial intelligence—"and large segments of the general public as well"—have come to accept the propositions "that men and computers are merely two different species or a more abstract genus called 'information processing systems,'" that reason is nothing more than logic, and "that life is what is computable and only that."

A society that accepts in any degree such equivalences of human beings and machines must become impoverished in the long run in those aspects of the human spirit which can never be fully quantified, and which machines may be able in some distant future to linguistically "understand" but will never be able to experience, never be able to bring to life, never be able therefore to communicate: courage, love, integrity, trust, the touch of flesh, the fire of intuition, the yearning and aspirations of what poets so vaguely but so persistently call the soul—that bundle of qualities we think of as being embraced by the word humanity.

This concern is by no means irrelevant to the issue of whether computer programs should be copyrighted. It is the heart of the matter.

RECOMMENDATION

The logical conclusion of this dissent, then, is a recommendation to Congress that:

> The Act of 1976 should be amended to make it explicit that copyright protection does not extend to a computer program in the form in which it is capable of being used to control computer operations.

Congress could obtain any technical advice necessary to assist it in reaching an appropriate definition of the cutoff point, the point at which a program ceases being a copyrightable writing and becomes an uncopyrightable mechanical device.

In our discussions, several possibilities have presented themselves:
(1) the moment of transformation from "source" to "object" program;
(2) the moment of input into a computer or microprocessor; or (3) at
the point where a program goes from "natural language," which any
expert reader can at once grasp, to higher-level, formal computer
language—this last deriving from Professor Weizenbaum, who writes "A
higher-level formal language is an abstract machine." With rapidly
advancing technology, natural language does in some programs already
reach to the very moment of entry into the computer. In every case,
however, Professor Weizenbaum makes clear, a transformation to a
machine state takes place, with a result that when the program is run,
communication as we understand it ceases and what he calls
"behavior"—an opening and closing of electronic gates—sets in. Where
his book is most eloquent, for our purposes, is in its powerful warning
of our loss of humanity if we come to believe, as many already do, that
anything like human communication is still taking place, or ever can
take place, after this mechanical stage has set in.

Congress should weigh most carefully the heavy responsibility of
breaking with tradition and enabling, by law of the land, for the first
time ever, copyright protection for communication, not with our fellow
human beings, but with machines—thus equating machines with human
beings as the intended recipients of the distribution that copyright was
designed to foster.

Surely it is especially vital, in a time of hurtling and insatiable
technology, that the nation's laws reflect, whenever possible, a
distinction between the realm and responsibility of human beings and
the realm and responsibility attributed to machines.

MODEL PROVISIONS ON THE PROTECTION
OF COMPUTER SOFTWARE*

INTRODUCTION

A) History of the Model Provisions

1. The Model Provisions on the Protection of Computer Software contained hereunder (referred to as "the model provisions") are the result of
six years' work carried out by the International Bureau of WIPO with the
assistance of experts.

2. In 1971, an Advisory Group of Governmental Experts on the Protection of Computer Programs met to advise the International Bureau on the
steps to be taken in order to prepare a study, requested by the United
Nations,[1] on the appropriate form of legal protection for computer programs
and on the possibilities in the field of international arrangements, with a
view to facilitating the access of developing countries to information on
computer software. This study was continued by the International Bureau
with the help of an Advisory Group of Non-Governmental Experts on the Protection of Computer Programs, which met in 1974, 1975, 1976 and 1977.

3. Before and during the elaboration of the model provisions, the
following questions were also discussed by the Advisory Group:

   (a) the need for special legal protection for computer programs
   and their related documentation (such programs and documentation are
   covered by the term "computer software"); and

   (b) the desirability that any system of legal protection should
   incorporate a system for the registration or deposit of computer software or for the compliance with other formalities.

The results of the discussions on these two questions are outlined below
(see paragraphs 5 to 8 and 9 to 21, respectively).

4. Moreover, the Advisory Group considered, in its 1976 session, the
question of an international treaty for the protection of computer software. Such a treaty could provide for a minimum level of protection for

* Prepared by the International Bureau of the World Intellectual
Property Organization, Geneva 1978.

[1] See the Report of the United Nations Secretary-General on the Application of Computer Technology for Development (UN document E/4800 of May
20, 1970), paragraph 202 in particular.

SOURCE: Reprinted from *Law and Computer Technology.* 11: 2-27 (1978) by
permission of the copyright holder. Copyright © 1978 by the World Peace Through
Law Center.

computer software and a system of recognition of the effects of an international registration or deposit of computer software by the Contracting States. Whereas the latter aspect of a possible treaty would depend on the establishment of registration or deposit systems on the national level (see hereinafter paragraphs 9 to 21), an obligation to provide for minimum protection presupposes that legal decisions on the protection to be granted on the national level have stabilized to some extent, an effect which could be achieved through the adoption of the present model provisions.

B) Need for Special Legal Protection

5. Before adopting or amending its legislation so as to provide special protection for proprietors and users of computer software, each country will almost certainly consider two basic questions: Is computer software in need of legal protection? Are the various forms of protection that are already available under its law insufficient?

6. Legal protection of computer software is desirable for the following reasons:

(a) Investment and time required. The investment in computer software is large: under a recent estimate, based on the number of computers currently in use, and the past and expected increase in that number, together with estimates of the staff employed on programming activities and the cost of software, it is possible that a sum of the order of 13 billion US dollars is spent annually on the creation and maintenance of software systems.[2] Although this must vary considerably, the time required for the planning and preparation of computer programs is long, often amounting to many man-months of total effort. The need for legal protection of computer programs should be seen not only in terms of the large-scale investment in computer software but also from the viewpoint of the small software enterprise or individual creator of software. The existence of strong legal protection would encourage the dissemination of their creations and enable such creators to avoid duplication of work. Without such dissemination, numerous programmers may spend considerable time and effort in order to accomplish, in parallel work, the same objective; although the programs created by them may be different, any one of those programs would probably fully accomplish the said objective. In any case, legal protection will encourage exploitation of software for purposes other than internal use.

(b) Likely future developments. Already, software is estimated to account for by far the greater part of the total cost of computer systems. The proportions of 70% and 30% representing the expenditure on software and hardware, respectively, would seem to be a reasonable estimate. In any case it can be expected that the software elements will, in the future, account for a substantial, if not a predominant, proportion of the expenditure and that the total expenditure on computer software will constantly increase. At present, the largest amount of expenditure on computer software seems to be devoted to

---

2 Estimate quoted in the (United Kingdom) Report of the Whitford Committee on Copyright and Designs Law (1977 -- London, Her Majesty's Stationery Office, Cmnd 6732), paragraph 477.

the creation and maintenance of specific purpose user programs, not of general applicability; since such programs are not of direct interest to third parties, their misappropriation is relatively unlikely in view of the adaptation required. However, there is a trend towards the creation of computer programs that are of interest to more than one user or even of general and widespread utility and thus can help to save expenditures; such a trend towards standardized user software is likely to increase as computers become more accessible to the public and easier to operate and as the proportion of the cost of the hardware components in computer operations decreases. In the context of the increasing accessibility of computer software, reference should be made to two important developments: the creation of computer networks among nations aided by sophisticated telecommunications systems (a trend which highlights the need for international protection), and the move towards new programming techniques facilitating the use of computers by persons other than trained programmers.

(c) Protection as an incentive to disclosure. The importance of ensuring the ready accessibility of the important form of modern technology represented by computer software has been referred to on many occasions, particularly in the context of the needs of developing countries (see, for example, the Report of the UN Secretary-General mentioned in footnote 1, above). Although some computer programs would not be made publicly available in any event (for example, programs revealing a trade secret of an enterprise or those designed to complement computer hardware and transferred only with the corresponding computer), it is reasonable to suppose that many proprietors of the rights in other programs would at present rely primarily on secrecy either in order to exclude all others from using the software or to permit only selected persons to use it under a confidential disclosure contract. Where effective legal protection is available, the proprietors of rights could instead rely on that protection and disclose the software.

(d) Protection as a basis for trade. The lack of legal protection may be particularly harmful in the context of trade. Both the seller and the buyer of computer software are interested in legal protection because it increases the legal security of their relationship. A system of protection would also be of advantage to developing countries; such a system would encourage dissemination of software to those countries, not only because the publication of the software would not defeat protection but also the protection would eliminate the uncertainty of enforcing a confidential disclosure contract. Also, legal protection would enable dissemination on favorable terms in some cases; for example, the proprietor of the rights in computer software might be encouraged to license it in a developing country at an especially low royalty if he could be sure of being able to take action against users in other countries if his software were accidentally disclosed by the licensee in the developing country. Moreover, the greater disclosure in the advertisement of software which, it is hoped, will result from legal protection may help such countries to evaluate the alternatives on the international market.

(e) Vulnerability of computer software. Consideration should also be given to the vulnerability of some forms of computer software; for instance, a "computer software package," consisting of a computer program and related descriptive and explanatory documentation, is expensive to prepare and easy to copy as soon as the prototype is available.

7. It may be that computer software can, in a few countries, be adequately protected without any change in existing laws. But, due to the newness of computer technology and the consequent scarcity of judicial decisions, and to disagreement among legal experts, there is a considerable state of uncertainty in this field. Two forms of legal protection may be specifically directed to the results of the intellectual creativity in computer software: they are <u>patent protection</u> and <u>copyright protection</u>. In addition, there are other branches of law which can provide means for protecting computer software, especially where it constitutes a trade secret.

(a) <u>Patent protection</u>. The patent would seem to be an appropriate form of legal protection of computer software since it covers new and inventive technical solutions. It can thus apply to programs embodying the same concept as a patented program, but in a completely different form; it can also be relied on to prevent others using the same program in a computer. However, in many countries computer programs and other items of computer software, in particular algorithms, cannot be regarded as patentable inventions; the European Patent Convention, for example, contains an express provision to that effect (Article 52(2)(c)). In some countries, a computer program would seem to be at least indirectly protectable by, for example, a patent granted for a computer programmed in a new way or for a process relating to the use of a program as a means of operating a computer in a new manner or as a means of control in the manufacture of articles. In most countries the question of patentability cannot be answered with any degree of certainty. Moreover, even if patent protection were generally available, it would probably cover only a minute proportion of computer programs since it is considered that only in very few cases (perhaps 1%) would a program have sufficient inventiveness to satisfy the requirements of patent law, although a large amount of time, effort and resources may have been devoted to its creation. There are also serious practical difficulties to be taken into account: difficulties in conducting the examination relating to the novelty and inventiveness of a computer program, in establishing the documentation on the prior art and in finding qualified examiners. One further difficulty is that, under patent procedures, any person has access to a full disclosure of the invention enabling a person skilled in the art to make the patented product or use the patented process; in view of the relative difficulty of detecting misappropriations of a computer program, it could be argued that such an unrestricted disclosure to the public is not desirable; and yet, to make an exception in the case of computer programs might prejudice a fundamental principle of patent law: disclosure to the public.

(b) <u>Copyright protection</u>. Whereas patent law protects the technical idea underlying an invention, copyright law focusses on protecting the form in which ideas are expressed, although protection is not limited to that form. Thus, copyright protection would seem to be particularly appropriate for computer software as a whole (and not merely computer programs) since a large amount of computer software consists of descriptive or explanatory matter; even a computer program (consisting, for example, of magnetic tape) is a form of expression -- of the ideas contained in the software leading up to the program. In most cases the intellectual creativity in computer software resides in the skill and effort used to make those ideas "understandable" to a computer, as economically and as effectively as possible. However, although some kinds of computer software (especially those in verbal form) are clearly protectable under copyright laws, experts disagree on whether other kinds (particularly a computer program, on magnetic tape for example) can be considered a literary, artistic or scientific work, which are the traditional subjects of copyright protection. Moreover, such protection may be of very limited value since it essentially covers only copying (or related acts such as translation or adaptation); thus, in itself, the use of a program to operate a computer cannot be prevented by copyright law (just as the making of a cake cannot be an infringement of the copyright in the recipe). It is essential that use in a computer should be covered by the rights in computer software; it is, in fact, possible that copyright law can provide a remedy in this case since it is probable that the use of a program always involves its copying in the computer memory, but the courts may not regard such internal reproduction as sufficient for the purposes of copyright law. The model provisions essentially adopt a copyright law approach which takes account of their subject matter's affinity with copyright protection and overcomes the possible limitations indicated above.

(c) Other forms of protection. The laws of certain countries provide a number of means of preventing the unauthorized disclosure or use of secret information. There are a number of laws which directly penalize or provide civil law remedies against the misappropriation of a trade secret or of information obtained in breach of confidence. A common means of protecting information concerning computer software, which is provided by all laws, is by contract. Even in the absence of an express term in a contract, persons in a fiduciary relationship with a computer enterprise, such as its employees, can be prevented from disclosing secret information. Secret information can also be indirectly protected by certain provisions in criminal law, by general provisions in civil codes or by certain actions in the law of torts. Even in the absence of secrecy, the misappropriation of computer programs may, in certain circumstances, be actionable in the context of unfair competition law. However, even in countries where trade secrets can be protected directly, there is uncertainty or differences as to the scope of protection and as to the conditions (for example, whether disclosure to a licensee or to a restricted number of other third parties would prejudice the secrecy of the know-how protected). The disadvantage of protection under contract law is that in most cases it will be difficult to prevent persons outside the contractual relationship from disclosing or using a program. Moreover, one of the advantages of the establishment of clear and adequate legal protection for computer software is to encourage greater disclosure of information on computer software which would otherwise be vulnerable to misappropriation. The aim of such protection is therefore precisely to avoid any necessity to rely on secrecy and on laws and legal measures safeguarding secrecy.

8. In conclusion, it can be said that computers are becoming more and more important in the fields of science, technology and commerce and other spheres of human activity; computer software accounts for the greater part of investment in computer technology and its creation requires a high degree of intellectual effort. It would therefore seem to need and deserve a guarantee of legal protection, which should encourage investment and trade in computer software and promote its wider accessibility. However, there is at present a state of uncertainty as to the protection of computer software under various legal systems. The purpose of the model provisions is to eliminate that uncertainty.

C) Deposit of Computer Software

9. The model provisions do not make the protection of computer software dependent upon its deposit or registration with a national authority or upon compliance with other formalities, such as the marking of the computer software. Countries interested in the model provisions might like to consider the desirability of including in their laws a mandatory provision of the kind indicated or of at least providing for an optional system for the deposit or registration of computer software. The arguments for and against such a mandatory system are outlined below, followed by those for and against an optional system.

10. The basic argument in favor of a mandatory system of deposit is that, in return for the special protection accorded, the proprietor of the rights in computer software should be obliged to deposit the software. Such a requirement would ensure the eventual disclosure of the software to the public with the consequent advancement of the art. It would also enable third parties to direct their efforts to creating computer software in new fields. Moreover, the deposit would promote the dissemination of computer software, facilitate its sale or licensing and increase certainty concerning the object of protection in each case, which would otherwise be difficult to define. These arguments apply to some extent also to the less strict requirement for the registration of computer software, under which the proprietor would simply have to provide particulars of the computer software, together with an abstract of it, which would be disclosed to the public.

11. A further argument in favor of a mandatory system of deposit or registration is that the proprietor should give notice to the public that a certain item of software is protected as well as an indication of when the term of protection expires, a date that is not easily ascertainable due to the fact that computer software is not normally published. In this connection, a number of experts feel that computer software, including additions updating a computer program, should at least be marked with an indication of the name of the proprietor of the rights and the date of their expiration.

12. The requirement of adequate disclosure to the public in return for the rights granted by the State is a fundamental obligation under patent law. Supporters of the basic argument, outlined in the first sentence of paragraph 10, above, are thus adopting a patent law approach. If such an approach is adopted, it is reasonable that it should apply to the system of legal protection of computer software as a whole, in particular to the rights granted under the law. However, for the reasons indicated in paragraph 7 (a) and (b), above, the model provisions are essentially based on a copyright law approach; the rights granted are consequently less extensive than those of a patentee: they do not protect the concepts underlying computer software and cannot prevent a person from independently creating the same computer software and using it. The primary purpose of the protection granted is not to allow proprietors to profit from a period of exclusive rights as a reward for the creation and disclosure of computer software, but simply to encourage creation and dissemination of computer software and to prevent the misappropriation of the results of another's valuable work, thus introducing legal security which should both facilitate trade in computer software and encourage proprietors to make it more generally available.

13. The advantages of a mandatory deposit system have also been questioned. Countries adopting it would have the difficult task of devising and administering a system for the classification and indexing of computer software; otherwise, in view of the vast amount of computer software created each year, the advantages of disclosure and notice to the public would be nugatory. Such a system would be facilitated if it were established at the international level. Furthermore, in order to fully achieve its purposes, a deposit system would have to provide for a time limit after which the depositor could no longer prevent disclosure of the software to the public. The fixing of such a time limit may, however, give rise to problems: if, taking into account the vulnerability of the proprietor's position in the case of complete disclosure, the time limit is fixed in a way that allows for a period of substantial secrecy, the advantages of disclosure for the public would be reduced or even eliminated.

14. With regard to a requirement for compliance with formalities in general, a number of disadvantages have been referred to. It has been stated that compulsory formalities would not be in the interest of the small software enterprises or individual users, who might be unaware of the need to comply with them; they might also render the system of protection unattractive since some people would seem to be in favor of such a system but opposed to deposit. A mandatory deposit might even have a discouraging effect on creators if they have to make a full disclosure of their creations. In view of the copyright law approach that has been adopted, it is above all logical that the protection provided by the model provisions should not be made dependent in any way (as far as either the existence or its enforcement before the courts is concerned) upon compliance with formalities, since there is no such requirement under the copyright laws of the majority of countries. On the other hand, if the copyright law of a country adopting the model provisions does contain a requirement for the deposit and/or marking of protected works, such a country would presumably include the same requirement in any law based on the model provisions. Moreover, any formalities would create problems in view of the fact that computer programs -- and even commercialized standard software -- are frequently updated.

15. In conclusion, it is suggested that countries considering the question discussed above should first decide the basic approach to the system of protection to be established. If a patent law approach were adopted, it would be logical for a requirement for compliance with formalities to be included in legislation based on the model provisions, which, as a whole, would have to be examined in the light of such an approach. If the principle of the model provisions (copyright law approach) were adopted: countries whose copyright law contains no requirement for compliance with formalities would have to consider, on the balance of convenience, whether and to what extent such a requirement should be introduced for forms of computer software that are not protected by copyright; other countries would presumably adopt the same solution as that contained in their copyright law.

16. Some of the arguments outlined above also apply to the question whether a system of optional deposit of computer software should be adopted. Under one possible system that has been discussed, the proprietor of the rights in computer software would be able to deposit with a national authority a computer program and/or any or all the documentation constituting software and relating to the program. Within that optional deposit system there would be a registration system which would be mandatory in the sense

that, if a deposit were made, a certain amount of information would have to be furnished for the purpose of publication; one of the most important requirements in this connection would be the furnishing of an abstract of the computer program which had been deposited or, if it had not been deposited, to which the deposited software related. To the extent that they had not been subjected to secrecy by the depositor, the contents of deposits would be accessible to the public. The deposit would not confer any legal rights but merely certain presumptions as to the time of the creation of the software.

17. An optional deposit system of the kind referred to would have three main purposes:

(1) to enable the public to have direct access to non-secret computer software;

(2) to provide the depositor with evidence of the prior existence of this computer software;

(3) through publication of an abstract of the computer software, to enable the public to know the kind of software available.

18. Doubts have been expressed, however, as to whether the first-mentioned purpose could be achieved through a deposit system of the kind indicated. It might be impracticable to require the deposit of computer programs in machine-readable form, and would be impossible for a depositary authority to provide copies of such programs unless it had a wide range of machinery for doing so, and it might not, in any event, be desirable that the public should be given copies of programs in machine-readable form (even if they are not secret) owing to the danger of infringement of the rights in the program; the deposit would be of limited value if only hard copies of the program or its related software were available to the public. Moreover, the public could never be sure that a computer program had not been updated since its deposit; thus, potential users would in any event have an interest in directly establishing contact with the depositor. Doubts have also been expressed concerning the second purpose mentioned in the preceding paragraph; the same evidential advantages could perhaps be achieved through the deposit of the computer software elsewhere, with a notary public for instance. If all that remains is the third purpose mentioned, this could be achieved through the simpler registration system (see paragraph 20, below).

19. It has been suggested that a full deposit system could be more meaningful if it were made more attractive to potential depositors by the enhancement of advantages to them, for example by the grant of a longer term of protection to deposited software. In addition, the question could be considered of providing for an international priority right to be based on deposit. However, it should be borne in mind that too great incentives for deposit would have the same effect as making deposit compulsory, a question that has been discussed above.

20. Some of the advantages mentioned above could be obtained through an optional registration system without any legal effects; the information registered could include an abstract of the computer program, the machines on which it could be used and the languages, possibly the price and other terms for the use of the software and possibly also the date of expiration of the protection.

21. The usefulness of an optional deposit or registration system would have to be examined in the context of the needs of software producers and users, and of the services already existing in that field. Any such system having no legal effects would probably have to be considered outside the framework of a system of legal protection of computer software.

D) Purpose and Structure of the Model Provisions

22. The purpose of the model provisions is to assist countries in complementing, or introducing certainty into, their laws applicable to the protection of computer software. They endeavor to regulate their subject matter in as complete a way as possible so that they could form the basis of a special law on the protection of computer software; they would of course have to be adapted to the legal system of the country adopting them and supplemented with the usual provisions in its legislation (transitional provisions and entry into force, for example).

23. At the same time, the model provisions should not be understood as necessarily requiring adoption in a separate law on the protection of computer software. In many countries, the principles contained in the model provisions may simply amount to clarifications or extensions of existing legal rules and could be incorporated -- in so far as they are not already included -- in existing laws, for example partly in the copyright law and partly in the law on trade secrets or unfair competition. Even in such a case, the complete presentation in the model provisions has the advantage that it draws attention to the various problems which may exist under particular national systems and indicates possible solutions to those problems.

24. The structure of the model provisions is as follows:

Section 1 defines the protected subject matter ("computer program," "program description," "supporting material" and "computer software," the latter consisting of one or more of the first-mentioned items) and the term "proprietor."

Section 2 deals with the question to whom the rights in respect of computer software belong, in particular in the case where computer software has been created by an employee; moreover, Section 2 regulates the transfer and devolution of rights in respect of computer software.

Section 3 defines the requirement of originality of computer software.

Section 4 makes clear that concepts (as opposed to the form in which they are expressed) are outside the protection of the Law.

Section 5 lists the acts covered by the rights of the proprietor; the list can be divided into two parts: items (i) and (ii) deal with the unauthorized disclosure of, and the unauthorized access to, computer software, while items (iii) to (viii) relate to acts of unauthorized copying, use, sale, etc., of computer software.

Section 6 defines infringement and specifies two cases that are not to be considered infringement (the independent creation of computer software and the particular situation of foreign vessels, aircraft, spacecraft or land vehicles entering the territory of the country).

Section 7 regulates the duration of the rights under the Law.

Section 8 establishes the relief available in the case of infringement.

Section 9 makes clear that protection on the basis of other provisions is not excluded.

25. The establishment of effective protection for computer software in as many countries as possible is desirable, not only from the point of view of each country but also from the point of view of the international community. The use of computer software frequently concerns more than one country; in particular, in view of the fact that modern technology enables the operation of a machine having information-processing capabilities to be controlled by signals transmitted from a distant place, it may well happen that the user of software is in one country while the machine which performs certain functions under control of the software is in another country. If, under such circumstances, effective protection of computer software existed only in one of those countries, it might happen that no protection whatsoever is granted since, in the country with the effective protection, it may not be possible to prove that the unauthorized act was committed on its territory and not in the other country. To fill those gaps and to achieve international harmonization of national laws is another important purpose of the model provisions for the protection of computer software.

THE CABLE TELEVISION PROVISIONS OF THE REVISED COPYRIGHT ACT

Susan C. Greene*

Copyright law is founded upon the premise that, for a limited period of time, authors and creators of intellectual works have the exclusive right to their products. This right can be sold or distributed as the creators wish, and those seeking use of copyrighted material must negotiate a satisfactory royalty payment with the copyright owner. As a result of judicial interpretations of the Copyright Act of 1909,[1] the cable television industry was not obligated to make royalty payments to copyright owners for the privilege of carrying their programs to subscribers in other television markets.[2] For twenty-five years, the cable industry has flourished by picking up broadcast signals from distant television markets and retransmitting them by wire to subscribers who pay a monthly fee for this service.[3] Historically, the cable industry has been almost entirely

---

* Regional Director, Cable Television Information Center of The Urban Institute, Washington, D.C. The opinions are those of the author and do not reflect the policies or positions of The Urban Institute.

1. Copyright Act of 1909, ch. 320, 35 Stat. 1075 (1909).

2. The inapplicability of the 1909 Act was determined by Fortnightly Corp. v. United Artists Television, Inc., 392 U.S. 390 (1968) and Teleprompter Corp. v. CBS, 415 U.S. 394 (1974). *See* notes 30-40 & accompanying text *infra*.

3. The first commercial cable television system is generally believed to have started operation in 1950 in Lansford, Pennsylvania. Early systems flourished in rural areas by bringing television signals from distant television markets to communities with little or no local broadcast service. By mounting a large antenna on the highest point in the area, the cable system could pick up broadcast signals, strengthen them, and deliver them to subscribers who paid a monthly fee for this service. Today distant signals are available off-air, by microwave relay or by satellite distribution. For example, WTCG-TV, Channel 17, Atlanta, now sells its programing to cable systems throughout the country and distributes the signal by satellite.

Initially, the technology of a cable system permitted a maximum channel capacity of five channels. In recent years capacity in a new system has expanded to 20 or more channels, thereby permitting cable systems to develop nonbroadcast services such as pay TV, shopper's guides, and public access. Future services may include security alarm services and digital communications hookups with computers. The cable television regulations of the Federal Communications Commission (FCC) are concerned in part with

---

SOURCE: Reprinted from the *Catholic University Law Review.* 27: 263-303 (Winter 1978) by permission of the author and the copyright holder. Copyright © 1978 by the Catholic University of America Press, Inc.

dependent upon the retransmission of broadcast signals for its service,[4] and it is this carriage of distant broadcast signals which is at the center of the ongoing cable-copyright controversy.

In October 1976, Congress passed a comprehensive revision to the 1909 Copyright Act.[5] The revised Act, which became effective on January 1, 1978, is the result of a thorough reevaluation of the contemporary shortcomings of the former Act.[6] The revision was necessitated by the development of radio, broadcast television, photocopying, and other electronic technology which, by making access to information rapid and convenient, precipitated a crisis in copyright law. The fundamental goal of copyright—to institutionalize the balance between the author's right to control the use of his property and the public's right of access to information—was rendered ineffective by the former statute's inapplicability to new forms of distribution. The revised Act will require cable television systems to make royalty payments for the privilege of retransmitting distant broadcast signals. Although this change will resolve a long-standing dispute between the copyright owners and original broadcasters on the one hand, and the cable television industry on the other, the revised Act promises to generate extensive litigation as a result of

encouraging the development of nonbroadcast services. *See* Cable Television Report and Order, 36 F.C.C.2d 143 (1972). The scope of this article, however, is limited to the copyright implications of the signal carriage function of cable television systems.

4. The economics of broadcast television are best understood by reference to the concept of "television market." A television market is a theoretical allocation bounded by a radius of 35 miles from a television station or from some specified point in the community. Markets are delineated by size and roughly correlate with the size of urban metropolitan areas (*e.g.*, New York is the first market, Los Angeles is the second market. The fiftieth market is Little Rock, the one hundredth is Columbia, S.C.). Ninety percent of all television households reside in the top 100 markets. When a cable system carries (or "imports") signals from a distant market it makes available signals which probably cannot be picked up in the cable system's home market. Through attraction to viewers, these additional signals compete with the local broadcast stations.

5. Copyright Law Revision, Pub. L. No. 94-553, 90 Stat. 2541 (1976) (codified at 17 U.S.C. §§ 101-810 (1976)) [hereinafter referred to as the revised Act].

6. Creators of intellectual property have long been protected by copyright laws. The first American copyright law, passed in 1790, was based upon the specific Constitutional requirement "to promote the Progress of Science and useful Arts, by securing for limited times to Authors and Inventors the exclusive Right to their respective Writings and Discoveries." U.S. CONST. art. I, § 8. Major revisions to the copyright law were promulgated in 1891 and 1909. Recently, the United States Register of Copyrights characterized the 1909 legislation as "essentially a 19th century copyright law, based on assumptions concerning the creation and dissemination of authors' works that have been completely overturned in the past 50 years." *Civil Liberties and the Administration of Justice: Hearings on H.R. 2223 Before the Subcomm. on Courts of the House Comm. on the Judiciary*, 94th Cong., 1st Sess. 99 (1975) [hereinafter cited as *1975 Subcommittee Hearings*]. Basically, the 1909 Act did not anticipate the spectacular growth in communication technology which occurred during the twentieth century.

ponderous implementation procedures and the creation of a new conflict between copyright law and national communications policy.

I. THE CABLE TELEVISION EXEMPTION UNDER THE COPYRIGHT ACT OF 1909

Traditionally, the Copyright Act of 1909 has been interpreted in such a way as to confer copyright liability on the broadcast media.[7] The courts have never read the Act, however, to make cable television systems similarly liable.[8]

Both broadcasters and copyright owners have challenged the cable industry's exemption from copyright liability. Their contentions can best be understood in the context of the program distribution market. Local television stations may be either network affiliates[9] or independent stations.[10] An affiliate fills most of its broadcast day with programing supplied by a network. The networks obtain most of their programing from independent producers and pay royalty fees to the producers based upon such factors as the number of affiliates expected to broadcast the program. Independent stations purchase programs directly from the pro-

---

7. This liability stemmed from judicial interpretation of the meaning of "performance" within the meaning of the 1909 Copyright Act. 17 U.S.C. § 1(e) (1970). *See* Jerome H. Remick & Co. v. American Auto. Accessories Co., 5 F.2d 411 (6th Cir. 1925). A radio station was sued for playing a copyrighted work without a license. In holding the station liable, the court stated:

> A performance . . . is no less public because the listeners are unable to communicate with one another, or are not assembled within an enclosure, or gathered together in some open stadium or park or other public place. Nor can a performance . . . be deemed private because each listener may enjoy it alone in the privacy of his home. Radio broadcasting is intended to . . . reach a very much larger number of the public at the moment of rendition than any other medium of performance. The artist is consciously addressing a great, though unseen and widely scattered, audience, and is therefore participating in a public performance.

Id. at 412. See also notes 25-40 & accompanying text *infra*.

8. *See, e.g.*, Teleprompter Corp. v. CBS, 415 U.S. 394 (1974); Fortnightly Corp. v. United Artists Television, Inc., 392 U.S. 390 (1968). *See* notes 30-40 & accompanying text *infra*.

9. A full network station is defined by the FCC as "[a] commercial television broadcast station that generally carries in weekly prime time hours 85 percent of the hours of programing offered by one of the three major national television networks with which it has a primary affiliation (i.e., right of first refusal or first call)." 47 C.F.R. § 76.5(l) (1976). Of the 960 commercial broadcast stations in operation in 1976, 701 are network affiliates. 46 TELEVISION FACTBOOK 67-a (1977).

10. An independent station is a commercial television broadcast station which generally carries not more than 10 hours of programing per week offered by the three major national television networks during prime time. 47 C.F.R. § 76.5(n) (1976).

ducers in the syndication market.[11] Network affiliates also purchase programs in the syndication market to fill nonnetwork time. The program producer sells the local broadcast station the exclusive rights to the program in the particular television market during the life of the contract. In return, the station pays a royalty fee based on market size, potential audience, and desirability of the program.

When a cable system retransmits a program televised by a local station, no economic harm ensues. The local broadcast station has purchased exclusive rights in the same market from the copyright owner, and the cable system merely enhances this programing by bringing a better quality picture to a larger local viewing audience. The improved picture and larger audience is reflected in the ratings for the local station, and it is thus able to command higher advertising rates from its sponsors. The copyright owner, in turn, is able to negotiate a higher royalty fee from the local station. The problem occurs with programing from distant markets. When a cable system carries programing from a broadcast station in a distant market, it undermines the exclusivity of the local contract agreement. For the copyright owner, the retransmission of a distant signal by a cable system diminishes the value of the program in the local market since the owner receives a reduced royalty fee from the local broadcast station because he can no longer guarantee an exclusive right to transmit the program in the local market.

Copyright owners asserted that the cable industry must pay royalties for the use of television programs because the cable industry's nonpayment amounted to commercial piracy and that use of programing from broadcast stations in distant markets violated the exclusive nature of copyright contracts.[12] On the other hand, the cable industry insisted that

---

11. A syndicated program is "any program sold, licensed, distributed or offered to television station licensees in more than one market within the United States for non-interconnected (i.e., nonnetwork) television broadcast exhibition, but not including live presentations." 47 C.F.R. § 76.5(p) (1976). Programs enter the syndicated market in one of two ways. Traditionally, a series completes its network run and is then sold on a market-by-market basis, as, for example, *The Mary Tyler Moore Show*. A more recent development is the syndication of new programing without ever using the networks, as, for example, *Mary Hartman, Mary Hartman*.

12. *1975 Subcommittee Hearings, supra* note 6, at 704-14. Jack Valenti, President of the Motion Picture Association of America, summarized the copyright owner's position as follows:

Cable television does something else to attract viewers away from local television stations. It imports signals—programs—from distant television stations to its cable subscribers in its own local market. Thus cable television is not only using local signals free of any cost, but by importing distant signals free of charge it fragments the market of the local television station with which it is competing for audience. In so doing, it not only competes unfairly with the television station

it was not liable for copyright under the judicial interpretation of the 1909 Copyright Act.[13] It further argued that since it merely expanded the viewing audience for broadcast programing, the copyright owner could seek greater compensation from broadcast stations rather than from the cable industry.[14] The broadcast industry, concerned with the ability of a cable system to fragment the local viewing audience and thereby affect station revenues, seized upon the copyright issue as an additional weapon with which to seek restrictions on the cable television industry.[15] Additionally, the broadcasters argued that the cable industry's resistance to royalty payments amounted to an unfair method of competition since the broadcast industry, and not the cable industry, was liable for copyright payments.[16]

The broadcasters were the earliest litigants. Local stations attempted to seek sole control of the use of their signals on the basis of the exclusive contracts which the station held. Had they been successful, the broadcast stations could then have restricted the use of their signals by a

---

which must pay for programming, but it destroys, or at the very least impairs, the copyright owner's ability to sell his product to the television station in that market. In short, if cable television is not subject to copyright liability, the Congress would not only be giving cable a free ride, but it would, in effect, be subsidizing cable at our expense and to our subsequent economic disadvantage. In so doing, the Congress would legitimize unfair competition against television— an unsubsidized free market enterprise.
Id. at 708.

13. *See* text accompanying notes 25-40 *infra*.

14. *1975 Subcommittee Hearings, supra* note 6, at 849-56. The cable industry's position was that cable service enlarged the audience of a broadcast station in two situations: first, when cable serves communities with no television stations; and second, when cable provides two or more additional channels to communities that have only one channel. The industry asserted that cable carriage expanded audiences by over five million households and that the copyright owner's product was therefore more valuable. *Id.* at 853. For additional discussion of these themes, see Blair, Book Review (reviewing S. LADAS, PATENTS, TRADEMARK, AND RELATED RIGHTS—NATIONAL AND INTERNATIONAL PROTECTION (1975)), 17 IDEA, Summer 1975, at 59.

15. Commercial broadcasting is economically based upon the size of the viewing audience which the station can deliver to advertisers. The greater the viewing audience, the higher the advertising rates which the station can charge. By bringing additional stations from other markets to the viewing audience, the broadcast industry contended, the cable systems fragmented the local audience and reduced station profitability. This issue is now the subject of an economic inquiry at the Federal Communications Commission. *See* Notice of Inquiry in Docket No. 21284, 4 RAD. REG. DIG. (P-H) ¶ 85:325 (released June 28, 1977).

16. The National Association of Broadcasters asserted that, according to FCC figures, the typical television station paid 33% of its total revenue for nonnetwork program material. *1975 Subcommittee Hearings, supra* note 6, at 775. In 1973 the broadcasting industry paid approximately 25% of its entire gross revenues of $4 billion for copyrighted material. *Id.* at 709.

cable system, thereby maintaining some control over the growth of the cable television industry. Nevertheless, the broadcasters failed to establish their exclusive right to copyrighted broadcast programing in two interrelated cases.

In *Intermountain Broadcasting & Television Corp. v. Idaho Microwave Inc.*,[17] three Salt Lake City network affiliates sued an Idaho microwave company and the Twin Falls, Idaho cable system for carrying their signals to Twin Falls subscribers when the local Twin Falls broadcast station held exclusive contracts to carry programing from the three Salt Lake City signals. The plaintiffs' argument, based on unfair competition and unjust enrichment, rather than copyright theory, was rejected at the district court level. The court stated that the plaintiff broadcasters received their profit from the sponsors of the program and "do not and cannot charge the public for their broadcasts."[18] The public was entitled to receive the broadcasts directly and indiscriminately. The court went on to hold that the defendants' cable system was, in principle, no more than an antenna. It "is simply a more expensive and elaborate application of the antenna principle needed for all television reception. It does not otherwise differ from what the owners could do for themselves."[19] The court did note, however, that if the action had been brought by the local Twin Falls broadcast station, the holding might have been in its favor.

Subsequently, in *Cable Vision, Inc. v. KUTV, Inc.*,[20] when the Twin Falls cable system brought suit against the local broadcast station for antitrust violations and the broadcaster counterclaimed for tortious interference with contractual rights and unfair competition, the district court found that the cable system was interfering with the exclusive nature of the broadcaster's contract with the Salt Lake City stations.[21] The implication of this decision was that a cable system could not import distant signals to a market in which the local broadcaster held an exclusive contract to import the same signals into the same market.

While this case was on appeal, the Supreme Court decided *Sears Roebuck & Co. v. Stiffel Co.*[22] and *Compco Corp. v. Day-Brite Lighting Inc.*,[23] two patent cases which settled certain issues relevant to the *Cable*

17. 196 F. Supp. 315 (S.D. Idaho 1961).
18. *Id.* at 325.
19. *Id.* at 327.
20. 211 F. Supp 47 (S.D. Idaho 1962), 335 F.2d 348 (10th Cir. 1964).
21. *Id.* at 56.
22. 376 U.S. 225 (1964).
23. 376 U.S. 234 (1964).

Vision case. *Sears* and *Compco* held that anyone may copy an unpatented design subject only to the limited protections provided the creator by federal patent law. Applying the *Sears-Compco* rationale to a copyright setting, the Tenth Circuit in *Cable Vision* reversed the district court and noted that "only actions for copyright infringement or such common law actions as are consistent with the primary right of public access to all in the public domain will lie."[24] Thus, the broadcast industry was left with no legal rights against the use of distant signals by cable television systems.

Copyright owners have also had their day in court against the cable industry. Interestingly enough, the issue of liability for retransmission of copyrighted programs predates the development of cable systems by over thirty years. The issue first arose in *Buck v. Jewell-LaSalle Realty Co.*[25] when the owner of a copyrighted song sued the management of a Kansas City hotel for distributing the program from a central radio to all public and private rooms by means of a wire distribution system. Finding that the hotel's distribution constituted a "performance" within section 1(e) of the Copyright Act, the Supreme Court held that the retransmission violated the Copyright Act. The Court's analysis was based upon the function which the hotel served. By "(1) installing, (2) supplying electric current to, and (3) operating the radio receiving set and loudspeakers,"[26] the hotel went beyond the limits of mere reception of the signal. This "reproduction" was deemed a performance. The Court also indicated that the fact that the hotel had no knowledge of the copyright violation by the radio station was immaterial. The risk of a copyright violation was assumed by the hotel when it distributed the broadcast signal for its own commercial purposes.[27] In a footnote, the Court hinted that if the radio station had not violated the copyright law, an implied license for its reception and further distribution might have arisen in favor of the hotel.[28] That particular issue was never clearly decided, and

---

24. 335 F.2d at 350.
25. 283 U.S. 191 (1931). In this case, neither the radio station nor the hotel had obtained a license to perform the copyrighted song.
26. *Id.* at 201.
27. *Id.* at 198-99.
28. *Id.* at 199 n.5. *Cf.* Buck v. DeBaum, 40 F.2d 734 (S.D. Cal. 1929) (a radio played for the enjoyment of customers in a cafe held not to be an infringement). In *Buck*, the radio station had obtained a license for the use of the copyrighted piece. The court noted that "when the plaintiffs licensed the broadcasting station . . . they impliedly sanctioned and consented to any 'pick up' out of the air that was possible in radio reception." *Id.* at 735. The performance occurs in the radio station, and the voluntary playing of the radio is "far from 'performing' the copyrighted work." *Id.*

Jewell-LaSalle set the precedent for copyright liability of programing retransmitted by wire for forty years.[29]

The *Jewel-LaSalle* standard was severely limited in *Fortnightly Corp. v. United Artists Television, Inc.*,[30] the first case that specifically challenged the cable industry's asserted exemption from copyright liability. In *Fortnightly*, copyright owners sued two cable television systems for retransmitting motion pictures which had been licensed exclusively to local television stations. United Artists argued that the cable systems performed the same function as the hotel in the *Jewell-LaSalle* case, and therefore should be liable for infringement of the Copyright Act. Both the district court and court of appeals found the cable systems liable under the *Jewell-LaSalle* doctrine. The Supreme Court, however, in a surprisingly unsophisticated analysis of the functions of the cable television system, reversed the lower courts. Justice Stewart, writing for the majority, reasoned that a "performance" takes place only when the broadcaster transmits electronic signals over the air. The viewer who merely converts to sight and sound with his receiving equipment can not be said to be "performing." In sum, he explained: "Broadcasters perform. Viewers do not perform."[31] The Court decided that cable's function is most like that of a viewer.[32] Acknowledging that a cable system, unlike a viewer's rooftop antenna, is a complex electronic system, the court nonetheless concluded that "the basic function the equipment serves is little different from that served by the equipment generally furnished by a television viewer."[33] The *Jewell-LaSalle* doctrine was distinguished in a series of footnotes as a "questionable 35 year old decision" which should be limited to its facts.[34] In the sole dissent, Justice Fortas castigated the majority for its ready abandonment of precedent and for the "disarmingly simple" analysis which the Court

---

29. Melville B. Nimmer, one of the foremost commentators on copyright law, has stated that:

> [T]he two major performing right societies, ASCAP and BMI, do not choose to enforce the Jewell-LaSalle doctrine to its logical extreme in that they do not demand performing licenses from commercial establishments such as bars and restaurants which operate radio or television sets for the amusement of their customers. However, such demands are made of hotels which operate in the manner of the La Salle Hotel.

1 M. NIMMER, NIMMER ON COPYRIGHT § 107.41 n.204 (1976).

30. 392 U.S. 390 (1968).

31. *Id.* at 398.

32. *Id.* at 399.

33. *Id.*

34. *Id.* at 401 n.30.

adopted, and warned of the "disruptive consequences" in copyright law outside the area of CATV.[35]

Fortnightly established that cable television systems carrying only local broadcast signals were not liable for copyright payments for re-transmitting local signals. In a subsequent case, *Teleprompter Corp. v. CBS*,[36] the Court determined that under the 1909 Copyright Act, cable systems were not liable for copyright infringement for importing distant broadcast signals, even though the cable television system provided services which were arguably more similar to a broadcaster than a mere retransmitter. The court of appeals in *Teleprompter* had determined that a cable system which distributes distant signals which are beyond the capabilities of any local antenna should be held to have performed the works so provided to its subscribers.[37] The rationale of the appeals court was obviously to limit the effect of *Fortnightly* and to revive the *Jewell-LaSalle* doctrine with respect to distant television signals.

The Supreme Court flatly rejected these efforts. Instead, it applied the *Fortnightly* analysis to determine that the distance between the broadcast station and the ultimate viewer is irrelevant to the determination of whether the retransmission is a broadcaster or viewer function.[38] The Court concluded that "a CATV system does not lose its status as a nonbroadcaster and thus a 'nonperformer' for copyright purposes when

---

35. *Id.* at 405. Those "disruptive consequences" were realized in Twentieth Century Music Corp. v. Aiken, 422 U.S. 151 (1975), in which the *Fortnightly* analysis was applied for the first time to a radio case. The Court considered whether the reception of a radio broadcast of a copyrighted musical piece which was transmitted through a speaker system in a fast-food restaurant was an infringement of the Copyright Act. Although the *Jewell-LaSalle* decision seemed the appropriate precedent, the Court limited it to "a factual situation like that in which it arose," *id.* at 160, and instead adopted the *Fortnightly* distinction between broadcaster and viewer functions. *Id.* at 161. The Court reasoned that if there was no finding of copyright infringement when sophisticated communications technology was involved, there could be no finding of liability by the mere activation of a radio. In addition, the Court stated that merely holding that a listener had "performed" the copyrighted piece would not result in enforcement because of the futility of policing all business establishments, and would be "inequitable" since a listener could never know if the broadcaster had obtained a license to perform the work. *Id.* at 162. The Court also concluded that to require individual licenses for listeners would exact multiple tribute for what was basically a single rendition of a public work. In a concurring opinion, Justice Blackmun argued that *Fortnightly*, which had been decided 5-1, should be limited to its facts, while *Jewell-LaSalle*, which had the unanimous backing of the Court and had served as the basis for radio licensing agreements for 40 years, should have been granted precedential effect.

36. 415 U.S. 394 (1974). CBS sued several Teleprompter systems, all of which imported broadcast signals from distant markets. At the same time, these cable systems performed additional services such as the origination of local programing.

37. 476 F.2d 338, 349 (2d Cir. 1973).

38. 415 U.S. at 408.

the signals it carries are from distant rather than local sources."[39] Although the Court chose to adhere to a superficial analysis, it clearly indicated the necessity for a congressional remedy in its recognition that the Copyright Act never contemplated the technology at issue in the cable television cases.[40] Thus, *Teleprompter* effectively denied copyright holders any cause of action against the cable industry under the 1909 Copyright Act.

II.   THE FCC CABLE RULES: THE LINK TO THE COPYRIGHT ACT

At the same time that the cable industry's exemption from copyright liability was being formulated in the courts, the broadcast industry was pressing its case against cable at the Federal Communications Commission (FCC). As a result of those efforts, the FCC promulgated a series of regulations through which it asserted increasingly more control over the retransmission of broadcast signals by cable systems. This exercise of jurisdiction by the FCC over cable remains significant today because of the relationship of the FCC rules to the revised Act. The applicability and scope of several of the revised Act's provisions are expressly tied to the content of the FCC rules and there is a distinct possibility of a conflict between those rules and both policy statements and the intended effect of the revised Act.

Because cable television started in 1950 as a master antenna service, providing television signals to communities without local broadcast stations, it was initially perceived by broadcasters as a boon since it increased the size of viewing audiences. In the 1950's and 1960's, however, as both the broadcast and cable industries prospered, it became apparent that cable television was a potential economic threat to the broadcast industry.[41] As cable systems began to carry broadcast signals from beyond the local television market, these distant signals competed with other broadcast signals for the available viewing audience. The greater the number of signals carried, the greater the fragmentation of a given viewing audience. Under these circumstances, local broadcasters argued that their stations lost much of the former viewing audience, thereby affecting advertising rates and, ultimately, station revenues. This economic injury was presumed to be most severe in small communities which had only one or two local broadcast stations and a small potential audience.

---

39. *Id.* at 409.
40. *Id.* at 414.
41. *See* notes 12-16 & accompanying text *supra*.

When this threat to local broadcasters became apparent, the broadcast industry petitioned the FCC for rulemaking to regulate the cable industry, particularly the unrestricted carriage of distant signals. Initially, the Commission refused to assert jurisdiction because it presumed that its authority under the Communications Act of 1934[42] was doubtful and because the broadcasters were able to offer no demonstrable proof of economic harm.[43] Shortly thereafter, however, the Commission reconsidered this policy due most probably to a few new appointments to the FCC.[44] Its first act was to assert jurisdiction over a particular cable system which used a microwave relay system to bring distant signals into a community with one local broadcast signal. In *Carter Mountain Trans-*

---

42. 47 U.S.C. §§ 151-155 (1970).

43. Report and Order in Docket No. 12443, 26 F.C.C. 2403 (1959). This inquiry was the first federal attempt to evaluate the economic consequences of competition between media in small markets. On the basis of its own research and comments filed, the FCC determined that, "of the 96 stations which have gone off the air since 1952, 89 UHF and 7 VHF, in only three cases has the existence of an auxiliary service . . . been mentioned as a factor." A factor in the FCC's decision was the holding in FCC v. Sanders Bros. Radio Station, 309 U.S. 470 (1940), in which the Court found that the Communications Act "does not essay to regulate the business of the licensee. The Commission is given no supervisory control . . . of business management or of policy." *Id*. at 475. The Court continued, "resulting economic injury to a rival station is not, in and of itself, . . . an element which [the FCC] must weigh . . . in passing on an application for a broadcast license." *Id*. at 473. The Court reasoned: "If such economic loss were a valid reason for refusing a license this would mean that the Commission's function is to grant a monopoly in the field of broadcasting, a result which the Act itself clearly negatives . . . ." *Id*. at 476.

However, in a more recent decision, the United States Court of Appeals for the District of Columbia stated that potential economic injury was a factor which the FCC must consider:

> [W]hether a station makes $5,000, $10,000 or $50,000 is a matter in which the public has no interest as long as service is not adversely affected. . . . But if the situation in a given area is such that available revenue will not support good service in more than one station, the public interest may well be in the licensing of one rather than two stations.

Carroll Broadcasting Co. v. FCC, 258 F.2d 440, 443 (D.C. Cir. 1958).

The question of the FCC's jurisdiction over cable was finally resolved in United States v. Southwestern Cable Co., 392 U.S. 157 (1968) in which the Court sustained FCC restrictions on the use of distant signals by a San Diego cable system, stating, "the authority which we recognize . . . is restricted to that reasonably ancillary to the effective performance of the Commission's various responsibilities for the regulation of television broadcasting . . . ." *Id*. at 178.

44. The Commission's about face seemed to be due mostly to a change of commissioners, including the addition of a new chairman, Newton Minnow. *Hearings on H.R. 7715 Before the Subcomm. on Communications and Power of the House Comm. on Interstate and Foreign Commerce*, 89th Cong., 1st Sess. 138-39 (1965).

mission Corp. v. FCC,[45] the FCC imposed regulations on the types of signals which the cable system could carry and the manner in which they could be carried in order to protect the local broadcaster from economic injury. The purpose of the regulation was to protect local broadcasters and, to a more limited extent, the owners of copyrighted program material. Although *Carter Mountain* was limited to the regulation of distant signals in this one cable system, shortly after this initial decision the FCC chose to assert jurisdiction over all microwave-fed cable systems.[46] Finally, in 1966, the Commission took jurisdiction over all cable systems whether or not microwave was actually used.[47]

Having assumed cable jurisdiction, the FCC proceeded to promulgate, between 1966 and 1970, three regulatory structures designed to control distant signal carriage by cable system.[48] These regulations were developed primarily to protect the local broadcaster and the exclusivity of the local market, but because copyright is also based on the concept of local markets, the FCC regulations also had the secondary effect of protecting the copyright owner as well. In 1966, the FCC promulgated procedures whereby cable systems in the top one hundred markets[49] could carry a distant television signal only with the consent of the Commission upon a showing that cable service would not injure the local broadcast stations.[50] The result of this policy was to impede significantly the growth of cable television since a cable system could commence service only after going through a costly and time consuming hearing before the FCC. Many systems chose not to enter local markets for this reason.

Therefore, the Commission reversed its policy in 1968. Not only were too many cable systems prevented from entering markets, but the backlog of cases for FCC action was too great. As an alternative, the FCC

---

45. 32 F.C.C. 459 (1962), *aff'd*, 321 F.2d 359 (D.C. Cir.), *cert. denied*, 375 U.S. 951 (1963).

46. First Report and Order in Dockets Nos. 14895 & 15233, 38 F.C.C. 683 (1965).

47. Second Report and Order in Dockets Nos. 14895, 15233 & 15971, 2 F.C.C.2d 725 (1966).

48. For a general review of the regulatory history of cable television see KRASNOW & LONGLEY, THE POLITICS OF BROADCASTING (1973); LeDuc, CABLE TELEVISION AND THE FCC: A CRISIS IN MEDIA CONTROL (1973); SEIDEN, CABLE TELEVISION U.S.A.: AN ANALYSIS OF GOVERNMENT POLICY (1972).

49. The top 100 television markets is frequently used as a cut-off point for the applicability of FCC rules and provisions under the revised Act. Ninety percent of the nation's television viewing audience lives in the top 100 markets. See note 4 *supra*.

50. Notice of Proposed Rulemaking and Notice of Inquiry in Docket No. 18397, 15 F.C.C.2d 417 (1968). It had generally been believed by Commission staff that the Supreme Court, in *Fortnightly*, would find cable liable under the 1909 Copyright Act. To the surprise of the staff, the Court held that cable was not liable. Interview with Henry Geller, former FCC General Counsel, in Washington, D.C. (February 10, 1977).

proposed the "retransmission consent plan" which replaced the hearing with a requirement compelling cable systems to seek retransmission consent on a program-by-program basis from the broadcast station which transmitted the program.[51] This plan was doomed from the outset. Because broadcasters and cable systems were bitter enemies, it was extremely unlikely that consent would ever be granted. Accordingly, this plan was never implemented.

In 1970 the Commission tried once again, initiating the "public dividend plan."[52] Under this policy, cable systems would be permitted to carry four distant nonnetwork stations. In exchange, the cable systems were required to pay five percent of their subscription revenues to public broadcasting. Furthermore, they were forced to substitute local broadcasters' advertisements for the advertisements from the distant stations. This plan was never implemented due largely to its great complexity.

In 1971, under the leadership of a new chairman, the Commission again reviewed the problem of cable television regulation. Chairman Dean Burch attempted to develop a new set of regulations to permit the entry of cable television into the top one hundred markets while neutralizing the broadcast and copyright opposition. Burch's plan was unveiled in a letter submitted in response to a request from then Senator John Pastore, Chairman of the Senate Subcommittee on Communications. This "letter of intent" outlined the proposed FCC cable television regulations which were to go into effect in 1972.[53] It indicated that the FCC believed cable regulation and copyright should be considered separately. The Commission stated that, although it was competent to handle the economic ramifications of the cable problem, it felt that "copyright policy is most appropriately left to the Congress and the courts."[54]

Copyright interests objected to the letter of intent because it left the cable industry's liability completely unresolved. Chairman Burch attempted to reach a compromise among the cable, broadcast, and copy-

---

51. *See* Notice of Proposed Rulemaking and Notice of Inquiry in Docket 18397, 15 F.C.C.2d 417 (1968). The retransmission consent plan was promulgated shortly after the *Fortnightly* decision. The Commission's action, in effect, circumvented the *Fortnightly* holding by imposing procedures which protected copyright interests.

52. Second Further Notice of Proposed Rulemaking in Docket No. 18397-A, 24 F.C.C.2d 580 (1970). The FCC indicated that comments regarding cable's copyright liability would be accepted but stated that only Congress could act on copyright legislation.

53. For the full text, see Cable Television Report and Order, App. C, 36 F.C.C.2d 140, 260-84 (1972). The proposed regulations are divided into four areas: television broadcast signal carriage; access to, and use of nonbroadcast cable channels; technical standards; and federal versus state local jurisdiction.

54. *Id*. at 261.

right interests in order to minimize opposition to his plan, but the negotiations soon broke down.[55] Burch then turned to the White House Office of Telecommunications Policy which proved successful in developing an agreement acceptable to all interests.[56]

This document, known as the Consensus Agreement,[57] satisfied both copyright owners and broadcasters basically because of the added "syndicated exclusivity" rules. [58] These rules were developed in the Consen-

55. Burch, in a concurring statement, explained his behavior as follows:
[I]t seemed to me that the time was right for another try. Broadcasters were understandably nervous that this program would go into effect and the Teleprompter [sic] case might go against them; cable was equally concerned about the outcome of litigation and the need to put itself on a solid base; and copyright owners were anxious to protect their major source of revenue in the top television markets. Then, too, the Office of Telecommunications Policy had a cable study underway, and all the principals were pressing their viewpoints in that forum.
Id., App. E at 291.

56. In the early and mid-1970's several major studies, funded by foundations, private industry, the White House, and Congress, looked at the growth potential of the cable industry. The studies were unanimous in recognizing a copyright obligation on the part of the industry. Thus, while it was not legally bound to copyright liability, the general institutional and government support for copyright payments helped persuade the industry to "voluntarily" agree to a copyright obligation. *See* SLOAN COMMISSION ON CABLE COMMUNICATIONS, ON THE CABLE: THE TELEVISION OF ABUNDANCE (1971); CABINET COMMITTEE ON CABLE COMMUNICATIONS, CABLE: A REPORT TO THE PRESIDENT (1974); COMMITTEE FOR ECONOMIC DEVELOPMENT, BROADCASTING AND CABLE TELEVISION: POLICIES FOR DIVERSITY AND CHANGE (1975); STAFF OF HOUSE SUBCOMM. ON COMMUNICATIONS OF COMM. FOR INTERSTATE AND FOREIGN COMMERCE, 94TH CONG., 2ND SESS., CABLE TELEVISION: PROMISE VERSUS REGULATORY PERFORMANCE (Comm. Print 1976).

57. *See* 36 F.C.C.2d at 284-86.

58. The syndicated exclusivity rule reads as follows:
(a) No cable television system, operating in a community in whole or in part within one of the first 50 major television markets shall carry a syndicated program pursuant to § 76.61(b), (c), (d), or (e) for a period of 1 year from the date that program is first licensed or sold as a syndicated program to a television station in the United States for television broadcast exhibition;
(b) No cable television system, operating in a community in whole or in part within a major television market, shall carry a syndicated program, pursuant to §§ 76.61(b), (c), (d), or (e), or 76.63(a) (as it refers to § 76.61(b), (c), (d), or (e)), while a commercial television station licensed to a designated community in that market has exclusive broadcast exhibition rights (both over-the-air and by cable) to that program: *Provided, however*, that if a commercial station licensed to a designated community in one of the second 50 major television markets has such exclusive rights, a cable television system located in whole or in part within the market of such station may carry such syndicated programs in the following circumstances:
(1) If the program is carried by the cable television system in prime time and will not also be broadcast by a commercial market station in prime time during the period for which there is exclusivity for the program;
(2) For off-network series programs:
(i) Prior to the first nonnetwork broadcast in the market of an episode in the series;

sus Agreement to protect the market exclusivity of copyright owners and to reflect programing market patterns. They constituted the heart of the Consensus Agreement and even today remain the core of the FCC's copyright rules. They are, as well, the most complex, least understood, and most controversial provisions of the cable rules.[59]

(ii) After a nonnetwork first-run of the series in the market or after year from the date of the first nonnetwork broadcast in the market of an episode in the series, whichever occurs first;
   (3) For first-run series programs:
     (i) Prior to the first broadcast in the market of an episode in the series;
     (ii) After two (2) years from the first broadcast in the market of an episode in the series;
   (4) For first-run, nonseries programs:
     (i) Prior to the date the program is available for broadcast in the market under the provision of any contract or license of a television broadcast station in the market;
     (ii) After two (2) years from the date of such first availability;
   (5) For feature films:
     (i) Prior to the date such film is available for nonnetwork broadcast in the market under the provisions of any contract or license of a television broadcast station in the market;
     (ii) Two (2) years after the date of such first availability;
   (6) For other programs: 1 day after the first nonnetwork broadcast in the market or 1 year from the date of purchase of the program for nonnetwork broadcast in the market, whichever occurs first.
Note 1: For purposes of § 76.151, a series will be treated as a unit, that is:
   (i) No episode of a series (including an episode in a different package of programs in the same series) may be carried by a cable television system, pursuant to §§ 76.61(b), (c), (d), or (e) or 76.63(a) (as it refers to § 76.61(b), (c), (d), or (e)) while any episodes of the series are subject to exclusivity protection.
   (ii) In the second 50 major television markets, no exclusivity will be afforded a different package of programs in the same series after the initial exclusivity period as terminated.
Note 2: As used in this section, the phrase "broadcast in the market" or "broadcast by a market station" refers to a broadcast by a television station licensed to a designated community in the market.
47 C.F.R. § 76.151 (1976).
59. In addition to the syndicated exclusivity provisions, the FCC signal carriage rules developed in the Consensus Agreement for cable systems included restriction on the number of signals a cable system could import from network affiliates, independent stations, and educational stations, all based on the market size of the cable system location, known as the signal carriage rules. See 47 C.F.R. §§ 76.57, .59, .61, .63 (1976). The rules also restricted the carriage by cable systems of network programing when a network affiliate in the same market as the cable system planned to air that programing. 47 C.F.R. § 76.91 (1976). These rules are of note because the revised Act provides that violation of the FCC rules constitutes a copyright infringement.
The syndicated exclusivity rule encourages broadcasters in the top 50 markets to seek longer exclusive contracts, simply to keep products off the cable system. In addition, the cable system, which is only permitted to import two distant signals, is required to black out any programing for which there is a contract between the local broadcaster and the copyright owner. Thus, the attractiveness of a distant signal may be severely diminished. Finally, the cable system must comply with a cumbersome and time consuming procedure requiring knowledge of local contracts, distant signal program schedules, and the like.

The rules prohibit the cable system from retransmitting certain programs from distant markets if they would interfere with exclusive contracts held by local broadcasters for the same programing. Specifically, the rules establish a graduated scheme of restrictions on the retransmission of distant signals based on the size of the local market. The rules for the top fifty markets are the most rigorous, imposing an absolute ban on cable retransmission of new syndicated programing for one year. After that, the cable system can import the program only if a local broadcast station does not hold an exclusive contract for the specific program. The practical effect of these rules is to curtail the importation of syndicated programing into the largest markets, because the most attractive programs will have exclusive contracts in those markets.

In markets fifty-one to one hundred, the rules, though less restrictive, are more complex. Depending on the nature of the programing, the prohibition on importation may last from one to two years. Syndicated programing, however, may not be imported during prime time if a local station with an exclusive contract for the program also plans to broadcast the program in prime time. The rules do not apply in the markets above one hundred. Thus, the syndicated exclusivity rules provide substantial copyright protection for local broadcasters in the largest television markets.

Although the amended Copyright Act is designed to remedy the objections of programmers and broadcasters, the issue is far from resolved. The FCC recently issued an inquiry to reassess the need for its syndicated exclusivity provisions.[60] The response has been typical of the controversies between the broadcast and cable industries, and both sides have taken diametrically opposed positions.[61] The FCC syndicated exclusivity rules were designed to appease the intransigent copyright and broadcast interests. The cable industry believed, not unreasonably, that the passage of new copyright legislation would eliminate the need for the FCC syndicated exclusivity rules, and thus the rules themselves could be discarded. In reality, however, the cable industry is presently saddled with both a new copyright law and with the FCC exclusivity provisions. The difficulty posed by this situation results from areas of conflict in the operation and purposes of the FCC rules and the amended copyright act.[62] Thus, instead of equitably resolving long-standing disputes be-

60. First Report and Order in Docket No. 20553, 58 F.C.C.2d 422 (1976).
61. Notice of Inquiry in Docket No. 20988, 61 F.C.C.2d 746, (1976).
62. *See, e.g.*, BROADCASTING, March 7, 1977, at 59-60. Broadcasters argue for greater exclusivity in markets 51-100 in order to protect the quality of local broadcast services. Program suppliers also seek additional exclusivity protection to ensure high quality

tween copyright owners and broadcasters with the cable industry, the new Act may have multiplied the possibilities for continued controversy.

III.   The Revised Copyright Act

The development of acceptable provisions to institutionalize copyright payments for the cable industry was a major obstacle to the passage of a revised copyright law.[63] For more than a decade, the battle over the copyright liability of the cable television industry had been fought in Congress,[64] the courts, and the FCC. In fact, passage of the revised Act in the 94th Congress was in serious doubt until the closing days of the session when the copyright interests and the cable television industry finally developed a mutually acceptable royalty fee schedule for cable.[65] Once the cable issue was resolved, the Copyright Act was enacted into law and became effective on January 1, 1978. For the first time the revised Act[66] addresses the copyright liability of the mass media and

---

programing in and to protect local markets. The cable industry seeks complete deletion of the rules since it now pays copyright fees. While it appears that exclusivity is a particular hardship for some cable systems (e.g., the Wauwatosa, Wisc., CATV system must black out 60% of its imported programing), there is some feeling that the rule is only enforced in 20 of the top 50 markets against 50 systems and it is generally not enforced in markets 51-100. Stengel, *Syndicated Exclusivity*, Vue, February 28, 1977, at 6-7.

63.   *See generally* Brennan, *An Overview of Copyright and the Copyright Bill*, 17 Idea, Fall 1975, at 5.

64.   The progression of copyright bills has been as follows: H.R. 11947, S. 3008, 88th Cong., 2d Sess. (1964); H.R. 4347, 5680, 6831, 6835, 89th Cong., 1st Sess. (1965); S. 1006, 89th Cong., 2d Sess. (1966); H.R. 2512, 90th Cong., 1st Sess. (1967); S. 597, 90th Cong., 1st Sess. (1967); S. 543, 91st Cong., 1st Sess. (1969); S. 644, 92d Cong., 1st Sess. (1971); S. 1361, 93d Cong., 1st Sess. (1973); H.R. 8186, 93d Cong., 1st Sess. (1973); S. 22, H.R. 2223, 94th Cong., 1st Sess. (1975). For a comprehensive discussion of the legislative history of the copyright bill, see Brennan, *Legislative History and Chapter 1 of S. 22*, 22 N.Y.L. Sch. L. Rev., 193 (1976).

65.   See Broadcasting, April 19, 1976, at 48 for a description of the last minute negotiations between the parties. This royalty fee schedule, with some modifications, is incorporated in the new Act. *See* Broadcasting, August 2, 1976, at 28.

66.   According to the United States Register of Copyrights:

The new Act is rather a completely new copyright statute, intended to deal with a whole range of problems undreamed of by the drafters of the 1909 Act . . . . [T]he new statute makes a number of fundamental changes in the American copyright system, including some so profound that they may mark a shift in direction for the very philosophy of copyright itself. Properly designated, the new act is not a "general revision," but is as radical a departure as was our own first copyright statute, in 1790.

Ringer, *First Thoughts on the Copyright Act of 1976*, 22 N.Y.L. Sch. L. Rev. 477, 479 (1977).

extends copyright liability to the cable industry.[67] As the House Committee on the Judiciary indicated, "cable systems are commercial enterprises whose basic retransmission operations are based on the carriage of copyrighted program material and . . . copyright royalties should be paid by cable operators to the creators of such programs."[68] The revised Act provides a new and perhaps less ambiguous definition of a "performance," and defines a public performance as one which is open to the public, or to any "substantial" number of persons outside of a normal family or social circle. The means of display or performance, as well as the time and place at which all members of the public receive it are not factors in determining whether a performance has occurred.[69] Of particular note here is that the House Report specifically states that "a cable television system is performing when it retransmits the broadcast to its subscribers."[70]

Under the framework of the revised Act, the copyright owner is granted five exclusive rights to his product. These include the right to reproduce and prepare derivatives of the work, to distribute copies, and to perform or display the work publicly.[71] Thus, under section 106, the

---

67. For additional analyses of the cable television provisions, see Botein, *The New Copyright Act and Cable Television—A Signal of Change*, 24 BULL. COPYRIGHT SOC'Y 1 (1977), and Meyer, *The Feat of Houdini or How the New Act Disentangles the CATV-Copyright Knot*, 22 N.Y.L. SCH. L. REV. 545 (1977).

68. H. R. REP. NO. 94-1476, 94th Cong., 2d Sess. 89 [hereinafter cited as HOUSE REPORT], *reprinted in part in* [1976] U.S. CODE CONG. & AD. NEWS 5659, 5704.

69. Revised Act § 101 provides in pertinent part:

To "perform" a work means to recite, render, play, dance, or act it, either directly or by means of any device or process or, in the case of a motion picture or other audiovisual work, to show its images in any sequence or to make the sound accompanying it audible.

. . . .

To perform or display a work "publicly" means—

(1) to perform or display it at a place open to the public or at any place where a substantial number of persons outside of a normal circle of a family and its social acquaintances is gathered; or

(2) to transmit or otherwise communicate a performance or display of the work to a place specified by clause (1) or to the public, by means of any device or process, whether the members of the public capable of receiving the performance or display receive it in the same place or in separate places and at the same time or at different times.

70. HOUSE REPORT, *supra* note 68, at 63.

71. *See* revised Act § 106, which provides that:

Subject to sections 107 through 118, the owner of copyright under this title has the exclusive rights to do and to authorize any of the following:

(1) to reproduce the copyrighted work in copies or phonorecords;

(2) to prepare derivative works based upon the copyrighted work;

(3) to distribute copies or phonorecords of the copyrighted work to the public by sale or other transfer of ownership, or by rental, lease, or lending;

copyright owner can generally withhold or sell his product as he sees fit. To obtain the use of such materials, potential users must negotiate with the owner on an appropriate royalty or licensing fee based on the manner and number of times the work will be used. If an agreement is reached, the user receives a license stating the terms of use and the owner receives royalty fees. However, this "bundle of rights" is not without restrictions. As the House Report points out, these rights granted the copyright owner in section 106 are subject to limitations in subsequent sections which set forth exemptions from the Act and certain restrictions on the basic rights granted by section 106.[72] What Congress gave in section 106 is, to some extent, taken away in the other sections.

One of the major limitations on the rights of the copyright owner is the imposition of the compulsory license, which will eliminate the market place determination of royalty payments for the cable industry. The mechanism requires the granting of a license in exchange for royalty payments as determined by a fee schedule. Accordingly, a copyright owner cannot withhold his material from a cable system as long as the system complies with the requirements for the license. To this extent, the compulsory license severely limits the copyright owner's control of his material and effectively removes the licensing process from the marketplace of supply and demand.[73] The use of a compulsory license

----

(4) in the case of literary, musical, dramatic, and choreographic works, pantomimes, and motion pictures and other audiovisual works, to perform the copyrighted work publicly; and

(5) in the case of literary, musical, dramatic, and choreographic works, pantomimes, and pictorial, graphic, or sculptural works, including the individual images of a motion picture or other audiovisual work, to display the copyrighted work publicly.

72. *See* HOUSE REPORT, *supra* note 68, at 61.

73. There is some feeling that the compulsory license concept is inappropriate in copyright law. The United States Register of Copyrights has stated:

[T]he interweaving of four full scale compulsory licensing schemes into the main fabric of the United States copyright system may have ominous implications for the future. Copyright has heretofore been considered a bundle of exclusive rights that can be withheld or sold as the owner sees fit. Does our experience in the development of the 1976 Act suggest that in the future, whenever a new right is granted by Congress, it will necessarily be subject to compulsory licensing? Does this mean that eventually compulsory licensing will supplant traditional copyright, and that all rights under a copyright law will in time consist entirely of the right to collect royalties?

Ringer, *supra* note 66, at 495.

There is disagreement among commentators over whether the compulsory license should have been used for cable television. One group believes that compulsory licensing for cable television will ultimately have negative economic consequences upon the program production market and increase the amount of program regulation. S. BESEN, W. MANNING JR. & B. MITCHELL, COPYRIGHT LIABILITY FOR CABLE TELEVISION: IS COMPUL-

was instituted for practical reasons. The House Report recognized the impracticality of requiring every cable system to negotiate with every copyright owner whose work was distributed by a cable system.[74] A compulsory license will be granted "for the retransmission of those over-the-air broadcast signals that a cable system is authorized to carry pursuant to the rules and regulations of the FCC."[75] Specifically, the Copyright Act focuses on cable system liability for the use of distant signal programs, which most severely affect the program distribution market.

Section 111 of the revised Act has gained a well-deserved reputation as the most prolix section in the statute. It outlines the requirements for a cable system to obtain a compulsory license, lists the exemptions from copyright liability, delineates the acts and omissions which are infringements of the Act, sets forth the statutory copyright fees, and establishes the reporting requirements for cable systems. Despite the comprehensive nature of this section, it can be divided into three relatively clear components: secondary transmissions exempted from copyright liability; secondary transmissions granted a compulsory license; and secondary transmissions subject to full copyright liability.[76]

The revised Act legislates the obligations of cable television systems in arcane and confusing terminology. A "primary transmission" and a "secondary transmission"[77] are defined in relation to one another. A primary transmission is a transmission made to the public by a broadcasting facility such as a television or radio station. A secondary transmission is the simultaneous further carriage and distribution of the signal by

---

SORY LICENSING THE SOLUTION? v-vi (1977). Another observer states that any copyright liability for cable television is inappropriate. Since it affects national communications policy, regulation of cable is better left to the FCC. B. KAPLAN, AN UNHURRIED VIEW OF COPYRIGHT, 106 (1967). The House Report recognizes the interplay between the copyright and the communications elements of the legislation but cautions

> [t]he Federal Communications Commission, and others who make determinations concerning communications policy, not to rely upon any action of this Committee as a basis for any significant changes in the delicate balance of regulation in areas where the Congress has not resolved the issue. Specifically, we would urge the Federal Communications Commission to understand that it was not the intent of this bill to touch on issues such as pay cable regulation or increased use of imported distant signals. These matters are ones of communications policy and should be left to the appropriate committees in the Congress for resolution.

HOUSE REPORT, *supra* note 68, at 89.

74. *Id*.
75. *Id*.
76. *See* revised Act § 111(a)-(e).
77. *See* revised Act § 111(f).

a cable system.[78] The "local service area of a primary transmitter"[79] is defined to be the area in which, under FCC rules, the television station can insist that the cable system carry its signal. Secondary transmissions which are granted general exemptions are delineated in section 111(a).[80]

---

78. A nonsimultaneous transmission, such as would occur if a cable system videotaped a program for later distribution, has traditionally been an infringement of copyright. *See* Walt Disney Prod. v. Alaska Television Network, Inc., 310 F. Supp. 1073 (W.D. Wash. 1969). Under the revised Act, a nonsimultaneous transmission is permitted for a cable system located outside the continental United States, with the exception of Puerto Rico and to a limited extent, Hawaii, provided that the system also complied with § 111(e) which prescribes strict standards for retransmission of a primary transmission. Any retransmission which does not conform with § 111(e) is an infringement of the new Act. The complexity of these measures is necessary to accommodate cable television systems which are located at too great a distance from the continental United States to receive simultaneous programing. These systems generally experience a lag of up to several days until duplicate videotapes can be delivered for transmission on the cable system.

79. *See* revised Act § 111(f). Under the FCC rules, a cable system in the first 50 television markets must carry the signals of:

(1)   Television broadcast stations within whose specified zone the community of the system is located, in whole or in part . . . ;

(2)   Noncommercial educational television broadcast stations within whose Grade B contours the community of the system is located, in whole or in part;

(3)   Television translator stations with 100 watts or higher power serving the community of the system . . .;

(4)   Television broadcast stations licensed to other designated communities of the same major television market . . .;

(5)   Commercial television broadcast stations that are significantly viewed in the community of the system. . . .

47 C.F.R. § 76.61 (1976). *See also* 47 C.F.R. §§ 76.57, .59, .63.

80. *See* revised Act § 111(a), which provides that:

(a)   CERTAIN SECONDARY TRANSMISSIONS EXEMPTED.—The secondary transmission of a primary transmission embodying a performance or display of a work is not an infringement of copyright if—

(1)   the secondary transmission is not made by a cable system, and consists entirely of the relaying, by the management of a hotel, apartment house, or similar establishment, of signals transmitted by a broadcast station licensed by the Federal Communications Commission, within the local service area of such station, to the private lodgings of guests or residents of such establishment, and no direct charge is made to see or hear the secondary transmission; or

(2)   the secondary transmission is made solely for the purpose and under the conditions specified by clause (2) of section 110; or

(3)   the secondary transmission is made by any carrier who has no direct or indirect control over the content or selection of the primary transmission or over the particular recipients of the secondary transmission, and whose activities with respect to the secondary transmission consist solely of providing wires, cables, or other communications channels for the use of others: *Provided*, That the provisions of this clause extend only to the activities of said carrier with respect to secondary transmissions and do not exempt from liability the activities of others with respect to their own primary or secondary transmission; or

(4)   the secondary transmission is not made by a cable system but is made by a governmental body, or other nonprofit organization, without any purpose of

The first set of exemptions applies to those apartment and hotel master antenna systems carrying local broadcast signals to the private rooms of the guests or residents of such buildings which do not impose a direct charge for this service.[81] If the programing is distributed through the building by a cable television system, however, the exemption does not apply.[82] The House Report makes clear that the exemption also does not apply if the transmission consists of anything more than the mere relay of broadcasts.[83] This exemption finally resolves the long-standing tension between the *Jewell-LaSalle* doctrine and the Supreme Court's recent holdings in *Fortnightly* and *Teleprompter*. The new Act limits the exclusion from liability to the distribution of signals to the private rooms in commercial establishments. Dining rooms, meeting halls, theatres, ballrooms, and similar places do not fit within the exemption.[84] Thus, if broadcast signals are transmitted in major public rooms, a hotel would once again be required to seek a copyright license. By this legislation, Congress has expressly rejected the recent decisions and has reestablished the vitality of *Jewell-LaSalle*. Section 110(5),[85] however, does provide an exemption from copyright liability for a small commercial establishment which provides radio or television entertainment to customers. Even though the transmission is public, as long as the receiving equipment is like that used in private homes, no direct charge is made to customers and the signal is not further distributed.[86] The distinction between this exemption and the liability provided in section 111(a)(1) appears to be principally predicated on the sophistication of the receiving equipment, a determination which must, by necessity, be made on a

---

direct or indirect commercial advantage, and without charge to the recipients of the secondary transmission other than assessments necessary to defray the actual and reasonable costs of maintaining and operating the secondary transmission service.

81. *See* revised Act § 111(a)(1).

82. *Id.*

83. *See* HOUSE REPORT, *supra* note 68, at 91.

84. *Id.*

85. The revised Act § 110(5) states:
Notwithstanding the provisions of section 106, the following are not infringements of copyright:
    (5) communication of a transmission embodying a performance or display of a work by the public reception of the transmission on a single receiving apparatus of a kind commonly used in private homes, unless—
      (A) a direct charge is made to see or hear the transmission; or
      (B) the transmission thus received is further transmitted to the public; . . .

86. *See* HOUSE REPORT, *supra* note 68, at 87. See the discussion of Twentieth Century Music Corp. v. Aiken, note 35 *supra*, for those facts which constitute the outer limits of this exemption.

case-by-case basis. It is therefore likely that the courts will be called upon by copyright owners to clarify the boundaries of this exemption.

Section 111(a)(2)[87] provides a general exemption from copyright liability for secondary transmissions of instructional programing of any government or nonprofit educational institution which meets certain conditions.[88] The relatively narrow limits of this exemption reflect the well-established relationships between public television and copyright owners, since public television, the source of most instructional programing, has traditionally paid royalty fees tied to certain conditions relating to the nature of the broadcast.[89]

A third group of exemptions relates to "passive" carriers which "provide wires, cables, or other communications channels for the use of others,"[90] such as leased telephone lines or other common carriers. A fourth category of exemptions includes boosters and translators which are operated on a nonprofit basis.[91] An overriding proviso to all four categories of exemptions is that the transmission may not be limited but must be available to the general public, at least within the confines of the area permitted by any given exemption.[92] Thus, any controls which restrict the viewing audience, such as scrambling a pay television signal[93]

---

87. *See* revised Act § 111(a)(2).

88. *See* revised Act § 110(2), which provides that the following are not infringements of copyright:

(2)   performance of a nondramatic literary or musical work or display of a work, by or in the course of a transmission, if—

(A)   the performance or display is a regular part of the systematic instructional activities of a governmental body or a nonprofit educational institution; and

(B)   the performance or display is directly related and of material assistance to the teaching content of the transmission; and

(C)   the transmission is made primarily for—

(i) reception in classrooms or similar places normally devoted to instruction, or

(ii) reception by persons to whom the transmission is directed because their disabilities or other special circumstances prevent their attendance in classrooms or similar places normally devoted to instruction, or

(iii) reception by officers or employees of governmental bodies as a part of their official duties or employment;

89. *See* revised Act § 118 for the copyright obligations of noncommercial television.

90. *See* revised Act § 111(a)(3). A common carrier is any communications medium which is available to the public at fixed rates on a first come, first served basis. The telephone is the most widely used common carrier. Other examples include domestic satellites and microwave relays.

91. *See* revised Act § 111(a)(4). A booster is an electronic device which strengthens a weak broadcast signal and retransmits it for off-air reception. A translator serves a similar function, but in addition it alters a signal from one frequency to another.

92. *See* revised Act § 111(b).

93. Pay television is a special program service which provides additional programs for a fee, such as first run films and major sports events, which are unavailable to the general

so that only special paying subscribers could have access to the program, would invoke full copyright liability.

Cable transmissions which do not qualify for the above exemptions are subject to full copyright liability. This liability, however, can be avoided by the cable system through the mechanism of the compulsory license, which is easily the most distinctive and controversial feature of the Copyright Act's regulation of cable television.[94] The filing and notice requirements for obtaining a compulsory license are delineated in section 111(d). Acts that are infringements of the compulsory license, which, in essence, are violations of the FCC's signal carriage rules are set forth in section 111(c).[95] The regulatory scheme permits a cable system to receive

viewing public. The operators of these services typically create interference, or "scramble" the picture, which only paying customers can unscramble.

94. See notes 73-74 & accompanying text *supra* for a discussion of compulsory licenses. The revised Act confers liability only upon secondary transmissions by cable companies. Therefore, it is critical to determine whether the retransmission systems falls within the definition of a cable system, which is defined as "a facility, located in any State, Territory, Trust Territory or Possession, that in whole or part receives signals transmitted or programs broadcast by one or more television broadcast stations licensed by the Federal Communications Commission, and makes secondary transmissions of such signals or programs by wires, cables, or other communications channels to subscribing members of the public who pay for such service . . . ." Revised Act § 111(f).

95. The revised Act §§ 111 (c)-(d) provide:

(c) SECONDARY TRANSMISSIONS BY CABLE SYSTEMS.—

(1) Subject to the provisions of clauses (2), (3), and (4) of this subsection, secondary transmissions to the public by a cable system of a primary transmission made by a broadcast station licensed by the Federal Communications Commission or by an appropriate governmental authority of Canada or Mexico and embodying a performance or display of a work shall be subject to compulsory licensing upon compliance with the requirements of subsection (d) where the carriage of the signals comprising the secondary transmission is permissible under the rules, regulations, or authorizations of the Federal Communications Commission.

(2) Notwithstanding the provisions of clause (1) of this subsection, the willful or repeated secondary transmission to the public by a cable system of a primary transmission made by a broadcast station licensed by the Federal Communications Commission or by an appropriate governmental authority of Canada or Mexico and embodying a performance or display of a work is actionable as an act of infringement under section 501, and is fully subject to the remedies provided by sections 502 through 506 and 509 . . . .

. . . .

(d) COMPULSORY LICENSE FOR SECONDARY TRANSMISSIONS BY CABLE SYSTEMS.—

(1) For any secondary transmission to be subject to compulsory licensing under subsection (c), the cable system shall, at least one month before the date of the commencement of operations of the cable system or within one hundred and eighty days after the enactment of this Act, whichever is later, and thereafter within thirty days after each occasion on which the ownership or control or the signal carriage complement of the cable system changes, record in the Copyright

a compulsory license for the secondary transmission of broadcast stations licensed by the FCC or the appropriate Mexican or Canadian authorities, so long as the carriage of the signal is permissible under FCC regulations and the cable system refrains from changing or altering the signal.[96]

To obtain a compulsory license, the cable system must supply the Copyright Office with extensive information concerning the operations and ownership of the system. Specifically, each system must submit a statement account on a semiannual basis, specifying the number of channels retransmitted, the names and locations of each broadcast channel carried, the total number of subscribers served by the cable system, and the gross receipts which the system received for this retransmission service. The Register of Copyrights may require any additional information which it deems necessary by promulgating appropriate regulations.[97] The cable systems must also file both a special statement of account for any nonnetwork programs from distant signals which have been added or substituted under special circumstances permitted by the FCC,[98] and a notice listing ownership of the cable system, the signals carried, and their location.[99] In addition to these reporting requirements, the cable system must carry only FCC authorized signals[100] and may not alter, delete, or add to any advertising or station announcements.[101] Finally, the system must deposit with the Register of Copyrights a royalty fee as computed by a statutory formula.[102]

The prohibition against additions, changes, and deletions is based on the perceived economic impact which such content alterations have on

---

Office a notice including a statement of the identity and address of the person who owns or operates the secondary transmission service or has power to exercise primary control over it, together with the name and location of the primary transmitter or primary transmitters whose signals are regularly carried by the cable system, and thereafter, from time to time, such further information as the Register of Copyrights, after consultation with the Copyright Royalty Tribunal, shall prescribe by regulation to carry out the purpose of this clause. . . .

96. *See* revised Act § 111(c)(1).

97. *See* revised Act § 111(d)(2)(A). Regulations establishing the form, content, and filing requirements for cable television systems were adopted, effective February 10, 1978. *See* 43 Fed. Reg. 960-64 (1978) (to be codified in 37 C.F.R. §§ 201.11, 201.17).

98. *Id.*

99. *See* revised Act § 111(d)(1).

100. *See* revised Act § 111(c)(2)(A).

101. *See* revised Act § 111(c)(3). An exception is made for market research companies that have obtained the prior consent of the advertiser who paid for the commercial, the television station which broadcasts the commercial, and the cable system which carries the commercial, so long as no further income is obtained from commercial time used in this manner.

102. *See* revised Act § 111(d)(2)(B).

the copyright owner. In the Committee's view, any willful alteration of the content of the broadcast material has a drastic effect on the nature of the cable retransmission, making the cable system function very much like a broadcaster. In particular, the substitution of advertising is believed to create the greatest harm because it injures the original advertiser, and this indirectly injures the copyright owner, whose compensation is dependent on the willingness of sponsors to pay for air time based on a particular audience size. Substitute advertising injures the broadcaster by forcing him to compete for advertising dollars with a cable system which does not have comparable programing costs.[103] Noncompliance with any of the above requirements or restrictions constitutes an infringement of the Act, provided, however, that the breach is "willful or repeated."[104] Accordingly, the cable system is protected from liability for unintended acts.

As noted above, in order to obtain a compulsory license, a cable system must pay a royalty fee to the Register of Copyrights. This fee is computed by using a formula based on the cable system's gross receipts and the number of distant signal equivalents. A distant signal equivalent (DSE) is a numerical value assigned to the secondary transmission of nonnetwork television programing beyond the local service area of the primary transmitter by a cable system.[105] In other words, a DSE is assigned only to the retransmission of distant signals. The value assigned a signal depends upon the nature of the station which originates the distant programing. The highest value is assigned to independent stations, and the lowest is assigned to network affiliates and noncommercial educational stations.[106] Although cable systems pay royalty fees only for retransmission of nonnetwork syndicated programing, network affiliates

103. *See* HOUSE REPORT, *supra* note 68, at 93-94.
104. *Id*. at 94.
105. *See* revised Act § 111(f).
106. *See id*. This provision also requires that fractional values be determined for any substituted programing or special program categories or part time retransmission as permitted under FCC rules. An independent station is allocated the highest value because its programing is comprised mostly of syndicated programing sold on a market-by-market basis. By retransmitting an independent signal beyond its local service area the cable system reduces the attractiveness of the program in its market since a local broadcaster will be less willing to pay for a program which has previously been viewed by retransmission on the cable system. In addition, the copyright owner's licensing fee does not reflect the additional viewers in distant markets who see the program on a cable system. A lower value is assigned to network as well as educational stations since copyright owners sell licenses for network programing on the basis of a national viewing audience. Therefore, the cable system need not compensate copyright owners for network programs. Network affiliates, however, also carry several hours per day of nonnetwork programing, which is reflected by the low value assigned to the network station.

are included in the computation of DSE's because they usually broadcast some nonnetwork programing.

Gross receipts include only those arising from the basic service of retransmission, and do not include receipts from other sources, such as pay cable or installation charges.[107] Royalty payments are made only for retransmission of distant signals composed of nonnetwork programing, because the economic harm caused by retransmission by cable systems essentially affects only copyright owners whose works are distributed in that manner. The copyright owner whose works are transmitted through network programing is not harmed by cable retransmission because he is compensated on the basis of a national (network) audience,[108] which is not increased by the cable retransmission. In the case of nonnetwork programing, however, the copyright owner is injured because he does not receive full compensation for his work. He is not credited with the increased audience size which results from presentation of his work by the cable system. Cable retransmission of a purely local signal is similar to the distant network programing. If the cable retransmission is to the same market audience for which the copyright owner is compensated by the primary transmitter, there is no economic injury to the copyright owner. Thus, cable systems do not make any royalty payments for local or network programing.

The procedure for determining royalty payments is set forth in section 111(d) of the revised Act.[109] First, the total number of distant signal

---

107. *See* HOUSE REPORT, *supra* note 68, at 96. Royalty payments are made only for secondary transmissions of distant signals, specifically, programs from independent stations and nonnetwork programs of network affiliates.

108. Revised Act § 111(f) defines a network station as

a television broadcast station that is owned or operated by, or affiliated with, one or more of the television networks in the United States providing nationwide transmissions, and that transmits a substantial part of the programing supplied by such networks for a substantial part of that station's typical broadcast day.

This same section defines an independent station as "a commercial television broadcast station other than a network station."

109. Revised Act § 111(d)(2)(B) states:

(B) except in the case of a cable system whose royalty is specified in subclause (C) or (D), a total royalty fee for the period covered by the statement, computed on the basis of specified percentages of the gross receipts from subscriber to the cable service during said period for the basic service of providing secondary transmissions of primary broadcast transmitters, as follows:

(i) 0.675 of 1 per centum of such gross receipts for the privilege of further transmitting any nonnetwork programing of a primary transmitter in whole or in part beyond the local service area of such primary transmitter, such amount to be applied against the fee, if any, payable pursuant to paragraphs (ii) through (iv);

(ii) 0.675 of 1 per centum of such gross receipts for the first distant signal equivalent;

equivalents carried by the cable system is determined. Then, each successive DSE, or any fraction thereof, is multiplied by a declining progression of fractional percentages of the system's gross receipts, and the sums thus obtained are added together to give the cable system's royalty payment. If a cable system is located partly within and partly without the local service area of a broadcast station, the fee is computed on gross receipts from subscribers outside the local service area.[110]

Due to the FCC's signal carriage rules, cable systems which are located outside all television markets are permitted to carry unrestricted numbers of distant signals[111] and are therefore required to pay a greater percentage of gross receipts as a royalty payment than are larger cable systems located in the major television markets where distant signal carriage is restricted. In order to minimize the financial burden on small cable systems, the revised Act includes two separate provisions which reduce the royalty fee for such cable systems. Section 111(d)(2)(C)[112] provides a special computation for systems with less than $80,000 in semiannual revenues, and section 111(d)(2)(D)[113] provides a formula for

---

   (iii) 0.425 of 1 per centum of such gross receipts for each of the second, third, and fourth distant signal equivalents;
   (iv) 0.2 of 1 per centum of such gross receipts for the fifth distant signal equivalent and each additional distant signal equivalent thereafter; and
in computing the amounts payable under paragraphs (ii) through (iv), above, any fraction of a distant signal equivalent shall be computed at its fractional value and, in the case of any cable system located partly within and partly without the local service area of a primary transmitter, gross receipts shall be limited to those gross receipts derived from subscribers located without the local service area of such primary transmitter;
   110. It is estimated that total copyright fees from the cable industry will amount to only $8.7 million or approximately $.81 per subscriber per year. HOUSE REPORT, *supra* note 68, at 91.
   111. 47 C.F.R. § 76.67 (1976).
   112. The revised Act § 111(d)(2)(C) declares:
   [I]f the actual gross receipts paid by subscribers to a cable system for the period covered by the statement for the basic service of providing secondary transmissions of primary broadcast transmitters total $80,000 or less, gross receipts of the cable system for the purpose of this subclause shall be computed by subtracting from such actual gross receipts the amount by which $80,000 exceeds such actual gross receipts, except that in no case shall a cable system's gross receipts be reduced to less than $3,000. The royalty fee payable under this subclause shall be 0.5 of 1 per centum, regardless of the number of distant signal equivalents, if any.
   113. The revised Act § 111(d)(2)(D) states:
   [I]f the actual gross receipts paid by subscribers to a cable system for the period covered by the statement, for the basic service of providing secondary transmissions of primary broadcast transmitters, are more than $80,000 but less than $160,000, the royalty fee payable under this subclause shall be (i) 0.5 of 1 per centum of any gross receipts up to $80,000; and (ii) 1 per centum of any gross

systems with semiannual revenues of between $80,000 and $160,000. Both formulas are based solely on a percentage of gross receipts without regard to the number of DSE's which the system carries.[114]

To administer the complexities of the compulsory licensing provisions and royalty fee schedules, the revised Act established the Copyright Royalty Tribunal.[115] Its function is to consider adjustments in royalty rates for cable[116] and certain other uses of copyrighted works, to distribute royalty fees[117] to owners of copyrighted works,[118] and to resolve conflicts over fee distribution.[119] The Tribunal is an independent entity in the legislative branch[120] and is now composed of five commissioners appointed for seven-year terms by the President with the consent of the Senate.[121] Unlike the substantive provisions of the new Act which became effective on January 1, 1978, the Tribunal was to be appointed within six months after the enactment of the law on October 19, 1976.[122] It is anticipated that much of its work will be the reevaluation of cable royalty fees. Section 801(b)(2) sets forth in great detail the basis for these rate reevaluations.[123] The Tribunal may readjust royalty rates to reflect

receipts in excess of $80,000 but less than $160,000, regardless of the number of distant signal equivalents, if any.

114. Under § 111(d)(2)(C), systems with semiannual revenues of $80,000 or less pay 1/2% of gross revenues as a royalty fee, with a minimum payment of $30 seminnually; under § 111(d)(2)(D), systems with semiannual revenues of between $80,000 and $160,000 pay 1/2% of gross revenues on receipts below $80,000 and 1% on gross receipts in excess of $80,000 but less than $160,000. In both cases no additional fee is assessed for DSE's.

115. See revised Act §§ 801-810. The United States Register of Copyrights calls the royalty tribunal an "ingenious" device for regulating compulsory licenses "without constant and unwarranted litigation and need for congressional action." Despite perceived benefits, the Register states that "the existence of a government body that is paying out royalties, settling disputes among copyright owners, reviewing royalty rates of licenses, seems an open invitation to further government control." See Ringer supra note 66, at 495.

116. See revised Act § 801(b)(2).

117. See revised Act § 801(b)(3).

118. See revised Act § 111(d)(3-5).

119. See revised Act § 801(b)(3).

120. See revised Act § 801(a).

121. See revised Act § 802(a).

122. See revised Act § 801(c). The appointments to the Tribunal were recently made. The appointees are Thomas C. Brennan, Douglas Coulter, Mary Lou Berg, Clarence L. James, Jr., and Frances Garcia.

123. The revised Act § 801(b)(2) provides:

(b) Subject to the provisions of this chapter, the purpose of the Tribunal shall be—. . . .

(2) to make determinations concerning the adjustment of the copyright royalty rates in section 111 solely in accordance with the following provisions:

(A) The rates established by section 111(d)(2)(B) may be adjusted to reflect (i) national monetary inflation or deflation or (ii) changes in the average rates charged cable subscribers for the basic service of providing secondary

national inflation or deflation or changes in the average subscriber fee charged for basic service "to maintain the real constant dollar level of the royalty fee per subscriber."[124] However, two limitations are imposed: first, if increases in the average subscriber rates for basic service exceed the inflation rate, any change in royalty fees cannot exceed the inflation rate. In addition, the royalty fee cannot be increased to reflect any reduction in the number of DSE's which a cable system may carry in

transmissions to maintain the real constant dollar level of the royalty fee per subscriber which existed as of the date of enactment of this Act: *Provided*, That if the average rates charged cable system subscribers for the basic service of providing secondary transmissions are changed so that the average rates exceed national monetary inflation, no change in the rates established by section 111(d)(2)(B) shall be permitted: *And provided further*, That no increase in the royalty fee shall be permitted based on any reduction in the average number of distant signal equivalents per subscriber. The Commission may consider all factors relating to the maintenance of such level of payments including, as an extenuating factor, whether the cable industry has been restrained by subscriber rate regulating authorities from increasing the rates for the basic service of providing secondary transmissions.

(B) In the event that the rules and regulations of the Federal Communications Commission are amended at any time after April 15, 1976, to permit the carriage by cable systems of additional television broadcast signals beyond the local service area of the primary transmitters of such signals, the royalty rates established by section 111(d)(2)(B) may be adjusted to insure that the rates for the additional distant signal equivalents resulting from such carriage are reasonable in the light of the changes effected by the amendment to such rules and regulations. In determining the reasonableness of rates proposed following an amendment of Federal Communications Commission rules and regulations, the Copyright Royalty Tribunal shall consider, among other factors, the economic impact on copyright owners and users: *Provided*, That no adjustment in royalty rates shall be made under this subclause with respect to any distant signal equivalent or fraction thereof represented by (i) carriage of any signal permitted under the rules and regulations of the Federal Communications Commission in effect on April 15, 1976, or the carriage of a signal of the same type (that is, independent, network, or noncommercial educational) substituted for such permitted signal, or (ii) a television broadcast signal first carried after April 15, 1976, pursuant to an individual waiver of the rules and regulations of the Federal Communications Commission, as such rules and regulations were in effect on April 15, 1976.

(C) In the event of any change in the rules and regulations of the Federal Communications Commission with respect to syndicated and sports program exclusivity after April 15, 1976, the rates established by section 111(d)(2)(B) may be adjusted to assure that such rates are reasonable in light of the changes to such rules and regulations, but any such adjustment shall apply only to the affected television broadcast signals carried on those systems affected by the change.

(D) The gross receipts limitations established by section 111(d)(2)(C) and (D) shall be adjusted to reflect national monetary inflation or deflation or changes in the average rates charged cable system subscribers for the basic service of providing secondary transmissions to maintain the real constant dollar value of the exemption provided by such section; and the royalty rate specified therein shall not be subject to adjustment.

124. Revised Act § 801(b)(2)(A).

order to compensate copyright owners for the consequent decrease in revenues.[125] The Tribunal is also free to consider any other factors deemed pertinent to the rate issue.

The Tribunal may adjust royalty payments if the FCC changes any of its rules on signal carriage.[126] In particular, the carriage of additional distant signals by cable systems based on changes in FCC regulations is a basis for reevaluating royalty rates. Upon any such change in signal carriage, the Tribunal is to assess "the economic impact on copyright owners and users."[127] In addition, it may consider rate revisions for changes in syndicated and sports exclusivity rules, but any adjustments will apply only to the broadcast signals affected by the change.[128]

The Tribunal is to evaluate the royalty fees for cable television in 1985 and every five years thereafter.[129] During this time schedule any user or owner of copyrighted material may request a rate adjustment upon a determination by the Tribunal that the applicant has a "significant interest" in the proceeding.[130] In a similar vein, a copyright owner or user with a significant interest may petition for an adjustment of royalty rates upon any change in the FCC signal carriage, sports, or snydicated exclusivity rules.[131] Any change made by the Tribunal may be reconsidered in 1980 and every fifth year thereafter.

The procedure for the collection and distribution of royalty payments is established by the Act through a joint operation of the Copyright Office and the Royalty Tribunal.[132] Cable companies are to make semi-annual royalty payments to the Register of Copyrights, who will deduct the administrative costs for the Copyright Office and deposit the balance in the Treasury for later distribution by the Tribunal. The Register will

---

125. Copyright owners expressed concern that cable systems might reduce the number of distant signals as special services such as pay cable systems increased in number. This shift in revenue would reduce royalty fees. The House Report indicated "such shifts of revenue sources, if they do occur, should be taken into account by the [Tribunal] in adjusting the basic rates." HOUSE REPORT, *supra* note 68, at 175.

126. *See* revised Act § 801(b)(2)(B).

127. *Id.*

128. *See* revised Act § 801(b)(2)(C). The intent of this provision is to protect the copyright owner if the FCC deletes or modifies its syndicated exclusivity or sports program exclusivity rules. The exclusivity rules protect the copyright owner by restricting the carriage of certain types of programing from distant signals. In case of any rule changes, the royalty rates may be adjusted to "assure that such rates are reasonable in light of the changes to such rules and regulations." HOUSE REPORT, *supra* note 68, at 177. See notes 60-61 & accompanying text *supra* for a discussion of the recent FCC notice of inquiry on revising the syndicated exclusivity rules.

129. *See* revised Act § 804(a)(2)(A).

130. *See* revised Act § 804(a)(2).

131. *See* revised Act § 804(b).

132. *See* revised Act § 111(d)(3).

submit to the Tribunal semiannually a compilation of the statements of accounts which the cable systems have supplied, and the Tribunal will then distribute the fees among copyright owners. Those eligible for royalty fees are owners whose works were carried on distant nonnetwork programs, programs from distant signals carried because of special substitution rules permitted by the FCC, and distant nonnetwork programing consisting exclusively of audio signals.[133]

To apply for compensation, a copyright owner must file a claim annually in July. The Act specifically preempts the antitrust laws and permits claimants to agree among themselves as to an appropriate division of compulsory licensing fees.[134] After August 1, the Tribunal decides if there is any disagreement regarding the distribution of fees.[135] If discord exists, the Tribunal must resolve it before the disputed fees may be distributed. Any licensing fees not in dispute may be distributed.[136] The Act does not specify the manner in which the Tribunal is to set an appropriate division of compulsory licensing fees, but leaves that determination to the Tribunal's discretion.[137]

Even a brief glance at the foregoing material reveals an extensive laundry list of acts and commissions by a cable system which may constitute infringements of the Copyright Act. The possibilities for infringement are summed up in sections 111(b) and 111(c).[138] Violations include secondary transmissions not permitted by the FCC rules, failure to file the required reports and statements of account or to pay a royalty fee, willful alteration of program content or substitution of commercials, or any other act contrary to a command or prohibition of the Act.[139]

Section 501 permits any legal or beneficial owner of a copyright to institute an action for breach of copyright.[140] In the case of the cable

---

133. *See* revised Act §§ 111(d)(4)(A)-(C).
134. *See* revised Act § 111(d)(5)(A).
135. *See* revised Act § 111(d)(5)(B).
136. *See* revised Act § 111(d)(5)(C).
137. *See* HOUSE REPORT, *supra* note 68, at 97.
138. *See also*, HOUSE REPORT, *supra* note 68, at 92.
139. *See* revised Act §§ 111(c)(2)(A), (B), 111 (c)(3).
140. The revised Act § 501 states:
    (a) Anyone who violates any of the exclusive rights of the copyright owner as provided by sections 106 through 118, or who imports copies or phonorecords into the United States in violation of section 602, is an infringer of the copyright.
    (b) The legal or beneficial owner of an exclusive right under a copyright is entitled, subject to the requirements of sections 205(d) and 411, to institute an action for any infringement of that particular right committed while he or she is the owner of it. The court may require such owner to serve written notice of the action with a copy of the complaint upon any person shown, by the records of the

television provisions, the Act creates two additional classes of plaintiffs who may seek remedies for infringement of section 111. A television station located in the cable system's market which holds the copyright on a particular program is treated as a legal or beneficial owner, and has a cause of action against a cable system which willfully or repeatedly imports the same program into the broadcaster's local service area in violation of the FCC's signal carriage rules.[141] In addition, a distant broadcast station originating a program, and any broadcast station in whose local service area the cable system's retransmission occurs, may sue a cable system which substitutes or otherwise changes the programs, commercials or announcements of the distant signal.[142]

Both legal and equitable remedies are available for violations of the Copyright Act. The legal or beneficial holder of a copyright may seek an injunction, impoundment of illegal copies, actual or statutory damages, and recovery of costs and reasonable attorneys fees.[143] In addition, copyright owners and local broadcasters have available a special remedy in the case of willful alteration of programing by the cable system; namely, a court may deprive the cable system of its compulsory license for one or more distant signals, for a period not to exceed thirty days.[144] Finally, criminal penalties are available against willful infringement for commercial advantage or private gain, and are particularly severe for infrigement of the copyright of a sound recording or motion picture.[145]

Copyright Office or otherwise, to have or claim an interest in the copyright, and shall require that such notice be served upon any person whose interest is likely to be affected by a decision in the case. The court may require the joinder, and shall permit the intervention, of any person having or claiming an interest in the copyright.

(c) For any secondary transmission by a cable system that embodies a performance or a display of a work which is actionable as an act of infringement under subsection (c) of section 111, a television broadcast station holding a copyright or other license to transmit or perform the same version of that work shall, for purposes of subsection (b) of this section, be treated as a legal or beneficial owner if such secondary transmission occurs within the local service area of that television station.

(d) For any secondary transmission by a cable system that is actionable as an act of infringement pursuant to section 111(c)(3), the following shall also have standing to sue: (i) the primary transmitter whose transmission has been altered by the cable system; and (ii) any broadcast station within whose local service area the secondary transmission occurs.

141. *See* revised Act § 501(c). Such a television station may also sue when the cable system has failed to comply with the procedures for filing notice, statements of account, or royalty fees with the Register of Copyrights. *Id*.

142. *See* revised Act § 501(d).

143. *See* revised Act §§ 502-505.

144. *See* revised Act § 509(b).

145. *See* revised Act § 506.

IV. THE REVISED ACT: SOME PROBLEMS

Whether the revised Act provides a satisfactory resolution to the copyright issue and whether it eliminates the obstacles to the growth of major market cable systems is uncertain. The Act is essentially a legislative compromise between competing interests. Neither broadcasters, copyright owners, nor cable system operators find the Act totally to their liking.[146] Yet the legislation does achieve a major goal merely by its institutionalization of copyright liability for the cable industry. The potential difficulty with the Act lies in its implementation. Problems of interpretation, enforcement, and jurisdictional overlay are both readily apparent and already developing. Furthermore, aside from the more or less internal problems with the Act, which are natural outgrowths of any substantial change in the law, the Act introduces a new and unsettling factor into the FCC's already difficult process of developing national communications policy.

Although the revised Act relies on the FCC's signal carriage rules to determine the liability of a cable system, the terms used in the Act do not parallel the definitions in the FCC's cable television rules. Moreover, the copyright definitions are often ambiguously drafted. For example, the revised Act defines a cable system as a "facility . . . that in whole or in part receives signals transmitted . . . and makes secondary transmissions of such signals . . . to subscribing members of the public who pay for such service."[147] It appears that this definition would include any system, regardless of size. In comparison, the FCC recently revised its definition of a cable system to exempt systems with fewer than 500 subscribers from compliance with its regulations. The result is that retransmission systems which are not bound by the FCC regulations will be held liable for copyright infringements as cable systems.[148]

---

146. For example, the final language on the fee schedules was hammered out in last minute sessions between the copyright and cable interests. The broadcasters had previously walked out of the sessions, but were forced to accept the terms once an agreement was reached between the two other parties. *See* BROADCASTING, April 19, 1976, at 48.

147. Revised Act § 111(f).

148. *See* First Report and Order in Docket No. 20561, 63 F.C.C.2d 956 (1976). The copyright definition provides no exemption for small systems. Section 111(a)(1) does exempt secondary transmissions of local signals within a hotel, apartment house or similar establishment when no charge is made for this service. If, however, a master antenna system in a large apartment complex also carries signals from another television market, such as Baltimore, it may be subject to copyright liability.

The situation was further confused by the Copyright Office's most recently promulgated regulations, which expressly declared that any FCC rule, regulation, or practice "which excludes facilities from consideration as a 'cable system' because of the number or nature of subscribers or nature of the secondary transmisions made shall not be given

The revised Act states that for purposes of computing the royalty fee, two or more cable systems in contiguous communities under common ownership or control or operating from one "headend"[149] are to be considered as one system. Although its precise meaning is uncertain, this statement has the potential to affect royalty fees dramatically. If, for example, it means that small systems in contiguous communities under common ownership or operating from the same headend are considered as one system, then gross receipts would be aggregated, and most likely the revenues would be in excess of the $320,000 annual gross receipts limit for small systems. The resulting difference in royalty payments could have a significant effect on the economic viability of small cable systems.[150]

The revised Act creates copyright liability for cable systems which carry broadcast signals beyond the local service area of the primary transmitter.[151] The statute's definition of local service area relies on the FCC's signal carriage rules.[152] Thus, a cable system would be required to make royalty payments for any distant signals carried. Read in conjunction with the Act's definition of a cable system, this liability would also seem to extend to master antenna systems in apartment houses, condominiums, and trailer parks, thereby imposing copyright liability on retransmission facilities which are not cable systems under the FCC rules. For example, the owner of a large apartment building in Washington, D.C. would be required to pay royalty fees if the master antenna system in the building distributed television signals from nearby cities, such as Baltimore, which are not a part of the Washington market. It is not clear whether Congress intended the Act to have such a broad scope.

---

effect" for the purposes of the new regulations. *See* 43 Fed. Reg. 961 (1978) (to be codified in 37 C.F.R. § 201.11 (a)(3)).

149. *See* revised Act § 111(f). A headend is the electronic processing center of a cable system. All signals, both broadcast signals and those originated on the cable system, are processed and transmitted through the cable system from the headend. Frequently one cable system operating with one headend serves several municipalities.

150. *Id*. This issue has been under consideration at the Copyright Office. *See* Transcript of Proceedings, Hearings on Cable Television, Docket No. RM 77-2 (Apr. 12, 1977) at 167 (unpublished transcript in Copyright Office). Many cable systems are designed so that one physical plant services many separate communities. The effect of aggregated revenues would be particularly severe on these systems. The Copyright Office recently acknowledged this problem but concluded that any "modification . . . would be an inappropriate addition to the language of the act." 43 Fed. Reg. 958 (1978).

151. *See* revised Act § 111(c).

152. The revised Act § 111(f) defines the " 'local service area of a primary transmitter', in the case of a television broadcast station, . . . [as] . . . the area in which such station is entitled to insist upon its signal being retransmitted by a cable system pursuant to the rules, regulations, and authorizations of the Federal Communications Commission . . . ."

If a cable system serves subscribers both within and without the local service area of the primary transmitter, the system must compute the number of subscribers beyond the local service area and make royalty payments on revenues from those subscribers.[153] An accounting problem is apparent since the boundaries of a television market cannot be accurately measured.[154] Thus, it will be difficult, if not impossible, for a cable system to determine the correct percentages. Given the inherent inaccuracies in measurement techniques, this requirement seems certain to foster disputes between cable systems, copyright owners, and broadcasters, and conflict between copyright law and communications policy.

The Copyright Act defines a network station as one that is "owned or operated by, or affiliated with, one or more of the television networks . . . and that transmits a substantial part of the programing supplied by such networks for a substantial part of that station's typical broadcast day."[155] The FCC definition requires that the television station carry in weekly prime time 85 percent of the hours of programing offered by the major network with which it is affiliated.[156] It is not clear whether the "substantial programing" requirement of the copyright definition is congruent with the more specific FCC definition, but it is entirely possible that certain signals which the FCC would categorize as independent stations may well be considered network affiliates under the Copyright Act.

Another problem is that the term "gross receipts" is defined as revenues received from "the basic service of providing secondary transmissions of primary broadcast transmitters."[157] The calculation is limited to fees from carriage of distant broadcast signals, although it may be difficult for a cable operator to determine what portion of his revenues are derived from that service. Traditionally, system operators charge a basic monthly fee for all services except pay cable, for which an additional fee is paid. The basic fee includes charges for nonbroadcast signals such as news, tickers, sports channels, shoppers guides, and the like. Allocating this fee among channels may be an impossibility.

In addition to the potential definitional conflicts between the revised Act and the FCC cable rules, problems have already developed with respect to what very well should be the simpler and more mechanical aspects of the Act. The revised Act establishes detailed reporting state-

---

153. *See* revised Act § 111(d)(2)(B).
154. For a discussion of "television market," see note 4 *supra*.
155. Revised Act § 111(f).
156. 47 C.F.R. § 76.5(l) (1976).
157. HOUSE REPORT, *supra* note 68, at 96.

ments which must be submitted to the Register of Copyrights. The information required, however, does not comport with the information which the industry already submits to the FCC, although much of it has duplicative content. The cable industry may easily become burdened with excessive filing requirements.[158] The Act states that noncompliance with the filing or fee provisions renders the cable system liable for copyright infringement. The more onerous the filing requirements, the more likely that cable systems will be liable for infringements of the Act. The statutory requirements are particularly troublesome, since some appear to be technically impossible to perform. Some of these problems, however, have recently been remedied by the Copyright Office.[159] Furthermore, the statute grants the Register of Copyrights certain latitude in developing specific reporting requirements.[160] Predictably, this has resulted in a continuation of longstanding arguments among the cable, copyright, and broadcast interests, with the copyright owners and broadcasters pressing for more detailed and extensive reporting procedures, and the cable industry fighting for lesser requirements. This clash of interests is also apparent in conflicting interpretations of other sections of the Act. The copyright owners support regulations which permit them to review the financial accounts of cable systems in order to verify gross receipts, while the cable industry resists such regulations. In addition, the copyright owners urge that filing fees be imposed on the cable industry to pay for the administrative costs of the act.[161]

158. The cable television industry has recommended that the Copyright Office utilize the same filing forms as the FCC. This suggestion has been opposed by the copyright owners and broadcasters who assert that additional information necessitates the use of different reporting forms. In a recent rulemaking proceeding, the Copyright Office determined that it would not be advantageous to utilize the FCC forms; however, the office did not have alternative reporting forms available and ultimately suggested that the cable industry devise its own forms. 42 Fed. Reg. 15,065-68 (1977). The Copyright Office has stated that it is continuing to explore the possibility of providing standardized reporting forms. 43 Fed. Reg. 960 (1978).

159. For example, the Act requires that the cable system submit a log of all radio signals which the system carries. The cable system which utilizes an all-band FM radio receiver cannot list with accuracy all signals since available radio signals depend to a large extent on weather and topographical conditions. Yet under the revised Act's § 111(c)(2)(B), a cable system may be violating the Act for failure to accurately file a statement of account as required in the revised act § 111(d). The Copyright Office has modified the filing requirement so that all-band FM signals "generally receivable" as a result of monitoring at reasonable times and intervals are listed in statements of account. 43 Fed. Reg. 963 (1978) (to be codified in 37 C.F.R. § 201.17 (e)(9)(iii)).

160. The revised Act § 111(d) permits the Register to require by regulation submission of any additional data by cable systems.

161. *See* testimony of Jack Valenti, President of Motion Picture Association of America, and Daniel Aaron, Chairman of National Cable Television Association in Hearings on Cable Television, *supra* note 150. The Copyright Office has determined that the Act

A further problem is one of available revenues. It is anticipated that the cable industry will pay approximately $8.7 million annually in royalty fees,[162] from which will be deducted the costs of administration for the Register of Copyrights and the Royalty Tribunal. In other words, the copyright holders bear the costs of administering the Act, since the deductions reduce the size of the fund out of which they are eventually paid. It is likely that in the early years of the Act there will be a considerable number of disputes as to the validity of fees submitted by the cable industry and the manner in which royalty fees will be distributed. These disputes will increase administrative costs and thereby reduce the monies available for distributions. Consequently, it is likely that copyright owners and broadcasters will soon seek additional compensation by requesting increases in the royalty fee schedule. Despite these easily anticipated difficulties, the Act provides only minimal guidance to the Tribunal on standards for changing the fee schedule.[163]

Finally, there exists the potential for abuse of the remedy provisions by copyright owners and broadcasters seeking redress for alleged infringements. The Act requires infringements to be willful or repeated, in order to protect the cable industry against harassment suits.[164] Section 501, however, indicates that any violation is an infringement of the Act, and until the meaning of "willful" or "repeated" is determined, there are likely to be numerous test suits, which may be perceived by cable interests as harassment.

Perhaps of even greater concern than these essentially internal interpretation problems is the potential for discord in the interaction of the Act with FCC policy. Because of the interrelationship between the FCC and copyright regulation, the FCC may at times find its policy determinations stymied by conflicting copyright considerations. For example, the FCC is now considering changes in the distant signal and syndicated exclusivity rules. A change in the FCC's signal carriage or syndicated exclusivity requirements automatically triggers an immediate reevalua-

---

prohibits the imposition of filing fees for cable systems submitting mandatory statements of account. However, filing fees will be imposed for permissive amendments. 43 Fed. Reg. 959 (1978).

162. *See* HOUSE REPORT, *supra* note 68, at 91.

163. *See* revised Act § 801(b); HOUSE REPORT, *supra* note 68, at 175-76.

164. The HOUSE REPORT, *supra* note 68, indicates that:

> The words "willful or repeated" are used to prevent a cable system from being subjected to severe penalties for innocent or casual acts ("Repeated" does not mean merely "more than once," of course; rather, it denotes a degree of aggravated negligence which borders on willfulness. Such a condition would not exist in the case of an innocent mistake as to what signals or programs may properly be carried under the FCC's complicated rules).

Id. at 5708.

tion of the cable fee schedule in the Copyright Act.[165] This mechanism makes sense from the standpoint of copyright regulation, since cable systems pay royalties only for retransmissions which are not currently prohibited by the FCC rules, but it could subject the cable industry to intensive and conflicting pressures. If royalty fees are unreasonably increased, the cable industry might refrain from carrying additional distant signals, despite the fact that the agency charged with creating communications policy has determined that such carriage is in the public interest. Thus, the Royalty Tribunal could become a court of last resort for competitive interests unhappy with FCC regulations.

A further example of this problem is the carriage of foreign broadcast signals. The FCC has determined that it is in the public interest to encourage carriage of foreign language stations on cable systems.[166] Cable systems located in the southern tier of the country, and serving substantial Spanish populations, often import broadcast signals from Mexico. Under the Copyright Act, a compulsory license for Mexican signals is given only if the signal can be received by "direct interception" or if carriage was grandfathered prior to April 15, 1976.[167] Presumably, only signals that can be picked up off-air will be subject to a compulsory license. Any Mexican signal which is transported by microwave or satellite would require the cable company to negotiate directly with the copyright owner or the broadcast station. Given the generally small audience for foreign language programing and the high cost of negotiating copyright agreements, it is foreseeable that cable systems will refrain from carrying Mexican signals. Therefore, the effect of the copyright

---

165. *Id.* The revised Act § 804(b) permits any owner or user of a copyrighted work to request an immediate review of royalty rates upon any change in the FCC's signal carriage, syndicated or sports exclusivity rules. In filings on the FCC's notice of inquiry on revision of signal carriage and syndicated exclusivity rules, the Motion Picture Association of America has already indicated that the cable industry's copyright fees are not high enough and has requested certain changes in the rules. *See* TELEVISION DIGEST, August 15, 1977, at 5.

166. *See* Cable Television Report and Order, 36 F.C.C.2d 143, 180-81 (1972).

167. *See* revised Act § 111(c)(4)(B). A cable system would be subject to full copyright liability if it used any receiving equipment other than an antenna which can pick up the signal directly from the transmitting station. Since an antenna can only receive signals transmitted over a limited distance, those cable systems located at too great a distance for direct pickup of the signal would be required to negotiate separately for copyright fees in order to carry a Mexican signal.

"Grandfathering" a signal is a procedure used by the FCC to permit a cable system which was in operation prior to the 1972 cable television rules to continue to carry broadcast signals which are not permissible under the 1972 rules. The term applies to any act by a cable system which is not permissible under current regulations but which the FCC permits because the practice was established prior to the imposition of the FCC regulations.

provision would contravene the FCC's stated public interest determination to encourage carriage of such signals. In addition, it may conflict with the FCC's determination that the distance between an originating signal and an importing cable system should not be a factor in choosing which distant signals will be carried. Finally, since the revised Act makes every program carried on a distant signal contrary to the FCC rules a copyright violation,[168] most determinations as to whether a cable system has violated FCC rules will be made in the context of copyright suits in which the FCC is not a party. Hence, communications policy may be made without the benefit of the FCC's input.

V. Conclusion

Under the new Copyright Act of 1976, the cable television industry will be subject to copyright liability for retransmission of distant broadcast signals. The revised Act is long overdue. Although judicial interpretations of the predecessor Act have exempted the cable industry from copyright payments, its use of broadcast programing without compensation to the copyright holder has been consistently in conflict with federal copyright objectives. Indeed, payment of royalty fees should benefit the cable industry. It should eliminate harsh criticism from the competing industries as well as from certain policymakers in both the FCC and Congress who have maintained that the industry has been pirating programing. At the same time, passage of the Copyright Act should signal the end of the FCC's syndicated exclusivity rules which were enacted as a substitute for copyright legislation. The deletion of the rules would certainly be in keeping with the FCC's recently stated policy of deregulation of the cable industry.

These benefits may never accrue, however, because of the inherent character of the revised Act. The cable television provisions are the result of endless negotiations between industries with conflicting interests. Accordingly, the provisions represent political compromises and, therefore, are only marginally acceptable to some of the parties. It is quite foreseeable that each industry will seek changes in the rules in order to further its self-interest. Consequently, hostilities between the cable, copyright, and broadcast industries may continue unabated on issues such as the extent of copyright liability and the level of royalty payments. Because the copyright provisions are closely linked with the FCC's signal carriage rules, it is likely that the pressures for change in the new law will be felt in Congress, the Copyright office, and the FCC.

---

168. *See* revised Act § 111(c)(2).

In addition, the Act may encourage a blurring of jurisdictional boundaries between the FCC and the Copyright Office. It is likely, for example, that the FCC rules will be interpreted by courts deciding copyright cases without the benefit of input from the FCC.

The revised Act creates a substitute for marketplace negotiations of royalty fees, and should, therefore, aim to duplicate marketplace behavior as closely as possible. Unfortunately, the new Act fails in this respect, particularly with regard to the royalty fee schedule. The fee schedule is extremely low and appears to bear little relationship to the fees which would be generated in the marketplace. Consequently, it is likely that copyright and broadcast interests will request increased royalty payments by the cable industry at every available opportunity.

Other weaknesses in the conceptualization of the cable television provisions suggest that these provisions may become needlessly difficult to implement, obey, and enforce. Whether the Act will ultimately provide an effective resolution of the cable-copyright issue will depend upon the outcome of judicial interpretations, the development of working procedures in the Copyright Office, possible legislative amendments, and, ultimately, the passage of time.

WILL BETAMAX BE BUSTED?

Steven Brill

Within the next two or three years television will probably stop dictating the schedules of even the worst tube addicts. If your favorite show is on at nine and you want to go out, you'll just set your video tape recorder to catch the program.

VTRs allow you to tape-record a television show while you're away, or while you're there watching it, or even while you're watching something else on the same set. With handy cassettes they're as easy to use as a tape recorder.

Some half million Americans already have these wonderful machines. As the technology shakes down and competition stiffens, the price—about $900 at a discount store—will probably drop. VTR sales are expected to triple this year, from last year's 250,000, and perhaps double again next year. You can even buy a regular TV set with the gadget built in. Within the next ten years, 50 to 60 percent of all American TV households are expected to have VTRs.

Why is this in a law column? Because there is a suit quietly grinding along that may stop everything.

In September 1976, Universal City Studios and Walt Disney Productions sued the Sony Corporation, charging that Sony's Betamax VTR, the most popular one now on the market, infringed on the copyright rights of Universal and Disney to control the use of the pictures they produce.

The basics of copyright law are simple. If I write a book, you have to buy it from me (or my publisher). You can't just copy or reprint your own. It's the same with all creative works, including television programs and motion pictures.

"What right do Sony and home viewers have to appropriate our products without paying for them?" asks John Davies, a dapper 1950s Australian Olympic swimmer who is a partner at the Beverly Hills firm of Rosenfeld, Meyer & Susman and is leading the fight against Betamax.

SOURCE: Reprinted from *Esquire Fortnightly* 89(11): 19, 20, 22 (June 20, 1978) by courtesy of the publisher. Copyright © 1978 by Esquire Magazine Inc.

On the other side, there's veteran star litigator Max Freund, of New York's Rosenman Colin Freund Lewis & Cohen. Along with Dean Dunlavy of Gibson, Dunn & Crutcher in Los Angeles, Freund is quarterbacking Sony's defense, which in the legal community makes this a much-gossiped-about coast-to-coast battle between two large prestige firms and one small prestige firm. (Rosenfeld, Meyer has only twenty-nine lawyers.)

Freund says that "video tape recorders are no different than the audio tape recorders that have been on the market for years. You can't tell me that someone who tape-records a record in his own home, or a song on the radio, is breaking the law," he explains. "The analogy is clear and so is the law."

According to independent experts, neither the analogy nor the law is clear. First, songs on the radio or on record albums can be heard frequently or purchased inexpensively; and they last only a matter of minutes, anyway. So taping them is not nearly as advantageous as taping something on television. TV movies present a special problem. Most are sold to television for repeated airings. The second showing of *Gone with the Wind* will have a diminished audience if masses of people can set a Betamax to record it the first time. (Davies says that Betamax sales surged the week before *GWTW* was televised last fall, and that many Betamax buyers are building libraries of movies shown on TV.)

Most important, records do not rely on advertisers buying an audience. TV shows do, and the Betamax has a speed-up switch that allows you to bypass commercials when you play back a show you missed the night before. This may scare advertisers. So might the fact that they will not know what time of day, or week, or month, they are reaching their potential customers. (What if they're promoting a one-day-only sale?)

Besides, it is not at all clear that taping a song from a radio or record is *not* a copyright violation. "What's the difference between us and our claim and the record industry and a claim against audio recorders?" asks Davies. "I'll tell you what it is. It's that *they* sat on their hands when they should have sued . . . . If the record industry had jumped in, maybe there would be some law now on this."

"Exactly," agrees Harvard Law School copyright professor Arthur Miller. "The record industry should have sued. No one ever established that audio recorders are not copyright infringements. If you read the law strictly, they probably are."

Miller notes that one reason the record industry has not sued *yet* is that "everyone has been waiting around for ten or fifteen years for the new copyright law to be passed. Now that it has [it took effect on January 1], there may be such a suit. Or," he adds intriguingly, "you may even see a suit against Xerox machines."

If photocopying machines are copyright infringing devices, then video recorders are worse. Photocopiers cannot produce a book in the same form, the way a Betamax can reproduce a TV performance. The apt comparison with a Betamax would be a machine that could take a book and instantly make a perfectly cloned bound copy of it.

On the other hand, Sony's lawyers argue that there is a "home use" exception to the law that allows people to make recordings—video or audio—in the privacy of their homes for their own use.

This memorandum of law for Sony, and the one filed by Rosenfeld, Meyer for Universal and Disney the same day, are exceptionally well done. But the one by Rosenfeld, Meyer, drafted by Davies's junior partner Stephen Kroft, is better because it does such a good job of anticipating and batting down Sony's defenses, including this home use claim. Put simply, there isn't any "home use" exception in the law, and no court has ever found that there is.

The Universal-Disney anti-Betamax memo further asserts that home recording by a single person becomes a public, commercial practice when viewed in the context of millions of such individuals buying the Betamax from Sony—which is being sued for alleged "contributory" and "vicarious" infringements in selling the VTRs to home users. It also notes that the only other possible saving exception for a Betamax—a "fair use" doctrine allowing parts of certain materials to be copied or otherwise used without permission if it's for educational or creative purposes—excludes copying that is done just for entertainment. The fair use privilege is so sternly defined that a federal court recently ordered a school board in New York to stop video-taping for classroom use a program shown on public television.

Where does all this leave those of us who want the freedom to plan our TV schedules and save our favorite movies? If we rely just on the law we're in trouble. "If you read the law strictly, there can be no doubt that there's an infringement," says Harvard professor Miller.

Thus, Sony's lawyers won't be relying just on the law when Federal District Court Judge Warren Ferguson hears the case next January or February. A section of their pretrial memorandum, taking up more space than the home use and fair use claims and a silly First Amendment argument, addresses the "public interest." It's a long, lawyerly way of saying, "If science has developed a way for Junior to watch *Monday Night Football* the next day, why should some greedy movie companies be able to use a stubborn reading of the law to stand in the way?" This is Sony's only real chance. As Miller puts it, "In the end, the judge may look beyond the law to the competing values and interests involved."

Universal and Disney are meeting these public interest arguments with dire predictions that video tape recorders will scare away so many advertisers that TV programs or movies will not be sold profitably to television stations. Thus, this seemingly beneficial machine will wipe out the industry. Some of the doomsday claims seem farfetched, such as the one that financially crucial syndication rights (to sell old prime-time shows to stations for daytime reruns) won't be sold because millions of Americans who now watch the reruns will instead record libraries of shows like *I Love Lucy*. Other claims are more convincing—such as the possibility of people storing movies and of advertisers not being able to count on the time their ads will be viewed, or even that they'll be seen at all, given the speed-up switch.

Between now and the trial, the nine lawyers working full time on the case will be gathering ammunition for these public interest-versus-industry damage claims. Already 120 depositions (pretrial testimony sessions) have been taken from marketing and other experts prepared to testify for one side or the other on the effects of Betamax on the TV programming industry.

Everyone agrees that the case presents such a novel either-or issue that it will go all the way to the Supreme Court. This doesn't mean that the trial judge, if he decides for Universal and Disney this winter, couldn't order all Betamax sales suspended while the appeal drags on.

That, of course, raises the remedy problem. "The remedy question is another thing that makes this case so interesting," says one lawyer involved in the case. "The judge could order them to buy back all the machines; he could just tell them to stop selling them but not buy them back; or he could simply tell them to figure out some kind of money compensation for the plaintiffs. The range of possibilities is limitless." Another possibility is that the judge will order technology changes—a tape that erases itself the first time it replays, for example, would eliminate that "library" problem while allowing for the time-shift convenience.

It sounds crazy. A company having to modify or drop a major product that makes life more fun for the rest of us. But, with the law as it is now written, I cannot imagine a way the judge could write a credible opinion upholding the Betamax. The case creeping along this summer may end up being a classic example of law not keeping up with progress. Then it will be up to Congress to give us back the Betamax. With all the opposition lobbying—from performers' groups, from the industry, and from others who claim that VTRs will do to the television business what my mythical book-cloning machine would do to the book business—that could take a long time.

COPYRIGHT AND DESIGNS LAW:
REPORT OF THE COMMITTEE TO CONSIDER THE
LAW ON COPYRIGHT AND DESIGNS

Reprography: Introduction

General

204. Reproduction of literary works by photographic and like means on a large scale is a comparatively recent phenomenon. Until the 1960s the usual means of obtaining multiple copies of textual matter was by carbon copying, stencil duplicating, photostat copying or contact photography. Photographic processes based on silver halide sensitized materials were essentially two stage (negative and positive) and involved wet processing and the use of dark rooms. They were therefore slow, inconvenient and relatively expensive. Thermographic copying processes and other developments at about the same time enabled office-type machines to be introduced, but it was not until the 1960s that electrophotographic or xerographic machines became available in this country to any appreciable extent. At first these tended to be large and expensive, but gradually smaller machines suitable for use in offices by non-specialised staff became available. The modern office copier machine is clean, dry and rapid in operation, with operator skill being limited to the ability to turn a dial and press a button. Coin-operated machines are now available in many places.

205. Over the last two decades the cost of photocopies has decreased considerably in relation to that of conventional printing. Not surprisingly publishers of books and periodicals have been watching these developments closely.

206. The widespread copying of textual matter is clearly here to stay. It would be out of the question to try to restrict the sale of copying machines. Photocopying is something authors and publishers must come to terms with in the best way possible. The question of a practical solution to the photocopying problem was one of the most difficult issues facing us and is therefore dealt with in some detail. Although the submissions were in the main concerned with the copying of textual matter we are aware that the techniques are applicable to the copying of any graphical material.

Definitions

207. The terms 'photographic copying' or 'photocopying' undoubtedly cover the majority of the processes used for permanent reproduction of text. Non-light processes, of which there are now a growing number of examples, are not however properly covered by these terms. Output can now be produced from computers by direct 'writing' onto film using electron beams. A number of facsimile transmission systems utilize non-light techniques. Laser techniques and systems of holographic reproduction are being developed. In view of these developments there has been a growing tendency to use the term 'reprography' or 'reprographic reproduction' as a more appropriate generic term. All these processes involve what may conveniently be called 'facsimile copies'.

SOURCE: Reprinted from *Copyright and Designs Law: Report of the Committee to consider the Law on Copyright and Designs*, Cmnd. 6732, by permission of the Controller of Her Britannic Majesty's Stationery Office. Copyright © 1977 by Her Majesty's Stationery Office.

208. The prefix 'micro' is used to indicate that images are recorded at a reduction ratio such that the resultant image is unreadable, or at least difficult to read, with the unaided eye. 'Microfilm' relates to lengths of film (usually 35 or 16mm wide) and 'microfiche' to cards of film (usually 105mm × 148mm in size). 'Microform' and 'microcopy' are generic terms. Microcopying techniques are now used to record between sixty and several thousand pages of text on a single sheet or reel of film at reduction ratios between 18:1 and 150:1.

209. The difference between micro and same size copying is mainly only a matter of degree. The preparation of a master microcopy is relatively expensive, but once produced it presents a ready means of copying. Further copies, possibly representing whole books, can be 'run-off' for a very small sum or selected frames may be 'blown-up' and reproduced in hard copy form.

210. A number of works are now being published in the form of microcopies, very often on an on-demand basis, particularly where demand is likely to be low or at least uncertain. Apart from its use in publishing, microcopying is, of course, now widely used for archival and security purposes and to save storage space. Copyright is a potential problem in these applications if the microcopying is not done with the authority of the copyright owner.

211. In our deliberations we have taken into consideration possible future developments, such as the wider use of computers. Accordingly we shall use the term 'reprographic reproduction' to cover the making of any visually perceivable facsimile copy by such means as are outlined above or any similar means.

The Gregory Committee and the 1956 Act

212. The Gregory Committee, in its consideration of 'fair dealing' (Gregory Report, paragraphs 43 to 54) took note of 'technical developments such as contact photography and micro-photography' which had changed the conditions under which transcripts and extracts from copyright works might be obtained for the purpose of research or private study. They also considered the conflict of interest between authors and publishers on the one hand and research organisations and libraries on the other, and made recommendations which found their way, almost without change, into Section 7 of the Copyright Act 1956. The 'fair dealing' exception which allows a student to make copies himself, if for research or private study, remained unaltered in Section 6, leaving unresolved the difficult question whether he was allowed to make photocopies as distinct from copies by hand.

213. In its consideration of the question of 'fair dealing' the Gregory Committee took careful note of the evidence from the Royal Society, in particular the oft-quoted Royal Society statement:

'Science rests upon its published record, and ready access to public scientific and technical information is a fundamental need of scientists everywhere. All bars which prevent access to scientific and technical publications hinder the progress of science and should be removed.

'Making single copies of extracts from books or periodicals is essential to research workers, and the production of such single extract copies, by or on behalf of scientists, is necessary for scientific practice.'

214. The Gregory Committee divided the problem of copying by libraries into three parts. First, as regards copying from periodicals, they recommended a provision permitting designated non-profit-making libraries to provide single copies of single articles for research or private study purposes, as long as the recipient paid an economic charge to the library. This is covered by Section 7(1) and (2) of the Copyright Act 1956. It was assumed that the charge requirement would safeguard publishers against abuse.

215. Second, as regards copying from books, the permission of the copyright owner was to be sought, and only if the owner could not be traced were designated libraries to be allowed to provide copies of reasonable parts of books under similar conditions as specified above (viz single copies at an economic charge for research or private study only). Provision was recommended for inter-library copying of books or periodicals. These matters are covered by Section 7(3) to (5) of the 1956 Act. It should be noted that in neither of these cases is the library obliged to pay anything to the copyright owner.

216. Third, as regards copying from old unpublished manuscripts accessible to the public, copying for private purposes was proposed but only if the author had been dead 50 years and the document itself was at least 100 years old. In a separate section on 'posthumous works' (Gregory Report, paragraphs 32 to 35) the Gregory Committee recommended that publication of these old documents should be allowed, subject to advertisement in a prescribed manner, and the right of the copyright owner to object. These matters are covered by Section 7(6) to (8) of the 1956 Act.

217. In paragraph 54, they recommended that reproduction of documents in connection with judicial proceedings or reports of such proceedings should not constitute infringement of copyright. This recommendation was adopted and forms Section 6(4) of the 1956 Act. A similar provision in respect of artistic works is to be found in Section 9(7).

218. The Gregory Committee does not appear to have had any submissions from educational institutions and did not make any specific recommendations for educational exceptions. However, during the passage through Parliament of the Bill to implement the Gregory recommendations, representations were made which resulted in certain restricted educational exceptions, incorporated in Section 41. These allow, as far as copying literary and other works are concerned, for reproduction in, and in answer to, examination test papers and for reproduction by a teacher or pupil in the course of instruction, but, in this latter case only, otherwise than by the use of a duplicating process.

219. The Copyright Act 1956 does not define the scope of 'fair dealing' (which only becomes relevant when a 'substantial part' has been copied) nor how large a part of a book may be copied by a library under Section 7(3). Case law however does provide some criteria in deciding these matters. Furthermore, some guidance has been given by the Society of Authors and the Publishers Association as to their views in a joint statement entitled *Photocopying and the Law*. According to this statement, they have agreed that they would not normally regard it as 'unfair' if, for the purposes of research or private study, a single copy is made from a copyright work of a single extract not exceeding 4,000 words or a series of extracts (of which none exceeds 3,000

words) to a total of 8.000 words, provided that in no case the total amount copied exceeds ten per cent of the whole work; poems, essays and other short literary works to be regarded as whole works in themselves. This however has apparently been misunderstood as setting limits having the effect of law rather than as indicating the level below which authors and publishers would rather not be troubled with requests for permission to copy.

International Situation

Berne Convention

220. Article 9(1) of the Paris text of the Berne Convention provides that authors shall have the exclusive right of authorising the reproduction of their protected works in any manner or form. Article 9(2) however allows countries to permit the reproduction of works in certain special cases, provided that the reproduction does not conflict with normal exploitation of the work and does not unreasonably prejudice the legitimate interests of the author. The intention of this provision, the interpretation of which is considered in paragraph 60, is that there should be no compulsory licences in fields in which works are normally exploited (for example publishing a book); and, if national laws permit copying on any scale without permission in other fields, they should ensure that the author is reasonably remunerated.

Universal Copyright Convention

221. The Universal Copyright Convention provides in Article IV *bis* 1 that the protection of the author's economic interests should include the exclusive right to authorise reproduction by any means. Paragraph 2 of that Article however allows states to make exceptions which do not conflict with the 'spirit and provisions' of the Convention and offer 'a reasonable degree of effective protection'.

International working group on reprographic reproduction of works protected by copyright

222. The problem of the photographic reproduction of copyright works has been under study at the international level since at least 1961. The interest which the discussions have aroused reflects the almost universal desire to find a *modus vivendi* between, on the one hand, the legitimate copyright interests of authors and publishers to control or at least receive remuneration in respect of reproduction of their works and, on the other hand, the equally legitimate interests of those engaged in research, in servicing research (for example libraries) and education who are mainly interested in the dissemination of information. Recent international activity in this area has included a working group set up jointly by the Intergovernmental Copyright Committee (IGC) of the UCC, which is administered by UNESCO, and by the Executive Committee of the Berne Union, which is administered by WIPO.

223. The working group considered that the regulation of reprography in detail is essentially a matter for national laws. They felt it unlikely that internationally agreed rules could be formulated except in broad generalities; each state would then be free to adopt any appropriate measures which, while respecting the provisions of the conventions, establish whatever system is best adapted to meet its own educational, cultural, social and economic

requirements. The working group reported that, in the case of states where reprographic reproduction is widespread, it seems likely that the general approach will be through the establishment of a limited number of agencies to exercise and administer the right of copyright owners to remuneration.

Position in individual countries

224. A number of countries abroad have sought to deal with the problem of reprography in different ways. We outline below what we understand to be the position in three countries which have taken steps to tackle the problem.

Sweden

225. Under the Swedish Copyright Law of 1960, archives or libraries may produce copies of literary or artistic works 'for the purpose of their activities' (Article 12). Further, copies of published works may be produced 'for personal use' (Article 11). Libraries do not pay royalties in respect of their photocopying but must inform the Swedish Fund for Authors of copies made (and books lent). Through the Fund, the State pays certain sums depending on the extent to which works are lent or reproduced.

226. Photocopying of copyright works in schools was the subject of an agreement concluded in 1973 between the Government of Sweden and a group of organisations representing authors and publishers. The practice of photocopying in Swedish schools had reached such proportions that a Commission to study the problem was appointed and a statistical study undertaken. This revealed that, by 1968, in Swedish schools alone 150 million impressions were made by photocopying each year. Of these, over 60 per cent involved copies of text books and school books, 14 per cent involved copies of newspapers and periodicals, and only 3 per cent involved copies of novels, plays and general literature.

227. Under the agreement, the organisations representing authors and publishers give general permission to teachers in Swedish schools to photocopy protected works within certain limits, without having to ask the copyright owner's permission, and the Swedish Government undertakes to pay a substantial fee for this permission, based on actual copies made, to a new author's and publisher's organisation called BONUS. The Swedish agreement appears to be unique in the history of copyright, since for the first time a Government is declaring its willingness to pay for photocopying in schools.

228. Distribution of the remuneration, which varies depending upon the nature of the work copied, is not prescribed in the agreement, although the funds are expected to be divided between authors and publishers, with some provisions for pensions and fellowships. A simple sampling system is utilized to determine which authors should benefit. The agreement is applicable initially only to Swedish works, and is to last for a renewable period of three years. It appears that a violation of the agreement by a teacher (for example, making 200 copies when only 100 are allowed) would constitute an act of infringement under the copyright law rather than a mere violation of contract. The restriction of the agreement to Swedish works is possible as a practical matter because most of the works involved are likely to be text books and school books which are largely Swedish in origin. In Swedish universities the proportion of foreign to

Swedish books is just the reverse and this factor would, it is acknowledged, have to be considered if, as originally planned, the agreement is extended to reproduction there.

Germany (*Federal Republic*)

229. Germany has tackled the problem in a somewhat different way. After a decision of the Federal Court of Justice in a case involving the photocopying by an industrial firm of articles from scientific journals, an agreement (effectively a blanket licence agreement) was concluded between the Federation of German Industry and the Exchange Association of the German Book Trade on photographic reproduction from scientific and technical periodicals of domestic origin carried out for the internal use of firms. Periodicals of foreign origin may be included within the scheme if reciprocal arrangements are negotiated; but so far this has not happened. The scheme is now based on the provision in Article 54(2) of the German Copyright Act 1965 that authors have a right to remuneration in respect of reproduction for commercial purposes. (It is only for strictly personal use that the law allows single copies to be made free.)

230. The administration of the scheme is in the hands of a collecting society, WISSENSCHAFT, which represents authors of scientific works. In common with other German collecting societies WISSENSCHAFT is subject to scrutiny by the German Patent Office. Authors wishing to participate assign their right to claim compensation to their publishers and the publishers in turn assign their rights to the collecting society. Licence fees may be paid by any of the following methods:

(i) Attachment to each photocopy made from a periodical covered by the scheme of a fee stamp to value 15 or 40 Pfennig depending on the subscription rate of the periodical being copied.

(ii) Payment of an annual fee of 30 per cent of the subscription rates for the periodicals regularly obtained and from which on the basis of experience photocopies are expected to be made; periodicals obtained in multiple copies only counting once.

(iii) Payment of an annual fee of 20 per cent of the subscription rates for all periodicals regularly obtained (whether to be copied from or not); periodicals obtained in multiple copies only counting once.

(iv) Payment of an annual fee determined by special agreement—applicable only to larger commercial enterprises.

Under the lump sum methods, commercial enterprises are required to make an annual return of periodicals regularly received.

231. After deducting its administrative expenses, the collecting society divides the fees collected into two equal parts for the benefit respectively of publishers and authors. The authors' portion is distributed to authors' associations for general welfare purposes. The publishers' portion is distributed to publishers according to the likely level of copying from each publisher's periodicals. The scheme is said to represent the best practical solution that could be devised under the threat of a complete breakdown of copyright observance resulting from technological progress.

232. A second blanket licensing scheme for reprographic reproduction is operating in Germany. In this case an agreement has been entered into between the Government and the collecting society WORT, which mainly represents authors of literary works including journalists, in respect of photocopying of newspapers for 'press-digests' in Government offices. A fee of 1·75 Pfennig is paid for each A4 size photocopy on the basis that double this figure would be the appropriate rate but only about half the material copied is likely to be material in which WORT would have a copyright claim. In order to facilitate distribution of the revenue to copyright owners according to the copying actually done WORT is given a copy of each digest and a note of the total number of copies produced. Although the future of this Government-based press-digest system is apparently under review (by the Government) the possibility of extending the system to other organisations is being considered.

Netherlands

233. The Netherlands Copyright Act 1912 was amended, as from 7 January 1973, to deal with the question of reprographic reproduction. There are three basic categories:

(i) Under fair dealing provisions allowing copying free of any copyright fee, a person may make, or order a third party, such as a library, to make, for his personal practice study or use, a few copies of any work which is out of print, any newspaper or periodical article or a 'small portion' of any other book, pamphlet or musical score.

(ii) The need for photocopies in the public services, which includes libraries and educational establishments, is met by a blanket licensing system incorporated in a decree effective from 1 January 1975. In this case there are much the same sort of limitations as in (i) above on what may be copied. But here payment is prescribed. The rates of payment are generally 0·10 Guilders per page of copyright material copied. A special rate of 0·025 Guilders is laid down for schools.

(iii) Commercial enterprises may also make copies under similar conditions as in (i) above on payment of 'equitable remuneration to the author of the work or his successors in title'. But in this case it is only in respect of 'scientific' books and articles that the copying is permitted.

In the case of categories (i) and (iii) no onward transmission of copies is permitted. In order to allow for the possibility that the setting up of collecting societies might be delayed, not only in the Netherlands but in other countries as well, a three-year time limit on claims has been laid down.

234. A study in the Netherlands has shown that, out of the total volume of photocopies made, the percentage of copies containing copyright material is about 5 per cent in both Government offices and commercial enterprises, about 25 per cent in educational establishments and about 65 per cent in libraries. This and other studies elsewhere have also shown that in libraries it is predominantly scholarly, scientific and technical publications which are copied.

Study of reprography in other countries

235. Other countries besides ourselves have the problem under study, for example Australia, Canada and the United States of America.

236. In June 1974, following the case of *Moorhouse & Anr v University of New South Wales*, the Attorney-General of Australia appointed a committee under the chairmanship of Mr Justice Franki of that country's Industrial Court to examine the question of the reprographic reproduction of works protected by copyright in Australia. It is understood the committee will recommend alterations to the Australian copyright law or any other measures necessary to maintain a proper balance between owners of copyright and users of copyright material.

237. It was reported to the UNESCO/WIPO working group referred to in paragraph 222 that Canadian authors and book publishers were planning to form a voluntary association for the collection of royalties to be paid to authors and publishers in return for a limited right to photocopy protected works in schools, colleges and universities and libraries.

238. The American Copyright Law Revision Bill of 23 February 1976[1] proposes extensive limitations to the general exclusive reproduction right under two headings, (1) 'fair use' and (2) reproduction by libraries and archives.

239. The 'fair use' exception (Section 107) specifically refers to reproduction in copies for purposes such as criticism, comment, news reporting, teaching, scholarship or research. In determining whether the use made of a work in any particular case is a fair use the factors to be considered include:

(i) 'The purpose and character of the use;

(ii) 'The nature of the copyrighted work;

(iii) 'The amount and substantiality of the portion used in relation to the copyrighted work as a whole; and

(iv) 'The effect of the use upon the potential market for or value of the copyrighted work.'

240. The library and archive exceptions (Section 108) cover the making, without payment to the copyright owner, of single copies of works for non-commercial purposes by libraries or archives which are open to the public or to researchers generally in a specialised field, subject to the inclusion with the reproduction of a notice of copyright. These provisions specifically apply to the making of copies of unpublished works for purposes of preservation and security or for research use in another library. Similarly they expressly allow for the replacement of copies of published works which are damaged, deteriorating, lost or stolen if replacement copies are not available elsewhere at a fair price. Copies of single articles from periodicals or extracts of other works for private study, scholarship or research are covered, as are complete copies of books which are not available elsewhere at a fair price. It is proposed that libraries should be absolved of all liability for copyright infringement on unsupervised reproducing equipment located on library premises provided a copyright notice in suitable terms is displayed. However, the making of multiple copies by the systematic reproduction of single copies is to be illegal and the exceptions in respect of musical or artistic works are to be more limited than for literary works.

---

[1] The American Copyright Revision Bill (S22) was signed on 19 October 1976 and will take effect, with some exceptions, on 1 January 1978.

Conclusions to be drawn

241. The international conventions allow a fair amount of discretion as regards national exceptions to the requirement that copyright works should be protected against unauthorised reproduction. There is no likelihood of international measures to deal with the reprography problem being agreed upon in the near future. In countries that have taken action already, the approach has generally been to introduce, or make provisions for, blanket licensing in specific restricted fields and to make some provision for private copying either by the person requiring a copy or by a third party, such as a library. It is understood however that this provision for making single copies free of royalty is having an undermining effect on the blanket scheme in at least one country. In fact many of the blanket schemes so far introduced seem to be experiencing some difficulty in practice. We do not interpret this as an indication that blanket licensing is unworkable, but rather that the details need careful consideration.

Evidence

General

242. Reprographic reproduction is a topic which in some aspect or another was touched upon in over seventy of the written submissions. It was also a major topic for discussion in oral evidence. Educational and library interests were particularly prominent in making submissions on the subject.

243. There was a general call from librarians for simplification. The declarations required by Section 7 of the Copyright Act 1956 are irksome to them and, it was suggested, probably of little or no value. Under the regulations anybody wanting a copy from a library has to sign a declaration by which he undertakes only to use the copy for the purposes of research or private study. He further declares that he has not been previously supplied with a copy of the work in question by any other library. We were given an instance of a procedure which it was suggested is not uncommon. A librarian was requested by one individual to supply 25 copies of one and the same article. This request was supported by 25 declarations bearing 25 different signatures. No doubt the copies, when handed over, were going to be used by 25 students in connection with some course of instruction. It is thought, at least by some librarians, though opinions are divided on this, that a librarian is justified in supplying 25 copies of one and the same article on such a request on the basis that if the copies are, on the face of the declarations which have been signed, for the purposes of private study or research then the provisions of the Act and the regulations have been complied with. We were given a further example of a librarian approached by an individual known by him to be a research worker in a commercial undertaking. This individual asked for a copy of an article and put in a declaration saying that the article was going to be used by him for the purposes of research. Opinion again is divided as to whether or not it is proper in such circumstances under the Act to supply a copy of the article. Under the Act study has to be 'private' study. There is no such qualification on the word 'research' and it is suggested there is certainly no express exclusion under the Act or the regulations which would debar the librarian from supplying a copy of an article to an individual who he is aware is going to use it for the purposes of research notwithstanding the fact that the research is going to be carried out for the business ends of a commercial organisation.

244. The need to make a charge and collect money is burdensome on librarians. Copyright owners on the other hand suggested that the charges which are made are derisory. At most, it was said, they only cover the cost of the copy paper and in no way represent the true cost of the copy. This, they said, enables individuals to get copies for private or possibly even for commercial purposes at, in the case of prescribed libraries, the public expense without any return to the copyright owner. For this and other reasons it was urged upon us that the cost of copies should cover full overheads.

245. It seems clear that the existing regulations only offer protection of a very limited nature to copyright owners. They may not altogether stop what is effectively multiple copying (a person with 25 requests separately signed). The declarations on which copies are provided may be quite untrue but there is no sanction attaching to the making of false declarations. The only effect of the declaration is to give clearance to the librarians. It is difficult to form anything approaching a precise assessment of the total amount of library copying and the extent of its effect upon the interests of the copyright owners. In one submission we were provided with a careful statistical analysis from which it might be concluded that the revenue which would accrue to copyright owners from a levy on library copying would be too small to justify the expenses of collection and distribution. What has to be considered however is not the revenue which might derive from any one library but the total revenue which might be derived from all libraries providing photocopying services, and on this there are no figures available on which estimates can be based.

246. It is worth noting in relation to one of the statistical analyses with which we were provided that, of the journals considered, the larger number were periodicals containing articles likely to be of interest to chemical or pharmaceutical organisations. One copy from any such journal obtained by one individual for 'research' might well be re-copied within a large establishment understandably requiring copies for distribution among various branches and possibly to a number of individuals. Using the library facilities a manufacturer could avoid subscribing to a considerable number of periodicals. The slow process of circulating a single copy of an original, or even a single photocopy, to all individuals interested could likewise be avoided.

247. The main concern of libraries is that they should continue to be able to offer a high level of service to their users, including a copying service, and in this respect several made reference to the continuing relevance of the Royal Society declaration submitted to the Gregory Committee (paragraph 213).

248. It appears that most libraries would welcome a blanket licensing scheme as long as they are not required to make returns. Some would only like it if they had the freedom to decide whether copyright fees were charged to customers or not. The British Library is against blanket licensing and hopes to be excluded from its scope even if a scheme is introduced elsewhere.

249. Libraries are the only major category of organisation in which lending plays a major role in providing services. There is, however, evidence that libraries are tending to replace lending by copying or duplication on an increasing scale. The reasons for this are administrative economy and greater stock control or file integrity. Savings, for example on postage, are not inconsiderable.

Libraries say they are concerned that no periodical's survival should be jeopard-ised by library copying and that copying should not reduce the proper income of publishers. Indeed, some librarians hold that there is little or no evidence that authors or publishers suffer any loss through library copying. In their opinion most of this copying is of periodical issues which are out of print and the most copied periodicals are the ones with the largest circulations. It is even suggested that publishers derive benefit from the publicity which libraries provide.

250. Librarians say they are put under considerable pressure to 'bend the rules'. In the case of industrial and educational libraries the librarian may not be in a position to withstand this pressure. Readers are generally not prepared to wait for the formal procedures to be followed and regard them as quite unreasonable if only a few pages are required to be copied. Libraries are particularly sensitive on the matter of responsibility in view of the growing tendency to provide photocopying facilities on a coin-operation basis. Smaller libraries operate with a minimum of staff and librarians feel that it should be no part of their duties to supervise what is being copied or to collect fees. Librarians feel users rather than themselves should be made responsible for compliance with the law.

251. Apart from the wish on the part of libraries to have greater freedom of action under the general 'fair dealing' umbrella there is also a call for more latitude in particular areas, notably the following:

(i) *Conservation.* Some publications in libraries are used more than others and receive more wear and tear. Libraries would like to be able to photo-copy in order to prevent problems occurring.

(ii) *Loss and Damage.* Libraries would like to be able to add to stocks and make good their collections by means of photocopies—usually from other libraries. This is mainly a problem where publications are out of print since most libraries are willing to buy new copies whilst these are still available.

(iii) *Security.* Where the security of documents, mainly manuscripts, is important, libraries would like to be able to lend photocopies rather than originals.

(iv) *Out-of-Print Works.* Libraries would like a general exception covering out-of-print works, particularly if required for research or private study. Some libraries have suggested that copying should only be allowed after the work has been out of print for some specified period, the period suggested ranging from three to thirty years. On the other hand publishers feel that they should continue to know which works are in demand.

(v) *Manuscripts and Archival Records.* Where manuscripts and records are open to public inspection, libraries feel they should be allowed to provide photocopies for research or private study.

(vi) *Space Saving.* Libraries would like, in certain circumstances, to be able to make microform copies of works in order to save space.

(vii) *Periodicals.* The provisions which restrict the allowable copying to a single article in any one publication are criticised as being obscure and unduly restrictive.

Documentation centres

252. Documention centres present special problems. Articles of possible future interest are often stored on microfilm. The articles may be indexed and/or abstracts recorded on microfilm or magnetic tape. Information from a number of sources may be collated. In response to requests for information, searches are made and information retrieved. In many cases this will involve the reproduction of articles from microfilm master copies. Whatever the exact details of any particular system there is likely to be infringement of copyright by way of reprographic reproduction. A compulsory or blanket licence was seen as the best solution by the documentation centres themselves.

Education

253. Educationalists on all sides called for greater freedom of action. Teachers felt they, and their support staff also, ought to be able to make copies without the delay of having to obtain permission. The submissions were divided however as to whether education should have to pay for the privilege requested or whether it should be free or paid for by some central subsidy or tax relief. A survey of copying in schools, jointly sponsored by the Council for Educational Technology and the Publishers Association, suggests that almost 70 per cent of the work copied in schools is internally generated. Nevertheless some schools are equipped to copy on a large scale and a great deal of infringing copying is taking place. The potential for infringement is enormous. The making of slides and other visual aids in teaching or lecturing may be regarded as a particular aspect of the general reprography problem.

254. The needs of education in modern society are changing. In the new teaching situation, exemplified we were told by the emergence of new curricula, the development of integrated studies, the emphasis on independent enquiry and the growth of mixed ability groupings, it is no longer considered appropriate for text books to be issued to each pupil. We were told that new methods of teaching and learning require the use of a wide range of teaching material to meet the particular needs of a student or a group of students. This concept of 'resource-based learning', whether applied to independent or class activity, was said to require the availability of a diversity of material, extracted from a great variety of sources. The development of educational thinking and philosophy has coincided with, and has been stimulated by, the availability of a range of technical devices capable of increasing the amount and variety of resource material. The use of these appliances is not peculiar to education, but inevitably both teacher and pupil have been quick to appreciate the potential of such innovations.

255. In the case of reprography the only provision in the Copyright Act 1956 of direct application to the educational field is the Section 6(6) provision making an exception (classified as fair dealing) in favour of the copying of short passages for inclusion in collections intended for schools. The exact extent of this exception must be a matter of doubt. Section 41, which gives a limited right of reproduction, expressly excludes (except in the case of examination questions) reproduction by any process 'involving the use of an appliance for producing multiple copies'. Section 41 was attacked both on the grounds of uncertainty and because, it was said by educationalists, it is too narrow in scope.

256. A factor which distinguishes the educational problem from the library one is that usually a teacher will want multiple copies whereas a researcher will need only a single copy. This factor was recognised by the Council for Educational Technology who suggested a dual approach for education—extended fair dealing provisions and a blanket licensing system. The Council has in fact been negotiating a blanket licence agreement with the Publishers Association for some time.

257. Only the Inner London Education Authority urged that all copying for educational purposes should be permitted as 'fair dealing'. Recognising however that authors may be worthy of some reward, it suggested that they (but not publishers) should be given some sort of direct subsidy, possibly by way of tax relief, to compensate them for the use of their work in educational institutions.

Industry

258. It is probably the case that most copying within companies is of internally generated documents. Even so, the amount of copying of copyright material may well be considerable, especially in industrial libraries for the purposes of research. Under present conditions the dissemination of published information is a *sine qua non* for successful research and development work in industry, and it was claimed that the provisions of the Copyright Act 1956, if fully observed, impose an unnecessary restriction on such dissemination without concomitant benefit to the copyright owner. It was suggested to us that, within any industrial organisation, there should be freedom within the law for one or more copies of a published literary work which has been purchased by the organisation to be made and distributed to the organisation's personnel. It was argued that this facility would in no way be detrimental to the copyright owner, for its denial would not result in further copies of the published text being purchased but simply cause frustration and waste of time within industry.

Other user interests

259. On the use of photocopies by other interests, the legal profession urged that 'fair dealing' should cover the making of copies for personal or professional use and that 'fair dealing' should be allowed in so far as the copying is not in competition with the copyright owner's exploitation. There was a general plea that, whatever the final decisions, the system should be simple to understand and operate. A simple code of practice on the lines of the *Highway Code* was suggested. Guidance as to what is allowable as 'fair dealing' and what constitutes 'a reasonable proportion of a work' was also requested. We are however doubtful whether any simple and equitable formula can be devised which will cover all cases.

Publishers

260. Publishers, not surprisingly, took a different line from libraries. They felt that library copying is seriously affecting the subscriptions to learned journals and other specialised periodicals to the extent that such publications are no longer viable or have to adopt practices which have hitherto been avoided, such as publishing papers in summary form with microform back-up. Educational books, it was said, were also being endangered. Publishers therefore concluded that any exceptions in favour of any class of copying

should be so defined as clearly to exclude at least multiple copying, copying by libraries under Section 6 of the Copyright Act 1956 (fair dealing) and the supply of copies at less than economic charges. It was also suggested that it should be emphasised that commercial libraries do not have any rights under Section 7 of the Act.

261. Publishers were alive to the possibilities of blanket licensing but although there was wide support for it in general terms they were divided as to how far they were prepared to go along with the idea. One licensing scheme does already operate, run by the Ordnance Survey in respect of the maps they publish. As mentioned above, the Publishers Association has been negotiating for some years with the Council for Educational Technology with a view to introducing an educational licensing scheme but it is quite clear that not all publishers are in favour of the proposal. As proposed, fees under this scheme would be charged on a capitation basis; but so far nothing concrete has emerged. The Publishers Association felt that a successful blanket licensing scheme should replace even the right to make single copies for research or private study.

Authors and composers

262. Authors' and composers' representatives were generally in favour of blanket licensing. In the categories of publications most photocopied, namely the scholarly, scientific and technical periodicals, there is little evidence of a demand for royalties by authors. These authors generally are not dependent on royalties from their writings for a living and on the whole are more interested in the esteem of their colleagues. It is the publisher rather than the author who normally enjoys the periodical rights. But the authors would be far from happy to see the publications in which their, and their colleagues' works appear, fail for financial reasons.

Arbitration

263. The British Copyright Council, which expressed itself in favour of a blanket licensing solution to the photocopying problem, whether for education or otherwise, suggested that the jurisdiction of the Performing Right Tribunal should be extended to deal with disputes between users and collecting societies as to the terms and costs of licences. This recommendation was supported by the Publishers Association and others. With education particularly in mind the Council for Educational Technology suggested that a statutory body should be set up to arbitrate in cases of dispute, for example as to whether a particular licensing scheme is in the public interest bearing in mind the interests of both the rights owners and the educational users and as to the terms and conditions of licensing schemes. The Industrial Council for Educational and Training Technology expressed similar views. The Inner London Education Authority considered that a statutory body should be set up with powers to consider any matter of dispute over the use of copyright material, including cases where access to copyright material is alleged to be withheld against the public interest.

Costs

264. The economics of reprography seems to be very elastic. It was claimed, on the one hand, that photocopies can be produced for as little as 1·2p per single sheet. Indeed we have seen a commercial price list with prices for multiple

copies going as low as 1·14p per copy. This must clearly represent little more than the cost of the materials used. On the other hand, it has been estimated by accountants that the true cost to an organisation of a photocopying machine is between 10p and 15p per page if overheads, including staff costs, are taken into account. But the cost of obtaining copies by alternative means may be even higher. Take for example a four-page artilce from a popular scientific magazine. At 15p per page the cost of photocopying the article would be 60p. However the cost of purchasing a back number may be 50p, to which must be added postage and a considerable administrative cost in writing a letter, dealing with the book-keeping and handling the periodical when received. The total cost could well be over £1. Furthermore the whole operation is likely to take at least a week to complete.

265. There are many commercial agencies where the standard charge for copies is still 5p or 6p per page. Prices for offset litho printing using a master produced by reprography can be less than 1p per sheet if runs of over 200 are considered. The charge for using coin-operated machines in libraries, stations, etc is generally 5p; attempts being made to place the responsibility for compliance with the copyright law in the case of these machines on the user by the posting of notices such as 'The responsibility for reproduction of copyright matter lies with the customer' or 'Users should not reproduce copyright material unless authorised to do so'.

266. Although designated libraries are required to charge for overheads under Section 7 of the Copyright Act 1956 it appears that charges generally may be quite low. The charge for while-you-wait A4 copies at the Science Reference Library (part of the British Library) was raised in March 1975 from 4p to 6p (plus VAT). It seems that educational establishments are sometimes lax in the matter of financial control, with libraries in some places offering students a free service. Apparently copiers may sometimes be used simply because they represent the easiest way out, irrespective of economics.

Prevention of copying

267. Efforts to devise ways of physically preventing copying, for example by coating documents with a fluorescent dye in order to 'dazzle' photocopying machines, are not meeting with much success. It appears that the latest photocopying machines are immune to such tactics. In any case we are satisfied that, as a solution, this is neither practicable nor desirable.

Conclusions
Education

268. In view of the growth of reprography as a problem in the educational field since the time of the Gregory Committee, we have considered first the question whether there should be any express exceptions in favour of educational establishments at all. We feel that the fact that 'education' is a good cause is not in itself a reason for depriving copyright owners of remuneration. Nobody suggests that the makers of note books, compasses and rulers should supply these products to educational establishments free of charge. Although the types of material used in such places today are very different from the text books of the past and indeed are much more diverse, education is still in a large measure dependent upon the work of authors, artists and composers. Education

is equally dependent upon the work of the publishers who first produced the material which the authorities want to copy for educational purposes. The majority of educational submissions were in fact of the view that, although they should be completely free to copy, it is right that they should pay copyright owners a reasonable fee in respect of the reproduction of copyright material. Copyright owners, with some exceptions, appeared to be prepared to accept the need for freedom of action in educational establishments, and to abandon any claims to a need for copyright clearance in advance, provided they are paid a fair sum for the use of their work. They were perhaps forced into this position because of the sheer impossibility of policing infringements and the probability that the detection of any individual instance of infringement and the institution of proceedings for such infringement would cost far more than any sum which might be recouped by way of damages.

269. On this first question therefore, we accept the general view that if copyright material is used in education then copyright owners are entitled to payment. They should not, as a class, be expected to make some exceptional contribution in this field. However large scale copying is here and nothing is going to stop it. Facilities for such copying are now generally available, and it is clear that any acceptable solution to the copyright problems involved must take account of the natural desire of educational establishments to make use of them. A second question therefore arises, whether education should be treated as a special problem requiring its own peculiar solution or whether it should be looked upon as a part only of the more general problem for which a correspondingly general solution will be necessary. We are in favour of the latter course since in general we are against special provisions to meet particular cases unless absolutely necessary. We do not think this applies here and therefore now turn our attention to the problem in its more general sense as it affects library, educational, industrial and other users alike.

General

270. The widespread availability of simple-to-operate and relatively cheap-to-use photocopiers has made the law unworkable. The complication and delay in obtaining permission from copyright owners is such that many people do not bother. Since detection is virtually impossible in many cases, there is no incentive to do so. It is pointless for the law to lay down prohibitions which are unenforceable.

271. On the other hand unless something is done there is a serious danger that, in some fields at least, publication will cease. We can envisage a vicious circle: the increase in library and other copying means smaller circulations; which means higher costs; which in its turn means more copying. In the end publication ceases. Some way must be found to reverse the trend.

272. We believe that most people requiring photocopies have no real wish to harm the interests of authors and publishers and would much prefer to be honest citizens. What they will not do is accept the trouble and delay involved in seeking permission for each copy. But they would welcome a system which, for a modest sum and with no great formality, would enable them, within the law, to meet their need for copies.

273. On the evidence before us it seems to be generally accepted that society in general, and education in particular, should be able to enjoy the fullest possible measure of benefit from modern reprographic devices and that the solution of the problems posed by photocopying should lie not in any suppression of the use of modern technology but in the adoption of arrangements which ensure that authors and publishers continue to enjoy sufficient financial incentives to write and publish. Negotiated blanket licences are seen as the only practicable solution by the majority of interested parties. Majority opinion is against, and we think rightly against, the idea of a levy (such as we are recommending for tape recorders) on sales of photocopying machines since many of these may never, or only infrequently, be used to infringe copyright. Unless one simply accepts that it is unnecessary or impossible to control photocopying the only possible solution lies in blanket licensing.

Blanket licensing

274. It is clear that different people have different ideas about what blanket licensing means, so this question will be considered first. Essentially blanket licensing involves a group of copyright owners foregoing their rights to take individual action, in the case now being considered, in respect of the reprographic reproduction of their works. Instead of individual authors or publishers being responsible for collecting their own royalties, remuneration at a standard rate is collected by a central collecting agency or society which undertakes the task of distribution of the revenue to the individual copyright owners whose works are reproduced. To facilitate this distribution in an equitable manner some sort of return of usage or sampling is inevitably involved. From the user's point of view the essence of a blanket licence is that it covers all the works he wants to copy. For a single annual fee he gets permission to use any or all of the works in the licensor's repertoire. The Performing Right Society is a good example of a blanket licensing scheme in operation in the field of the public performance of music. The amount of the fee is based on the extent to which copyright works within the repertoire are likely to be used.

275. It has been estimated that on a world-wide basis some 4,500,000 publications are issued annually involving some 100 million pages of new printed literature. It is probably impractical to introduce, certainly in a single step, a scheme to cover the whole of the published field. Nevertheless, given favourable conditions and a willingness of authors and publishers to collaborate, we see no reason why viable schemes should not in time operate over most of the field.

276. Apart from one factor, there is nothing in the present Act to prevent blanket licensing schemes from operating now. The one factor is the existing exception in Section 7 of the 1956 Act allowing the making of single copies, coupled with the low charges which libraries make in practice. We have already discussed the difficulties of deciding what is a single copy (paragraph 243). While this loophole exists there is little incentive for a library to take a licence. The librarian no doubt feels that the law excuses him from any need to do so. We therefore recommend that as and when blanket licensing schemes are in existence, the latitude given by Section 7 should no longer apply. At the same time it should be made clear that Section 6 of the 1956 Act (fair dealing for research or private study) should not allow the making of facsimile copies but only those made by hand or by using a typewriter.

277. It would in our view be impracticable to attempt to write into a new Copyright Act the details of a blanket licensing scheme. It ought however to be possible to enact provisions which would encourage the introduction of blanket licensing and enable it to operate successfully.

278. The Act should we think go no further than make provisions along the following lines:

(i) Reprographic reproduction should still be a restricted act.

(ii) However, within particular areas to be designated by regulation a period should be allowed in which copyright owners, through recognised collecting societies, can promulgate blanket licensing schemes. If they fail to do so within that period then, until such schemes are promulgated, reprographic reproduction within that area should not be an infringement.

(iii) The areas referred to under (ii) would include copying by libraries, educational establishments, Government departments, industry and professional interests and indeed by copying agencies. No copying should be allowed which would conflict with the copyright owner's normal modes of exploitation, eg the distribution of copies to the public.

(iv) The number of societies must be kept as low as possible to avoid the need for users to have to take out a multitude of licences and to keep administrative costs to a minimum. In the literary field there should at most be one society for books and one for periodicals. We think therefore that ministerial recognition of those societies allowed to operate is essential.

(v) All negotiations between collecting societies and users should be subject, in case of dispute, to appeal to a copyright tribunal.

279. Users of copyright material cannot be expected to give up the facilities offered by Section 7 of the 1956 Act without a guarantee that their needs will be met by blanket licensing schemes. It is for this reason that we suggest in (ii) above that, in order to encourage copyright owners to form collecting societies, after due time for negotiations there should in effect be a free-for-all unless a blanket licensing scheme is offered. By a free-for-all we mean the right to make copies free of payment, otherwise than for issue to the public at large, for instance either for one's own use or for supply to one's pupils or to the order of one's employees or library users.

280. The advantage of the above approach would be, we think, that it would allow considerable flexibility in the arrangements the collecting society or societies could make with different groups of users. No doubt different rates would apply for different classes of users. Rates could be reduced in return for statistics on usage (sampling) which the licensing bodies will need in order to know how to distribute their takings among their members. The scheme would replace the exceptions in Section 7 of the 1956 Act. It is likely that some at least of the other exceptions, as indicated in Chapter 14, should remain, certainly as regards non-reprographic reproduction. But all copies made by reprographic means by or within the institutions and agencies referred to above, whether for private use or otherwise, should be subject to the blanket licence terms.

281. The general terms and conditions, including whether returns would be required, would all be subject to negotiation. Obviously the administration should be as simple as possible in order to avoid the cost of collection and distribution exceeding the sums collected. In the early stages costs may indeed swallow up most of the income, but this is unlikely to last for long. It may be possible to arrange for charges to be made on a capitation basis, particularly in education. We see no reason why, when the teething troubles are over, the administration costs should exceed the 10 to 15 per cent which holds in other fields.

282. The stipulation that collecting societies should be subject to ministerial recognition would enable the number of societies to be controlled. The Minister would wish to be satisfied on two criteria: first that any collecting society participating represented, or was capable of representing, a reasonable proportion of copyright owners in a particular class and could offer a reasonable administrative machinery for distributing the payment received. Secondly the Minister would have to be satisfied that a copyright owner with a reasonable claim would not be excluded from membership of the collecting society licensing his kind of work since, when a scheme has been promulgated and comes into effect, membership will be the only way in which copyright owners can receive remuneration in respect of reprographic reproduction.

283. No doubt the proposal that the scheme should cover single-copy facsimile copying, even for private purposes and even to some extent for non-copyright material (since libraries may find it difficult to differentiate), will be unpopular, particularly if users have to pay more for their copies. On the other hand, for the reasons given in paragraph 276, the success of blanket licensing will depend largely on this proposal. Libraries owe their very existence to authors and publishers and ought accordingly to be mindful of their interests. It may be one thing to allow a research worker to copy, by hand, part or even the whole of a work in a library, but if, to avoid the labour, he is content to pay for a photocopy the price paid we think in fairness ought to include not only the true cost of the photocopy but also a royalty element for the copyright owner. In the case of works available on the market it is scarcely 'fair dealing' to get, even for private study, a cheap copy with no return to the author, more particularly when much of the cost of copying is borne by the ratepayers or taxpayers.

284. Many users claim that a large part of the material copied by them is out of copyright or is internally generated, for which there is no copyright problem. It would be up to users to negotiate appropriate licence fees to allow for this. In one of the schemes operating in Germany the appropriate rate was halved on the basis that half the works copied were likely to be free anyway. Special terms might be negotiated for 'out-of-print' works. The scheme should be sufficiently flexible in practice for these factors to be taken care of. It is likely that this would meet the EEC Commission's objection to the practice of collecting societies charging for non-copyright material.

285. Coin-operated machines would have to operate under a special licence, and we envisage the person who permits the installation of the machine as being the person who should be responsible for taking out a licence. If such a machine is used to infringe copyright he will be responsible and it should be no defence that he has affixed a copyright notice to the machine. We think that the licence

for coin-operated machines will of necessity have to differ from other licences. In particular, it should cover use for copying any category of work (although the licence will of course only be a licence to reproduce). The licences will be issued by a single body with the proceeds being split between the different societies concerned, and the licence should, we think, take into account the fact that the licence covers any category of work. It may also be possible for the licence fee to be varied according to the location of the machine and hence the likely extent of its use to reproduce copyright material. In the event of the prospective licensee and collecting society being unable to agree terms there would be a right of appeal to the copyright tribunal.

286. The new Act should make it clear that microcopies are simply facsimile copies and that the relevant provisions apply accordingly. It will be open to the parties involved to negotiate special terms and conditions for this category of copying if this is thought to be appropriate.

287. This brings us to considering the upper limits of blanket licensing. We envisage the details of the schemes, the rates of payment and the restrictions and other conditions, being worked out in consultation between licensing bodies and organisations representing users; and, in the not unlikely event of disagreement, the tribunal having power to decide not only on rates of payment, but also on terms and conditions, having regard to what is reasonable in all the circumstances. (We would urge this approach rather than an approach based on 'public interest' so called, since the latter might produce a result unduly biased against the interests of copyright owners in, for example, the field of education.) But to allow licences which would invade the normal fields of exploitation of works, namely, publishing them, would be contrary to our obligations under the Berne Convention (paragraph 220). Nor have we any intention of allowing one publisher the right to demand a compulsory licence to reproduce works which are the exclusive right of another. The tribunal's jurisdiction to settle terms and conditions should not therefore include the making of copies with a view to publication (in the copyright sense of issuing copies to the public).

288. So far we have considered blanket licensing schemes only in relation to works which have already been published. The question arises whether blanket licences (and in default the free-for-all) should apply to some or all unpublished works. We are recommending in Chapter 13 that the term of copyright protection for works contained in Part I of the 1956 Act should never exceed 50 years after the death of the author. But there may be cases in which, before this time elapses, letters and other documents are deposited in public archives with open access to them. The arguments as regards them are nicely divided. There will be the undoubted demand by scholars to be able to get facsimile copies without the trouble of copying by hand. On the other hand the copyright owners should not be deprived of their right to exploit their property, and blanket licensing schemes are unlikely to provide them with much, if any, remuneration. On the whole we do not feel that there would be any serious injustice in allowing librarians who are licensees under blanket licensing schemes to supply facsimile copies of those unpublished works which are on open access. Clearly also the copying of manuscripts or other unpublished copyright material should be permitted if this is required as a condition for the issue of an export licence.

289. Convention nationals would of course enjoy the same rights in this country as Britons, subject to the same condition that they too exercise their rights through a collecting society. The extent to which they will benefit in practice will depend on whether suitable reciprocal agreements can be negotiated with collecting societies in other countries, or even whether suitable terms can be worked out for their joining the appropriate British society.

290. Future trends are difficult to predict. The economics of one method of reproduction relative to another may change and facsimile transmission systems may well be improved upon. Since, however, our suggested blanket licensing procedures would be prescribed without reference to any particular technology and with only a minimum of detail actually in the Act we see no obvious reason why they should not continue to provide a workable solution to the reprography problem for many years to come.

Summary of Recommendations

291. In relation to reprographic reproduction:

(i) **There should be a flexible system of blanket licensing to cater for all user requirements for facsimile copies, including library, educational, Government, industrial and professional copying; but there should be no compulsory licence to publish (paragraph 278).**

(ii) **To encourage copyright owners to set up schemes, the Act should provide that, within particular areas to be designated by regulation and after due time for schemes to be promulgated, reprographic reproduction shall not be an infringement unless and until a blanket licensing scheme is in fact promulgated (paragraphs 278 and 279).**

(iii) **The number of separate blanket licensing schemes should be limited by providing that they may only be administered by collecting societies recognised by the Minister (paragraphs 278 and 282).**

(iv) **All negotiations between collecting societies and users should be subject, in the case of dispute, to appeal to a copyright tribunal (paragraphs 278 and 287).**

(v) **Once a scheme is in operation, the present latitude for the making of single copies under Section 7 of the Copyright Act 1956 should no longer apply; nor should Section 6 (fair dealing for the purposes of research or private study) permit the making, even by the student himself, of reprographic (facsimile) copies (paragraph 276).**

(vi) **Persons installing coin-operated machines would require a special licence and it would be no excuse that the machine bore a notice forbidding its use for infringement of copyright (paragraph 285).**

(vii) **Schemes should, in principle, cover all published works and also certain unpublished ones (paragraph 288).**

COPYRIGHT IMPACTS OF FUTURE TECHNOLOGY [†]

MADELINE M. HENDERSON

Institute for Computer Sciences and Technology,
National Bureau of Standards,
Washington, D.C. 20234

Received February 9, 1976

Dynamic developments in computer and communication technologies, and in reprography and micrographics, are yielding systems and equipment that render better and faster access to information that has been copyrighted in traditional formats. Procedures and mechanisms must be worked out to permit us to take advantage of these technologies without destroying our basic systems of information dissemination.

Scientific information services and systems today, including chemical information systems, are characterized by developing network capabilities and cooperative activities aimed at improving resource sharing. Many of the administrative and economic considerations underlying these developments have been described in the earlier papers in this symposium: the greater volume of papers offered for publication in primary journals, the increasing numbers of specialized journals, the

[†] Presented at the 171st National Meeting of the American Chemical Society, New York, N.Y., April 5, 1976, in a Joint Symposium of the Committee on Copyrights and the Division of Chemical Information on "Impacts of Copyright Developments on Chemical-Information Transmission and Use".

spiraling costs of publication which contribute to increased subscription charges, and the development of efficient but relatively expensive computer-based information searching services and of services offering on-line access to a number of data bases.

Mention has also been made that tight budgets for library and information centers, coupled with inflationary costs, are forcing the search for alternative ways to maintain service to users in providing access to as many needed books and journals as possible, and as quickly, efficiently, and cheaply as possible. The obvious way for users and their intermediaries is through resource sharing and cooperative activities. For many years, libraries and (more recently) some information services have been cooperating on formal grounds and through informal agreements. Particular success has been achieved in the areas of interlibrary lending, bibliographical access (union lists of holdings), agreements for specialization in collection development, and cooperative technical processing of materials.

These cooperative activities and interlibrary network developments have been accelerated by recent technological advances. For example, interlibrary loan is facilitated by improved photocopying techniques, union lists are maintained in current and easily accessible form in computer files, specialized collections are shared by several cooperating libraries via on-line catalogs and photocopied exchanges, and cooperative processing has become more attractive with on-line access to computer files of cataloging data.

Such advances in the technologies of computers, communications, and reprography have had fundamental impacts on scientific and technical information services. Trends in these technologies will affect even more the patterns of user access to information resources. These patterns include even greater reliance on the services of the libraries or information centers for subscriptions to primary journals and secondary journals, for access to data bases, for photocopies, and for computer-produced bibliographies. Improvements in computer hardware and software, reduced operating costs, and increased use of newer recording media for space and cost savings will contribute to more efficient and effective applications in networking.

The impacts of these trends on copyright protection, already touched upon by previous speakers, bear further careful consideration.

TRENDS IN TECHNOLOGICAL DEVELOPMENTS

Computer Technology. Advances in computer technology have resulted in dramatic reductions in hardware costs. Thus, economical quantity production of computer hardware is enhanced by developments in solid-state technologies. This is supplanting the economies of scale that had been the dominant factor for large centralized computer systems. Cost benefits resulting from such quantity production will cause computer architects and designers to promote configurations involving distributed computing. This trend to dispersing computing power from a central processor out to peripheral devices began in the 1960's and is accelerating.

Processing costs have also decreased; indeed, the trend in reduction of such costs is expected to continue into the 1990's. Developments in basic central processors have resulted in far more computing power than is necessary for ordinary information-handling applications. But as machine processes are applied more and more to content analysis and the automatic organization of information, this cheap processing power will be even more important.

Another important development trend is the increasing power, decreasing cost, and reduced size of minicomputers. These are important in computer networks and for low-cost local handling of small files or small portions of large files. The price-performance ratio of minis has been improving steadily since they were first introduced in 1963. This trend is expected to continue and will have considerable impact on intelligent terminals and for decentralizing many functions. Recently, much more improvement in performance has been achieved in small computers than in large ones. This suggests again that the more attractive configuration is going to be the combination of a large centralized facility for common functions, coupled to smaller computers for support of local operations.

It has long been recognized that the speeds of available storage devices are not adequately matched to the logic circuitry used for computations. Many of the applications in scientific information handling make computation practically incidental to the storing, retrieving, and manipulating of data. Great effort and ingenuity have been devoted to the question of improved storage devices, resulting in an extensive hierachy of devices and technologies. This is still an extremely active field, one in which developments are proceeding on many fronts. The evolution of solid-state components fabricated in extremely dense form, requiring exceedingly low power per storage element, has resulted in the broad-scale replacement of traditional core memories with active storage devices. The elements used for these devices are typically able to be turned on and off at speeds comparable to the speed of the logic circuitry used elsewhere in the computer. Core memories eventually reached speeds in the hundreds of nanoseconds; solid-state memories now can operate in tens of nanoseconds.

In addition, numerous large-scale information-storage media are being developed and will enter the systems marketplace in the next few years. The basic physical properties of such materials, which utilize magnetic phenomena, conventional or new photographic processes, or laser-actuated storage mechanisms, will provide for very much higher densities than now employed. These mass-memory storage techniques allow greater packing densities, which in turn promise more rapid retrieval and display of selected data elements or whole pages of information.

Perhaps the most dramatic developments in computer technology have occurred in terminals, input/output devices, or local processors, man's primary communication links to the computer. The terminal marketplace is dynamic and competitive. For example, CRT-based terminals are already available for $1000; some projections show a cost for a basic terminal of only a few hundred dollars in a very few years. Major cost-performance improvements of digital logic using large-scale integrated circuitry are major factors in bringing down costs for terminals and their related logic.

High-performance terminal devices are becoming available that offer video-screen textual and graphic presentations, on-line correction and data-manipulation capabilities, and final output through printers or data-output stations. Such terminals, for example, can be used very effectively in editorial processing centers to provide reductions in the costs and increases in the efficiency of publication of primary scientific journals.

Minicomputer-based or microcomputer-based terminals have a certain amount of local processing capability and can be adapted to different communication protocols and user requirements. As the cost of microprocessors continues to go down, more and more terminals will incorporate them, leading to a trend toward specialized terminals which will cost little more than today's general-purpose terminals. This is important, because some of the requirements of library and information services exceed those of most scientific and business applications, for example, the need to handle scientific notations and multiple alphabets of non-English characters. The minimum library character set for bibliographic information alone includes 176 different characters, according to the Library of Congress. It is now technically feasible, and it will be increasingly economically viable, to build equipments to handle such a range. This, of course, is of great importance for computerized publishing, which in turn can provide the content of machine-readable publications for storage in information systems.

Communications Technology. Developments in computer networking rely on data-communications technology. Communications links of importance in scientific information systems include links between the individual user and the system, from a centralized distribution point to a particular service center, and among nodes in a store-and-retrieve network. Until recently the system could embody only two choices for these communications links: the telephone network and leased private telephone lines between two points, both designed primarily for voice (not data) transmission. Now, many different services are available, and improvements in both performance and cost of data transmission can be clearly foreseen. Digital transmission services will be used increasingly and will become the prime data communications carrier. These networks will be able to operate in the mode most suitable for the particular terminals or computers involved, that is, either store-and-forward or real-time.

Whereas today the user worries about modulating systems to maximize the number of bits per second that can be transmitted over an analog phone line of fixed bandwidth, in the future the user will be concerned with finding the optimum coding scheme to maximize the number of conversations that can be sent over a digital data channel of fixed transmission rate.

In addition to developments in digital transmission services, facsimile data communications will involve more use of specialized carriers, satellite channels, and packet switching services. For example, satellite links will be used increasingly for textual-information transmission, as is done now by the *Wall Street Journal* in transmitting complete newspaper pages from its main printing plant in Massachusetts to its regional plant in Florida.

These developments in communications technology will not reduce basic costs to any large extent, however. Various changes in tariffs will give the user some price breaks. The cost of logic circuitry will decrease at a faster rate than the cost of basic communications. So developmental efforts today reflect an emphasis on distributed systems having multiple, specialized processors. There will be an incentive to carry out more processing at the local level, or to carry out sufficient preprocessing to reduce the amount of information to be transmitted.

The potential of cable TV is high for local distribution of information of all types. The technical capabilities of new CATV facilities to provide two-way communications to over 50 channels can supply an enormous amount of information. Of course, the legal and regulatory questions involved constitute major concerns in realizing these potentials.

In summary, the components exist for expanding the current skeleton national computer network into a full-fledged computer utility, one which could make possible great gains in service efficiencies at low costs. However, a number of regulatory and policy questions remain to be answered.

Reprographic and Microgaphic Technologies. Reprography and micrographics involve technologies of major importance in scientific information systems. New and unusual recording media are being developed which will permit meaningful space and cost savings and will guarantee faster and better copies for the user.

The most popular types of microforms in use today are roll film, microfiche (sheet film containing images in a grid pattern, with reduction ratios of 24 to 48), jackets (plastic carriers holding strips of microfilm, which permits addition or updating of material), and ultrastrips and ultrafiche (with reduction ratios of up to 250 to 1).

The use of micrographics should be encouraged as a means of conserving scarce and expensive paper. However, use patterns today usually result in blowing back the micro-image to full-size copies, resulting, of course, in using paper. In general, today's paper problem will not affect copying operations as much as original publishing; in any case, it will accelerate the development curve of micrographics and reprography.

As regards the role of micrographics in publishing, we see the use of microfilm for micro-republishing, where copyright arrangements or agreements are worked out satisfactorily; for original publishing in micro editions concurrent with traditional editions; and for micro editions as sole outputs because of printing and distribution costs.

Newer microforms include photochromic, photopolymeric, electrostatic, and thermoplastic materials, and holographic techniques.

The distribution or dissemination of information within or between information service centers and networks will be accomplished more economically in the future by facsimile transmission. The technology is already well developed, but commercial scanners and display modules need to be improved. I have mentioned the use of facsimile transmission of page masters for the *Wall Street Journal*; in this the material is scanned with a high-quality scanner, transmitted, and re-generated at the target site with high-quality equipment. One link is by satellite, and ten others are by microwave trans-missions. It is at present an expensive procedure, owing to the costs of appropriate hardware as well as to data trans-mission. For ordinary library and information-service users, the expense cannot now be justified in terms of time constraints or requirements. In general, also, image resolution or quality is not good: for office copying or newspaper material the system proves satisfactory, but it might not be for scientific and technical publications containing smaller type sizes and detailed graphical material.

For technical journals, present TV-type display technology is also not satisfactory. There are, for example, an average of 15,000 characters per page of *Index Medicus*, but the usual character generator displays 30 lines of 36 characters each, or 1080 total characters on the CRT screen. However, techniques have been demonstrated for using laser or electron beam scanning to drive another scanner to activate display modules. Material stored on 16-mm microform were re-generated as 35-mm microforms with good success by Project Intrex.

Computer-output-microfilm (COM) is another technology for the production of micrographics of interest to scientific information systems. COM, which first appeared in 1958, offered the promise of being faster than the computer impact printer and more compact than bulky paper reports. Today, technological advances in equipment and supplies have vastly improved reliability, quality, and cost effectiveness. COM recorders have average output capability of 20,000 lines/min, approximately 20 times faster than most computer impact printers. Even the latest innovation in computer in-line printing, a laser printer, operates at 13,000 lines/min.

In addition to savings in storage (270 tab-sized pages of printed data on a microfiche) and handling (4 fiche weigh less than an ounce and can be inserted into a 4 × 6 in. envelope), COM can be economically reproduced and rapidly duplicated: up to 1300 microfiche can be produced in an hour. COM can be considered, then, as a substitute for the line printer, a technique for photocopying for micro editions (mentioned earlier), or a means for photocomposing for subsequent blow-up to produce macro (regular size) publications. Such uses will proliferate in the near future and will contribute to faster and cheaper dissemination and distribution of information throughout library and information-service networks.

IMPACTS ON COPYRIGHT PROTECTION

Concern has been expressed, and properly so, about the use of copyrighted works in traditional formats in computers and computer networks. As has been pointed out, a work stored in a computer network accessible to users all over the country means that one copy could serve needs which previously could be met only by, perhaps, 10,000 copies. Much of the abstracting and indexing material in today's data banks is the result of computer typesetting of conventional secondary publications. There are few real problems in obtaining the copyright owner's permission for their use.

But computers also store raw data which are not copyrighted. So we have two groups of problems.

The first group concerns use of computer files which contain materials that are protected by copyright. What kinds of uses of what sorts of works should require permission of the copyright owners? Should permission be required and royalties paid when the work is input to the computer system? Or when it is displayed or printed out by the system? Should the copyright owner have control over the input of abstracts or digests of his work, or over use of the computer system to index his work? If the digest is so detailed as to constitute a derivative work, it would seem that permission should be required. And if the abstract was prepared by the author himself, it is copyrighted. But if the condensation is so brief that consultation of the original work is not precluded, as in an annotated bibliography or catalog, should permission to use be required?

The arguments for permission at input vs. permission at output revolve around the probable use patterns of such material in computer files. For example, permission and royalty payment at input would cover situations where a particular work might never be printed out in its entirety, or might be used only in fair-use situations. On the other hand, having to pay royalties at the input stage might inhibit computer-file development; material that is judged to be of marginal interest might well be left out.

Of course, permission and payment at input are easier to control than use at the output stage. But does scanning a file to search for material constitute use of the material? If material stored in a computer is used to generate or create a new work, who is the author and copyright owner? To quote, "The distinction between author or producer of stored material and the user of that material tends to be blurred".[1]

The second copyright problem centers on protection in computer banks of raw data and unpublished material. Unpublished material that is the product of "creative and original intellectual endeavor" should have the same copyright protection as published works. Raw data, however, may not involve such intellectual effort, although it may have required large investments in time and funds. So the question centers on how the investment in gathering masses of new data to be stored in a computer can be protected.

Another problem entirely is that of maintaining the integrity of data and information in computer systems and in computer networks. The ready availability of remote terminals connected through convenient communication services, and coupled with sometimes carelessly designed log-in and password schemes, provides ready access to all of the data in many networks with a minimum of effort. Careful attention to the design of individual computer systems, including all of the resources maintained within them, and to their coupling with communications services and terminals, is necessary to establish complete control over data accessibility.

This problem of controlling network access is coupled with one that is almost exactly the opposite. It is essential that those individuals and organizations which need resources know where to find them and be able to access them readily. Here, however, it is nontechnological problems of providing access that are creating our concern. We are all familiar with, and users of, various indexing services that reflect our fields of interest. The growth of information makes the development of even better retrieval tools imperative. Indeed, when we consider this need along with the developments in computer, communications, and reprographic technologies outlined previously, we can see a time in the not-too-distant future when the use of larger retrieval systems available to more users will become more common. We must work to develop procedures and mechanisms to take advantage of all these technologies without destroying our basic systems of information dissemination and exchange.

LITERATURE CITED

(1) Cambridge Research Institute, "Omnibus Copyright Revision: Comparative Analysis of the Issues", American Society for Information Science, Washington, D.C., 1973, 280 pp.

(2) G. Lapidus, "Fascimile Systems Begin to Link Up with Computer Networks", *Data Commun.*, **5** (1), 51–64 (1976).

(3) B. L. Linden, "Copyright, Photocopying, and Computer Usage", *Bull. Am. Soc. Inf. Sci.*, **1** (10), 12–14 (May 1975).

(4) National Academy of Sciences, Computer Science and Engineering Board, Information Systems Panel, "Libraries and Information Technology, a National System Challenge", Report to CLR, Inc., National Academy of Sciences, Washington, D.C., 1972, 84 pp.

(5) R. Shank and M. M. Henderson, "Federal Library Cooperation", in "Library Cooperation" issue, *Library Trends*, **24** (2), 157–423 (Oct 1975).

SUMMARY OF LIBRARY PHOTOCOPYING
IN THE UNITED STATES

King Research, Inc.

This report presents the results of a study of the amount of photocopying of library materials by library staff in United States libraries. A national survey was conducted from a sample of Public, Academic, Special and Federal libraries to determine the annual volume of photocopying undertaken for interlibrary loans, local users, and intrasystem loans. Since interpretations of the Law concerning eligibility for royalty payment appear to vary, data are also given for the amount of photocopying that occurs under various hypothetical conditions of eligibility as they might be interpreted in the new Copyright Law and in guidelines set forth by the National Commission on New Technological Uses of Copyrighted Works (CONTU) for photocopying for interlibrary loans. The report documents the effects of these hypothetical conditions from the perspective of both libraries and publishers. In addition, the report describes alternative royalty payment mechanisms and discusses some advantages and disadvantages of each from the standpoints of small and large libraries and small and large publishers. This summary presents estimates of total volume of photocopying, analyzes implications of the new Law from the perspectives of libraries and publishers, and describes alternative payment mechanisms.

Sampling and Data Collection

The sample of libraries for collection of data on the volume and characteristics of photocopies of library materials made on library staff-controlled equipment was a stratified random selection representing the five categories of libraries: Academic, Public, Federal, Special associated with profit-seeking organizations, and Special

---

SOURCE: Reprinted from *Library Photocopying in the United States: With Implications for the Development of a Copyright Royalty Payment Mechanism.*

libraries associated with not-for-profit organizations. The target minimum number of participating libraries by type were: 100 Academic, 100 Public, 62 Federal, 108 Special (74 Profit associated, 34 Non-Profit associated). These target numbers were based in part on the estimated volumes of interlibrary lending for 1972, the most recent year for which comprehensive data could be assembled at the time.

Some large libraries were included in the sample with certainty, to represent themselves. The remaining libraries of each type were stratified by significant variables to facilitate selection of a representative sample from which to estimate totals for the non-certainty libraries. Academic libraries were stratified by size (measured by volumes in collection) and type of institution (University, four year, two year). Public libraries were stratified by population served and by region. Federal libraries were stratified by agency and by volume of interlibrary loans. Special libraries were stratified by size. Participation was invited from a sample larger than the minimum target number, so that ineligible libraries, refusals, and nonresponse would not disrupt the very tight time table.

In order to avoid excessive burden on any library, short sample periods were specified for collecting each major category of information. Each library was asked to record and report information on photocopying volumes for a sample period, to describe characteristics of library materials photocopied for selected days, and to report on requests made during a specified period for interlibrary loans, and on the disposition of those requests. These sample periods ranged from one day to three weeks, and were specified in light of volume reported on a preliminary screener form.

Subsequently, participating libraries were also asked to respond to a questionnaire which addressed questions of costs of photocopying operations, preferences among possible royalty payment mechanisms, judgments concerning relative costs of hypothetical recordkeeping procedures, and a few volume items. Thus, the data collection from libraries involved an initial screener inquiry and four separate, but closely related, requests for information.

In addition, the time limitation on the project did not permit data collection to be spread throughout the year. Therefore, it was important to find adjustment factors to correct for the difference between periods (days of the week and months of the year) when data were collected and the average activity over the year. Such adjustment weights were derived in the course of an analysis of interlibrary loan data for the MINITEX system for the year 1976. The MINITEX data were also used to verify a mathematical model used to project estimates of the distribution of photocopying to the entire year.

A total of 37,032 individual photocopy transactions were reported by the sampled libraries and analyzed. These reports of photocopying included information about each individual photocopy transaction such as type of material (serials, books, other materials), whether copyrighted, type of transaction (interlibrary loan, local user, intrasystem loan) as well as other relevant information.

Total Volume of Photocopying

In 1976, one full year prior to implementation of the new Copyright Law, a substantial amount of photocopying took place in libraries in the United States. It is estimated that there were 36.8 thousand paper-to-paper photocopying machines in the 21,280 libraries from which the sample was chosen. Of 35.3 thousand machines used regularly for photocopying of library materials, 15.4 thousand were used exclusively by patrons for photocopying library and other materials and 19.9 thousand were used by library staff. Thus, the average number of machines per library is less than one. This study addressed only the volume of photocopying performed by library staff of library materials. Even with this limitation, an estimated 114 million photocopy items were made by library staff in that year. Less than one-half of this volume, however, was from copyrighted materials. This means that the per library average is about 2,500 copyrighted items from 54 million photocopies made from copyrighted materials.

Public libraries accounted for the largest share of photocopying of all library materials, with 64 million photocopy items. Special libraries were next, with 26 million photocopy items, followed by Academic libraries, with 17 million, and Federal libraries, with 7 million. (See Figure 1.) The 8,310 Public libraries in the population averaged 7,700 photocopy items per library. The 3,030 Academic libraries averaged 5,500 photocopy items per library, with Special libraries (8,510) averaging 3,100 and Federal libraries (1,430) averaging 4,900 items. The proportion of photocopying from copyrighted materials varied somewhat among the types of libraries. Public libraries had the lowest

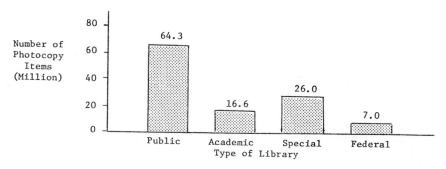

Figure 1. Number of Photocopy Items by Type of Library (1976)

proportion of photocopying from copyrighted materials (37%) and Special libraries had the highest proportion (69%). Academic libraries did 48 percent and Federal libraries did 58 percent of their photocopying from copyrighted materials. This variation among types of libraries reflects differences in the types of materials photocopied by different types of libraries.

Over all the libraries, serials accounted for 48 million photocopy items; books 14.9 million; and other materials 50.8 million. (See Figure 2.) Only 7 percent of the other materials, however, were identified as being copyrighted, whereas, 79 percent of the photocopy items of serials and 84 percent of the photocopy items made from books were from copyrighted materials. Public libraries accounted for nearly three-fourths of all the photocopying of other materials, which is why they had a low proportion of photocopying from copyrighted materials.

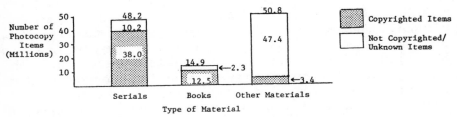

Figure 2.   Number of Photocopy Items by Type of Material (1976)

Volume of Serial Photocopying

This report pays particular attention to volume of photocopying of serials. Serials accounted for the largest number of items photocopied from copyrighted materials, at about 38 million photocopy items. Also, libraries and publishers appear to be more concerned about serials than about books or other materials. Special and Public libraries have the largest number of photocopy items from copyrighted serials, about 16 million and 14 million respectively. Academic and Federal libraries made, respectively, about 5 million and 4 million photocopy items from copyrighted serials. The disparity among the types of libraries is largely accounted for by the number of libraries within each type. When one considers the average number of photocopy items per library, the disparity is much less. Although Federal libraries averaged 2,500 photocopy items per library, the other three types ranged from 1,600 to 1,800 items per library.

It is especially important to observe the categories in which serial photocopying breaks down according to use (interlibrary loan, local use by patrons or library staff, and intrasystem loan to a branch library) since both the Copyright Law and CONTU Guidelines may have different implications for each. Most photocopy items of copyrighted serials (about 22 million) are made for local users. Twelve million items of copyrighted serials are made for intrasystem loans and about 4 million are made for interlibrary loan. (See Figure 3.) For each of the three types of transactions mentioned above, the amount of photocopying performed under different conditions of eligibility is summarized below.

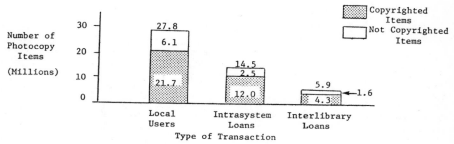

Figure 3.   Number of Photocopy Items of Serials That Are Copyrighted by Type of Transaction (1976)

Filled serial interlibrary loan requests for domestic serials account for 3.8 million photocopy items, of which 3.1 million are estimated to be copyrighted. When CONTU guidelines are applied to the 3.1 million, it is estimated that 2.4 million are under six years old and 2.0 million are both under six years old and not used for replacement or classroom use. If the rule of six copies or more is applied, about 500 thousand photocopy items are subject to royalty payment. (See Figure 4.) This total increases to 1.9 million items if all photocopy items from serials over five years old are also considered eligible.

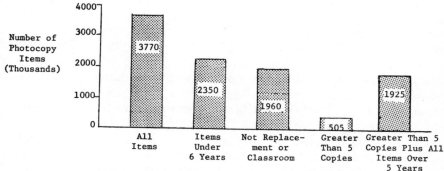

Figure 4.   Number of Photocopy Items of Domestic Serials Requested for Interlibrary Loans—All Items, Items Under 6 Years, Items Not for Replacement or Classroom, Items With Greater Than Five Copies (1976)

Considering all interlibrary loan photocopy items, it is estimated that 81 percent of all U.S. libraries will have less than 250 items per year. These libraries, however, account for only 41 percent of the total interlibrary loan photocopy items, for there is a high degree of centralization of photocopying for interlibrary loans. Twenty percent of the libraries request 73 percent of the photocopied interlibrary loans. (See Figure 5.)

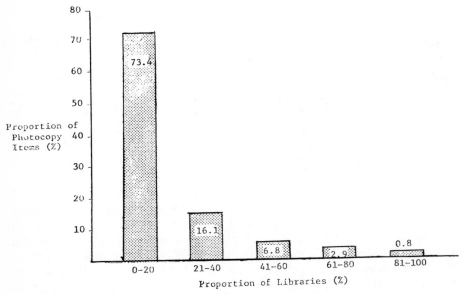

Figure 5. Distribution of Interlibrary Loan Photocopy Items by Proportion of Libraries (1976)

Local use accounts for the largest amount of photocopying at 28 million serial photocopy items. Of these, about 22 million are copyrighted and 19 million are from copyrighted domestic serials. If one hypothetically applies CONTU's eligibility conditions for local use as well as for interlibrary loan, one finds that 15 million photocopy items are from serials under six years old, 17 million are from serials having five or more copies made in a library, and 13 million are from serials under six years old with five or more copies made in a library. One also finds that 800 thousand photocopy items for local users were made for replacement or for classroom use by faculty. Another hypothetical condition of eligibility from Section 108(d) of the Law, involves single copies made for individuals. It is estimated that 82 percent of the photocopy items made for local users involve single copies made for individuals or institutions. Considering all photocopy items made for local use, it is estimated that 62 percent of all U.S. libraries will have less than 250 photocopy items. These libraries account for only seven percent of the total photocopy items made for local use, with the remaining 93 percent made by 40 percent of the libraries. A total of 78 percent of the photocopies made for local use are made by 20 percent of the libraries. (See Figure 6.)

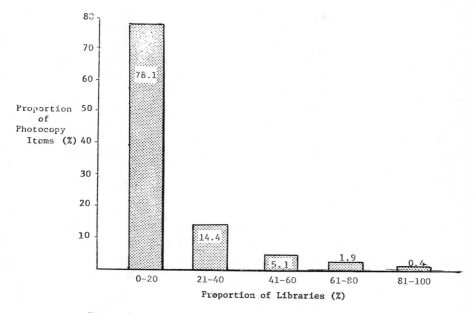

Figure 6. Distribution of Local Use Photocopy Items by Proportion of Libraries (1976)

Photocopying for intrasystem loan of serials comes to a total of 14 million photocopy items, of which 10 million are from copyrighted domestic serials. One-half million of these items involve replacement or classroom use. Approximately 7 million of the intrasystem loan photocopy items are from serials under six years old. Finally, it is estimated that about 76 percent of the items photocopied for intrasystem loan are single copies made for individuals or other institutions. Over one-third of the transactions for intrasystem loan involve multiple copies of one or two pages, which may be photocopies of tables of contents or title pages made for current awareness.

Libraries and Photocopying Operations

Depending upon final legal interpretation of the conditions of eligibility for royalty payment, libraries may be required to screen outgoing interlibrary loan requests to check for possible exemptions. A majority of libraries report that they would not incur extra costs which could not be absorbed if they were required to perform various screening operations for outgoing serial interlibrary loan requests. Depending upon the specific screening operation, this answer varies among libraries from 84 percent of all libraries to 62 percent of all libraries.

In similar proportions, libraries indicated that they would not incur higher costs if required to screen requests from local patrons. There is an exception, however. About 60 percent of responding libraries reported that extra non-absorbable costs would be incurred in the event that they were required to check for previously made photocopies from a requested title.

No single royalty payment mechanism stood out as being preferred over the others. Libraries in the survey rated as "most preferred" four mechanisms: higher subscription prices for all serials, purchase of royalty stamps or coupons, photocopying machine fees, and purchase of multiple copies or reprints from a single agency. No more than one-third of the libraries, however, rated any of these mechanisms as "most preferred."

In some instances, libraries charge their users for photocopying services. The average annual gross income per library for operation of photocopying machines is $3,085. The largest average annual gross income is $11,544 for Academic libraries, followed by $3,648 for Federal libraries, $2,964 for Public libraries, and $96 for Special libraries. The largest average annual income per machine is $3,607 for Academic libraries, followed by $2,432 for Federal libraries, $1,744 for Public libraries, and $87 for Special libraries. On the average, however, photocopying operations cost Public libraries $4,080 per year and Academic libraries $16,260 per year. This suggests that some libraries, on the average, may currently be incurring net losses for their photocopying operations when their gross income is compared to their operational costs. Sufficient data were not available to estimate annual costs for Federal and Special libraries.

Publishers and Photocopied Serials

Publishers have information needs unlike those of libraries. For example, they need to know how much photocopying of individual serials occurs across all libraries. The estimate is that, over all libraries, the total number of interlibrary loan photocopy items per serial title is 50 or less for 40 percent of serial titles, with these titles accounting for three percent of the total photocopy items. About seven percent of the serials have more than 500 photocopy items made from them. Considering only those photocopy items that are not for replacement or classroom use, that are less than six years old, and that have more than five copies, 91 percent of serial titles have 50 or fewer photocopy items and very few, if any, have more than 100 photocopy items made of them. There is, in fact, a high concentration of photocopying serials: 86 percent of the photocopying of serials occurs on only 20 percent of the serials. (See Figure 7.)

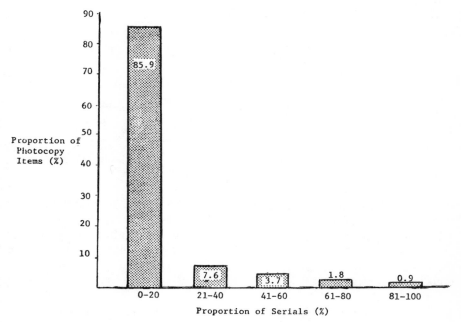

Figure 7. Distribution of Interlibrary Loan Photocopy Items by Proportion of Serials (1976)

For local user photocopying, the estimate is that 67 percent of the copied serials have less than 1,000 photocopy items and a small, but significant, five percent of the titles have more than 5,000 items made of them. Considering only those photocopy items of serials less than six years old and with more than five copies, nearly all of the serials have less than 500 photocopy items. Here, also, a significant proportion of the serials accounts for a major proportion of the photocopy items. About 68 percent of the photocopy items come from 20 percent of the serials. (See Figure 8.)

According to the recent Indiana University survey of publishers, nearly 50 percent of responding journals expected to receive no royalty payments from a clearinghouse arrangement supplying authorized copies. The average expected payment was about $1.50 per item for

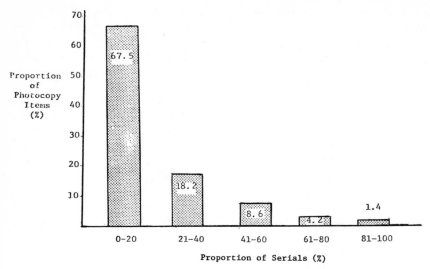

Figure 8. Distribution of Local Use Photocopy Items by Proportion of Serials

those publishers who expected payment. Many publishers appeared to prefer direct licensing of photocopying to clearinghouse arrangements. This survey, however, was made before the Association of American Publishers, Inc. had announced its intention to set up a Copyright Clearance Center. After that announcement, the response may have been different.

Implications for the Development of Royalty Payment Mechanisms

Although the implications of royalty payment mechanisms for libraries and publishers are different, it appears that only a minority of either group would be appreciably affected by the actual payment of royalties, since a large proportion of photocopying takes place in 20 percent of the libraries and with 20 percent of the serials.

No single mechanism appears suitable for all photocopying which might be eligible for royalty payment. Depending upon the final resolution of the eligibility question and the volume of photocopying involved, it is likely that a combination of mechanisms will be required.

Generally speaking, royalty payment mechanisms become more expensive to design and operate as the matching of eligible photocopying volume and royalty payments requires more accuracy and precision. As evidenced by their relatively high ranking of higher subscription prices as an alternative royalty payment mechanism, libraries appear willing to exchange some accuracy for a simplification of their mode of participation in a royalty payment mechanism.

Because of the low number of eligible photocopy items per serial for the majority of copyrighted domestic serials, and because of the potentially low proportion of eligible photocopy items at any one library, it may be more cost-effective, at least initially, for a central agency, clearinghouse, or payment center to concentrate on serving high-volume serials and high-volume libraries. Low-volume libraries and low-volume serials may also find it inexpensive when compared to their own monitoring, depending upon the proportion of photocopying in their libraries which was actually eligible for payment.

Monitoring and enforcing royalty payment may be among the most expensive components of a royalty payment mechanism. If publishers desire monitoring, these functions may be handled most effectively by a central agency if legal questions such as anti-trust can be resolved.

The impact of royalty payments in terms of subscription cancellations is uncertain. We hypothesize that, if this occurred, it would have the most negative impact on small, specialized journals.

Caveats and Statistical Precision of Results

One should keep in mind that behavior of libraries and publishers may be different after the Copyright Law goes into effect in 1978. A change in behavior could substantially alter the number of photocopy items eligible for royalty payment from the estimates made in the sample. Also, attitudes of libraries and publishers toward alternative royalty payment mechanisms may change (from those observed in recent surveys) after they become familiar with operating under the Law.

Since the data were obtained from a sample of libraries, there is some chance of estimates being higher or lower than those given in this report. In order to give some indication of the statistical precision of the results, standard errors of typical estimates are stated here. Statistical precision estimates made for all libraries are higher than those made by type of library because of the difference in sample sizes. The standard error for interlibrary loan for all photocopies made in all four types of libraries is 3.8 ± .58 million. The interpretation is that the number of photocopies made in all four types of libraries for interlibrary loan requests is between 4.4 million and 3.2 million at 66 percent level of confidence, or, 3.8 ± 1.16 million at 95 percent level of confidence. The number of photocopies made for interlibrary loans by Public libraries would be 1.0 ± .16 million, and for Academic libraries 1.1 ± .13 million. The standard errors for Special and Federal libraries are 1.3 ± .54 million and 0.4 ± .012 million respectively. The estimate for local users is 19.0 ± 3.4 million. The estimates for Public, Academic, Special and Federal libraries are 7.4 ± 3.7; 1.8 ± 1.4; 7.9 ± 2.2; and 2.0 ± 0.6 respectively. It is noted that estimates that involve the proportion of transactions such as the proportion of serials that are copyrighted, the proportion that are from domestic publishers, age of the publications and so on have a substantially higher statistical precision since the sample sizes are over 10,000.

Finally, the estimates derived from the MINITEX data base serve as an excellent verification of estimates of photocopying for interlibrary loans made from the national library survey. It appears that the national library survey data closely resemble those obtained from MINITEX. Also, data from another National Science Foundation study of scientific and technical publishing yield very similar overall results to estimates of total photocopying of scientific and technical serials observed in this study.

SCHOLARLY AND RESEARCH JOURNALS: SURVEY OF PUBLISHER PRACTICES AND PRESENT ATTITUDES ON AUTHORIZED JOURNAL ARTICLE COPYING AND LICENSING

Bernard M. Fry, Herbert S. White, and Elizabeth L. Johnson

PROJECT BACKGROUND AND SUMMARY OF FINDINGS

History

In the late summer of 1976 the Research Center for Library and Information Science at the Indiana University Graduate Library School was approached by the National Commission on New Technological Uses of Copyrighted Works (CONTU) about the feasibility of distributing, tabulating and analyzing a questionnaire to be provided by CONTU to the publishers of United States scholarly and research journals. The IU Graduate Library School was selected for this task because, in an earlier study for the National Science Foundation*, it had developed a core list of 2,459 U.S. scholarly and research journals. Inclusion criteria for this list are explained later in this report. It was believed that this list, initially developed in 1974, could be updated to serve as the basis for this survey. Moreover, since the IU GLS Research Center had already established contacts with these journal publishers in the completion of the NSF questionnaire, it was felt that this familiarity would improve cooperation and response rates.

The agreement for Indiana University to distribute and analyze the questionnaire was completed on September 27, 1976. The development and pre-testing of the proposed questionnaire by CONTU (one for publishers of scholarly and research journals, one for each journal included) after the new copyright act was signed on October 19, 1976, did not permit these questionnaires to be distributed until February 15, 1977, with a requested response date of March 25, 1977. At the request

---

*   Fry, Bernard M. and White, Herbert S. "Economics and Interaction of the Publisher-Library Relationship in the Production and Use of Scholarly and Research Journals." Final Report on NSF Grant GN-41398, PB 249108, 1975. Also available as: Fry and White—"A Study of Scholarly and Research Journals." D.C. Heath & Co., Lexington, Mass., 1976.

of CONTU, a follow-up mailing was made on April 15, 1977, and all responses received by May 10, 1977 are included in these tabulations.

The list of 2,459 journals published by 1,634 publishers used in the NSF survey was updated through a review of *Ulrich's International Periodicals Directory*, 16th edition (1975-76), which lists both cessations and new journal starts. The list was modified in the light of the responses of publishers themselves, some of which indicated that journals still listed had actually ceased publication, while others called our attention to journals not in our survey for a variety of reasons, including the fact that they were too new to be listed in *Ulrich's*. The result of these changes was a revised survey population of 2,552 U.S. scholarly and research journals, distributed by 1,672 publishers.

Project Personnel

Bernard M. Fry, Dean of the Indiana University Graduate Library School, has served as Principal Investigator for this project. Herbert S. White, Professor in the Graduate Library School and Director of its Research Center for Library and Information Science, has served as Co-Principal Investigator. Elizabeth L. Johnson has served as Research Associate.

Purpose of Investigation

The questionnaires, which were distributed with explanatory and background material also developed by CONTU, were designed to elicit information concerning attitudes toward photocopying and various methods for dealing with licensing or the supply of authorized photocopies for such article copying not exempt under the provisions of the 1976 Copyright Revision Act, and which would require auhorization of the copyright owner. It was felt that these would help the National Commission to fulfill its statutory responsibility to make recommendations to the Congress and the President "as to such changes in copyright law or procedures that may be necessary to assure . . . access to copyrighted works and to provide recognition of the rights of copyright owners." (Public Law 94-553)

Response Rates

The response rate for publishers was 31.8% (531 of 1,672); for journals they published it was 38.2% (974 of 2,552). Some additional responses have also been received since the May 10, 1977 cut-off date, and the data taken from these have been retained in case further analysis is desired.

There is clear evidence, moreover, that a large portion of the non-response comes from journals which are not copyrighted, and which may therefore have felt relatively unaffected by the questions being posed. A total of 872, or 89.5% of responding journals indicated that they were copyrighted. By contrast, analysis of the records of the Copyright Office indicates that only about 60% of the non-responding journals are copyrighted. The response levels therefore represent, in all probability, a greater proportion of those journals whose views and decisions concerning copyright policies are of significance in the measurement of attitudes. Confidentiality of all responses has been strictly maintained, and the completed questionnaires are being returned to the respondents.

Techniques of Analysis

Responses to the questions provided by CONTU were analyzed in total for the publisher or journal group responding. As appropriate, responses were also analyzed to determine differences between the for-profit and non-profit publications sectors; between the subject disciplines of pure science, applied science and technology, social science, and humanities; and by size of circulation for each journal. At the request of King Research, Inc., an organization involved in a related study for the National Science Foundation, National Commission on Libraries and Information Science, and CONTU, publisher responses were also broken down as between those who published only one journal, and those who published more than one.

SUMMARY OF FINDINGS

General

Although the tabular and descriptive data which follow present a wealth of information, it is somewhat difficult to draw clearcut generalized conclusions. There are several reasons for this. At the time of the distribution and completion of these questionnaires, the new copyright law had been enacted only a few months earlier and will not come into effect until January 1, 1978. In addition, no specific proposals for the establishment of clearinghouses or royalty payment centers had as yet been promulgated, let alone publicized.

Of the responses, 449 come from publishers who publish only one journal in the survey. This represents 84.6% of the responding publisher population, and 46.5% of the responding journal population. Of responding publishers in the survey, 95.5% distribute five or fewer journals, and these in turn include 61.3% of the responding journals. Scholarly and research publishing consists predominantly of relatively small non-profit journals, whose publishers probably have little knowledge of or have paid little attention to the complex and lengthy provisions of the new copyright act. Clearly, a number of major publishers, both in the for-profit and non-profit sectors, have done so, but this number represents only a small minority. The inexperience and lack of prior thought by the larger proportion of the response group shows up clearly in responses which are somewhat difficult to track. Appended comments, which provide valuable insight, indicate that many of these respondents are reluctant to be involved at all. Many of them have little if any expectation of receiving payment through any copyright mechanism. They have no particular interest in involvement in any system which they might consider complex, and they expect no remuneration of any sizeable proportions. At the same time, many of these same respondents are apparently suspicious of considering agreements the implications of which they do not fully understand. This leads to a contrasting posture in many cases of unwillingness to give permission, while at the same time having no expectation of return. They supply reprint copies to authors, or assign back issue rights to agents, and they would just as soon be left out of what they fear might become a substantial entrapment in bureaucratic routine. It is, of course, interesting, and perhaps ironic, that many libraries have expressed this as their greatest fear as well, rather than the potential payment cost.

At the other extreme there are few publishers who give voice to payment expectations which are undoubtedly unrealistically high. The most significant finding, in general terms, is the need for further information and education, which must reach in particular the small journal and fringe publisher who is such an important part of this field. Proposals made by the Association of American Publishers and others must be widely publicized, and there is a major educational and dissemination role which must be undertaken, perhaps by or with the cooperation of CONTU. Such assistance could include the development and explanation of alternative specimen statements as part of copyright notices, as well as the calculation of assessment of the impact of implementation of the new copyright law, in particular for small journals and individual publishers. For publishers wishing to copyright but who are willing to adopt a liberal policy on copying, specimen terminology to be distributed as potential notices in journals could deal with concepts such as "for private study and research," "willing to let non-profit users copy," "restrictions limited to the first year following publication," but in much more specific form. To a substantial degree respondents are willing to grant rights to non-profit users that they are not willing to grant to commercial users, whether out of principle or expectation of return. They do not appear to know, however, how to go about implementing this preference, or others which they may feel.

Journal Survey

1.   Publication Frequency: The survey indicates differences in publication frequency not only as between the commercial and non-profit sectors, but also as among subject disciplines. Better than half of non-profit journals publish quarterly or even less frequently, while the same holds true for commercial journals in only 36% of cases. Humanities journals appear quarterly or less frequently in 73% of responding cases, which is more than twice the reported rate for pure and applied science journals, which appear with considerably greater frequency.

2.   Size of Journals: Scholarly and research publishing is heavily populated by small journals. Better than half of the journals in the survey had a circulation of under 3000 copies, and this figure is even higher for commercial than for non-profit journals. However, large (between 10,000 and 100,000 circulation) journals, while representing only 19.5% of the journals, include 74.2% of the issues distributed.

3.   Foreign Circulation: Less than half of responding journals report a foreign circulation which exceeds 20% of the total, and only 27% have foreign circulation of above 30%. However, smaller circulation journals are more heavily dependent on foreign subscribers.

4.   Copyrighting: The great majority of journals which responded to this survey, in particular commercial journals, copyright each issue published. They do not, however, include individually copyrighted articles in many cases, and commercial journals tend to avoid this in particular.

5.   Page Charges: About three fourths of the journals responding do not employ page charges at all, and only 3.5% have mandatory page charges. Commercial journals make less use of page charges, and large commercial journals responding don't use them at all.

6.   Selling Reprints of Articles: Better than half of responding journals currently sell reprints directly (although it is not known if minimum quantity limitations are applied), but only about one third sell reprints through an agent. The use of such agents is fairly concentrated among commercial journals to two agents (Xerox University Microfilm and Information Unlimited), and dominated by Xerox University Microfilm for non-profit journals.

7.   Current Prices of Reprints: Rates charged by journals which presently sell reprints vary widely, although most non-profit journals

are willing to accept $3 or less for a ten page article, and better than half of commercial journals are willing to accept orders for $5. However, a sizeable minority, particularly in the commercial sector, charges $7 or even more for a ten page article, supplied on pre-payment to domestic customers.

8.   Comparative Prices of Reprints: Perhaps surprisingly, and indicative of lack of informed judgement mentioned earlier, journals which do not sell reprints express themselves as satisfied with lower payments, in response to a hypothetical question, than journals which do sell them.

9.   Volume of Reprint Sales: Two thirds of the responding journals indicate no reprint sales at all or sales which average under 6 reprints a week. Only 13% of responding journals sell more than thirty reprints per average working day, and can be considered to be "in the business of selling reprints." Responses indicate that more than half of the journals fill orders within five days of receipt, although over 17% take a month or longer to comply.

10.   Expected Prices for Authorized Copies: More than 50% of responding copyrighted journals expect no payment to them from the operation of a clearinghouse, or from an agent, and this lack of expectation was particularly pronounced among commercial journals. Where compensation was expected, 50 cents was acceptable in about half of the cases. However, a small but insistent minority indicates considerably greater expectations, in some cases well above $5.

11.   Expected Prices for Licensed Photocopying: At the same time, perhaps because of lack of information, responding journals hesitate to commit themselves to licensing directly or through an agent or clearinghouse. Where there was willingness, 50 cents is an acceptable payment in more than half the respondents, but a small minority (See no. 10 above) hold out for as much as $7 or more.

12.   Microform Editions: By a substantial margin, journals prefer to sell microform editions through an agent rather than directly. At the same time, they are not willing to authorize copying from microform during the current year of publication, and only slightly more willing to permit unrestricted copying from past year microforms.

13.   Policies on Liberal Provisions to Copy: Although many journals do not presently exact payment charges from libraries, they are overwhelmingly unwilling to grant blanket permission for copying, or blanket permission for interlibrary loan. This negative reaction to

"carte blanche" subsides only to some extent for back year permission, and is particularly strong with relation to libraries in for-profit organizations. Where there is willingness for back year unlimited copying, the cut-off is most frequently set at one year.

Publisher Survey

14.   International Standard Serial Numbers (ISSN): Only a small percentage of responding publishers feel that the inclusion of ISSN numbers would facilitate the provision of reprints or photocopies at a lower price. This may be true in part because only slightly more than one third of responding journals presently identify their journals with ISSN numbers, and some responding publishers may not even have been aware of what ISSN numbers were.

15.   Licensing Preferences: Under licensing preferences, all types of publishers indicate a strong preference for direct licensing, as against the use of either agents or clearinghouses. It should be stressed that this question was answered as something of an abstraction, since no specific clearinghouse mechanism proposal had as yet been promulgated and distributed, either by the AAP, or by any other organization.

16.   Use of Agents: For what are probably some of the same reasons, responding publishers expressed a strong preference for supplying authorized copies directly, rather than through clearinghouses or agents. As stressed in the general comments, the use of clearinghouses and agents is a concept which is probably little understood by some of the publishers of small and scattered journals, and it would require explanation and publicity to gain wider acceptance.

17.   Teletype Equipment for Ordering Reprints: Responding publishers saw little practical utility in teletype equipment for receiving orders, in large part because very few publishers have such equipment at present. Additionally, few publishers foresaw the usefulness of another form of electronic communication.

18.   Telephone Orders: Better than two thirds of responding publishers, and in particular commercial publishers, indicated a willingness to accept telephonic orders, with a majority also willing to do this at a standard charge.

19.   Preferred Methods of Payment: The receipt of individual one-time payment for the filling of a one-time order is the most preferred method of handling copy requests, since it avoids either billing or record keeping. Only about one fifth of the responding

publishers found open accounts or deposit accounts acceptable, and this positive response is largely limited to large commercial publishers, who might have reason to expect a larger volume of business, and the same response patterns held for the use of stamps or coupons. Slightly less than half of the responding publishers were agreeable to billing with shipment of the order, although it is not certain that all of these would be willing to do this for single copy orders as well as multiple copies. Large non-profit publishers were particularly reluctant to endorse this approach.

20. Future Policies: Of the 43.5% of publishers who responded to a question which implied that they did not presently sell reprints or photocopies directly or through an agent, about three fourths continued to express their unwillingness to do so in the future.

THE EFFECT OF A LARGE-SCALE
PHOTOCOPYING SERVICE ON JOURNAL SALES

MAURICE B. LINE and D. N. WOOD★
(with the assistance of C. B. Wootton and C. A. Bower)
British Library Lending Division, Boston Spa

The proposition is examined that large-scale photocopying, such as that practised by the British Library Lending Division, affects the sales of journals. There is little evidence of a reduction in journal circulation figures. In spite of large increases in journal prices (which have risen much faster, in terms of cost per page, than the Retail Price Index), university libraries have, since the NLLST was established, devoted an increasingly high proportion of their budgets to journals, though recent financial pressures are now forcing cancellations. An extensive survey of demand for journals at BLLD shows a heavy concentration on a relatively small number of titles, most of them well established journals, widely held by libraries and with large circulations. The demand for in-print issues of the average journal is small. It is concluded, in the absence of any evidence to the contrary, that economic difficulties experienced by journal publishers and the increased demand on the BLLD are unrelated, though both owe something to the economic pressures on libraries.

INCREASINGLY IN recent years, particularly since the Whitford Committee on Copyright was set up, suggestions have been made that the great extension of photocopying over the last decade, especially that done at the British Library Lending Division, is affecting the sales of journals. This is an important issue, on which arguments can be adduced on both sides, but on which there are few available facts. This paper attempts to collect some relevant evidence.

The two basic claims are that 1) journal subscriptions are either declining, or not increasing in proportion to the potential market, and 2) there has been a vast increase in photocopying, particularly at the British Library Lending Division. To take the latter first, there is no disputing this.

Not only did the total demand on the British Library Lending Division (and its predecessor the National Lending Library for Science and Technology) increase from 41,000 to 2,104,000 between 1961 and 1974, but the proportion of demands from British libraries met by photocopies also increased during the period, from 7% to over 40%. Table 1 shows the increase in the number of articles photocopied over the last 12 years. At the same time, far more photocopying has been carried out in other libraries of all kinds, as a result of the ready availability of cheap copying machines, whether in the library or elsewhere, though no hard figures are available. It is however, known that total photocopying, in terms of sheets copied, in university libraries increased by about 36% between 1970–1 and 1972–3—these figures include secretarial and other copying, but one would not expect the proportion of journal copying to have changed greatly, unless some libraries acquired in the interval machines capable of cheap multiple copying, which took over work formerly done on stencil duplicators.

★ The views expressed are those of the authors and not necessarily those of the British Library Board.

SOURCE: Reprinted from the *Journal of Documentation* 31: 234-245 (1975) by permission of the copyright holders. Copyright ©1975 by Aslib and contributors.

For a loss in potential journal sales less evidence is available. Circulation figures of a sample of 100 journals showed an overall increase of over 10% between 1967–8 and 1973–4, only 18 of the 100 showing a decrease. A separate sample, of 50 British journals only, showed an overall increase of 5% (37 increased, 13 decreased); society and commercial journals were not dissimilar in this respect. It is hard to guess what the *potential* increase in sales might have been. For comparison, the increase in the total population of the UK between 1966 and 1972 was less than 3%. It might be expected that sales would increase roughly in proportion to the number of research libraries, perhaps even in proportion to the increase in research personnel, but few reliable figures are available for these.

However, the size of the potential market is only one factor. Its ability to pay for the product is another, and since the actual number of current journals has been increasing exponentially (see Table 2)—an increase that has only recently shown signs of fading—any individual library would have had to increase its budget at a fast exponential rate to keep up. (It may be noted that there has been no noticeable increase in the mortality rate of serials; indeed, this has remained remarkably constant, at any rate until very recently.)

TABLE 1. *Items photocopied by BLLD, 1963–74*

Year	No. of items photocopied
1963	13,307
1964	18,244
1965	23,856
1966	30,735
1967	36,598
1968	53,781
1969	100,716
1970	251,000
1971	343,000
1972	439,845
1973	664,692
1974	893,801

TABLE 2. *Current serials received by BLLD*

	received	on order
1963	18,175	8,287
1964	20,783	4,790
1965	22,619	3,616
1966	26,284	3,826
1967	29,693	4,901
1968	31,904	5,278
1969	34,300	5,374
1970	35,824	4,607
1971	36,980	4,950
1972	40,192	4,484
1973	42,934	4,723
1974	44,767	4,673

In addition, the average cost of journals has been increasing rapidly. Some of this increase can be attributed to a general increase in costs, especially paper and postage, and some of it to a supposed increase in size of individual journals. It is therefore reasonable to calculate cost per page of text, and allow for the increase in the Retail Price Index, in order to arrive at an indication whether 'value for money' has changed over the past 10 or 15 years. Table 3 presents figures for British journals to show that the value for money has declined substantially since 1960, much more sharply for journals published by societies than for commercial journals. However, it should be noted that the effect has been to bring the two types of journal more in line with one another; 'society' journals were relatively underpriced until recently. [On average academic journals have shrunk in size slightly since 1970, and this accounts for some of the decline in 'value'. Some of the fall in value (or rise in cost) is probably due to a decline in advertising: this has dropped considerably in science journals, from 34% of pages in 1960 to 8% in 1973].

Taking all factors into account, therefore, any library that wanted to keep up fully with the literature would have had to increase its journal budget at an average annual rate of 17% over the period 1965–71. Figures for industrial libraries are not readily available, but figures for universities show that the increase in the income of the average established university library was about 17 or 18% per annum over the same period 1965–71. They thus kept pace with the increased cost of journals, but economic circumstances have changed radically since 1971, and continued growth of expenditure at this rate would be inconceivable.

It may be argued that institutions might be expected to devote an increased proportion of their budget to libraries. In fact, universities have slightly increased their allocations to the library over the past 15 years; but again, it is hard to see how this trend could be continued for long. It is also possible that libraries could allocate more of their budgets to journals, and less to books and other items of expenditure. Table 4 shows that the percentage of university library expenditure devoted to serials has increased somewhat over the past 15 years—all of the increase having occurred since the establishment of the NLLST in 1961. Since during this period monographs have also increased greatly in price, and the number published each year has also increased substantially until recently,

TABLE 3. *Changes in real 'value' of serials, 1960–73*

	Commercial	Society	All
Science	− 6% (22)	−30% (18)	−17% (40)
Social Sciences	− 4% (6)	+10% (5)	− 3% (11)
Humanities	−21% (3)	−21% (7)	−21% (10)
All	− 7% (31)	−28% (30)	−17% (61)

Figures in brackets represent numbers of journals sampled.

This table is based on the detailed analysis of a sample of serials taken by BLLD. Number of pages of text (i.e. excluding advertising matter, etc) was related to the subscription price of each journal, and allowance was made for increases in the Retail Price Index, so that the figures represent changes in real 'value for money'.

monograph publishers would appear to have a stronger cause for complaint than journal publishers. Indeed, several university libraries have recently had to cancel journal subscriptions, for the highly practical reason that to continue with all their present subscriptions would lead in 3 or 4 years' time to an inability to buy any other library materials whatever. Other academic and special libraries have also stated that wherever possible journal subscriptions have been maintained and increased, often at the expense of monographs.

These figures seem to suggest that libraries could hardly be spending more than they do on journals, whether or not photocopies were being provided from the British Library Lending Division or anywhere else. It is possible, indeed probable, that they would plead a stronger case for larger funds if photocopies could not be supplied, but it is very doubtful indeed whether their institutions could provide them.

Despite the overall increases in sales reported above, it is certainly true that libraries are now beginning to look critically at their journal holdings and to make extensive cancellations. Furthermore, this trend is likely to continue. This must be due almost entirely to current economic pressures, and may in time cause serious problems for some journals. British libraries are only a relatively

TABLE 4. *University Libraries: Relative Expenditure on Books and Periodicals 1950/51–1971/72*

Year	Books (B)	Periodicals (P)	Total (T)	B/P	B/T	P/T	Total Library Expenditure as % of University Expenditure
		Expenditure on Libraries					
1950–1	197,062	103,305	891,385	1·90	·221	·116	3·7
1951–2	202,567	118,702	988,029	1·71	·205	·120	3·8
1952–3	276,852	135,907	1,118,482	2·02	·234	·115	3·9
1953–4	290,581	147,669	1,203,231	1·94	·242	·123	4·0
1954–5	310,102	154,963	1,352,244	2·00	·230	·114	3·8
1955–6	324,983	170,404	1,468,512	1·91	·222	·116	3·9
1956–7	371,504	196,884	1,620,978	1·89	·229	·121	3·9
1957–8	383,137	212,478	1,821,943	1·80	·210	·117	3·8
1958–9	434,254	231,458	1,979,945	1·88	·219	·117	3·8
1959–60	599,977	271,663	2,350,294	2·20	·255	·115	4·0
1960–1	626,214	297,530	2,624,625	2·10	·238	·113	3·9
1961–2	640,354	329,774	2,831,500	1·95	·227	·117	3·8
1962–3	753,317	401,302	3,285,575	1·86	·229	·122	3·8
1963–4	957,017	461,855	3,946,646	2·08	·242	·117	3·9
1964–5	1,158,424	599,035	4,813,092	1·93	·240	·125	3·9
1965–6	1,615,638	878,170	6,306,565	1·84	·256	·139	3·9
1966–7	1,911,572	1,106,227	7,401,028	1·73	·258	·149	3·9
1967–8	2,072,420	1,236,180	8,161,068	1·68	·254	·151	3·9
1968–9	2,323,323	1,478,394	9,468,973	1·58	·246	·156	4·0
1969–70	2,603,398	1,749,569	10,927,118	1·49	·239	·160	4·0
1970–1	2,939,016	2,010,799	12,683,594	1·46	·232	·159	4·0
1971–2	3,505,300	2,340,730	14,996,259	1·50	·234	·156	4·1

Sources: UGC Returns
DES Statistics of Education, v. 6: Universities

small proportion of the market for most academic journals, but similar trends are being observed in other countries, including the United States of America. A recent note in *The Times*, for instance, stated that the economic situation in France had obliged university libraries to cut back on their journal purchases by as much as 40%.

A recent survey of libraries of various kinds by the Library Association attempted to discover the extent and nature of cancellations of journal subscriptions by UK libraries of different kinds. The survey showed that the thirty libraries which responded cancelled in all 1,221 journals in the current financial year—an average of over forty per library—compared with 646 in the previous year. It is noteworthy that very few journals were cancelled by more than one library, that about 12% were in foreign languages, and that not many were British. Among criteria for cancellation, extent of use, content, and quality were mentioned as often as price. Availability from other sources was mentioned by four libraries, but they appeared to be referring to availability in other libraries in the locality. BLLD was not mentioned by any library. Some libraries, particularly large industrial libraries, take several copies of some journals, and these tend to be prime candidates for cancellation. The journals likely to be affected most rapidly are therefore 'fringe' journals that can easily be spared (perhaps because academic interests have shifted), and journals with large circulations of which multiple copies have been bought by some libraries.

Institutions are of course only one market for journals; individuals are another. However, few individuals have ever purchased more than a very few journals, and several of those they do acquire have often been received as part of their membership of a learned society. Though there is no real evidence, it is extremely doubtful if individuals would have bought more journals if their libraries had not had them or been able to provide copies of required articles. Indeed, it is most improbable that an individual would buy for himself journals to which he needed access so rarely that his local library was able to supply his needs by photocopies rather than by purchase.

The growth of photocopying at the BLLD was illustrated above. However, much of this growth in demand has been due neither to the growing volume of publication nor to the economic problems of libraries, but simply to the effect of a good fast service. The reason why Britain has a higher figure of ILL requests per head than most other countries is not because its libraries are less well endowed but because a good supply system is available: the supply has created the demand. Much, if not most, of the present ILL demand would not exist if BLLD did not exist. We are not therefore talking about an *alternative* to local purchase, but an *extra* demand. It may be noted that at a time when economic pressures are affecting libraries much more radically than ever before, the rate of increase in demand on the BLLD shows signs of slackening, as these same economic pressures cause libraries to limit interlibrary borrowing.

In any case, crude figures of total requests tell only a portion of the full story. More details are provided by a large survey of 61,333 requests for serials, carried out early in 1975. The first point to note is that over 50% of requests were for articles from volumes more than 3 years old, and therefore likely to be unobtainable from publishers' stock. They can hardly therefore affect sales of current journals. Secondly, 40% of satisfied requests for serials are met by loans rather than photocopies. Only 30% therefore of requests for serials result in photocopies of articles from issues in print. Thirdly, some requests appear to come from libraries that subscribe to journals but want issues that are at binding, mislaid, or otherwise unavailable locally.

Of a total of 14,967 serial titles appearing altogether in the survey, 3,800 are estimated to be defunct, leaving about 10,200 current titles, of the 45,000 currently received. Since the survey covered only 12 weeks and a very long 'tail' was revealed (the last 10% of demands were spread over 6,000 titles), the total number of titles requested over the whole year would be a good deal larger.

The distribution of demand is shown in Table 5 and Fig. 1. The top 210 titles that accounted for 20% of all demand would each have on average fewer than 260 copies each made in 1974 from the last 3 years' issues.

Since BLLD has 5,100 libraries registered as borrowers, the probability that any library is having more than two or three copies a year made from most of these journals is small. Certainly journals requested less than this can be ignored for present purposes: for if copying on this scale (on average 1·24 copies per article) is threatening the continued existence of such journals, their value to the community must be called in question.

We may therefore confine our discussion to the eighty-one journals that, by extrapolation from the survey, will have 300 or more copies made annually of articles published in the last 3 years. These are listed in Table 6. There are several points we may note about these journals. The first is that only twelve are British. The second is that many of those for which recent circulation figures could be found have large circulations which would hardly be threatened even by a much larger quantity of copying than that carried out by BLLD. The third is that nearly all are in science, and 'pure' science at that. The fourth is that they all appear to be high status journals that rank high on any criteria and that will be taken by any library with a particular interest in a field. Indeed, a check in the *British Union Catalogue of Periodicals* of the fifty titles most in demand from BLLD in 1969 showed that on average each was taken by thirty-three libraries—and it must be remembered that *BUCOP* records the holdings of only a limited number of libraries, mainly academic.

TABLE 5. *Distribution of demand for serials at BLLD*

% of demand	No. of titles
10	58
20	210
30	450
40	800
50	1,400
60	2,150
70	3,300
80	5,200
90	8,300
100	14,967

It is estimated that 3,800 of the titles requested are no longer current.

Based on a 12-week survey in 1975 of 61,333 requests.

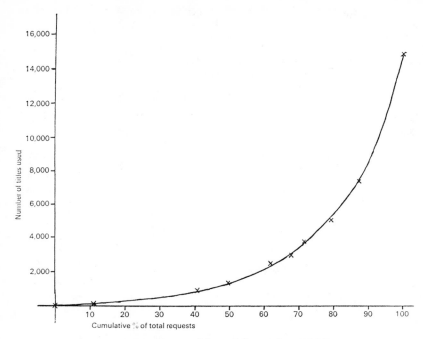

FIG. I. *Distribution of demand for serials at BLLD*

These results may appear puzzling. Why do libraries request such common journals? Certainly most of them must be taken by most academic libraries (which incidentally account for 38% of all demand on BLLD). The explanation is that what is a standard journal to an academic community is a marginal item to a specialized industrial library; and industrial libraries comprise the great majority of BLLD's registered borrowers. Even a few hundred of these requesting *Nature* occasionally can easily account for the 850 or so requests for copies of articles published in the last 3 three years. Some of the demand may well be from industrial libraries that acquire a journal currently but keep it only for a year, preferring to save space at the cost of having to apply to BLLD for issues over a year old.

It is unfortunate that information is not available on the distribution of demand among libraries to confirm (or contradict) these hypotheses. However, a brief look at the economics of purchase vs. borrowing suggests that, for the average academic journal, any library expecting more than seven or eight uses a year to be made of the current year's issues would find it cheaper to buy than to borrow, as each satisfied interlibrary loan (or photocopy) costs the borrowing library £1.50. On the other hand, no library would normally buy a journal of which only two or three uses of the current volume were expected in a year, whether or not it was available from elsewhere. In theory, a current volume wanted more than two or three times but fewer than seven or eight could be a candidate for purchase, but in the first place the number of libraries requesting a given journal between three and seven times is not likely to be very large, and secondly the alternative of purchase or borrowing for many desirable items (books as well as journals) is not now open to such libraries—they do not have the money to buy, and are becoming increasingly unable to borrow.

TABLE 6. *Serials estimated to have 300 or more photocopies a year made by BLLD of articles published in the last 3 years*

Rank order	Title	Estimated no. of photocopies p.a. of articles in print	Circulation (as given by Ulrich 1973/4)
1	Science	1,288	154,200
2	Biochimica et Biophysica Acta	1,078	4,500
3	New England Journal of Medicine	959	140,000
4	Annals—New York Academy of Sciences	917	
5	Nature	854	21,000
6	Journal—American Chemical Society	798	
7	Journal of Biological Chemistry	784	7,200
8	Analytical Chemistry	700	~36,000
8	Journal—American Medical Association	700	239,000
10	Clinical Chemistry	693	7,505
11	Proceedings—National Academy of Sciences	679	8,600
12	Scientific American	630	500,700
13	Journal of Chromotography	623	
14	Analytical Biochemistry	609	
15	British Medical Journal	595	84,748
15	Lancet	595 (N. American ed.) (British ed.)	221,577 29,366
17	Clinica Chimica Acta	588	
18	Journal—Acoustical Society of America	546	6,300
19	Journal of Clinical Investigation	525	6,600
20	Brain Research	518	
21	Biochemical Journal	511	~6,100
21	Life Sciences	511	
23	Journal—Optical Society of America	497	9,600
24	American Journal of Physiology	490	4,655
25	Medical Journal of Australia	483	17,500
26	Journal of Chemical Physics	469	6,200
26	Journal of Pharmaceutical Sciences	469	13,350
26	Journal of Physiology	469	3,700
29	Applied Microbiology	462	10,800
29	Biochemical Pharmacology	462	
31	Journal of Applied Physics	455	10,000
32	Journal of Bacteriology	441	12,000
33	Proceedings—Royal Society A	427	3,250
34	Journal of Agricultural and Food Chemistry	420	4,982
34	South African Medical Journal	420	9,400
36	Biochemical and Biophysical Research Communications	413	
36	Proceedings—Society for Experimental Biology and Medicine	413	7,740
38	Journal—Water Pollution Control Federation	406	22,000

Rank order	Title	Estimated no. of photocopies p.a. of articles in print	Circulation (as given by Ulrich 1973/4)
39	Analytica Chimica Acta	385	
39	Communications—ACM	385	
39	Federation Proceedings	385	16,500
39	Journal of Pharmacy and Pharmacology	385	3,000
43	Journal of Physical Chemistry	378	5,500
43	Pediatrics	378	22,500
45	Archives of Biochemistry and Biophysics	364	
45	Biochemistry	364	6,600
45	Environmental Science and Technology	364	30,000
45	Journal of Applied Physiology	364	3,860
49	American Journal of Obstetrics and Gynaecology	357	17,033
49	Febs Letters	357	(controlled)
49	Journal of Infectious Diseases	357	3,500
52	Journal—Electrochemical Society	350	7,500
52	Research Communications in Chemical Pathology and Pharmacology	350	1,000
54	American Journal of Psychiatry	343	25,569
54	Psychological Bulletin	343	10,500
56	Proceedings—Institution of Mechanical Engineers	336	
57	Annals of Internal Medicine	329	63,000
57	Cancer (Philadelphia)	329	13,155
57	Chemical Engineering	329	70,000
57	Journal of Ecology	329	3,488
57	Journal of Laboratory and Clinical Medicine	329	6,723
57	Journal of Pharmacology and Experimental Therapeutics	329	3,038
57	Machine Design	329	110,000
57	Research Quarterly—American Association for Health, Physical Education, and Recreation	329	
65	Child Development	322	6,300
65	Oil and Gas Journal	322	48,000
65	Water Research	322	
68	Chemistry and Industry	315	8,627
68	Experientia	315	
68	Journal—American Ceramic Society	315	9,900
68	Journal—National Cancer Institute	315	2,500
68	Journal of Investigative Dermatology	315	3,513
73	American Sociological Review	308	~18,000
73	Gastroenterology	308	8,263
73	Journal of Clinical Pathology	308	
73	Journal of Colloid and Interface Science	308	
73	Journal of Urology	308	11,633
78	Advances in Chemistry Series	301	
78	Chemical Engineering Science	301	
78	Journal—American Water Works Association	301	26,000
78	Journal of Geophysical Research	301	9,500

Looking again at the gross figures, let us assume for a moment that articles from 20,000 different current journals will be copied this year. At an average of seventy articles per journal* per year, the total number of articles published in the last 3 years in these journals is about 4·2 million. The total number of copies made of articles in print will be about 0·5 million. Thus, each article in print has a less than one in eight chance of being copied.

This is of course an overall average. But even for *Science*, the most requested of all journals, the average will be only 0·37 copies per article (1,162 articles were published in 1974). Equivalent figures for the two top British journals, *British Medical Journal* and the *Lancet*, are respectively 0·2 (0·4 if 'short communications' are excluded) and 0·27 (0·5 excluding 'short communications'). Copies per issue for each of the three journals are respectively 8·3, 3·8, and 2·6. These calculations help to put the figures in perspective.

In parenthesis, a fair amount of demand on BLLD is for 'any recent issue' of a specific journal, especially one newly published. These requests are of course for loans rather than photocopies, but it is known that most of them arise from a desire to sample a journal in order to decide whether to purchase or not. Thus the BLLD is actually *assisting* journal publishers to some extent by helping libraries to select journals they might otherwise have difficulty in seeing.

Let us consider what would happen if the British Library Lending Division did not supply photocopies. If it received a request and did not photocopy, it would lend the issue. There is a good chance that it would be copied at the borrowing library, but there is certainly no greater probability that the local library would buy it if it could be obtained on loan rather than by photocopy. Availability from the BLLD would be somewhat reduced, as items would be on loan quite often when required, whereas if articles are photocopied the issues are always available. In theory, the BLLD could buy additional copies of journals in heavy demand, but the amount of money available for this would be strictly limited, and it would be the high-status journals of which more copies were bought; perhaps at the expense of low-use journals. All that would happen therefore is that the user would get a worse service, because he would have to wait longer than he does now for an article he wants, and some more obscure journals might become unavailable altogether. It should be noted that the BLLD buys large numbers of journals that are bought by no other library in Britain. To cancel journals that are rarely wanted, and transfer the money to buying duplicates of heavily used journals would do more harm to journal publishers than the present situation.

Some articles in the library press have suggested that libraries could and should cancel some of their journal subscriptions, in view of the service available from the BLLD. However, no librarian is likely to ask for a smaller budget because BLLD exists. The BLLD's service means rather that if and when a library does have to cancel a journal, its users suffer much less than if the BLLD did not exist. If the BLLD did not exist at all, libraries would revert to the old system whereby journals were borrowed from other libraries by the use of union catalogues, speculative inquiry, and other cumbersome and inefficient methods. If even this failed, individuals could still go to reference libraries, including the libraries of professional associations. The only thing that one can be fairly sure would not happen

---

* Based on an average of eighty-five per journal per year for science and technology[1] and forty-seven for social sciences[2].

is that sales of journals to libraries or individuals would increase more than fractionally.

The truth is that the market for learned journals has always been limited. It has not grown enough to sustain the great increase in the number and cost of journals in recent years, and the problem has been aggravated by the economic constraints now facing libraries. If a book publisher is in economic difficulties, he can cut the number of titles published, and concentrate on those more likely to sell. If a journal publisher is faced with similar difficulties—and it must be remembered that many publishers issue only a small number of journals—he has far less freedom of movement. He can reduce the size of the journal while charging the same or a higher price—and, as we have seen, this has actually happened. Or his journal can be discontinued; the fairly consistent annual mortality noted earlier shows as yet few signs of increasing.

Supposing the publishers were in a position to do anything about the BLLD's photocopying service, what they could do would not benefit them. For example, they could charge a higher price to BLLD than to ordinary libraries for their journals. In this case, the BLLD, not having inexhaustible funds, would simply buy fewer journals; or, alternatively, it would buy fewer books, which would hardly suit book publishers. Alternatively, the publishers could stop selling journals to BLLD at all. Quite apart from the question whether this would be legal, it would merely result in their having one (often more than one) sale the fewer. The BLLD could in theory pass on additional costs to user libraries. This would almost certainly act as a brake on the growth of demand for copies and loans, since most libraries would not be able to find the extra finance required; thus the net result would be a restriction on the dissemination of knowledge.

It may be argued that, although the sales of journals are not being seriously affected, in fairness a royalty ought to be paid to publishers for each article copied. It is not difficult to calculate the amount of money this might bring in. If 5p a copy were charged, *Science*, the most requested of all journals, would receive £220 if all articles were taken into account, £110 if only articles in print were considered. *Nature* would receive £147 (or £74 for articles in print). Only eighty-nine journals would receive as much as £50 (£25 for articles in print). Nearly all of these journals, as we have observed, are high-status journals with medium or large circulations, and their continued existence cannot be affected one way or the other by sums of this order.

Accepting the problems facing journal publishers, and knowing that the BLLD's photocopying service has expanded greatly in recent years, it is tempting to put the two together as effect and cause. It is far more likely that both are due to the same cause—an increasingly constrained library and individual market at the same time as the volume and cost of publication have continued to increase. Libraries have been able to buy less, and this has resulted in a) economic difficulties for publishers, and b) increased demand on the BLLD—though, as noted above, the rate of increase appears now to be slowing. There is no evidence to suggest that if the BLLD went out of existence tomorrow, any more money could be made available to libraries to buy more journals.

Undue concern with photocopying on the part of journal publishers may divert some of their attention from seeking a solution to their very real problems, which are quite unrelated to photocopying.

Although there may be little hard evidence of declining journal sales so far, recent economic factors have led to a critical situation for many journals. Increases in costs have become so severe that even a very large increase in sales could hardly be expected to cover them. In the present state of the market, such an increase is impossible to achieve.

The last 2 or 3 years have seen the publication of several papers discussing such alternatives as synopsis journals, microform journals, abstracts backed up by hard copy on demand, and so on. Some of these alternative forms of publication are now being used. They will pose their own problems for libraries, but that is another matter.

What is important is the increasing recognition that solutions to the economic problems of publishing must be found, and that there is no evidence that they have anything to do with photocopying by libraries.

ACKNOWLEDGEMENT

Much of the data used in this paper was derived from a survey of serial requests to BLLD, carried out on behalf of the Swedish Council for Scientific Information and Documentation (SINFDOK).

REFERENCES

1. VICKERY, B. C. Statistics of scientific and technical articles. *Journal of Documentation, 24*(3), September 1968, 192–6.
2. WOOD, D. N. *and* FERGUSON, J. Statistics of social science periodicals. *BLL Review, 2*(3), July 1974, 92–5.

THE EFFECT OF A LARGE-SCALE PHOTOCOPYING SERVICE ON JOURNAL SALES

E. VAN TONGEREN
Associated Scientific Publishers (ASP), Amsterdam

I WOULD LIKE to comment on the article by Mr M. B. Line and Mr D. N. Wood on 'The Effect of a Large-Scale Photocopying Service on Journal Sales', which was published in the December 1975 issue of the *Journal of Documentation*, as I feel that the authors have achieved the enviable feat of obscuring the real problems facing the dissemination of scientific information through a haze of generalities.

The reader is informed of the fact that the BLLD received in 1963 18,175 serials and copied 13,307 articles from these serials and that the figures for 1974 were: 44,767 serials, from which 893,801 articles were reproduced. This staggering increase in the gratis use of the contents of scientific journals is then declared to be of little or no influence on the fate of these journals. In the body of the article the authors are seldom specific and do not ever attempt to distinguish between more general scientific publications such as *Nature* and *Scientific American* and the highly specialized 'core' journals which are devoted to the dissemination of advanced research findings, and which by their nature have a small circulation. There are thus strange omissions and the impression is inevitably created that the authors have been pulling out all stops to try to 'whitewash' the large-scale free use by BLLD of an information system which has been set up, by others, at great intellectual and financial cost.

The activities of BLLD and organizations similarly occupied should be a matter of the greatest concern not only to those who publish scientific information (and it should be remembered that a large part is published by non-profit scientific organizations), but equally—no, even more so—by the scientific community itself.

Under threat is the whole system of the dissemination of scientific information and this threat has been very clearly formulated by the Editor of *Chemical and Engineering News* as follows:

> The act of copying is not the damaging element. The use of modern technology to speed and increase the dissemination of knowledge is desirable and to be encouraged. But dissemination from an expensive information base without contributing to its support is certain to lead to erosion of something of great value: the information base itself or, in simpler terms, the scientific journal system.

All who are involved in maintaining this information base must take issue with Line and Wood over their article in the *Journal of Documentation*, not only because of the detrimental repercussions which such an article might have on the very basis of information dissemination, but also, and more significantly, because of the underlying misinterpretation of many of the basic facets of journal publishing.

SOURCE: Reprinted from the *Journal of Documentation* 32: 198-204 (1976) by permission of the copyright holders. Copyright © 1976 by Aslib and contributors.

At a critical stage in scientific publishing such an article is diverting attention away from the really important issues, immersing the reader in a morass of justification of BLLD's activities and imbuing him with a false sense of the stability of journal publishing. Contrary to their (expressed) belief, scientific journal publishing *is* facing a critical future. Journal subscriptions are falling; costs are rising. Each of these trends would, in isolation, force subscription prices up, but in conjunction they result in an escalating spiral of prices as compensation is sought for the diminishing sales basis.

(This, incidentally, gives some explanation for journal price rises being in excess of the Retail Price Index as pointed out by Messrs Line and Wood.) A recent NSF-funded study, 'Economics and Interaction of the Publisher-Library Relationship in the Production and Use of Scholarly and Research Journals' (B. Fry, November 1975), gives a fairly detailed analysis of the increasing financial problems confronting journal publishers in the USA. There is no reason to believe that the situation in the UK or Europe is any better. In fact, the scientific community—including publishers, librarians and authors—is currently faced with the fundamental problem of how to prevent the total collapse of scientific information dissemination.

Early in their article, the authors claim that they could detect no reduction in journal subscriptions, whereas most STI publishers estimate the cancellation rate of journals during the last five years to be at least of the order of 5% per annum. This in spite of a growth in the numbers of the UK post-graduate studentship awards in science between 1968–73 of about 28%. The number of students in tertiary education increased by 28%, the number of awards of special research grants in science rose by 81% and the number of current special research grants rose by 46%; all these seem to me more relevant yardsticks than the 3% growth in population used by Messrs Line and Wood (p. 235).

Line's assertions on journal subscription appear to be based entirely upon a scant investigation of some 50/100 journals out of a possible 45,000 journals on order at BLLD. It would be valuable, indeed it is essential, to know more of this sample if Mr Line's basic hypothesis is to be supported. What types of journal were included? Were they society journals, 'general' journals—such as *Nature* and *Science*—review journals, letter journals, journals in the sciences, humanities, social sciences, or multidisciplinary? Were they specialized 'core' journals containing the research results from a scientific subdiscipline?

It is this latter group that is most seriously in danger as a result of photocopying. BLLD's list of most frequently photocopied journals contains six of our own journals in the top fifty. All of these are highly specialized 'core' journals in the research fields of either chemistry or the biosciences. All of them are large in number of pages and small in circulation. Their average subscription is 2,250 worldwide, but two of them—highly reputable and, in terms of the submission of quality articles, well supported by the academic research fraternity—have subscription levels barely over the 1,000 mark. There is no margin left for safety. If, as scientific publishers believe, the 'super' libraries worldwide are adversely influencing subscriptions to these 'core' journals, then it is on BLLD's shoulders that some of the responsibility for any future collapse must be placed. Are we really to believe that the striking increase in journal cancellations from ten university libraries (seventy-six in 1973–4 rising to 782 in 1974–5, as reported in the Library Association's submission to the Whitford Committee) is in no way related to an awareness by academic libraries of BLLD's service? And what is there to take over the present role of the specialized scientific research journals which could face extinction? We believe, not without reason, that BLLD's activities are indeed influencing cancellation decisions. We wrote to a number of institutes that had cancelled subscriptions to the specialized Elsevier/North-Holland journals and several (from the UK at least) indicated that the BLLD service had influenced their decision. I should add that the naming of BLLD was entirely unsolicited.

The following diagram indicates the cancellation trend in fourteen of our major highly specialized research journals:

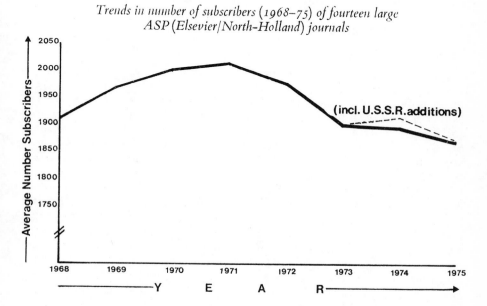

Trends in number of subscribers (1968–75) of fourteen large ASP (Elsevier/North-Holland) journals

More recent evidence has indicated that several UK libraries have adopted the practice of circulating the contents pages of select journals among their readers offering to order photocopies of the articles, which they wish to see, from Boston Spa.

Another example is that of a large British chemical concern that has issued instructions to its overseas divisional libraries that all requests should go to BLLD rather than to their own headquarters. Line and Wood attribute some of the growth to BLLD's activities to their good and fast service, but carefully avoid mentioning its cheapness. In the BLLD news sheet for April 1975 the marginal cost of BLLD of each loan or photocopy was estimated at about 75p. while it is now being sold at about 46p. (plus VAT). The difference is funded by the British Library Board. In fact, therefore, BLLD is able to be generous to its clients (*a*) at the expense of the journals, whose material is used without any compensation and without any regard for the tremendous outlay of money which was necessary to get the material refereed, edited, rewritten, styled, redrawn, subedited, typeset, proofread, printed, and distributed, and (*b*) at the expense of the British taxpayer.

Apart from considerations of finance and survival, there are, it seems to me, also important legal (copyright) issues at stake. One could question whether it was the law's intention that anyone (not necessarily on the staff of the receiving library) could be the nominated person to receive the copy—or whether the 'contribution to the general expenses' can also consist of a token contribution. One could ask what exactly is the definition of 'libraries established or conducted for profit', which are excluded from UK copying facilities etc. These are all hazy and grey areas of the law which BLLD is currently interpreting to their own advantage.

Internationally speaking, however, there is no doubt that the international activities of BLLD form a serious threat to national copyright law as they can render the rules and regulations which, for example, are imposed in The Netherlands by law on the reproduction of literature, null and void.

A few further comments should be made on the article.

1. *Library purchases of ST literature*
In Table 4 the article implicitly equates the total book and periodical budget of University libraries (=40% of BLLD's customers) to the sum which they spend on scientific/technical literature specifically. This of course is not necessarily true, as it does not take into account that these libraries collect the arts, humanities, social sciences and general-interest publications as well. In fact, in the United States, it has been found (Baumol and Marcus, Economics of Academic Libraries, 1973, pp. 83–4) that the public and private academic institute libraries spend only between 16 and 25% of their book budget on science and the remainder on humanities, social sciences etc. Also, only some 39% of the university library expenditure is on books and periodicals (a small decline from the 40% levels of 1966–9); salaries and other expenditure items constitute a much larger spending outlay. As far as the industrial and commercial libraries are concerned, it is well-known that they spend a growing amount on topical economic, commercial, and trade information and our researches show that they can do this at the cost of scientific literature readily available from photocopying services. This means that there is a considerable 'cushion' of subjects whose allocation could be cut. This assumes no BLLD however, which—as can be seen in Table 6 of the article—is especially in demand for the sciences. With this service the whole picture, as related to libraries, becomes distorted. BLLD's existence means that academic libraries can be assured of ready and quick access to the expensive small-circulation journals on specialized scientific subjects.

Of course their contents are in great demand: these journals have a worldwide authorship and a worldwide interest and audience, which is not the case for many subjects in other fields of study which are frequently directed to a much greater degree towards a national readership. The ability to borrow science periodicals from BLLD does have an influence on library budgeting. The service provided means that academic librarians (again: 40% of BLLD's clientele) will have at the back of their minds that a cancellation does not mean a cut-off from the information base. Therefore BLLD loads the dice against STI publications.

2. *Libraries should not spend more (p. 236)*
The authors—who do not seem to have realized that in the UK the growth in the number of students between 1968 and 1973 was about 30%—seem to feel that the funds allowed to libraries have expanded enough. Yet in Table 4 one sees that in 1950 the total library costs were 3·7% of the total University expenditure and that in 1972 they had crept up by only 0·4%. Taking into account that the

book and journal purchases form only part of the library costs, one can certainly not say that the libraries have been—relatively speaking—over-endowed.

3. Changes in 'real value' of serials (p. 236)

Elsevier/North-Holland are represented in BLLD's 'top'-list in Table 6, page 241, by four titles in the first twenty and six among the first fifty. Line and Wood state (p. 236) that 'any library that wanted to keep up fully with the literature would have had to increase its journal budget at an average annual rate of 17% over the period 1965–1971.' The actual prices per page of the above six journals are given below with—between brackets—what they would have cost at an increase of 17% annually. The discrepancy is obvious!

Table of ASP journals price per page (1965–71)

Journal	1965	1966	1967	1968	1969	1970	1971
Biophysica et Biochimica Acta	9·1	9·7 (10·6)	8·9 (12·5)	8·9 (14·6)	9·5 (17·1)	10·0 (19·9)	10·3 (23·3)
Journal of Chromatography	9·3	11·4 (10·9)	10·3 (12·7)	12·7 (14·9)	11·0 (17·4)	11·5 (20·4)	13·5 (23·8)
Clinica Chimica Acta	7·3	6·3 (8·5)	10·6 (10·0)	9·5 (11·7)	10·2 (13·7)	8·5 (16·0)	9·6 (18·7)
Brain Research	—	10·8	8·9 (12·6)	14·6 (14·8)	12·1 (17·3)	14·9 (20·2)	15·1 (23·6)
Analytica Chimica Acta	9·7	11·8 (11·3)	11·2 (13·3)	11·1 (15·5)	13·0 (18·2)	10·9 (21·3)	12·6 (24·9)
FEBS Letters	—	—	—	—	18·9	19·2 (22·1)	19·2 (25·9)
Average of above journals	8·9	10·0 (10·4)	10·0 (12·2)	11·4 (14·3)	12·5 (16·7)	12·5 (19·5)	13·4 (22·8)

4. Relative expenditure on books and periodicals (Table 4)

From this Table it appears that books lost rather heavily relative to journals in the period 1960–70. Since 1969 the loss has become less steep and indeed a change in favour of books developed in 1971–2. It should be noted that the number of photocopies provided by BLLD increased from 100,716 in 1969 to 439,845 in 1972.

5. Signs of slackening

The authors state (p. 238) that 'the rate of increase in demand on the BLLD shows signs of slackening as these same economic pressures cause libraries to limit inter-library borrowing.'

It is in this respect interesting to examine Table 1 in the Line and Wood article, which shows that in 1972 about 96,000 more items were produced than in 1971, in 1973 225,000 more than in 1972, and in 1974 229,000 more than in 1973. What is slackening?

6. *Using without contributing (p. 240)*

The authors seem to support the view that 'occasional use' of a very expensive information base should be free. Apparently airlines should allow the occasional passenger to fly free. Apparently engine manufacturers should give away parts of engines to those who do not need the entire engine, etc. It is precisely this attitude which I wish to fight with all my strength. There would appear to be a widespread feeling that the whole structure of copyright protection can be disregarded without the production of possibly catastrophic side-effects. No account is taken of the fact that enormous efforts have been made by learned societies and scientific publishers to create the structures and service organizations by means of which the publication of the primary scientific literature has become possible.

7. *Literature from back volumes*

Provision of photocopies of material from back volumes may indeed be said not to exert great effect on the current subscription list. But most or all publishers have stocks of back volumes, so why should they simply be by-passed?

8. *New journal subscription build-up*

It is stated on page 243 that BLLD is actually *assisting* journal publishers to some extent by helping libraries to select journals they might otherwise have difficulty in seeing.

I wonder how frequently this happens as it is well known that each society or commercial publisher who brings out a new periodical, makes free sample copies available on a very large scale to potentially interested subscribers.

9. *Compensation*

It does occur to the authors that in fairness a royalty ought to be paid to publishers, but the thought is rejected as soon as it is born. A fee of 5p. per copied article is mentioned, but with no indication of how this derisory amount is arrived at. It is perhaps in line with BLLD's interpretation of a 'contribution to the general expenses' which has been questioned above. Why 5p. and not 25p.? Why not charge the full cost of request fulfilment (75p.) and contribute the difference to the source? Why is payment per article preferable to payment per page?

It is undeniable that the present economic climate is very unfavourable and has led to a critical situation for many ventures, and certainly for the publishing of books and journals. This being the case it is hard to understand why the authors think it justifiable to hasten the decline by the creation of super- and networking-libraries who without thought for the future expect their raw materials to be supplied free of charge. They must know that there are large numbers of specialized research journals that have 1,000–2,000 subscribers. Many of these find themselves in lists of most-consulted periodicals. But they are in imminent danger of collapse which, should it be brought about, could have incalculable consequences for scientific progress.

In the opinion of most STI publishers, extensive photocopying presents a serious and immediate threat to the existing role of specialized scientific/technical journals. I am convinced that laws must be eventually passed for the sake of the entire scientific community and its information needs, which result in proper control of photocopying. Fundamentally, this means that entitlement to make single copies *as a matter of right* should be removed from the existing law. This and other wider problems of copyright infringement (of which BLLD's activities are only part) must be settled to allow time for the longer-term development of a system of information dissemination satisfactory to author, publisher, librarian, and user.

It is hoped that legislators will recognize the threat which hangs over the future of scientific publishing before irreparable harm has thoughtlessly been caused.

PHOTOCOPYING AND JOURNAL SALES:
a reply by
M. B. LINE *and* D. N. WOOD

We will try to take up Mr van Tongeren's points as briefly as we can.

i The rapid growth in photocopying at Boston Spa has been a consistent factor since the NLLST was started. During the 1960s journal publishing appeared to be booming, and only in the last two or three years has there been any serious suggestion of any relationship to photocopying. If there had been any relationship it should have become apparent much earlier. What has happened in the last two or three years is that libraries—all over the world, in countries where there is no equivalent of BLLD—have had less money to maintain their journal purchases, and it is this factor that is creating problems for publishers.

ii The information system has, as Mr van Tongeren says, 'been set up by others at great intellectual and financial cost'. We have seen no suggestions that the intellectual effort of the authors should be rewarded; indeed, their efforts depend on the ready availability of information, in which BLLD plays a critical part in the UK. The 'subsidy' on BLLD request forms is ultimately to the authors, without whom journals would not exist.

iii It is quite probable that economic factors will force changes in the present pattern of publishing. There are several alternative possibilities. Conventional publication is a very expensive way of reaching the very few readers that most articles have. Non-publication in a conventional journal need not mean unavailability; for example, 'report literature' is quite widely disseminated. Trying to squeeze more money out of libraries (which don't have it anyway) would at best merely postpone the radical review of journal publication which will be needed.

iv The Fry study is cited by Mr Van Tongeren. This study of the US situation concludes that, while interlibrary availability may affect the way libraries spend their money on journals, it makes no difference to the money they spend.

v We suspect that the increase in student numbers has not been reflected by many new science and technology courses, just more students on each course. Libraries do not normally increase their journal subscriptions merely in response to more users studying the same subjects.

vi The subscription figures we quoted were for the most used journals. We could see no point in collecting figures for journals that were little used. Our

SOURCE: Reprinted from the *Journal of Documentation* 32: 204-206 (1976) by permission of the copyright holders. Copyright © 1976 by Aslib and contributors.

full rank list is available if anyone wishes to collect subscription figures for further titles, but it is difficult to see what this could prove.

vii It is true that some high-use journals do not have large subscriptions. These are mostly very expensive journals, which libraries would not buy if they could not obtain from BLLD. What has been the experience with these journals in countries which have no BLLD?

viii Most academic libraries would confirm that their cancellations have nothing to do with BLLD. A recent survey by the Library Association Industrial Libraries Group indicates that, while they have to make cuts, these are not related to BLLD's service. As in the USA, the availability of journals from elsewhere may affect the way any cuts are allocated, but not the extent of cuts.

ix The circulation of contents pages has no more to do with BLLD than the publication of current awareness services. If the items in question are asked for often enough, libraries will buy them. Some libraries are known to have taken out subscriptions to journals because they were asked for frequently from BLLD—thus, BLLD sometimes stimulates demand and encourages purchase.

x Since there is a government committee considering copyright, any discussion of legal aspects is best left until it reports. The BLLD's operations are entirely within the present law.

To take Mr van Tongeren's numbered comments:

1. *Library purchases of ST literature*
Our article does *not* implicitly equate university library budgets with expenditure on scientific and technical literature. Our discussion was not confined to any one subject field. Much of the 'topical economic, commercial and trade information' required by industrial and commercial libraries is also available from BLLD, so that any switch of expenditure to this can hardly be due to BLLD. It is true that 'BLLD's existence means that academic libraries can be assured of ready and quick access to the expensive small-circulation journals on specialized scientific subjects'. It is also true that few of these are much requested from BLLD.

2. *Libraries should not spend more*
No one pretends that libraries are over-endowed, or that their funds have expanded as fast as might have been desirable. One of us (Line) was previously a university librarian, continually pressing for more money. That very little extra was obtained was due simply to the fact that the university did not have the money to give.

3. *Changes in real value of serials*
Our figure of 17% per annum growth in expenditure required to 'keep up' allowed for growth in the number of titles as well as price increase.

4. *Relative expenditure on books and periodicals*
If libraries had not begun to devote a little more attention to their book budgets their entire budgets would have been spent on journals in a few years.

5. *Signs of slackening*

We did not say that demand on BLLD was falling, but that *the rate of increase* is slackening, as Mr van Tongeren will see if he calculates percentage increases from year to year.

6. *Using without contributing*

As explained, libraries contribute a great deal, indirectly to the input into scientific literature, directly to its communication.

7. *Literature from back volumes*

Our experience in chasing missing parts does not suggest a wide availability of back runs.

8. *New journal subscription build-up*

The use of BLLD to assess demand is mentioned above. It may be easier to ask BLLD than to obtain a free sample—it is hard otherwise to see why libraries so often ask for 'any recent issue' for a journal.

9. *Compensation*

Why not 25p? Because, as we suggested, libraries would then borrow instead— and once the user had it in his hands he would probably copy it at once. The NLLST first started to photocopy because it was noticed that many journals were being returned as soon as they had been received, and it was clear that they were being copied and sent straight back. As for payment per page, this would penalize journals with large pages and high densities of print per page; and thus discourage sensible production economies.

We understand the concern of many publishers at the effect on them of the economic recession, and agree that their situation needs careful study. A review of trends in scholarly publishing has recently been carried out on funds from the British Library R&D Department, and this will help to provide some perspective. Questions such as the effect of photocopying on sales require *facts*. We provided what factual evidence we could; Mr van Tongeren offers none.

COPYRIGHT, RESOURCE SHARING, AND HARD TIMES:

A VIEW FROM THE FIELD

by Richard De Gennaro

The following article is the first-place, $1,000 winner in Round II of American Libraries' Prize Article Competition. It questions the impact of the new copyright law and warns librarians against expecting too much from resource sharing.

Richard De Gennaro is director of the University of Pennsylvania Libraries. He also serves on ALA's White House Conference Planning Committee.

Remember the bumper stickers from the Vietnam peace movement that read: SUPPOSE THEY GAVE A WAR AND NOBODY CAME? We could use a slogan like that to help end the long and tedious war of words between publishers and librarians over the fair use and photocopying provisions of the new copyright act scheduled to take effect Jan. 1, 1978. Our line might read: SUPPOSE THEY GAVE A NEW COPYRIGHT ACT AND NOBODY CARED?

That is what may happen once the unfounded fears of publishers and librarians are allayed, after they live with the new law for a time and discover that it changes virtually nothing for the vast majority of them. But right now, many librarians are worried sick about complying with the new act. It is complex and unfamiliar and they are afraid of the adverse effects that its provisions, particularly sections 107 and 108(g), may have on their capacity to continue to serve their users in the usual ways. These fears stem in part from the publicity given to early proposed versions of these sections which threatened to seriously limit or even put an end to "fair use" and photocopying in interlibrary loan operations.

But that is behind us now. I believe the final versions of Sections 107 and 108 and the CONTU (National Commission on New Technological Uses of Copyrighted Works) guidelines are fair to authors, publishers, and librarians. I can foresee no real difficulties in complying with them, and I do not believe they will significantly affect the way most libraries serve their readers. Most librarians in public and academic libraries need not try to master the legal intricacies of the new law or make elaborate preparations to implement it. The leaders of library associations and their legal counsel should and will continue to monitor and influence the implementation and administration of the new law; the rest of us should set the copyright issue aside and turn our attention and energies to other more critical matters.

The continued preoccupation of the entire profession with the copyright issue will keep us from coming to grips with such pressing problems as escalating book and journal prices, mounting losses from theft and mutilation, rising personnel costs, and steadily declining budgetary support. In comparison to these and other problems facing us, the impact of the new copyright law on libraries will be relatively slight.

This article has three aims. One is to put the matter of copyright and its possible effects on libraries and publishers into better perspective by offering some data and insights based on practical experience. Another is to urge librarians to exercise freely all the considerable rights the new law grants them. They should not permit themselves to be bullied or bluffed by hard-sell publishers into buying copyright privileges they have always had and which the new law reinforces.

The third is to dispel some of the exaggerated fears and hopes that many publishers and librarians have about the harmful or beneficial effects that increasingly effective inter-library loan, networking, and other resource sharing mechanisms will have on their finances and operations. Some publishers fear that library resource sharing will seriously diminish their sales, and some librarians hope it will save them from the crunch that is coming. Both views are quite unrealistic.

A special issue of the ALA *Washington Newsletter* on the new copyright law is a readily available and indispensable guide through the complexities of the law.[1] It contains brief highlights of the new law, a librarian's guide to it, recommended preparations for compliance, and excerpts from the law and the Congressional Reports, including the CONTU guidelines. (Also of interest is the May 1977 issue of *American Libraries*, which has two excellent articles—one by librarian Edward G. Holley and the other by attorney Lewis I. Flacks).

Our interest here is not the entire copyright law but the Fair Use provisions and CONTU guidelines.

In Section 107 of the new law, the Fair Use doctrine is given statutory recognition for the first time. Section 108 defines the conditions and limitations under which libraries can make copies for their internal use and for interlibrary loan. Nothing in Section 108 limits a library's right to fair use of copyrighted works; the new law reconfirms most of the rights librarians had before and even extends some. It prohibits "systematic copying," but this is no problem since

few academic or public libraries engage in systematic copying as defined in Section 108(g)(2) and the CONTU guidelines. Librarians are not liable for the unsupervised use of
photocopying machines by the public provided certain conditions are observed. This is no change from the existing
situation.

The most serious limitation appears not in the law itself
but in the CONTU guidelines. They recommend that libraries
refrain from copying for interlibrary loan purposes more than
five articles a year from the last five years of a periodical title.
They also stipulate that libraries must maintain records to
document this use, placing responsibility for monitoring it
on the requesting library.

What do these limitations really mean in practical terms?

If the University of Pennsylvania Library's experience is
in any way typical, then the five-copy limitation will not
seriously interfere with present interlibrary loan operations
and services to users. Why not? Because interlibrary loan
photocopying constitutes a relatively insignificant portion of
our total library use to begin with. Once we exclude from our
total interlibrary loan photocopying requests those that are
from monographs, from journals more than five years old,
and from journals to which we subscribe, those that are left
will be a fraction of the total—probably on the order of 20
percent. As much as 90–95 percent of this remaining 20 percent will be requests for less than six articles from the same
title in a year. Of the 5–10 percent that may exceed the
guideline limitation, some will be for articles from journals
whose authors and publishers have no interest in collecting
royalties and from foreign journals which may not be part
of the copy payment system. In the end, a library could simply
decline to request more than five copies from any journal
which required the payment of royalties.

The record keeping required by the guidelines is a trivial
matter and involves only maintaining and analyzing a file of

the third copy of a new three-part interlibrary loan form being developed. It could produce some interesting and unexpected consequences by reminding librarians that their subscription decisions should be based more heavily on actual rather than potential use. Librarians may identify some journals whose use will justify a subscription and a great many others whose lack of use will invite cancellation.[2]

These conclusions are based on statistics gathered at the University of Pennsylvania and on a report of a sampling of photocopy statistics from Cornell.

Applying the CONTU guidelines (no more than five copies in a year from the last five years of any title), the Penn Interlibrary Loan Office (excluding law and medicine) reported the following experience during the year from July 1976 through June 1977.

Articles were requested from 247 different journal titles. Of these, 173, or 70 percent, of the journals had requests for only one article. Five had five requests, two had six requests, and one had seven requests.[3]

In every case where five or more articles were requested from a single journal, all were requested by one person working on a specific project or an annual review article. A total of four scholars were responsible for all these requests; two of them were working on annual review articles. The authors and publishers of the papers requested for mention in annual review articles should be grateful to have their works cited and not ask for royalties. Indeed, there were only two commercial journals listed which might qualify for royalty payments. The rest were nonprofit, scholarly journals. In any event, this type of occasional use hardly justifies a library subscription.

Last year Penn circulated nearly a half million volumes from its libraries, not including periodical volumes, which do not circulate. The total of home loans and in-building use is estimated at well over 2 million. During that year, we borrowed 2,941 volumes and received 3,726 photocopies from other libraries for a total of 6,667 items (less than one half of one percent of our total use). We lent 7,748 volumes to other libraries and filled 7,682 photocopy requests—a total of 15,430 items. The sum of all such extramural transactions— borrowings as well as loans—was 22,000, or about one percent of our intramural use.

Penn is not unusual in this regard. The median for all university members of the Association of Research Libraries in 1975–76 was 11,053 loans and 4,505 borrowings for a total of 15,558 transactions. All these libraries together borrowed a half million originals and photocopies in 1975–76 and lent about two million.[4] Even if this traffic doubled or tripled in the next few years, it would still be relatively insignificant.

What can we conclude from these gross statistics? Simply that the total amount of interlibrary loan and photocopying in lieu of interlibrary loan is and will always remain a relatively small fraction of total library use. The point is not to denigrate the value of interlibrary loan or resource sharing but to emphasize the overriding importance of the local use of local collections. Publishers, librarians, and particularly network planners should keep this basic truth in mind.

Last year Penn spent $1.3 million on books and journals, and we would spend considerably more if we had it. We *saved* virtually nothing by using interlibrary loan and photocopying; in fact, we incurred substantial additional costs using interlibrary loan channels to obtain some important little used materials for a small number of users who might otherwise have done without.

The Cornell experience with the five-copy limit is similar to Penn's. Madeline Cohen Oakley, Cornell interlibrary loan librarian, reports it as follows:

> The new restrictions on photocopying pose a number of questions of policy and procedure for Cornell interlibrary loan

operations. Although the five article per journal photocopy limit may seem low, our experience in interlibrary borrowing (the term covers both requests for loans and for photocopy) at Olin Library has not, for the most, borne this out. We consider a journal for which we have four or more photocopy requests to be "frequently ordered," and all such journals are considered for purchase. To give an example, in the 1975–76 fiscal year, out of a total of 188 different journal titles represented in one group of requests, only 15 involved multiple copies of four or more from one journal. (Of those 15, nine were for more than five articles.)[5]

She remarks that the five-copy limit is likely to be a problem when a single individual or research project requires a number of articles from one journal. This is Penn's view as well. In such cases some restrictions will have to be worked out, and our users will have to be more selective in what they request. In those few cases for which we need to exceed the five-copy limit, we can presumably choose to pay a reasonable royalty to a payments center or do without. The mechanism for paying such fees may be in place by next year.

Ben H. Weil of Exxon has been appointed to serve as program director of the Association of American Publishers/Technical-Scientific-Medical Copy Payments Center Task Force, which is expected to design and implement a payments system by Jan. 1, 1978. The center would periodically invoice the users and allocate the payment, less a processing charge, to the appropriate publisher. I wish the center luck, but my guess is that the processing charges will far exceed the royalty payments, making it a financially precarious service.

It is important that librarians exercise all the rights and privileges the new law gives them, uninhibited by the fear of lawsuits or by an exaggerated or misplaced sense of fair play and justice. Section 504(c)2 relieves employees of non-profit libraries from personal liability in case of infringement if they had reasonable grounds for believing their use of the work was a fair use under section 107. Librarians must comply with the law as best they understand it, but they are not obliged to do more. Even the Internal Revenue Service encourages taxpayers to take all the deductions to which they are legally entitled and to pay no more taxes than the law requires.

Some librarians are already going to great lengths to establish elaborate and far more restrictive procedures than the law or the guidelines require in order to demonstrate their intent to comply with the spirit as well as the letter of the law and to show their good faith. By so doing, they appear defensive and guilty and run the risk of losing the rights they are too cautious to exercise. It is a time for boldness and courage.

Based on past performance, we can be sure that the publishers will not be cautious or diffident about exercising all the rights the law allows them—and even a bit more on occasion. Last fall, for example, one publisher misrepresented the provisions of the new law in a letter to his library customers offering to sell copying privileges that the law already gives them as a right.

Libraries that buy subscriptions with strings attached may forfeit their rights under the law. "Section 108(f)(4) states that the rights of reproduction granted libraries by Section 108 do not override any contractual obligations assumed by the library at the time it obtained a work for its collections. In view of this provision, libraries must be especially sensitive to the conditions under which they purchase materials, and before executing an agreement which would limit their rights under the copyright law, should consult with their legal counsel." (ALA *Washington Newsletter*, Nov. 15, 1976, p. 5)

Actually, urging librarians to consult legal counsel in copyright matters may not be very helpful advice. Because of its vagueness and complexity, the new copyright law is already being called the "full employment act" of the legal profession. The typical general counsel that the typical librarian can turn to will know little about copyright law and will, as lawyers customarily do when asked for advice by cautious clients on unfamiliar matters, give the most conservative opinion possible in order to be on the safe side. Librarians might be better advised in general to study the appropriate sections of the law and have the courage to make their own interpretations and decisions.

The vast majority of academic and public librarians have nothing to fear from the new copyright law. The amount and kind of copying that is done in their libraries will not require the payment of any significant amount of royalties, and the dollar amounts involved will be trivial to publishers and library users alike. I think that time and experience will show that the whole publisher-librarian controversy over copyright, interlibrary loan, and photocopying was the result of fear and misunderstanding—largely on the part of the publishers.

Resource sharing and networking give publishers nightmares and librarians hope, but both groups are seriously overestimating the impact these developments will have on their financial status and operations. Inflationary trends and market forces at work will soon change much of our current thinking about these matters.

Libraries are cutting their expenditures for books and journals because they do not have the acquisition funds, not because they are able to get them on interlibrary loan or from the Center for Research Libraries or the British Library Lending Division. Publishers still have the idea that if they can discourage interlibrary loan and photocopying, libraries will be forced to spend more money to buy books and journals. This is bunk. Libraries can't spend money they don't have. The fact is that with or without effective sharing mechanisms, with rising prices and declining support, libraries simply do not have the funds to maintain their previous acquisitions levels. If we cannot afford to buy the materials our users need, and if the law prohibits us from borrowing or photocopying what we do not own, our users will simply have to do without. Moreover, there is an increasing recognition that librarians and faculty members alike have developed highly exaggerated notions of the size, range, and depth of the library collections that are actually needed by most library users.

Studies have repeatedly shown that in general roughly 80 percent of the demands on a library can be satisfied by 20 percent of the collection. Journal use is a Bradford type distribution where a small number of journal titles account for a large percentage of the use. Eugene Garfield's numerous studies using citation analysis and the Institute for Scientific Information's *Journal Citation Reports* also corroborate it. A recent University of Pittsburgh Library School study showed that 44 percent of the books acquired by one major research library in 1969 were never used in the succeeding five-year period.[6] A recent study at Penn produced a comparable finding. Earlier studies on library use by Fussler,[7] Trueswell,[8] and Buckland[9] showed similar use patterns.

Large collections confer status and prestige on librarians and faculty members alike, but when the budget crunch comes to a library, many of these status purchases will be foregone or dropped and the essentials will be maintained. Although we will rely on interlibrary loan or a National Lending Library to obtain these missing items when needed, they will rarely be called for, for they are rarely, if ever, used.[10] Libraries will continue to buy and stock as many of the high use books and journals as they can possibly afford.

It is also worth noting here that the word "research" is much overused to describe what professors do and what libraries support. This is another legacy of the affluent 1960s when there was seemingly no end to the increase in the numbers of Ph.D. candidates and professors in our universities and the wide variety of their research needs and interests. The economic decline in the 1970s is changing this attitude. Apart from those located at the major research-oriented universities, the primary mission of most academic libraries is or should be to support the instructional needs of their students and faculty. This function can be documented by a quote from the 1975 Ladd-Lipset survey of U.S. faculty members reported by the authors in an article entitled "How Professors Spend Their Time," which appeared in the *Chronicle of Higher Education* (Oct. 14, 1975, p. 2).

The popular assumption has been that American academics are a body of scholars who do their research and then report their findings to the intellectual or scientific communities. Many faculty members behave in this fashion, but that overall description of the profession is seriously flawed.

Most academics think of themselves as "teachers" and "intellectuals"—and they perform accordingly.

Although data on the number of scholarly articles and academic books published each year testify that faculty members are producing a prodigious volume of printed words, this torrent is gushing forth from relatively few pens:

—Over half of all full-time faculty members have never written or edited any sort of book alone or in collaboration with others.

—More than one third have never published an article.

—Half of the professoriate have not published anything, or had anything accepted for publication in the last two years.

—More than one quarter of all full-time academics have never published a scholarly word.

They summarize as follows:

American academics constitute a teaching profession, not a scholarly one. There is a small scholarly subgroup located disproportionately at a small number of research-oriented universities.

These conclusions about how faculty members spend their time correlate well with what library statistics show about faculty use of libraries—namely, that it is on the order of ten percent of the total and that much of it is for instructional purposes rather than research.

As for the publishers, they may make themselves feel better by blaming journal cancellations and shrinking book orders on increasingly effective library resource sharing via systematic photocopying and interlibrary loan rather than on inflation and declining library budgets, but they will be deceiving themselves.

Resource sharing will not seriously erode publishers' profits, nor will it help libraries as much as they think. Interlibrary loan will increase, but it will still continue to be a very small percentage of total library use. The high cost of interlibrary loan and the needs and demands of library users will not permit it to grow into something major. Its importance will always be as much in the capability for delivery as in the actual use of that capability. Like the Center for Research Libraries, it serves as an insurance policy. We do not justify our annual membership fee in the center by the number of items we borrow every year but by the fact that our membership gives us access—if and when we need it—to several million research items which might otherwise not be available to us.

In the long run, librarians cannot count on interlibrary loan or their regional consortia or networks for the major economies they will need to make to weather the hard times that are ahead. This is as true for the many small college library consortia as it is for the prestigious Research Libraries Group and the now defunct Five Associated University Libraries cooperative. All too frequently, cooperation is merely a pooling of poverty. Many consortia members are vulnerable because the magnitude of the cuts they will have to make to counter inflation and declining support will far outweigh the relatively minor savings regional cooperation will yield in the end. In fact, like many automation projects, regional consortia may actually be costing their members far more than the benefits they derive if one includes the very substantial cost of staff time needed to make them work. This cost will become more apparent when the grant money that supports many consortia runs out.

Why can't consortia and resource sharing fulfill their promise? Because they focus almost exclusively on reducing expenditures for books and journals and only incidentally on reducing expenditures for personnel. But in the end, any significant savings in library expenditures must come from eliminating positions, because that is where the money goes.

A typical large academic or public library spends 70–75 percent of its budget for personnel and benefits, 20–25 percent for books and journals, and only 5 percent for other purposes. Thus, the amount of cost savings that can be made through resource sharing in any one year is necessarily only a small percentage of the book and journal budget. With these costs rising at the rate of 15 percent a year, the savings will be largely absorbed by inflation.

The unpleasant fact is that we must eliminate positions if we are to make significant cost reductions to cope with inflation and no-growth budgets. To reduce staff will require a drastic curtailment of the intake of materials, reduced services, and increased productivity. There is no other way. Resource sharing is essential but it is not a panacea.

The cheap and easy victories come early in library cooperation, but what do we do that is cost effective after we have agreed to reciprocal borrowing privileges with our neighbors and saved a few positions by joining OCLC? What do we do for an encore after we have reduced our staff, journal subscriptions, and book acquisitions by five or ten percent through cooperation, resource sharing, automation, and improved management? In the year 1975–76 inflation and declining support caused a 10 percent decrease in the median number of volumes added to ARL libraries and a 5 percent decrease in the number of staff employed.

Academic libraries are sharing the financial troubles of their parent institutions, and public libraries those of the local governments that support them. These troubles come from long-term economic, social, and demographic trends; they will probably get worse in the decade ahead. The troubles that publishers have are caused by rising costs and changing market conditions and not by library photocopying or deficiencies in the copyright law. These troubles will not be resolved by the collection of royalties on a few journal articles or the sale of a few more library subscriptions.

The library market is shrinking and hardening, and publishers—both commercial and scholarly—will have to accept that fact and make adjustments. Librarians will have to accept that the savings they make through networking, cooperation, and resource sharing in the next several years will be quickly absorbed by the continuing inflation in book and journal prices and rising personnel costs. Moreover, library budgetary support will continue to decline and the pressures to reduce expenditures will increase.

The fact is, libraries can no longer afford to maintain the collections, staffs, and service levels that librarians and users have come to expect in the last two decades. Libraries are experiencing a substantial loss in their standard of living as a result of inflation, increasing energy costs, and changing priorities in our society. We can rail against it and search for scapegoats, but it would be better if we came to terms with this painful reality and began to reduce our excessive commitments and expectations to match our declining resources.

The importance of resource sharing mechanisms, and particularly the most cost-effective ones—the centralized libraries' libraries, such as the Center for Research Libraries and the

British Library Lending Division—is not so much that they will save us funds we can reallocate to other purposes, but that they will permit us to continue to have access to a large universe of materials we can no longer afford, spending our diminishing funds on the materials we need and use most. In sum, effective resource sharing will help ease the pain that will accompany the scaling-down of commitments and expectations we face in the years ahead. ☐

Notes

1. Special Issue *ALA Washington Newsletter* on the New Copyright Law, Nov. 15, 1976. (Reprinted and available from **ALA** Order Dept. for $2.)

2. For more on the need for a new attitude toward journals in libraries see: Richard De Gennaro, "Escalating Journal Prices: Time to Fight Back," *American Libraries*, February 1977, p. 68–74.

3. The eight titles which had five or more requests are *American Orchid Society Bulletin*, Harvard University, Botanical Museum, Cambridge; *Fizika*, Yugoslavia; *Journal of Electroanalytical Chemistry*, Elsevier Sequoia, Lausanne; *Nukleonika*, Polska Akad. Nauk, Ars Polona Ruch, Warsaw; *Pramana*, Indian Academy of Science, Bangalore; *Revue Roumaine de Physique*, Bucharest; *Synthesis*, George Thiene Verlag & Academic Press; and *Worldview*, Council on Religion and International Affairs, New York.

4. ARL Statistics, 1975–76. Washington, D.C., Association of Research Libraries, 1976, p. 14.

5. Madeline Cohen Oakley, "The New Copyright Law: Implications for Libraries," Cornell University Libraries *Bulletin*, No. 202, October-December 1976, p. 5.

6. Stephen Bulick, and others, "Use of Library Materials in Terms of Age," *Journal of the American Society for Information Science*, May-June 1976, pp. 175–8.

7. Herman H. Fussler, *Patterns in the Use of Books in Large Research Libraries*, Chicago, Univ. of Chicago Press, 1969.

8. Richard W. Trueswell, "User Circulation Satisfaction vs. Size of Holdings at Three Academic Libraries," *College & Research Libraries*, May 1969, pp. 204–13.

9. Michael H. Buckland, *Book Availability and the Library User*. New York, Pergamon Press, 1975.

10. For a more extended discussion of these points see: Richard De Gennaro, "Austerity, Technology, and Resource Sharing: Research Libraries Face the Future," *Library Journal*, May 15, 1975, pp. 917–23.

LIBRARY PHOTOCOPYING†

James M. Treece*

INTRODUCTION**

Determining the proper statutory treatment for library uses of copyrighted works involves the intricate problem of balancing the needs of libraries and their users against the claims of copyright owners for compensation for various uses of their works. In formulating a statutory scheme, two fundamental inquiries must be resolved: the extent to which library lending shall stand free of any obligation to compensate the copyright owner of the borrowed work; and the extent to which libraries and their users shall be permitted to photocopy without compensating the copyright owner of the work. Whether fees should be charged for library lending of copyrighted works poses difficult questions. Such compensation would conflict with library practice in the United States, which traditionally has not involved a fee. However, several European nations have given, or are considering giving, copyright owners remuneration when copies are loaned. The West German copyright law provides for a lending royalty, entitling authors to an equitable remuneration when copies of their copyrighted works are loaned to users by corporate libraries, public libraries, or book-

---

† A license is hereby granted to students, teachers, librarians and journal publishers to reproduce copies of this Article by any means, and to distribute copies of this Article to the public, provided that copies reproduced for distribution to the public include a notice of copyright in the following form: Copyright © 1977 by James M. Treece.
   * Professor of Law, University of Texas. Barbara Marquardt and John Christensen facilitated and guided the research underlying this Article. Barbara Marquardt, John Christensen, Robert Berring and Roy Mersky graciously read and constructively criticized an early draft of the manuscript.
   ** Certain citation conventions are used throughout this Symposium. These conventions are presented at page vii.

SOURCE: Reprinted from the *UCLA Law Review* 24: 1025-1069 (1977) by permission of the copyright holders. Copyright © 1977 by James M. Treece and by the Regents of the University of California.

stores.[1]   The United Kingdom is seriously considering a public lending right[2] which would compensate authors according to the number of times their works are loaned or the number of copies of their works purchased by libraries.[3]   In Sweden, the state pays authors sums which depend on the number of times their works are loaned.[4]   Somewhat similarly, in Denmark since 1946, the Minister for Education has granted Danish authors one crown per year for each copy in excess of fifty copies of their works in public libraries.[5]

A country that compensates copyright owners when their works are loaned must, to be consistent, also compensate copyright owners when their works are photocopied and the photocopy is transferred to the user in lieu of a loan.   However, a country that does not enforce a lending right, especially a country with a strong commitment to free lending, might not wish to impose a royalty for photocopies that substitute for library loans, regardless of its position on other types of photocopies.

Two aspects of the photocopying controversy have been adjudicated in the courts of several countries: the liability of libraries that photocopy for their own purposes or for their users, and the liability of libraries whose users photocopy for themselves. The former aspect emerged dramatically in this country in the well-known case of *Williams & Wilkins v. United States*,[6] in which the practice of two government libraries of providing photo-

---

[1]   UNESCO, COPYRIGHT LAWS AND TREATIES OF THE WORLD, COPYRIGHT STATUTE, FEDERAL REPUBLIC OF GERMANY, art. 27.   *See* Reimer, *The Right of Distribution with Special Reference to the Hiring and Lending of Books and Records*, 9 COPYRIGHT 56, 60-61 (1973).   This lending royalty right was secured for public library lending when federal, state and local governments agreed to compensate authors through 1984 by paying royalties to named authors' societies, as representatives of the authors, for the lending activities of publicly funded libraries.   *See* Dietz, *The Public Lending Right in the Federal Republic of Germany: Evolution and Regulation*, 7 INT'L REV. INDUS. PROP. & COPYRIGHT L. 220 (1976).

[2]   *See* PUBLIC LENDING RIGHT: AN ACCOUNT OF AN INVESTIGATION OF TECHNICAL AND COST ASPECTS (London: HMSO 1975).

[3]   *See* PUBLIC LENDING RIGHT: FINAL REPORT OF AN INVESTIGATION OF TECHNICAL AND COST ASPECTS (London: HMSO 1975).

[4]   UNESCO, COPYRIGHT LAWS AND TREATIES OF THE WORLD, SWEDEN, COPYRIGHT ROYALTIES FROM LIBRARIES, Royal Decree No. 464 of 1955.   *See* Desjeux, *Photocopying and Copyright*, 9 COPYRIGHT 51, 53 (1973).

[5]   UNESCO, COPYRIGHT LAWS AND TREATIES OF THE WORLD, DENMARK, COPYRIGHT ROYALTIES FROM LENDING LIBRARIES.   *See* Desjeux, *supra* note 4, at 53.

[6]   172 U.S.P.Q. (BNA) 670 (Ct. Cl. 1972), *rev'd*, 487 F.2d 1345 (Ct. Cl. 1973), *aff'd per curiam by an equally divided court*, 420 U.S. 376 (1975).

copies of articles contained in copyrighted journals to their patrons and other libraries was held to constitute fair use.[7] The latter question recently arose in Australia[8] and France,[9] whose courts

---

[7] Williams & Wilkins, a commercial publisher of 37 technical and scientific journals, sued the United States for the copying activities of two of its institutions, the National Institute of Health and the National Library of Medicine. The library at the National Institute of Health is open to the public and, at the time of the action, subscribed to 3,000 journals, two subscriptions each, including the allegedly infringed copyrighted journals published by Williams & Wilkins. The National Library of Medicine functioned primarily as a librarian's library, filling requests for interlibrary loans from its collection, which included the journals published by Williams & Wilkins and much of the world's medical literature.

The library at the National Institute of Health photocopied journal articles for users upon request without inquiring into their reasons for acquiring photocopies. In 1970, the Institute made photocopies of about 93,000 articles. The National Library of Medicine also photocopied articles for requesting libraries and for other users without regard to user purpose. In 1968 it filled 120,000 requests for copies of journal articles.

Williams & Wilkins sued the United States for infringing the copyright in four of its journals by photocopying articles in their entirety without the consent of the publisher. The United States argued that reproducing and distributing single copies of journal articles to users and to libraries requesting interlibrary loans constituted a fair use under the Copyright Act of 1909. The Commissioner who first heard the case concluded that the fair use defense could not justify the comprehensive duplication systems operated by the defendant libraries. *See* 172 U.S.P.Q. (BNA) 670, 678-79 (Ct. Cl. 1972). But the majority of the judges of the Court of Claims, with three judges dissenting, reversed the Commissioner's decision, emphasizing that the defendant libraries kept photocopying for users within "reasonable" bounds and that their photocopying served the public interest by contributing affirmatively to medical research in the United States. 487 F.2d 1345, 1356-59 (Ct. Cl. 1973). The Supreme Court divided evenly on the infringement versus fair use question and consequently affirmed the judgment of the Court of Claims. 420 U.S. 376 (1975). Thus, the sixteen judicial officers who voted on the issue of library photocopying of journal articles split evenly on its resolution, thereby indicating the balanced appeal of the competing claims.

[8] In Moorhouse v. Univ. of New South Wales, [1974] 3 Austl. L.R. 1 (N.S.W. Sup. Ct. 1974), *judgment set aside*, [1975] 6 Austl. L.R. 193 (High Ct. 1975), the author and copyright proprietor of a book of short stories filed a copyright infringement suit against the University of New South Wales for authorizing a borrower to make two photocopies of one of the 20 short stories in the book. The Supreme Court of New South Wales declared that although the library did not explicitly authorize the user to reproduce the particular copies, it did, in general, authorize infringements by library users through its indifference to voluminous copying by students and others from 140,000 books on open stacks in proximity to eight unsupervised copying machines. [1974] 3 Austl. L.R. 1, 17 (N.S.W. Sup. Ct. 1974). On appeal, the Australian High Court entered a declaration that the library had authorized the user's act of copying and had thereby infringed the copyright in the plaintiff's book. The High Court stated that a library could not offer an unlimited supply of books and an unlimited opportunity to use copying machines to users of the library without qualification or supervision. [1975] 6 Austl. L.R. 193, 208-10 (1975).

[9] In Société Masson v. CNRS, [1974] D.S. Jur. 337 (Trib. gr. inst. 1974), *abstracted*, 5 INT'L REV. INDUS. PROP. & COPYRIGHT L. 332 (1974), the plaintiff was a publisher of medical journals and the defendant library subscribed to 1,400

held liable for damages libraries that provided unsupervised and unlimited photocopying facilities to their patrons on the theory that, in effect, the libraries had authorized infringements by their patrons.

This recent spate of litigation suggests that photocopying poses a more substantial threat to the security of publishers of copyrighted works than did the past methods of copying by hand or with stenographic aids.   Such litigation, coupled with the diverse judicial treatments of the photocopy question, provides impetus for legislative consideration of the problem.   A legislature must initially decide whether to provide any exceptions to the copyright owner's exclusive right to reproduce copies in the case of library photocopying.   The more difficult task is then to formulate exceptions which adequately balance the goal of encouraging the dissemination of information against the principle of compensating the copyright owner for use of his work.

Various European countries have made the legislative decision to protect the interests of copyright owners by imposing a surcharge on photocopying.   The fees for copying ultimately inure, directly or indirectly, to the benefit of authors or publishers.[10]   In countries where the Anglo-American concept of fair use

---

periodicals.   The suit arose when the library loaned an issue of one of the plaintiff's journals to a user whose credentials and purpose the defendant did not investigate.   The user made copies of two articles in the journal, using unsupervised library copying machines.

Under its charter, the defendant library was implicitly authorized to provide copies of documents in its possession to requesting scientists.   Moreover, under French copyright law, a copyright proprietor cannot prohibit users from making copies strictly reserved for the private use of the copier.   UNESCO, COPYRIGHT LAWS AND TREATIES OF THE WORLD, COPYRIGHT STATUTE, FRANCE, art. 41(2). Nevertheless, the library was held to have infringed.   The Tribunal agreed that a user has a privilege under French copyright law to make a photocopy of a copyrighted work for private use on machines provided by a library.   A library will, however, find itself culpably associated in the infringement by a user who copies for a nonprivate purpose.   Under French copyright law, the defendant's practices failed to insulate it from liability because it did not require proof of its user's identity or purpose before lending him a copyrighted journal from which any number of unsupervised copies could be made.

[10] See generally Kolle, Reprography and Copyright Law: A Comparative Law Study Concerning the Role of Copyright Law In the Age of Information, 6 INT'L REV. INDUS. PROP. & COPYRIGHT L. 382 (1975).

In Sweden, for example, the State, through the Swedish Fund for Authors, compensates authors for the reproduction of their works by or in libraries. Records of copying are kept by the libraries.   UNESCO, COPYRIGHT LAWS AND TREATIES OF THE WORLD, SWEDEN, COPYRIGHT ROYALTIES FROM LIBRARIES, Royal Decree No. 464 of 1955; see also Desjeux, supra note 4, at 51, 53.

exists as an exception to the copyright owner's exclusive right to reproduce his work, enacting legislation poses more complex problems. First, those uses of the new photocopying technology that exceed fair use and that unreasonably interfere with economic and other interests secured by copyright must be identified. Second, an administratively feasible scheme to forbid such excess uses, or to charge users with a fee for the benefit of authors and copyright proprietors, must be devised.[11]

Against this background of varying legislative and judicial treatment of library lending and photocopying, and mindful of the result in *Williams & Wilkins v. United States*,[12] Congress set out to revise the American copyright law. In his remarks before the House of Representatives on September 22, 1976, when the House voted to pass the Copyright Act of 1976, Representative Kastenmeier noted that the issue of photocopying by public libraries was one of the most troublesome issues before the House Judiciary Committee and Subcommittee. He stated his belief "that we have successfully balanced the needs of libraries against the rights of copyright proprietors by providing that libraries may photocopy copyrighted material, including for purposes of interlibrary loans, as long as such photocopying is not systematic and a substitute for purchase or subscription."[13]

In this Article, the effectiveness of this legislative balance is assessed. Exposition of the statutory scheme is followed by analysis of the impact of the new provisions on such library activities as lending, photocopying, offering secondary services, and operating library networks and consortia.

France has recently introduced a tax on the sale of copying machines under the Finance Law of December 31, 1975. The proceeds are to be kept in a National Book Fund to finance orders by government libraries for scientific, technical and cultural books. *See* Kerever, *The International Copyright Conventions and Reprography*, COPYRIGHT 188, 196 (1976).

[11] The United Kingdom, for example, restricts photocopies which public libraries may provide to users to single copies of limited portions of copyrighted works, requires users to declare in writing that a photocopy is needed for purposes of research or private study, and treats all other photocopies of copyrighted works as infringing. UNESCO, COPYRIGHT LAWS AND TREATIES OF THE WORLD, UNITED KINGDOM, THE COPYRIGHT (LIBRARIES) REGULATIONS (1957).

[12] *See* note 7 *supra*.

[13] 12 CONG. REC. H10,874 (daily ed. Sept. 22, 1976) (remarks of Rep. Kastenmeier).

I. COPYRIGHT ACT PROVISIONS GOVERNING LIBRARIES

Section 106 of the Copyright Act gives the owner of a copyright in a work the following exclusive rights: (1) to reproduce the copyrighted work in copies or phonorecords; (2) to prepare derivative works; (3) to distribute copies or phonorecords of the copyrighted work by sale or by lending; (4) to perform the copyrighted work publicly; and (5) to display the copyrighted work publicly.[14] Section 106, standing alone, severely limits a librarian's or archivist's freedom to lend, display or reproduce copyrighted works. Sections 107 through 118, however, place limitations on the exclusive rights of copyright owners. Some of these limitations enable librarians to perform more than just their traditional functions. Sections 107, 108 and 109 in particular describe the extent to which libraries and their users may utilize copyrighted works without liability for infringement.

A. Lending by Libraries

1. Section 109: The Lending Privilege

Section 109(a) dispels the notion that libraries can no longer freely lend works in their collections. By its terms, the owner of a particular copy or phonorecord or any person authorized by such owner is permitted to "sell or otherwise dispose of the possession of that copy or phonorecord" without the authority of the copyright owner.[15] Thus libraries and archives may own a copy or phonorecord of a work and can authorize employees to "dispose of the possession of that copy or phonorecord," by lending it for a limited time. Any concern that the phrase "sell or otherwise dispose" permits the owner of a copy or phonorecord only to transfer possession permanently is dispelled by the House Report's explicit recognition of the right of "a library . . . to lend [copies of works and phonorecords] under any conditions it chooses to impose."[16]

Under section 109(b), the owner of a copy or phonorecord or any person authorized by the owner also may, without the authority of the copyright owner, "display that copy publicly . . . to viewers present at the place where the copy is located."[17] This

---

14 NEW ACT § 106(1)-(5).
15 Id. § 109(a).
16 H. REP. at 79; S. REP. at 71-72.
17 NEW ACT § 109(b).

language confirms the traditional right of the owner of a work to exhibit it to others, but the words carefully restrict libraries to the use of outmoded technology. While a library may place a painting in a public room or project a slide or transparency onto a large screen, it may not transmit an image to another library, transmit an image to viewers not present where the copy is located, or retrieve an image of a work stored in a computer file or a data bank. According to the House Report, "The committee's intention [in drafting section 109 was] . . . to preserve the traditional privilege of the owner of a copy to display it directly, but to place reasonable restrictions on the ability to display it indirectly in such a way that the copyright owner's market for reproduction and distribution of the copies would be affected."[18]

2.   Liability for Infringement by Users

Not only may libraries and archives circulate their holdings by lending without the necessity of compensating the copyright owner, they may do so free of any potential liability for infringements of the copyrights in the loaned works which may be committed by borrowers. Section 108(f)(1) provides that libraries and archives may maintain reproduction equipment on library premises for the *unsupervised use* of library users, provided that the equipment bears a notice that the making of a copy of a work may be subject to the copyright law.[19]

3.   Copying by Users

Libraries, including libraries and archives that are closed to the public and operated by profit-making firms, are relieved by section 108(f)(1) from vicarious liability for infringement by users who reproduce unsupervised photocopies of borrowed works using properly labeled copying machines. However, nothing in the photocopying portion of the Act excuses from liability for copyright infringement the user who uses library copying machines to reproduce photocopies. A user who photocopies substantial portions of copyrighted works violates the copyright owner's exclusive right "to reproduce the copyrighted work in

---

[18]   H.Rep. at 80; *accord*, S. Rep. at 72.
[19]   For regulations regarding copyright notice, see 37 C.F.R. § 202.2 (1976). Compare the recent decisions of courts in Australia and France, *see* notes 8-9 & accompanying text *supra*, with this limited liability under the new law.

copies,"[20] unless the user can justify his reproduction of a photo-copy or photocopies as a fair use of a copyrighted work, for pur-poses of criticism, comment, news reporting, teaching, scholarship or research.[21]

The Act does not specifically say whether reproducing a single copy of an entire article or a full chapter from a copyrighted work for use as a record to prepare a news report or a scholarly or critical article is a fair use of the copyrighted work. The Act does say that "reproduction in copies" for such purposes is an example of a fair use.[22] It also lists general factors that identify fair uses, such as whether the purpose and character of the use are nonprofit educational, and whether the use affects the potential market for the copyrighted work.[23]

A user who reproduces a single photocopy of a copyrighted article or chapter for use as a record to prepare a scholarly article, a paper for a course or a set of notes for an examination is prob-ably implicitly a fair user since he manifests no commercial pur-pose and no negative effect upon the potential market for the coprighted work is apparent.[24] Furthermore, section 108(d), which allows a library to provide a user with a photocopy of an article in a periodical if it "has had no notice that the copy . . . would be used for any purpose other than private study, scholar-ship or research,"[25] supports the view that a patron who photo-copies for such purposes is a fair user.

---

[20] NEW ACT § 106(1).

[21] *Id.* § 107.

[22] *Id.* In discussing works excluded from § 108, the House Report states: Although subsection (h) generally removes musical, graphic and audio-visual works from the specific exemptions of section 108, it is important to recognize that the doctrine of fair use under section 107 remains fully applicable to the photocopying or other reproduction of such works. In the case of music, for example, it would be fair use for a scholar doing musicalogical research to have a library supply a copy of a portion of a score or to reproduce portions of a phonorecord of a work. Nothing in section 108 impairs the applicability of the fair use doctrine to a wide variety of situations involving photocopying or other reproduction by a library of copyrighted material in its collections, where the user requests the reproduction for legitimate scholarly or research purposes. H. REP. at 78-79.

[23] NEW ACT § 107.

[24] Students and scholars cannot and will not buy copies of works they bor-row and photocopy. Instead, they will make notes if they cannot photocopy. George Fry & Associates, *Survey of Copyrighted Material Reproduction Practices in Scientific and Technical Fields*, 11 BULL. COPYRIGHT SOC'Y 69, 117-20 (1963). It is no answer that they would pay a photocopying royalty rather than rely on notes, for no royalty is owed for uses that are fair.

[25] NEW ACT § 108(d)(1) (emphasis added).

Of course, a library need not concern itself with the status of its patrons. A library can comply with the New Act simply by lending its holdings freely, from open or closed stacks, and by providing borrowers with access to properly labeled photocopying machines. Only when a library goes further and itself reproduces and distributes photocopies to its patrons must it become concerned that its patrons are fair users under section 107 or that its photocopying program complies with requirements for library photocopying set forth in section 108.

B. *Copying by Libraries*

Section 108 of the Copyright Act describes in detail the circumstances in which libraries and archives may reproduce and distribute copies of works without infringing their copyrights. In order to make use of the photocopying privileges for libraries enumerated in section 108, a library must satisfy the qualifying criteria set forth in subsection (a). The collection of the library or archives must be open to the public or available to persons doing research in a specialized field, in addition to the researchers formally affiliated with the institution.[26] Only these "subsection (a)" libraries qualify for the rights of reproduction in section 108; libraries and archives that do not fulfill the subsection (a) "open or available" requirement cannot take advantage of the privileges.

Additionally, subsection (a) provides that a particular act of reproduction or distribution must satisfy three other criteria in order to qualify for a section 108 privilege: the copy reproduced or distributed must be a single copy;[27] it must be "made without any purpose of direct or indirect commercial advantage";[28] and it must include a notice of copyright that communicates the copyright owner's claim of copyright.[29]

The apparent difficulty in assigning meaning to the requirement that the copy reproduced or distributed be made without any purpose of direct or indirect commercial advantage is somewhat mitigated by the guidance provided by the House Report. This Report states that "the 'advantage' referred to in this clause must attach to the immediate commercial motivation behind the repro-

---

[26] *Id.* § 108(a)(2).
[27] *Id.* § 108(a).
[28] *Id.* § 108(a)(1).
[29] *Id.* § 108(a)(3).

duction or distribution itself, rather than to the ultimate profit-making motivation behind the enterprise in which the library is located."[30] Thus libraries in profit-making medical clinics, law firms and manufacturing corporations, upon qualifying as subsection (a) libraries by making their collections "open or available," may reproduce a single copy and distribute it to an employee of the organization for use in his work, or may reproduce a copy for another purpose, without thereby evidencing a purpose to achieve an indirect commercial advantage by reason of the copying itself.[31] In addition, the Conference Report states explicitly that a subsection (a) library or archives in a for-profit organization may make single copies or phonorecords under the protection of a section 108 privilege if the other conditions of section 108 are met.[32]

While meeting the subsection (a) requirements is a condition to qualifying for photocopying privileges, the requirements do not themselves define the section 108 privileges. The availability of each privilege depends on satisfying additional requisites. The remainder of this section describes these copying privileges.

1. Reproducing Single Copies for Library Purposes

Section 108 permits a subsection (a) library or archive which meets the other three subsection (a) requirements to make a copy or phonorecord of a copyrighted work in certain circumstances to secure or maintain its collection or to enrich another collection. These very limited "library purpose" privileges fall into two categories: those pertaining to published works,[33] and those pertaining to unpublished works.[34]

The sole purpose for making a copy or phonorecord of a published work must be to replace a work that is damaged, deteriorating, lost or stolen, a new copy of which is not obtainable at a reasonable price.[35] To qualify in the case of an unpublished work, the purpose for making a copy or phonorecord must be to preserve the original work from wear, to secure against loss, or to deposit the copy or phonorecord for research use in another subsection (a) library or archives.[36] Although the privilege to

---

30 H. REP. at 75.
31 Id.
32 CONF. REP. at 74.
33 NEW ACT § 108(c).
34 Id. § 108(b).
85 Id. § 108(c).
36 Id. § 108(b).

copy a published work for library purposes is available regardless of whether the work is in the collection of the copying library, an unpublished work may be reproduced only when the copying library currently holds the work in its collection.[37]

Library purpose copies of both published and unpublished works must be "in facsimile form" to qualify under section 108.[38] This limitation requires that copies be in eye-readable form.[39] Thus, library purpose copies may be reproduced in microform format but they may not employ a machine-readable format for storage in an information system.[40]

2.   Reproducing Single Copies for Distribution to Users

As the *Williams & Wilkins* case suggests,[41] the aspect of library copying which creates the most tension among affected interest groups is copying by libraries for users. In certain circumstances, section 108 of the new Copyright Act permits a subsection (a) library or archive to make and distribute to a user a single copy or phonorecord that meets the three subsection (a) requirements.[42] This right of reproduction and distribution, however, does not apply to musical works, pictorial, graphic, or sculptural, works, motion pictures, or non-news audiovisual works.[43] Thus, libraries holding musical works must negotiate a license to photocopy, rely on the privilege of fair use,[44] or provide users with properly labeled copying machines to reproduce copies for themselves.[45]

The "user copy" privileges in section 108 divide into two categories: (1) those pertaining to a copy of a small portion of a copyrighted work, or of no more than one entire article in an issue of a periodical ("small portion or article" copy);[46] and (2) those

---

[37] *Compare* § 108(c) *with* § 108(b).

[38] NEW ACT § 108(b)-(c).

[39] H. REP. at 67-68.

[40] *Id.* at 75-76.

[41] *See* note 7 & accompanying text *supra*. *Williams & Wilkins* generated emotional turmoil for some United States publishers. *See* note 127 *infra*.

[42] NEW ACT § 108(d)-(e).

[43] *Id.* § 108(h). But pictorial or graphic works published as descriptions of works which can be copied and distributed may be copied and distributed. *Id.*

[44] *Id.* § 107.

[45] *Id.* § 108(f)(1).

[46] *Id.* § 108(d).

pertaining to a copy of a substantial portion or all of an out-of-print work other than an article in a periodical ("entire work" copy).[47]

Both the small portion or article copy and the entire work copy may be made in response to a request by a user or by another library pursuant to a request for an interlibrary loan,[48] but the entire work copy may be made only if a new or used copy of the work cannot reasonably be obtained in the trade.[49] In addition, the distribution of both categories of user copies must occur in the context of three user copy conditions in order to obtain the privilege: (1) The library or archive must prominently display at its copy order desk and in its order form a "warning of copyright";[50] (2) The library or archive must have no notice that the user copy being distributed will be used for any purpose other than private study, scholarship or research;[51] and (3) The copy distributed must become the property of the user.[52] Section 108 as thus described enables libraries and archives that wish to do so to provide single copies of periodical articles and single copies of excerpts from textbooks to most users, thereby freeing the users from the schedules, circulation rules and physical surroundings of libraries and archives.

Congress foresaw potential harm to copyright interests and ultimately to the public interest in the cumulative effect upon periodical subscriptions of large numbers of library-distributed single copies.[53] It therefore placed in section 108(g) another set of limitations designed to restrict the total number of single copies that can be reproduced for distribution to users from the same periodical or other copyrighted work. Section 108(g) permits a library or archive to distribute isolated, unrelated single copies of the same material to users on separate occasions but forbids a library to distribute "related or concerted" copies of the same materials or to engage "in the systematic reproduction or distribution" of photocopies of copyrighted works. Libraries are also

---

[47] *Id.* § 108(e).
[48] *Id.* § 108(d); H. REP. at 76.
[49] NEW ACT § 108(e); H. REP. at 76.
[50] NEW ACT §§ 108(d)(2), (e)(2). The warning must be in accordance with requirements that the Register of Copyrights prescribes by regulation.
[51] *Id.* § 108(d)(1), (e)(1).
[52] *Id.*
[53] *See generally*, N. HENRY, 2 COPYRIGHT—INFORMATION TECHNOLOGY—PUBLIC POLICY (1976) (a full discussion of the concerns and positions of the various interest groups affected by the Copyright Act during the revision period).

precluded by section 108(g)(2) from reproducing and distributing interlibrary loan copies "in such aggregate quantities" that the copies distributed substitute in purpose or effect[54] for a subscription to or purchase of the copied work by the library requesting the interlibrary loan photocopy.

The House Report frankly acknowledges that the prohibitions against the concerted reproduction of multiple copies and the systematic reproduction of single copies for users or for interlibrary loans offer little specific guidance to those seeking to comply with them.[55] However, the Conference Report sets forth some guidelines for complying with section 108(g)(2) which in its view[56] "are a reasonable interpretation" of the section as it applies to the situations covered by the guidelines.[57]

Although the guidelines are highly specific, they cover only inter-library transactions. They state that a library or archive that does not have a subscription may request up to five photocopies per calendar year of an article or articles published in the same periodical within five years prior to the date of the request.[58] This limitation of five copies per year per periodical per requesting library is quite stringent: The guidelines do not allow five copies of articles in a given issue or volume of a periodical; The limitation applies to all issues of a given periodical published within the five year period preceding the request.[59]

This guideline does not apply to interlibrary requests for photocopies of articles in periodicals whose publication date is

---

[54] Libraries that are members of networks may forfeit their privileges to request inter-library photocopies from other members of the network. *See* notes 151-84 & accompanying text *infra*.

[55] H. Rep. at 78.

[56] Conf. Rep. at 72-74. These guidelines were proposed by CONTU, The National Commission on New Technological Uses of Copyrighted Works, and "accepted" by certain author, publisher and library organizations.

[57] *Id*. at 72.

[58] *Id*. at 72-73 (Guidelines § 1(a)). Thus, the sixth request in a calendar year for a copy of an article from an issue of *National Geographic* published within five years preceding the request filled by one library for another for distribution to a user may constitute an infringement of copyright.

[59] *Id*. at 72 (Guidelines § 1(a)). However, when a library requests from another library a copy of an article in a periodical which the library has ordered or subscribes to but which is unavailable, the "request shall be treated as though the requesting entity made such copy from its own collection." *Id*. at 73. It must then be determined whether the appropriate provisions of § 108 permit the copying. If the requesting library could make a copy from its own collection, it may request the copy from the supplying library.

more than five years prior to the date of the request.[60]   Thus interlibrary requests from one library during one calendar year for photocopies of eight articles published in the same periodical, four articles with publication dates within five years preceding the request and four articles with publication dates more than five years prior to the request, would not violate the guidelines because the guidelines do not speak to requests for photocopies of articles with publication dates more than five years prior to the request.

The guidelines do, however, state that a library may supply to a requesting library up to five photocopies per calendar year of material from a copyrighted work other than a periodical, including works of fiction, books of poems and collective works such as encyclopedias.[61]   This suggests that issues of periodicals with publication dates more than five years old could be treated like other copyrighted works, so that interlibrary requests by a library for photocopies of articles from any such source would be limited to five per calendar year, with additional requests providing evidence that interlibrary requests for photocopies had substituted for a purchase of the issue of the periodical, as opposed to a subscription to the periodical.   Such an approach permits interlibrary requests for photocopies of articles with publication dates within five years of the request to be evaluated in cumulative effect as substituting for a subscription and permits requests for photocopies of articles with publication dates more than five years prior to the request to be evaluated in cumulative effect as substituting for a purchase of a back copy.

The guidelines thus emphasize that a library may, for the use of its patrons, request from other libraries a limited number of photocopies of articles from recent issues of a periodical to which it does not subscribe and a limited number of photocopies of portions of other works that it has not purchased.   Beyond these limits, a library must subscribe to the periodical, purchase the work, purchase a license to photocopy or give up requests for interlibrary loans.[62]   Of course, a library that has purchased a work or subscribed to a periodical will, in many cases, desire to

---

60   *Id.*

61   *Id.* (Guidelines § 1(b)).

62   The guidelines also impose two clerical burdens upon interlibrary loan requests: a request must carry a representation that it conforms to the guidelines; and a requesting library or archives must maintain records of requests made and filled "until the end of the third complete calendar year after the end of the calendar year in which the respective request shall have been made." *Id.* at 73 (Guidelines §§ 3-4).

distribute to users, directly or through interlibrary loans, more than five copies in a calendar year of articles from recent issues of the periodical or excerpts from the other work. The question naturally arises whether upon receiving the sixth request from a user for a photocopy, such a library must refuse to fill it or, if it fills it, must enter a second subscription for the periodical or purchase a second copy of the work in question. The guidelines do not address this situation, but the common sense answer is no. Many more than five users can and will use a single issue of a periodical or single copy of another work when access occurs through circulation. Thus, it would seem that the number of user copies of material from the same source that constitutes in cumulative effect related, concerted or systematic reproduction is a number that exceeds a reasonable circulation rate for the photocopied work. Thus, if ten users can and will use a circulated copyrighted work in a period of time, and a library provides access to such a work, both loans and photocopies, to no more than ten users in such a period, then the photocopies can be described as substituting for loans rather than substituting for a purchase or subscription. Therefore, such photocopies appear to be privileged by analogy to the language in section 108(g)(2) expressing a limitation on privileged interlibrary loan photocopies that substitute in cumulative effect for purchases or subscriptions.

3. News Programs

Subsection (a) libraries or archives may reproduce a limited number of copies of the whole or a portion of an audiovisual news program for library or archival purposes, and may lend such copies to other libraries or to users, provided the copies include a notice of the owner's copyright and are not distributed with any purpose of commercial advantage.[63] The Conference Report interprets this privilege broadly, stating that it extends to copies of "local, regional or network newscasts, interviews concerning current news events, and on-the-spot coverage of news events."[64]

---

[63] NEW ACT § 108(f)(3).
[64] CONF. REP. at 73.

C. *Privileged Library Photocopying and Fair Use*

1. In General

Section 108 explicitly provides that the photocopying privileges granted in that section are in addition to, not in lieu of, any library photocopying which might be privileged as fair use.[65] Thus a library or archive charged with copyright infringement, if it has no other privilege, may be able to defend on the basis of fair use by showing that the general criteria of fair use were met and that the allegedly infringing copies were "for purposes such as . . . scholarship, or research . . . ."[66]

2. Library Copying for Teachers

As a general rule, a library or archive can reproduce and distribute user copies or phonorecords in accord with section 108 without inquiring into a user's identity or purpose. But users in many instances will themselves have a fair use privilege to reproduce and, more rarely, to distribute copies or phonorecords of copyrighted works for purposes such as teaching, scholarship or research.[67] What a user may do for himself, he may have another do for him.[68] Thus "copy shops," "other" libraries and subsection (a) libraries and archives may, in a particular transaction, reproduce and distribute single or multiple copies or phonorecords of a copyrighted work, not as a library or archive exercising a privilege under section 108, but as the agent of a user possessing a fair use privilege.

One common example is library copying for teachers. Section 107 provides that reproduction and distribution of multiple copies or phonorecords for classroom use for purposes of teaching may constitute fair use in proper circumstances. The House Report concludes that "a *specific* exemption freeing certain reproductions of copyrighted works for educational and scholarly purposes from copyright control is not justified . . . [even though] there is a 'need for greater certainty . . . for teachers.' "[69] Ac-

---

[65] NEW ACT § 108(f)(4).

[66] *Id.* § 107. *See* notes 20-25 & accompanying text *supra*.

[67] *Id.*

[68] A handicapped fair user surely may ask another to reproduce a copy for him. A corporate fair user would by definition exercise a privilege of fair use through the agency of another entity. Nothing in the statute suggests that a user with a privilege to photocopy must himself operate the machine or lose the privilege.

[69] H. REP. at 66-67 (emphasis added).

cordingly, the House Committee did not draft a specific fair use exemption for teachers but referred to and included in its report guidelines for classroom copying of books and periodicals and for educational uses of music. The Conference Report accepts these guidelines as reflecting the conferees' understanding of fair use.[70]

These guidelines are too detailed for a full description here. In general, they identify the types of works that may be reproduced and the circumstances, typically involving a spontaneous decision to copy, in which multiple copies for classroom use may be reproduced and distributed. They also suggest limitations based on length (up to 250 words from a poem), frequency (not more than nine instances of multiple copying per term) and other aspects of copying (not more than one essay from the same author per term). These guidelines are highly arbitrary, but when combined with the reasonable and equitable concept of fair use, the result is a flexible rule allowing the distribution of a whole work or a whole portion of a work if the length of the distributed portion approximates the limits in the guidelines. Consequently, libraries, if they choose to do so, will have freedom to fill teachers' requests for multiple copies for teaching purposes without any genuine fear that requests from "unfair users" will be difficult to identify,[71] or that such copying will raise an obligation to purchase additional periodical subscriptions, as would systematic copying by a library for users other than teachers.[72]

---

[70] *Id.* at 70.

[71] Teachers requesting multiple copies for use in teaching that are within the guidelines can be assumed by library employees to be acting well within the limits of fair use; teachers requesting multiple copies for use in teaching that are not far outside the guidelines can reasonably be assumed by library employees to be acting within the limits of fair use; and teachers requesting multiple copies for use in teaching that are far outside the guidelines may nevertheless be acting within the limits of fair use, depending upon the circumstances. Thus libraries, archives and their employees need not in deciding to honor teachers' requests for multiple copies actually count words; in most instances a *coup d'oeil* will inform the employee that a request can be filled.

In the unlikely event that a library infringes a copyright by reproducing multiple classroom copies at the request of a teacher, § 504(c)(2) instructs the court to remit (reduce to zero) any statutory damages recoverable by the copyright proprietor. The likelihood that a proprietor could show that substantial actual (as opposed to statutory) damages occurred by a library's good faith copying of his work or complying with a teacher's request for classroom copies is remote enough to be beyond reasonable concern.

[72] *See* note 42 & accompanying text *supra.* A library that reproduces photocopies for teachers for classroom use should keep a record containing such information as the date the teacher first learned of the contents of the copied work, the date of the request to copy, the date of the contemplated use, the

II. COMMENTARY ON THE COPYRIGHT ACT PROVISIONS

A. *Lending by Libraries*

As previously noted,[73] a number of European countries have moved toward using the copyright laws to regulate library lending. Refusing to follow this European trend, Congress, in the new Copyright Act left unaffected the traditional privilege of libraries to lend copies of copyrighted works without being required to compensate the copyright owners.[74]

Free public lending libraries first opened in the United States during the middle of the nineteenth century.[75] The industrial revolution provided light, literature, leisure time and tax base for the free library movement,[76] and the main currents of nineteenth century American thought supported it.[77] The democratic premise justified a government of the people spending public funds to make information freely available to the people, particularly the underprivileged, whose interest in information was stirred in free public schools. Even industrialists supported public libraries, hoping that the education of the masses would have a stabilizing influence upon their aspirations.[78]

Congress' reconfirmation of the privilege of a library or other owner to lend a copyrighted work[79] carries forward an important

---

number of copies reproduced, the number of students in the class, and the title of the course. The burden of persuading a judge or jury that a use of a copyrighted work was fair is upon the party charged with infringement. Note that if a library's records show that photocopies were provided for patrons who are fair users, these photocopies need not be included in the cumulative totals of § 108 photocopies, if the library is treated as an agent of the user. *See* notes 20-25 & accompanying text *supra*.

73 *See* notes 1-5 & accompanying text *supra*.

74 *See* notes 15-18 & accompanying text *supra*.

75 Durbidge, *Lending Libraries*, 14 ENCYCLOPEDIA LIB. & INFORMATION SCI. 247 (1975). In 1850, the New Hampshire legislature gave local governments taxing authority to raise money for public libraries. Thompson, *Library: History of Libraries from 1600 to World War II*, 17 ENCYCLOPEDIA AMERICANA 307, 314-17 (1977). Other states emulated New Hampshire. Public libraries opened in Boston in 1854, in Cincinnati in 1856 and in Chicago in 1873. *Id.* at 317. There were 963 public libraries in the United States by 1900, McMuller, *The Distribution of Libraries throughout the United States*, 25 LIB. TRENDS 31 (1976), and more than 8,300 by 1975. NATIONAL COMM'N ON LIBRARIES & INFORMATION SCIENCE, TOWARD A NATIONAL PROGRAM FOR LIBRARY AND INFORMATION SERVICES: GOALS FOR ACTION 13 n.4 (1975).

76 *See* S. DITZION, ARSENALS OF A DEMOCRATIC CULTURE 30-49 (1947).

77 J. SHERA, FOUNDATIONS OF THE PUBLIC LIBRARY 200-44 (1949).

78 *See* O. GARCEAU, THE PUBLIC LIBRARY IN THE POLITICAL PROCESS 33-43 (1949).

79 *See* NEW ACT § 109(a).

democratic institution that has become hallowed custom in the United States. The European suggestion that library lending should be regulated for the benefit of authors and copyright owners cannot currently stand in the face of that strong tradition.

B.   *Photocopying by Library Patrons*

Photocopying of copyrighted works by library patrons occurs daily in most of the world's large libraries, including American libraries. The courts of Australia and France have placed a responsibility upon libraries to supervise on-premises photocopying by library users.[80] Congress, however, quite firmly chose not to impose such a requirement upon American libraries.[81] This legislative decision to free libraries from a supervisory role enables libraries to provide users the convenience of copying machines while avoiding the direct or indirect commitment of an additional portion of library resources to supervising the use of the machines or keeping records of their use. The administrative difficulties that libraries charged with supervising user copying would encounter are apparent: Stacks might have to be closed; photocopying machines would have to be supervised, operated by library employees, or excluded from library premises altogether; and library employees might be required to ascertain user identities and purposes, and evaluate them, using such imprecise and expansive terms as "research," "scholarship," "private use," and "fair use."

Relieving libraries from an obligation to supervise photocopying, on the other hand, enables portions of library collections to be made accessible through open stacks and to circulate on and off premises without library supervision. Moreover, users may have access to copying machines in conjunction with open stacks where it is most efficient. As a result, users can conserve time and avoid loans with the attendant potential inconveniences of lost and overdue books.

Although relieving libraries and archives from supervisory roles will probably lead to more frequent infringing photocopying, Congress' decision seems justified. The detriment to copyright owners from such infringements appears preferable to the administrative barriers which supervision would place between users,

---

[80]   *See* notes 8-9 & accompanying text *supra*.
[81]   *See* note 19 & accompanying text *supra*.

and, in the case of public libraries, the books which were purchased with users' tax dollars. Furthermore, the interests of copyright owners are accommodated to some extent. Some photocopying of some copyrighted materials (those published in new
scientific and technical journals and photocopied for possible citation by scholars, for example) contributes directly to the prestige
of the materials photocopied and indirectly to user demand for and
library purchases of or subscriptions to the materials.[82] Moreover,
many users who reproduce single photocopies of articles and short
portions of other works for personal use for purposes of scholarship or research probably are fair users, not infringers.[83] Finally,
all users, including those who are potential infringers, must be
warned by a notice placed on the photocopying machines in libraries that photocopying may not be privileged.[84] Presumably
such signs will deter some potential infringers.

C. *Photocopying by Libraries and Archives*

1. In General

Congress did more than simply free libraries and archives
from an obligation to supervise user photocopying; it also permitted certain libraries and archives themselves to photocopy
copyrighted works for their own purposes and for the benefit of
their users. Only those libraries and archives qualifying under
section 108 as subsection (a) institutions may invoke the copying
privileges. To qualify, a library—however funded and controlled
—must be open to the public, its copying must be without any purpose of commercial advantage, and it must reproduce and distribute only single copies that contain a notice of copyright.[85]

This statutory scheme reflects a congressional decision to accommodate copyright owners minimally, without significantly limiting user access to copyrighted information. By singling out libraries open to the public for the privilege of photocopying, Congress encourages user access to copyrighted works. There are

---

[82] *See* Geo. Fry & Associates, *supra* note 24, at 120-23.

[83] *See* notes 20-25 & accompanying text *supra*. When Congress passed the
Sound Recordings Act of 1971, the House Report stated that "it is not the intention of the Committee to restrain the home recording, from broadcasts or from
tapes or records, of recorded performances, where the home recording is for
private use and with no purpose of reproducing or otherwise capitalizing commercially on it." 1971 U.S. CODE CONG. & AD. NEWS 1566, 1572 (1972).

[84] NEW ACT § 108(f)(1).

[85] *Id.* § 108(a)(1)-(3). *See* notes 26-32 & accompanying text *supra*.

more than 15,000 private, special and academic libraries and archives in the United States.[86]   Insofar as the different treatment
accorded subsection (a) libraries and archives motivates essentially private libraries to open their collections to the general public, Congress will have increased user access to copyrighted and
uncopyrighted information.[87]

However, the availability of the section 108 privileges to special libraries in private firms does not alter the potential liability
of those firms for infringing photocopying by its employees.   If
a firm includes in its organization an engineering department and
a subsection (a) library, and if one of its engineers enters the library
and reproduces an infringing photocopy on a properly labeled machine, the firm will be unable to rely on the immunity from personal liability of its librarian, for the firm will be vicariously liable
for the engineer's infringement in the course of his employment.
Nor will the firm's position change if its engineer requests its librarian to reproduce the photocopy.   Section 108(f)(2) expressly
imposes liability for infringement upon one who, without a privilege, requests a section 108 photocopy, regardless of the immunity
of the librarian who reproduces and distributes the copy.[88]

Copyright owners are also afforded some protection in that
the section 108 privileges of reproduction and distribution are limited to single copies.   Thus the statutory approach seeks to accommodate the desire of users for convenient access to information and the desire of copyright owners for severe, if not absolute,
limitations on user photocopying by striking a balance that does
not significantly increase library costs or impair library services to
users.

While copyright owners in many instances would doubtless
prefer that Congress have disabled libraries and archives from
photocopying for themselves or for users, the decision to grant limited photocopying privileges to institutions that open their collections accords with the American tradition of making information,

---

[86] NATIONAL COMM'N ON LIBRARIES & INFORMATION SCIENCE, *supra* note 65,
at 13 n.4.

[87] NEW ACT § 108(f)(1), relieving libraries from responsibility for user
photocopying and § 107, describing fair use, apply to all libraries, not just subsection (a) libraries.   Some libraries, however, might find in § 108(d) sufficient
additional incentive to open their collections.

[88] NEW ACT § 108(f)(2).

including copyrighted information, widely and inexpensively available.[89]   On this basis alone, limited, uncompensated copying of copyrighted works by libraries with open collections is supportable in the absence of data indicating that photocopying privileges deter authors and publishers from generating new information.[90] The balance struck by Congress seems correct.

2.   Photocopying by Libraries for Library Purposes

a.   *Published Works.*   Because they are open to the public, subsection (a) libraries and archives are more likely than other libraries and archives to suffer loss or damage to works in their collections.   Librarians must of course keep track of and care for the works they purchase.   If they nevertheless suffer a loss, it is theirs.   They must purchase another copy, if purchase is reasonably possible; and searching for replacement copies is something that libraries and most archives do routinely.   The legislature decided, however, that once a library has reasonably but unsuccessfully attempted to purchase a replacement from "the trade," including reprint houses and out-of-print sources, it should be absolved of any duty to the copyright owner.   Placing the burden of investigating the possibility of repurchase upon the institution whose copy is lost or damaged seems obviously correct given the nature of the relations of most libraries and archives with their trade sources.   Likewise, allowing subsection (a) libraries and archives the privilege of reproducing for replacement purposes a copy of a published work that is damaged, deteriorating, lost or stolen, if a replacement copy is not reasonably available for purchase in the trade,[91] seems quite sensible.   Seeking permission from copyright owners of out-of-print works is always burdensome and often expensive, particularly when the whereabouts or identity of the copyright owner is unclear.

---

[89]   The copyright statutes of the American colonial period are interesting in this regard.   The Massachusetts statute required every author to present two printed copies of his book to the library of the University at Cambridge for the use of the university.   North Carolina required the author to deliver one copy of his work for the use of the executive branch of government.   The statutes in Connecticut, Georgia, New York, North Carolina and South Carolina required that copyrighted books be published at a low price and in "sufficient" quantity. *See* Crawford, *Pre-Constitutional Copyright Statutes*, 23 BULL. COPYRIGHT SOC'Y 11 (1975).

[90]   *See, e.g.*, Mazer v. Stein, 347 U.S. 201 (1954).

[91]   NEW ACT § 108(c).   *See* notes 33-39 & accompanying text *supra*.

b. *Unpublished Works.* Congress has also authorized subsection (a) libraries and archives to reproduce copies of previously unpublished works to preserve the original version of the works
or to deposit a copy for research use in another subsection (a)
library or archives.[92] This group of privileges, in conjunction with
the provisions which preempt common law copyright in unpublished works and place all works fixed in a tangible medium of
expression under federal protection,[93] has altered the law of copyright significantly.

Prior to the Gutenberg era, preserved works of authors existed with very few exceptions in single manuscript form.[94] Scholars depended on monasteries to collect and preserve manuscripts,
and travelled from scriptorium to scriptorium to read and to
learn.[95] Property rights in collected manuscripts became a
source of wealth. The more exact the handmade copy, the more
valuable it was.[96] Sometimes a fee was charged for access to read
the manuscripts. Other times a monastery would exchange a privilege to copy for land, cattle or services.[97] This basic property
right in parchment that carried text was in effect the first western
copyright.

The invention of paper, ink and the printing press made it
possible for the first time to produce identical copies of manuscripts. The printing press spelled doom for the old system of
wealth based on the possession of manuscripts. After its invention, a manuscript owner who parted with control of even a single
copy parted with something easily and accurately multiplied. The
law responded to the printing press by articulating the concept of
copyright, which separates from the basic property rights in a manuscript the right to copy and to publish the form of the message
contained in the manuscript. An author may part with copies of
an original work without impairing its potential for generating
wealth, as long as others respect the exclusive right of the owner

---

[92] *Id.* § 108(b). *See* notes 37-38 & accompanying text *supra.*

[93] *See id.* § 301(a); Brown, *Unification: A Cheerful Requiem for Com-
mon Law Copyright,* 24 UCLA L. REV. 1070 (1977); Goldstein, *Preempted
State Doctrines, Involuntary Transfers and Compulsory Licenses: Testing the
Limits of Copyright,* 24 UCLA L. REV. 1107 (1977).

[94] *See* G. PUTNAM, 2 BOOKS AND THEIR MAKERS DURING THE MIDDLE AGES
477-78 (1898).

[95] *Id.*

[96] *Id.* at 481.

[97] *Id.*

of the copyright in the work to reproduce and distribute copies. Because courts eventually applied the new concept of copyright to all works of authorship, including unpublished documents, it became possible for one party to own the basic property rights in an uncopied, uncirculated and unpublished document while another party owned the copyright in the message contained in the document.[98] Thus an author-owner can, as in the case of personal letters, transfer his interest in the physical property in documents while retaining a literary interest that embraces the right to copy or to authorize copying and the right to publish or to authorize publication.[99]

The problem for librarians, archivists and other custodians of unpublished documents under the traditional copyright scheme has been to determine the rights of an owner of a physical property interest in an unpublished work. Since common law copyright protection is perpetual, an archivist with a possessory interest in unpublished documents who did not also control the common law copyrights in those same works had great difficulty in determining what sort of access, if any, could be given to a scholar, and what sort of use, if any, the scholar could make of the documents and their contents.[100]

An author's decision to part with possession of a copy of a work, such as a letter, has suggested to some courts that the person who receives it, and by extension, those who succeed to the receiver's interests, may make some uses of the work, short of reproduction and distribution of full text copies.[101] Yet the number

---

[98] Chamberlain v. Feldman, 300 N.Y. 135, 89 N.E.2d 863 (1949).

[99] Baker v. Libbie, 210 Mass. 599, 97 N.E. 109 (1912). *Cf.* United States v. First Trust Co., 251 F.2d 686 (8th Cir. 1958) (journals of William Clark, who traveled west on the Missouri, Clearwater, Snake and Columbia Rivers with Meriwether Lewis).

[100] *See* Lovett, *Property Rights and Business Records*, 21 AM. ARCHIVIST 259 (1958); Preston, *Problems in the Use of Manuscripts*, 28 AM. ARCHIVIST 367 (1965); Winn, *Common Law Copyright and the Archivist*, 37 AM. ARCHIVIST 375 (1974).

[101] *See, e.g.*, Baker v. Libbie, 210 Mass. 599, 97 N.E. 109 (1912). Concerning the letters of Mary Baker Eddy, the court said

> [T]he receiver [of a personal letter] . . . may destroy or keep at pleasure. Commonly there must be inferred a right of reading or showing to a more or less limited circle of friends and relatives. But in other instances the very nature of the correspondence may be such as to set the seal of secrecy upon its contents. . . . On the other hand, the conventional autograph letters by famous persons signify on their face a license to transfer.

Id. at 606, 97 N.E. at 112. The court said further that the extent of the right of an author of ordinary letters "is to make or restrain a publication but not to

and extent of permissible uses is far from clear.[102] A number of cases permitting scholars and others to make limited unconsented uses of portions of works that have been reproduced in published copies invested with statutory copyright[103] may support the proposition that a scholar may make similar uses of portions of "unpublished" works, especially unpublished but circulated works. A few cases even suggest that in proper circumstances, involving risks to public health or safety, extensive use, including reproduction and distribution of full text copies, may be made of the contents of previously uncirculated documents.[104]

---

prevent a transfer . . . [using publication] in the sense of making public through printing or multiplication of copies." *Id.* at 607, 97 N.E. at 112.

[102] Some years ago, an author writing a biography of Warren G. Harding discovered originals of letters written by Harding in the collection of the library of the Ohio Historical Society. He gained access to the letters, but was thwarted from quoting from them in the published version of his manuscript as a result of a lawsuit commenced by Harding's heir, who owned the exclusive rights to publish the contents of the letters, as opposed to the letters themselves. *See Ohio Court Enjoins Use of Harding Letters*, 186 PUBLISHER'S WEEKLY, Aug. 10, 1964, at 32. The Ohio Historical Society had custody of the letters only temporarily, but during that time the curator made a complete set of photocopies of the letters and delivered them to the editor of the American Heritage for "historic safekeeping." *Id.* at 32. *See also* Duckett & Russell, *The Harding Papers: How Some Were Burned and Some Were Saved*, 62 AM. HERITAGE 24 (Feb. 1965). The Ohio Historical Society, as the owner of the physical letters, should, at common law, have at least the same rights that the addressee had before transferring the letters to the Society. Thus, exhibiting the letters to limited numbers of people and transferring the possession of the letters to another should be permissible. Whether the Society could photocopy the original letters and provide access to or lend such photocopies as a means of preserving the originals, is unclear under common law. Such activities seem wholly unlikely to interfere with the basic economic interest secured by the copyright in the letters, especially if those who receive access to photocopies of originals from the Ohio Historical Society themselves acquire no possessory interest in the photocopies. *But cf.* SmokEnders, Inc. v. Smoke No More, Inc., 184 U.S.P.Q. (BNA) 309, 318 (S.D. Fla. 1974) ("Both unauthorized use of an original document and unauthorized photocopying of the document protected by common law copyright . . . [are] piracy.") Regardless of the method by which a Harding biographer gains access to information in Harding's uncopied, unpublished letters, the copyright proprietor's right to exploit the original letters commercially by means of copies should preclude the Society, and the biographer who receives legitimate access to the letters, from commercially or otherwise exploiting copies of the letters until they pass into the public domain by operation of the new preemptive provisions. *See* NEW ACT § 303.

[103] *See, e.g.*, Rosemont Enterprises, Inc. v. Random House, Inc., 366 F.2d 303 (2d Cir.), *cert. denied*, 385 U.S. 1009 (1966); McMillan & Co. v. King, 223 F. 862 (D. Mass. 1914); Folsom v. Marsh, 9 F. Cas. 342 (C.C.D. Mass. 1841) (No. 4,901); Meeropol v. Nizer, 361 F. Supp. 1063 (S.D.N.Y. 1963); New York Tribune, Inc. v. Otis & Co., 39 F. Supp. 67 (S.D.N.Y. 1941).

[104] *See, e.g.*, Hubbard v. Vosper, [1972] 2 W.L.R. 389, [1972] 1 All E.R. 1023 (C.A.) (Speech of Lord Denning, M.R.). *But see* British Oxygen Co. v. Liquid Air, Ltd., [1925] 1 Ch. 383.

However, the cases justifying extensive uses of unpublished works without the consent of the copyright owner have not occurred with regularity, and their principle does not in any event appear to apply to cases where persons with access wish to reproduce copies of unpublished documents without or against the consent of the copyright owner in pursuit of some purpose less acute than protecting public health or safety. And the fair use cases involving unconsented uses of portions of published works are also regarded as doubtful guides: "The law by bestowing a right of copyright on an unpublished work bestows a right to prevent its being published at all; and even though an unpublished work is not automatically excluded from the defense of 'fair dealing' it is yet a much more substantial breach of copyright than publication of a published work."[105] The Anglo-American law of unpublished documents is in truth not refined, and statutory guidance on the subject is therefore welcome. Section 108(b) now authorizes subsection (a) libraries to reproduce and distribute single full text copies of unpublished works, without the consent of the copyright owner.

This new statutory privilege to reproduce copies of unpublished works will help guard against destruction of the originals, or will at least ensure the existence of copies in the event of such destruction. Those who own a possessory interest in original uncopied manuscripts have a power to destroy them. Franz Kafka directed Max Brod to destroy all copies of Kafka's unpublished manuscripts.[106] Had Brod obeyed, German and Austrian literature would have been denied Kafka's influence. Conversely, Isabel Arundell Burton gratuitously burned the works of her husband, Sir Richard Burton, in progress at his death.[107] After writing a highly romanticized biography, she also burned most of Sir Richard's diaries and journals, at some cost to the literature of history and anthropology.[108]

Significant unpublished business, personal and government records that are beyond public access[109] are also vulnerable to efforts to destroy them, or to revise their contents. Both American

---

105 Beloff v. Pressdram Ltd., [1973] 1 All E.R. 241 (Ch.).
106 F. KAFKA, THE TRIAL 326-35 (Modern Lib. ed. post script to 1st ed. 1925).
107 F. BRODIE, THE DEVIL DRIVES: A LIFE OF SIR RICHARD BURTON (1967).
108 *Id.*
109 Access to the records of the agencies and offices of the federal government of the United States, despite recent legislation increasing accessibility, is, in

and British governments impose substantial barriers to access to the records of the offices and agencies of government by electors and by critics.[110] If in addition a copyright law or a custom among archivists inhibits the reproduction of copies of secret, private, un-circulated, unduplicated or unpublished documents, films, and phonorecords the likelihood increases that significant records will be edited, altered, censored or destroyed to serve a transient per-sonal interest. In fact, past custodians of official documents, in-cluding professional historians, have consistently recharacterized reports of their contents to accommodate notions of propriety or loyalty.[111]

Altering and destroying original sources are prime crimes against history. Accordingly, professional custodians who acquire the physical possession of unduplicated documents but not the copyright should be privileged to reproduce a copy immediately upon obtaining possession to insure the preservation of the origi-nals, and to distribute a copy or copies to make destruction and alteration more difficult.[112]

Section 108(b) permits subsection (a) libraries that ob-tain the possessory interest in Nixon's tapes, Plath's letters, Ein-stein's notebooks, General Motors' dossiers, the Atomic Energy Commission's files, and the records of the Continental Congress to reproduce and distribute copies, for the enumerated purposes. The new Copyright Act therefore contributes significantly to the likelihood that professional historians will consult fewer altered sources and will have fewer opportunities to alter sources them-selves. Moreover, giving a privilege to libraries and archives to produce and distribute copies of unpublished works to other li-braries and archives increases the probability that the information in such documents will become widely available: Some copyright owners will publish copies of such works formally, rather than sub-mit to the royalty-free distribution of copies to libraries and ar-chives authorized by section 108(b); and when formal publication does not occur, the informal process authorized by section 108(b) can operate.

---

the judgment of some, woefully inadequate for the purposes of democratic rule. *See* Miller & Cox, *On the Need for a National Commission On Documentary Access*, 44 GEO. WASH. L. REV. 213 (1976).

[110] *See* Feis, *The Shackled Historian*, 45 FOREIGN AFF. 332 (1967).

[111] *See* NATIONAL HISTORICAL PUBLICATIONS COMMISSION, A REPORT TO THE PRESIDENT CONTAINING A PROPOSAL 9 (1963).

[112] *Id.*

c. *A Limitation on Copies for Library Purposes: Facsimile Form.* Sections 108(b) and 108(c) limit the right of reproduction and distribution of copies by libraries and archives for library purposes to copies duplicated in facsimile form.[113] While library copies may be made of photographs and motion pictures as well as of printed information, the copies must be in eye-readable, rather than machine-readable format.[114]

This limitation is consistent with Congress' decision, reflected throughout the Act, to refuse to define the scope of copyright as it relates to computerized data base systems.[115] The facsimile form limitation allows libraries and archives to use the various photocopying and microform processes when exercising section 108 privileges. Thus a library may reproduce from its own microform holdings a microform user copy for use in a home reader and may reproduce facsimile copies from a cathode tube or other display unit attached to a computerized data base system.[116] However, transfer of copyrighted information from an original medium onto magnetic tape or any similar means of storing information in a computerized system is not permitted without the consent of the copyright owner.

3. Photocopying by Libraries and Archives for Individual Users

In section 108(d), Congress authorized libraries and archives to reproduce and distribute to users directly or by interlibrary loan single copies of no more than one article or other contribution to a copyrighted periodical, or a small part of other types of copyrighted works.[117] This controversial privilege has several conditions: the library or archives must place language informing users about the law of copyright on a prominent sign at the place where orders are accepted and on its order forms;[118] the library cannot have notice that the copy it distributes to the user will be used for any purpose other than "private study, scholarship or research";[119] and the copy must become the property of the user.[120]

---

[113] *See* notes 38-40 & accompanying text *supra*.
[114] NEW ACT § 108(b)-(c).
[115] *See id.* § 117.
[116] For a discussion of present and future microform technology, see N. HENRY, 1 COPYRIGHT—INFORMATION TECHNOLOGY—PUBLIC POLICY 30-33 (1976).
[117] *See* notes 42-49 & accompanying text *supra*.
[118] NEW ACT § 108(d)(1).
[119] *Id.*
[120] *Id.*

These conditions are not overly burdensome. The cost of a sign and the cost of a couple of sentences on an order form are insignificant. The regular use of order forms might itself entail more substantial costs, especially if the forms are stored after use. The statute, however, does not require that forms be used, or if they are used, that they be stored. The condition that the library have no notice of a user's improper purpose in seeking a copy does not require the library affirmatively to seek any information about his identity, status or affiliation, or to make any judgments as to a user's intended purpose.[121] All that is necessary is that a library not distribute a copy to a user after receiving actual notice that he will use it improperly.

The ability of subsection (a) libraries to reproduce and distribute to users copies of articles and small parts of other works free from serious restraints illustrates Congress' decision to favor the interests of libraries, archives and users over the interests of many authors and most publishers. It cannot be assumed, however, that all authors are opposed to royalty-free reproduction of their copyrighted works.

A large number of authors make a living from their writing. They consider their creations to be private property as much as land titles or oil leases are, and think it fair that those who use any portion of their work pay for the privilege. Poets, short story writers, novelists and essayists whose works are anthologized and excerpted for texts often earn relatively substantial amounts of income by granting permissions.[122] Such authors think it pernicious that a book store could be persuaded to reproduce and distribute a photocopy of a book or a portion of it to a user whose purpose is studying the photocopy, or using it for research or scholarship.[123] To such authors, library photocopies do not present a dramatically different case.[124]

---

[121] Note that records of photocopies provided for users that describe the users' identity and purpose may enable a library to justify user photocopies as produced for the fair use of another. *See* note 22 *supra*. While § 108 user photocopies need not be so justified, user photocopies that can be so justified need not be included in the cumulative totals of § 108 photocopies.

[122] *See* Karp, *Copyright—the Author's View*, COPYRIGHT—THE LIBRARIAN AND THE LAW 44 (G. Lukac ed. 1972).

[123] *See id.* at 39-45.

[124] This position on library photocopying is best stated by David Catterns: "As I see it, the principle is simple: as a result of reprography, the authors' work is useful in a new way; he ought to share in the benefits of this new usefulness." Catterns, The American's Baby *by Moorhouse: An Australian Story of Copyright and the New Technology*, 23 BULL. COPYRIGHT SOC'Y 213, 226 (1976).

Other groups of authors, especially those employed by colleges, universities, government agencies and industrial firms, express a greater concern for the dissemination of information. The usual goals of these authors, who often write in scientific and technical fields, are to disseminate information, to advance art and science and to increase the prestige of the author or the employing institution.[125] Most of these authors write for professional journals, receive no fee or royalty for their effort and in some cases even pay page charges to publishers to help finance the publication of their contributions. Their desire is that the contents of their work receive wide distribution, including distribution by formal republication in texts and journals as well as by photocopying single copies of the original publication for individual users. These authors are often willing to let others make such uses of their work without payment of royalties.[126]

However, editors and publishers are, as a group, opposed to royalty-free copying.[127] In fact, many publishers of scientific journals have developed a dual price system for their journals under which institutions, such as libraries, pay a much higher subscription charge than individual subscribers. This higher charge is designed in part to compensate publishers for photocopying by and for users in libraries.[128] Textbook publishers also resist uncompensated photocopying of portions of their materials. Publishers of advanced treatises and encyclopedias depend upon libraries for sales. They regard the imposition of photocopying

---

[125] George Fry & Assoc., *supra* note 24, at 81-84; L. HATTERY & G. BUSH, REPROGRAPHY AND COPYRIGHT LAW 120 (1964).

[126] According to one view,

[The scientific researcher] utilizes other people's results in order to achieve a usually tiny advance in the field of human knowledge. In the same way, he places the results of his work at the disposal of everyone . . . so that his findings can in turn be plundered to form the basis of future progress. The mutual renunciation of copyright is implicit in this process . . . .

Arntz, *Reprography and Copyright*, 11 COPYRIGHT 95, 96 (1975).

[127] Indeed, after the Court of Claims decided that the photocopying involved in the *Williams & Wilkins* case did not constitute copyright infringement, the Emergency Care Research Institute announced publicly that it would deny the National Institute of Health and the National Library of Medicine any further purchases of its publication, *Health Devices*, until NIH and NLM agreed to pay a fee for photocopying in addition to the subscription charge. White, *Copyright Decision*, 183 SCIENCE 698 (1974). *See also* Passano, *How Photocopying Pollutes Sci-Tech Publishing*, TECHNOLOGY AND COPYRIGHT 266 (G. Bush ed. 1966).

[128] Walsh, JOURNALS: *Photocopying Is Not the Only Problem*, 183 SCIENCE 1274, 1275 (1974).

royalties in addition to sales prices as a means of recouping the high costs of preparing and publishing such books.[129]   Elementary school, high school and college texts require substantial prepublication expenditures[130] that usually are not recovered for several years; moreover, even when profits are finally generated, they typically are not high.[131]   Publishers of such texts believe that the expense and risk of publication are so great as to justify a rule against royalty-free photocopying, even of small parts of a work and for the use of students.[132]

However, some editors and publishers, primarily those who publish scientific, technical and professional journals, consider limited photocopying of their publications justified and even desirable.   "A large number [of journal editors] believe[s] that the results of research should be made freely available to all scholars."[133]   In fact, although most scientific and technical journals published by commercial publishers are copyrighted, many noncommercial editors and publishers do not attempt to control the use of their journals' contents by copyrighting the journal.[134]

An examination of the privilege to copy and distribute articles thus reveals that this privilege does not deviate substantially from the desires of authors and publishers.   The authors and publishers most willing to permit royalty-free copying of their works are those connected with scholarly works.   Common sense supports a tentative conclusion that the privilege will usually be invoked by users of just such works.   In the case of current commercial magazines, it would probably often be cheaper to purchase a given issue than to pay photocopying charges.

It must also be emphasized that without such a privilege for library copying and distribution, the interests of scholars and students would be severely undermined.   As a group, researchers,

---

[129]   L. HATTERY & G. BUSH, *supra* note 125, at 108-09.

[130]   These costs range from $50,000 for a simple text to $7 million for an encyclopedia.   Henry, *Copyright, Public Policy and Information Technology,* 183 SCIENCE 384, 388 (1974).

[131]   McGraw-Hill's 1000-title list of science and high technology titles returns only 2% of the company's profits.   *Soaring Prices and Sinking Sales of Science Monographs,* 183 SCIENCE 282 (1974).   Profits in elementary and high school texts declined slightly in 1972-75.   *Economic Review of the Book Industry,* PUBLISHER'S WEEKLY, July 26, 1976, at 58.

[132]   L. HATTERY & G. BUSH, *supra* note 125, at 109-10.   George Fry & Assoc., *supra* note 24, at 84-89.

[133]   NATIONAL SCIENCE FOUNDATION, CHARACTERISTICS OF SCIENTIFIC JOURNALS 1949-1959, at 8-9 (1964).

[134]   *Id.* at 8.

teachers and students agree that published information should be freely available for copying for private use. While most users could probably pay a photocopying royalty without unduly altering the portion of their personal resources allocated to essential goods and services, almost no user from the listed groups could afford to purchase from publishers the books and journals containing the articles and chapters they photocopy as part of a program of research or study. Even the most dedicated professional scientists subscribe to only a small number of professional journals, usually from two to four.[135] They depend on libraries and archives for information, and they photocopy much of what they find useful in the collections. It is, moreover, difficult to conclude that this practice of royalty-free photocopying unfairly uses the work of the author and publisher. For years, users have been able to go to libraries, borrow materials and take notes of their contents. Now users make photocopies in lieu of fallible notes. They underline, mark-up, annotate and otherwise use photocopies of articles, chapters and sections.[136] They free themselves not only from library schedules and surroundings, but from errors in quotations and citations and from inexact summaries.[137] The result of their use of the copyrighted materials they consult is not much different than would have been the case had they sat in the library making careful notes. Their efficiency and independence increase because of developments in the technology of reprography, for which they as consumers pay. In such cases, an additional payment to copyright owners is unwarranted.

It is probably the case that students use library collections somewhat differently than professional scholars and researchers. The new legislation takes this difference into account. Like professional researchers, students cannot afford to purchase from publishers much of what they read in pursuit of their studies.[138] Unlike professional researchers, they tend to request from libraries and read materials that are basic to a field and therefore much in demand by their fellow students. Materials consulted by students are often "on two hour reserve," and students may choose

135 George Fry & Assoc., *supra* note 24, at 118.
136 L. HATTERY & G. BUSH, *supra* note 125, at 69-72.
137 *See id.* at 49.
138 *Cf.* Letter, From Assoc. of American Law Schools to Rep. Kastenmeier, *excerpted*, 122 CONG. REC. H10,881 (daily ed. Sept. 22, 1976).

to photocopy those materials to free themselves from such strictures on circulation, or to ask the library to reproduce and distribute a photocopy in lieu of a two-hour loan. Libraries that photocopy articles and chapters for students probably reproduce more copies of the same articles and chapters than libraries that photocopy articles and chapters for professional researchers. Thus copying for student users may have aggregate effects on library purchases and subscriptions that copying for professional users does not have. Libraries that photocopy articles and chapters for students without restraint may purchase fewer duplicates of books and journals from publishers than would be the case were copying machines unavailable.

Congress was sensitive to that possibility. Section 108(g)(2), therefore, limits the privilege of a library or archives to reproduce and distribute copies of the same material to the making of *isolated and unrelated copies in an unsystematic way*. Although this limitation does not delineate what constitutes systematic reproduction, it is possible to suggest guidelines by considering other legislative provisions. In the case of user photocopies reproduced and distributed in inter-library transactions, Congress prohibits the receipt by a requesting library or archives of such a number of copies of the same material that the photocopies "substitute for a subscription to or purchase of such work."[139] The Conference Report interprets this language to limit requests for inter-library loans to five photocopies per year of articles published within the preceding five years from issues of the same periodical.[140] One may infer from the five copy guideline for photocopies of articles from journals to which a library does not subscribe, that the permissible number of photocopies of articles from journals to which a library does subscribe that may be reproduced and distributed to users is greater than five. A book or an issue of a periodical possessed by a library that circulates every two weeks can be used without restriction by twenty-five borrowers a year; a book or an issue of a periodical that circulates every two hours can be used freely by twenty-five to fifty borrowers a week. This suggests that when the combined instances of loans and library reproduced photocopies of a work approach the approximate circulation rate for that type of work that would obtain in the absence of photocopying, the photocopying is substituting for a purchase or subscription. At

[139] NEW ACT § 108(g)(2). *See* notes 54-62 & accompanying text *supra*.
[140] CONF. REP. at 72-73.

that point, the library should acquire an additional copy or subscription. As a rule of thumb, a library that reproduces and distributes to users more than twenty-five single copies in any one week of an article or excerpt from a work on reserve, or more than twenty-five single copies in any one year of a work circulated for two week periods, should purchase a second subscription to the periodical or a second copy of the book or compilation.

Until now, libraries have generally tended to purchase multiple copies of books and periodicals based upon actual or anticipated use by borrowers. Lists of users waiting to borrow copies of best sellers usually induce public libraries to purchase additional copies.[141] Inclusion of a book or article on an assigned reading list for a course has normally moved academic librarians to acquire additional copies according to the number of students in the course. A sudden and unexpectedly heavy demand by borrowers to use the sole copy of a work in a library in most cases causes librarians to resort to photocopies only in the short run, and thereafter to purchase additional copies from the publisher, assuming the demand continues. Therefore the possibility of a library that depends primarily upon circulation engaging in systematic photocopying which substitutes for an additional subscription to a given work is not great.

An apparently difficult problem arises where an instructor recommends an article or chapter to students in his class. Librarians should respond by reproducing for students only that number of photocopies upon which the librarians have previously settled as acceptable. If more copies are demanded, students can borrow the materials and make their own photocopies or ask the instructor to exercise his fair use privilege to reproduce copies for them. If the instructor's fair use privilege does not apply and the library cannot provide a sufficient number of photocopies to meet the demand, the library will know that it must buy additional copies to meet similar requests the next time the course is taught. The library that adheres to a rule of thumb on the number of photocopies of the same work it will make for student users in a one week period puts pressure upon itself to purchase additional copies of materials in continual demand. Publishers cannot reasonably expect anything more, especially since a library may simply choose

---

[141] Telephone Interview, Acquisitions Department, Austin Public Libraries, Austin, Texas.

to circulate works in heavy demand knowing that many student borrowers will themselves reproduce photocopies of the borrowed work, probably with a privilege, and in any event with a practical guarantee of freedom from challenge by copyright owners.[142]

Copyright owners may find some satisfaction in learning that the use of photocopies to substitute for original material sometimes generates subscriptions. Indeed, in the *Williams & Wilkins* case, an expert witness testified that many professional researchers will not put their names on library waiting lists for journals, sit in libraries and take notes by hand, or write to publishers to request reprints.[143] In short, they will not read some articles that they would read if photocopies were available.[144] Such unread articles then become uncited articles; uncited articles remain unread articles; and journals of unread and uncited articles remain journals with limited subscription lists. In this sense photocopies of articles reproduced and distributed to professional researchers in lieu of loans of published copies[145] can, through the process of citation, contribute indirectly to an increase in subscriptions. The mere request for photocopies of articles can also lead to subscriptions by libraries. Often a librarian photocopies articles that could be delivered less expensively by purchase.[146] Inter-library loan transactions involving photocopies of articles or small portions of books often cost both libraries eight or ten dollars.[147] Whenever the annual cost of photocopying materials from a particular journal exceeds the journal's yearly subscription fee, common economic sense dictates that the librarian subscribe to the journal.[148]

---

[142] In the legislative history of the Sound Recording Amendment passed in 1971, the House Judiciary Committee stated that it had no intention to restrain the home recording of recorded performances for private use, saying "This practice is common and unrestrained today . . . ." 1971 U.S. CODE CONG. & AD. NEWS 1566, 1572 (1972).

[143] Williams & Wilkins Co. v. United States, 487 F.2d 1345, 1358 (Ct. Cl. 1973), aff'd per curiam, 420 U.S. 376 (1975).

[144] *Id.*

[145] One empirically supported survey of library photocopying practices, doubtless somewhat outdated, concluded that as of the early 1960's, photocopies did not often act as replacements for subscriptions. In most cases, the photocopy served as a substitute for a loan of the original material. George Fry & Assoc., *supra* note 24, at 117, 119-20.

[146] *Id.* at 105.

[147] Stevenson, *The Doctrine of Fair Use as It Affects Libraries*, 68 LAW LIB. J. 254, 267-69 (1975).

[148] *See* NATIONAL COMM'N ON LIBRARIES & INFORMATION SCIENCE, *supra* note 75, at 55-57. "A library expecting six or more uses of any material is

Copyright owners fear that under the new Copyright Act, librarians will rely more heavily upon photocopies than subscriptions because of the explicit privilege to photocopy for users. Yet Congress' decision to permit libraries and archives to photocopy articles and small portions of larger works for users is consistent with its decision to permit users in libraries to photocopy for themselves.[149] Permitting librarians to photocopy for users, with attendant flourishes of copyright notices and warnings, and strictures against systematic copying, insures a greater general regard for the interests of copyright owners than would result from placing the matter wholly in the hands of users. At the same time, it incidentally enables librarians and archivists to provide full user services without losing physical control of all of the materials in their collections.

Doubtless the new Copyright Act will lead to more photocopying by libraries and archives for users than occurred under the Copyright Act of 1909. Under the New Act, instances will occur where librarians will reproduce and distribute a photocopy to users in circumstances where, under the old law, they would have provided the user with nothing, purchased an authorized copy, or depended upon the user to reproduce the work.[150] The photocopying privileges in the Act extend the basic policy of free lending and unsupervised use of library collections. The Act is not without limitations, however. The five copy per year per requesting library guideline on interlibrary transactions protects copyright owners against one of their persistent fears: that a central library will purchase single copies of books and periodicals then reproduce an endless number of photocopies at the request of hundreds of affiliated libraries who serve users primarily by distributing photocopies reproduced by the central library. Only experience will show whether future library photocopying for users will lead to a decrease in multiple subscriptions by each library. In the meantime, Congress cannot be seriously faulted for anticipating that a decrease will not occur, and for permitting librarians and

---

better off buying it." Baker, Grannes & Reuter, *Scholarly Publishers Survey Their "Interdependence,"* PUBLISHER'S WEEKLY, Aug. 9, 1976, at 35.

[149] *See* text accompanying notes 20-25 *supra.*

[150] The policy of the Library of Congress in recent years has been not to photocopy copyrighted materials without the signed authorization of the copyright owner. *See* Williams & Wilkins Co. v. United States, 487 F.2d 1345, 1355 n.16 (Ct. Cl. 1973), *aff'd per curiam,* 420 U.S. 376 (1975); V. CLAPP, COPYRIGHT—A LIBRARIAN'S VIEW (1968).

users to enjoy the many side benefits that accrue to both libraries and users when photocopies substitute for library loans, but not for library purchases or subscriptions.

D. *Library Networks and Consortia*

At the beginning of 1976, there were more than sixty library networks in the United States, the members of which shared resources through inter-library loan transactions or shared information about catalog contents, materials location and acquisitions through printed compilations or by on-line access to a computerized data base containing such information.[151] The community libraries of suburban Chicago,[152] the libraries of Harvard, Yale and Columbia Universities and New York City,[153] and the libraries of the many campuses of the California State University System[154] constitute three of the sixty networks.

The usual goal of a library network is to provide resources to users when and where requested at low cost.[155] Networks pursue this goal in different ways, and so the characteristics of networks differ. Nevertheless, networks can be classified into two groups: Those that exchange information to enable members to rationalize acquisitions, and those that do not exchange information to enable members to rationalize acquisitions.

In a network that does not rationalize members' acquisitions, members share computers and programs to locate, order, pay for and catalog acquisitions; to store and retrieve bibliographic information and to accomplish other purposes.[156] For example, the acquisitions department at Stanford University uses a computer

---

[151] ERIC CLEARINGHOUSE ON INFORMATION RESOURCES, ACRONYMS AND INITIALISMS OF LIBRARY NETWORKS (2d version 1975). *See also* NATIONAL COMM'N ON LIBRARIES & INFORMATION SCIENCE, *supra* note 75, at 57; Mayhew, *Computerized Networks Among Libraries and Universities: An Administrator's Overview*, 5 INFORMATION REP. & BIBLIOGRAPHIES 2 (1976).

[152] *See* Frisbie, *Revolution on the Prairie: Library Networking in Suburban Illinois*, PUBLISHER'S WEEKLY, June 21, 1976, at 66.

[153] *See* Weinberg, *The Photocopying Revolution and the Copyright Crisis*, 38 PUB. INTEREST 99, 101 (1975).

[154] Kountz, *Library Support Through Automation: The California State University and Colleges Plan For Library Automation*, 8 J. LIB. AUTOMATION 98 (1975).

[155] Kilgour, *Library Networks*, PROCEEDINGS, EDUCOM FALL CONFERENCE 38 (1973).

[156] See Mayhew, *supra* note 151, at 2-8.

based system, called BALLOTS which enables the various libraries at Stanford to use the system to order a book or periodical, record the arrival of the acquisition, trace its progress until it is shelved, make a catalog card describing its contents and record full bibliographic information about the acquisition in the appropriate files of the computerized data base.[157]   Each library in the network can consult the data base to learn about the status of the acquisitions in process or the holdings of its own library or any other library using the BALLOTS program and data base.

PHILSOM is a program and data base originating at the Washington University School of Medicine and used presently by eight geographically dispersed medical libraries.[158]   Its primary purpose is to share bibliographic information rather than to facilitate acquisitions. PHILSOM provides members with bibliographic information about the contents of approximately 11,000 periodicals even though about half of the described periodicals are not held by any member library.[159]

Information about the contents of bibliographies and catalogs, the titles and status of acquisitions in process and the location of holdings is not protected by copyright.[160]   Therefore its exchange does not interfere with any legally protected interest of copyright owners.   Thus, members of networks can use such information to make decisions about purchases and subscriptions. For example, one library in a University or one library in a metropolitan area may learn that three other libraries in the University or metropolitan area subscribe to the American Economic Review and may decide to forego or cancel its own subscription, reasoning that the needs of potential borrowers of issues of the American Economic Review can be met by other libraries, either by direct loans from their collections, or indirectly, through inter-library transactions.

The decision to forego or cancel a subscription, based on an exchange of information in a library network, though it results in fewer subscriptions to the American Economic Review by the libraries in the University or in the metropolitan area, is a decision within the power of the librarian making it, and the resulting diminution in subscriptions is beyond redress by the owner of the

---

[157] *Id*. at 6.
[158] *Id*. at 7.
[159] *Id*.
[160] *See* notes 186-87 & accompanying text *infra*.

copyright in the affected periodical, for the law of copyright does not compel purchases or subscriptions or forbid members of library networks to "rationalize" acquisitions.

Indeed, in a network that rationalizes members' acquisitions, members can save thousands of dollars in subscriptions to little-used journals and books by eliminating uncoordinated subscriptions or purchases by each member of the network and substituting subscriptions or purchases by one member, or several, in the minimum quantity necessary to meet the needs of all the members' users, either through direct requests for loans by users entered at a member library holding the works or through indirect requests for inter-library loans for users by members whose holdings have been rationalized to exclude the requested works.[161] While the number of networks that presently rationalizes acquisitions is small, it is growing larger.[162]

Under the new Copyright Act, it is clear that one member of a rationalizing network may inform its patrons of the location of works held by other members of the network, and may direct them to the appropriate library.[163]   Just as certainly, one member of a rationalizing network may request that another member deliver the physical possession of a held work to the requesting member, on inter-library loan for the use of a patron.[164]   Quite probably, in certain circumstances, one member of a rationalizing network may supply another member with a section 108 photocopy, in lieu of an inter-library loan of the physical possession of a copyrighted work, if the members exchanging the photocopy jointly purchased and jointly own the photocopied work.[165]

It is also possible that a member of a rationalizing network may request for the use of its patron a section 108 inter-library loan

---

[161]   *See* LIBRARY NETWORKS '74-'75 (S. Goldstein & M. Miller eds. 1974).

[162]   *Id.*

[163]   *See* note 160 *supra.*

[164]   NEW ACT § 109(a).

[165]   Assume a work of limited interest and expensive to purchase. Assume that circulation of one copy of the work could meet the needs of all of the potential patrons of each of the members of a rationalizing network, if the potential patrons would travel to the library holding the work. Assume no single library can afford to purchase a copy. If all or some of the members of the network purchase a single copy of the work jointly, and provide patrons with access by direct loans and § 108 inter-library loan photocopies, then the photocopies, though greater in number than five, would not appear to substitute, in purpose or effect, for a purchase of the work.

photocopy of a work excluded from its holdings from a library not a member of a rationalizing network.[166]

The availability to members of rationalizing networks of relatively inefficient inter-library loan possibilities would have little significance if members are permitted by the New Act simply and freely to exchange section 108 photocopies. The fact is, however, that the New Act emphatically disables network members who exchange information to rationalize acquisitions from sharing resources through inter-library loan transactions involving photocopies. Section 108(g) states that the limited privilege of one library to reproduce single copies of journal articles and small parts of other copyrighted works and distribute them does not extend

> to cases where the library or archives . . . is aware . . .
> that it is engaging in the related or concerted reproduction or
> distribution of multiple copies . . . of the same material
> . . . over a period of time . . . or engages in the systematic reproduction or distribution of single or multiple
> copies . . . of material described in subsection (d) [periodical articles and small parts of other copyrighted works] . . . .

The words "concerted reproduction" in section 108(g)(1) plainly prohibit the reproduction and distribution of photocopies by members of a network that has as one of its goals rationalizing the acquisitions of its members. If two libraries agree that one will purchase titles A through M, that the other will purchase titles N through Z, and that each will supply the other's users with photocopies, the reproduction and distribution of even a single photocopy of a portion of a single work by one library for the other would be the product of a plan accomplished together and would therefore be a "concerted" copy.

The Senate Report confirms the view that unprivileged reproduction and distribution occurs "when a library makes copies . . . available to other libraries or to groups of users under formal or informal arrangements whose purpose or effect is to have the reproducing library serve as their source of material."[167] Among the examples of unprivileged copies listed in the Report are: a

---

[166] This result requires that § 108(g), which states that the section 108 privileges do not extend to cases where a library is aware that it is engaging in the related or concerted reproduction or distribution of multiple copies, be interpreted to apply to the state of mind of the sending library and not the requesting library, and upon the sending library in the particular case not being "aware," etc.

[167] S. REP. at 70.

copy distributed to one library by another library that has announced that it will maintain and build its own collection in a particular field and make copies of materials in that field available to other libraries on request; and a copy distributed to one branch of a library system by another branch under an agreement that the one branch will purchase particular materials and distribute photocopies to the other in lieu of each branch's purchasing the same materials separately.[168]

The House Report acknowledges that section 108(g) "provoked a storm of controversy centering around the extent to which the restrictions on 'systematic' activities would prevent the continuation and development of inter-library networks and other arrangements involving the exchange of photocopies."[169] However, the only addition to section 108(g)(2) in response to this controversy was language stating that nothing in section 108(g)(2) "prevents a library or archives from participating in inter-library arrangements that do not have, *as their purpose or effect*, that the library or archives receiving such copies or phonorecords . . . does so in such aggregate quantities as to substitute for a subscription to or purchase of such work."[170]

Thus the language of section 108(g) and its history indicate that the exchange of photocopies by members of networks formed to permit libraries to concentrate on maintaining and expanding particular sections of their collections while depending upon other members to supply royalty-free photocopies of copyrighted materials which the requesting members do not own themselves is not permissible. The privilege of libraries to distribute in an inter-library loan transaction a royalty-free photocopy of a published copyrighted work in print is limited to copies of journal articles and small portions of other works, reproduced and distributed without substituting in purpose or in effect for a purchase or subscription.

---

[168] *Id.*

[169] H. REP. at 77-78.

[170] *Id.* at 78. The Report of the Conference Committee states only that § 108(g)(2) of the Act deals with limits on interlibrary arrangements for photocopying and permits arrangements involving journal articles and small parts of other works that do not in purpose or effect substitute for purchases or subscriptions. CONF. REP. at 72. The five copy guideline, *see* notes 54-57 & accompanying text *supra*, defines "effect" in the phrase "purpose or effect" and the one copy analysis, *see* note 168 & accompanying text *supra*, defines "purpose".

Library networks are not confined by technology to inter-library loans of originals and photocopies.

Interlibrary networking which utilizes modern technology to provide to members and users on-line access to data banks containing full texts of copyrighted works is currently feasible.[171] The contents of printed works can be stored in computer data banks and made available for display and photocopying to all libraries, firms and homes that wish to link into the system. The National Library of Medicine has already developed significant programs to make bio-medical information widely available. Its Medlars program provides regional medical libraries with access to a computerized data base containing titles to articles and studies in the bio-medical field, and to index terms for retrieval of the titles. In 1972, a portion of this data base was made accessible throughout the country, through a commercial time-sharing service, to physicians and medical librarians having computer terminals.[172] Since 1972, the data base has been improved and enlarged. The system—now Medlars II—still provides users with primarily bibliographic information, but can also communicate full texts of articles, abstracts, summaries and digests.[173]

In the legal field, two automated search and retrieval systems usable by libraries, firms and individuals already exist. WEST-LAW utilizes as a data base the West Publishing Company's head-notes to reported cases, the bulk of which are protected by statutory copyright. When fully operational, the system will permit keyboard access, cathode tube visual display and IBM copier print-out wherever a terminal is located.[174] LEXIS uses a data bank of files containing the full text of statutes and reported opinions. It permits subscribers to search for, display, and retrieve copies of any information in the system, wherever they choose to

---

171 *See* SOPHAR & HEILPRIN, THE DETERMINATION OF LEGAL FACTS AND ECONOMIC GUIDEPOSTS WITH RESPECT TO THE DISSEMINATION OF SCIENTIFIC AND ECONOMIC INFORMATION AS IT IS AFFECTED BY COPYRIGHT—A STATUS REPORT 49 (1967).

172 R. HAYES & J. BECKER, HANDBOOK OF DATA PROCESSING FOR LIBRARIES 43-44 (1974).

173 Katter & Pearson, *Medlars II: A Third Generation Bibliographic Production System*, 8 J. LIB. AUTOMATION 87 (1975).

174 *See* J. SPROWL, A MANUAL FOR COMPUTER-ASSISTED LEGAL RESEARCH 55-57 (1976); Dee & Kessler, *The Impact of Computerized Methods on Legal Research Courses: A Survey of LEXIS Experience and Some Probable Effects of WESTLAW*, 69 LAW LIB. J. 164 (1976).

locate a terminal.[175] Neither of these systems, as described, utilizes a data base of material in which others own copyrights, but each system would be enhanced by the inclusion of the contents of copyrighted texts and journals.

It would be strange indeed if Congress had disabled libraries and archives from forming networks to utilize photocopies of copyrighted works delivered by mail or courier[176] but had permitted libraries and archives to form networks to utilize computerized transmissions of the text of copyrighted works. Congress, of course, did no such thing. The facsimile form limitation on copying for library purposes[177] effectively eliminates most electronic delivery systems. By prohibiting reproduction of the work "in 'machine-readable' language for storage in an information system,"[178] distribution of the work in machine readable language to a user of another library would also seem to be precluded. Moreover, while the provisions governing copying and distribution for users[179] do not explicitly confine libraries and archives to copies duplicated in facsimile form, the limitation on privileged interlibrary loan arrangements to those that are the product of unconcerted and unsystematic transactions places a nearly total prohibition on library loan transactions involving the communication of copies in any form.[180] Indeed, the whole thrust of section 108(g) is to prevent libraries from permanently or systematically sharing copyrighted resources through the use of modern technology without the consent of copyright owners. Thus the provisions of section 108 offer no basis for supposing that a library or archives may purchase a terminal, tie into a data base at another library or archives and, without the owners' consent, systematically provide its users with transmitted copies of the contents of copyrighted works in that other library's collection.[181]

---

[175]   See J. SPROWL, supra note 174, at 10-15; Dee & Kessler, note 174 supra.

[176]   See notes 167-70 & accompanying text supra.

[177]   See notes 38-40, 114-16 & accompanying text supra.

[178]   H. REP. at 75.

[179]   NEW ACT § 108(d)-(e), (g). See generally notes 41-62 & accompanying text supra.

[180]   See notes 167-70 & accompanying text supra.

[181]   Indeed, it is very doubtful that a library may ever freely transfer information from copyrighted works in its own collection in traditional format to a machine-readable format for use at its own facility. Section 117 of the New Act states that the use of copyrighted works in automatic systems capable of storing, retrieving and transferring their contents shall be governed by the law as it has evolved under the Copyright Act of 1909 and the common law and statutes of

A national network of libraries, archives and information services using automated systems would be wonderfully convenient and may even become indispensable.[182]   However, libraries may not begin the transition from the present information system of paper, print and mechanical delivery to computerized systems at the expense of copyright owners.   Nor may a system of networking using facsimile transmission or hand delivery of photocopies be established without a license from copyright owners.[183] While some fear that these limitations will impede existing and future network programs, the legislation in fact strikes a balance between the public interest in the wide availability of information and the copyright owner's economic well-being that is difficult to criticize as unwarranted, unwise, unrealistic or improper. Networks may use automated information systems to allocate resources efficiently among members and members may share physical resources through inter-library loans, without consulting the copyright owners of the shared works.   Library networks that rationalize acquisitions and that share resources using electronic and reprographic technology may do so only by negotiating licenses with copyright owners.[184]   However, even if the members of such networks had the full privileges of section 108 given to non-members of networks, the network members would almost certainly have to negotiate licenses in any event, or sacrifice efficiency, for it seems highly unlikely that when empirical data becomes available that it will show that an efficient rationalizing network could operate within the five copy per year guideline

---

the several states, as of December 31, 1977.   It is most unlikely that § 117 will be construed to permit libraries or others freely to store, retrieve and transfer the contents of copyrighted works. *See also*, Project, *New Technology and The Law of Copyright: Reprography and Computers*, 15 UCLA L. REV. 939 (1968); R. Kastenmeier, *Automated Information Systems and Copyright Law*, 114 CONG. REC. 16,852-58 (daily ed. June 11, 1968).

[182] *See* NATIONAL COMM'N ON LIBRARIES & INFORMATION SCIENCE, *supra* note 75, at 35-68.

[183] *See* notes 167-70 & accompanying text *supra*.   122 Cong. Rec. S2040-42 (daily ed. Feb. 19, 1976) (remarks of Sen. Magnuson).

[184] Congress has stated its expectation that the competing interests will collaborate on guidelines to facilitate a smooth continuation and expansion of networks:

> The photocopying needs of such operations as multi-county regional systems must be met.   The committee therefore recommends that representatives of authors, book and periodical publishers and other owners of copyrighted material meet with the library community to formulate photocopying guidelines to assist library patrons and employees.   Concerning library photocopying practices not authorized by this legislation, the committee recommends that workable clearance and licensing procedures be developed.

for the exchange of section 108 photocopies in interlibrary transactions.

In sum, Congress has chosen to protect copyright owners against unlicensed uses of their materials by library networks whose members share use through mechanical delivery of photocopies or the transmission of signals from which photocopies can be produced. Through this legislative proscription, not only are the traditionally protected economic interests of copyright owners shielded but copyright owners are assured that material published in the printed medium will not, during the life of the copyrights in the materials, become exploited in electronic media without the copyright owners' consent.

S. REP. at 70-71.

One manner in which networks might choose to proceed would be to establish clearing houses to exchange permissions and payments to copyright owners. *First Annual Report of the Committee to Investigate Problems Affecting Communication In Science and Education*, 10 BULL. COPYRIGHT SOC'Y 18 (1962); SOPHAR & HEILPRIN, *supra* note 171, at 48-55. Arranging clearinghouses for networks of libraries with similar specialized interests is the most feasible possibility. All of the copyrighted journals held by the National Library of Medicine and the National Institute of Health are provided by only 1000 publishers. Williams & Wilkins Co. v. United States, 172 U.S.P.Q. (BNA) 670, 680 (Ct. Cl. 1972), *rev'd*, 487 F.2d 1345 (Ct. Cl. 1973), *aff'd per curiam* 420 U.S. 376 (1975). There are less than forty primary journals in such fields as physics and electrical engineering. Carter, *The Library and Informational Service Needs of Scientists*, TECHNOLOGY AND COPYRIGHT 223, 232 (G. Bush ed. 1972). The cost of administering a clearing house for permissions and payments for a specialized network should therefore be low, relative to what the administration costs would be if they were born individually by each library. Weinburg, *The Photocopying Revolution and the Copyright Crisis*, 30 PUB. INTEREST 99, 114-16 (1975); AMERICAN LIBRARY ASSOCIATION, LIBRARIES AND COPYRIGHT: A SUMMARY OF THE ARGUMENTS FOR LIBRARY PHOTOCOPYING 20 (1974).

Clearinghouses will not come into existence immediately. In the meantime, networks that exchange information to rationalize acquisitions face an administrative dilemma. They could temporarily alter their programs to exclude rationalization of acquisitions, thereby restoring to each member its privilege to request up to five photocopies of a copyrighted work per year from other members (if five photocopies per year will enable a member to meet the requests of its users); they could continue to rationalize acquisitions and direct members to request the privileged number of inter-library loan photocopies from non-members of the network; they could negotiate licenses with individual copyright owners and exchange only licensed photocopies; they could share ownership of particular works and exchange photocopies of jointly owned works up to that number which indicates that photocopies are substituting for a second purchase or subscription of jointly owned works by the joint owners; or they could place in an escrow account sums of money that approximate reasonable fees for unprivileged photocopies and hold the accumulating fees for delivery to a copyright owners' society after a workable clearinghouse arrangement emerges (with the assumption that one feature of a clearinghouse arrangement will be a release by copyright owners of libraries from liability for past infringements and with the hope that a suit for infringement will not be filed in the interim against the members of the network by an owner of copyright in photocopied materials).

E. *Secondary Services*

Librarians routinely provide users with secondary services such as lists of titles of books recently purchased, bibliographies of titles in specialized fields and photocopies of the tables of contents of recently received issues of periodicals.[185] The copyright in a book does not protect its title.[186] Thus, libraries, including libraries in networks, may prepare and distribute lists of titles of recently acquired materials and bibliographies without the consent of copyright owners. One court has explained that the copyright owner cannot exclude others from using the title of a copyrighted work "since it is . . . a means of description which aids in identifying a literary production . . . ."[187] The table of contents of most periodicals contains a list of the titles of the articles, comments, features, and reviews contained in the issue. The rule excluding titles from the protection of copyright seems plainly to permit libraries to photocopy periodical tables of contents since issues of periodicals are nearly always collections of separately copyrightable works bearing their own titles.[188] Even periodical tables of contents that include a brief abstract of the contents of articles appear to fall within the category of materials that librarians can photocopy freely, either because the abstracts, like the titles, are aids in identifying the literary work,[189] or because the abstracts "describe facts and nothing more"[190] and are on that basis not protected by copyright.[191]

Information that is not protected by copyright can of course be used in computerized information systems, and secondary services are particularly suitably produced through automated information systems because they are most valuable to users when they

---

[185] George Fry & Assoc., *supra* note 24, at 100-02. In some fields, scientific fields in particular, scholars find it so difficult to remain informed of recent literature in their area of specialization that they rely very heavily upon secondary services. Carter, *supra* note 184, at 223-25.

[186] Affiliated enterprises, Inc. v. Rock-Ola Mfg. Corp., 23 F. Supp. 3 (N.D. Ill. 1937); M. NIMMER, NIMMER ON COPYRIGHT § 34 (1976).

[187] Becker v. Loew's, Inc., 133 F.2d 889, 891 (7th Cir. 1943).

[188] NEW ACT § 404(a).

[189] Becker v. Loew's, Inc., 133 F.2d 889 (7th Cir. 1943).

[190] Consumers Union of United States, Inc. v. Hobart Mfg. Co., 199 F. Supp. 860, 861 (S.D.N.Y. 1961).

[191] *Id. See also* Kane v. Pennsylvania Broadcasting Co., 73 F. Supp. 307 (D. Pa. 1947) "[I]t would almost seem as though the plaintiff's books were intended to be used in some manner similar to that in which the defendant has used them." *Id.* at 308.

provide current and comprehensive information.[192] Thus, the National Library of Medicine publishes *Index Medicus*, an annual printed compilation of the titles of and citations to journal articles concerning medical science published in several thousand periodicals.[193] The same information, currently updated, is available through the Medline information system.[194] The American Chemical Society, with the financial support of the National Science Foundation, sponsors the Chemical Abstracts Service, which provides a computer-based total information system with terminal access in libraries and elsewhere to articles, titles, authors' names, patent numbers, article abstracts and index entries.[195] The Institute for Scientific Information also stores bibliographic information from 5,000 scientific and technical journals in a computerized data base accessible to the user through terminals.[196] The number of secondary services, both computerized and printed, offered by libraries and other institutions is currently increasing very rapidly.[197]

In sum, the New Act does not inhibit librarians from providing full secondary services to users or to other libraries or members of a network by using photocopying alone or in conjunction with automated information systems. Librarians may use electronic and reprographic technology to provide users with full information about the contents of published works available at other libraries and to enable themselves to "spend" their section 108 photocopying privileges and scarce acquisitions dollars more efficiently than would be the case if users were less well informed about the contents of requested materials.

III. CONCLUSION

In the Copyright Act of 1976, Congress has dealt with the problem of library and archival photocopying by establishing a

---

[192] *See* Squires, *Copyright and Compilations in the Computer Era: Old Wine In New Bottles*, 24 BULL. COPYRIGHT SOC'Y 18, 20-24 (1976).

[193] *Id.* at 22.

[194] *Id.*

[195] Carter, *supra* note 184, at 227.

[196] Ulmer, *Automatic and, in Particular, Computerized Information and Documentation Systems and the Copyright Law*, 11 COPYRIGHT 239, 243 (1975).

[197] *See* R. CHRISTIAN, THE ELECTRONIC LIBRARY: BIBLIOGRAPHIC DATA BASES 1975-76 (1975) (listing well over 100 available data bases); Artundi, *On-Line Information Systems In Perspective*, 16 J. CHEM. INFO. & COMPUTER SCI. 80 (May 1976); Cooper & DeWath, *The Cost of On-Line Bibliographic Searching*, 9 J. LIB. AUTOMATION 195 (1976).

complex statutory scheme which provides three fundamental guidelines: Photocopies of copyrighted journal articles and small portions of other copyrighted works that substitute for library loans of the copied material are privileged.[198]   Photocopies made by users of copyrighted works borrowed from a library or archives are not the responsibility of the library or archives.[199]   Photocopies of copyrighted works that substitute for library purchases or subscriptions are not privileged.[200]   The probable cumulative effects of this legislation are impressive.   The Act certainly will increase library users' ease of access to copyrighted information, thereby assuring its wider dissemination, with attendant direct and indirect benefits to the public generally,[201] and to publishers.   It will facilitate the task of administering libraries and archives, giving librarians and archivists a basis in law for increasing or decreasing their physical control of collections as good librarianship demands, a method of meeting user needs other than through the circulation of holdings and a means of protecting materials from loss, wear and tear.   The provisions will also allow libraries and archives to provide their patrons easier access to unpublished documents, while in the process protecting against their alteration or loss through destruction of original copies.

It is not clear whether the library photocopying authorized by the Copyright Act will bankrupt any journals.   Photocopying has apparently not had that effect in the past.[202]   It is equally unclear whether the net revenues to publishers generated by photocopying royalties would save any journals.   Many publishers' problems are too complex and severe to solve with photocopying royalties.[203]   Even if photocopying revenues prolonged the life of

---

[198]   *See* notes 41-62, 117-97, 135-50 & accompanying text *supra.*
[199]   *See* notes 19, 80-84 & accompanying text *supra.*
[200]   *See* notes 35-39, 91-93, 105-16, 151-84 & accompanying text *supra.*
[201]   *See* B. KAPLAN, AN UNHURRIED VIEW OF COPYRIGHT 75 (1967); Breyer, *The Uneasy Case for Copyright: A Study of Copyright in Books, Photocopies, and Computer Programs,* 84 HARV. L. REV 281, 318 (1970).
[202]   George Fry & Assoc., note 24 *supra.*
[203]   Some publishers perceive photocopying as a threat to sales and subscription revenues. PASSANO, *supra* note 127, at 266.   Others do not. SOPHAR & HEILPRIN, *supra* note 184, at 6.   Many of the affected publications have financial problems.   Production costs are rising.   Abelson & Ormes, *Supporting Society Journals,* 193 SCIENCE 9 (1976).   Profits depend upon sales to libraries, but library budgets do not keep pace with their own rising operating costs.   Benjamin, *Soaring Prices and Sinking Sales of Science Monographs,* 183 SCIENCE 282 (1974). Much of the problem lies in the multiplication of sources.   In this century, the number of "hard core" scientific journals has doubled every fifteen years. NATIONAL SCIENCE FOUNDATION, *supra* note 133, at 17.   There were 34 new scien-

a few journals, the correlative inconveniences to users would surely overshadow any gain.[204]   The available information suggests that there is little to gain and much to lose by denying librarians, archivists and borrowers at least some limited benefits from reprography.   Congress wisely avoided restrictions on copying as a means of alleviating publishers' problems which were not caused by reprography in the first place.   Congress also avoided giving librarians and archivists so much leeway that their use of reprography and related technology would be likely to create substantial new problems for publishers.   Given the large number of interest groups affected, the line Congress drew between permitted and prohibited uses of reprography is remarkably clear, and should be easily administrable in the vast majority of situations.

---

tific journals introduced every ten years between 1919 and 1949, 74 new journals introduced between 1949 and 1959.   *Id.*   In fact there are too many journals. A group of internationally prominent scientists wrote in 1973 that there were too many publications in chemistry, resulting in the dissemination of much inferior work, often produced merely to create the appearance of scholarship for university administrators and other sources of funds.   Walsh, *Journals: Photocopying Is Not the Only Problem*, 183 SCIENCE 1274, 1275 (1974).   Nearly 15 years ago, the President's Science Advisory Committee said, "A simple but urgent suggestion to authors is to refrain from unnecessary publication."   THE PRESIDENT'S SCIENCE ADVISORY COMMITTEE, SCIENCE, GOVERNMENT AND INFORMATION: THE RESPONSIBILITIES OF THE TECHNICAL COMMUNITY AND THE GOVERNMENT IN THE TRANSFER OF INFORMATION 25 (1963).   Journals, in the meantime, have proliferated, and not only in the sciences: Scientists also double at a fast pace, and become specialized and sub-specialized and establish journals for specialties and sub-specialties.   Benjamin, *Soaring Prices and Sinking Sales of Science Monographs*, 183 SCIENCE 282 (1974).

[204]   Breyer, *supra* note 201, at 332-37.

FAIR USE AND THE NEW ACT

STEPHEN FREID*

I. FAIR USE

The Constitution gives Congress the power "[t]o promote the Progress of Science and useful Arts, by securing for limited Times to Authors and Inventors the exclusive Right to their respective Writings and Discoveries . . . ."[1] The primary purpose of any copyright statute enacted under this Constitutional mandate is to improve the state of knowledge in the arts and sciences for the benefit of the public. The Constitution clearly provides the method by which this purpose is to be achieved—individuals are to be encouraged in their research and writing by laws providing economic incentives.[2] The 1909 Copyright Law provided a system of economic incentives by giving copyright owners the exclusive rights to "print, reprint, publish, copy, and vend the copyrighted work . . . ."[3] Despite the wording of this statute, courts have always realized that a literal reading of the exclusiveness of these rights would defeat the statute's purpose in many situations by unduly restricting the dissemination and use of copyrighted works. In order to avoid unnecessary hindrances of progress in the arts and sciences, and results contrary to the purpose of the constitutional mandate, courts have relied on a concept of "fair use" to allow reasonable uses of copyrighted materials under certain circumstances.[4]

---

* Attorney, Office of General Counsel, U.S. Department of Health, Education, and Welfare. This article was written in the author's private capacity. No support or endorsement by the Department of Health, Education, and Welfare is intended nor should be inferred.

1. U.S. CONST. art. I, § 8.

2. Mazer v. Stein, 347 U.S. 201, 219 (1954).

3. 17 U.S.C. § 1(a) (1970).

4. The definition of fair use that has received the most widespread acceptance is that it constitutes a "privilege in others than the owner of a copyright to use the copyrighted material in a reasonable manner without his consent, notwithstanding the monopoly granted to the owner by the copyright." H. BALL, THE LAW OF COPYRIGHT AND LITERARY PROPERTY § 125 (1944). On the other hand, the House Committee Report relating to the New Act states that "no real definition of the concept has ever emerged." H.R. REP. No. 1476, 94th Cong., 2d Sess. 65 (1976) [hereinafter referred to and cited as HOUSE REPORT].

SOURCE: Reprinted from *The Complete Guide to the New Copyright Law* by permission of the publisher and the copyright holders. Published by Lorenz Press, Inc., Dayton, Ohio. Copyright © 1977 by Stephen Freid and by the New York Law School.

The standards for determining the applicability of this concept, however, have not always been clearly articulated. One court has referred to fair use as "the most troublesome [issue] in the whole law of copyright . . . ."[5]

In section 107 of the New Act,[6] Congress has given statutory recognition to the fair use of a copyrighted work for the first time. A copyright owner's exclusive rights[7] are now limited as follows:

> [T]he fair use of a copyrighted work, including such use by reproduction in copies or phonorecords or by any other means specified by that section, for purposes such as criticism, comment, news reporting, teaching (including multiple copies for classroom use), scholarship, or research, is not an infringement of copyright. In determining whether the use made of a work in any particular case is a fair use the factors to be considered shall include—
>
>   (1) the purpose and character of the use, including whether such use is of a commercial nature or is for nonprofit educational purposes;
>
>   (2) the nature of the copyrighted work;
>
>   (3) the amount and substantiality of the portion used in relation to the copyrighted work as a whole; and
>
>   (4) the effect of the use upon the potential market for or value of the copyrighted work.[8]

These four factors are the crux of the statutory provision for determining whether a particular use of a copyrighted work is so reasonable that it should be allowed as a fair use. They are, however, basically the same factors that have been used by courts for many

---

There has been a lack of agreement over whether fair use is a technical infringement of the copyright laws or whether it is a non-infringing use. *Compare* Holdredge v. Knight Pub. Corp., 214 F. Supp. 921, 924 (S.D. Cal. 1963) *with* Eisenschiml v. Fawcett Pub., Inc., 246 F.2d 598, 604 (7th Cir.), *cert. denied*, 355 U.S. 907 (1957). Section 107 of the New Act clarifies this matter by providing that fair use is not an infringement of the owner's copyright.

5.   Dellar v. Samuel Goldwyn, Inc., 104 F.2d 661, 662 (2d Cir. 1939).

6.   Pub. L. No. 94-553 (October 19, 1976) [hereinafter referred to as the New Act and cited as Pub. L. No. 94-553].

7.   The "exclusive" rights of a copyright owner are now set forth in Pub. L. No. 94-553, § 106. However, these "exclusive" rights are not only limited by section 107 but also by sections 108-18. The limitation in section 108 concerning reproduction of copyrighted works by libraries and archives is closely related to the issues of fair use discussed in this article. See notes 68-74 *infra* and accompanying text.

8.   Pub. L. No. 94-553, § 107. These enumerated examples are not exhaustive, but "give some idea of the sort of activities the courts might regard as fair use . . . ." HOUSE REPORT at 65.

years in making fair use determinations.[9] In fact, the HOUSE RE-
PORT relating to the New Act provides that section 107 "is intended
to restate the present judicial doctrine of fair use, not to change,
narrow, or enlarge it in any way."[10] Nevertheless, the legislative
history of section 107 does provide more specific guidance than
anything found in prior court decisions on what the *minimum* standards of fair use are in certain limited circumstances.[11]

The more difficult problem of defining the outer limits of the
fair use concept has not been solved by the enactment of the New
Act. There remains, however, a sound basis for developing a
reasonable approach to these cases. The next section of this article
will review the judicial doctrine of fair use and suggest such an
approach.

II. THE LEGACY OF *Williams & Wilkins Co.*

Two of the four factors for determining fair use now embodied
in section 107—the nature of the use[12] and the economic effect the
use has on the copyright holder[13]—have been the decisive factors
in most court decisions involving fair use.[14] The other two
factors—the nature of the copyrighted work[15] and the amount and
substantiality of the portion used[16]—have a secondary effect in that
they only become significant when the two major factors are inap-
plicable or not decisive.[17] It is not surprising that the use and

---

9. *See, e.g.*, Williams and Wilkins Co. v. United States, 487 F.2d 1345, 1352 (Ct.
Cl. 1973), *aff'd by an equally divided Court*, 420 U.S. 376 (1975).

10. HOUSE REPORT at 66.

11. See text accompanying notes 54-67 *infra*.

12. Pub. L. No. 94-553, § 107(1).

13. *Id*. § 107(4).

14. For a good discussion of the primary factors and their interrelationship *see*
Note, *Copyright Fair Use-Case Law and Legislation*, 1969 DUKE L.J. 88-99. At least
one commentator feels that court decisions relating to fair use can be best explained
by just looking at the economic effect factor. 2 M. NIMMER, COPYRIGHT § 145, at 646
(14th ed. 1976) [hereinafter cited as 2 NIMMER].

15. Pub. L. No. 94-553, § 107(2).

16. *Id*. § 107(3).

17. The amount and substantiality of the copyrighted material that is used will
usually decide the cases where the major factors are not decisive. *See* note 25 *infra*.
However, there is substantial authority for the proposition that the fair use concept
cannot be used to justify copying which is "virtually complete or almost verbatim."
2 NIMMER, § 145, at 650-51. *See* Wihtol v. Crow, 309 F.2d 777 (8th Cir. 1962); Robert
Stigwood Group Ltd. v. O'Reilly, 346 F. Supp. 376, 384-85 (D. Conn. 1972), *rev'd on
other grounds*, 530 F.2d 1096 (2d Cir. 1976). Of course, if substantially all of a
copyrighted work is copied it will be a near perfect substitute for the original and
will tend logically to reduce the potential market for the original. Consequently, the

economic effect factors have come to control the decisions in this area, because they relate closely to the purpose behind the copyright laws and the method that is used to achieve that purpose. If copyrighted material is used in such a way that the arts and sciences are benefited, the purposes of the copyright laws are being furthered despite the apparent invasion of the copyright owner's "exclusive" rights. In order to avoid frustrating progress in the arts and sciences, courts will often cite the benefits and allow the use.[18] The economic effect factor is used to protect the economic incentive system which the copyright laws have established; if the use has an adverse economic effect on the copyright owner, the incentive to write or publish copyrighted works is diluted and consequently the use is unlikely to be designated as a fair use by the courts.[19]

The two major factors will interrelate in one of four ways in any particular situation depending upon whether the use hastens progress in the arts and sciences (a positive use as compared to an ordinary use) and whether the use will have an adverse economic effect on the copyright owner (a detrimental effect):

(a) detrimental effect—ordinary use

(b) no detrimental effect—positive use

---

real thrust of these cases might actually be the economic effect the use had on the copyright holder. *But see* Williams and Wilkins Co. v. United States, 487 F.2d 1345, 1353-54 (Ct. Cl. 1973), *aff'd by an equally divided Court*, 420 U.S. 376 (1975) discussed in the text accompanying notes 26-53 *infra*.

The nature of the copyrighted work usually only becomes important as it relates to the economic effect factor. If the copyrighted work does not have a useful nature (*i.e.*, if it does not serve the public interest or further progress in the arts and sciences), the economic effect factor will not be a significant determinant in deciding the fair use issue.

18. *See, e.g.*, Rosemont Enterprises, Inc. v. Random House, Inc., 366 F.2d 303 (2d Cir. 1966), *cert. denied*, 385 U.S. 1009 (1967); Time, Inc. v. Bernard Geis Associates, 293 F. Supp. 130 (S.D.N.Y. 1968). These cases also illustrate the point that the arts and sciences should be interpreted in broad terms. The former case involved the use of a copyrighted article in a biography about Howard Hughes; the latter involved the use of frames of a copyrighted motion picture in a book about the assassination of President Kennedy. Although neither use involved what would normally be classified as an art or science, both served the public interest and were allowed on that basis. Section 107 of the New Act lists the following as being among those purposes that can fall within the fair use doctrine: criticism, comment, news reporting, teaching (including multiple copies for classroom use), scholarship, or research . . . ."

19. *See, e.g.*, Marvin Worth Prods. v. Superior Films Corp., 319 F. Supp. 1269 (S.D.N.Y. 1970); Addison-Wesley Pub. Co. v. Brown, 223 F. Supp. 219 (E.D.N.Y. 1963); Henry Holt & Co. v. Liggett & Myers Tobacco Co., 23 F. Supp. 302 (E.D. Pa. 1938).

(c) no detrimental effect—ordinary use

(d) detrimental effect—positive use.

Courts have had little difficulty in deciding the fair use question when a case falls in one of the first two categories, because consideration of both major factors leads to the same result. *Henry Holt & Co. v. Liggett & Myers Tobacco Co.*,[20] where a quote from a copyrighted book was used in a cigarette advertisement, is a good example of the easy type of case that is found in the (a) category. Once the court concluded that the copyright owner suffered economic harm from the use, it had no difficulty in holding that the use was outside the concept of fair use, because the use was only ordinary (i.e., a cigarette advertisement does nothing to further progress in the arts and sciences).

An easily decided case that fits into the (b) category is *Rosemont Enterprises, Inc. v. Random House, Inc.*[21] where information from a copyrighted magazine was used in a biography. The court found that the use served the public interest (a positive use),[22] and that the copyright owner did not suffer any detrimental economic effects from the use.[23] As a result of these conclusions the court had little difficulty in holding that the use should be allowed.[24] In cases that fall into the (c) category, the major factors do not force a definite conclusion, since there is neither a positive use nor a detrimental effect from the use. As a result, courts facing this situation will often use other factors, such as the amount of the use, to decide whether it should be allowed.[25]

The type of cases that fall into the (d) category pose the most troublesome situation for courts to handle, because the two major factors call for divergent results; the use is a positive one indicating

---

20.   23 F. Supp. 302 (E.D. Pa. 1938).

21.   366 F.2d 303 (2d Cir. 1966), *cert. denied*, 385 U.S. 1009 (1967).

22.   *Id.* at 309. See note 18 *supra*.

23.   366 F.2d at 310-11.

24.   *Id.* at 311.

25.   Good examples of situations where the major factors might not be decisive are found in the typical parody cases; the use is not usually looked upon as a positive one but it would not tend to harm the copyright holder as long as the two works serve distinct markets. The amount of the copyrighted work that is used in the parody can be decisive in these cases. *See, e.g.,* Berlin v. E.C. Publications, Inc., 329 F.2d 541 (2d Cir.), *cert. denied*, 379 U.S. 822 (1964); Benny v. Loew's, Inc., 239 F.2d 532 (9th Cir. 1956), *aff'd sub nom.*, Columbia Broadcasting Sys., Inc., v. Loew's, Inc., 356 U.S. 43 (1958). Looking at the amount of the copyrighted work that is used also serves another purpose; if there is not a substantial taking from the copyrighted material to begin with there can be no infringement in any event. *See, e.g.,* Mathews Conveyor Co. v. Palmer-Bee Co., 135 F.2d 73 (6th Cir. 1943).

that it should be allowed, but its detrimental economic effect on the copyright owner undermines the incentive system set up by the copyright laws. In reaching any result in this situation the courts should engage in a delicate weighing process. Cases involving massive library photocopying would seem to fall within this last, most difficult category, but in the major court decision in this area, *Williams & Wilkins Co. v. United States*,[26] the court conveniently avoided analyzing the situation as it would logically seem to exist. A close analysis of this case is necessary to any complete discussion of the judicial doctrine of fair use. The case illustrates, in particular, the importance of the economic effect factor in the more difficult fair use cases.

In *Williams & Wilkins Co.* the United States Court of Claims promulgated the first major court decision concerning whether the photocopying of copyrighted materials on a massive scale constitutes an actionable infringement under the copyright laws. Williams & Wilkins, a major publisher of medical journals and books, brought the action against the United States for infringements allegedly committed by the Department of Health, Education, and Welfare through the National Institutes of Health (NIH) and the National Library of Medicine (NLM). Both the NIH and the NLM had liberal photocopying policies; articles from numerous copyrighted journals, including some published by the plaintiff, were routinely photocopied for the benefit of researchers and libraries.[27]

---

26.   487 F.2d 1345 (Ct. Cl. 1973), *aff'd by an equally divided Court*, 420 U.S. 376 (1975). Justice Blackmun did not participate in the Supreme Court's decision and the remaining eight justices split four to four.

27.   487 F.2d at 1347-49. The NIH operates a library for the benefit of its research staff. Researchers upon request could receive a copy of an article from any journal in the library. The researcher did not have to state the reasons for his request nor did he have to return the photocopy to the library when he was finished using it. Usually, however, only one photocopy was made per request, each request was limited to forty or fifty pages, and only a single article could be photocopied from one issue. Exceptions to these rules were frequently made if the proper approval was obtained, however. In one year, 1970, the library photocopied about 93,000 articles. *Id.* at 1348.

The NLM is a librarian's library in that most of its loans are made to other libraries. Instead of loaning journals, the NLM sends photocopies of requested articles. These photocopies are not requested to be returned. The NLM, like the NIH, had some self-imposed limitations; it would only loan one copy per request and it would not photocopy entire issues. It also would not generally photocopy journals if they were among one hundred four journals that were on a list of widely available journals. Exceptions to these limitations were made, however, and government library requests were never refused on the basis that the journal was widely available. In 1968 about 127,000 photocopies were made by the NLM. *Id.* at 1348-49.

The government defended the policies primarily by trying to prove that the practices involved constituted nothing more than a fair use of the materials and that such uses are never held to be infringements under the copyright laws.[28] The case was heard in the first instance by a Commissioner of the Courts of Claims who decided that the defendants, the NLM and the NIH, had infringed upon exclusive rights owned by the plaintiff and were liable for infringement.[29] The Court of Claims, however, accepted the government's fair use defense and reversed the Commissioner's decision.[30] The court managed to avoid answering the most troublesome questions of massive photocopying by concluding that Williams & Wilkins never proved any economic injury from the photocopying practices;[31] once this conclusion was reached the case neatly fit into a category of cases that have been clearly decided. The conclusion and the resulting categorization, however, are subject to criticism and undermine the basis of the court's decision.[32] The Supreme Court affirmed the Court of Claims' decision by an equally divided Court.[33]

In deciding that the photocopying practices of the NIH and the NLM were a fair use, the Court of Claims in *Williams & Wilkins* relied on findings that the use was especially important to medicine and medical research, that the plaintiff did not prove a detrimental economic effect from the use, and that the problems involved called for legislative solutions.[34] Once these findings were made, the result was clearly dictated by the major factors; a case that involves a positive use that has no detrimental economic effects on the copyright owner fits into the (b) category where courts have no trouble in deciding that the use should be allowed.[35] Ad-

---

It should also be noted that the exact number of photocopies that were made from the four journals involved in the lawsuit was not ascertained. The defendants conceded that they made at least one photocopy of each of eight articles from the journals involved in the lawsuit. *Id.* at 1349.

28. *Id.* at 1350. The defendants also had other defenses, but the decision was based on the fair use issue. The other defenses included contentions that the Williams & Wilkins Company was not the proper plaintiff and that the proscription against copying in the copyright laws should not apply to books and periodicals. *Id.* at 1349-52.

29. *Id.* at 1347.

30. *Id.* at 1362-63.

31. *Id.* at 1357-59.

32. *See* text accompanying notes 34-53.

33. 420 U.S. 376 (1975).

34. 487 F.2d at 1353-54.

35. *See* text accompanying notes 21-24. The court made a valid point when it

mittedly, there is no reason not to allow a use that will significantly help medicine or medical research if the copyright owner does not suffer any economic harm. The conclusion, however, is only valid if the findings concerning the major factors are sound. If the court had concluded otherwise on the issue of economic harm it would have faced the type of case found in the (d) category where a difficult weighing process would have to be used to decide the issue of fair use.[36] Although the result may have hinged on the issue of economic harm, the court's findings that the Williams & Wilkins Company suffered no economic harm is the weakest part of its opinion.

Although courts are frequently faced with the problem of determining whether a copyright owner has been harmed from a use of his works, the criteria for making this determination are far from clear. There does seem to be a generally accepted framework from which to begin the analysis, however. Adverse economic harm has been put in the context of a more workable test; if the use of a copyrighted work "tends to diminish or prejudice the potential sale of the plaintiff's work" there is sufficient economic harm for it to become a key factor in the determination of the validity of a defense based upon fair use.[37] The relevant comparison under this test is between the actual market for the copyright owner's work and the market that would have existed if the use in question had never occurred. If the actual market is less than the hypothetical one there has been an adverse economic effect from the use. The obvious problem in using this test, however, is that while the actual market can be determined easily, the hypothetical market can rarely be calculated with any precision. In some cases it may be possible for a copyright owner to show that he lost a certain number of sales because of a specific use of his work; in most cases, however, there will be numerous economic factors influencing the demand for the work and it will be almost impossible to produce concrete evidence that the use caused the actual market to be less than the hypothetical market.

Many court decisions reflect a realization that to require concrete proof of economic harm in copyright infringement cases

---

stated that some legislative action was needed in this area. *Id.* at 1363. That, however, should not have prevented the court from deciding the issues that were presented in the case, especially since fair use was a judicially-created doctrine.

36. *See* text following note 25.

37. 2 NIMMER, § 145, at 646.

would defeat the purpose of the copyright laws.[38] Since most plaintiffs would have a very difficult time in proving the matter, to require such proof would cause economic harm to cease to be a factor in most fair use cases and the economic incentive system that was designed to further progress in the arts and sciences would become ineffective. A copyright would no longer be an adequate incentive, because it would be impossible to enforce in many situations. In order to avoid this result, some courts will allow a copyright owner to prove economic harm in fair use cases by use of a "probable effects test"—the copyright owner need show only that the *probable* economic effect from the use will be economically harmful to him.[39] By using a test based upon logic rather than concrete evidence, courts have usually been able to maintain the vitality of the economic incentive system that the copyright laws have established.

The loose causal connection between use and economic harm that is required under a probable effects type of test can be illustrated from previous court decisions. In *Henry Holt & Co. v. Liggett & Myers Tobacco Co.*[40] the court held that the use of three sentences from plaintiff's book in a cigarette advertisement was not a fair use. The court found that plaintiff suffered economic harm by reasoning that the demand for his book was likely to decrease because the use would harm his reputation.[41] Although there was no concrete evidence that the use caused any actual damage, the court

---

38. As a result, statistics that show an upward trend in the sales of a publication notwithstanding a certain use, are by themselves meaningless to determine whether a copyrighted work has been harmed by the use. The use may tend to decrease the sales, but other factors not related to the use may be simultaneously working to increase the sales. Despite an increase in sales a copyright owner is still harmed if the sales are less than they would be without the use. *See* Inge v. Twentieth Century-Fox Film Corp., 143 F. Supp. 294, 301 (S.D.N.Y. 1956).

39. *See, e.g.,* Marvin Worth Prods. v. Superior Films Corps., 319 F. Supp. 1269 (S.D.N.Y. 1970); Addison-Wesley Pub. Co. v. Brown, 223 F. Supp. 219 (E.D.N.Y. 1963); Henry Holt & Co. v. Liggett & Myers Tobacco Co., 23 F. Supp. 302 (E.D. Pa. 1938). The term "probable effects test" is not found in the case law; it does, however, accurately describe the process by which these courts reach a decision on the issue of economic harm. One method of determining whether the probable economic effect of any particular use of a copyrighted work will be harmful is to look at whether the two works serve the same market or function. 2 NIMMER, § 145, at 646-48. If defendant's work can be used as a substitute for the copyrighted material the probability of economic harm to the copyright owner is great. *See, e.g.,* Wihtol v. Crow, 309 F.2d 777 (8th Cir. 1962); Robert Stigwood Group Ltd. v. O'Reilly, 346 F. Supp. 376 (D. Conn. 1972).

40. 23 F. Supp. 302 (E.D. Pa. 1938).

41. *Id.* at 304.

found that there was sufficient economic harm for it to be a factor in defeating a fair use defense.[42] In another case, *Addison-Wesley Publishing Co., Inc. v. Brown*,[43] an action for infringement was brought by the holder of a copyright on a college physics book; the allegedly infringing use was a publication containing the solutions to the problems in the textbook. One factor that influenced the court's decision to grant injunctive relief was the finding that the use would adversely affect the market for the copyrighted book. The finding was based on evidence from previous sales of textbooks and marketing research—although the proof did not show with any certainty that the copyright owner was or would be damaged, the court found enough economic harm for it to be a consideration in the fair use determination.[44] In cases where the copyright owner is found not to have suffered any economic harm courts still will frequently reach a result by a probable effects type of analysis; for example, courts will often conclude that no economic harm has been suffered by the copyright owner when the copyrighted material and the use serve different markets.[45]

Despite the acceptability and utility of determining economic harm by something less than concrete evidence, the court in *Williams & Wilkins* required something more than a probable effects test:

> In the face of this record, we cannot mechanically assume such an effect, or hold that the amount of photoduplication proved here "must" lead to financial or economic harm. This is a matter of proof and plaintiff has not transformed its hypothetical assumption, by evidence, into a proven fact.[46]

---

42. This case is obviously distinguishable from *Williams & Wilkins* in that the use does not further progress in the arts and sciences. The use, however, should have no effect upon how economic harm is determined.

43. 223 F. Supp. 219 (E.D.N.Y. 1963).

44. *Id.* at 222.

45. Rosemont Enterprises, Inc. v. Random House, Inc., 366 F.2d 303 (2d Cir. 1966), *cert. denied*, 385 U.S. 1009 (1967); Berlin v. E.C. Pub., Inc., 329 F.2d 541 (2d Cir.), *cert. denied*, 379 U.S. 822 (1964); Time, Inc., v. Bernard Geis Associates, 293 F. Supp. 130 (S.D.N.Y. 1968).

46. 487 F.2d at 1359. The Court of Claims decision in *Williams & Wilkins* has been criticized on the ground that "[it] confused the issues of damages and liability." Nimmer, *Photocopying and Record Piracy: Of Dred Scott and Alice in Wonderland*, 22 U.C.L.A.L. Rev. 1052, 1053 (1975). Nimmer points out that the inherent difficulty in copyright infringement cases in proving actual damages is the reason that the copyright laws have provided for recovery of statutory damages when

If this type of rigid approach had been used by the courts in *Henry Holt* or in *Addison-Wesley* they would have been forced to conclude that the copyright owners did not suffer any economic harm, because the harm was not a proven fact—it was only the logical effect of the use. Those courts, however, realized that a flexible approach in determining the issue of economic harm would help to protect the economic incentive system that was set up by the copyright laws. The court in *Williams & Wilkins* would have employed a better approach, both in terms of the purposes underlying the copyright laws and legal precedent, if it had chosen to do likewise. The court should have determined the probable effect that the use had on the copyright owner instead of insisting that economic harm be established by proven facts.[47]

Under a probable effects test it is clear that the photocopying practices of the NIH and the NLM were harmful to the Williams & Wilkins Company. Although some people that use the photocopies would not purchase the article even if the photocopies were not available,[48] it seems inevitable that some people will photocopy articles in lieu of purchasing the journals that contain them. Certain factors compel the conclusion that the actual market for the journals that the plaintiff publishes must be less than the hypothetical market that would exist if no photocopying was allowed. First, there is the fact that the defendants photocopied thousands of articles every year. Even though only a small percentage of the total number of articles being photocopied may have replaced purchases, the large numbers involved indicate that a significant number of purchases were being replaced.[49] Second, the fact that it is

---

actual damages cannot be proven. *Id.* Section 504 of the New Act provides the copyright owner the right to elect "to recover, instead of actual damages and profits, an award of statutory damages . . . ." Requiring a plaintiff to prove economic harm by concrete evidence when a defendant raises a fair use defense is not consistent with the idea of statutory damages. See the text accompanying notes 78-81 *infra.*

47.   Some commentators have suggested that the flaw in the Court of Claims decision is that the court placed the burden of proof as to the fair use issue on the plaintiff rather than the defendants. *See, e.g.,* Comment, 26 MERCER L. REV. 1401, 1409 (1975). Placing the burden of proving fair use on the defendant would seem to have nearly the same effect as a probable effects test.

48.   The court erred in its analysis by only focusing on those people who would never buy the journal. 487 F.2d at 1358. The focus should have been on the people that would purchase the journal if there were no photocopying; the court never showed why this number would not be substantial.

49.   The fact that large numbers of photocopies were made indicates that the defendants' self imposed limitations were ineffective. *See* note 27 *supra.* The limitations may have decreased the amount of harm involved but it did not eliminate it.

cheaper to photocopy a single article than it is to purchase the entire journal will influence the rational consumer to photocopy when he might otherwise purchase.[50] When these two facts are considered along with the obvious consideration that a photocopy is a perfect substitute for an original article, the probable economic effect upon the copyright owner becomes clear. The trial judge astutely analyzed the situation in his opinion:

> The photocopies are exact duplicates of the original articles; are intended to be substitutes for, and serve the same purpose as, the original articles; and serve to diminish plaintiff's potential market for the original articles since the photocopies are made at the request of, and for the benefit of, the very persons who constitute plaintiff's market.[51]

The conclusion that the plaintiff suffered economic harm is supported by logic, if not by concrete evidence. Since this economic harm was not offset by any substantial economic benefits,[52] it should have been a major consideration in the determination of the

---

50. Nimmer, *Project, New Technology and the Law of Copyright: Reprography and Computers*, 15 U.C.L.A.L. REV. 931, 941-42 (1968).

51. 487 F.2d at 1378.

52. Arguments that plaintiff benefited from the massive photocopying are specious. Any increased interest in the journals as a result of the photocopying will only lead to more photocopying, since it is much more economical to photocopy than it is to purchase. The few people that would be influenced to purchase the journal would seem to be greatly outnumbered by those that have stopped purchasing the journal because of the alternative of photocopying.

It should also be noted that since the inquiry into economic harm is primarily for the purpose of determining what effect the use will have on the copyright owner's incentive, it should include an analysis of the copyright owner's business or financial situation. Only then can it be determined whether the use hinders the dissemination of information or defeats an author's incentive to write. If a copyright owner has a large scale operation, a small decrease in sales will not influence his actions to any significant degree but the same decreases could have serious effects on a small or marginally profitable enterprise (or author). The Williams & Wilkins Company is the type of enterprise that should be afforded the most protection under any economic harm analysis, because it published marginally profitable journals that are extremely useful to the scientific community. The precarious financial situation of the journals is evidenced by their low profit margins; they have never been large and usually range from $1,000 to $15,000. 487 F.2d at 1357. While the four journals involved in the suit only constitute part of the plaintiff's publishing business, the profit margin on each journal is the key consideration since the plaintiff cannot be expected to continue publishing journals that run a deficit. Since the journals are susceptible to losing money and becoming extinct, each lost purchase constitutes grave economic harm; this situation furthers the probability that the plaintiff must have suffered economic harm from the defendants' photocopying practices.

validity of defendants' fair use defense.[53] While the Court of Claims failed to properly address the question of the economic harm to the copyright holder in the *Williams & Wilkins* case, there is adequate flexibility under the New Act for a probable effects test to be adopted in future fair use cases. In this way courts can protect the viability of the economic incentive system set up by the copyright laws and provide a basis for the proper balancing of the major factors in fair use cases.

III.   Section 107 of the New Act

When section 107 of the New Act is viewed against the judicial doctrine of fair use discussed in the preceding section of this article two main points become apparent: (1) section 107 is a step forward from the judicial doctrine of fair use because it illuminates, through its legislative history, minimum standards for the applicability of the fair use concept in certain limited circumstances (relating to educational uses of copyrighted materials) and provides some

---

53. If the court in *Williams & Wilkins* had found that the plaintiff suffered economic harm from the defendant's photocopying practices, it would have faced a much more difficult task in deciding the validity of the fair use defense. The major factors no longer clearly indicate the proper result; the factors now have to be reconciled. The use is a positive one in that it serves the public interest by facilitating progress in medicine and medical research—the use factor by itself clearly indicates that the photocopying should be allowed as a fair use. The same use, however, is harmful to the copyright owner; the economic harm factor indicates that the use should not be allowed because it impedes the economic incentive to write and to publish. In order to reconcile these conflicting policies a weighing process will have to be employed. The process will seek to find the result that will best serve the purposes underlying the copyright laws.

While the original categorization of fair use cases depended upon a qualitative analysis, a weighing process contemplates a quantitative comparison—the questions are no longer whether the use is positive and whether the copyright owner suffers economic harm, but rather how much the use benefits and harms progress in the arts and sciences. Since the amounts of harm and benefit will differ in every situation, the utility of a general rule is minimal. Nevertheless, a useful distinction can possibly be made between those cases where the harm imperils the existence of a publication and the somewhat less harmful situations where the use merely serves to limit the profits of a still profitable enterprise. The harm in the two cases affects the purposes of the copyright laws in differing degrees. The harmful effects of the use in the first situation are direct and immediate—the publication ceases to exist (or will cease to exist in the foreseeable future) and useful information is no longer being published. On the other hand, when the publication will clearly continue to exist, the harmful effects of the use are more indirect. While they lessen the economic incentive to write or publish in the future, the threat of immediate harm is not present. Under any weighing test that determines the issue of fair use, the benefit needed to outweigh direct harm would have to be greater than that needed in cases where the harmful effects are only indirect.

degree of certainty for those individuals who limit their copying practices accordingly; and (2) while section 107 fails to explicitly define the outer limits of fair use, the statute does leave the door open for courts to ·take a reasonable approach in the more difficult fair use cases. These two significant points will be the focus of the discussion in the remainder of this article.

IV. MINIMUM STANDARDS

It was pointed out at the beginning of this article that section 107, on its face, does not provide more precise standards for making fair use determinations than previous court decisions.[54] Rather, section 107 is "intended to restate the present judicial doctrine of fair use"[55] and does so by listing the four general factors that have been used by the courts for years in fair use cases.[56] This was done in recognition of "the endless variety of situations and combinations of circumstances that can rise in particular cases."[57]

Nevertheless, Congress also recognized that there was a need for certainty and protection for certain users of copyrighted works, especially teachers.[58] At the June 1975 House Judiciary Subcommittee Hearings on revision of the copyright laws, committee members urged the interested parties to meet to achieve agreement concerning permissible uses of copyrighted works for educational purposes.[59] This suggestion led to meetings held by three groups dealing with the problems of classroom reproduction of printed material, music, and audio-visual material. Two of the groups were successful in agreeing upon guidelines stating the minimum standards of "educational" fair use for printed material and music. The adoption of these agreements are quite significant since the House Committee stated its belief that "the guidelines are a reasonable interpretation of the minimum standards of fair use"[60] in these situations and incorporated the agreements into the HOUSE REPORT.[61]

---

54. See text accompanying notes 9-10 *supra*.
55. HOUSE REPORT at 66.
56. See, e.g., Williams & Wilkins Co. v. United States, 487 F.2d 1345, 1352 (Ct. Cl. 1973), *aff'd by an equally divided Court*, 420 U.S. 376 (1975).
57. HOUSE REPORT at 66.
58. Id. at 67, 72.
59. Id. at 67.
60. Id. at 72. See also 122 CONG. REC. 10880 (daily ed. Sept. 22, 1976) (remarks of Congressman Drinan).
61. HOUSE REPORT at 68. The full agreements read as follows:

AGREEMENT ON GUIDELINES FOR CLASSROOM COPYING IN
NOT-FOR-PROFIT EDUCATIONAL INSTITUTIONS

WITH RESPECT TO BOOKS AND PERIODICALS

The purpose of the following guidelines is to state the minimum standards of educational fair use under Section 107 of H.R. 2223. The parties agree that the conditions determining the extent of permissible copying for educational purposes may change in the future; that certain types of copying permitted under these guidelines may not be permissible in the future; and conversely that in the future other types of copying not permitted under these guidelines may be permissible under revised guidelines.

Moreover, the following statement of guidelines is not intended to limit the types of copying permitted under the standards of fair use under judicial decision and which are stated in Section 107 of the Copyright Revision Bill. There may be instances in which copying which does not fall within the guidelines stated below may nonetheless be permitted under the criteria of fair use.

GUIDELINES

I. *Single Copying for Teachers*

A single copy may be made of any of the following by or for a teacher at his or her individual request for his or her scholarly research or use in teaching or preparation to teach a class:

A. A chapter from a book;

B. An article from a periodical or newspaper;

C. A short story, short essay or short poem, whether or not from a collective work;

D. A chart, graph, diagram, drawing, cartoon or picture from a book, periodical, or newspaper;

II. *Multiple Copies for Classroom Use*

Multiple copies (not to exceed in any event more than one copy per pupil in a course) may be made by or for the teacher giving the course for classroom use or discussion; *provided that:*

A. The copying meets the test of brevity and spontaneity as defined below; *and,*

B. Meets the cumulative effect test as defined below; *and,*

C. Each copy includes a notice of copyright

Definitions

Brevity

(i) Poetry: (a) A complete poem if less than 250 words and if printed on not more than two pages or, (b) from a longer poem, an excerpt of not more than 250 words.

(ii) Prose: (a) Either a complete article, story or essay of less than 2,500 words, or (b) an excerpt from any prose work of not more than 1,000 words or 10% of the work, whichever is less, but in any event a minimum of 500 words.

[Each of the numerical limits stated in "i" and "ii" above may be expanded to permit the completion of an unfinished line of a poem or of an unfinished prose paragraph.]

(iii) Illustration: One chart, graph, diagram, drawing, cartoon or picture per book or per periodical issue.

(iv) "Special" works: Certain works in poetry, prose or in "poetic prose" which often combine language with illustrations and which are intended sometimes for children and at other times for a more general audience fall short of 2,500 words in their entirety. Paragraph "ii" above notwithstanding such "special works" may not be reproduced in their entirety; however, an excerpt comprising not more than two of the published pages of such special work and containing not more than 10% of the words found in the text thereof, may be reproduced.

Spontaneity

(i) The copying is at the instance and inspiration of the individual teacher, and

(ii) The inspiration and decision to use the work and the moment of its use for maximum teaching effectiveness are so close in time that it would be unreasonable to expect a timely reply to a request for permission.

Cumulative Effect

(i) The copying of the material is for only one course in the school in which the copies are made.

(ii) Not more than one short poem, article, story, essay or two excerpts may be copied from the same author, nor more than three from the same collective work or periodical volume during one class term.

(iii) There shall not be more than nine instances of such multiple copying for one course during one class term.

[The limitations stated in "ii" and "iii" above shall not apply to current news periodicals and newspapers and current news sections of other periodicals.]

III. *Prohibitions as to I and II Above*

Notwithstanding any of the above, the following shall be prohibited:

(A) Copying shall not be used to create or to replace or substitute for anthologies, compilations or collective works. Such replacement or substitution may occur whether copies of various works or excerpts therefrom are accumulated or reproduced and used separately.

(B) There shall be no copying of or from works intended to be "consumable" in the course of study or of teaching. These include workbooks, exercises, standardized tests and test booklets and answer sheets and like consumable material.

(C) Copyright shall not:

    (a) substitute for the purchase of books, publishers' reprints or periodicals;

    (b) be directed by higher authority;

    (c) be repeated with respect to the same item by the same teacher from term to term.

(D) No charge shall be made to the student beyond the actual cost of the photocopying.

Agreed MARCH 19, 1976.

Ad Hoc Committee on Copyright Law Revision:

                By SHELDON ELLIOTT STEINBACH.

Author-Publisher Group:

Authors League of America:

                By IRWIN KARP, *Counsel.*

Association of American Publishers, Inc.:

                By ALEXANDER C. HOFFMAN,

                Chairman, Copyright Committee.

GUIDELINES FOR EDUCATIONAL USES OF MUSIC

The purpose of the following guidelines is to state the minimum and not the maximum standards of educational fair use under Section 107 of HR 2223. The parties agree that the conditions determining the extent of permissible copying for educational purposes may change in the future; that certain types of copying permitted under these guidelines may not be permissible in the future, and conversely that in the future other types of copying not permitted under these guidelines may be permissible under revised guidelines.

Moreover, the following statement of guidelines is not intended to limit the types of copying permitted under the standards of fair use under judicial decision and which are stated in Section 107 of the Copyright Revision Bill. There may be instances in which copying which does not fall within the guidelines stated below may nonetheless be permitted under the criteria of fair use.

A. Permissible Uses

1. Emergency copying to replace purchased copies which for any reason are not available for an imminent performance provided purchased replacement copies shall be substituted in due course.

2. (a) For academic purposes other than performance, multiple copies of excerpts of works may be made, provided that the excerpts do not comprise a part of the whole which would constitute a performable unit such as a section, movement or aria, but in no case more than 10% of the whole work. The number of copies shall not exceed one copy per pupil.

(b) For academic purposes other than performance, a single copy of an entire performable unit (section, movement, aria, etc.) that is, (1) confirmed by the copyright proprietor to be out of print or (2) unavailable except in a larger work, may be made by or for a teacher solely for the purpose of his or her scholarly research or in preparation to teach a class.

3. Printed copies which have been purchased may be edited or simplified provided that the fundamental character of the work is not distorted or the lyrics, if any, altered or lyrics added if none exist.

4. A single copy of recordings of performances by students may be made for evaluation or rehearsal purposes and may be retained by the educational institution or individual teacher.

5. A single copy of a sound recording (such as a tape, disc or cassette) of copyrighted music may be made from sound recordings owned by an educational institution or an individual teacher for the purpose of constructing aural exercises or examinations and may be retained by the educational institution or individual teacher. (This pertains only to the copyright of the music itself and not to any copyright which may exist in the sound recording.)

B. Prohibitions

1. Copying to create or replace or substitute for anthologies, compilations or collective works.

2. Copying of or from works intended to be "consumable" in the course of study or of teaching such as workbooks, exercises, standardized tests and answer sheets and like material.

3. Copying for the purpose of performance, except as in A(1) above.

4. Copying for the purpose of substituting for the purchase of music, except as in A(1) and A(2) above.

5. Copying without inclusion of the copyright notice which appears on the printed copy.

The agreement relating to the educational use of printed materials is worthy of special attention. The "Agreement on Guidelines for Classroom Copying in Not-For-Profit Educational Institutions"[62] with respect to books and periodicals covers the making of a single copy of a copyrighted work for use by a teacher[63] and the making of multiple copies for classroom use. Before summarizing the guidelines for these two types of situations, certain general prohibitions should be noted. The guidelines do not allow copying which is (a) used to create, replace or substitute for anthologies, compilations or collective works, (b) from "consumable" works such as workbooks, (c) a substitute for a purchase, (d) directed by a higher authority, (e) repeated by one teacher from term to term, or if (f) the student is charged beyond the actual cost of copying.[64]

The guidelines do allow a teacher to make a *single* copy of a chapter in a book; an article from a periodical; a short story, short essay, or short poem from a collective work; a graph, diagram, a drawing, cartoon or picture from a book, periodical or newspaper for purposes of research, teaching, or classroom preparation.[65] The guidelines concerning multiple copies for classroom use are more complicated, however. A teacher giving a course may make multiple copies for classroom use if each copy has a copyright notice and certain requirements relating to brevity, spontaneity and cumulative effect are met.[66] The tests concerning brevity and cumulative effect are sufficiently precise; for example, the guidelines only allow multiple copies of a complete poem to be made if it is less than two hundred and fifty words and printed on one or two pages. One of the cumulative effect requirements is that there cannot be more than nine such instances of multiple copying in a course during a class term. In contrast, however, the spontaneity requirements are defined in somewhat less definite terms; thus, among

---

62. *Id.* at 68-71. Not all affected parties concurred in these guidelines. The Association of American Law Schools and the American Association of University Professors both took exception to the guidelines as being too restrictive at the university and graduate school levels. *See* 122 CONG. REC. 10880-81 (daily ed. Sept. 22, 1976); HOUSE REPORT at 72. However, the objections of these groups should be looked at in light of the fact that the guidelines are intended to be interpretations of the *minimum* standards of fair use.

63. An instructional specialist working with a classroom instructor is considered to be a teacher. 122 CONG. REC. 10875 (daily ed. Sept. 22, 1976).

64. Section III of the *Agreement on Guidelines for Classroom Copying in Not-For-Profit Educational Institutions* quoted in full in note 61, *supra*.

65. *Id.* at Section I.

66. *Id.* at Section II.

other things, the copying must be at the "inspiration" of the teacher involved.

Nevertheless, the ambiguities that are bound to surface with respect to these guidelines are tempered by the fact that they are only interpretations of the minimum standards of fair use in the educational setting. A teacher who fails to stay within the precise parameters of the guidelines can still assert a fair use defense based on the general factors listed in section 107. In addition, teachers (as well as other employees or agents of nonprofit educational institutions, libraries or archives) acting within the scope of their employment are afforded certain protection in section 504 of the new New Act. This provision provides that a "court shall remit statutory damages in any case where an infringer believed and had reasonable grounds for believing that his or her use of the copyrighted work was a fair use under section 107 . . . ."[67] While the infringer could still be liable for actual damages, this provision adds a significant safeguard for a limited class of users deserving special protection.

While this article has focused on the judicial concept of fair use and its embodiment in the new section 107, any discussion of these matters would not be complete without a short deviation into section 108 of the new New Act. Section 108 allows libraries and archives, as well as their employees "acting within the scope of their employment, to reproduce [or distribute] no more than one copy or phonorecord of a [copyrighted] work" under certain circumstances without infringing the owner's copyright.[68] It is important to realize, however, that the concept of fair use applies to library photocopying despite section 108. While section 108 authorizes certain photocopying practices which go beyond the confines of fair use,[69] it explicitly does not in any way affect "the right of fair use as provided by section 107."[70] While section 108 does not prescribe minimum standards of fair use for library photocopying, it does provide protection to certain limited library photocopying practices in a manner similar to the guidelines for classroom copying discussed above.

An important limitation on the copying practices allowed under section 108 is that the protections of this section do not ex-

---

67.   Pub. L. No. 94-553, § 504(c)(2).
68.   *Id.* § 108(a).
69.   HOUSE REPORT at 74.
70.   Pub. L. No. 94-553, § 108(f)(4).

tend to the "systematic reproduction or distribution of single or
multiple copies . . ."[71] of the relevant works. While full interpretation of this limitation will undoubtedly be the subject of future
litigation, it should be noted that the legislative history of the New
Act indicates that photocopying practices are systematic when
there is a deliberate substitution of photocopying for the purchase
of the copyrighted work.[72] In addition, the HOUSE REPORT provides that section 108

> does not authorize the *related* or *concerted* reproduction
> of multiple copies or phonorecords of the same materials,
> whether made on one occasion or over a period of time,
> and whether intended for aggregate use by one individual
> or for separate use by the individual members of a
> group[73] (emphasis added).

It is evident that section 108 is not as precise as one might hope.[74]
However, it is a more advantageous approach to the problem of
library photocopying than leaving the allowability of these practices
entirely to the concept of fair use.

V.   THE OUTER LIMITS OF FAIR USE

It was pointed out earlier in this article that section 107 does
not precisely define the outer limits of the fair use doctrine. Instead, section 107 restates the judicial doctrine of fair use by
enumerating the four factors that courts have used for years in
making fair use determinations. Since these factors have sometimes
led to inconsistent results in the more difficult fair use cases,[75] it

---

71. *Id.* § 108(g)(2).

72. HOUSE REPORT at 75.

73. *Id.* at 77.

74. There was a strong reaction to the restrictions on "systematic" copying set
forth in section 108(g) of the Senate Bill. One concern was that it would impede
development of interlibrary networks or arrangements. In response to this concern
the House added the proviso found in section 108(g)(2):

> *Provided,* That nothing in this clause prevents a library or archives from
> participating in interlibrary arrangements that do not have, as their purpose
> or effect, that the library or archives receiving such copies or phonorecords
> for distribution does so in such aggregate quantities as to substitute for a
> subscription to or purchase of such work.

Interested parties have agreed to "Guidelines for the proviso of subsection 108(g)(2)"
which the Conference Committee adopted as reasonable interpretations of the proviso. 122 CONG. REC. 11728-29 (daily ed. Sept. 29, 1976).

75. *Compare* Williams & Wilkins Co. v. United States, 487 F.2d 1345 (Ct. Cl.
1973), *aff'd by an equally divided Court,* 420 U.S. 376 (1975), *with* Wihtol v. Crow,
309 F.2d 777 (8th Cir. 1962).

would appear that little progress has been made in defining the outer limits of the fair use doctrine. Nevertheless, section 107 is significant in that it gives courts adequate leeway to adopt a reasonable approach in the more difficult fair use cases by using a probable effects test in regard to the issue of economic harm. It is important that there is nothing in the New Act or its legislative history which indicates approval of the approach used by the Court of Claims in the *Williams & Wilkins* case; that approach being that a plaintiff in a copyright infringement action must prove economic harm by concrete evidence for that to be a factor in the court's determination of the validity of a fair use defense. In fact, there are some indications, discussed below, that adoption of a probable effects test would be consistent with congressional intent.

While section 107 is intended to restate the judicial doctrine of fair use, the legislative history is still quite significant because it indicates what Congress thinks the doctrine of fair use is. In regard to the importance of the economic harm factor in fair use cases the SENATE REPORT provides that:

> [w]ith certain special exceptions (use in parodies or as evidence in court proceedings might be examples) a use that supplants any part of the normal market for a copyrighted work would ordinarily be considered an infringement . . . . Fair use is essentially supplementary by nature . . . . Isolated instances of minor infringements, when multiplied many times, become in the aggregate a major inroad on copyright that must be prevented.[76]

This language does not explicitly accept or reject a probable effects test, nor does it illustrate how a court should determine if the use supplants the normal market for a copyrighted work. However, the language does indicate that Congress intended that *any* reduction in the market for a copyrighted work, no matter how small, be considered a major factor in fair use determinations. One way to ensure that the economic harm factor is given the weight contemplated by Congress in any fair use determination is for courts to adopt a probable effects test. If a plaintiff is required to prove economic harm by concrete evidence, as happened in the *Williams*

---

76. S. REP. NO. 473, 94th Cong., 1st Sess. 65 (1975) [hereinafter referred to and cited as SENATE REPORT]. The later House Committee Report states that "[t]he Committee has reviewed this discussion, and considers that it still has value as an analysis of various aspects of the problem . . . ." of fair use. HOUSE REPORT at 67.

& *Wilkins* case, it will often become a non-factor despite congressional intent that fair use should normally supplement, and not supplant, the normal market for the copyrighted work.[77]

The damages section of the New Act also lends support to the adoption of a probable effects test.[78] The New Act, like the 1909 version, gives plaintiff the option of recovering statutory or actual damages in an infringement action.[79] By allowing a plaintiff to prevail in an infringement action without submitting proof of actual damages, Congress gave recognition to the obvious fact that it is often difficult, if not impossible, for a plaintiff to prove the precise harm caused because of an infringement. It is hard to reconcile allowing a plaintiff to recover statutory damages without proof of actual harm with an approach that requires a plaintiff to submit concrete proof of economic harm before that can be considered a major factor in a fair use determination. The Court of Claims' opinion in the *Williams & Wilkins* case was criticized for this inconsistency,[80] but under section 107 of the New Act courts have the opportunity to apply a more reasonable standard when judging whether a particular use has caused economic harm to the copyright owner.[81] If a probable effects test is used by the courts, eco-

---

77. Once economic harm becomes a non-factor courts would normally allow the use if it is construed to hasten progress in the arts and sciences. If the use does nothing to further progress in the arts and sciences but does no harm to the copyright owner, courts will rely on the other factors in making a fair use determination. See the text accompanying notes 20-25 *supra.*

78. Pub. L. No. 94-553, § 504. A provision for statutory damages was also part of the 1909 Copyright Law. 17 U.S.C. § 101(b) (1970).

79. The SENATE REPORT clearly provides that under both the new and old copyright laws "the plaintiff in an infringement suit is not obliged to submit proof of damages and profits if he chooses to rely on the provision for . . . statutory damages." SENATE REPORT at 143 (1975).

80. *See, e.g.,* Nimmer, *Photocopying and Record Piracy: Of Dred Scott and Alice in Wonderland,* 22 U.C.L.A.L. REV. 1052, 1053 (1975); Comment, 26 MERCER L. REV. 1401, 1409 (1975); Significant Developments, 54 B.U.L. REV. 689, 693-95 (1974).

81. Lower courts need not feel constrained by the fact that the Supreme Court affirmed the Court of Claims decision in *Williams & Wilkins Co.* While the affirmance of a lower court decision by an equally divided court is conclusive as between the parties, it is not binding authority in future cases. Hertz v. Woodman, 218 U.S. 205, 213-14 (1910). In fact, it has been suggested that Wihtol v. Crow, 309 F.2d 777 (8th Cir. 1962), is more persuasive authority in regard to the fair use issue than *Williams & Wilkins.* Nimmer, *Photocopying and Record Piracy: Of Dred Scott and Alice in Wonderland,* 22 U.C.L.A.L. REV. 1052, 1059 (1975). One interesting aspect of these two cases is that while Justice Blackmun was the Justice not participating in the Supreme Court's affirmance of *Williams & Wilkins* he did vote with the majority in *Wihtol* when he was a judge on the Eighth Circuit.

nomic harm to the copyright holder will remain a key factor in the difficult balancing process that occurs in the more difficult fair use cases. By doing this, courts will be protecting the economic incentive system set up by the copyright laws and be able to more fairly delineate the outer boundaries of the fair use concept.

In the United States Court of Claims

No. 73-68

(Decided November 27, 1973)

THE WILLIAMS & WILKINS COMPANY v. THE UNITED STATES

Alan Latman, attorney of record, for plaintiff. *Arthur J. Greenbaum* and *Cowan, Liebowitz & Latman*, of counsel.

Thomas J. Byrnes, with whom was *Assistant Attorney General Harlington Wood, Jr.*, for defendant.

Irwin Karp, for The Authors League of America, Inc., amicus curiae.

Philip B. Brown, for the Association of Research Libraries, Medical Library Association, American Association of Law Libraries, American Medical Association, American Dental Association, Mayo Foundation, Robert H. Ebert, M.D. (in his capacity as Dean of the Faculty of Medicine, Harvard University), The University of Michigan Medical School, The University of Rochester, School of Medicine and Dentistry, American Sociological Association, Modern Language Association of America, and History of Science Society, amici curiae. *Cox, Langford & Brown* and *John P. Furman*, of counsel.

Harry N. Rosenfield, for The National Education Association of the United States, amicus curiae.

William D. North, for the American Library Association, amicus curiae. *Perry S. Patterson, Ronald L. Engel, James M. Amend, John A. Waters, Thomas B. Carr*, and *Kirkland & Ellis*, of counsel.

Charles H. Lieb, for the Association of American Publishers, Inc. and The Association of American University

Presses, Incorporated, amici curiae. *Paskus*, *Gordon & Hyman*, and *Elizabeth Barad*, of counsel.

Arthur B. Hanson, for The American Chemical Society, amicus curiae. *Hanson*, *O'Brien*, *Birney*, *Stickle & Butler*, of counsel.

Davies, *Hardy*, *Ives & Lawther*, for The American Institute of Physics Incorporated, amicus curiae. *Robert E. Lawther*, of counsel.

Robert B. Washburn, *Virgil E. Woodcock*, and *Woodcock*, *Washburn*, *Kurtz & Mackiewicz*, for American Society for Testing and Materials and National Council of Teachers of Mathematics, amici curiae.

Before COWEN, *Chief Judge*, DAVIS, SKELTON, NICHOLS, KASHIWA, KUNZIG and BENNETT, *Judges*.

OPINION

DAVIS, *Judge*, delivered the opinion of the court:

We confront a ground-breaking copyright infringement action under 28 U.S.C. § 1498(b), the statute consenting to infringement suits against the United States.[1] Plaintiff Williams & Wilkins Company, a medical publisher, charges that the Department of Health, Education, and Welfare, through the National Institutes of Health (NIH) and the National Library of Medicine (NLM), has infringed plaintiff's copyrights in certain of its medical journals by making unauthorized photocopies of articles from those periodicals. Modern photocopying in its relation to copyright spins off troublesome problems, which have been much discussed.[2] Those issues have never before been mooted or determined by a court. In this case, an extensive trial was held before former Trial Judge James F. Davis who decided that the Government was liable for infringement. On review, helped by the briefs and agreements of the parties and the amici curiae,

---

[1] Prior to 1960, § 1498 provided only for patent infringement suits against the Federal Government. In that year, Congress amended the section to make the United States liable in money for copyrighted infringement, pursuant to Title 17 of the United States Code, the general copyright statute. This is the first copyright case to reach trial in this court.

[2] We list in the Appendix, *infra*, several considerations to these problems.

we take the other position and hold the United States free
of liability in the particular situation presented by this
record.

I [3]

Plaintiff, though a relatively small company, is a major
publisher of medical journals and books. It publishes 37
journals, dealing with various medical specialties. The four
journals in suit are *Medicine, Journal of Immunology, Gastroenterology,* and *Pharmacological Reviews. Medicine* is
published by plaintiff for profit and for its own benefit. The
other three journals are published in conjunction with specialty medical societies which, by contract, share the journals'
profits with plaintiff. The articles published in the journals
stem from manuscripts submitted to plaintiff (or one of the
medical societies) by physicians or other scientists engaged
in medical research. The journals are widely disseminated
throughout the United States (and the world) in libraries,
schools, physicians' offices, and the like. Annual subscription
prices range from about $12 to $44; and, due to the esoteric
nature of the journals' subject matter, the number of annual
subscriptions is relatively small, ranging from about 3,100
(*Pharmacological Reviews*) to about 7,000 (*Gastroenterology*). Most of the revenue derived from the journals comes
from subscription sales, though a small part comes from
advertising.[4] The journals are published with notice of copyright in plaintiff's name. The notice appears at the front of
the journal and sometimes at the beginning of each article.
After publication of each journal issue (usually monthly or
bimonthly) and after compliance with the requisite statutory
requirements, the Register of Copyrights issues to plaintiff
certificates of copyright registration.

NIH, the Government's principal medical research organization, is a conglomerate of institutes located on a
multi-acre campus at Bethesda, Maryland. Each institute is
concerned with a particular medical specialty, and the insti-

---

[3] We borrow, with some modifications, the statement of facts from the
opinion of Trial Judge James F. Davis.

[4] *E.g.,* the November 1956 issue of *Medicine* has 86 pages, four of which
carry commercial product advertising. The August 1965 issue of *Journal of
Immunology* has 206 pages, nine of which carry commercial product
advertising.

tutes conduct their activities by way of both intramural research and grants-in-aid to private individuals and organizations. NIH employs over 12,000 persons—4,000 are science professionals and 2,000 have doctoral degrees. To assist its intramural programs, NIH maintains a technical library. The library houses about 150,000 volumes, of which about 30,000 are books and the balance scientific (principally medical) journals. The library is open to the public, but is used mostly by NIH in-house research personnel. The library's budget for 1970 was $1.1 million; of this about $85,000 was for the purchase of journal materials.

The NIH library subscribes to about 3,000 different journal titles, four of which are the journals in suit. The library subscribes to two copies of each of the journals involved. As a general rule, one copy stays in the library reading room and the other copy circulates among interested NIH personnel. Demand by NIH research workers for access to plaintiff's journals (as well as other journals to which the library subscribes) is usually not met by in-house subscription copies. Consequently, as an integral part of its operation, the library runs a photocopy service for the benefit of its research staff. On request, a researcher can obtain a photocopy of an article from any of the journals in the library's collection. Usually, researchers request photocopies of articles to assist them in their on-going projects; sometimes photocopies are requested simply for background reading. The library does not monitor the reason for requests or the use to which the photocopies are put. The photocopies are not returned to the library; and the record shows that, in most instances, researchers keep them in their private files for future reference.

The library's policy is that, as a rule, only a single copy of a journal article will be made per request and each request is limited to about 40 to 50 pages, though exceptions may be, and have been, made in the case of long articles, upon approval of the Assistant Chief of the library branch. Also, as a general rule, requests for photocopying are limited to only a single article from a journal issue. Exceptions to this rule are routinely made, so long as substantially less than an entire journal is photocopied, i.e., less than about half of the journal. Coworkers can, and frequently do, request single copies of the same article and such requests are honored.

Four regularly assigned employees operate the NIH photocopy equipment. The equipment consists of microfilm cameras and Xerox copying machines. In 1970, the library photocopy budget was $86,000 and the library filled 85,744 requests for photocopies of journal articles (including plaintiff's journals), constituting about 930,000 pages. On the average, a journal article is 10 pages long, so that, in 1970, the library made about 93,000 photocopies of articles.

NLM, located on the Bethesda campus of NIH, was formerly the Armed Forces Medical Library. In 1956, Congress transferred the library from the Department of Defense to the Public Health Service (renaming it the National Library of Medicine), and declared its purpose to be "* * * to aid the dissemination and exchange of scientific and other information important to the progress of medicine and to the public health * * *." 42 U.S.C. § 275 (1970). NLM is a repository of much of the world's medical literature, in essence a "librarians' library." As part of its operation, NLM cooperates with other libraries and like research-and-education-oriented institutions (both public and private) in a so-called "interlibrary loan" program. Upon request, NLM will loan to such institutions, for a limited time, books and other materials in its collection. In the case of journals, the "loans" usually take the form of photocopies of journal articles which are supplied by NLM free of charge and on a no-return basis. NLM's "loan" policies are fashioned after the General Interlibrary Loan Code, which is a statement of self-imposed regulations to be followed by all libraries which cooperate in interlibrary loaning. The Code provides that each library, upon request for a loan of materials, shall decide whether to loan the original or provide a photoduplicate. The Code notes that photoduplication of copyrighted materials may raise copyright infringement problems, particularly with regard to "photographing *whole issues* of periodicals or books with *current copyrights*, or in making *multiple copies* of a publication." [Emphasis in original text.] NLM, therefore, will provide only one photocopy of a particular article, per request, and will not photocopy on any given request an entire journal issue. Each photocopy reproduced by NLM contains a statement in the margin, "This is a single photostatic copy made by the National Library of Medicine for purposes of study or research in lieu of lending the original."

In recent years NLM's stated policy has been not to fill requests for copies of articles from any of 104 journals which are included in a so-called "widely-available list." Rather, the requester is furnished a copy of the "widely-available list" and the names of the regional medical libraries which are presumed to have the journals listed. Exceptions are sometimes made to the policy, particularly if the requester has been unsuccessful in obtaining the journal elsewhere. The four journals involved in this suit are listed on the "widely-available list." A rejection on the basis of the "widely-available list" is made only if the article requested was published during the preceding 5 years, but requests from Government libraries are not refused on the basis of the "widely-available list."

Also, NLM's policy is not to honor an excessive number of requests from an individual or an institution. As a general rule, not more than 20 requests from an individual, or not more than 30 requests from an institution, within a month, will be honored. In 1968, NLM adopted the policy that no more than one article from a single journal issue, or three from a journal volume, would be copied. Prior to 1968, NLM had no express policy on copying limitations, but endeavored to prevent "excessive copying." Generally, requests for more than 50 pages of material will not be honored, though exceptions are sometimes made, particularly for Government institutions. Requests for more than one copy of a journal article are rejected, without exception. If NLM receives a request for more than one copy, a single copy will be furnished and the requester advised that it is NLM's policy to furnish only one copy.

In 1968, a representative year, NLM received about 127,000 requests for interlibrary loans. Requests were received, for the most part, from other libraries or Government agencies. However, about 12 percent of the requests came from private or commercial organizations, particularly drug companies. Some requests were for books, in which event the book itself was loaned. Most requests were for journals or journal arti-

cles; and about 120,000 of the requests were filled by photocopying single articles from journals, including plaintiff's
journals. Usually, the library seeking an interlibrary loan
from NLM did so at the request of one of its patrons. If
the "loan" was made by photocopy, the photocopy was given
to the patron who was free to dispose of it as he wished. NLM
made no effort to find out the ultimate use to which the photocopies were put; and there is no evidence that borrowing
libraries kept the "loan" photocopies in their permanent
collections for use by other patrons.

Defendant concedes that, within the pertinent accounting
period, NLM and the NIH library made at least one photocopy of each of eight articles (designated by plaintiff as the
Count I-to-Count VIII articles) from one or more of the
four journals in suit. These requests, as shown at the trial,
were made by NIH researchers and an Army medical officer
(stationed in Japan) in connection with their professional
work and were used solely for those purposes. In seven of the
eight counts in the petition, the article requested was more
than two years old; in the eighth instance it was 21 or 22
months old.

II

We assume, for the purposes of the case, but without
deciding, that plaintiff is the proper copyright owner and
entitled to sue here,[5] and we agree with plaintiff that, on
that assumption, it can sue for infringement of the eight
separate articles.[6] This faces us squarely with the issue of
infringement.

Perhaps the main reason why determination of the question is so difficult is that the text of the Copyright Act of
1909, which governs the case, does not supply, by itself, a

---

[5] Defendant vigorously contests the publisher's claim to be the copyright
"proprietor" and its right to sue in this court. The argument is that the
individual authors of the articles are the owners and they have not assigned
their rights to plaintiff.

[6] Section 3 of the copyright statute, 17 U.S.C. § 3, says that, "* * * [t]he
copyright upon composite works or periodicals shall give to the proprietor
thereof all the rights in respect thereto which he would have if each part were
individually copyrighted under this title." This means, and was intended
to provide, that each article in the journals is protected from infringement
to the same extent as the entire issue. *Advertisers Exch., Inc.* v. *Laufe*, 29 F.
Supp. 1 (W.D. Pa. 1939) ; *King Features Syndicate* v. *Fleischer*, 299 F. 533
(C.A. 2, 1924).

clear or satisfactory answer. Section 1 of the Act, 17 U.S.C.
§ 1, declares that the copyright owner "shall have the exclusive right: (a) To print, reprint, publish, copy, and vend
the copyrighted work; * * *." Read with blinders, this
language might seem on its surface to be all-comprehensive—
especially the term "copy"—but we are convinced, for several
reasons, that "copy" is not to be taken in its full literal
sweep. In this instance, as in so many others in copyright,
"[T]he statute is hardly unambiguous * * * and presents
problems of interpretation not solved by literal application
of words as they are 'normally' used * * *." *DeSylva* v.
Ballentine, 351 U.S. 570, 573 (1956). *See, also, Fortnightly
Corp.* v. *United Artists Television, Inc.*, 392 U.S. 390, 395–96
(1968).

The court-created doctrine of "fair use" (discussed in Part
III, *infra*) is alone enough to demonstrate that Section 1
does not cover all copying (in the literal sense). Some forms
of copying, at the very least of portions of a work, are uni-
versally deemed immune from liability, although the very
words are reproduced in more than *de minimis* quantity.
Furthermore, it is almost unanimously accepted that a
scholar can make a handwritten copy of an entire copyrighted article for his own use, and in the era before photoduplication it was not uncommon (and not seriously questioned) that he could have his secretary make a typed copy
for his personal use and files. These customary facts of copy-
right-life are among our givens. The issue we now have is
the complex one of whether photocopying, in the form done
by NIH and NLM, should be accorded the same treatment—
not the ministerial lexicographic task of deciding that
photoduplication necessarily involves "copying" (as of course
it does in dictionary terms).

One aspect of the history and structure of the 1909 Act
offers another reason for refusing to give "copying" in Section 1, as applied to these articles, its simplest "ordinary"
reach. It is pointed out to us, on the basis of analysis of the
copyright laws from 1790 to 1909,[7] that the early statutes

---

[7] Congress enacted the first copyright statute in 1790 (Act of May 31, 1790,
ch. 15, 1 Stat. 124). Thereafter, the statute was revised from time to time,
notably in 1802, 1831, 1870, and 1891. In 1909, the present statute was
passed (Act of March 4, 1909, ch. 320, 35 Stat. 1075) and later was codified
as 17 U.S.C. (Act of July 30, 1947, 61 Stat. 652).

distinguished "copying" from "printing," "reprinting," and "publishing," and provided that the copyright in books is infringed by "printing," "reprinting" and "publishing," while the copyright in other works (*e.g.*, photographs, paintings, engraving, drawings, etc.) is infringed by "copying." *Cf. Harper* v. *Shoppell*, 26 F. 519, 520 (C.C.S.D.N.Y. 1886). The 1909 Act obliterated any such distinction in its text. It provides in § 5 a list of all classes of copyrightable subject matter (including books and periodicals), and says in § 1 that the owner of copyright shall have the exclusive right "to print, reprint, publish, copy and vend the copyrighted work." Thus, the 1909 Act, unlike the earlier statutes, does not expressly say which of the proscribed acts of § 1 apply to which classes of copyrightable subject matter of § 5. Defendant and some of the amici say that, to be consistent with the intent and purpose of earlier statutes, the "copying" proscription of § 1 should not apply to books or periodicals; rather, only the proscribed acts of "printing," "reprinting" and "publishing" control books and periodicals. The proponents of this view stress that the legislative history of the 1909 legislation does not suggest any purpose to alter the previous coverage.[8]

This is quite a serious argument. However, in view of Congress's general inclusion of the word "copy" in Section 1 and of the practice under the Act since 1909, we are not ready to accept fully this claim that infringement of periodical articles can come only through "printing," "reprinting" or "publishing." But we do believe this point—that there is a solid doubt whether and how far "copy" applies to books and journals—must be taken into account in measuring the outlines of "copying" as it involves books and articles.

Adding to this doubt that "copy" blankets such printed matter is the significant implication of a special segment of the background of the 1909 statute, a sector of history which is peripheral but revealing. The then Librarian of Congress,

---

[8] For instance, H.R. Rep. No. 2222, 60th Cong., 2d Sess. 4 (1909) states: "Subsection (a) of section 1 adopts without change the phraseology of section 4952 of the Revised Statutes, and this, with the insertion of the word 'copy,' practically adopts the phraseology of the first copyright act Congress ever passed—that of 1790. Many amendments of this were suggested, but the committee felt that it was safer to retain without change the old phraseology which has been so often construed by the courts."

Herbert Putnam, was the leading public sponsor of that Act (outside of Congress itself), and was intimately involved in its preparation from at least 1906 on. While the bill was being considered in Congress, the Library's 1908 "Rules and Practice Governing the Use and Issue of Books," p. 6, specifically provided:

> "*Photographing.* Photographing is freely permitted. The permission extends to the building itself and any of its parts, including the mural decorations. *It extends to articles bearing claim of copyright*, but the Library gives no assurance that the photograph may be reproduced or republished or placed on sale. These are matters to be settled with the owner of the copyright" (emphasis added).

After the 1909 Act became law, the Library continued the same provision. The 1913 version of the "Rules and Practice" [9] added the following on "Photostat," after the above paragraph on "Photographing":

> Photo-duplicates of books, newspapers, maps, etc. can be furnished at a reasonable rate by means of the photostat, installed in the Chief Clerk's Office. Apply to the Chief Clerk for a schedule of charges.

Later editions, throughout Dr. Putnam's tenure (which ended in 1939), contained the same or comparable provisions.[10] Indeed, when he left his post in 1939, he was honored by the American Council of Learned Societies because (among other things) "You have led in adapting the most modern photographic processes to the needs of the scholar, and have * * * made widely available for purposes of research copies of your collections * * *." This illuminating slice of history, covering the time of enactment and the first three decades of the 1909 Act, should not be ignored.

These are the leading reasons why we cannot stop with the dictionary or "normal" definition of "copy"—nor can we extract much affirmative help from the surfacial legislative text. As for the other rights given in Section 1, "vend" is clearly irrelevant (since NIH and NLM do not sell), and the applicability to this case of "print," "reprint" and "publish" is more dubious than of "copy." The photocopy process

---

[9] There was an 1911 edition, but no copy has been located.
[10] The Library's current practice is described in Part III, 3, note 16, *infra*.

of NIH and NLM, described in Part I, *supra*, does not even amount to printing or reprinting in the strict dictionary sense; and if the words be used more broadly to include all mechanical reproduction of a number of copies, they would still not cover the making of a single copy for an individual requester. If the requester himself made a photocopy of the article for his own use on a machine made available by the library, he might conceivably be "copying" but he would not be "printing" or "reprinting." The library is in the same position when responding to the demands of individual researchers acting separately.

For similar reasons there is no "publication" by the library, a concept which invokes general distribution, or at least a supplying of the material to a fairly large group.[11] The author of an uncopyrighted manuscript does not lose his common law rights, via publication, by giving photocopies to his friends for comment or their personal use—and publication for Section 1 purposes would seem to have about the same coverage. In any event, the hitherto uncodified principles of "fair use" apply to printing, reprinting, and publishing, as well as to copying, and therefore the collocation of general words Congress chose for Section 1 is necessarily inadequate, by itself, to decide this case.

III

In the fifty-odd years since the 1909 Act, the major tool for probing what physical copying amounts to unlawful "copying" (as well as what is unlawful "printing," "reprinting" and "publishing") has been the gloss of "fair use" which the courts have put upon the words of the statute. Precisely because a determination that a use is "fair," or "unfair," depends on an evaluation of the complex of individual and varying factors bearing upon the particular use (see H.R. REP. No. 83, 90th Cong., 1st Sess., p. 29), there has been no exact or detailed definition of the doctrine. The courts, congressional committees, and scholars have had to be content

---

[11] To the extent that *Macmillan Co.* v. *King*, 223 F. 862 (D. Mass. 1914), may possibly suggest that "publication" can occur through simple distribution to a very small restricted group, for a special purpose, we think the opinion goes too far.

with a general listing of the main considerations—together
with the example of specific instances ruled "fair" or "unfair." These overall factors are now said to be: (a) the purpose and character of the use, (b) the nature of the
copyrighted work, (c) the amount and substantiality of the
material used in relation to the copyrighted work as a whole,
and (d) the effect of the use on a copyright owner's potential
market for and value of his work.

In addition, the development of "fair use" has been influenced by some tension between the direct aim of the copyright privilege to grant the owner a right from which he
can reap financial benefit and the more fundamental purpose
of the protection "To promote the Progress of Science and
the useful Arts." U.S. Const., art. 1, § 8. The House committee which recommended the 1909 Act said that copyright
was "[n]ot primarily for the benefit of the author, but primarily for the benefit of the public." H.R. REP. No. 2222,
60th Cong., 2d Sess., p. 7. The Supreme Court has stated that
"The copyright law, like the patent statutes, makes reward
to the owner a secondary consideration." *Mazer* v. *Stein*, 347
U.S. 201, 219 (1954); *United States* v. *Paramount Pictures*,
334 U.S. 131, 158 (1948). *See* Breyer, *The Uneasy Case for
Copyright: A study of Copyright in Books, Photocopies, and
Computer Programs*, 84 Harv. L. Rev. 281 (1970). To serve
the constitutional purpose, " 'courts in passing upon particular claims of infringement must occasionally subordinate
the copyright holder's interest in a maximum financial return
to the greater public interest in the development of art,
science and industry.' *Berlin* v. *E.C. Publications, Inc.*, 329
F. 2d 541, 544 (2d Cir. 1964). Whether the privilege may
justifiably be applied to particular materials turns initially
on the nature of the materials, e.g., whether their distribution
would serve the public interest in the free dissemination of
information and whether their preparation requires some use
of prior materials dealing with the same subject matter.
Consequently, the privilege has been applied to works in the
fields of science, law, medicine, history and biography."
Rosemont Enterprises, Inc. v. *Random House, Inc.*, 366 **F. 2d**
303, 307 (C.A. 2, 1966).

It has sometimes been suggested that the copying of an
entire copyrighted work, any such work, cannot ever be

"fair use," but this is an overbroad generalization, unsupported by the decisions [12] and rejected by years of accepted practice. The handwritten or typed copy of an article, for personal use, is one illustration, let alone the thousands of copies of poems, songs, or such items which have long been made by individuals, and sometimes given to lovers and others. Trial Judge James F. Davis, who considered the use now in dispute not to be "fair," nevertheless agreed that a library could supply single photocopies of entire copyrighted works to attorneys or courts for use in litigation. It is, of course, common for courts to be given photocopies of recent decisions, with the publishing company's headnotes and arrangement, and sometimes its annotations. There are other examples from everyday legal and personal life. We cannot believe, for instance, that a judge who makes and gives to a colleague a photocopy of a law review article, in one of the smaller or less available journals, which bears directly on a problem both judges are then considering in a case before them is infringing the copyright, rather than making "fair use" of his issue of that journal. Similarly with the photocopies of particular newspaper items and articles which are frequently given or sent by one friend to another.[13]

---

[12] *Leon* v. *Pacific Tel. & Tel. Co.*, 91 F. 2d 484, 486 (C.A. 9, 1937) and *Public Affairs Associates, Inc.* v. *Rickover*, 284 F. 2d 262, 272 (C.A.D.C. 1960), *vacated and remanded,* 369 U.S. 111 (1962), which are often cited in this connection, both involved actual publication and distribution of many copies, not the simple making of a copy for individual personal or restricted use. In *Wihtol* v. *Crow*, 309 F. 2d 777 (C.A. 8, 1962), 48 copies of the copyrighted song were made and distributed, and there were a number of public performances using these copies. It was as if the defendant had purchased one copy of sheet music and then duplicated it for an entire chorus.

On the other hand, *New York Tribune, Inc.* v. *Otis & Co.*, 39 F. Supp. 67 (S.D.N.Y. 1941), shows that copying of an entire copyrighted item is not enough, in itself, to preclude application of "fair use." Although it was already plain that an entire copyrighted item (a newspaper editorial) had been reproduced, the court ordered further proceedings to take account of other factors.

[13] Verner Clapp, former Acting Librarian of Congress, has pointed out some of the uses of a photocopy for which the library copy original is unsuited (*Can Copyright Law Respond to the New Technology?*, 61 Law Lib. J. 387, 407 (1968)):

"I cannot submit the original conveniently in a court, in a suit of law. I cannot put the original into my filing cabinet. I can't shuffle it with notes in preparation for an address. I can't make notes on it. I can't conveniently give it to a typist. I can't use it as printer's copy. I can't send it through the mail without serious risk of loss of an original. With a photocopy I can do all these things and more, and this is the reason I want a copy."

There is, in short, no inflexible rule excluding an entire copy-righted work from the area of "fair use." Instead, the extent of the copying is one important factor, but only one, to be taken into account, along with several others.

Under these over-all standards, we have weighed the multiplicity of factors converging on the particular use of plaintiff's material made by NIH and NLM, as shown by this record. There is no prior decision which is dispositive and hardly any that can be called even close; we have had to make our own appraisal. The majority of the court has concluded that, on this record, the challenged use should be designated "fair," not "unfair." In the rest of this part of our opinion, we discuss *seriatim* the various considerations which merge to that conclusion. But we can help focus on what is probably the core of our evaluation by stating summarily, in advance, three propositions we shall consider at greater length: First, plaintiff has not in our view shown, and there is inadequate reason to believe, that it is being or will be harmed substantially by these specific practices of NIH and NLM; second, we are convinced that medicine and medical research will be injured by holding these particular practices to be an infringement; and, third, since the problem of accommodating the interests of science with those of the publishers (and authors) calls fundamentally for legislative solution or guidance, which has not yet been given, we should not, during the period before congressional action is forthcoming, place such a risk of harm upon science and medicine.

1. We start by emphasizing that (a) NIH and NLM are non-profit institutions, devoted solely to the advancement and dissemination of medical knowledge which they seek to further by the challenged practices, and are not attempting to profit or gain financially by the photocopying; (b) the medical researchers who have asked these libraries for the photocopies are in this particular case (and ordinarily) scientific researchers and practitioners who need the articles for personal use in their scientific work and have no purpose to reduplicate them for sale or other general distribution; and (c) the copied articles are scientific studies useful to the requesters in their work. On both sides—library and requester—scientific progress, untainted by any commerical gain from the reproduction, is the hallmark of the whole enterprise of duplication. There has been no attempt to misappropriate the work of earlier scientific writers for forbidden ends, but rather an effort to gain easier access to the material for study and research. This is important because it is settled that, in general, the law gives copying for scientific purposes a wide scope. *See, e.g., Rosemont Enterprises, Inc.* v. *Random House, Inc., supra,* 366 F. 2d at 306–07; *Loew's, Inc.* v. *Columbia Broadcasting System, Inc.,* 131 F. Supp. 165, 175 (S.D. Cal. 1955), *aff'd,* 239 F. 2d 532 (C.A. 9, 1956), *aff'd by an equally divided Court,* 356 U.S. 43 (1958); *Greenbie* v. *Noble,* 151 F. Supp. 45, 67–68 (S.D.N.Y. 1957); *Thompson* v. *Gernsback,* 94 F. Supp. 453, 454 (S.D.N.Y. 1950); *Henry Holt & Co.* v. *Liggett & Myers Tobacco Co.,* 23 F. Supp. 302, 304 (E.D. Pa. 1938).

2. Both libraries have declared and enforced reasonably strict limitations which, to our mind, keep the duplication within appropriate confines. The details are set forth in Part I *supra,* and in our findings. Both institutions normally restrict copying on an individual request to a single copy of a single article of a journal issue, and to articles of less than 50 pages. Though exceptions are made, they do not appear to be excessive, unwarranted, or irrational. For instance, though on occasion one person was shown to have ordered or received more than one photocopy of the same article, the second copy was for a colleague's use or to replace an illegible or undelivered copy. Some care is also taken not to have excessive copying from one issue or one volume of the periodical. While a certain amount of duplication of articles does, of course, occur, it does not appear to be at all heavy.[14] There is no showing whatever that the recipients use the libraries' photocopying process to sell the copies or distribute them broadly.

NIH responds only to requests from its own personnel, so that its entire photoduplication system is strictly "in-house"—in the same way that a court's library may supply

---

[14] One survey of NIH operations shows only 4 instances of duplication in over 200 requests; at NLM, as of 1964, duplication occurred at a 10% rate in the 102 most heavily used journals (constituting one-third of total requests); if all requests were considered, the rate would be less. The Sophar & Heilprin report (see Appendix), which is not friendly to library photocopying, estimates that for libraries generally the duplication rate was about 3% (p. 111).

a judge of that court with a copy of a law journal article or a reported decision. NLM fulfills requests more generally but it has adopted the practice of not responding (outside of the Government) where the article appears in a recent (preceding 5 years) issue of a periodical on its "widely-available list". The result is that the duplication of recent issues of generally available journals is kept within the Government, and distribution to the larger medical public is limited to older, less available issues and to journals which are harder to obtain from medical libraries. It is a fair inference, supported by this record, that at the very least in the latter classes the demand has been inadequately filled by reprints and the publisher's sale of back issues. *See, also,* Part III, 4, *infra.* In those instances not covered by "five year" policy, the impression left by the record is that, on the whole, older rather than current articles were usually requested.

Brushing aside all such breakdowns, plaintiff points to the very large number, in absolute terms, of the copies made each year by the two libraries. We do not think this decisive.[15] In view of the large numbers of scientific personnel served and the great size of the libraries—NIH has over 100,000 volumes of journal materials alone, and NLM is currently binding over 18,000 journals each year—the amount of copying does not seem to us to have been excessive or disproportionate. The important factor is not the absolute amount, but the twin elements of (i) the existence and purpose of the system of limitations imposed and enforced, and (ii) the effectiveness of that system to confine the duplication for the personal use of scientific personnel who need the material for their work, with the minimum of potential abuse or harm to the copyright owner. The practices of NIH and NLM, as shown by the record, pass both of these tests, despite the large number of copies annually sent out.

Without necessarily accepting the full sweep of the concept that the library is nothing more than the individual requester's ministerial agent, we do agree that the NIH and NLM systems, as described in the evidence, are close kin to the current Library of Congress policy, *see* note 16, *infra,*

---

[15] In 1970, NIH copied 85,744 and NLM 93,746 articles.

of maintaining machines in the library buildings so that readers can do their own copying. The principal extension by NLM and NIH is to service requesters who cannot conveniently come to the building, as well as out-of-town libraries. But the personal, individual focus is still present. The reader who himself makes a copy does so for his own personal work needs, and individual work needs are likewise dominant in the reproduction programs of the two medical libraries— programs which are reasonably policed and enforced.

3. We also think it significant, in assessing the recent and current practices of the two libraries, that library photocopying, though not of course to the extent of the modern development, has been going on ever since the 1909 Act was adopted. In Part II, *supra*, we have set forth the practice of the Library of Congress at that time and for many years thereafter.[16] In fact, photocopying seems to have been done in the Library at least from the beginning of this century. *Can Copyright Law Respond to the New Technology?* 61 Law. Lib. J. 387, 400 (1968) (comments of V. Clapp). In 1935 there was a so-called "gentlemen's agreement" between the National Association of Book Publishers (since defunct) and the Joint Committee on Materials for Research (representing the libraries), stating in part: "A library * * * owning books or periodical volumes in which copyright still subsists may make and deliver a single photographic reproduction * * * of a part thereof to a scholar representing in writing that he desires such reproduction in lieu of loan of such publication or in place of manual transcription and solely for the purposes of research * * *." Though this understanding discountenanced photoduplication of an entire book it was regularly construed as allowing copying of articles. There have been criticisms of this pact, and we cite it, not as binding in any way on plaintiff or any other pub-

---

[16] Currently, and for some time, the Library of Congress has said that copyright material will "ordinarily" not be photocopied by the Library "without the signed authorization of the copyright owner," but "[e]xceptions to this rule may be made in particular cases." The Library does, however, maintain machines which readers may themselves use for photocopying; these machines contain notices saying that "a single photocopy of copyrighted material may be made only for the purpose of study, scholarship, or research, and for no other purpose" and "the sale and/or further reproduction of any photocopied copyrighted materials is illegal."

lisher, or as showing universal recognition of "single" photocopying, but as representing a very widely held view, almost 40 years ago, of what was permissible under the 1909 statute.

There is other evidence that, until quite recently, library photocopying was carried on with apparent general acceptance. Witnesses in this case testified that such photocopying has been done for at least fifty years and is well-established. The National Library of Medicine Act, in 1956, by which NLM was created (42 U.S.C. § 275, *et seq.*), provided at § 276(4) that the Secretary of Health, Education, and Welfare, through NLM, should "make available, through loans, photographic or other copying procedures or otherwise, such materials in the Library as he deems appropriate * * *"; and the Medical Library Assistance Act of 1965 (42 U.S.C. § 280b–1, *et seq.*) provided that grants be made to medical libraries for, among other things, "acquisition of duplicating devices, facsimile equipment * * * and other equipment to facilitate the use of the resources of the library." 42 U.S.C. § 280b–7. These two pieces of legislation indicate to us that Congress knew in 1956 and 1965 of the practice of library photocopying, and assumed that it was not beyond the pale. The General Interlibrary Loan Code (revised in 1956), *see* Part I, *supra,* is a similar indication of the extent of the practice, and of the general position of the libraries (at the least) that such copying is permissible.

The fact that photocopying by libraries of entire articles was done with hardly any (and at most very minor) complaint, until about 10 or 15 years ago, goes a long way to show both that photoduplication cannot be designated as infringement *per se,* and that there was at least a time when photocopying, as then carried on, was "fair use." There have been, of course, considerable changes in the ease and extent of such reproduction, and these developments bear on "fair use" as of today, but the libraries can properly stand on the proposition that they photocopied articles for many years, without significant protest, and that such copying was generally accepted until the proliferation of inexpensive and improved copying machines, less than two decades ago, led to the surge in such duplication. The question then becomes whether this marked increase in volume changes a use which was generally accepted as "fair" into one which has now become "unfair."

4. There is no doubt in our minds that medical science would be seriously hurt if such library photocopying were stopped. We do not spend time and space demonstrating this proposition. It is admitted by plaintiff and conceded on all sides. *See, e.g. Varmer, Photoduplication of Copyrighted Material by Libraries,* Study No. 15, "Copyright Law Revision," Studies Prepared for the Subcommittee on Patents, Trademarks and Copyrights, Senate Judiciary Committee (1959), p. 49; Memorandum of General Counsel Willcox, Department of Health, Education and Welfare, June 7, 1965, Hearings before Subcommittee No. 3, Committee on the Judiciary, H. of Reps., 89th Cong., 1st Sess., on H.R. 4347, H.R. 5680, etc., "Copyright Law Revision," Part 2, 1132, 1133. The trial testimony of a number of the requesters and authors documents the point. The supply of reprints and back numbers is wholly inadequate; the evidence shows the unlikelihood of obtaining such substitutes for photocopies from publishers of medical journals or authors of journal articles, especially for articles over three years old.[17] It is, moreover, wholly unrealistic to expect scientific personnel to subscribe regularly to large numbers of journals which would only occasionally contain articles of interest to them. Nor will libraries purchase extensive numbers of whole subscriptions to all medical journals on the chance that an indeterminate number of articles in an indeterminate number of issues will be requested at indeterminate times. The result of a flat proscription on library photocopying would be, we feel sure, that medical and scientific personnel would simply do without, and have to do without, many of the articles they now desire, need, and use in their work.[18]

5. Plaintiff insists that it has been financially hurt by the photocopying practices of NLM and NIH, and of other libraries. The trial judge thought that it was reasonable to infer that the extensive photocopying has resulted in some

---

[17] Plaintiff itself publishes a notice to the effect that it does not attempt to keep a stock of back issues, and it refers requests for reprints to the author.

[18] We think the alternative of compulsory licensing is not open to us under the present copyright statute. *See, infra,* Parts III, 6, and IV.

loss of revenue to plaintiff and that plaintiff has lost, or failed to get, "some undetermined and indeterminable number of journal subscriptions (perhaps small)" by virtue of the photocopying. He thought that the persons requesting photocopies constituted plaintiff's market and that each photocopy user is a potential subscriber "or at least a potential source of royalty income for licensed copying." [19] Studies rejecting as "fair use" the kind of photocopying involved here have also assumed, without real proof, that the journal publishers have been and will be injured. *See, e.g., Project— New Technology and the Law of Copyright: Reprography and Computers*, 15 U.C.L.A. L. Rev. 931 (1968); *Sophor & Heilprin, "The Determination of Legal Facts and Economic Guideposts with Respect to the Dissemination of Scientific and Educational Information as It Is Affected by Copyright—A Status Report"* (1967).

The record made in this case does not sustain that assumption. Defendant made a thorough effort to try to ascertain, so far as possible, the effect of photoduplication on plaintiff's business, including the presentation of an expert witness. The unrefuted evidence shows that (a) between 1958 and 1969 annual subscriptions to the four medical journals involved increased substantially (for three of them, very much so), annual subscription sales likewise increased substantially, and total annual income also grew; (b) between 1959 and 1966, plaintiff's annual taxable income increased from $272,000 to $726,000, fell to $589,000 in 1967, and in 1968 to $451,000; (c) but the four journals in suit account for a relatively small percentage of plaintiff's total business and over the years each has been profitable (though 3 of them show losses in particular years and in all years the profits have not been large, varying from less than $1,000 to about $15,000, some of which has been shared with the sponsoring

---

[19] It is wrong to measure the detriment to plaintiff by loss of presumed royalty income—a standard which necessarily assumes that plaintiff had a right to issue licenses. That would be true, of course, only if it were first decided that the defendant's practices did not constitute "fair use." In determining whether the company has been sufficiently hurt to cause these practices to become "unfair," one cannot assume at the start the merit of the plaintiff's position, *i.e.*, that plaintiff had the right to license. That conclusion results only if it is first determined that the photocopying is "unfair."

medical societies) ; [20] and (d) plaintiff's business appears to have been growing faster than the gross national product or of the rate of growth of manpower working in the field of science. Defendant's expert concluded that the photocopying shown here had not damaged plaintiff, and may actually have helped it.[21] The record is also barren of solid evidence that photocopying has caused economic harm to any other publisher of medical journals.

Plaintiff has never made a detailed study of the actual effect of photocopying on its business, nor has it refuted defendant's figures. It has relied for its assumption (in the words of the chairman of its board) on "general business common sense and things that you hear from subscribers, librarians and so forth." Its argument—and that of the other supporters of its position [22]—is that there "must" be an effect because photocopies supplant the original articles, and if there were no photocopying those who now get the copies would necessarily buy the journals or issues. But this untested hypothesis, reminiscent of the abstract theorems beloved of the "pure" classical economics of 70 or 80 years ago, is neither obvious nor self-proving. One need not enter the semantic debate over whether the photocopy supplants the original article itself or is merely in substitution for the library's loan of the original issue to recognize, as we have already pointed out, that there are other possibilities. If photocopying were forbidden, the researchers, instead of subscribing to more journals or trying to obtain or buy back-issues or reprints (usually unavailable), might expend extra time in note-taking or waiting

---

[20] Defendant explains the loss years and the fall-off in some subscriptions in some years as due to particular circumstances (which are spelled out) other than photocopying.

[21] The trial judge referred to two instances in which subscribers cancelled subscriptions because of the availability of photocopying. Defendant is correct that both instances rest on hearsay, and in any event this small number of purported cancellations is *de minimis* in view of the more solid and detailed proof as to the health of plaintiff's journals and the increase in their subscription lists.

[22] The published literature does not reveal any careful, thorough, impartial study of this question. Often there is no attempt to ascertain the actual economic impact on the publishers and authors; when inquiry has been made of the latter, their conclusory generalizations of injury have been accepted uncritically.

their turn for the library's copies of the original issues—or they might very well cut down their reading and do without much of the information they now get through NLM's and NIH's copying system. The record shows that each of the individual requesters in this case already subscribed, personally, to a number of medical journals, and it is very questionable how many more, if any, they would add. The great problems with reprints and back-issues have already been noted. In the absence of photocopying, the financial, time-wasting, and other difficulties of obtaining the material could well lead, if human experience is a guide, to a simple but drastic reduction in the use of the many articles (now sought and read) which are not absolutely crucial to the individual's work but are merely stimulating or helpful. The probable effect on scientific progress goes without saying, but for this part of our discussion the significant element is that plaintiff, as publisher and copyright owner, would not be better off. Plaintiff would merely be the dog in the manger.

Since plaintiff and those who take the same view have not attempted any hard factual study of the actual effect of photocopying, it is not surprising that others have concluded against an adverse impact. The 1962 Fry Report (George Fry & Associates, "Survey of Copyrighted Material Reproduction Practices in Scientific and Technical Fields," March 1962) states that the "basic conclusion of this report is that at the present time, no significant damage occurs to the copyright holders in the scientific and technical fields although duplication of this material is widespread and is growing rapidly." In March 1965, Dan Lacy, Managing Director, American Book Publishers Council, told a House of Representatives committee: "It has been pointed out that recent technological developments have enormously increased the amount of photocopying in libraries and technology is continuing to change rapidly. Most of this photocopying, at least at present, probably consists of excerpts and probably mostly of journal articles. *Most of it at present is probably undertaken in lieu of manual note taking, typing, or handwriting a copy, and in lieu of library loan rather than in lieu of buying a copy*" (emphasis added). Hearings before Subcommittee No. 3, Committee on the

Judiciary, H. of Reps., 89th Cong., 1st Sess., on H.R. 4347, H.R. 5680, etc., "Copyright Law Revision," Part 1, p. 120. The record in this case does not prove that the situation was any different at the time of the trial.

To us it is very important that plaintiff has failed to prove its assumption of economic detriment, in the past or potentially for the future. One of the factors always considered with respect to "fair use," *see supra*, is the effect of the use on the owner's potential market for the work. This record simply does not show a serious adverse impact, either on plaintiff or on medical publishers generally, from the photocopying practices of the type of NIH and NLM. In the face of this record, we cannot mechanically assume such an effect, or hold that the amount of photoduplication proved here "must" lead to financial or economic harm. This is a matter of proof and plaintiff has not transformed its hypothetical assumption, by evidence, into a proven fact.

In this connection it is worth noting that plaintiff does not have to concern itself, with respect to these journals, with authors or medical societies who are interested in a financial return. The authors, with rare exceptions, are not paid for their contributions, and those societies which share profits do not press for greater financial benefits. Indeed, some of the authors of the copied articles involved in this case testified at the trial that they favored photocopying as an aid to the advancement of science and knowledge.

6. Added to the powerful factors we have been considering is another (already suggested by the discussion in Part II, *supra*)—the grave uncertainty of the coverage of "copy" in Section 1 of the 1909 Act and the doubt whether it relates at all to periodicals.[23] The latitude for "fair use" is of course lessened to the extent Congress has been explicit in spelling out protection to the copyright owner. But Congress has, up to now, left the problem of photocopying untouched by express provision and only doubtfully covered to any extent by the generalizations of Section 1. The statute must, of course, "be applied to new situations not anticipated by Congress, if, fairly construed, such situations come within its intent and meaning" (*Jerome H. Remick & Co.* v. *American Automobile*

---

[23] The same is true of "print," "reprint," and "publish," as applied to the challenged practices of NLM and NIH.

Accessories Co., 5 F. 2d 411 (C.A. 6, 1925), *cert. denied*, 269 U.S. 556), but our problem is with the latter part of this quotation. That being so, we think that, in evaluating "fair use," we should give the benefit of the doubt—until Congress acts more specifically—to science and the libraries, rather than to the publisher and the owner.

While, as we have said, this record fails to show that plaintiff (or any other medical publisher) has been substantially harmed by the photocopying practices of NIH and NLM, it does show affirmatively that medical science will be hurt if such photocopying is stopped. Thus, the balance of risks is definitely on defendant's side—until Congress acts more specifically, the burden on medical science of a holding that the photocopying is an infringement would appear to be much greater than the present or foreseeable burden on plaintiff and other medical publishers of a ruling that these practices fall within "fair use."

Plaintiff's answer is that it is willing to license the libraries, on payment of a reasonable royalty, to continue photocopying as they have. Our difficulty with that response—in addition to the absence of proof that plaintiff has yet been hurt, and the twin doubts whether plaintiff has a viable license system and whether any satisfactory program can be created without legislation [24]—is that the 1909 Act does not provide for compulsory licensing in this field. All that a court can do is to determine the photocopying an infringement, leaving it to the owner to decide whether to license or to prohibit the practice. Plaintiff and other publishers cannot enjoin governmental libraries (because 28

---

[24] Defendant and its amici strongly attack plaintiff's so-called licensing plan as nothing more than a shell. The American Library Association points out, for instance, that the Williams & Wilkins license would apparently not apply to inter-library loans or to requests from persons not physically present in the library building.

There is also debate over whether a feasible ASCAP-type or clearinghouse system can be developed without legislation, and if so whether it would be desirable. *See, e.g.,* Note, *Education and Copyright Law: An Analysis of the Amended Copyright Revision Bill and Proposals for Statutory Licensing and a Clearinghouse System,* 56 Va. L. Rev. 664 (1970) ; also published as MacLean, *Education and Copyright Law: An Analysis of the Amended Copyright Revision Bill and Proposals for Statutory Licensing and a Clearinghouse System,* in ASCAP, *"Copyright Law Symposium, Number Twenty,"* 1 (1972) ; Breyer, *The Uneasy Case for Copyright: A Study of Copyright in Books, Photocopies and Computer Programs,* 84 Harv. L. Rev. 281, 330 *ff.* (1970) ; Note: *New Technology and the Law of Copyright: Reprography and Computers,* 15 UCLA L. Rev. 939, 961 *ff.* (1968).

U.S.C. § 1498, *supra* note 1, is the sole remedy), but if photo-copying of this type is an infringement the owners are free under the law to seek to enjoin any and all nongovernmental libraries. A licensing system would be purely voluntary with the copyright proprietor. We consider it entirely beyond judicial power, under the 1909 Act,[25] to order an owner to institute such a system if he does not wish to. We think it equally outside a court's present competence to turn the de-termination of "fair use" on the owner's willingness to license—to hold that photocopying (without royalty pay-ments) is not "fair use" if the owner is willing to license at reasonable rates but becomes a "fair use" if the owner is adamant and refuses all permission (or seeks to charge excessive fees).

The truth is that this is now preeminently a problem for Congress: to decide the extent photocopying should be allowed, the questions of a compulsory license and the pay-ments (if any) to the copyright owners, the system for col-lecting those payments (lump-sum, clearinghouse, etc.), the special status (if any) of scientific and educational needs. Obviously there is much to be said on all sides. The choices involve economic, social, and policy factors which are far better sifted by a legislature. The possible intermediate solu-tions are also of the pragmatic kind legislatures, not courts, can and should fashion. But Congress does not appear to have put its mind directly to this problem in 1909, undoubt-edly because the issue was not considered pressing at that time. That statute is, unfortunately, the one we must apply, and under it we have the choice only of thumb's up or thumb's down, for the photocopying practice involved in this litiga-tion, without any real Congressional guidance. Intermedi-ate or compromise solutions are not within our authority.[26] The theme of this subpart 6 of Part III of the opinion is that, on balance and on this record, thumb's up seems to us less dangerous to the varying interests at stake during the pe-riod which remains before Congress definitively takes hold of the subject.

---

[25] A court's powers under the anti-trust legislation is another matter.

[26] It has been suggested, however, that publishers now have the power to adopt the intermediate solution of charging more for subscriptions sold to libraries or other entities which engage regularly in photocopying.

7. The revision of the 1909 Act is now under consideration and has been for several years. The House of Representatives passed a bill in the 90th Congress (in April 1967), but the Senate has not acted.[27] In its report on the bill which the House adopted (H.R. REP. No. 83, 90th Cong., 1st Sess.), the House Committee on the Judiciary discussed the existing doctrine of "fair use" at some length (pp. 29–37). We cite these comments, not as binding on us, but as the official views on the extent of "fair use" of the committee of the House of Representatives with cognizance over copyright; as such, they are and should be influential.

The report makes it very clear that photocopying can be a "fair use", in proper circumstances; it negatives the notion that copying of a complete work can never be a "fair use"; and it obviously believes that the doctrine is flexible, depending upon the particular situation.[28] The report does not, however, express a categorical or clear view whether photocopying of the sort we have in this case is or is not a "fair use" under the doctrine as it has been developing. Rather, the committee's observations are delphic, with each side being able to quote to us one or another passage, or to argue by analogy from the specific situation (classroom teaching) considered in greatest detail in the report.

Specifically on library photocopying the committee says (p. 36) that it does not favor a specific provision dealing with that subject, and it adds: "Unauthorized library copying, like everything else, must be judged a fair use or an infringement on the basis of all of the applicable criteria and the facts of the particular case. Despite past efforts, reasonable

---

[27] A synopsis of the revision effort (up to 1968) is set forth in *Fortnightly Corp.* v. *United Artists Television, Inc.,* 392 U.S. 390, 396 n. 17 (1968).

[28] The report says (p. 29) that "* * * since the doctrine is an equitable rule of reason, no generally applicable definition is possible, and each case raising the question must be decided on its own facts"; that (p. 32) the committee endorses "the purpose and general scope of the judicial doctrine of fair use, as outlined earlier in this report, but there is no disposition to freeze the doctrine in the statute, especially during a period of technological change. Beyond a very broad statutory explanation of what fair use is and some of the criteria applicable to it, the courts must be free to adapt the doctrine to particular situations on a case-by-case basis; and that (p. 32) "Section 107, as revised by the committee, is intended to restate the present judicial doctrine of fair use, not to change, narrow, or enlarge it in any way."

arrangements involving a mutual understanding of what
generally constitutes acceptable library practices, and providing workable clearance and licensing conditions, have not
been achieved and are overdue. The committee urges all concerned to resume their efforts to reach an accommodation
under which the needs of scholarship and the rights of
authors would both be respected."

We read this report, as a whole, as recognizing affirmatively that, under the existing law, library photocopying can be
"fair use" in proper circumstances, and as leaving the determination of whether the particular circumstances are proper
ones to an evaluation "of all the applicable criteria and the
facts of the particular case." That is, of course, the overall
standard we are using, and therefore we consider our approach to be consistent with that of the Committee. Although
one cannot say that the report places its sanction directly on
the photocopying practices now before us, neither does it
suggest or intimate that they are "unfair." That question is
left open. The report is nevertheless helpful because it indicates the correctness of our general approach, and also
because it contradicts the concept, urged by plaintiff, that
photocopying of an entire article is necessarily an infringement.

8. The last component we mention, as bearing on "fair
use", is the practice in foreign countries. The copyright legislation of the United Kingdom, New Zealand, Denmark, Finland, Italy, Norway, Sweden, France, the German Federal
Republic, Lichtenstein, Mexico, the Netherlands, and the
U.S.S.R. have specific provisions which we think would
cover the photocopying activities of NLM and NIH. Canada,
India, Ireland and South Africa, while having no specific
provisions permitting copying of copyrighted works for the
purposes of private research and study, do provide, more
generally, that fair dealing for purposes of private study or
research shall not be an infringement.[29] These provisions in
foreign countries with problems and backgrounds comparable to our own are highly persuasive that the copying done

---

[29] The foreign laws are compiled in *Copyright Laws and Treaties of the
World*, published by UNESCO.

here should be considered a "fair use," not an infringement.[30] Where Congress has left such a large void to be filled entirely by the courts, it is appropriate for us to consider what other jurisdictions have done either by way of legislation or judicial decision.

IV

Fusing these elements together, we conclude that plaintiff has failed to show that the defendant's use of the copyrighted material has been "unfair," and conversely we find that these practices have up to now been "fair." There has been no infringement. As Professor (now Mr. Justice) Kaplan observed, it is "fundamental that 'use' is not the same as 'infringement' [and] that use short of infringement is to be encouraged * * *. " Kaplan, *An Unhurried View of Copyright* 57 (1967); *see Fortnightly Corp.* v. *United Artists Television, Inc.,* 392 U.S. 390, 393–95 (1968).

So as not to be misunderstood, we reemphasize four interrelated aspects of our holding. The first is that the conclusion that defendant's particular use of plaintiff's copyrighted material has been "fair" rests upon all of the elements discussed in Part III, *supra,* and not upon any one, or any combination less than all. We do not have to, and do not, say that any particular component would be enough, either by itself or together with some of the others. Conversely, we do not have to, and do not, say that all the elements we mention are essential to a finding of "fair use." They all happen to be present here, and it is enough for this case to rule, as we do, that at least when all co-exist in combination a "fair use" is made out.

Connected with this point is the second one that our holding is restricted to the type and context of use by NIH and NLM, as shown by this record. That is all we have before us, and we do not pass on dissimilar systems or uses of copyrighted materials by other institutions or enterprises, or in other

---

[30] The general report of the Committee of Experts on the Photographic Reproduction of Protected Works [a joint committee of UNESCO and the United International Bureau for the Protection of Intellectual Property (BIRPI)] recommended that libraries should have the right to provide one copy free of copyright for each user provided that such copy, in the case of a periodical, shall not be more than a single article. 4 *Copyright* 195, 197 (1968).

fields, or as applied to items other than journal articles, or with other significant variables. We have nothing to say, in particular, about the possibilities of computer print-outs or other such products of the newer technology now being born. Especially since we believe, as stressed *infra*, that the problem of photo and mechanical reproduction calls for legislative guidance and legislative treatment, we feel a strong need to obey the canon of judicial parsimony, being stingy rather than expansive in the reach of our holding.

The third facet articulates the same general premise—our holding rests upon this record which fails to show a significant detriment to plaintiff but does demonstrate injury to medical and scientific research if photocopying of this kind is held unlawful. We leave untouched, because we do not have to reach them, the situations where the copyright owner is shown to be hurt or the recipients (or their interests) would not be significantly injured if the reproductions were ruled to infringe.

Finally, but not at all least, we underline again the need for Congressional treatment of the problems of photocopying. The 1909 Act gives almost nothing by way of directives, the judicial doctrine of "fair use" is amorphous and open-ended, and the courts are now precluded, both by the Act and by the nature of the judicial process, from contriving pragmatic or compromise solutions which would reflect the legislature's choices of policy and its mediation among the competing interests. The Supreme Court has pointed out that such a "job is for Congress" (*Fortnightly Corp.* v. *United Artists Television, Inc.*, 392 U.S. 390, 401 (1968)), and in an earlier copyright case in which it was recognized that the owner might be morally or economically entitled to protection the Court applied "the act of Congress [as it] now stands," saying that the other "considerations properly address themselves to the legislative and not to the judicial branch of the Government." *White-Smith Music Co.* v. *Apollo Co.*, 209 U.S. 1, 18 (1908). Hopefully, the result in the present case will be but a "holding operation" in the interim period before Congress enacts its preferred solution.

On this record and for these reasons, we hold the plaintiff not entitled to recover and dismiss the petition.

Appendix

SOME DISCUSSIONS OF LIBRARY PHOTOCOPYING

B. Varmer, Photoduplication of Copyrighted Material by Libraries, Study No. 15, Copyright Law Revision, Studies Prepared for Senate Comm. on the Judiciary, 86th Cong., 2d Sess. (1960); G. Sophar and L. Heilprin, The Determination of Legal Facts and Economic Guideposts with Respect to the Dissemination of Scientific and Educational Information as it is Affected by Copyright—A Status Report, Final Report, Prepared by The Committee to Investigate Copyright Problems Affecting Communication in Science and Education, Inc., for the U.S. Department of Health, Education, and Welfare, Project No. 70793 (1967); Report of the Register of Copyrights on the General Revision of the U.S. Copyright Law to the House Comm. on the Judiciary, 87th Cong., 2d Sess. at 25–26 (1961); Project—New Technology and the Law of Copyright: Reprography and Computers, 15 U.C.L.A. L. Rev. 931 (1968); V. Clapp, Copyright—A Librarian's View, Prepared for the National Advisory Commission on Libraries, Association of American Libraries (1968); Schuster and Bloch, Mechanical Copyright, Copyright Law, and the Teacher, 17 Clev.–Mar. L. Rev. 299 (1968); "Report on Single Copies"—Joint Libraries Committee on Fair Use in Photocopying, 9 Copyright Soc'y Bull. 79 (1961–62); Breyer, "The Uneasy Case for Copyright: A Study of Copyright in Books Photocopies, and Computer Programs," 84 Harv. L. Rev. 281 (1970); Note, "Statutory Copyright Protection for Books and Magazines Against Machine Copying," 39 Notre Dame Lawyer 161 (1964); Note, Education and Copyright Law: An Analysis of the Amended Copyright Revision Bill and Proposals for Statutory Licensing and a Clearinghouse System," 56 Va. L. Rev. 664 (1970); Hattery and Bush (ed.), Reprography and Copyright Law (1964).

COWEN, *Chief Judge*, dissenting:

It is my opinion that our former Trial Judge James F. Davis fully and correctly resolved the difficult and perplexing issues presented by this case in his scholarly and well-reasoned opinion. I would therefore adopt his opinion, findings of fact, and recommended conclusions of law as a basis for a judgment by the court in favor of the plaintiff.

In its discussion of the grounds for the decision which rejected the trial judge's conclusions, the court has, in my opinion, unduly emphasized the facts that are favorable to the defendant and has given inadequate consideration to other facts which led the trial judge to reach a contrary result. For these reasons, I am incorporating in this dissent those portions of the trial judge's opinion which I think are particularly pertinent to the grounds upon which the case has been decided. In view of the court's extensive discussion of the issues and its consideration of some matters not argued to the trial judge, I am supplementing his opinion with the material that follows.

As a preface to my disagreement with the court, I think it would be helpful to point out that this is not a case involving copying of copyrighted material by a scholar or his secretary in aid of his research, nor is it a case where a teacher has reproduced such material for distribution to his class. Also, it is not a case where doctors or scientists have quoted portions of plaintiff's copyrighted articles in the course of writing other articles in the same field. We are not concerned here with a situation in which a library makes copies of ancient manuscripts or worn-out magazines in order to preserve information. What we have before us is a case of wholesale, machine copying, and distribution of copyrighted material by defendant's libraries on a scale so vast that it dwarfs the output of many small publishing companies. In order to fill requests for copies of articles in medical and scientific journals, the NIH made 86,000 Xerox copies in 1970, constituting 930,000 pages. In 1968, the NLM distributed 120,000 copies of such journal articles, totalling about 1.2 million pages. As the trial judge correctly observed, this extensive operation is not only a copying of the copyrighted articles, it is also a reprinting by modern methods and publication by a very wide distribution to requesters and users.

I

Photographic Reproduction of Plaintiff's Journal Articles Is An Abridgement of the Copyright Owner's Exclusive Right To Copy

The majority maintains there is a "solid doubt" whether and how far the word "copy" in Section 1(a) of the 1909 Copyright Act applies to books and journals. The argument continues that the infringement of periodical articles can come only through "printing," "reprinting," or "publishing."

Certainly few things in the law are beyond all doubt or qualification. I think it is apparent, however, from the wording of the 1909 Act, and from the cases interpreting that Act, that Congress intended the word "copy" to apply to books and journals as well as other copyrightable materials. Section 1(a) of the 1909 Act gives the copyright proprietor the exclusive right to "print, reprint, publish, copy, and vend the copyrighted work." 17 U.S.C. § 1 (1970). It follows that copying of a substantial portion of the copyrighted work by someone other than the copyright owner would be an infringement.

I think the trial judge correctly concluded that there is nothing in the legislative history of the 1909 Act which indicates that a restrictive definition of the word "copy" was intended. A significant change in the 1909 Act was the elimination of sections 4964 and 4965 of the prior copyright statute, which it is claimed, are the source of the distinction between the copying of books and the copying of other copyrighted material.[1] By removing those two sections and by adopting the general classification of "copyrighted works" in Section 1(a) and a general listing of all copyrightable works in Section 5 of the 1909 Act, Congress obliterated the distinction, if there ever had been one, between the copying of books and the copying of other materials.[2]

As a result of the simple clarity in the phrasing of the copyright owner's exclusive rights in the 1909 Act, it is not surprising that numerous court decisions interpreting that Act have focused on the copying of copyrighted material (including books and other items of this type) as the infringing act. *See. e.g., Harold Lloyd Corp.* v. *Witwer*, 65 F. 2d 1, 16–19 (9th Cir. 1933) ; *King Features Syndicate* v. *Fleischer*, 299 F. 533, 535 (2d Cir. 1924).

---

[1] These sections had been in the copyright law since 1831 and had been twice re-enacted. Act of February 3, 1831, ch. 16, §§ 6 and 7, 4 Stat. 436 ; Act of July 8, 1870, ch. 230, §§ 99 and 100, 16 Stat. 214 ; Act of March 3, 1891, ch. 565, §§ 4964 and 4965, 26 Stat. 1109.

[2] The trial judge observed that it was the intent of Congress in all the copyright acts to proscribe the unauthorized duplication of copyrighted works. The words used in the various statutes were simply attempts to define the then-current means by which duplication could be effected. I believe this is a fair statement, but it is not necessary to debate the statutory history in light of the changes in the 1909 Act.

I have not been able to find one decision since the 1909 Act which has held that the word "copy" in section 1(a) would not apply to the making of one or a number of copies of a book or other material of this type. The cases have simply not recognized the claimed distinction between copying and printing or publishing. For example, in *New York Tribune, Inc.* v. *Otis & Co.*, 39 F. Supp. 67 (S.D.N.Y. 1941), the court found the making of photostatic copies of plaintiff's newspaper editorial and masthead to be a "good cause of action on its face," and denied defendant's motion for summary judgment. *Id.* at 68. The defendant in that case had distributed the photocopies to a selected list of public officials, bankers, educators, economists and other persons. The court drew no distinction between printing, publishing, or copying. By comparison, the copying and distributing of the newspaper editorial and masthead in that case is very similar to the copying and distributing of the journal articles in the present action.[3]

Therefore, I do not think there is substantial doubt that the photocopying by defendant's libraries is a copy of the plaintiff's journal articles in violation of the copyright owner's exclusive right to copy or to multiply copies of his work under section 1(a). I can see no reason to draw a distinction between copying of "books" and copying of other materials when the distinction is expressly rejected on the face of the copyright statute, has not been observed in numerous cases applying the 1909 Act, and has no reasonable basis in light of the purposes of copyright protection.[4]

---

[3] For cases involving the copying of segments from a copyrighted catalog by photographic reproduction, *see* Hedeman Products Corp. v. Tap-Rite *Prods. Corp.*, 228 F. Supp. 630, 633–34 (D.N.J. 1964) ; R. R. Donnelley & Sons Co. v. Haber, 43 F. Supp. 456, 458–59 (E.D.N.Y. 1942).

[4] The fact that Dr. Putnam, the Librarian of Congress at the time of the 1909 Act, interpreted the word "copy" not to include library photoduplication is no indication that the Congress drafted the statute with this intent. The absence of any provision allowing library photoduplication in the statute or the legislative history indicates, as much as anything else, that Congress did not consider it to be exempt from the Act. The many efforts to amend the law to authorize photocopying by libraries provide a strong indication that existing law was not intended to grant this exemption to libraries. See n. 14, trial judge's opinion.

II

The Photocopying of Plaintiff's Copyrighted Articles Was Not Fair Use

1. Realizing the necessity for showing that the defendant's unauthorized copying of plaintiff's articles was both reasonable and insubstantial, the court relies heavily on policies which were adopted by the libraries in 1965. Although these policies were designed to limit the extent of copying that had been done in prior years, the trial judge's opinion and the findings of fact show the exceptions are routinely granted by the defendant's libraries, that there is no way to enforce most of the limitations, and that defendant is operating a reprint service which supplants the need for journal subscriptions.

In particular, the trial judge has, I think, clearly demonstrated that the claimed "single-copy-per-request" limitation is both illusory and unrealistic. He has found, and it is not disputed, that the libraries will duplicate the same article over and over again, even for the same user, within a short space of time. NLM will supply requesters photocopies of the same article, one after another, on consecutive days, even with knowledge of such facts. I find great difficulty in detecting any difference between the furnishing by defendant's libraries of ten copies of one article to one patron, which he then distributes, and giving each of ten patrons one copy of the same article. The damage to the copyright proprietor is the same in either case.

2. The law is well settled, and I believe not questioned by the court in this case, that under Section 3 of the Copyright Act, plaintiff's copyrights of the journals cover each article contained therein as fully as if each were individually copyrighted. Section 3 expressly mentions periodicals, and for the purpose of determining whether there has been infringement, each copyrightable component is to be treated as a complete work. *Markham* v. *A. E. Borden Co.*, 206 F. 2d 199, 201 (1st Cir. 1953).

It is undisputed that the photocopies in issue here were exact duplicates of the original articles; they were intended to be substitutes for and they served the same purpose as the original articles. They were copies of complete copyrighted works within the meaning of Sections 3 and 5 of the Copyright Act. This is the very essence of wholesale copying and, without more, defeats the defense of fair use. The rule to be applied in such a situation was stated in *Leon V. Pacific Telephone & Telegraph Co.*, 91 F. 2d 484, 486 (9th Cir. 1937) as follows:

> Counsel have not disclosed a single authority, nor have we been able to find one, which lends any support to the proposition that wholesale copying and publication of copyrighted material can ever be fair use.

For other cases to the same effect, *see Public Affairs Associates, Inc.* v. *Rickover*, 284 F. 2d 262, 272 (D.C. Cir. 1960), *judgment vacated for insufficient record*, 369 U.S. 111 (1962) ; *Benny* v. *Loew's Inc.*, 239 F. 2d 532, 536 (9th Cir. 1956), *aff'd by an equally divided court sub nom., Columbia Broadcasting System, Inc.* v. *Loew's Inc.*, 356 U.S. 43 (1958) ; *Holdredge* v. *Knight Publishing Corp.*, 214 F. Supp. 921, 924 (S.D. Cal. 1963). *See also* M. Nimmer, *Nimmer on Copyright* § 145 at 650–51 (1973 ed.).

Although the majority states that the rule announced in the cases cited above is an "overbroad generalization, unsupported by the decisions and rejected by years of accepted practice," the court cites no decisions in support of its position.

3. I recognize that the doctrine of fair use permits writers of scholarly works to make reasonable use of previously copyrighted material by quotation or paraphrase, at least where the amount of copying is small and reliance on other sources is demonstrated. *See, e.g., Rosemont Enterprises, Inc.* v. *Random House, Inc.*, 366 F. 2d 303 (2d Cir. 1966), *cert. denied,* 385 U.S. 1009 (1967) ; *Simms* v. *Stanton,* 75 F. 6, 13–14 (C.C.N.D. Cal. 1896). However, I think the basic error in the court's decision is its holding that the fair use privilege usually granted to such writers should be extended to cover the massive copying and distribution operation conducted by defendant's libraries. The articles are not reproduced by the libraries to enable them to write other articles in the same field. In fact, booksellers and licensed copiers of plaintiff's journals sell copies of journal articles to the same class of users and for the same purposes as the copies reproduced by defendant's libraries.

I do not believe that anyone would contend that the ultimate use of the purchased articles by scientists, doctors, or
drug companies would permit the commercial concerns mentioned to reproduce copies without plaintiff's permission. In
an effort to overcome this obstacle, the majority relies in part
on the nature and function of the NIH and the NLM and the
fact that the articles are reproduced and distributed free of
charge. I do not know of any case which holds that an unauthorized reproduction which is made without profit
amounts to fair use by the infringer, and there are decisions
to the contrary.[5]

Moreover, as plaintiff has pointed out, almost every service
provided by Government agencies is financed by appropriated
funds and furnished without charge to the recipient. If Congress had intended to relieve Government agencies from liability for copyright infringement whenever the material is
copied or otherwise reproduced without charge to the recipient, there would have been no need for the enactment of the
1960 Amendment, now 28 U.S.C. § 1498(b), which gives us
jurisdiction of this action.

Defendant also argues that its libraries are entitled to the
fair use privilege of scientists, researchers, or scholars, because the libraries act as their agent in making the photocopies at their request. This argument is so far-fetched that
the majority balks at embracing it completely. It collides
with reality. The libraries installed and operate the reproduction and distribution operation on their own initiative
and without any kind of an agreement with the ultimate
users of the copies. There is no showing that these alleged—
and in the case of NLM generally unknown—principals have
any say in the formulation of the policies and practices of the
photocopying operation. The libraries decide, without consulting or obtaining the consent of the alleged principals,
whether to loan the original of the journals or to provide

---

[5] It has been held that the copying or printing of something which has been
lawfully copyrighted is an infringement "without any requirement that there
be a sale or that profits be made from sale of the copies." Chappell & Co., Inc. v.
Costa, 45 F. Supp. 554, 556 (S.D.N.Y. 1942). In Wihtol v. Crow, 309 F. 2d
777 (8th Cir. 1962), the First Methodist Church was found to be liable for a
choral instructor's copying of a copyrighted song.

photocopies. The libraries are no more the agent of the users of the material than are the venders of plaintiff's magazines and the commercial concerns which are licensed by plaintiff to make and sell copies to doctors and scientists. The essential elements of agency are wholly lacking.

4. The trial judge found that it is reasonable to infer from the evidence that the extensive unauthorized copying of plaintiff's journal has resulted in some loss of revenue and serves to diminish plaintiff's potential market for the original articles. Since the inferences made by the trial judge may reasonably be drawn from the facts and circumstances in evidence, they are presumptively as correct as his findings of fact. *Bonnar* v. *United States*, 194 Ct. Cl. 103, 109, 438 F. 2d 540, 542 (1971). *See also Baumgartner* v. *United States*, 322 U.S. 665, 670 (1944) ; *Penn-Texas Corp.* v. *Morse*, 242 F. 2d 243, 247 (7th Cir. 1957). Accordingly, under the standards which we employ for reviewing the findings of our trial judges, I would adopt these findings. *Davis* v. *United States*, 164 Ct. Cl. 612, 616–17 (1964) ; *Wilson* v. *United States*, 151 Ct. Cl. 271, 273 (1960).

Although the court states that it rejects the trial determinations as to both actual and potential damage to plaintiff, I think the opinion shows that the court's conclusion is based primarily on its finding that plaintiff failed to prove actual damages. In so doing, the majority relies heavily on evidence that the plaintiff's profits have grown faster than the gross national product and that plaintiff's annual taxable income has increased. This evidence is irrelevant to the economic effects of photocopying the journals in this case, because these periodicals account for a relatively small percent of plaintiff's total business. Moreover, the extent of plaintiff's taxable income for the years mentioned does not reflect the effect of defendant's photocopying of plaintiff's journals, and particularly the effect it will have on the prospects for continued publication in the future.

By the very nature of an action for infringement, the copyright proprietor often has a difficult burden of proving the degree of injury. It is well established, however, that proof of actual damages is not required, and the defense of fair use may be overcome where potential injury is shown. *See, e.g., Henry Holt & Co., Inc.* v. *Liggett & Myers Tobacco Co.*, 23 F. Supp. 302, 304 (E.D. Pa. 1938). As Professor Nimmer has stated, the courts look to see whether defendant's work "tends to diminish or prejudice the potential sale of the plaintiff's work." M. Nimmer, *Nimmer on Copyright* § 145 at 646 (1973 ed.).

The problem posed by library photocopying of copyrighted material has long been a subject of controversy. Several studies of this problem have pointed out that extensive photocopying by libraries is unfair because of its potential damage to the copyright owner. The trial judge has quoted from the reports of several of these studies.[6]

In a thorough and thoughtful discussion of the effects of reprography, prepared at the University of California, Los Angeles, and funded by the National Endowment for the Arts, it is stated:

> It has long been argued that copying by hand "for the purpose of private study and review" would be a fair use. Users are now asserting that machine copying is merely a substitute for hand copying and is, therefore, a fair use. But this argument ignores the economic differences between the two types of copying. Copying by hand is extremely time consuming and costly, and is not an economic threat to authors. *Viewing reprography as though it were hand copying, however, overlooks the effect of the total number of machine copies made. Few people hand copy, but millions find machine copying economical and convenient. Allowing individual users to decide that their machine copying will not injure the author and will thus be a fair use fails to take into account the true economic effect when thousands of such individual decisions are aggregated.*

The problem is vividly presented by the practice of

---

[6] *See* the trial judge's opinion for quotations from B. Varmer, Photoduplication of Copyrighted Material by Libraries, Study No. 15, Copyright Law Revision, Studies Prepared for the Senate Comm. on the Judiciary, 86th Cong., 2d Sess. 62–63 (1960) ; Report of the Register of Copyrights on the General Revision of the U.S. Copyright Law, House Committee Print, 87th Cong., 1st Sess. 25–26 (1961). M. Nimmer, *Nimmer on Copyright* § 145 at 653–54 (1973 ed.). *See also* Crossland, *The Rise and Fall of Fair Use: The Protection of Literary Materials Against Copyright Infringement by New and Developing Media,* 20 S. Car. L. Rev. 153, 154 (1968).

the National Library of Medicine. The Library justifies its distribution of reprographic copies of journal articles to biomedical libraries (without permission of the copyright owner) on the basis of a 1939 understanding between publishers and libraries called the "Gentlemen's Agreement." Under this agreement photocopies are permitted whenever the user would have made a hand copy himself, the rationale being that no purchases of the author's work are displaced under these circumstances. When an individual would actually copy by hand, the theory is valid; there is no sound reason to force him to do the work. But many people obtain copies from the library who would not copy by hand, and who might in fact buy a copy of the work if they were unable to receive an inexpensive machine reproduction of it. Thus, the library interprets the Gentlemen's Agreement in its favor and thereby "justifies" a substantial amount of copying. (Emphasis supplied.) *Project, New Technology and the Law of Copyright: Reprography and Computers*, 15 U.C.L.A. L. Rev. 931, 951 (1968).

As the majority points out, one study, made in 1962, concluded that photocopying did not result in economic damage to publishers at that time: Fry & Associates, Survey of Copyrighted Material Reproduction Practices in Scientific and Technical Fields, 11 Bull. Cr. Soc. 69, 71 (1963). This study also stated:

One situation was reported during the survey in which economic damage may occur. A prominent university library in a small town with several corporate research and development centers gives excellent service on its collection. This library felt that these corporate libraries are subscribing to only the minimum number of journals. They rely on the university to supply photocopies of other material.

  *   *   *   *   *

This is the one clear-cut example disclosed during the survey of dilution of the publishers' circulation market. *Id.* at 119.

Indeed, this example is very nearly the situation presented by this case. Government institutions, medical schools, hospitals, research foundations, drug companies, and individual physicians are supplementing their collections, if they subscribe to any journals, by acquiring free photocopies of articles from the NLM.[7]

In addition to the conclusions of those who have studied the problem extensively, there are other facts and circumstances in this record which I think amply support the views of the trial judge that the system used by defendant's libraries for distributing free copies of plaintiff's journal articles attracts some potential purchasers of plaintiff's journals.

Subscription sales provide most of the revenue derived from the marketing of plaintiff's journals. It is important to remember that each of plaintiff's journals caters to and serves a limited market. Plaintiff's share of the profits from these journals has varied from less than $1,000 to about $7,000 annually.[8] In the context of rising costs of publication, an inability to attract new customers, and the loss of even a small number of old subscribers may have a large detrimental effect on the journals. A representative of William & Wilkins Company testified that in recent years there have been journals that have failed, and in the opinion of those at Williams & Wilkins, photocopying has played a role in these failures.[9] The majority relies on the fact that subscriptions for the four journals in this case have shown a general increase over the last five years, but two of the journals, *Medicine* and *Phar-*

---

[7] It should be noted that the Fry survey was made when photocopying was not as prominent as it is today. Even at that time, the Fry Report notes that larger publishers (who were photocopied most heavily) complained about the effects of photocopying. Fry Report at 86–87. Secondly, the Fry Report operates on the dubious assumption that in most cases the photocopy serves as a substitute for loaning the original material and does no more damage than would loaning of the original material.

In addition to the Fry Report, the majority cites a statement by Dan Lacy, Managing Director, American Book Publisher's Council, to the effect that photocopying is undertaken in lieu of manual note taking, typing, or handwriting a copy, and in lieu of a library loan rather than in lieu of buying a copy. We can hardly expect a representative of an organization of book publishers to be an expert on the problems of journal publishers. Library photocopying of books does not pose the same threat to a book publisher as photocopying of journal articles does to its publisher. Rarely are books photocopied completely. At present, there appears to be no competition for the consumer market between libraries and book publishers.

[8] For example, in 1968, profit from *Pharmacological Reviews* was $1,154.44 (on sales of about $40,000). The profit was divided, $1,039 to the American Society for Pharmacology and Experimental Therapeutics and $115.44 to plaintiff. In 1969, net income from *Gastroenterology* was $21,312 (on sales of about $245,000) and $11,532.35 of that amount was offset by losses the previous year, leaving a balance of $9,779.73. The balance was split between plaintiff and the American Gastroenterological Association, plaintiff getting $4,889.86.

[9] Tr. at 73.

macological Reviews, have shown a slight decrease in subscriptions from 1968 to 1969. In addition, the *Journal of Immunology* showed losses in the period prior to 1961; *Gastroenterology* showed losses in 1967 and 1968; *Pharmacological Reviews* showed a loss in 1969. There is no evidence to show specifically whether any particular instance or instances of unauthorized photocopying of plaintiff's journals has or has not resulted in the loss of revenue to plaintiff. However, I think the record, as a whole, supports the determination of the trial judge that the photocopying in this case has had a tendency to diminish plaintiff's markets in the past.

The NLM publishes a monthly indexed catalog of journal articles in medicine and related sciences entitled "Index Medicus." The index is widely distributed to medical libraries, research centers, schools, hospitals, and physicians. The catalog announces its new publications and acquisitions and thus advertises to the medical and scientific community, which constitutes plaintiff's market, that certain articles are available free of charge in the form of a photocopy.

At the present time, the NIH purchases only two subscriptions to plaintiff's journals. If nothing else, it would certainly need more than the two copies to meet the requests of the large in-house staff. Although it has been argued that the photocopies are merely a substitute for the loan of an original and does no more harm than the loan of the original material, I think this argument is fallacious. One copy of the original material could not possibly be loaned to as many requesters as the numerous photocopies, the competitive effect of which is much greater. Also, the photocopies are not required to be returned and become the property of the possessor. They can be marked, cut into segments, placed in the files, and otherwise put to uses that would be impossible with a loan of the original. While the library may look at the giving of a photocopy as a substitute for a loan, the user and would-be purchaser gets an exact copy of the original article which is a substitute for a purchased copy.

One of the new sources of income to publishers is the supplying of back issues or providing copies of such issues. When plaintiff receives a request for an out-of-print article, the customer is generally referred to the Institute of Scientific Information, which is licensed by plaintiff to make the photo-

copies. If the same articles can be obtained from the NLM
without charge, it seems obvious that the supplying of free
copies by the defendant's libraries will tend to diminish
plaintiff's income from this source. NLM reproduces and
supplies copies of journal articles to the patrons of other
libraries. Therefore, the libraries who make the requests do
not have to buy subscriptions for the use of their own patrons.

III

Foreign Laws Do Not Justify an Exemption From the Copyright Laws

The court relies to some extent on the copyright laws of the
United Kingdom, New Zealand, Denmark, Finland, Italy,
and other countries. The plaintiff says there are many differences between our copyright laws and those of other countries, and plaintiff does not agree that the defendant would
be exempt from liability under the statutes of some of the
countries named. However, we need not delve into the details
of the copyright legislation of these foreign countries. There
is a shorter answer to the court's reliance on foreign laws.
Unlike the legislative bodies of these countries, the Congress
has not yet changed the Copyright Act of 1909 to permit the
same kind of copying by the NIH and the NLM. If the time
has come when the defendant's libraries should be exempted
from the provisions of the Copyright Act to the extent permitted by the court's decision, the exemption should be provided by legislative action rather than by judicial
legislation.

IV

A Judgment for Plaintiff Will Not Injure Medicine and Medical Research

The court has bottomed its decision to a very large extent
on its finding, which is not disputed, that medical science
would be seriously hurt if the photocopying by defendant's
libraries is entirely stopped. But the court goes further and
concludes that a judgment for plaintiff would lead to this
result. It is not altogether clear to me how the court arrives

at the second conclusion, and I think it is based on unwarranted assumptions.

The plaintiff does not propose to stop such photocopying
and does not desire that result. What plaintiff seeks is a
reasonable royalty for such photocopying and, in this case,
a recovery of reasonable compensation for the infringement
of its copyrights. Plaintiff has established a licensing system
to cover various methods of reproducing its journal articles,
including reproduction by photocopying. One of the licensees
is a Government agency, and on several occasions plaintiff
has granted requests from Government agencies and others
for licenses to make multiple copies (Finding 36). In May
1967, the photocopying of plaintiff's journal articles was
monitored by NLM for a 90-day period which was judged
to be a representative sample. As the trial judge has shown,
NLM found that it would have paid plaintiff from $250 to
$300 if it had granted plaintiff's request for royalty pay-
ments. The Director of NLM testified that this was, in his
opinion, a surprisingly small sum. He also testified (Part
III, trial judge's opinion) that the payment of a royalty to
plaintiff for photocopying "has nothing to do with the operation of the library in the fulfillment of * * * [its]
function. It is an economic and budgetary consideration and
not a service-oriented kind of thing." This is the only direct
testimony that I have found on how the payment of royalties
for photocopying will affect the functions of the library,
and it gives no indication or initimation that the payment
of royalties to plaintiff will force NLM to cease the
photocopying.

The court has laid heavy emphasis on the public interest
in maintaining a free flow of information to doctors and
scientists, and on the injury that might result if this flow
should be stopped. However, there is another facet to the
public interest question which is presented in this case. The
trial judge put it well in his statement:

> The issues raised by this case are but part of a larger
> problem which continues to plague our institutions with
> ever-increasing complexity—how best to reconcile, on
> the one hand, the rights of authors and publishers under
> the copyright laws with, on the other hand, the techno-
> logical improvements in copying techniques and the

> legitimate public need for rapid dissemination of scientific and technical literature. (Part III, trial judge's opinion)

In enacting the 1909 Act, the House Committee said:

> The enactment of copyright legislation by Congress under the terms of the Constitution is not based upon any natural right that the author has in his writings * * * but upon the ground that the welfare of the public will be served and progress of science and useful arts will be promoted by securing to authors for limited periods the exclusive rights to their writings. H.R. Rep. No. 2222, 60th Cong., 2d Sess. 7 (1909).

In *Mazer* v. *Stein*, 347 U.S. 201, 219 (1954), the Supreme Court emphasized that the copyright protection given to authors and publishers is designed to advance public welfare, stating:

> "The copyright law, like the patent statutes, makes reward to the owner a secondary consideration. * * *" However, it is "intended definitely to grant valuable, enforceable rights to authors, publishers, etc. * * *"
> The economic philosophy behind the clause empowering Congress to grant patents and copyrights is the conviction that encouragement of individual effort by personal gain is the best way to advance public welfare through the talents of authors and inventors in "Science and useful Arts."

In order to promote the progress of science, not only must authors be induced to write new works, but also publishers must be induced to disseminate those works to the public. This philosophy has guided our country, with limited exceptions, since its beginning, and I am of the opinion that if there is to be a fundamental policy change in this system, such as a blanket exception for library photocopying, it is for the Congress to determine, not for the courts. The courts simply cannot draw the distinctions so obviously necessary in this area.

The court recognizes that the solution which it has undertaken to provide in this case is preeminently a problem for Congress which should decide how much photocopying should be allowed, what payments should be made to the copyright owners, and related questions. Nowhere else in its opinion is the court on more solid ground than when it declares that the "choices involve economic, social, and policy factors which are far better sifted by a legislature. The possible intermediate solutions are also of the pragmatic kind legislatures, not courts, can and should fashion." In spite of this obviously correct statement, the court has bridged the gap which the inaction of Congress has left in the Copyright Act of 1909.

I agree with the court that we have no jurisdiction to order a copyright owner to institute a licensing system if he does not wish to do so, but I think we are equally powerless to assume the congressional role by granting what amounts to a blanket exemption to defendant's libraries. Without too much difficulty, however, we can determine the amount of just compensation that is due plaintiff for the infringement of its copyrights. If that should be done, it may very well lead to a satisfactory agreement between the parties for a continuation of the photocopying by defendant upon the payment of a reasonable royalty to plaintiff.

NOTE: The remainder of the dissent can be found in 487 F.2d 1372 (1973). It consists largely of excerpts from the trial judge's opinion which is presented in full in Bush, *Technology and Copyright: Annotated Bibliography and Source Materials*, 1972, pp. 374-437.

ACKNOWLEDGMENTS

My sincere thanks are due to the American Chemical Society, the American Library Association, Aslib, the Catholic University Law Review, the Copyright Society of the U.S.A., Her Majesty's Stationery Office, Lorenz Press, Inc., the N.E. Corporation, the New York Law School, the UCLA Law Review, and the World Peace through Law Center.

This occasion is taken to thank the individual or corporate authors of articles reprinted herein.

William J. Baumol, coauthor: *Economics of Property Rights as Applied to Computer Software and Data Bases.*

Yale M. Braunstein, coauthor: *Economics of Property Rights as Applied to Computer Software and Data Bases.*

Steven Brill, author: *Will Betamax Be Busted?*

Committee to consider the Law on Copyright and Designs, author: *Copyright and Designs Law: Report of the Committee to consider the Law on Copyright and Designs.*

CRC Systems Incorporated, author: *Impact of Information Technology on Copyright Law in the Use of Computerized Scientific and Technological Information Systems.*

Richard De Gennaro, author: *Copyright, Resource Sharing, and Hard Times: A View from the Field.*

Dietrich M. Fischer, coauthor: *Economics of Property Rights as Applied to Computer Software and Data Bases.*

Stephen Freid, author: *Fair Use and the New Act.*

Bernard M. Fry, coauthor: *Scholarly and Research Journals: Survey of Publisher Practices and Present Attitudes on Authorized Journal Article Copying and Licensing.*

Susan C. Greene, author: *The Cable Television Provisions of the Revised Copyright Act.*

Madeline Henderson, author: *Copyright Impacts of Future Technology.*

John Hersey, author: *Dissent from CONTU's Software Recommendation.*

International Bureau of the World Intellectual Property Organization, author: *Model Provisions on the Protection of Computer Software.*

Elizabeth L. Johnson, coauthor: *Scholarly and Research Journals: Survey of Publisher Practices and Present Attitudes on Authorized Journal Article Copying and Licensing.*

King Research, Inc., author: *Library Photocopying in the United States: With Implications for the Development of a Copyright Royalty Payment Mechanism.*

Maurice Line, coauthor: *The Effect of a Large-Scale Photocopying Service on Journal Sales* and *Photocopying and Journal Sales: A Reply.*

Janusz A. Ordover, coauthor: *Economics of Property Rights as Applied to Computer Software and Data Bases.*

Barbara Ringer, author: *Copyright in the 1980's.*

Jeffrey Squires, author: *Copyright and Compilations in the Computerized Era: Old Wine in New Bottles.*

James M. Treece, author: *Library Photocopying.*

E. Van Tongeren, author: *The Effect of a Large-Scale Photocopying Service on Journal Sales.*

Herbert S. White, coauthor: *Scholarly and Research Journals: Survey of Publisher Practices and Present Attitudes on Authorized Journal Article Copying and Licensing.*

D.N. Wood, coauthor: *The Effect of a Large-Scale Photocopying Service on Journal Sales.*

LIST OF PERIODICALS CITED

AAUP Bulletin
Air Force JAG Law Review
ALA Bulletin
ALA Washington Newsletter
Albany Law Review
America
American Documentation
American Journal of International Law
American Libraries
APLA Bulletin
Aslib Proceedings
Audiovisual Instruction
Billboard
Book Production Industry
Boston University Law Review
Brooklyn Law Review
Buffalo Law Review
Bulletin of the American Society for Information Science
Bulletin of the Copyright Society of the U.S.A.
Canadian Library Journal
Catholic University Law Review
Clearing House, The
Cleveland-Marshall Law Review
College and Research Libraries
College & Research Libraries News
Communications of the ACM
Computers and Automation
Computerworld
Computing Surveys
Congressional Record
Copyright
Copyright Management
Datamation
Dickinson Law Review
Duke Law Journal
Emory Law Journal
Esquire
Federal Bar Journal
Florida Bar Journal
Fordham Law Review
Gazette
Georgetown Law Journal
George Washington Law Review
Harvard Law Review
Honeywell Computer Journal, The
Howard Law Journal
IEEE Transactions on Professional Communication
Indiana Law Journal
Information Hotline
Information Retrieval and Library Automation
International Journal of Law Libraries
Iowa Law Review

John Marshall Journal of Practice & Procedure, The
Johns Hopkins Magazine
Journal of Chemical Information and Computer Sciences
Journal of Documentation
Journal of Education for Librarianship
Journal of Law & Economics
Journal of Library Automation
Journal of the American Society for Information Science
Kentucky Law Journal
Law and Computer Technology
Law Library Journal
Legal Briefs for Editors, Publishers, and Writers
LIBRA
Library Journal
Library Trends
Maine Law Review
MICRODOC
Microfiche Foundation Newsletter
Modern Data
National Journal Reports
New York Law School Law Review
New York University Law Review
Northern Kentucky Law Review
Notre Dame Lawyer
Performing Arts Review
Phi Delta Kappan
PS
Public Interest, The
Publishers Weekly
Rutgers Journal of Computers and the Law
Saturday Review
Scholarly Publishing
School Media Quarterly
Science
Serials Librarian, The
South African Libraries
Special Libraries
St. Louis University Law Journal
Teachers College Record
UCLA Law Review
Unesco Bulletin for Libraries
University of Western Australia Law Review
Utah Law Review
Valparaiso University Law Review
VideoNews
Wall Street Journal
Washington Post
Washington University Law Quarterly
Wilson Library Bulletin
Yale Law Journal, The

INDEX OF NAMES

SUBJECT INDEX*

---

*Pages 3-118 refer to bibliographic annotations; others to text of source materials.

INDEX OF CASES